HARDENING Network Security

John Mallery, Jason Zann
Patrick Kelly, Wesley Noonan
Eric Seagren, Paul Love
Rob Kraft, Mark O'Neill

MCGRAW-HILL/OSBORNE
New York Chicago San Francisco
Lisbon London Madrid Mexico City
Milan New Delhi San Juan Seoul
Singapore Sydney Toronto

The McGraw·Hill Companies

McGraw-Hill/Osborne
2100 Powell Street, 10th Floor
Emeryville, California 94608
U.S.A.

To arrange bulk purchase discounts for sales promotions, premiums, or fund-raisers, please contact McGraw-Hill/Osborne at the above address. For information on translations or book distributors outside the U.S.A., please see the International Contact Information page immediately following the index of this book.

Hardening Network Security

1234567890 CUS CUS 0198765

ISBN 0-07-225703-2

Editorial Director
Tracy Dunkelberger
Executive Editor
Jane K. Brownlow
Project Editors
Jody McKenzie
Jennifer Malnick
Acquisitions Coordinators
Athena Honore
Agatha Kim
Jessica Wilson
Technical Editor
Lee Imery

Copy Editor
Bill McManus
Proofreader
Linda Medoff
Indexer
Valerie Perry
Composition
Apollo Publishing Services
Illustrator
Sue Albert
Cover Series Design
Theresa Havener

This book was composed with Corel VENTURA™ Publisher.

I dedicate my work on this book to my family. Without their support I never would have made it through this project. Thank you Paula, Garrick, and Erika, you always understood when this book took me away from family events. I couldn't have a more wonderful family.

—John Mallery

I dedicate my work to my wife Cheryl, to our children Jessica Clark and Abby Manatt, grandchildren Ocean and Izaak Redmon, and to Bridget for teaching me the value of life, the value of play, and to never back down.

—Patrick Kelly

To my wife Dana, for the support that she gave me writing this book. And to my parents, David and Joan, who are a bigger part of this project than they will ever know.

—Jason Zann

About the Series Editor/Author

Roberta Bragg (Grain Valley, MO), CISSP, Security+, ETI Client Server, Certified Technical Trainer, IBM Certified Trainer, DB2-UDB, Citrix Certified Administrator, MCSE: Security, has been the columnist for "Security Advisor" for *Microsoft Certified Professional Magazine* for six years and for the "Security Watch" newsletter for three years. She is a Security Expert for SearchWindowsSecurity.com, for which she also writes the "Security Checklist" column. Roberta designed, planned, produced, and participated in the first Windows Security Summit, held in Seattle in 2002. Also in 2002, at TechMentor San Diego, Roberta gave the first production of "Security Academy," a three-day hands-on secure network-building workshop, which was subsequently scheduled for five repeat presentations in 2003. She presented for Microsoft during a series of 2004 Security Summits. Roberta has been an instructor for SANs and for the MIS Training Institute.

Roberta has participated in numerous security audits and has traveled all over the world as a security evangelist, consulting, assessing, and training on networks and network security. Roberta has served as adjunct faculty at Seattle Pacific University and at Johnson County Community College, teaching courses on information security design. Roberta is the lead author of two other McGraw-Hill/Osborne titles, *Network Security: The Complete Reference* (2003) and *Hardening Windows Systems* (2004), and *Designing Security for a Windows Server 2003 Network* (Microsoft Press, 2004).

About the Lead Authors

John Mallery is a Managing Consultant at BKD, LLP, and a veteran security specialist. Previously, he was CTO of Clarence M. Kelley and Associates, Inc, a private investigation and security consulting company founded by the former director of the FBI. John is a nationally recognized public speaker and trainer in the area of computer forensics and computer security. He has developed continuing legal education programs for the legal community and POST accredited programs for law enforcement. His presentations always receive excellent evaluations at national conferences.

John draws upon his unique experiences as an investigator, network security consultant, and comedian to provide presentations that are both informative and entertaining. John is a member of the Information Technology Security Council for ASIS International, a member of the High Technology Crime Investigation Association, Infragard, and a contributing editor for *Security Technology and Design* magazine.

Jason Zann, CISSP, is currently an Information Security Consultant for DST Systems, Inc. With more than nine years as an information security professional, he has been responsible for management, operational, and technical developments for information security products, systems, networks, and processes on a global scale. He has worked for corporate, product, and consulting organizations delivering a range of information security concepts and solutions.

Patrick W. Kelly, CISSP, CCSE, MCSE, MCP+I, currently serves as Information Assurance Engineer for ComGlobal Systems, Inc. Patrick has more than 15 years of combined application development and network security experience. In his current position he is responsible for Enterprise Security Awareness Programs, Vulnerability and Risk Assessment, and Security Component Design and Build. Throughout his career, Patrick has been responsible for implementation and development of network security programs. Some of these projects include Intrusion Detection and Reaction Systems, Firewall Technology Design and Implementation, Network Security Risk and Vulnerability Assessment, and Internet Security Programs.

About the Contributing Authors

Wesley J. Noonan (Houston, Texas), MCSE, CCNA, CCDA, NNCSS, Security+, has been working in the computer industry for more than 11 years, specializing in Windows-based networks and network infrastructure design and implementation. He is a Senior Network Consultant for Collective Technologies, LLC (http://www.colltech.com), a company that specializes in storage, server and network design, architecture, implementation, and security. Wes got his start in the United States Marine Corps working on its Banyan VINES network, and has since worked on building and designing secure networks ranging in size from 25 to 25,000 users. Wes previously worked in R&D for BMC Software, Inc., on their PATROL management solutions, architecting and testing their network and application management products. Wes is also an active trainer, developing and teaching his own custom, Cisco-based routing and switching curriculum. He has spoken at a number of technical conferences and user groups and is a member of the Ask the Experts panel at http://searchwindowssecurity.techtarget.com. Wes is also the author of *Hardening Network Infrastructure* (McGraw-Hill/Osborne, 2004).

Eric S. Seagren (Missouri City, TX), CISSP, ISSAP, SCNP, CCNA, CNE, MCP+I, MCSE, has nine years of experience in the computer industry, with the last six years spent in the financial services industry working for a Fortune 100 company. Eric started his computer career working on Novell servers and performing general network troubleshooting for a small Houston-based company. While working in the financial services industry, his duties have included server administration, disaster recovery responsibilities, business continuity coordination, and Y2K remediation responsibilities. He has spent the last four years as an IT architect, designing secure, scalable, and redundant networks. His design experience includes the implementation of intrusion detection systems, and the security evaluation of network designs and network device configurations.

Paul Love, CISSP, CISA, CISM, Security +, is a Security Manager for a large financial institution and has been in the IT field for 15 years. Paul holds a master of science degree in network security and a bachelor's degree in information systems. He is a coauthor of the book *Hardening Linux* (McGraw-Hill/Osborne, 2004) and has been the technical editor for over ten best-selling Linux and Unix books. Paul ran a successful Linux portal site during the dot com era.

Rob Kraft is the director of software development for KCX, Inc. Rob spent two years as a Microsoft Certified Trainer teaching classes on SQL Server and Visual Basic. He is also certified by IBM to teach DB2 and WebSphere. In addition to teaching, Rob spent 15 years developing applications on a range of platforms, development languages, and database management systems. Rob coauthored books on Microsoft SQL Server and has presented SQL Server, Internet Security, and Visual Basic at conferences and seminars. In his spare time, Rob assists local nonprofits with IT and other needs. You may contact Rob at http://www.RobKraft.org.

Mark O'Neill is the principal author of *Web Services Security* (McGraw-Hill/Osborne, 2003). Mark has written on the topic of XML and web services security in magazines such as *Web Services Journal, XML Journal, Java Pro, Enterprise Architect, Infoconomy,* and *Technology for Finance.* As Chief Technical Officer at Vordel, a pioneering vendor of XML security products, Mark has met many early adopters of XML, gathering and synthesizing their security requirements. Mark regularly presents training courses on web services security in London, California, and on the U.S. East Coast. For the past four years, he has been chosen as a speaker on the topic of XML security at the RSA Conference, the infosec industry's largest annual conference. Mark lives in an old house in Boston's up-and-coming Roslindale neighborhood, with Kristen and their two-year-old son Ben.

About the Technical Reviewer

Lee Imery, CISSP, CISA, CPP, is an information security specialist with the federal government, where he writes policies to secure critical and classified information, and works with various government organizations to implement practices and technological procedures consistent with those policies. Previously, he was Senior Communications Manager with (ISC)², where he edited and produced the (ISC)² newsletter, an electronic publication sent to over 20,000 information security professionals worldwide. He was also Lead Instructor for the CISSP CBK Review Seminar, which he taught internationally to private and public sector audiences. He has worked for telecommunications, retail, and consulting organizations, and continues to contribute to the profession in several volunteer capacities, including as a member of the ASIS Information Technology Security Council, and as Chair of the ISSA Committee on Professional Ethics.

Contents

PART IV How to Succeed at Hardening

Foreword

Network security is not just about applying technical controls and defending systems from attack. It's not just about hardening this operating system or that operating system or securing network infrastructure. Above all, it's not going to happen because we finally have bug-free code. When all is said and done, good network security rests on the ability and ethics of the people who run our networks and on that of the people who are able to access them.

Still, we cannot always pick a security dream team, nor expect our employees to all be saints, our customers to all be law abiding, and all the world's peoples to have the same beliefs as we do. Because humans are imperfect, we build information systems that fail, apply technical controls that other humans can subvert, and ignore some events that, if caught and corrected, could have prevented compromise.

The answer, however, is not to give up. The answer is not to insist that others do our job for us. The answer is to join together with others who we trust and develop solutions that, if not perfect, keep systems running, keep protection in place, and stay one step ahead of those who play by evil rules. Let's grab victory one bit at a time, one machine at a time, and one day at a time. There is a wealth of experience that can help us if we only listen. There is a lot we can do if only we will do it. There is knowledge to share, experiences to relate, truths to reveal.

This book is the result of such a joining together. Last year, six Kansas City security professionals met in a Starbucks with the goal of writing a book that would not just talk about our disparate information security experiences but would be the result of our sharing those experiences. We didn't want a book of isolated evidence; we wanted to talk about how everything was supposed to work together. While we wanted to express technical issues with the purpose of helping others understand how to technically secure their systems, we didn't want to ignore the people side of the process.

Like mythological warriors on a quest, we started down the road with lofty ideals. We met with tragedy and major life issues along the way. Some of the original team departed and others joined us. Just about every person involved with the book, from author to reviewer to publisher's editorial team, experienced some life-changing event during the book-writing process. People quit their jobs or were fired. Folks moved, a wedding took place, families were involved in accidents, life-threatening events ensued. As series editor I sometimes felt like I was a participant on *Survivor*. But survive this book did.

Today, you see the results of our quest. This book is not a panacea for what ails information security today, but perhaps it's something much more valuable. Remember, things change, people change, there are new problems every day. If you want to be part of your organization's information security solution, if you want to be part of the worldwide information security solution, you must be prepared to adapt to the future while protecting today. Take our words and instructions and apply them today as best you can. But look within this book and within your own hearts and minds for those things that will help our information systems survive tomorrow. Most of all, add your own voice and deeds to the battle—it's one that together we can win.

—Roberta "I don't think we're in Kansas anymore" Bragg
December 15, 2004

Acknowledgments

I wish to thank Michael Waid of Ameriquest, who was my very first mentor and didn't laugh too hard when I referred to DOS as "dose." I also wish to thank Mark Carney at Fishnet Security for his assistance with wireless network security concepts. Special thanks to Tom Dupriest at CMKA, who helped provide nearly all of my technical training. But I would like to especially thank Roberta Bragg for giving me the opportunity to work on this project. Her support and encouragement were spectacular. Thank you, Roberta, for giving me such a great opportunity.

—John Mallery

I must recognize Roberta Bragg for dedicating part of her life to making computing safer for the rest of us and providing this opportunity. For his encouragement and vision, I should thank Paul Pauesick, who should be on the cover of a magazine. I would like to thank Frank Hewitt, Chris Carspecken, Mike and Connie Woodward, Patricia Curtis, Leslie Griffith, and Rose Moore for having the wisdom to give me a fighting chance.

—Patrick Kelly

I want to thank all of the people who let me bounce ideas and thoughts off of them during this project, including Travis Marlow, Shane Kinsch, Oggy Vasic, James Sullivan, Bruce James, and the information security teams at DST Systems, Inc. I would also like to personally thank Roberta Bragg and the McGraw-Hill/Osborne team for making this project a reality.

—Jason Zann

Introduction

by John Mallery

I have been writing and speaking about computer security issues for six years. Initially, my perspective came from my experiences as a system administrator and then as Chief Technology Officer for a security consulting company. I gained additional insight working on consulting engagements that addressed numerous areas of computer security, such as policies and procedures, penetration testing, patch management, and end-user training. As my involvement in the industry progressed, I realized there were many people providing presentations and programs on computer security–related topics. With the amount of material being provided on security-related issues, I thought that security would become a priority for every firm and system administrator. But during the last year, I was blindsided by two experiences that convinced me that not everyone has "seen the light" regarding computer security.

The first experience started when I received a phone call from a client, "We think our internal accountant has stolen some money from us." Upon visiting the client's office, it was discovered that not only had she taken "some money," the amount was an astounding $3 million! Even more astounding to me was that the amount was not higher, since the network, which was directly connected to the Internet without a firewall, also required no passwords for authentication. In addition, each workstation had a modem, a phone line, and a remote access client that also required no password for authentication. I had to wonder if the owners of the company had been in a coma for the past six years. The weak security in the company allowed its internal accountant to access all financial records and programs at any time of day without any of her activities being logged. Her activities included deleting fraudulent transactions, modifying financial statements, and reclassifying expenditures.

The second incident was when I met a computer consultant who managed networks for six law firms. He informed me that not a single network had a firewall in place, in spite of the fact that each law firm handled numerous sensitive cases. When questioned about the lack of firewalls in place, he responded, "Do you think they should be installed?" I think I mumbled the word "clueless" under my breath.

After these experiences, I realized that there is more work to do to educate individuals and organizations regarding computer security, and this book is part of my efforts to do so. Unlike many books on computer security, this book was written by multiple experts in the field. This means that each author had a chance to contribute material on his or her area of expertise. They provided material based on personal knowledge and expertise; they didn't simply regurgitate other commonly held security beliefs. In addition, this book is all "substance." You will not have to wade through chapters on theory and Internet history to get to the material that you can actually use immediately to secure your systems and networks. This book is an excellent complement to the other books in the *Hardening* series. If you are new to computer security, the first chapter gives direct step-by-step directions on how to immediately begin to tighten the security in your organization. If you have some experience with security and are looking for some insight into a particular problem or some new ideas, you will find that information in this book as well.

So, it is time to begin securing your networks. There is little time to waste and so much yet to do.

In this Book

This book was written to offer practical knowledge and step-by-step directions to system administrators who are given the task of securing a diverse network with multiple devices and operating systems. It is assumed that the reader has good technical knowledge and expertise but might be well versed in only one operating system or platform. The material provided will enable system administrators with limited security training to immediately "tighten down" their networks and systems. As with all security books, this book is not a complete security solution, but is intended to be the best place to start when beginning to evaluate security in the enterprise. For system administrators who believe their systems are secure, this book can provide validation for your efforts, but will also provide a different perspective and alternative solutions that will allow you to strengthen your defenses.

Part I: Do This Now!

Chapter 1: "Do These Seven Things Before You Do Anything Else!" by John Mallery

The first chapter is designed to provide solutions that can be applied immediately to networks and computer systems. For those who don't know where to start, the information provided allows you to quickly and effectively start reducing vulnerabilities on your network. This chapter goes beyond recommendations, telling you exactly what to do and how to do it. It is intended to provide the type of information that experienced system administrators will look at and say, "Wow, I wish I had had this type of information when I started."

Part II: Take It from the Top: Systematically Hardening Your Enterprise

Chapter 2: "Break the Network into Common Areas of Functionality for Security" by John Mallery

One of the principal concepts of computer security is "defense in depth." This chapter begins addressing the layered approach to security by segmenting networks using specific criteria. Some of the criteria addressed will be new to many system administrators.

Chapter 3: "Hardening with Identity Management Systems" by Jason Zann

Identity management has many different interpretations; however, all of them are focused on the issues of user management. This chapter explores the common rationales for developing enterprise-wide identity management programs, from a desire to meet perceived legislative requirements and internal liability issues to an effort to reduce costs and improve productivity. This chapter also includes information on how current directory-based services fulfill the organization's need to manage the different identities of employees, customers, contractors, and vendors. It also offers advice on evaluating current identity management solutions.

Chapter 4: "Hardening Cross-Platform Authentication" by Jason Zann

When users access information systems, they must usually provide information such as a user account name and some proof that they are authorized to use that account for system access. This process of proving they are who they say they are is called authentication. The proof may take the form of a password, smart card, token, biometric, or some other type of proof. The security professional's job is usually to ensure that the strongest possible approach to authentication is used. This chapter explores how to do that job when multiple operating systems and platforms are part of the mix and users must access more than one of them.

Chapter 5: "Hardening Web Services" by Mark O'Neill

Systems that provide web services are constantly under attack, simply because they are often more readily accessible than other systems and their vulnerabilities are well publicized. Removing these vulnerabilities ensures that web services stay up and running, which often is the difference between success and failure for many businesses.

Web services provide application-integration solutions across computer systems using technologies such as XML and web services (WS) security. This chapter explores standards developed to support web services and WS-security and provides information on security practices and pitfalls for the web service developer and evaluator. Both those who are comfortable with developing and deploying web services and those who must make decision upon the adoption of web services will benefit from the clear definitions and explanations in this chapter.

Chapter 6: "Hardening Mobile Environments" by Jason Zann

This chapter discusses security solutions for mobile devices such as PDAs and smart phones, including authentication, antivirus protection, and encryption. It also addresses protection from security vulnerabilities present in infrared and Bluetooth technologies commonly used for communications between mobile devices and PCs, and between mobile devices and other wireless devices such as headphones, cameras, and printers.

Chapter 7: "Beyond Access Controls: Protecting Stored Data" by Jason Zann

Cryptography and encrypting data traditionally have been considered areas reserved for Ph.D.s in mathematics. Now, the use of encryption algorithms in computer networks is considered a security best practice. This chapter outlines quick and useful ways to understand the value of cryptography relevant to the needs of an organization. Cryptographic algorithms, key management, and rules for selecting specific algorithms or products are discussed. Specific instructions for the best uses of encryption are also provided.

Chapter 8: "Hardening Database Access from the Web" by Rob Kraft

Critical and sensitive data now resides in databases that are accessible from web-based applications exposed via the Internet. If the access is not secure, a company can inadvertently provide access to competitors and attackers. In addition to hardening Internet servers, more attention needs to be paid to considering how best to protect the data they provide access to. The major database vendors, Microsoft, Oracle, and IBM, all provide tools for this purpose; this chapter describes how you can use them to secure databases, and what you might do if you use more than one database vendor. This chapter has recommendations for all phases of database use, from installing the database securely, to setting permissions, using application partitions, following software development best practices, monitoring and auditing database activity, and securing backups.

Chapter 9: "Hardening Cross-Platform Access Controls" by Paul Love and Roberta Bragg

Both Windows and Unix-based operating systems provide access controls for file systems. However, these controls are not equivalent. The first step in providing a robust solution to cross-platform access control is to understand these differences and then approach integration solutions from the perspective of overall security. Controls for both systems are explained in this chapter, as are hardening options for various integration solutions such as Samba, SANs, and Microsoft Services for UNIX.

Chapter 10: "Hardening Data Transport Using Encryption" by Wes Noonan

Data is vulnerable to attack when it is "at rest," meaning while it is stored on a system, and while it is "in transit," being transmitted between systems. This chapter addresses different encryption mechanisms that can be utilized while data is in transit, including VPNs, SSL, and IPSec. However, a poorly implemented security solution can be worse than no security solution at all, because it provides a sense of false security. Best practices and knowledge of the issues can ensure robust and secure communications.

Chapter 11: "Hardening Remote Clients" by Eric Seagren

Organizations pay a great deal of attention to hardening remote access servers and using strong perimeter controls for the network, but then send employees across the world with unprotected laptops and allow them to remotely access networks from distant cities and lands. A comprehensive plan to secure the remote client is required, as discussed in this chapter. Whether the client is a traditional desktop PC, a laptop, a PDA, or a smart phone, following the best practices presented in this chapter will result in a more secure remote access solution. These steps include securing remote access services, securing remote access transports, and securing clients including using a secure remote access method, configuring client firewalls, restricting access privileges, using antivirus products, keeping clients and servers patched, and training end users in secure remote access practices.

Chapter 12: "Hardening Wireless" by Wes Noonan

Wireless networks have almost become standard operating environments for large and small businesses and even home users. Advice abounds on how to secure the single wireless access point network and those that span a few users. However, scant attention is paid to the use of wireless in a large organization or in the wireless WAN. The philosophy behind securing wireless is similar in all scenarios: adopt a wireless security policy, secure authentication and data transport, provide key management, detect and eliminate rogue wireless networks, and treat wireless networks as the untrusted networks that they are. However, the wireless WAN provides additional challenges. This chapter addresses these issues.

Chapter 13: "Hardening a Mixed Unix Network" by Paul Love

The Unix operating system is the culmination of over 30 years of constant development and tinkering by a disparate group of companies and developers. Over this time period, Unix has branched out into different variations, each of which implements protocols and system procedures differently. Although all Unix systems stay true to the core Unix philosophy, their implementations of security mechanisms differ enough to cause confusion among the untrained. This chapter's goal is to provide you with a thorough understanding of the differences and similarities in security implementations among the different flavors of Unix and Windows in a heterogeneous environment. A special emphasis is placed upon the emerging popularity of Linux in the work environment and the unique concerns when intermixing Linux with Unix and Windows.

Chapter 14: "Intrusion Detection and Response" by Patrick Kelly

Knowing when someone has breached your defenses is one of the most critical aspects of network security. An intrusion detection system (IDS) can act as a constant monitor of network and host access activity in an organization. These monitors can be configured to recognize malicious and unwarranted activity and provide a tangible audit trail. Properly handled, this audit trail can provide valuable evidence in identifying an attack and determining a course of remediation. But many administrators are not properly trained to respond effectively when the IDS alerts them of a breach. It is important to be able to identify whether the alert is the result of an attack or a false alarm. IT professionals need to understand the framework of IDSs and to what extent these systems can assist the organization in maintaining a reliable, safe, and productive technology environment. This chapter provides that information.

Chapter 15: "Managing Malicious Code" by Jason Zann

Malicious code, or malware, such as viruses, Trojans, and spyware is so prevalent that the only people who have never heard of it live in a place without computers. A layered approach, or providing defense in depth, also applies to protecting a system from malicious code. You can't simply install one product or application and be totally protected. You must layer your defenses by providing perimeter defenses and by protecting servers and clients. Malicious code is difficult to detect because, in many cases, it uses preexisting system settings in a manor in which they were not originally intended to be used to produce an adverse result. Adverse results range from threatening privacy, to compromising the value of a system, to a standard annoyance. This chapter introduces various types of malware and describes how to detect it, how to report it, and ways to attempt to block it altogether.

Chapter 16: "Hardening Wetware" by John Mallery

Security professionals often lament that their systems would be secure if they did not allow people to use them. Some even go so far as to say that the weakest link in security is the human factor. There are steps that can be taken to train and educate the "human" side of security, but it takes effort, planning, and constant management support, as described in this chapter.

Part III: Once Is Never Enough

Chapter 17: "Auditing and Testing the Security of a Mixed Network" by Eric Seagren

Creating and implementing a solid and comprehensive security policy is only the first step in hardening your network. The next step is to ensure that the end result is actually secure. As this chapter discusses, an information system audit can help you understand both where your network stands in its implementation of your security plan and how your security stands up against currently accepted practices. The audit evaluates the current security configuration for compliance with the security policy and, depending on the scope defined before the audit, may test the network for how well that security works. But an audit is more than penetration testing and making check marks on a list; an audit should show you how you can improve.

Chapter 18: "Change Management" by Patrick Kelly

The adoption of solid change management practices stretches across technology boundaries. As administrators of security systems begin to configure and maintain the infrastructure, documenting a baseline standard will assist in managing changes to software, hardware, and networking components. Providing examples of processes that consider forethought, deployment, and follow-up will reduce negative impact on the performance of the security environment.

Chapter 19: "Security Patching" by Patrick Kelly

For most system administrators, it is common knowledge that no operating system is secure "out of the box," but must be patched to reduce vulnerabilities on the system. They also know that new vulnerabilities are discovered on a regular basis, so systems must be constantly patched. Patching can be a simple process on a small network, but on a large network, patching could become an incredibly burdensome task. In fact, it can become so burdensome that it is no longer properly addressed. This chapter shows you practical methods for reducing the burden of patch management, from identifying systems in need of patching, verifying licenses, obtaining patches, and applying patches in an efficient manner.

Information systems have always required maintenance. Today's maintenance, however, is not the slow process of correcting errors or eventually adding features that were promised on delivery. Today's maintenance is dominated by the need to quickly and securely apply patches developed in response to identified vulnerabilities. This chapter will tell you how to do so.

Chapter 20: "Security Review" by John Mallery

Designing and implementing security mechanisms is only part of securing a network. Security is a dynamic process and requires periodic reviews of the security posture of an organization. Are policies and procedures being ignored or bypassed? Did the latest system upgrade cause more security problems than it solved? This chapter provides descriptions of the review process and includes some unique approaches.

Part IV: How to Succeed at Hardening

Chapter 21: "Politics of Security Management" by John Mallery

Often, securing a network is only possible with management support and buy-in. Gaining management support can be a difficult task, but if system administrators learn the language of management, the challenge can be overcome. In addition to management support and approval, there are other internal political issues that cannot be overlooked. In this chapter, you will learn the language of management and different methods to identify and address political challenges.

Chapter 22: "Security Apathy" by Patrick Kelly

Not everyone sees the benefit of security. To many people, it is restrictive, burdensome, expensive, and controlling. To others, security means safety, productivity, protection, and the removal of fear, uncertainty, and doubt. These mixed views of security can collide and produce problems for those charged with securing information systems. Perhaps the biggest roadblocks to security are individuals who absolutely refuse to believe that networks are vulnerable and are constantly under attack. Their attitude is that security practitioners exaggerate the security problem in an effort to sell security products and consulting services. This chapter provides insight into getting past this stubborn attitude. To successfully promote and provide impetus for secure information system practices, you must be able to provide information on the cost of security enhancements, identify and answer key objections to security programs, and include everyone in the security effort.

Part I

Do This Now!

Chapter 1

Do These Seven Things Before You Do Anything Else!

by John Mallery

- Change Default Account Settings
- Use Administrator Accounts for Administrator Tasks Only
- Identify Unused or Unnecessary Ports
- Disable/Shut Down/Remove Unused and Unnecessary Services and Daemons
- Remove Rogue Connections: Wireless and Dial-Up
- Set Up Filters for Malicious Content for Each OS
- Test Backup and Restore Procedures

For many individuals tasked with securing a corporate network, the job can seem overwhelming. There are multiple systems in place such as web servers, application servers, and database servers. There are firewalls, routers, and intrusion detection systems to configure and maintain. There are telecommuters, remote systems, and business partners requiring access to the corporate network. For most businesses, corporate systems and data are widely dispersed.

Corporate data and information is a "multitentacled beast" and is becoming increasingly difficult to corral and protect. Data resides not only on static devices such as servers and desktop computers, but also on more dynamic and mobile systems. Personal digital assistants (PDAs), cell phones, and removable storage devices such as USB flash drives all may contain valuable corporate data. And some of these mobile devices are becoming more "covert." USB flash drives are now taking the shape of pens and key fobs and can even be found in Swiss army knives.

In addition, "attack tools" are easily accessible to those who are intent on targeting a corporation's systems and data. Password-cracking tools, virus-creation programs, and wireless access point (WAP) detectors are just some of the tools available. Web sites such as Packet Storm, http://www.packetstormsecurity.org, and The Hacker's Choice, http://www.thc.org, provide easy access to numerous tools that can be used to circumvent security mechanisms.

NOTE There is great debate over the value of some of these sites and the tools they provide. Some argue that these sites are heinous because they provide those intent on destruction step-by-step directions and tools to bring down systems and networks. Others argue that these sites provide valuable information to those interested in securing their own systems. Keep in mind that tools have no ill intentions, only the people that use them do.

Web sites are not the only source of information. The long-established *2600* magazine often publishes step-by-step directions on how to break into particular systems. *2600: The Hacker Quarterly* (once known as *The Monthly Journal of the American Hacker*) has been published since 1984. Initially designed to share information on how to hack phone systems to get free phone calls, it eventually expanded into computer-related topics. It can be found at many major bookstores and online at http://www.2600.com.

It may seem that the odds are stacked against systems administrators. However, by following these seven basic steps, you can begin to shore up your system defenses:

- Change default account settings.
- Use administrator accounts for administrator tasks only.
- Identify unused or unnecessary ports.
- Disable/shut down/remove unused and unnecessary services and daemons.
- Remove rogue connections: wireless and dial-up.
- Set up filters for malicious content for each OS.
- Test backup and restore procedures.

Taking these steps, as more fully described in the sections that follow, may deflect attacks and may even provide enough of a defense that an attacker will give up and seek more vulnerable systems.

Change Default Account Settings

Nearly all devices and systems have default account settings that are utilized to get systems up and running quickly and efficiently. These account settings are usually published username and password combinations that are easy to remember or guess by technicians who must work on a variety of systems. Unfortunately, these default account settings are often never changed or reset, which can provide easy access for an attacker. This default account information is published and updated on a regular basis. A search on Google for the phrase "default passwords" yields more than 17,000 hits.

HEADS UP!

It is important to remember that changing default account settings will not necessarily stop the determined attacker. Changing default passwords will defeat only the unsophisticated attacker who is using automated or pre-scripted attack tools. Since numerous tools exist to capture and crack user accounts and passwords, changing default account settings is only a part of the hardening process. However, changing default account settings does prevent simple attacks that rely on default passwords, and may cause an attacker to seek easier prey.

Change Default Passwords

To understand the significance of default password settings, one only has to look at the Voyager Alpha Force worm that targeted Microsoft SQL Server implementations that had a null or blank system administrator sa account password, which is the default configuration for SQL Server. This worm spread by scanning for systems with port 1433 open, the default port for SQL Server. The worm would then try to log in as sa with a blank password. The scanning activity of this worm caused network slowdowns and, in some instances, denial of service situations for the infected host.

The other issue that this example illustrates is that there are often "unknown" accounts in place on a network that are configured with default settings that can leave systems vulnerable. Many businesses thought they were immune to this worm because they "were not running any version of SQL." Much to their chagrin, their systems were slowed down and their networks clogged because the worm had attacked them. Why? The worm attacked not only SQL Server 7 and SQL Server 2000 but also implementations of MSDE, the Microsoft Data Engine, which is the desktop version of SQL Server. MSDE is used to run small databases, often at the desktop level. It is used on small databases, those less than 2GB in size. Once installed on a system, it is scheduled to run at startup. And just like its SQL relatives, MSDE has a blank default sa account password.

To learn more about this worm, see Microsoft Knowledge Base Article KB313418, "PRB: Unsecured SQL Server with Blank (Null) SA Password Leaves Vulnerability to a Worm."

Other databases have well-known administrator account passwords as well:

	Account Name	Password
MySQL	root	Null
Oracle	sys	oracle
DB2	dlfm	ibmdb2

Default database passwords are not the only passwords that are easy to find. An attacker can simply connect to http://defaultpassword.com and search through the list of over 1100 default passwords, which includes default passwords for Cisco Systems, 3Com, Linksys, and Netgear devices (among others). The ability to search for default passwords is made even more convenient because this web site provides access to web-enabled phones at http://wap.defaultpassword.com.

Finding and changing default passwords can be challenging, because there is no single tool that checks all operating systems and all devices for default passwords. OS/400 has the Analyze Default Password tool, ANZDFTPWD, but there is nothing similar for other operating systems. Running password-cracking tools such as the latest version of L0phtCrack, LC 5 (http://www.atstake.com/products/lc/), or John the Ripper (http://www.openwall.com/john/) can detect weak and default passwords. Searching default password lists, such as the one found at http://www.phenoelit.de/dpl/dpl.html, can often point out systems that may be vulnerable. Routers, firewalls, switches, and WAPs are other places where default passwords might be left in place. Change all default passwords to a more robust password by following your firm's password policy. Creating password policies and robust passwords is addressed in Chapter 16.

HEADS UP!

When searching for accounts with default passwords, do not forget to check the phone system. Nearly all phone systems have default accounts and passwords configured for troubleshooting or configuration purposes. As an example, according to http://www.cirt.net, the Siemens Hicom 100E PBX has a default user ID of 31994 with a default password of 31994. When evaluating computer system default passwords, include your phone system as part of the audit.

Rename or Hide Administrator Accounts

Every hacker, cracker, and attacker knows the name of the "superuser" accounts for every major operating system, whether it is administrator, admin, or root. If someone truly wants to take over a system, they try to log in as one of these accounts or as a user or service that has the same system privileges. This is why a tool such as the Offline NT Password and Registry Editor, which can reset the administrator password, is so valuable for attackers.

NOTE The Offline NT Password and Registry Editor theoretically works on all Windows operating systems, but it cracks only the "local" administrator account. The tool can be found at http://home.eunet.no/~pnordahl/ntpasswd/.

Renaming or hiding these accounts may not slow down sophisticated attackers but can stop the less sophisticated ones.

Renaming the Administrator Account in Windows

In Microsoft Windows XP and Windows Server 2003, to rename a local administrator account, simply do the following:

1. Right-click the My Computer icon and select Manage.
2. Expand the Local Users and Groups folder in the left panel and select Users.
3. In the right panel, right-click Administrator and select Rename.
4. Change the name of the administrator account to something innocuous.

In Microsoft Windows 2000, to rename a local Administrator account, the steps are similar:

1. Click Start | Settings | Control Panel.
2. Double-click the Users and Groups folder.
3. Click the Advanced tab.
4. Click the Advanced button.
5. Expand the Local Users and Groups folder in the left panel and select Users.
6. In the right panel, right-click Administrator and select Rename.
7. Change the name of the administrator account to something innocuous.

To further the subterfuge, change the description of the Administrator account as well:

1. Right-click the renamed Administrator account and select Properties.
2. Enter a new description. Use a general description, like Basic Account or Limited Account.

HEADS UP!

Although renaming the Administrator account in Windows systems is helpful, it will not stop a determined attacker. Although the name is changed, the security identifier (SID) remains the same.

All accounts have SIDs associated with them, and built-in system accounts have well-known and well-publicized SIDs. According to Microsoft Knowledge Base Article 243330, "Well Known Security Identifiers in Windows Server Operating Systems," the SID for the Administrator account in Windows Server 2003 and Windows 2000 is S-1-5-*domain*-500. There are tools that will show an account's SID, so a sophisticated attacker will simply look at the SID to determine the significance of an account. Even with a renamed Administrator account, this type of attacker will not be fooled.

Many of these tools utilize anonymous access, which is occasionally locked down so that these types of attacks are thwarted. However, in some environments, locking down anonymous access is not possible, so these kinds of attacks could be successful.

If the name of the Administrator account is changed, be sure the name change is documented. This is critical if the person who made the change is no longer available. It would be prudent to keep a file of critical account names and passwords in case something happens to the system administrator, especially if there is no staff redundancy. This can be a paper file kept by a member of management—the higher up the "food chain" the better. This is a business continuity concept. In fact, one administrator used to call this file the "If I get hit by a bus" file.

Another important consideration for those administrators with numerous member servers on the network is to rename each administrator account. That way, if one administrator account is compromised, the rest of the servers still have unknown

ONE STEP FURTHER

Some individuals suggest that in addition to renaming the Administrator account, you can further confuse attackers by creating a new, "dummy" Administrator account. Simply create an account named "Administrator" and enter the default administrator description for this account. Then, create an exceptionally long and complex password for the account, so that if someone tries to crack the account password, it will take them significant time and resources to do so. Even if they do crack the password, they will not be able to gain system control since this is not really an administrator account.

administrator account names. There are some administrative issues to address if these changes are made on a large network with a large number of member servers. Trying to remember all the new administrator account names is cumbersome, which may cause people to write down the new account names. Writing down the names defeats the purpose of changing the names in the first place.

Hide Admin Account in NetWare

Versions of Novell NetWare from 4.*x* on up rely on an X.500 directory structure. In this type of environment, the admin account is installed in the root of the directory tree by default. This fact is known by attackers, who can either attempt to guess the admin password or, if allowed console access, use a tool such as setpwd.nlm (available at http://www.computercraft.com/noprogs/setpwd.zip) to reset the admin password. To prevent these types of attacks, it can be helpful to move the admin account to a different container so that attackers have to work a little harder to log in as admin. Creating a separate container such as H4A (Home for Admin) can be enough to cause an attacker to move somewhere else. Be sure to provide to management documentation of this new container object for the admin account, should they ever need access to the system in the event the system administrator is no longer available.

NOTE The NetWare Loadable Module, setpwd.nlm, has been used effectively on Novell NetWare 4.*x* and 5.*x* servers to reset the admin password when the system administrator leaves an organization "unwillingly." This is a quick way to lock a disgruntled system administrator out of a network. But keep in mind that many system administrators also have other accounts they use that can be "admin equivalents." These accounts need to be disabled as well.

Leave Root Alone

In the Unix world, it is possible to rename the root account; however, this is not practical. Many processes run as root, so changing the name could cause system problems. Also, renaming the account only slows down casual attackers, since the user identifier (UID) is not changed. It is best to leave root alone.

Disable Guest Accounts

Older operating systems had the Guest account enabled by default, often without a password in place. Keep this in mind if you are administering legacy systems. To disable the Guest account in Windows 2000 and NT:

Windows 2000

1. Click Start | Settings | Control Panel.
2. Click Users and Passwords.
3. Click the Advanced tab.
4. In the Advanced User Management window, click Advanced.

5. In the Local Users and Groups dialog box, expand the Users folder.
6. In the left panel, right-click the Guest account and click Properties.
7. Select the Account Is Disabled check box.
8. Click Apply.

Windows NT

1. Click Start | Programs | Administrative Tools (Common) | User Management.
2. In the User Manager window, click Guest to highlight it.
3. Open the User menu and click Properties.
4. In the User Properties window, select the Account Disabled check box, then click OK.
5. Restart the computer for the changes to take effect.

Newer operating systems either have the Guest account disabled by default or require the addition of the account if it is needed. To avoid automated attacks on your systems, if you need to provide temporary access to visitors, use a name other than Guest, such as visitor, friend, partner, or associate.

Use Administrator Accounts for Administrator Tasks Only

Many system administrators log in to their systems with an Administrator account or equivalent and use this account for all activities performed during the day. Normally this involves nonadministrator tasks such as viewing e-mails, creating documents, researching new software, and similar tasks.

Using an administrator account for these activities is dangerous. If an e-mail attachment or downloaded tool contains malicious code and gets executed, it will have unfettered access to the system or network because it will be running with administrator privileges.

It is very important to use administrator accounts or their equivalent only when performing administrator tasks. Many operating systems provide tools that allow this type of account switching to be done quickly and effectively.

Use the runas Command in Microsoft Windows

When logged in as a normal user, an administrator can use the **runas** command to log in as an administrator to run programs and applications that require administrator privileges. For Microsoft Windows XP, Windows 2000, and Windows Server 2003, simply navigate to the application within Windows Explorer and right-click the application (with Windows 2000, hold down the SHIFT key when right-clicking) and select Run As. In the Run As window, select The Following User radio button and enter the administrator account name and password. The program now runs with administrator privileges.

If you like to have more control over your commands, use the command-line tool **runas**. The standard syntax for this command is

```
runas  /user:ComputerName\administrator cmd
```

The default action is for the user's profile to be loaded when logging in. When running this command, you are asked to supply the administrator password. After you enter it, the system responds with

```
Attempting to run cmd as user "ComputerName\administrator..."
```

The application then runs. To learn more about **runas**, type **runas /?** at the command line.

NOTE For Microsoft Windows NT 4 administrators, use the **su** utility that is available with the Resource Kit.

ONE STEP FURTHER

Using the **runas** command is a very effective mechanism for increasing the security of system administrator machines. However, many system administrators find that right-clicking or typing long commands at the command prompt is too time consuming. To improve efficiency, create desktop shortcuts for frequently run programs. Right-click the desktop and select New | Shortcut. In the Create Shortcut dialog box, type **runas** followed by the command and the appropriate parameters (never include the admin password in the shortcut).

To run a command prompt with administrator privileges, simply enter

```
runas /user:ComputerName\administrator cmd
```

When saving the shortcut, enter a name that identifies what program will be running; in this case, a shortcut title of "Runas cmd" would make it easily identifiable. It is possible to create shortcuts for many administrative programs. To learn more, see "To Create a Shortcut Using the runas Command," at http://www.microsoft.com/resources/documentation/windows/xp/all/proddocs/en-us/windows_security_runas_shortcut.mspx.

Use su and sudo with Unix Systems

The **su** (substitute user identity) command can be found in all versions of Unix. It provides the opportunity to log in as a user and switch to root only when necessary. According to the **su** man page, "**su** requests the password for *login* and switches to that user and group ID after obtaining proper authentication."

NOTE After running a program using **su**, be sure to log out and return to using a normal user account.

Some people consider the **sudo** (superuser do) command to be even more valuable. The **sudo** command enables users identified in the /etc/sudoers file to run commands as root, with logging of all commands and modifiers. This logging ability provides the opportunity to see "who did what and when." Once a user has been added to the file /etc/sudoers, all that user has to do is begin a command with **sudo** and the system will ask for the user's password. The command then runs and is logged in the /var/log/messages file. To learn more about **sudo**, type **man sudo** at the command prompt or visit "Using Sudo," Chapter 13 of the online book *Linux Home Networking,* by Peter Harrison, http://www.siliconvalleyccie.com/linux-hn/sudo.htm.

Identify Unused or Unnecessary Ports

The concept of ports can be extremely confusing for new system administrators, but it is one of the most important concepts to understand. Ports can be considered "doors" that a computer has open to allow other computers to connect to it. Each port is given a number that is intended to coincide with a particular service or program. For example, if one computer wishes to connect to another computer so that a Telnet session can be initiated, the requesting computer searches to see if TCP port 23 is open. If it is, a connection is established.

It is important to be able to recognize common port numbers so that if you see an unusual port number open on a computer, you can take corrective action. Port numbers run from 0 to 65536, with numbers from 0 to 1024 being reserved for recognized or well-known ports. Table 1-1 lists several well-known ports.

Along with learning well-known port numbers, learning some of the ports that are opened by Trojans can be useful. For example, port 31337 is used by the back-door Trojan called "Back Orifice."

Keep in mind that sophisticated attackers will not necessarily use the program's default port. Also, newer Trojans (or "remote administration tools") like bo2k have no default port; the port used must be defined by the attacker.

Because of the ability of attackers to specify particular ports their tools can use, it is extremely important to be able to identify open ports that are running on a particular

Port	Service
21, 22	FTP
23	Telnet
25	Simple Network Mail Protocol (SMTP)
53	Domain Name Server (DNS)
80	HTTP
110	POP3 Mail
135, 137, 139	NetBIOS

Table 1-1. Well-Known Port Numbers

system. Benchmarking ports on a newly installed system can help administrators to identify unusual open ports in the future.

Use netstat to Identify Open Ports

The command-line tool **netstat** allows administrators to identify open ports on a system. Versions are available for nearly all operating systems, with the only difference between versions being the switches that are available.

netstat shows the network status of a system, identifying listening ports, established connections, and other network statistics. Common switches include the following, as quoted from Windows XP Professional Product Documentation: Netstat, at http://www.microsoft.com/resources/documentation/windows/xp/all/proddocs/en-us/netstat.mspx:

- **–a** Displays all active TCP connections and the TCP and UDP ports on which the computer is listening.
- **–n** Displays active TCP connections, however, addresses and port numbers are expressed numerically and no attempt is made to determine names.

Figure 1-1 shows typical **netstat** output using the **–a** and **–n** switches (only TCP ports are shown, for clarity).

For many system administrators, this output may be extremely intimidating and confusing, causing them to stop investigating any port security issues. However, if you look closely, some of the activity on this machine is easily identified. By looking at the last half dozen lines or so of Figure 1-1, you can see that several connections have been made to port 80 on several remote systems. This most likely indicates that the user of this machine has been accessing several web sites. Notice also that more than one connection has been made to several of the sites visited. This is because browsers often open more than one connection to facilitate the downloading of content.

```
F:\>netstat -an

Active Connections

  Proto  Local Address          Foreign Address        State
  TCP    0.0.0.0:135            0.0.0.0:0              LISTENING
  TCP    0.0.0.0:445            0.0.0.0:0              LISTENING
  TCP    0.0.0.0:1025           0.0.0.0:0              LISTENING
  TCP    0.0.0.0:1027           0.0.0.0:0              LISTENING
  TCP    0.0.0.0:1029           0.0.0.0:0              LISTENING
  TCP    0.0.0.0:1031           0.0.0.0:0              LISTENING
  TCP    0.0.0.0:1033           0.0.0.0:0              LISTENING
  TCP    0.0.0.0:1034           0.0.0.0:0              LISTENING
  TCP    0.0.0.0:1035           0.0.0.0:0              LISTENING
  TCP    0.0.0.0:1036           0.0.0.0:0              LISTENING
  TCP    0.0.0.0:1066           0.0.0.0:0              LISTENING
  TCP    0.0.0.0:1067           0.0.0.0:0              LISTENING
  TCP    0.0.0.0:1068           0.0.0.0:0              LISTENING
  TCP    0.0.0.0:1069           0.0.0.0:0              LISTENING
  TCP    0.0.0.0:1070           0.0.0.0:0              LISTENING
  TCP    0.0.0.0:4101           0.0.0.0:0              LISTENING
  TCP    0.0.0.0:4107           0.0.0.0:0              LISTENING
  TCP    0.0.0.0:5000           0.0.0.0:0              LISTENING
  TCP    0.0.0.0:5003           0.0.0.0:0              LISTENING
  TCP    0.0.0.0:12345          0.0.0.0:0              LISTENING
  TCP    127.0.0.1:1027         127.0.0.1:1029         ESTABLISHED
  TCP    127.0.0.1:1029         127.0.0.1:1027         ESTABLISHED
  TCP    127.0.0.1:1036         127.0.0.1:4101         ESTABLISHED
  TCP    127.0.0.1:4101         127.0.0.1:1036         ESTABLISHED
  TCP    127.0.0.1:6999         0.0.0.0:0              LISTENING
  TCP    192.168.100.15:139     0.0.0.0:0              LISTENING
  TCP    192.168.100.15:427     0.0.0.0:0              LISTENING
  TCP    192.168.100.15:1033    192.168.100.4:524      ESTABLISHED
  TCP    192.168.100.15:1034    192.168.100.5:524      ESTABLISHED
  TCP    192.168.100.15:1035    192.168.100.4:524      ESTABLISHED
  TCP    192.168.100.15:1066    216.239.41.99:80       CLOSE_WAIT
  TCP    192.168.100.15:1067    66.102.11.124:80       CLOSE_WAIT
  TCP    192.168.100.15:1068    216.239.41.99:80       CLOSE_WAIT
  TCP    192.168.100.15:1069    216.12.136.100:80      CLOSE_WAIT
  TCP    192.168.100.15:1070    216.12.136.100:80      CLOSE_WAIT
  TCP    192.168.100.15:1073    192.168.100.5:1677     TIME_WAIT
  TCP    192.168.100.15:9391    0.0.0.0:0              LISTENING
```

Figure 1-1. Typical netstat output using the –a and –n switches

Most system administrators recognize the IP addresses of principal devices on their network. The system administrator of this machine would notice that connections have been established with IP addresses 192.168.100.4 and 192.168.100.5, and would know that these are the file and print server and mail server, respectively. Even without knowing that 192.168.100.5 is a mail server, an experienced administrator would recognize the service provided by this system by looking at the next-to-last line, where a connection has been established on port 1677. Port 1677 is the default port for a Novell GroupWise mail server. The last initial item to note is that the system is listening on port 12345. This port is often used by the well-known Trojan Netbus.

NOTE There are ports that are used by both legitimate programs and Trojans. Seeing a port open that is used by a Trojan does not necessarily mean that your system has been compromised. In the situation described in the preceding paragraph, TrendMicro OfficeScan, an enterprise antivirus program, also uses port 12345.

It is important to learn to recognize the standard ports that are open on your system so that unusual open ports will jump out at you. In addition, becoming comfortable with the **netstat** command can be extremely helpful since it is available in many operating systems.

Learning to identify which processes utilize which ports can be a time-consuming task. Although conducting research to learn what processes open particular ports is time well spent, there are tools that will help map ports to processes for you. In Microsoft Windows XP and Windows Server 2003, the **–o** switch was added to **netstat** to show the process ID (PID) for each open port. Figure 1-2 shows the output of **netstat** on the previous system, but with the **–o** switch added.

Matching the PID to its respective process is fairly straightforward and is outlined as follows in Microsoft Knowledge Base Article 323352, "How To Determine Which

```
F:\>netstat -ano

Active Connections

  Proto  Local Address          Foreign Address        State           PID
  TCP    0.0.0.0:135            0.0.0.0:0              LISTENING       820
  TCP    0.0.0.0:445            0.0.0.0:0              LISTENING       4
  TCP    0.0.0.0:1025           0.0.0.0:0              LISTENING       872
  TCP    0.0.0.0:1027           0.0.0.0:0              LISTENING       1592
  TCP    0.0.0.0:1029           0.0.0.0:0              LISTENING       1592
  TCP    0.0.0.0:1031           0.0.0.0:0              LISTENING       4
  TCP    0.0.0.0:1033           0.0.0.0:0              LISTENING       576
  TCP    0.0.0.0:1034           0.0.0.0:0              LISTENING       576
  TCP    0.0.0.0:1035           0.0.0.0:0              LISTENING       576
  TCP    0.0.0.0:1036           0.0.0.0:0              LISTENING       460
  TCP    0.0.0.0:1066           0.0.0.0:0              LISTENING       1552
  TCP    0.0.0.0:1067           0.0.0.0:0              LISTENING       1552
  TCP    0.0.0.0:1068           0.0.0.0:0              LISTENING       1552
  TCP    0.0.0.0:1069           0.0.0.0:0              LISTENING       1552
  TCP    0.0.0.0:1070           0.0.0.0:0              LISTENING       1552
  TCP    0.0.0.0:4101           0.0.0.0:0              LISTENING       1592
  TCP    0.0.0.0:4107           0.0.0.0:0              LISTENING       1592
  TCP    0.0.0.0:5000           0.0.0.0:0              LISTENING       996
  TCP    0.0.0.0:5003           0.0.0.0:0              LISTENING       1628
  TCP    0.0.0.0:12345          0.0.0.0:0              LISTENING       1072
  TCP    127.0.0.1:1027         127.0.0.1:1029         ESTABLISHED     1592
  TCP    127.0.0.1:1029         127.0.0.1:1027         ESTABLISHED     1592
  TCP    127.0.0.1:1036         127.0.0.1:4101         ESTABLISHED     460
  TCP    127.0.0.1:4101         127.0.0.1:1036         ESTABLISHED     1592
  TCP    127.0.0.1:6999         0.0.0.0:0              LISTENING       2716
  TCP    192.168.100.15:139     0.0.0.0:0              LISTENING       4
  TCP    192.168.100.15:427     0.0.0.0:0              LISTENING       4
  TCP    192.168.100.15:1033    192.168.100.4:524      ESTABLISHED     576
  TCP    192.168.100.15:1034    192.168.100.5:524      ESTABLISHED     576
  TCP    192.168.100.15:1035    192.168.100.4:524      ESTABLISHED     576
  TCP    192.168.100.15:1066    216.239.41.99:80       CLOSE_WAIT      1552
  TCP    192.168.100.15:1067    66.102.11.124:80       CLOSE_WAIT      1552
  TCP    192.168.100.15:1068    216.239.41.99:80       CLOSE_WAIT      1552
  TCP    192.168.100.15:1069    216.12.136.100:80      CLOSE_WAIT      1552
  TCP    192.168.100.15:1070    216.12.136.100:80      CLOSE_WAIT      1552
  TCP    192.168.100.15:9391    0.0.0.0:0              LISTENING       268
```

Figure 1-2. PID displayed for open ports by using the –o switch with the netstat command

Program Uses or Blocks Specific Transmission Control Protocol Ports in Windows Server 2003":

1. Press CTRL-ALT-DELETE, and then click Task Manager.
2. Click the Processes tab.
3. If you do not have a PID column, click View, click Select Columns, and then click to select the PID (Process Identifier) check box.
4. Click the column header that is labeled "PID" to sort the process by PIDs. You should be able to easily find the process ID and match it to the program that is listed in Task Manager.

Figure 1-3 shows the Processes tab of Windows Task Manager, with the running processes sorted by PID number.

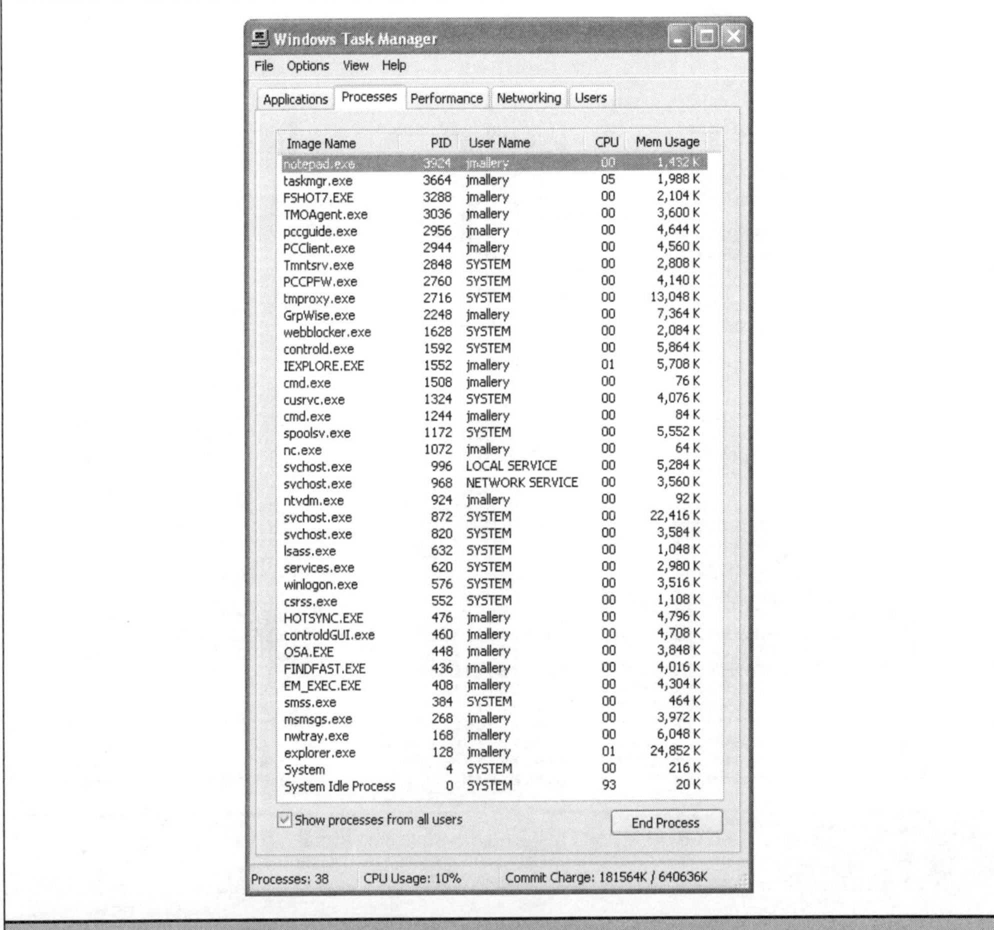

Figure 1-3. Task Manager showing running processes

To see how simple it is to map a port to a running process, look at Figure 1-2 and identify the PID for the process listening on port 12345. You will notice that the PID is 1072. Now look at Figure 1-3 and you can see that the PID is owned by nc.exe. This happens to be the executable for **netcat**, a very powerful network tool that can be used by attackers to read and write data to a target system. **netcat** can be configured to allow a remote connection to the command line (to download or learn more about **netcat**, visit http://www.atstake.com/research/tools/network_utilities/).

This application should not be running on the average system. If a "hostile" process is identified within Task Manager, it is possible to immediately disable the process by clicking the End Process button. However, this does not necessarily mean that the process will not start up again on a system reboot. Determining how the process is started is the next step.

Methods for identifying how applications or services are started are numerous. Click Start | Run and enter **services.msc** to see which services are available on the machine and how they are started. Other tools such as System Information and the System Configuration Utility can be accessed by entering **msinfo32** and **msconfig**, respectively, in the Run window. More detailed information is provided in the upcoming section "Disable/Shutdown/Remove Unused and Unnecessary Services and Daemons."

The **fport** tool, from Foundstone, is a Microsoft Windows tool for identifying which files start which process. This free tool, available at http://www.foundstone.com/index.htm?subnav=resources/navigation.htm&subcontent=/resources/intrusion_detection.htm, shows the PID, the associated process, the open port, and the path to the program that runs the particular process. This is a very helpful program. An example of its output is shown in Figure 1-4.

In addition to **fport**, there are also commercially available tools. These include products like X-NetStat, http://www.freshsw.com/xns/, and Network Monitor, which is part of the Advanced Administrative tools from G-Lock Software, http://www.glocksoft.com/aatools.htm. Many of these programs include the capability to conduct a search on a particular port number to determine the most common applications that utilize that port.

Utilize OS-Specific Tools to Identify Open Ports

netstat is available in many operating systems, the only difference being which switches are available. With Unix operating systems, to learn more about the capabilities of **netstat**, simply type **man netstat** at a command prompt. This opens the man page for **netstat**. It shows in great detail what can be done with the tool.

NOTE For those who are new to Unix, to exit a man page, press the Q key.

Useful switches include the following:

- **–a** Displays all sockets
- **–t** Displays TCP information

- **–v** (verbose) Displays more detailed information than the standard output
- **–p** Displays PID/program name

An example of the output of this command is shown in Figure 1-5.

The output of this command is extremely helpful and shows what processes are utilizing what ports. But the output is not complete. Notice in the first line that port 32768 is open, but no responsible process is listed. To determine what application or process has the port open, use the **lsof** (list open files) command:

```
lsof -i TCP:32768

COMMAND     PID    USER       FD   TYPE     DEVICE    SIZE  NODE   NAME
rpc.statd 3694   rpcuser  6u    IPv4     3330          TCP    *.32768 (LISTEN)
```

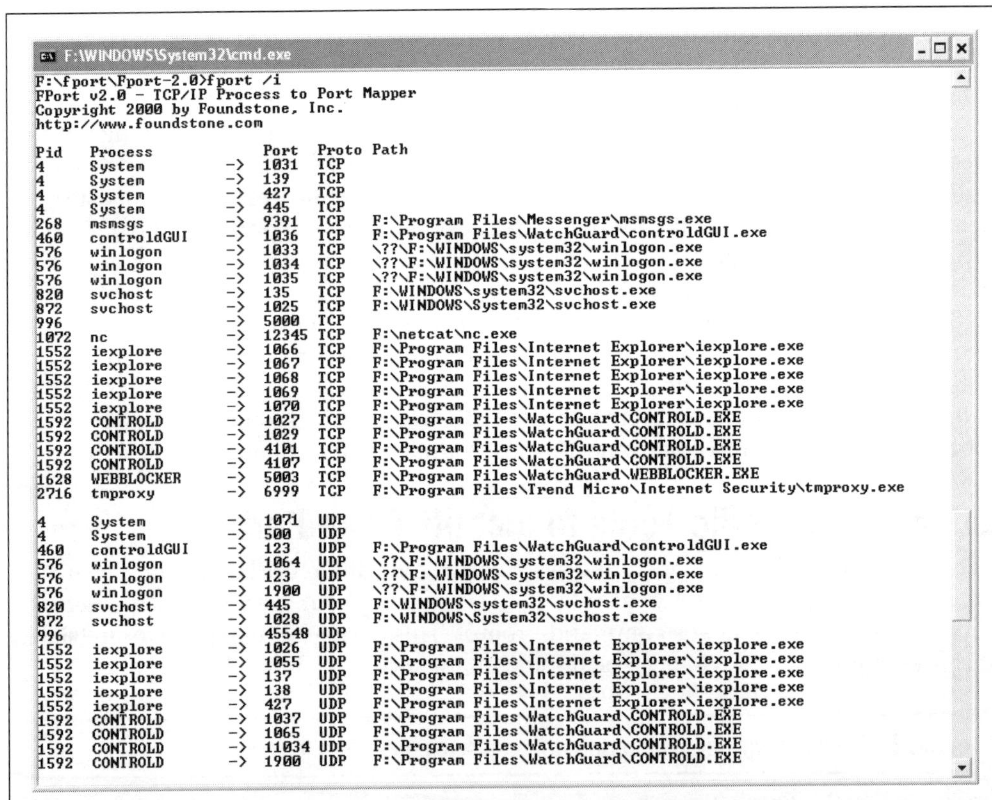

```
F:\WINDOWS\System32\cmd.exe
F:\fport\Fport-2.0>fport /i
FPort v2.0 - TCP/IP Process to Port Mapper
Copyright 2000 by Foundstone, Inc.
http://www.foundstone.com

Pid   Process            Port  Proto Path
4     System        ->   1031  TCP
4     System        ->   139   TCP
4     System        ->   427   TCP
4     System        ->   445   TCP
268   msmsgs        ->   9391  TCP   F:\Program Files\Messenger\msmsgs.exe
460   controldGUI   ->   1036  TCP   F:\Program Files\WatchGuard\controldGUI.exe
576   winlogon      ->   1033  TCP   \??\F:\WINDOWS\system32\winlogon.exe
576   winlogon      ->   1034  TCP   \??\F:\WINDOWS\system32\winlogon.exe
576   winlogon      ->   1035  TCP   \??\F:\WINDOWS\system32\winlogon.exe
820   svchost       ->   135   TCP   F:\WINDOWS\system32\svchost.exe
872   svchost       ->   1025  TCP   F:\WINDOWS\System32\svchost.exe
996                 ->   5000  TCP
1072  nc            ->   12345 TCP   F:\netcat\nc.exe
1552  iexplore      ->   1066  TCP   F:\Program Files\Internet Explorer\iexplore.exe
1552  iexplore      ->   1067  TCP   F:\Program Files\Internet Explorer\iexplore.exe
1552  iexplore      ->   1068  TCP   F:\Program Files\Internet Explorer\iexplore.exe
1552  iexplore      ->   1069  TCP   F:\Program Files\Internet Explorer\iexplore.exe
1552  iexplore      ->   1070  TCP   F:\Program Files\Internet Explorer\iexplore.exe
1592  CONTROLD      ->   1027  TCP   F:\Program Files\WatchGuard\CONTROLD.EXE
1592  CONTROLD      ->   1029  TCP   F:\Program Files\WatchGuard\CONTROLD.EXE
1592  CONTROLD      ->   4101  TCP   F:\Program Files\WatchGuard\CONTROLD.EXE
1592  CONTROLD      ->   4107  TCP   F:\Program Files\WatchGuard\CONTROLD.EXE
1628  WEBBLOCKER    ->   5003  TCP   F:\Program Files\WatchGuard\WEBBLOCKER.EXE
2716  tmproxy       ->   6999  TCP   F:\Program Files\Trend Micro\Internet Security\tmproxy.exe

4     System        ->   1071  UDP
4     System        ->   500   UDP
460   controldGUI   ->   123   UDP   F:\Program Files\WatchGuard\controldGUI.exe
576   winlogon      ->   1064  UDP   \??\F:\WINDOWS\system32\winlogon.exe
576   winlogon      ->   123   UDP   \??\F:\WINDOWS\system32\winlogon.exe
576   winlogon      ->   1900  UDP   \??\F:\WINDOWS\system32\winlogon.exe
820   svchost       ->   445   UDP   F:\WINDOWS\system32\svchost.exe
872   svchost       ->   1028  UDP   F:\WINDOWS\System32\svchost.exe
996                 ->   45548 UDP
1552  iexplore      ->   1026  UDP   F:\Program Files\Internet Explorer\iexplore.exe
1552  iexplore      ->   1055  UDP   F:\Program Files\Internet Explorer\iexplore.exe
1552  iexplore      ->   137   UDP   F:\Program Files\Internet Explorer\iexplore.exe
1552  iexplore      ->   138   UDP   F:\Program Files\Internet Explorer\iexplore.exe
1552  iexplore      ->   427   UDP   F:\Program Files\Internet Explorer\iexplore.exe
1592  CONTROLD      ->   1037  UDP   F:\Program Files\WatchGuard\CONTROLD.EXE
1592  CONTROLD      ->   1065  UDP   F:\Program Files\WatchGuard\CONTROLD.EXE
1592  CONTROLD      ->   11034 UDP   F:\Program Files\WatchGuard\CONTROLD.EXE
1592  CONTROLD      ->   1900  UDP   F:\Program Files\WatchGuard\CONTROLD.EXE
```

Figure 1-4. Output from fport

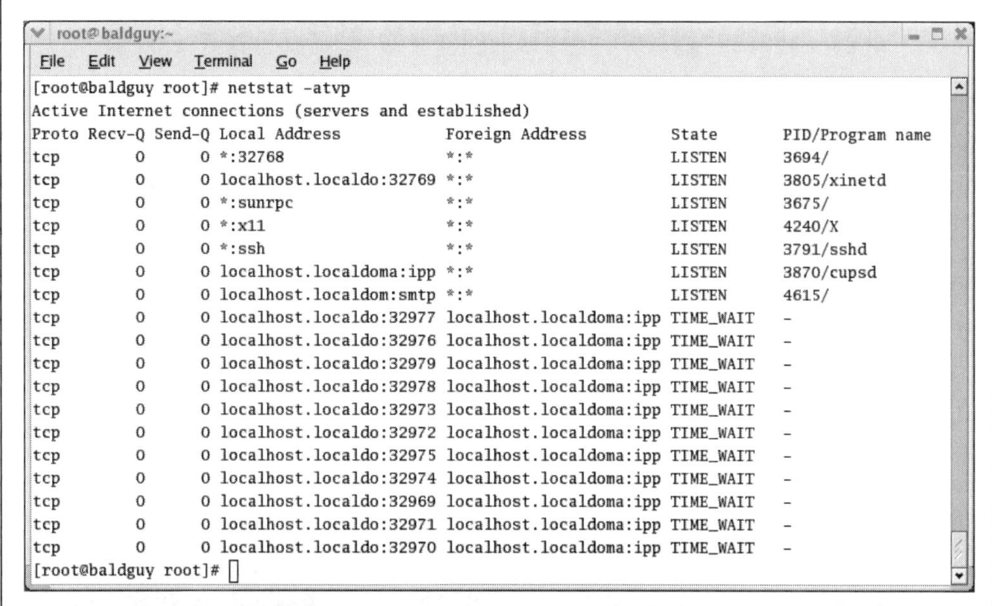
root@baldguy:~
File Edit View Terminal Go Help
[root@baldguy root]# netstat -atvp
Active Internet connections (servers and established)
Proto Recv-Q Send-Q Local Address Foreign Address State PID/Program name
tcp 0 0 *:32768 *:* LISTEN 3694/
tcp 0 0 localhost.localdo:32769 *:* LISTEN 3805/xinetd
tcp 0 0 *:sunrpc *:* LISTEN 3675/
tcp 0 0 *:x11 *:* LISTEN 4240/X
tcp 0 0 *:ssh *:* LISTEN 3791/sshd
tcp 0 0 localhost.localdoma:ipp *:* LISTEN 3870/cupsd
tcp 0 0 localhost.localdom:smtp *:* LISTEN 4615/
tcp 0 0 localhost.localdo:32977 localhost.localdoma:ipp TIME_WAIT -
tcp 0 0 localhost.localdo:32976 localhost.localdoma:ipp TIME_WAIT -
tcp 0 0 localhost.localdo:32979 localhost.localdoma:ipp TIME_WAIT -
tcp 0 0 localhost.localdo:32978 localhost.localdoma:ipp TIME_WAIT -
tcp 0 0 localhost.localdo:32973 localhost.localdoma:ipp TIME_WAIT -
tcp 0 0 localhost.localdo:32972 localhost.localdoma:ipp TIME_WAIT -
tcp 0 0 localhost.localdo:32975 localhost.localdoma:ipp TIME_WAIT -
tcp 0 0 localhost.localdo:32974 localhost.localdoma:ipp TIME_WAIT -
tcp 0 0 localhost.localdo:32969 localhost.localdoma:ipp TIME_WAIT -
tcp 0 0 localhost.localdo:32971 localhost.localdoma:ipp TIME_WAIT -
tcp 0 0 localhost.localdo:32970 localhost.localdoma:ipp TIME_WAIT -
[root@baldguy root]#

Figure 1-5. Sample output of the netstat command using –atvp

This command shows that the rpc.statd daemon is listening on port 32768.

Another option is to use the **ps** (process status) command with the **–p** switch and the PID to determine what command or process has that port open:

```
ps -p 3694
```

This also reveals that rpc.statd has the port open.

NOTE rpc.statd, also known as statd on some systems, is the file-locking status monitor and has known vulnerabilities.

Another helpful command is **top**, which displays top CPU processes. This is very similar to the Processes tab in Task Manager for Windows operating systems, which shows which applications are using what percentage of CPU resources. This can be helpful in identifying poor system performance as well as finding unauthorized programs.

Disable/Shut Down/Remove Unused and Unnecessary Services and Daemons

Identifying the applications, services, or processes that open unneeded or unnecessary ports is only the first half of removing "connection points" for attackers. The second half is to remove or disable the responsible applications, services, or processes.

Disable Unnecessary Services in Windows

The services that are disabled on a computer should be based on informed decisions and planning. There are lists of recommended services to disable, and they are relatively easy to find using the phrase "unnecessary services" (quotes required) followed by the name of the operating system. Pages 149–156 in *Hardening Windows Systems,* by Roberta Bragg (McGrawHill/Osborne, 2004), contains an extensive list of services to disable in a Microsoft environment. Disabling services can be accomplished in several ways, and the choice of which tools to use is based on how many systems need to be modified and the network environment.

Use the Services Console to Disable Services on an Individual System

The Services console is one of the easiest methods to stop or disable a particular service in Microsoft Windows 2000 or higher. To get to the Services console, follow these steps:

1. Click Start | Run.
2. Enter **services.msc** in the Open text field.
3. Click OK.
4. The Services console window opens.

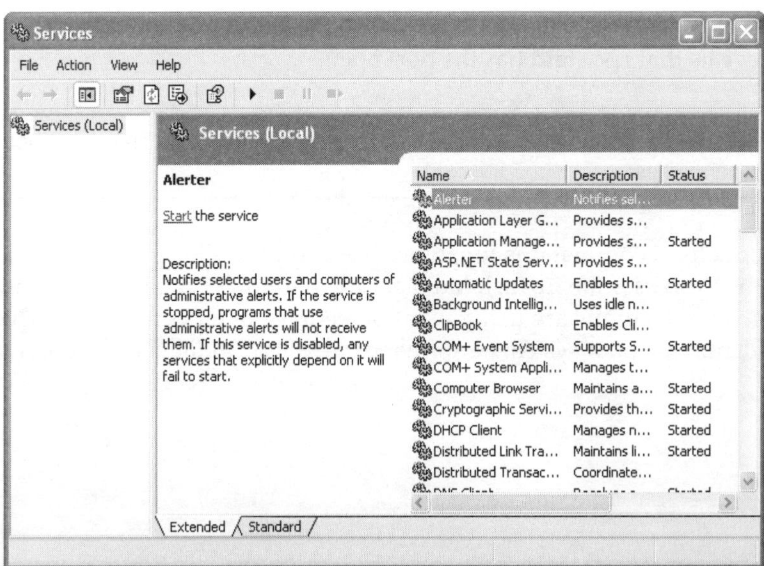

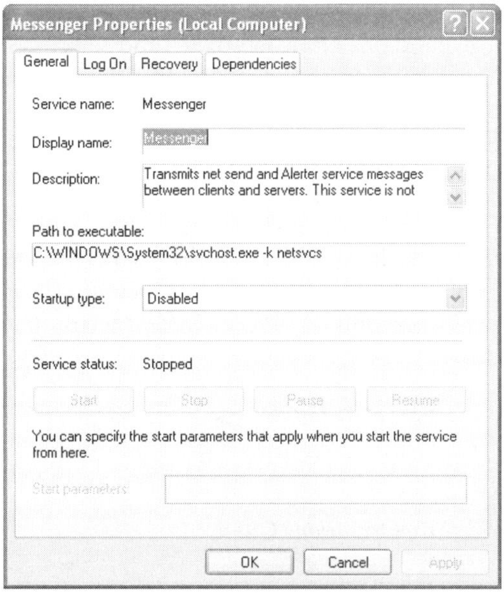

Figure 1-6. Properties window for the Messenger service

To stop a service, highlight the name of the service and click the Stop button—the small black square—on the toolbar. Or, you can right-click the name of the service and select Stop from the shortcut menu that appears.

Once the service is stopped, you want to ensure that the service will not start up again when the system is rebooted. To do this, simply double-click the name of the service and change the Startup Type to Disabled. Figure 1-6 shows the startup settings for the Messenger service (one of the recommended services to disable).

Use the MMC Security Templates Snap-In to Modify Services Across a Domain

The Microsoft Management Console (MMC) Security Templates snap-in enables you to create a custom security template that you can apply efficiently to multiple servers in a domain. Providing full step-by-step directions is beyond the scope of this discussion. However, if you have never worked with the MMC, the following steps enable you to begin "exploring."

To view and modify a security template in MMC:

1. Click Start | Run and enter **mmc** in the Open text box. Click OK.
2. The Console window will open. Click File (Windows Server 2003 and Windows XP) or Console (Windows 2000) and select Add, Remove Snap In.

3. Click Add and then select Security Templates. Click Close and then click OK.
4. In the left panel, expand one of the templates and select System Services, as shown in Figure 1-7. You can then use the right panel to select service permissions and startup options for the available services.

To make changes, simply double-click a service to open the window shown in Figure 1-8. Make the changes and click OK.

Using security templates in a production environment requires research and planning, and the ability to test the configuration in a nonproduction environment. The following resources can be extremely helpful in configuring security templates. They all can be found by going to http://www.microsoft.com and entering the name in the "Search microsoft.com for" text box.

- *Windows Server 2003 Security Guide*
- *Threats and Countermeasures: Security Settings in Windows Server 2003 and Windows XP*
- *Windows 2000 Security Operations Guide*

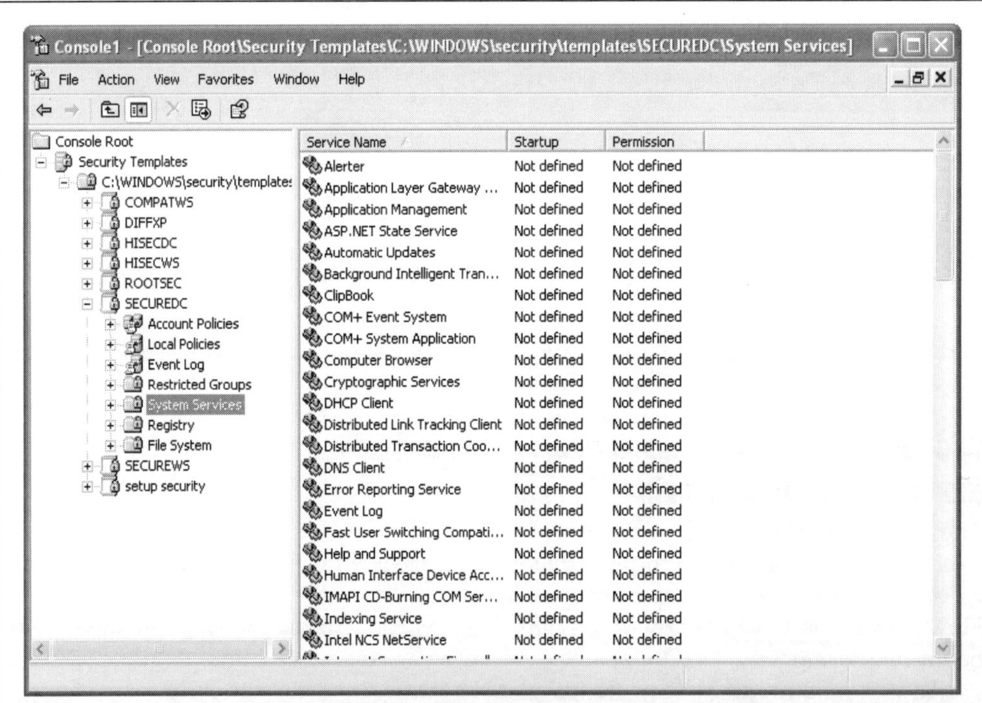

Figure 1-7. System Services view for the SECUREDC template in a Windows XP MMC

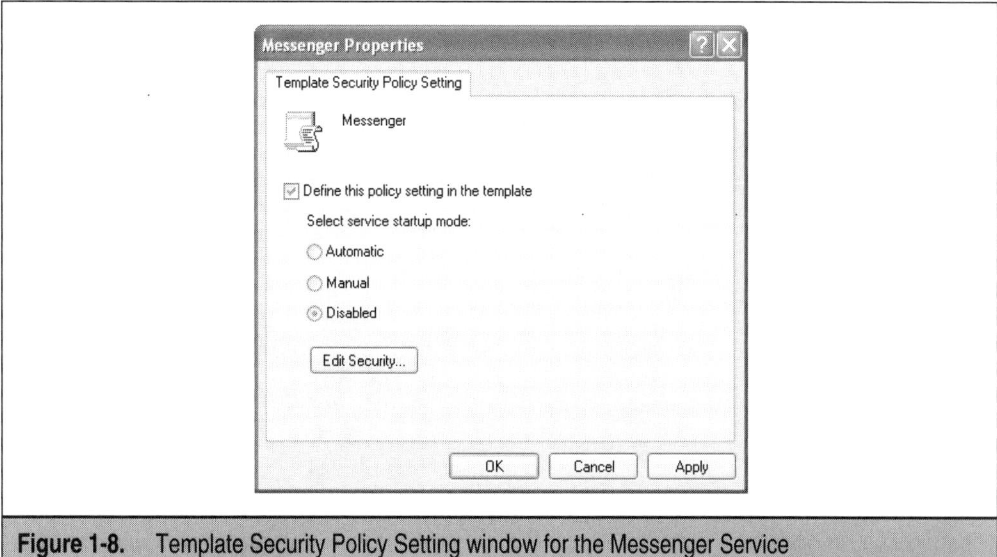

Figure 1-8. Template Security Policy Setting window for the Messenger Service

Use the System Configuration Utility to Disable Rogue Applications Scheduled to Run at Startup

Although this section does not necessarily relate to port issues, it does relate to unwanted and unauthorized applications that can be running on systems without the administrator's knowledge. There are many programs that are designed to run in a "stealthy" mode, in which they do not show up in Task Manager or in Add/Remove Programs in the Control Panel. Keystroke capture and monitoring applications are two types of programs that can be installed and configured to run in this fashion. No matter how stealthy they are, to be effective they must run at startup. Looking in the Startup tab of the System Configuration Utility, (Windows Server 2003 and Windows XP) enables you to find these applications. Access the System Configuration Utility by going to Start | Run and entering **msconfig** in the Open text box. Figure 1-9 shows the System Configuration Utility on a Windows XP system. The last two items (which have been deselected and no longer run at startup) are the executable files for two keystroke capture programs. The first is nvsr32, which is the executable for Invisible Keylogger; the second, syncagent, is the executable for Ghost Keylogger.

Disable Unnecessary Services in Unix

There are numerous methods available to configure services in Unix operating systems. For the new user, a graphical utility such as the Service Configuration program found in Red Hat is especially useful. This program can be accessed through the Start menu, by clicking System Settings | Server Settings | Services. Figure 1-10 shows an example of Service Configuration.

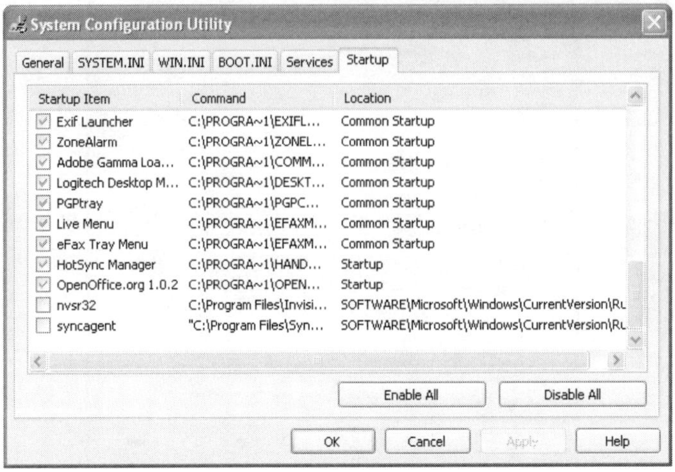

Figure 1-9. System Configuration Utility showing startup files for two keystroke-monitoring applications

With this tool, services can be stopped, started, or restarted by highlighting a particular service and clicking the appropriate button. You can also modify the startup configuration with this tool. Check or uncheck the box next to a service and then click File | Save Changes. The changes will take effect at the next system boot.

NOTE The tool Service+ from Active+ Software performs the same functions in the Microsoft Windows environment. To learn more, visit http://www.activeplus.com/us/products/sp/.

If a graphical interface is not available, several other tools are available. Entering **ntsysv** at the command line brings up a very simple interface that allows you to change the startup options for various services and daemons. For a system administrator who is not particularly familiar with Unix services, pressing the F1 key while a service is highlighted brings up a brief description of the service (this tool is available only on Red Hat–based distributions of Linux).

One of the most useful programs is **chkconfig**, which updates and queries run-level information for system services. To list the settings for a particular service, simply enter

```
chkconfig --list <service name>
```

As an example, to learn whether **sendmail** is configured to run for a particular run level, simply type

```
chkconfig --list sendmail
sendmail    0:off   1:off   2:on  3:on   4:off   5:off   6:off
```

This command shows that **sendmail** will start in run levels 2 and 3 only.

To change the configuration for a particular run level (in this case, run-level 2), enter

```
chkconfig sendmail --level 2 off
```

NOTE A run level is a particular system configuration that determines what services will run. A system can exist in only one run level at a time. In Linux the following run levels are available:
0—Halt/Shutdown
1—Single User
2—Multiuser, without network services
3—Multiuser, the default run level for most systems
4—Unused
5—Graphical Login
6—Reboot

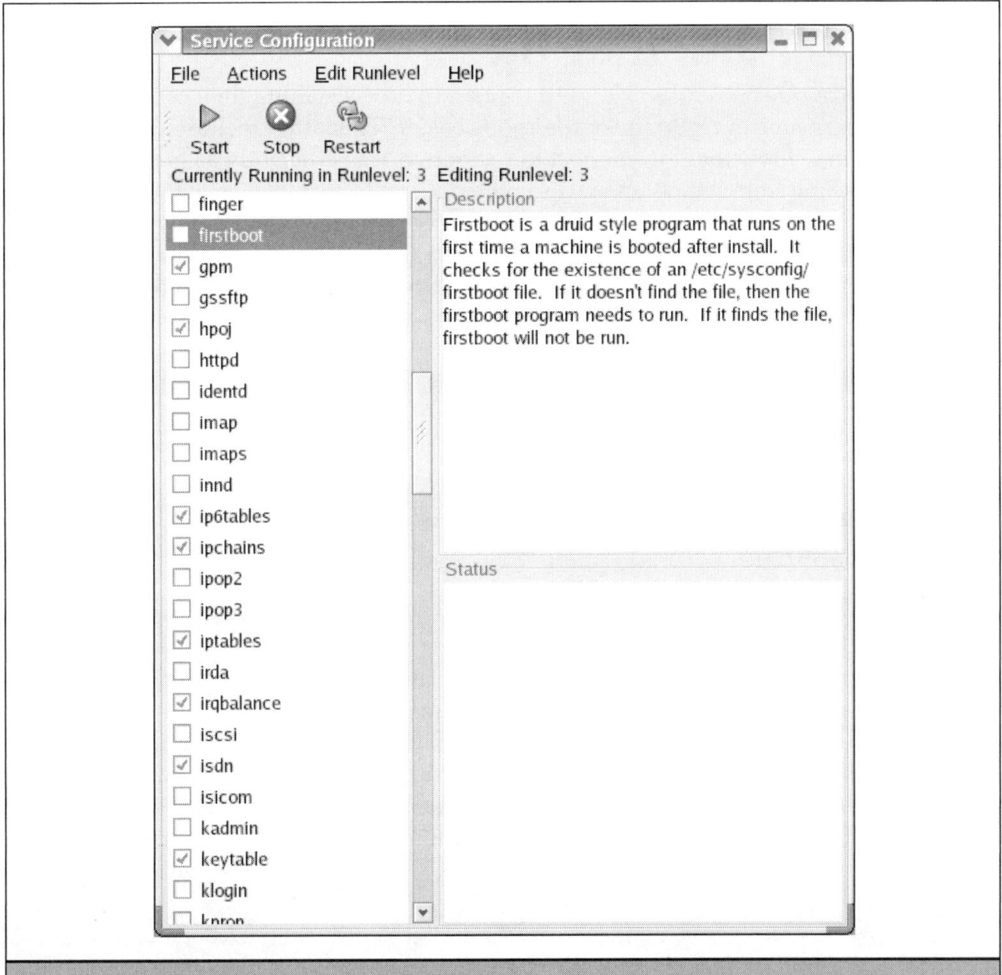

Figure 1-10. Service Configuration in Red Hat 9

HEADS UP!

Configuring services in Unix can be a complex task. The information provided here is designed to provide you with some basic information to get started. To learn more, numerous books are available, but one of the most detailed is *Real World Linux Security*, by Bob Toxen (Prentice Hall PTR, 2000). It also comes with a CD-ROM of useful tools, many of which were written and tested by Mr. Toxen. You can find information on the book at http://www.realworldlinuxsecurity.com.

Remove Rogue Connections: Wireless and Dial-Up

As long as corporate networks exist, end users will do everything they can to bypass security mechanisms to try to make their jobs easier. This often includes setting up mechanisms that allow them to connect to the network as efficiently as possible. This can mean anything from setting up WAPs in their offices so that they are not "tied down" to any particular location, to installing remote access software so that they can access their computer from home.

Because these mechanisms are installed without even the slightest thought of security, they make the corporate network extremely vulnerable.

Find All Wireless Access Points and Devices: 802.11 and Bluetooth

If you are new to the wireless revolution, a good place to start learning about its threats to corporate data is the Wireless Network Visualization Project, http://www.ittc.ku.edu/wlan/index.shtml. The site contains very detailed and accurate images of the range of many wireless networks in Lawrence, Kansas. While looking at the images, imagine how far beyond the physical confines of your building an unauthorized wireless network could spread.

There are numerous resources available for hardening wireless networks, including Chapter 8, "Hardening Wireless LAN Connections," of *Hardening Network Infrastructure* (Wesley Noonan, McGrawHill/Osborne, 2004). This section deals with finding and removing unauthorized devices only. If you are questioning the probability of having unauthorized wireless networks installed in your facility, keep several thoughts in mind. Wireless networks are deceptively easy to set up and are inexpensive. Marne E. Gordon of TruSecure put it quite simply in a recent presentation, "If you have a consumer electronics store in your community, you have a wireless network in your business."

Determining whether there is a rogue wireless network in your facility is extremely simple. You need the following equipment:

- A laptop computer.
- NetStumbler software, available for free from http://www.netstumbler.com.
- A wireless network interface card (NIC), one that can communicate with all current 802.11 technologies. When purchasing a NIC, be sure to check the NetStumbler readme file first to learn of NIC compatibility issues, http://www.netstumbler.org/showthread.php?t=10366.

If you have a large facility or campus, you may also need the following:

- An antenna, either an omnidirectional antenna or an inexpensive signal booster like Super Cantenna, http://www.cantenna.com.
- A DC-to-AC power inverter, like Radio Shack part #22-146, which provides power to your laptop through your automobile's power outlet.

This equipment allows you to drive around the perimeter of your facility or through your campus and find unauthorized WAPs. If you wish to scan the inside of the facility, it is possible to do so with additional portable equipment such as a Windows CE handheld device, a wireless network card, and MiniStumbler, the PDA version of NetStumbler.

HEADS UP!

It is important that you not underestimate the threat of rogue WAPs. The technology is inexpensive to purchase and extremely easy to get up and running. For some products, the only initial configuration required is to set the region in which the WAP will be operating. The setup manual that comes with one particular product specifically states "Do not change the other settings." The settings that are not to be changed include changing the default Service Set Identifier (SSID) or enabling WEP (Wired Equivalent Privacy), which are usually considered the first steps in securing a wireless network (although WEP is not considered an exceptionally strong encryption program). Few system administrators recognize how common wireless networks are. To emphasize this point, consider a 30-minute drive from Overland Park, Kansas, to midtown Kansas City, Missouri. This part of the country is not considered a high-technology center. But during the drive, 240 WAPs were discovered: 45 percent had no encryption, and 44 percent were using the default SSID. These WAPs were discovered without the use of an antenna or signal amplification device. Are you sure you don't have a wireless access point in your facility?

Scanning for networks is extremely simple. If your wireless NIC is installed and configured properly, simply opening NetStumbler begins the scanning process.

Taking the time to regularly scan the facility for rogue WAPs may be unrealistic for some system administrators. One solution is to engage the services of a trusted employee who moves throughout the entire facility as part of their job requirements. Wesley Noonan, in *Hardening Network Infrastructure,* suggests equipping the mail-delivery person with the appropriate technology and viewing the results of their "scanning" at the end of their shift. Other firms have enlisted cleaning crews as part of their security team.

Look for the Newest Threat: Bluetooth Devices The flexibility provided by wireless devices is prompting many individuals to embrace the concept of personal area networks, small networks of personal devices that communicate without wires or cables. The Bluetooth protocol is one of the driving forces behind this development. Both the 802.11 and Bluetooth protocols utilize the 2.4 GHz radio spectrum. However, the range for Bluetooth-enabled technologies is significantly smaller, although newer devices may have a much wider range.

There is some debate over the true vulnerabilities of Bluetooth-enabled devices; however, there is a threat that unknown and unauthorized devices on a network could "siphon off" proprietary data without the knowledge of system administrators or management.

The tools that are needed to scan for Bluetooth-enabled devices are similar to those needed for 802.11*x* devices. You need only a laptop with a Bluetooth adapter, such as those offered by TDK Systems, http://www.tdksystems.com/products/range.asp?id=1, and a scanning tool. Several Linux based tools include

- **Redfang** http://www.atstake.com/research/tools/info_gathering/
- **Bluesniff** http://bluesniff.shmoo.com/
- **btscanner** http://www.pentest.co.uk/cgi-bin/viewcat.cgi?cat=downloads§ion=01_bluetooth

TDK Systems provides a free Microsoft Windows–based tool, called BlueAlert, and the only requirement is that you must be using one of TDK Systems' adapters (see Figure 1-11). The BlueAlert help file describes the tool in this manner, "BlueAlert provides visual pop up notifications of the Bluetooth devices in range. When a device has come into range of your PC a pop up box will appear on your screen to inform you. This gives you the first opportunity to access its services."

It is important to look for Bluetooth devices on a regular basis. However, because they are mobile devices, you may not detect them when they are in use. Creating a strong "no tolerance" policy prohibiting the use of these devices, combined with regular scanning, is the only effective way to minimize the impact of these devices.

An excellent resource for learning about Bluetooth issues is the whitepaper by Ollie Whitehouse, "War Nibbling: Bluetooth Insecurity," which you can find at http://www.atstake.com/research/reports/acrobat/atstake_war_nibbling.pdf.

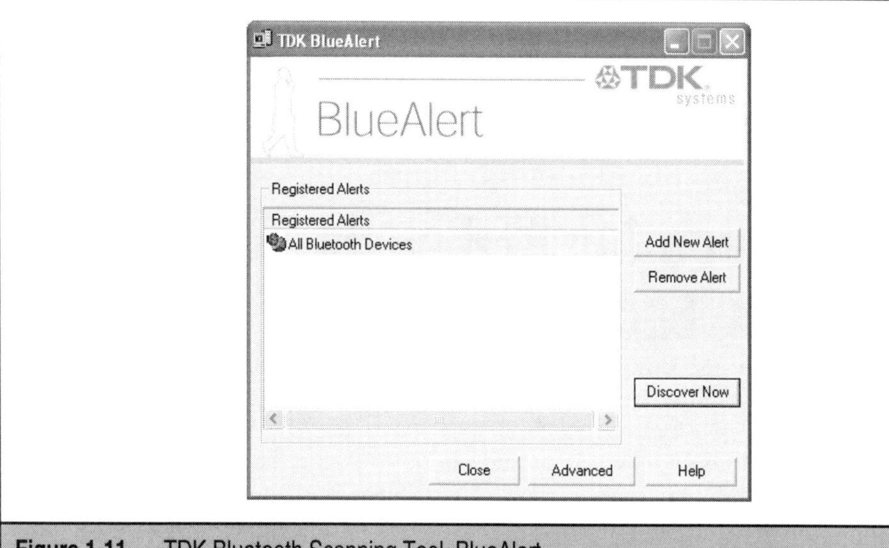

Figure 1-11. TDK Bluetooth Scanning Tool, BlueAlert

Remove Rogue Dial-Up Connections

For many system administrators and IT professionals, the thought of using a dial-up connection to accomplish any technical task is laughable. Although broadband access is widely accessible and inexpensive in some areas, dial-up networking is still the only option available in some areas. And for many users, the ability to dial into their office computer to gain access to the corporate network is enticing. Modems and phone lines are inexpensive, as is the software that makes dial-up networking possible. An end user can easily have a phone line installed in their office, with the bill coming directly to them, not to accounts payable. This type of dial-up access is usually not secure and can be a significant threat to an otherwise secure network.

Detecting and removing this type of access can be difficult. There is not a single surefire way of detecting rogue dial-up connections, other than visual inspection of the back of every desktop PC in a business. This may not be practical. The following steps should help you to eliminate this type of access:

1. Create a "no tolerance" program that begins with a strong policy—and enforce it.
2. Conduct periodic inspections of workspaces.
3. Create an anonymous reporting mechanism so that employees can report inappropriate modem usage.
4. If possible, review phone bills/invoices for unfamiliar numbers.
5. Utilize war-dialing tools to identify modems attached to known company phone lines.

NOTE War-dialing tools include, among others, ShokDial (http://www.securityfocus.com/tools/557), a popular Linux-based tool; Phone Tag (http://www.pelttech.com/security/tools.htm), a limited Windows-based tool; THC Scan, a DOS-based tool (same URL as Phone Tag); and ModemScan (http://www.wardial.net). Commercial tools include PhoneSweep (http://sandstorm.net/products/phonesweep/).

Set Up Filters for Malicious Content for Each OS

Many businesses and system administrators feel that if they have some form of protection from malicious code installed at the gateway, they do not have to protect additional systems or resources. For businesses with limited resources, this is the first step in providing protection from malicious code, but it should not be considered adequate protection. There is a significant amount of malicious code in existence, and newer and more creative code is being created on a regular basis. If a business relies on a gateway appliance alone, it has a single point of failure and may be extremely vulnerable if the device malfunctions or new code is written that bypasses the device. It is important to have programs in place on each system to identify, block, and remove malicious code.

Evaluating antivirus products can be a daunting task because of the large number of products available. One place to start looking for information is the ICSA Labs Anti-Virus site, http://www.icsalabs.com/html/communities/antivirus/index.shtml. ICSA Labs has an antivirus program certification process, which states that a product must do the following to be certified (http://www.icsalabs.com/html/communities/antivirus/certification.shtml):

1. Provide protection to computer systems and media from computer virus intrusion.
2. Provide detection of computer viruses on an infected computer system or media.
3. Provide for recovery from a computer virus's infection.

NOTE If a product has not received ICSA certification, it does not necessarily mean it is a faulty product. It may mean it has not been submitted for certification.

Purchasing a product that is ICSA-certified is a good way to protect against malicious code, because the testing process involves testing the product against a library of known viruses and Trojans.

If you implement a product that is not ICSA-certified, you can test its capabilities by using the eicar.com antivirus test file. The eicar.com test file is simply a string of ASCII characters that triggers the "virus detected" response of antivirus programs. The file can be downloaded at http://www.eicar.org/anti_virus_test_file.htm. If a system detects the file, it does not necessarily mean that the program is "robust," but if it doesn't detect the file, you should consider implementing another solution.

Test Backup and Restore Procedures

One of the constant rallying cries of security professionals is, "Back up your systems!" That cry is a valid one, but the one part that is often left unsaid is, "Make sure the backups are valid!" For a system administrator, there is no worse feeling in the world than trying to restore data after a system failure or malfunction and discovering that the backup tapes are empty. Many experienced administrators have spent long weekends manually restoring data after the restore process has failed. This is possible in a small business, but for a larger company, the inability to restore data can be extremely expensive, and usually costs one or more administrators their jobs. This testing should be done on a regular basis, with the schedule being determined by business needs and available resources. Having the ability to restore mission-critical applications is much more important than having the ability to restore archived internal memos (unless, of course, the firm is involved in some high-profile litigation).

CAUTION Many system administrators become rather complacent about testing the restore process because their systems are running with RAID arrays. Under no circumstances should a RAID array be considered a fallback position for the backup and restore processes. There have been many situations where multiple hard drives have failed at the same time. This happened to a utility company that had multiple hard drives fail on a server, and no valid backups. It cost the company $5 million to manually re-create the data that was lost.

For smaller companies, testing the restore process can be relatively simple:

1. Create a Restore folder on the server.
2. Copy multiple files into this folder.
3. Allow the backup process to run, making sure that the new folder is included in the backup.
4. After the backup has run, delete the folder and its contents.
5. Restore the data from the backup tape.
6. Verify that the data was restored.

If the data was restored, then the restore process was successful and the company can rest a little easier knowing that the process works. If the data is not restored, it may be necessary to run checks on the backup hardware and software and run the test again with a different tape.

For larger organizations, the process is similar, but it may be necessary to add additional steps to the process. If backup tapes are stored offsite, it would be prudent to run through the process of determining which tape is required for the restore and then request the tape from the storage facility. Even if the tapes are perfectly functional, if it takes an inordinate amount of time for the tapes to be delivered or the tapes cannot be found, it may not matter that the tapes contain valid backups.

These tests should be run on production systems, after taking appropriate precautions to minimize unplanned downtime. This is the only way to ensure that the process works on the equipment that may be called upon to conduct the restore. If you are unfamiliar with the backup and restore software, however, practicing with it on a test system or network first is advisable.

Part II

Take it From the Top: Systematically Hardening Your Enterprise

Chapter 2

Break the Network into Common Areas of Functionality for Security

by John Mallery

- Select a Segmentation Model
- Select Appropriate Methods for Segmenting Networks

The tendency in many organizations is to provide free and open access to all systems and data. On the surface this sounds like an excellent idea. By opening up the network, there are no impediments to restrict access to data, which in turn improves efficiency and significantly impacts the business's bottom line. Unfortunately, this is a fallacy. This type of thinking *will* impact the bottom line, but not in a positive manner. Such an organization may have robust security mechanisms in place at the gateway to its network, to protect itself from Internet threats, but fails to recognize that internal employees are the greatest threat to a network and its data.

Although estimates vary widely, many security professionals believe that as many as 80 percent of security compromises are caused by internal staff. Even if a company's own employees were not interested in attacking systems or stealing data, their lack of technical sophistication can cause security breaches. An employee who inadvertently opens a virus-laden e-mail attachment can shut down a network that is completely wide open. In addition, many companies provide access to personnel other than employees. Contractors, temporary employees, and consultants are often provided with access to corporate systems. A wide-open network provides opportunities for third parties to gain access to data and systems they have no reason to access. There have been instances where trusted third parties have actually "attacked" an organization. One company in particular was dismayed to discover that an IT security company had installed keystroke-capturing software on key employees' computers.

For these reasons, it is extremely important to segment a network into areas of common functionality. The concept of "defense in depth" that is often applied to protecting a business from external attacks applies to internal defenses as well.

NOTE "Defense in depth" is the concept of applying multiple layers of security to protect important assets. Many people utilize this concept to protect paper files and don't even realize it. Paper files often are kept in locked file cabinets, in a locked room, which is inside a locked building that sits behind a locked and gated fence. When applying this concept to IT security, imagine data that is encrypted, sits on a file server, which resides behind a firewall, which is behind a router with properly applied access control lists. Defense in depth should be applied to critical data, since it is not advisable to rely on only one defense mechanism for protection. Network segmentation is part of the defense-in-depth concept.

Select a Segmentation Model

Segmenting a network can be accomplished in many ways. As in all areas of network security, appropriate evaluation and planning should be conducted prior to segmenting a network. Determine what the impact will be if certain buildings, departments, and individuals are segmented from other parts of the network or network segments. When preparing for network segmentation, segments can be created based on the following criteria:

- Job responsibilities
- Threat level

- Risk level
- Service types
- Business needs

Segment Network Based on Job Responsibilities

Segmenting a network based on the job responsibilities of particular departments is a good first step in reducing threats to critical systems and data. This is not just a good idea from a security perspective, it also helps you to maintain compliance with numerous regulations. Many regulations such as HIPAA (Health Insurance Portability and Accountability Act) and GLBA (Gramm-Leach-Bliley Act) require businesses to take steps to restrict access to proprietary data. These regulations are designed to protect "nonpublic information" of clients and employees. These regulations are fairly specific and address different issues.

In the case of HIPAA, the primary concern is protecting personal healthcare information, as outlined in section 164.306 (see the upcoming sidebar for the complete text). Segmenting the network will help you to comply with the first two general requirements of HIPAA because it helps you to "ensure the confidentiality, integrity, and availability" of protected information and "protect against any reasonably anticipated threats."

HIPAA Section 164.306. Security Standards: General Rules

a. General requirements. Covered entities must do the following:
   1. Ensure the confidentiality, integrity, and availability of all electronic protected health information the covered entity creates, receives, maintains, or transmits.
   2. Protect against any reasonably anticipated threats or hazards to the security or integrity of such information.
   3. Protect against any reasonably anticipated uses or disclosures of such information that are not permitted or required under subpart E of this part.
   4. Ensure compliance with this subpart by its workforce.

In the case of GLBA, the requirements address financial records, including bank records, credit card information, and so forth, as stated in section 6801 (see the following sidebar for the complete text). As with HIPAA, placing confidential information in a separate network segment can help you to comply with GLBA. Network segmentation can help maintain confidentiality, protect against anticipated threats, and limit access to confidential information to authorized parties.

GLBA Section 6801. Protection of Nonpublic Personal Information

a. Privacy obligation policy

It is the policy of the Congress that each financial institution has an affirmative and continuing obligation to respect the privacy of its customers and to protect the security and confidentiality of those customers' nonpublic personal information.

b. Financial institutions safeguards

In furtherance of the policy in subsection (a) of this section, each agency or authority described in section 6805(a) of this title shall establish appropriate standards for the financial institutions subject to their jurisdiction relating to administrative, technical, and physical safeguards

1. to insure the security and confidentiality of customer records and information;
2. to protect against any anticipated threats or hazards to the security or integrity of such records; and
3. to protect against unauthorized access to or use of such records or information which could result in substantial harm or inconvenience to any customer.

HIPAA and GLBA are not the only regulations in effect. The Sarbanes-Oxley Act addresses corporate accountability and includes section 404, "Management of Internal Controls," which is designed to ensure the protection of financial records, specifically to prevent the modification of these records. Although initially focused on publicly traded companies, some believe that privately held firms will eventually be held to the same standards.

NOTE These regulations are quite detailed and impact many industries and businesses. If you are unfamiliar with these regulations, it is recommended that you take the time to learn as much as you can about them. Information on these regulations can be found at the following web sites: Sarbanes-Oxley Act (SOX), http://www.law.uc.edu/CCL/SOact/soact.pdf; Health Insurance Portability and Accountability Act (HIPAA), http://www.hhs.gov/ocr/hipaa/; Gramm-Leach-Bliley Act (GLBA), http://www.ftc.gov/privacy/glbact/index.html.

By isolating proprietary data in a separate network segment, access is significantly restricted. Because of the sensitive nature of personnel and financial records, many businesses begin segmenting their networks with the human resources (HR) and accounting departments. Servers running HR and accounting applications are placed in a separate network segment and only appropriate personnel are granted access to these systems. Although none of the legislation mentioned requires segmentation, it does require restricting access to confidential information. Placing confidential information in separate network segments is an excellent first step in restricting access.

HEADS UP!

Many businesses appropriately segment HR and accounting departments and their respective data and applications from the rest of the corporate network. However, these businesses often provide a workstation in a common area that allows employees to check on benefits, sick and vacation time accrued, etc. These workstations are often unsupervised and provide a direct link to proprietary information, bypassing security devices. One organization attempted to secure this connection by requiring employees to use a login name and employee ID to log in to the HR systems. What the organization failed to realize is that its employee badges contained not only a picture and name, but also the employee ID. Learning other employee IDs is a trivial matter in this environment. And, in fact, this oversight was exploited and an employee was able to access another employee's health history. Information regarding treatment for a mental illness was discovered and used against the unsuspecting employee when he ran for public office. Does your organization want to be involved in a lawsuit that stems from such negligence?

For many IT professionals, the concept of segmenting a network is simple, and can be done regardless of the physical location of employees. Moving cables in a wiring closet, adding a separate router for the segment, or configuring a virtual LAN (VLAN) are fairly straightforward tasks. However, isolating a department from a "digital perspective" is not enough. It is also important to restrict physical access to workstations and terminals if you want to maintain control of who accesses proprietary information. An unattended workstation that is turned on and logged into the network can allow unauthorized individuals access to confidential information. Many businesses physically separate HR and accounting personnel from the rest of the organization, providing office space in an area with very restricted access control. Employees from other departments are prohibited from entering this area without authorization or an escort.

HEADS UP!

VLANs are an excellent mechanism for segmenting networks, but should not be considered a solution in and of themselves. VLANs (which are addressed later in this chapter in the section "Use VLANs") should be considered one part of the segmentation process. Keeping in mind the phrase "defense in depth," VLANs must be combined with solid physical separation, firewalls, antivirus tools, Virtual Private Networks (VPNs), and so forth. Never rely on a single mechanism to protect a network segment.

Other departments that can be segmented from the rest of the organization include

- Legal
- Executive management
- Security
- Warehouse facilities
- Sales and marketing
- Telecommuters
- Departments with high-bandwidth requirements

Segment Network Based on Threat Level

Another mechanism to isolate mission-critical information is to provide separate network segments to departments or networks that pose the greatest threat. In educational facilities, students are often provided with network access so they have the resources necessary to pursue their education and complete assignments. With the inquisitive nature of many students ("I wonder what will happen if I do this?"), it is extremely important to restrict their activities to nonsensitive areas of the network. Many schools that do not isolate the student network from the administration network discovered that students could change grades, access personnel records of teachers, and wreak havoc on the network.

Computer labs that are used to test new hardware and software can also pose a significant risk. Software, even "shrink wrapped, fresh out of the box" software can perform unpredictably. Providing separate, isolated space for these labs can help protect mission-critical systems.

Wireless networks are notoriously vulnerable to attack. In fact, some organizations feel the risk is so great to the corporate network that wireless networks are completely banned. But some businesses find the flexibility provided by a wireless network to be such a benefit that they install one anyway. In this situation the wireless network should be isolated from mission-critical systems. Because of the threat that improperly configured wireless networks pose, they should be treated and segmented as another hostile, untrusted network. For additional information on the security of wireless networks, see Chapter 12.

NOTE Until recently there has been a shortage of vendor-neutral wireless network training available. Planet3 Wireless has created a series of Certified Wireless Network Professional training and certification programs. Additional information can be found at http://www.cwnp.com. This site is also a great repository of information on wireless networking.

Segment Network Based on Risk Level

Some departments in an organization are not only a significant threat to the organization, but can be high-risk targets as well. Research and development labs can pose a threat to a network because individuals that work in these labs are focused on their research alone and do not have the time or patience to be aware of what their systems are doing. But these R&D labs can also be a target, particularly because they are often the location where future projects and products are developed. In some instances, the future of a company depends on maintaining the confidentiality of this information.

In the legal industry, "war rooms" pose a similar problem. War rooms are areas where legal teams involved in litigation work together to create their strategies for court. Many of these war rooms are created during multidistrict litigation or class action law suits in which there is a significant amount of money at stake. In this situation, the nontechnical lawyers and paralegals pose a threat, but the material they are creating is also a target. Departments and network segments such as these are a double-edged sword when it comes to IT security issues. Maintaining security of network segments that include these departments requires multiple layers of security mechanisms.

Segment Network Based on Service Types

Segmenting a network based on job responsibilities and on threat level are two methods of segmenting a network. Another method is to segment the network based on service types. A typical example are the DMZs that businesses create for their public-facing services, such as web servers, FTP servers, and DNS servers. A DMZ (from the military phrase "demilitarized zone") is created to keep private and public assets separated and can be created in several ways. One of the most effective DMZs is to isolate the public-facing servers between two firewalls, as shown in Figure 2-1.

This type of configuration provides multiple benefits to an organization and system administrators:

- Internet-based services can be provided while reducing the threat to internal data and systems.
- Since public-facing services are separated from business systems, it is much easier to identify an attack aimed at business systems.
- The second firewall provides redundancy should the first firewall fail.
- Intrusions can be identified faster.

Segment Network Based on Business Needs

There are numerous advantages to segmenting a network. Some individuals may argue that the costs of segmenting a network outweigh the advantages, but this perspective is a little short sighted. Yes, initially it may require additional hardware and staff to install

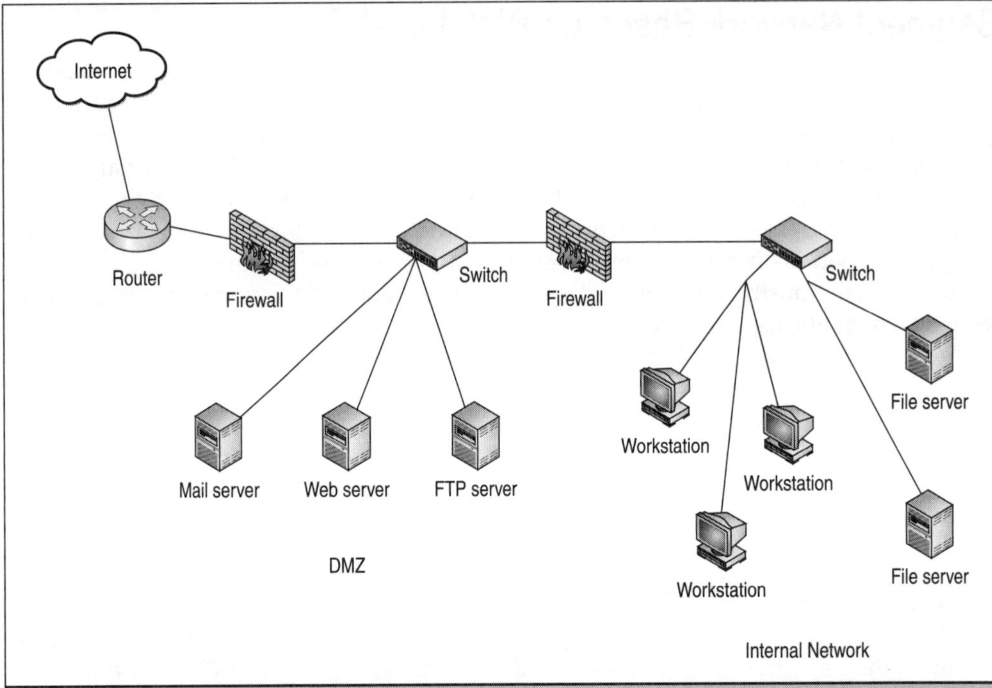

Figure 2-1. Simple DMZ configuration

and configure the devices, but over the long term the benefits will significantly outweigh the initial cost. Providing economic support for security recommendations can be difficult, and requires proper research and presentation of findings. This topic is addressed in greater detail in Chapter 21.

HEADS UP!

When setting up a DMZ, it is important to remember that the servers that are installed in this network segment should be hardened as much as possible. Some administrators feel that since the systems are between two firewalls, no hardening is necessary. Keep in mind that attacks can be mounted through what appears to be legitimate traffic, bypassing firewalls. Buffer overflows are an example. Shut down unnecessary services, configure the servers so that they can't "talk" to each other, and configure the firewall to prevent the servers from initiating a connection with a system on the Internet. If you remember that the servers are designed to serve requests from the Internet only, you will be able to significantly harden the DMZ.

NOTE When evaluating new security mechanisms and methodologies, it is extremely important to examine the financial impact any changes will have on your company. Executive management and stockholders are focused on anything that positively impacts the bottom line of the financial statement. Being able to demonstrate cost savings is the best way to get approval for any new security implementation. Determine cost savings from objective third parties or organizations that have implemented the identical solution being evaluated. Vendors of security products are more than willing to provide the cost savings of their particular products, but their data can often be skewed in their favor. These issues will be addressed in greater detail in Chapter 21.

Attack Containment

Perhaps the greatest advantage of segmenting a network is the ability to contain the impact of attacks or breaches to only a portion of a network. Isolating an attack means that the risk to data and systems is minimized and the cost of recovering from an attack is significantly reduced. Imagine an organization that adds a wireless segment to its corporate network to provide greater flexibility to its workforce. Wireless networks are notoriously insecure and provide access points outside the physical confines of the business. If a wireless network is not segmented from the rest of the corporate network, once the wireless network is compromised, the entire system is compromised. But if the wireless network is segmented from the rest of the network using a router and firewall combination, any breach of the wireless network will not necessarily mean a breach of the entire system.

Segmenting networks also reduces the impact of unintentional attacks caused by users. If a user introduces a virus into a wide-open network, the network will need to be completely shut down in order to recover. But if the virus is introduced into a network segment, only that segment of the network will be impacted. This will significantly reduce the cost to recover from the incident. The importance of segmenting a network to contain an attack can best be demonstrated by the Sasser Worm outbreak in May of 2004. It is believed that the Sasser Worm caused a disruption of RailCorp's radio network in Sydney, Australia, leaving 300,000 passengers stranded when only 20 percent of the system's trains were able to run (http://www.sophos.com/virusinfo/articles/sassertrain.html). In this type of situation, isolating the radio network from other systems might have reduced or eliminated the impact of the worm. There is no business reason for an e-mail–based worm to impact the railroad's radio network. Segmenting the "user" network from the radio network could have completely prevented this problem.

Although honeypots and honeynets have questionable value in containing an attack, they are extremely interesting and can provide excellent information on hacking methodologies and exploits. They can be a useful tool in a security professional's toolkit. Multiple tools exist, including the Deception Tool Kit (DTK), http://all.net/dtk/dtk.html, honeyd, http://www.honeyd.org, and the commercial product, Specter, http://www.specter.com. Several excellent resources include the Honeynet Project, http://www.honeynet.org, and *Honeypots: Tracking Hackers*, by Lance Spitzner (Addison-Wesley, 2002).

HEADS UP!

Some organizations have taken the concept of attack containment one step further by adding a honeynet or honeypot to their network. Quite simply, *honeynets* and *honeypots* are decoy systems, placed on a production network, that are designed to attract attackers like "bees to honey." The theory is that attackers will spend their time attacking the decoy and ignore the production systems. One of the leading experts on honeypots and honeynets (two or more honeypots connected together), Lance Spitzner, does not feel that honeypots should be used for prevention, but rather are better suited for detection: "A honeypot's greatest value lies in its simplicity, it's a device that is intended to be compromised. This means that there is little or no production traffic going to or from the device. Any time a connection is sent to the honeypot, it is most likely to be a probe, scan, or even attack." (From "The Value of Honeypots, Part One: Definitions and Values of Honeypots," by Lance Spitzner, *Security Focus,* October 10, 2001, http://www.securityfocus.com/infocus/1492.)

Some individuals do not consider honeynets and honeypots a form of attack containment, only attack misdirection. These individuals think that allowing any type of hostile traffic into a network, even a DMZ, is a very dangerous concept.

There are legal issues to consider before employing a honeypot or honeynet. Many individuals consider them a form of entrapment. Be sure to check with legal counsel before implementing a honeypot on a production network.

Reduce Monitoring Costs

Few organizations have a staff surplus in their IT department. IT staff members spend their days responding to immediate problems. They have limited time and resources to participate in proactive monitoring of systems. The direction they receive from management is to focus on functionality and efficiency; security responsibilities are often on the bottom of the priority list. Because of this, the IT staff has limited time available to monitor activity on the network, and has limited time to try to identify hostile attacks. If a network is segmented so that mission-critical systems are isolated, the IT staff members can focus their energies on monitoring traffic entering or attempting to enter the network segment that contains these mission-critical systems. They will have less information to review, making the task of detecting anomalous traffic much easier. Administrators should recognize that all systems need to be monitored periodically, not just network segments hosting critical systems. A segmented network provides the opportunity to prioritize monitoring activities, to essentially apply limited resources to critical areas first. This is similar to the triage concept used in hospital emergency rooms.

Reduce Access Points to Critical Data

A properly segmented network provides limited access to critical data. If traffic can travel through only one entry point into a network segment, it is much easier to restrict access. With wide-open networks, numerous resources have to be utilized to configure individual systems and multiple access points. Once again, it is important to keep in mind that although network segmentation provides the ability to limit network access and reduce monitoring needs, do not consider it to be a stand-alone solution. Reducing access points to critical data does not reduce the need for firewalls, intrusion detection, and log monitoring.

Select Appropriate Methods for Segmenting Networks

There are many methods to segment a network, from the incredibly simple to the extremely complex. As you establish the gateways to each particular segment, it is important to remember one concept, "default deny," which means to automatically deny all traffic unless it is specifically allowed. This goes against the grain for many businesses and system administrators that use the concept of "default allow," which allows all traffic unless it is specifically denied. This is a dangerous approach and can often leave holes and vulnerabilities if not configured properly. Default deny is a much safer concept, but can initially cause workflow problems if necessary traffic is not specifically allowed. But this can be adjusted as necessary, by opening up to traffic on an as-needed basis.

The default deny concept applies not only to gateway borders, but to nearly all network security implementations. Default deny is often a tough policy to sell to management. The following are a few approaches that often are effective when proposing the implementation of default deny:

- Quantify the cost to the business if a network breach occurs and mission-critical data is stolen or destroyed. Using questions like "Could the business survive the loss of the accounting server?" can often help strengthen the security stance of a business.
- Present a corollary of a nontechnical approach. This is perhaps the best approach, especially to those who are not technically sophisticated. There is not a business today that does not control access to its physical facilities. Signs such as "Authorized Personnel Only," "Keep Out: Employees Only Past This Point," and "Trespassers Will be Shot on Sight" are the equivalent of "gateway" security. No business would allow a hostile intruder into the executive suites, just as no business should allow a hostile intruder into the network.

Start by Segmenting at the Server

In all cases, support network segmentation by controlling access to data using file permissions. In a small business, the only network segmentation will probably be between the business network and the Internet, so using file permissions may be the only practical way that data can be partitioned and protected within the network.

Segmenting the network should begin with an evaluation of the permissions assigned to different files and applications at the server level. Although tightening permissions does not create a truly segmented network and all of its associated benefits, it addresses the issue of segmenting information so that users or groups have access only to the information that they need to perform their work. As an example, in most organizations, accounting records and software are accessible only by individuals in the accounting department, and possibly executive management. Denying access to additional members of the organization provides a good starting point to protecting financial records and information. But most importantly, "segmenting at the server" is essential to protecting information should an attacker get past perimeter defenses.

Some readers may argue that file permissions do not create true network segments. But in smaller networks, file permissions combined with other access-control mechanisms, such as login restrictions, may be the only way to create any form of segmentation.

Some guidelines for setting permissions include (from the *Implementing Microsoft Windows 2000 Professional and Server* course manual, Module 6, "Managing Data by Using NTFS"):

- Grant permissions to groups as opposed to users
- Group resources to simplify administration
- Only allow users the level of access that they require
- Create groups according to the access that the group members require

The concept behind permissions is nearly identical for most operating systems, but each operating system uses slightly different terminology for implementing permissions. From a security perspective, it is important to truly understand the concept of permissions for the operating systems for which you are responsible. Permissions are often overlooked or simply ignored because they can be time consuming to understand and configure. The significance of permission problems is appropriately addressed by Bob Toxen in *Real World Linux Security*, Second Edition (Prentice Hall, 2002): "Most of the Linux distributions carry on the proud yet inappropriate philosophy of defaulting to having much more permissive a set of file permissions than they should." It takes time to understand file permissions, regardless of the operating system.

Most operating systems have different levels of configuration options that allow administrators to be extremely specific as to who or what can access a particular folder or file. Both Microsoft Windows and Linux have graphical tools to view and set permissions on their resources. Simply select a file, right-click, and select Properties. Within the

Properties window, select either the Security tab or the Permissions tab, depending on the operating system. This is a great way to make changes when you need to make them quickly or need to make only a limited number of changes. Command-line tools included in batch files enable you to make changes more efficiently. For Microsoft Windows operating systems, the tool to use is cacls (NT 4.0, 2000, and XP) or xcacls (2000 and XP). xcacls is part of the Windows 2000 Resource Kit and can be downloaded from, http://www.microsoft.com/windows2000/techinfo/reskit/tools/existing/xcacls-o.asp. For Linux systems, there are numerous tools for working with file permissions, including getfacl, setfacl, chmod, and chown. For more detailed information regarding file permissions, see Chapters 9 and 13. Detailed information on Windows file permissions can be found in Chapter 10, "Harden Data Access," of *Hardening Windows Systems*, by Roberta Bragg (McGraw-Hill/Osborne, 2004).

Use Gateway Devices to Segment Networks

Although addressing file permissions at the server level is helpful, true segmenting of the network begins at the perimeter with "gateway routers." From a security perspective, routers are nearly identical to the security checkpoints located within airports. You must provide the proper "credentials" in order to pass through the checkpoint and continue on your journey. The same is true for network packets—they must provide the proper credentials to the router before the router will allow them to continue on their journey.

Use Access Control Lists

One of the easiest ways to segment a network is through access control lists (ACLs). These lists can be applied to both the inbound and outbound directions of a router interface, restricting traffic to only the traffic that is needed. ACLs are based on the source IP address of network packets. These ACLs enable routers to function as a mini-firewall. Many organizations utilize ACLs to block traffic from IP address blocks belonging to known spammers or countries that have a lenient attitude toward hackers. To see what address blocks other people and organizations consider hostile, search the Web with the phrase "IP address blacklist." An example of a blacklist can be found at http://www.kgb.to.

NOTE It is important to recognize that routers are not designed to be full-fledged firewalls and should never be considered a substitute for a firewall. It is possible for an attacker to spoof the IP address of an allowed source.

With Cisco routers, creating ACLs is fairly straightforward. Standard IP ACLs are numbered from 1–99 and filter on source IP address only.

HEADS UP!

When discussing gateway security devices, it is important to have a basic understanding of the Open Systems Interconnection (OSI) reference model. This is a theoretical model designed to represent the communications between computers and can be helpful in determining which security methodology is appropriate for your business. The OSI reference model, shown here, is a layered model with each layer communicating with the layers immediately above and below it.

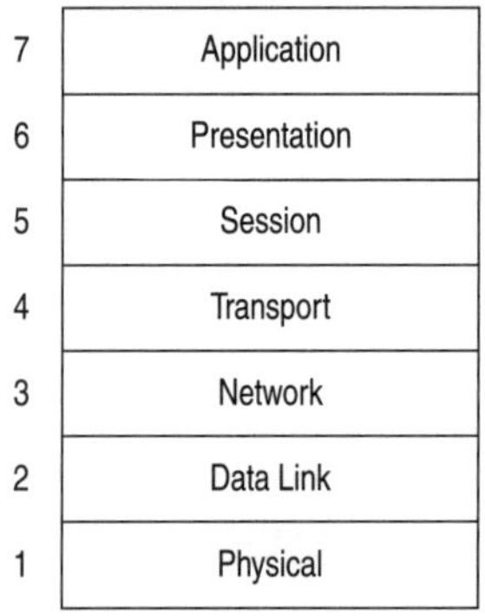

7	Application
6	Presentation
5	Session
4	Transport
3	Network
2	Data Link
1	Physical

When selecting methods to filter or segment traffic, take the time to understand at which level of the model these devices operate. The more levels at which they operate, the more protection they can provide, but they also require more processing power and add more latency to the traffic. In some instances, providing filtering at a lower level of the model is sufficient, such as blocking traffic based on IP address, while in other instances, such as blocking specific e-mail attachments, filtering at a higher level of the model is required. The OSI model truly embraces the concept of "defense in depth." For more detailed information on the OSI model, visit http://www.cisco.com/univercd/cc/td/doc/cisintwk/ito_doc/introint.htm#xtocid5.

When dealing with IP ACLs, there are two options that the router can consider for network packets, **permit** or **deny**. The syntax for an IP ACL looks like this:

```
access-list <access list number 1-99> <permit/deny> <source address>
<wildcard mask> <log>
```

When a packet reaches a router, the router reviews the ACL and acts on the first line that matches the packet's source. It then acts on the packet; it goes no further down the list. This is why it is extremely important to configure ACLs correctly, because if a rule is placed in the wrong position in the list, it is possible to block desired traffic. A simple ACL might look something like this:

```
CorpRouter(config)#access-list 5 deny host 192.168.100.32
```

This list will block all traffic originating from host 192.168.100.32. This list can also be written as

```
CorpRouter(config)#access-list 5 deny 192.168.100.32 0.0.0.0
```

The 0.0.0.0 is referred to as the *wildcard* or *wildcard mask* and tells the router which bits of the address to match and which to ignore. A mask of 0.0.0.0 requires the source IP address to match exactly.

Masks are often easier to understand if examined in dotted-decimal notation. A mask of 0.0.0.0 can be represented like this in dotted-decimal notation:

```
0000-0000.0000-0000.0000-0000.0000-0000
```

A mask of 255.255.255.255 is represented as all 1's in dotted-decimal notation:

```
1111-1111.1111-1111.1111-1111.1111-1111
```

The significance of 1's and 0's in a particular position in a mask is explained very well by Donald Lee in *Enhanced IP Services for Cisco Networks* (Cisco Press, 1999): "A zero in a bit position tells the router to match the bit; that is, to compare the bit in the packet's source address to the same bit in the pattern. Conversely, a one tells the router to ignore the bit—to skip a comparison of the bit in the packet to the same bit in the pattern."

Masks can be created to allow any or all portions of an address block to be acted upon. A list that will allow a range of addresses looks like this:

```
CorpRouter(config)#access-list deny 192.168.100.32 0.0.0.15
```

To identify the range of addresses denied, simply look at the address and the mask in dotted-decimal notation:

IP Address – 11000000.10101000.01100100.00100000
Mask – 00000000.00000000.00000000.00001111

This shows that the last four bits can be either a 1 or a 0, because the 1 tells the router to ignore the comparison of bits in that location. So the range would go from 192.168.100.32 to 192.168.100.47 or, in dotted-decimal notation,

```
11000000.10101000.01100100.00100000 to 11000000.10101000.01100100.00101111
```

Access control lists are created one line at time until the list is completed. Here is a simple list:

```
CorpRouter(config)#access-list 7 permit 0.0.0.0 255.255.255.255
CorpRouter(config)#access-list 7 deny 192.168.100.0 0.0.0.255
CorpRouter(config)#access-list 7 deny 172.16.3.3 0.0.0.0
```

This ACL accomplishes the following things. The first line allows all traffic to enter the router (it could also be written as "permit any"). The second line denies all traffic arriving from address block 192.168.100.0–192.168.100.255. And the last line denies traffic from host 172.16.3.3. There is actually one additional line that is not written and does not appear when reviewing the list. This is the **deny any** rule and it is included in every list as a security mechanism.

This is a simple example, but ACLs can be very detailed. However, exceptionally long ACLs can significantly impact network traffic. If a router has to go through a long list for every packet that enters it, slow throughput will be the result. It is recommended that ACLs be configured so that the majority of network traffic is matched in the beginning of the list. This will improve the efficiency of the router. Figure 2-2 demonstrates how an ACL functions.

HEADS UP!

When creating ACLs on a router port that faces the Internet, be sure to block any spoofing attacks by blocking inbound traffic originating from an internal IP address. Since private IP addresses should not be coming into a network from the Internet, blocking these addresses will help prevent a spoofing attack. The following ACL will block private IP addresses (as well as loopback addresses):

```
deny 10.0.0.0 0.255.255.255
deny 172.16.0.0 0.15.255.255
deny 192.168.0.0 0.0.255.255
deny 127.0.0.0 0.255.255.255
```

While standard IP ACLs provide filtering on source address alone, extended ACLs, which number from 100–199, can filter not only on source address, but also on destination address, protocol, destination port, precedence level, and type of service. The syntax for an extended ACL is

```
access-list <access list number 100-199> <permit/deny> <protocol>
<source address> <source wildcard mask> <source port><destination address>
<destination address mask> <destination port><log><options>
```

An example of an extended ACL that will allow mail traffic (Simple Mail Transfer Protocol, or SMTP, which opens port 25) from any host through to a mail server with IP address 192.168.100.75 looks like this:

```
permit tcp any 192.168.100.75 0.0.0.0 eq 25
```

In this example the list will allow traffic from any IP address to connect to port 25 on host 192.168.100.75 (eq is shorthand notation for "equal to").

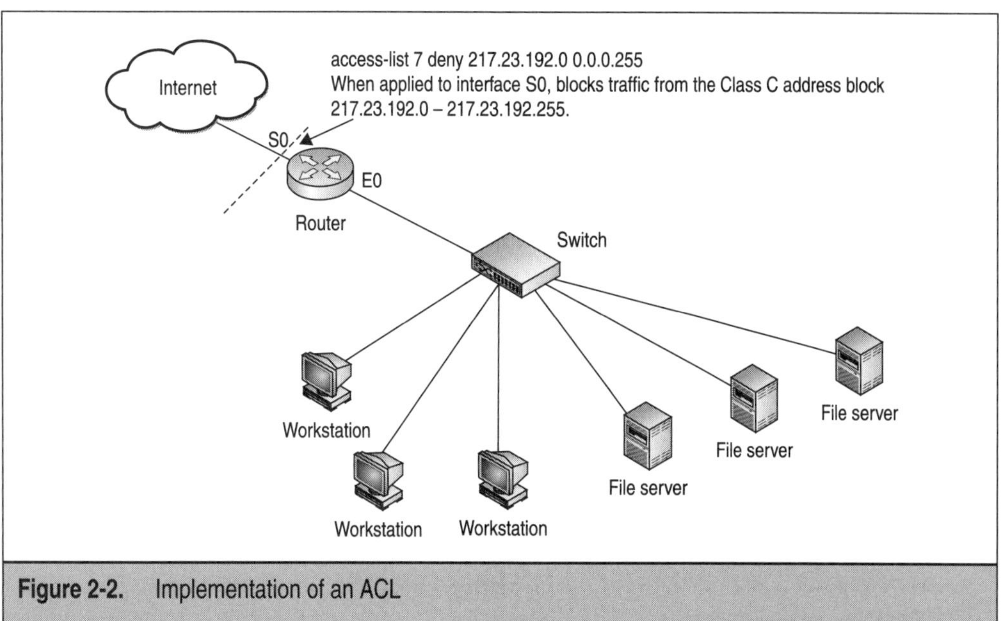
access-list 7 deny 217.23.192.0 0.0.0.255
When applied to interface S0, blocks traffic from the Class C address block
217.23.192.0 – 217.23.192.255.
Internet
S0
E0
Router
Switch
Workstation
Workstation
Workstation
File server
File server
File server

Figure 2-2. Implementation of an ACL

Extended ACLs enable you to add even more control over the types of traffic that can enter a network segment. The following list blocks FTP traffic from addresses 192.168.100. 5 through 192.168.100.15 to addresses 172.16.1.5 through 172.16.1.9 while allowing all IP traffic:

```
access-list 105 deny tcp 192.168.100.5 0.0.0.10 172.16.1.5 0.0.0.4 eq ftp
access-list 105 permit ip any any
```

Applying this list in a business environment could be very beneficial. Figure 2-3 shows how this specific ACL could be applied to prevent the sales department from connecting to the HR and accounting departments using FTP.

There are several resources available for those interested in learning more about ACLs. Matt Briddell's GCFW practical assignment, "A Comprehensive Perimeter Security Architecture for GIAC Enterprises," contains a very detailed section on ACLs; it can be found at http://www.sans.org/rr/papers/23/839.pdf. Chapter 6, "Deploying Basic Security Services," in *Enhanced IP Services for Cisco Networks* has some excellent information as well.

Use Firewalls

Utilizing routers and ACLs is a great way to begin segmenting a network, but they are simply not enough. Routers essentially perform only protocol-based filtering, and it is possible to spoof "accepted" addresses and attack systems by using acceptable protocols

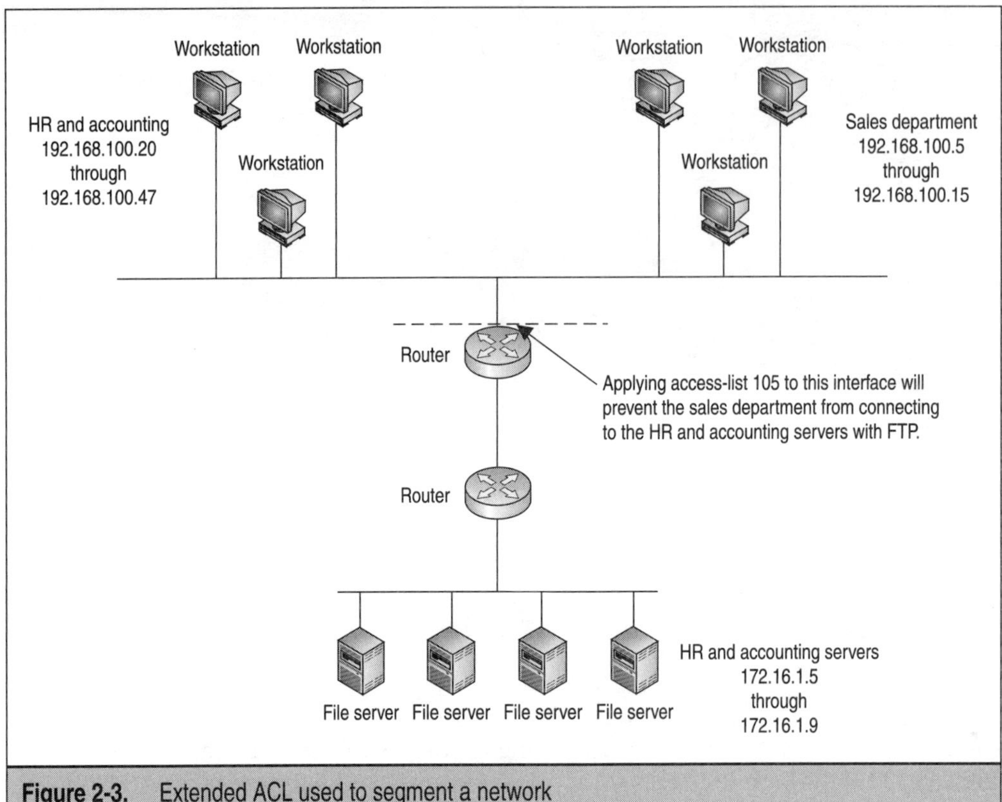

Figure 2-3. Extended ACL used to segment a network

or by spoofing acceptable protocols. The NetBIOS Name Server Protocol Spoofing vulnerability is an example of a protocol-spoofing attack (see Microsoft Security Bulletin MS00-047 for additional information). In addition, routers only work at Layer 3 of the OSI model, whereas firewalls have the ability to filter traffic at higher layers. Firewalls examine traffic in a similar manner to the way in which routers examine traffic, but firewalls have the ability to perform more intense examinations than routers and can more readily identify a malicious attack.

NOTE An appropriate firewall can offer incredible protection to an internal network or network segment; however, many firewalls also have vulnerabilities, so it is important to patch a firewall as needed. Firewalls need to be maintained in a similar manner to other network devices. They are not designed to be installed and ignored.

Installation of Firewalls Is Mandatory for All Businesses

It is absolutely imperative that networks and systems directly connected to the Internet be protected by a firewall. Systems are under attack constantly; in fact, tools to perform attacks are readily available at sites like Packet Storm (http://www.packetstormsecurity.org) and attack methods are outlined in publications like *2600 Magazine* (http://www.2600.com). It is blatantly irresponsible to connect a system to the Internet without implementing a firewall solution, but this is done on a regular basis. I recently encountered an organization from which an employee had embezzled $2 million over several years. The network was directly connected to the Internet without a firewall, the network operating system required no passwords for authentication, and every desktop had PCAnywhere installed with no password required. The company lost clients, lost its reputation, and struggled to survive. In this situation, most companies never recover from the financial loss or loss of reputation.

In addition to being more robust than routers when it comes to filtering incoming traffic, firewalls also provide more options to filter outbound traffic. This means that user activity can be monitored and inappropriate activities can be blocked. The average user does not need the ability to utilize FTP or Telnet services, and the ability to use these services can be blocked at the firewall.

NOTE Although firewalls are excellent products, they are not infallible and should not be relied upon as the only security mechanism put in place within an organization. Firewalls should be implemented in conjunction with additional tools and policies. As an example, implementing methods for preventing file sharing of music and videos is suggested since many file-sharing programs poke holes in firewalls.

A firewall is designed to filter traffic between trusted and untrusted networks, and there are different techniques for accomplishing this task. It is important to understand the different types of firewalls in existence so that you can select the appropriate solution for your organization. During your firewall selection process, keep in mind the following useful thoughts posted by Marcus J. Ranum on the firewall-wizards list at Insecure.org (Sept. 26, 2000), http://seclists.org/lists/firewall-wizards/2000/Sep/0317.html:

1. The easier it is for outside systems to talk to you, the less secure you are.
2. The more transparent operations are for users, the more transparent they will be for a trojan horse (and by extension, the less secure you are).

HEADS UP!

When evaluating firewalls (or any security product for that matter) be sure to ask for input from an objective third party. If possible, try to get feedback from other individuals or organizations that are currently using the product you wish to purchase. This may be somewhat time consuming, because many organizations are reluctant to discuss their security mechanisms. It is not recommended to rely strictly on the recommendations of a vendor. Some vendors have the tendency to "stretch" the capabilities of a particular product in order to make a sale.

What follows is a description of the basic firewall types currently in existence. Some current firewalls are hybrids of one or more of these types. Your selection should be based on the acceptable level of risk that your organization has determined suits its business needs.

Packet-Filtering Firewalls There are two types of packet filters, static and dynamic. A static packet filter is exactly what a router accomplishes when it is configured with ACLs. As traffic enters the firewall, it examines the source and destination addresses, protocol, and source and destination ports before forwarding the data. Using this filtering system is certainly more secure than a wide-open network, but it is not an extremely secure solution since it is possible to spoof the originating address and add malicious content to accepted protocols.

The dynamic packet filter (also called *stateful packet filter*) not only examines packets at Layer 3, it also reaches into Layer 4 to learn connection information. Dynamic packet filters are aware of the differences between new and established connections. If a connection is initiated from the internal network, the dynamic packet filter can examine the reply received, verify that it is part of an established "conversation," and then allow the verified reply into the network. Although this awareness makes dynamic packet filters more secure, they still are susceptible to spoofing and are not aware of packet contents.

Circuit-Level Firewalls Circuit-level firewalls work at Layer 6, the presentation layer, of the OSI model and provide one more security check than is provided by dynamic packet filters. Circuit-level firewalls verify the handshaking process of each connection (SYN, ACK, SYN-ACK) and the sequence numbers of "conversations." Although circuit-level firewalls add an additional level of security, they still are unaware of the contents of data packets.

Application-Level Firewalls Application-level firewalls copy, filter, and forward incoming and outgoing data packets and examine packet contents. This prevents direct connections between the trusted and untrusted networks. In addition, application-level firewalls handle data packets only for the services for which they are configured. Other services are blocked. Early implementations of this type of firewall (also called a *proxy server*) slowed system performance and were not transparent to users. With the advances in processor power and new developments by firewall manufacturers, application-level firewalls now have reduced impact on system performance. Figure 2-4 shows the incoming SMTP proxy configuration window for a WatchGuard Firebox II. Notice that it provides the ability to block e-mail attachments of specific file types.

Hybrid Firewalls New gateway products can no longer be classified as a specific firewall type since they perform multiple functions. A recent ad for a series of Symantec gateway appliances describes them as "…full inspection firewall appliances that integrate intrusion prevention and intrusion detection, antivirus, content filtering, anti-spam and VPN." These products can help reduce the cost of implementing gateway protection, but they can also introduce a single point of failure into the network.

Use VLANs

Segmenting a network can most readily be accomplished by setting up virtual LANs on a network. VLANs enable you to create separate networks regardless of the physical location of a user or system.

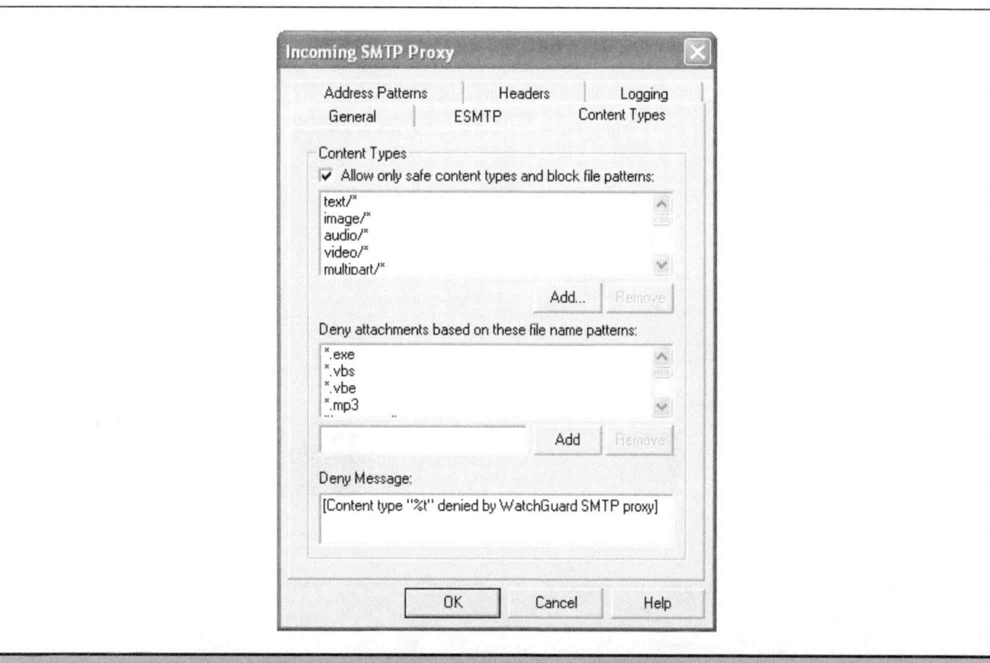

Figure 2-4. Incoming SMTP Proxy window from Watchgurad Firebox II, which has the capability to block incoming file types and attachments

Historically, one method of creating networks was to connect all system devices to a centralized hub. This provided connectivity but was not highly efficient because all traffic would be sent to all devices on the network. This created one large collision domain. With the advent of switches, it was possible to have each device be in its own collision domain. However, all devices were still in a single broadcast domain. Although the concept of "collisions" made it sound like it was amazing that network traffic could be transmitted at all, the technology worked extremely well, except perhaps in high-volume or extremely large networks. The ability to segment networks by creating VLANs provides the ability to create separate broadcast domains, which improves performance and creates a certain level of security. Figure 2-5 shows a network divided into two separate VLANs.

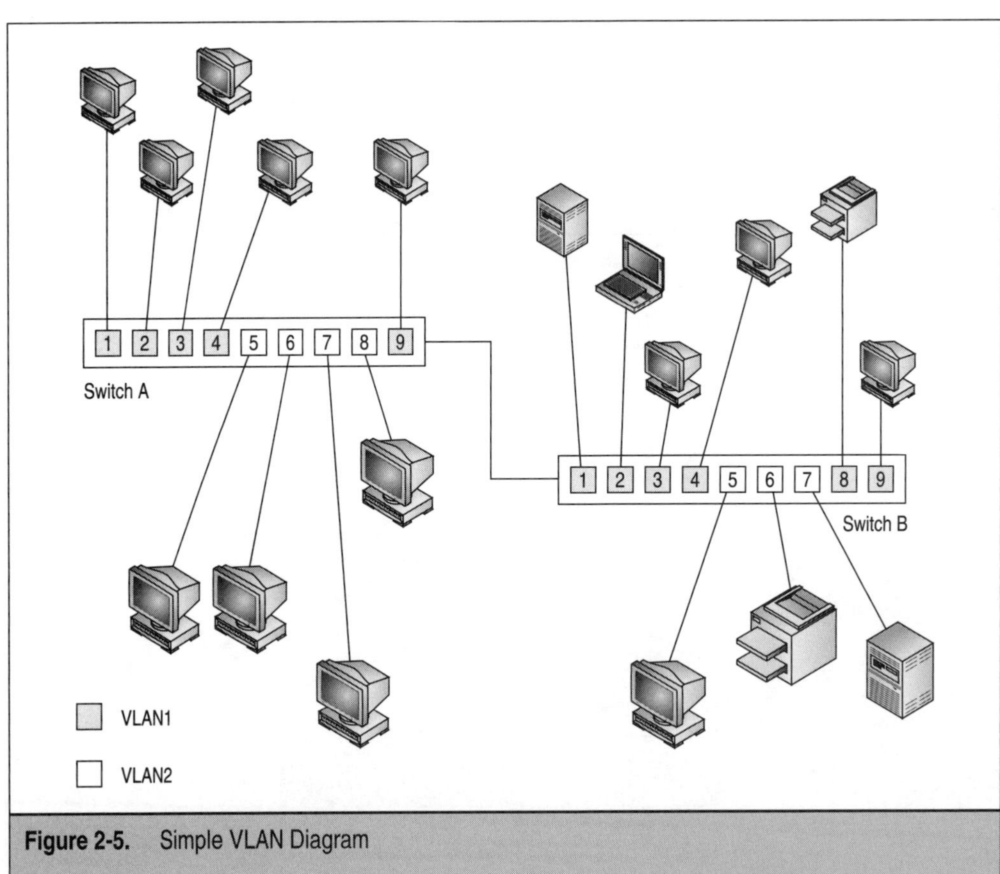

Figure 2-5. Simple VLAN Diagram

There are three ways to create a VLAN. The first is to create a VLAN based on ports, by assigning specific ports of a switch to a VLAN. As an example, Accounting could be assigned ports 1 to 5, R&D could be assigned ports 6 and 7, and Graphic Design could be assigned ports 8 to 10. Port-based VLANs are often referred to as *static* VLANs.

The second method is to create a VLAN based on MAC addresses. MAC addresses are entered into a centralized database that matches MAC addresses to specific VLANs. So if a device is moved from one switch port to another, the MAC address is looked up in the database and automatically assigned to the appropriate VLAN.

The third method is similar to creating a VLAN with MAC addresses, but the database is populated with protocol type and Layer 3 addresses. Once again, if a device is moved from one switch port to another, the switch can automatically assign the device to the appropriate LAN.

VLANs can be connected to one another using several methods. VLANs can be connected to a Layer 3 device, such as a router, or trunking can be used to make a switch port a part of multiple VLANs.

The capability to create multiple VLANs enables you to segment a network regardless of the physical location of a device, system, or user. VLANs can be implemented in a single facility or even expanded across a metropolitan area network.

HEADS UP!

When initially developed, VLANs were considered a security mechanism because systems were isolated from one another. Unfortunately, VLANs have their own security issues to be concerned with. Older switches could be fooled into allowing packets to hop from one VLAN to another without passing through a Layer 3 device. Steve A. Rouiller, in his detailed article "Virtual LAN Security: Weaknesses and Countermeasures" (http://www.sans.org/rr/papers/38/1090.pdf), lists nine Layer 2 attacks that can be mounted against VLANs. There is some controversy over the ability to actively carry out these attacks in a production environment. Regardless, it is important to recognize that segmenting a network using VLANs is not a "be all, end all" security solution.

Use VPNs to Transmit Between Protected Segments

Since their initial development, firewall products have become much more robust and can provide a variety of capabilities. Firewalls have the ability to block specific e-mail attachments, control spam, and block access to specific Internet URLs. But perhaps the most significant development, as far as segmenting networks is concerned, is the ability to provide Virtual Private Network (VPN) connections to remote clients. VPNs are designed to provide a low-cost, secure connection between networks and remote clients. VPNs enable you to provide a secure, private connection from a remote system or network without the costs associated with dedicated lines. VPNs can be exceptionally beneficial in helping to maintain a segmented network, but you need to consider these issues before you implement a VPN:

- What other systems are connected to the remote VPN client? Is the client connected to an unsecure network or system?
- Because VPN technologies use encryption to secure the connection, it is possible that some firewalls will not be able to adequately filter the data that passes through them from a VPN connection.

Chapter 3

Hardening with Identity Management Systems

by Jason Zann

- Understand Identity Management Drivers
- Establish an Identity Management Foundation
- Use Identity Management to Enforce Corporate Access Control Policies
- Manage Identities Through Workflow and Audit Processes

Identity management, the management of digital identities, is a critical measure for long-term security. Specifically, it refers to controlling the digital representation of users across an organization. Issues ranging from legal and regulatory forces to business requirements are driving your business toward an identity management solution. In most cases, this means adopting an identity management system to coordinate the management of the digital identities that define users on virtually every electronic system you use.

In the past, you've managed identities with point solutions. For example, when you build or buy a new application, you construct a new access management element and yet another new digital identity for your users. While most of these access management structures can be designed to be rather secure by themselves, they generally do not remain autonomous for long. They end up providing a piece of a larger solution, being accessed in ways that were not originally planned for, and possibly being replaced by a different application or system all together. Meanwhile, the users of these systems have multiple identities defined in multiple systems across your organization, making it difficult to determine the sum of each user's access among your information systems.

Today, your organization cannot afford to manage identities in this manner. Identity management is designed to address this issue and may be able to provide your organization with a more favorable course of action. This chapter gives you a step-by-step plan that you can use to build an identity management solution in your environment.

Understand Identity Management Drivers

The adoption of identity management systems is driven in different organizations by different needs. Different aspects of identity management solve different issues, and each organization has different needs. The first step in leveraging identity management systems to provide increased security is to understand what the business drivers are for your specific organization. For example, your organization may need to manage the identities for internal employees to improve your organization's security posture. Or, you may be looking for a method to manage the identities of your customers across multiple applications.

Identity management can mean a number of different things to a number of different organizations. Organizations such as casinos may use identity management to spot individuals who have been blacklisted from among the hundreds of thousands of people who are allowed to pass through their doors on a daily basis. Identity management systems have even been used to track fish in large aquariums to determine which ones are eating the others.

While there are many examples of what identity management could mean to an organization, this chapter looks at the most common requirements and analyzes the approaches that could be used to implement them. The most prevalent business drivers for identity management in corporations are liability and cost, time savings, and security.

Determine Identity Management Liability Drivers

A *liability* is an obligation or debt. It's often explained as the possibility of increased indebtedness. For example, if your organization does not follow standard safety procedures, it may be liable if employees are injured on the job. This liability may mean large monetary expenditures. Business liability can often be reduced by making changes in safety and security practices. Liability drivers are of two major types: external and internal. *External liability drivers* are laws or regulations that affect your specific industry. If laws are followed, a business's liability is reduced. Examples of an external liability would be legislation such as HIPAA (Health Insurance Portability and Accountability Act of 1996) or SOX (Sarbanes-Oxley Act of 2002). An *internal liability driver* is a driver that is inspired to be addressed internally without an external mandate. For example, an internal liability driver might be the threat posed by former employees. Your ability to effectively identify and remove the access to computer resources by ex-employees can reduce liability of those IDs being used for ill will.

Identify External Liability Issues to Resolve with Identity Management

How information security and privacy laws and regulations will affect the way you manage information is not yet clear. However, you should be knowledgeable of these laws and strive toward compliance. Laws and regulations are starting to focus on defining what should be common business best practices. Because business practices today tend to be coupled with electronic systems, new laws may mean modifications to those systems. For example, accounting has not been done by hand and on paper for a number of years now. As a result, controlling who has electronic access to accounting systems has taken the place of controlling who has access to a written ledger.

HEADS UP!

No law or pending legislation identifies the specific product or technology you must implement to be compliant. There are, however, vendors who say that you have to implement their technology to be compliant with a piece of legislation. This is simply not true. The laws and regulations focus on a particular point that needs to be addressed or a particular result that needs to occur. Some technologies will make it easier to facilitate that outcome, but you should never buy into the mindset that a technology by itself will make your environment compliant with a law or regulation. In the words of one of the security industry's thought leaders, Bruce Schneier, "Security is a process, not a product."

Recognize Laws that Do Not Specify Product Compliance Solutions While laws and regulations don't specify the exact hardware or software product that is needed for compliance, they do outline, at a minimum, what your business practices and processes should be. Because business practices have a number of interdependencies with technology, you may need to modify your technology implementations to align the business with the laws and regulations.

The recent wave of corporate scandals has highlighted the need for accountability. Specifically, organizations should be able to identify responsibility for actions that could affect the financial statements of the organization, whether the actions involve technology or not. This does not mean that new laws requiring accountability for financial statement information require identity management solutions, regardless of what a vendor may suggest or insist in their presentation. However, organizations must be able to provide some level of assurance that they can determine what affects the systems involved in processing financial information. In a majority of the corporate accounting scandals publicly discussed, the perpetrators have been identified. These individuals, for lack of a better term, were "trusted insiders" and could have accomplished their frauds even if a technical solution were in place. Identity management will not prevent dishonest people from doing dishonest things. Identity management may reduce the likelihood of an opportunist taking advantage of the system and may increase accountability.

Understand Current Legislation Because laws and regulations are written by politicians and lawyers, they require interpretation to identify the business and/or technological perspective. The interpretations of legislation throughout this section focus on potential technical liabilities that you may need to address. You should seek the same kind of interpretation for other laws and regulations, both those currently in force and those that may be ratified in the future. Examples of other laws and regulations that may affect your organization are the European Data Protection Directive, the Gramm-Leach-Bliley Act (GLBA), and the U.S. Patriot Act.

It is a good idea not to interpret the technical impacts of laws and regulations in a vacuum but rather to educate yourself as to what the potential technical impacts of a law or regulation could be on your organization. Generally, the best way to do this is to locate a subscription service that gives you information on how these regulations are evolving and what their immediate and future impact will be on IT. (Two such subscription services are SANS PrivacyBits and SANS AuditBits, both of which can be accessed at http://www.sans.org/newsletters/.) Additionally, your corporate counsel can generally offer valuable insight as to how these regulations can directly impact your specific organization.

Reviewing the different aspects of external liability sources will convince you that it is important to offer a method to effectively manage who has the capability to do what to information within your environment. With this in mind, consider two acts that may affect the management of digital identities (both carbon-based and noncarbon-based users) within your environment: the Health Information Portability and Accountability

Act (HIPAA) and the Sarbanes-Oxley Act. The following are examples of their impact on identity management:

- **HIPAA privacy directives** Define and direct who is permitted to access, view, and disclose what patient information. It poses questions such as these: Does a claims processor need to be able to view the entire medical history of a patient? What if the claims processor has multiple roles within a healthcare organization? How is the digital identity of a claims processor limited specifically to the information that they need to see for the specific role that they are performing?
- **HIPAA security directives** Address requirements for the audit of information access, including information on what is accessed and by whom. Auditing is one of the primary aspects that are needed to establish accountability for who has access and who has the ability to access what information.
- **Sarbanes-Oxley Act** Defines financial-based controls. It requires organizations to assess the effectiveness of their internal controls, which are those policies and procedures (both technical and nontechnical) that control the management of financial information. The management of identities that access financial systems is one such control.

Identify Internal Liability Issues to Resolve with Identity Management

Internal liability may share some of the same themes as external liability. Whereas external issues are items that impact all organizations within an industry or that fit a particular corporate profile, internal issues focus specifically on your organization. For example, an employee who has left your organization could pose a threat to your organization if they still have dial-in access to your network. While there might not be any specific fines that could be imposed on the organization if this occurs, there is a threat to the organization in that unauthorized access to the environment can be attained. The inability to properly manage identities affects not only current employees and their access but also individuals who no longer need access to the current environment.

Determine Identity Management Cost- and Time-Saving Drivers

Identity management can mean cost and time savings. Cost savings can result from reduced user administration overhead. Additional service offerings can affect the bottom line.

Increased customer satisfaction due to a better overall user experience with current and new systems can mean increased sales. Solving the problem of password resets can provide both benefits (cost- and time-saving drivers). No matter where in the world you ask, one of the top calls to any corporate help desk is for password resets. Password resets are required when users forget their passwords. Password resets consume the time (and possibly money) of both users and the personnel actually resetting the password. If users can reset their own passwords in a secure fashion, the time and frustration usually associated with password resets can be minimized. Fewer people are required to maintain the same service levels of the help desk, and users have a better experience because they neither have to wait nor be embarrassed by admitting to others that they forgot a password. An organization may find that this increases customer loyalty and possibly maintains a competitive edge.

NOTE Setting up self-help password resets requires collecting unique, private information from customers, to authenticate them if they attempt to reset their password. The best time to collect this information is during enrollment, because users rarely modify their personal information after they establish an account. During enrollment, allow users to choose their own confirmation questions and answers, and to choose multiple questions. This enables you to avoid posing generic questions that everyone can answer, like "What is your favorite color?" or "Where were you born?" Using these "conversational questions" increases the risk that an adversary might figure out a password, because a user might unwittingly relay their password reset information in a general conversation. Allowing users to create their own questions and answers reduces this risk significantly. Caution and train users to understand that the answers they provide for the questions hold the same value as a password. Therefore, as an administrator, you should confirm that these passwords are not retained in an insecure format, like in clear text in a database.

Another benefit of an identity management solution that can bring forth cost and/ or time savings in your environment is the ability to efficiently and quickly set up user access to systems and services. Setting up a user's accounts and providing them with appropriate resource access to information systems should not take multiple hours or days, but it often does when multiple unmanaged, unique systems are present. The potential for loss of business also exists because IT cannot quickly cater to user requests. User requests, and access to systems, may be the result of both employee and customer requirements. The easier you can make the customer login experience (including their password management experience), the more they may use the application and the more referrals you may receive from them.

These factors alone (decrease in support personnel required to service customers, the capability for users to support themselves, and the ability to efficiently set up users to use a service) are very significant when considering the political landscape of using IT more efficiently. While all of these points may not be tangible, they do lead to competitive advantages.

Determine Identity Management Security Drivers

Identity management has many different interpretations; however, all of them are focused on the age-old issue of user management. In the world of identity management, key points need to be determined long before a technological solution is introduced. One such point is the identification of which resources users require access to. You must define the directories that currently include both internal and external resources, perhaps Internet-facing data stores. Another key point is the ability to determine exactly what each unique user can access.

From a security perspective, it is also important to define the user's role on the network and how that translates to applications and data stores. You should be able to identify who has access to what on which system. Given a user ID, you should be able to determine which applications the user has access to and what roles within those applications the user has. This is a rather easy task if your organization has a limited number of systems that users can access, but the task is almost impossible in larger organizations. For example, if your organization is small and its users access the network operating system (NOS), one or two applications that are specific to their jobs, and maybe a human resources (HR) system, identity management can be pretty straightforward. In fact, in some cases, it might even be done manually with rather decent results. However, most users within a typical large organization have in excess of 16 different identities that actually represent them across the enterprise. In situations like this, it is very inefficient and often cost prohibitive to attempt to manually manage users with all of their various system accesses. This is the exact problem that identity management solutions are meant to solve.

The second thought from a security perspective is that you should be able to identify who has access to what on which system. This is different from the problem presented earlier in this section. In that example, you were interested in identifying what a user can do. Here, your concern is how to identify, for each resource, who can access it and what can they do with it. While this may seem fairly straightforward and something that should be offered on virtually any application or system, it's often not easy to obtain. In addition, other critical information about the user, the data, and the level of access is also difficult to determine from a multisystem perspective. You should, for example, be able to answer the following questions:

- Does this person need access to this system?
- Is this person still an employee?
- If this person is an employee, are they in a role that requires this access?
- If they got this access because they required it, do they still require it now? (In other words, have they been promoted, demoted, transferred, or otherwise moved into another role that no longer requires this access?)
- Does the access they require to one system actually contradict access that they may have to another system? (In other words, if a user has access to part of an accounts payable system, does that access also then give them access to an accounts receivable system?)

These questions are only a few of those that you must answer as you move toward an identity management solution.

Establish an Identity Management Foundation

Very rarely is the number of applications available to users reduced. Most likely, more applications will be added in the future, and you must be able to manage the identities of users of those applications.

Every application has its "own" method of identifying users and controlling access management, but the goal of identity management is to be able to centrally control all aspects of an individual's identity across all systems. In addition to current systems, you must be able to control the identities for new applications, platforms, and systems as they are added, and to extend identity management to apply to new customers and partners. The first step is to build the foundation on which identity management can be constructed.

Adopt a Standards-Based Directory Service

While it is difficult to predict the future, you should attempt to adopt standards that can be used in the future. When implementing a new application, use a standard directory service like an X.500 directory. Implementing an X.500-type directory or some other standard by itself will not give you identity management. However, as you progress down the path of implementing an identity management solution, having a standards-based directory service will give you the leverage and flexibility you may need to do the best job of building a centralized directory. Additionally, having a standard directory as your identity management underpinning will help prevent you from being locked into a vendor that uses a proprietary directory store, like a modified database. X.500 directories are compatible with each other; vendor modified database solutions do not carry the same guarantee.

NOTE A number of other standards are emerging and being used in the identity management arena. It is important that you monitor these standards and understand what impact they may have on your environment. Standards like the Security Assertion Markup Language (SAML) and Service Provisioning Markup Language (SPML) have been designed to promote interoperability between independent identity systems. Information on standards that affect the identity management space can be found by clicking the Standards button under the Industry Resources menu on the left side of the Digital Identity World web page located at http://www.digitalidworld.com/.

Match Identity Management Solutions with Organizational Needs

You may not be able to find an identity management solution that meets all of your needs. Standards for identity management are still being developed. Vendors have matured based on different roadmaps. As a result, product vendors have not yet integrated all of the elements of their solutions. Additionally, sometimes organizations will require a more flexible solution than any vendor offers. This is a maturing market and no vendor does everything well.

Identify Organizational Identity Management Needs

If you cannot identify the problems that identity management can solve for you, you will be implementing a solution that targets tasks and objectives that vendors and project managers know will be successful, rather then a solution that solves your specific requirements.

> **CAUTION** This approach of providing solutions to perceived problems rather than to real ones is widespread. If this is your organization's traditional approach, stop now and ask the question, do we really have a problem that identity management can solve?

To identify your requirements, start with identity issues of which you are already aware. Most organizations have internal issues with regard to effectively managing the identities of their employees. Do you? If so, then this is a good place to start. Customer-facing applications or external applications also require management of identities. If you can manage customer data, you can leverage the information across multiple applications. It is possible that your external applications may be the area in most need of identity management in your organization.

Identity management can mean different things to management, vendors, and implementers. To obtain a solution that matches your needs, you need to provide a detailed assessment of the problem you are trying to solve. Armed with this detail, the steps that you need to take and the components necessary for a solution can be more easily found. The alternative is also true. The more vague your understanding and expression of need is, the more useless your identity management solution will be.

The following table provides examples of four possible primary needs and the type of product that you should try to acquire for each primary need:

Primary Need	Recommended Product
Find out which users have access to what systems and what their user IDs are across those systems.	Look for a product that has strong directory and correlation capabilities.
Password synchronization. (Make passwords for user applications, platforms, or systems the same so that users have only one password to remember.)	After you review what the password requirements are for each of the systems, review the requirements for your environment and determine if it will be acceptable to force users to one location to make a password change or if users will need the ability to change their password in any location and have that change propagated to the rest of the applications, platforms, and systems. If you are looking to do the former, you will be able to use a system that uses agent or agentless technologies. (Agent vs. agentless is defined later in this chapter.) If you are looking for users to be able to change their password in any one location, you will need to look at a product, at least in part, that supports agent technology.

Primary Need	Recommended Product
Set up and remove users in your environment as they come and go. (Provisioning and de-provisioning)	Look for a product that has "hooks," or the ability to interface with the applications, platforms, and systems that are needed by users in your environment. All of the top-tier identity management products will offer hooks into common application suites (like Windows Active Directory, SAP, and PeopleSoft); however, there is often a need to interface with custom applications. Because most environments have a number of custom applications, you will need to understand how the product that you select will interface with those custom applications. For example, some products offer an SDK (software development kit) for you to program interfaces as needed, others will offer small applications that will allow you to "build" a connector to interface with a custom application, others will have professional services that will design agents for you, and others will work with third-party middleware to interface with your custom applications. The decision as to which is the best for your environment will depend on the resources that you have available to you, the programming experience that you have in house, and how many custom applications you will need to interface with.
Implement an entire identity management strategy using a single product or suite of products.	Look for a product that has the capability to fulfill directory services, provision users, service users, workflow, and the like while taking into account all the preexisting technologies within your environment and how they will be impacted. For this type of identity management implementation, a suite product will always work better than a "best-of-breed" product selection.

While there are many interpretations as to what identity management is, the only meaningful definition is the one that solves your problems with managing identities.

After you assess your organization's needs, match each one with an aspect or aspects of identity management. If users are burdened by large numbers of passwords that they must update frequently, implementing password synchronization across the environment may be the solution. If accountability for financial information is the issue, then being able to audit what users have access to what systems is important.

HEADS UP!

Identity management vendor solutions are maturing in different ways depending on vendor history, direction, growth, and customer demands. Your organization is also growing and may find new needs for identity management. It is possible that you may outgrow the vendor solution that appears to fit your needs today. Before locking yourself into a single vendor's identity management solution, be aware that different vendor solutions may not work seamlessly with others. Look for flexibility in product design and the use of standards that may make integrating with other products in the future easier. When evaluating products, consider your possible future needs, the vendor's track record and projected future abilities, and the flexibility of the solution.

Match Identity Management Needs to Vendor Solutions

Once you have identified your needs, you must determine if a specific vendor can fulfill them. This is not as simple as it seems. For example, every vendor of identity management products, from the mom and pop shops to the most sophisticated product companies in the world, provides a solution that can work with the authentication process and identity objects used in the most prevalent NOS. Additionally, most vendors' products can interoperate with major third-party software packages like PeopleSoft, SAP, and the like. While the requirements for managing identities embedded in these systems are of major concern to you, and their successful management will be the base elements for your first identity management wins within your environment, they are not the only integration issues you will have to address. It is the "other systems" that can become major impediments to successful identity management projects.

You need to determine what these systems are, and what percentage of your total identity management needs they represent. It may be that homegrown applications that serve a majority of your business and applications started out on someone's workstation as a proof of concept. It may be that they now control a major portion of your supply chain. Look for systems that manage the mission-critical aspects of your organization and ensure that the proposed identity management solution will work with them.

Mature vendors and mature vendor products may prove to be invaluable in providing solutions that address the integration of less-well-known products and those unique to your organization. A vendor's custom interfaces or product application programming interfaces (APIs) might easily be adopted by your organization. Alternatively, vendors may have a team that is involved with building interfaces for homegrown, nonstandard-based directories. Either option means that you are more likely to get a stronger identity management solution in the long term. While your unique or less-well-known applications may not be your primary focus as you seek a product to solve your identity management needs, and the results of managing the identities specific to these programs may not be realized for quite some time, it is very important that the vendor demonstrate to you that it has the ability to integrate with those programs and provide the flexibility that your environment requires.

Prepare to Implement an Identity Management Solution

Implementing an identity management solution is an enterprise-wide initiative. In order for it to succeed, you must properly prepare your organization. You must enlist the support of stakeholders, and accurately forecast cost and effort.

Enlist Support of All Stakeholders

When an identity management solution is implemented, it has an impact on the entire enterprise. Additionally, Identity Management implementations will require commitments from multiple parts of the organization for its continued success. This means that you need to obtain buy-in from a large number of groups and departments within your organization.

Application, platform, and systems administrators and developers should be educated early in the process. They need to have an understanding and see the benefits of an identity management solution, not only because their current roles may be affected by the implementation, but also because future developments have to take the identity management solution into account.

One of the best ways to enlist support is to educate stakeholders as to what the benefits will be to each of the stakeholders. For example, if you are speaking with a system administrator, ask them how much time they spend administering users or running user reports for auditors. With the implementation of an identity management solution, their administration of users could be significantly reduced. In turn, they could spend the time that they would normally spend on administrating users more productively doing other systems administration. Additionally, an identity management solution could reduce the time that they need to prepare for audits from days to hours.

If you are enlisting the support of business units or call center management, you could relay to them that an identity management solution could make a new hire productive in a day as opposed to the week that it takes to set up users now.

If you are enlisting the support of an executive, you could inform them that you will be able to provide reports in rather short order that outline exactly who has access to what systems and prove that employees do not have access to any more applications, platforms, and systems than what they need to get their job done. This is something that cannot normally be done with any degree of confidence without an identity management solution.

If you are enlisting the support of a help desk manager, you could share how an identity management system could reduce their call wait times by allowing passwords to be reset automatically.

Every stakeholder in an identity management project needs to see a personal benefit in order for them to commit to the project. Once you identify what problem you want your identity management solution to solve, you will then determine who the stakeholders are.

You will not succeed if executive management does not support the identity management solution. Executive management not only can deliver the support of downstream staff to the initiative but also can maintain that support over the extended time required to implement an identity management solution. Identity management is a journey, not a destination. If executive management does not back your identity management solution, it can easily provoke its failure by continuing to support autonomous solutions.

One way to gain the cooperation and backing of executives is to provide them with both the potential cost savings and ROI possible with identity management solutions and the redundant costs of providing identity management solutions that are unique to every application.

As a centralized identity management solution becomes more pervasive, the autonomous operation of applications, platforms, and systems is less of an option. The time to enlist support from those who are responsible for these items is before the identity management solution requires them to change the way of doing business. Everyone needs to be in agreement from a corporate perspective with regard to the goals and direction of identity management. Obtain this support and you will have less departmental or group resistance to using a corporate identity management solution for future initiatives. The bottom line is that executive management as well as their subordinates need to realize that if they continue to support building identity management into applications on a one-by-one basis, they will continue to incorporate redundant costs by rebuilding solutions and decrease the level of security and ROI because of the increased complexity of managing these solutions.

Correctly Forecast Identity Management Implementation Costs and Effort

Identity management products will not provide the entire identity management solution, so use the 80/20 rule to forecast cost and effort. Solutions are only about 20 percent product and product capabilities and about 80 percent backend consultative work. Understand that this work also includes internal resources. This also means that a purchase price of well under $1 million can swell to a multimillion-dollar investment. This is a fact that product vendors rarely divulge, because their compensation is traditionally based on the sale of the product.

Of the 80 percent of consultative work that is required for a successful implementation, approximately 30 percent of that should be done prior to actually purchasing a product. This may seem excessive at face value; however, in reality, it is probably a little low.

Identity management offers the ability to incorporate the management of multiple, widely disbursed directories. There are, however, many different ways that each of those directories are managed, developed, and used. To centrally manage all of those disbursed directories, you must become familiar with how they are utilized today. You have to know how users are set up and retired, how they are administered, what requirements the groups may have with regard to their directories, and who is actually in the directory (employees, customers, etc.). You must know this prior to selecting and purchasing an identity management product.

In addition, you need to know how current directory structures rely on other directories, what processes exist for documenting what is done to the directory (is there workflow that determines how users are set up, or is there a unique validation step that is used for user validation?), and if there are any aspects as to the history of the directory and how it evolved that make it unique. In sum, you have to have a firm understanding of your current environment prior to selecting an enterprise identity management solution.

NOTE The 80/20 rule also holds true for the costs of implementing an identity management solution. Initial product cost will vary depending on the size and scope of your implementation. Typical product pricing is in the $250,000–$750,000 range. Apply the 80/20 rule to forecast the actual cost to implement the product. It is not uncommon for an enterprise identity management solution to be a multimillion-dollar initiative.

Identify an Internal Authoritative Source

An *authoritative source* is one that is considered the primary authority for users within a security domain. It is the location where information about the identity of a majority, if not all, of the individuals within an organization will reside. For example, in an organization, an HR system, like PeopleSoft, will most likely be an authoritative source.

The identities in an authoritative system may have very limited electronic access within an organization or may have significant access to many of your digital information systems. Regardless of the extent of the access in the environment, the authoritative source should have a record of everyone and what their relation to the environment is.

HR systems are good authoritative sources because they normally include everyone that is receiving a paycheck within your organization. Since virtually every employee receives a paycheck, this is usually a good place to start. Other benefits to using HR systems as authoritative sources are as follows:

- HR systems, unlike most others, include individuals that have very limited electronic access to the environment. Examples of such employees are maintenance personnel and security guards. These individuals may have access only to an intranet site to update their insurance or retirement information, but it is important that you be able to identify and track every individual's system access.
- HR systems track employees as they move within the environment.
- HR systems are often designed to track contractors, consultants, and temporary personnel within your organization.

As a result, an HR system usually gives you the best visibility into all the potential identities that could exist within your environment.

HEADS UP!

Finding a widely used system that can be used as an authoritative source will usually require some thought. IT professionals generally assume that widely used systems like the NOS login make good authoritative sources.

The rational is that the only digital identities necessary to manage are the ones that have network access to begin with. This thought process is shortsighted because it does not account for kiosks or shared computers with limited access within the organization that are used for benefit enrollments and the like from non-network users such as maintenance personnel and security guards. Even users with limited access can create problems when the management of their digital identities is ignored.

Locate External Authoritative Sources

As you expand your identity management solutions to cover more information systems, and as identity management systems become more prevalent, you may need to consider the use of multiple authoritative sources. The HR system may not contain all the information and details that relate to the identity of every user. It may not contain information on some groups that are provided access to your systems. For example, tracking users such as customers may become very important, especially in organizations that are focused on the consumer arena or that come under the jurisdiction of privacy advocacy laws. It may even become important to track information about customers of your customers, and this information may be jealously guarded. Even when there is little hope of getting any accurate information about them, there are still issues that need to be resolved.

The authoritative sources for customer information may or may not be within your control. Therefore, you may need to develop a trusting relationship with the security domains that control prospective authoritative sources. Chapter 3 of this book provides details on how to secure the mechanics of interoperating authoritative sources and how to use federated identities (a single identity that can be used in multiple locations). For now, it is important to realize that you will eventually need to identify authoritative sources for information on all identities that have access to systems and data within your organization. Both internal and external authoritative sources may be identified. Figure 3-1 provides a general representation of the types of identities that will be accessing your systems and data.

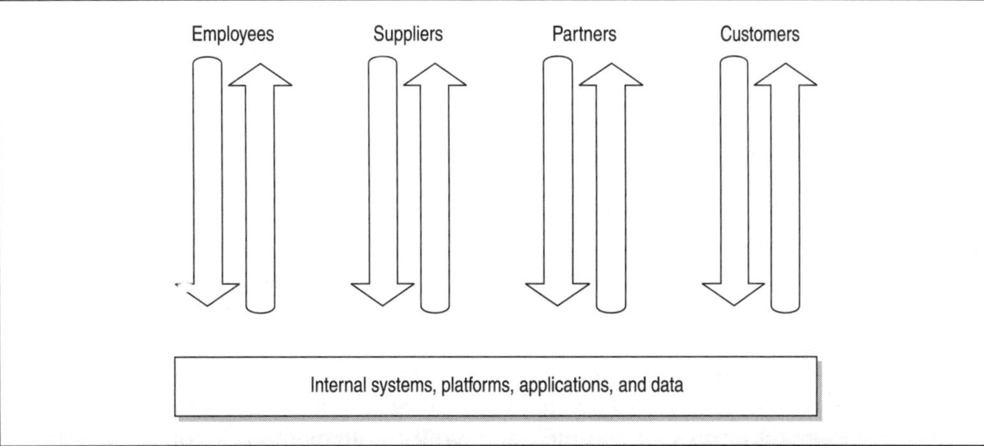

Figure 3-1. The virtual extensions of identity management within your organization

Use Identity Management to Enforce Corporate Access Control Policies

Identity management is designed to manage the digital identities throughout your organization. Centralized control over identity information is one aspect of digital identity management. Another is the enforcement of access controls. Your current policies and business reasons dictate which users and organizational roles have what access to which systems. Your identity management systems should have the ability to effectively and efficiently enforce those policies.

To ensure these policies are addressed, keep the following phases in mind:

- Inception
- Proliferation
- Management
- Termination

Control the Inception Process

The inception process is the procedure used to set up a new user's access to your information systems. This is often a rather time-consuming and thought-provoking task. The first step is to uniquely identify a user within your environment. Unique identification is not just associating the user with a unique identifier but also consists of associating the identifier with information that can further qualify or help identify who that user is.

Creating a unique identifier is actually pretty easy. Many organizations select certain consistent user properties and utilize those elements in combination with a sequential value to provide distinction. For example, an organization might use the first letter of a first name + the first letter of a last name + a five-digit value. If the user's name is John Doe, the unique identifier might be JD00001. When selecting the derivation of unique identifiers, do not limit the number of total users that can be created, regardless of your company size. If you use first initial + last initial + a one-digit identifier (JD1), you run the risk of running out of name combinations and ultimately needing to add another digit. Such a change may not lead to any confusion in the short term but might require significant cost and effort to adapt information systems built around the smaller identifier's footprint. It is better to settle on a naming standard that has room to grow.

Depending on the type of systems that you are creating identities for, you may need to create pseudonyms or provide complete anonymity. Both methods involve obfuscating the real information about a user to different degrees to provide a level of privacy. A pseudonym is often used when the full identity of a user should be obscured within your system but must be known to grant them access to your system. For example, suppose you are a back-office financial services firm that accepts requests from users that have been validated through other organizations. Because other organizations have already approved the users, you do not need to know their purchasing history, personal preferences, or details of their credit history. However, you may be required to review customer identity against a watch list for those suspected of violating the provisions in the U.S. Patriot Act. To do so, you require users' names and social security numbers. Using this limited information about a user (without all the details about the user) to establish an identity is an example of a creating a pseudonym.

In contrast, complete anonymity may be required in the systems of a medical disease-testing facility. Not only is the real identity of a participant unnecessary for the processing of related information, but there are valid privacy reasons to keep their identity confidential. It is important to realize that when you are creating an inception process for identity management, there may be situations where you cannot or should not tie any more information to an identity than minimally needed.

When designing an inception process, you will probably have to consider preexisting identities and how they are defined within your environment. This can be difficult. Many of your existing identities were created for single applications, platforms, or systems without a tremendous amount of thought to the relationship of other systems. The establishment of common identities among uncommon systems is a requirement for identity management. You need to find a way to match up all the identities for users across the environment. If user John Doe is jdoe on one system, johnd on another, and user123 on a third, all three identities have to be mapped to a single identity. An identity management product can provide the infrastructure for implementing this mapping but it cannot magically tell you which disparate identities map to a single real person. An attempt at figuring out which digital identities really represent the same person is a good exercise to do prior to purchasing any kind of an identity management product.

In fact, establishing continuity among identities is paramount in a successful identity management implementation. Major identity management vendors, like Computer Associates, IBM, and Novell, offer a directory service that can be used to replicate all the different aspects of identities (not only identities, but attributes of those identities) from multiple directories into one repository to assist you with those associations. An apt name for such a directory is "stealth directory." This is not meant to imply that there is something mischievous about the directory itself, just that it can be created without impacting any current system operations.

The creation of a stealth directory is usually noninvasive—that is, it does not change identities on your current systems. It is merely a method that can provide insight into what the identities are like throughout your environment. The term "stealth" in this context is used to indicate that the directory will not be seen by most users or administrators who are not directly involved with this step of the identity management project. It is normally done through the use of a metadirectory and does not impact production user administration. The use of a stealth directory method will allow you to pull information from preexisting directories into a common interface and correlate the information. From the stealth directory, you can actually see how identities look across multiple systems and start to make rudimentary judgments on how they can be associated. For example, you may see that one system uses first initial and last name to identify a user and another system uses the first name and the last initial. Because any modifications made in the stealth directory are not reciprocated back to the production environment, it is generally a safe method to use to become more technically intimate with the naming conventions that are used across multiple systems.

Another benefit of creating a stealth directory is that it enables you to see immediate deficiencies within the preexisting autonomous directory structures. For example, if you find that there are users who are not identified in the system that you chose to be your authoritative source, you can immediately investigate the problem. Remember, your authoritative source should be the master authority for identities throughout your environment. If the identity is not in the authoritative source but is in other systems, you should find out why. It could be something as simple as a temporary identity that was set up on a single system by an administrator for a test that has not been removed, or it could be that someone has compromised your environment and placed an identity on the system as a method to allow themselves access in the future. Additionally, if the stealth directory reveals that an identity is disabled in the authoritative source and not disabled on other systems, this could mean that a user has left the organization and the access associated with that user has not been removed across all the systems that they had access to.

NOTE Two primary methods can be used to attain identities from disbursed directories and collapse them into a single directory (stealth directory): agent and agentless. There are pros and cons to both. To decide which is best, focus on the type of technology that will satisfy your current requirements. Agent-based technology is very useful for determining real-time modifications made to the different directories referenced by the stealth directory. This may be a future need if you wish to dynamically manage and enforce policy with regard to identities in real time, but it is not a requirement for the initial steps of implementing identity management into your environment. In agent-based technology, a piece of software attaches itself to the application, platform, or system and monitors the health of identities based on preexisting directives from the identity management system. The impact of the agent software on the other process that runs on the system should be considered. Agentless technology refers to the ability of the identity management system to "log into" the application, platform, or system as an administrator and retrieve the specific data required. Agentless technology cannot react to changes on a native system as quickly as agent technology without producing significant overhead; however, it is not nearly as intrusive, because only a login is required. For the purposes of creating a stealth directory and becoming more familiar with the characteristics of identities within your environment, without installing software, agentless technology is recommended.

HEADS UP!

It is generally a good idea to disable, rather than delete, an account in the authoritative source when a user has left the organization. This allows management of the identity to continue if the user rejoins the organization at a later time. Additionally, if the authoritative source is producing unique identifiers for every individual identity, this will prevent the identity from being reused at a later time by a different individual. This is why it is important to develop a naming scheme that can grow with your organization.

Control the Proliferation Process

Proliferation is the process of taking an identity and applying it to the environment. This process includes tying access controls to the unique identifier so that each user's access is correctly established throughout your organization and each user has exactly the access they require to do their job and no more. The nirvana of proliferation is to establish a user in an authoritative source with a unique identifier and propagate that unique identifier throughout the environment. Proliferation can only be done after there is a firm understanding of how to identify users from the inception process. The proliferation has a dependency on the inception process.

Define the Current Proliferation Process

During proliferation, updates are made to the production environment based on the role that the identity assumes. The first step in improving this process is to identify how it is currently accomplished. In your present job, you most likely have access to the facilities that you need to access, the data resources (such as file shares) that you need, phone systems, and the like. How did you get that access? In addition to outlining the current process, you should ask the following questions:

- How long did it take for all the accesses to become a reality? In some organizations, it can take weeks or longer for a new employee to get all of their appropriate accesses to do their job. Normally, there is a soft cost here in lost or wasted time because an employee did not have the necessary access to start being productive.
- What is the impact on security of the current process? For example, are requests for certain accesses achieved through a phone call, e-mail, or a conversation at the water cooler? If this is how access is granted to certain systems, what criteria are verified to establish if the users ultimately required access to the system? How is the user account set up and credentials for that account disseminated to the user?

It is important to improve the identities proliferation process because there are cost savings and security implications that will not be attained if it is done incorrectly.

Define New Proliferation Phases

Proliferation of a new user within an organization should be examined in phases. It is not realistic to think that you will be able to simply flip a switch and automatically have all proliferation take place. Proliferation can and should be analyzed in a structured and methodical manner. Because a range of applications, platforms, and systems could be in your environment, you must have an identity management system that can accommodate and work with native user administration in your environment, ranging from legacy products (and some of the limitations of native products) to products that have not yet been designed.

Identify Major Systems Common to All or Many Users Your initial focus should be on the applications, programs, and systems that the majority of users will require access to, and then expand your offerings from there. For example, when creating your stealth directory, you may notice that

- Everyone in the organization has access to the HR system.
- A majority of the organization has access to the NOS, e-mail, and the intranet.
- Some groups require access to a host of different applications to provide customer service.
- Others, like administrators, do not need access to any of these applications, but may require access to the underlying platforms that the applications are using.
- There may be other systems, like an obscure payroll system, that only a handful of individuals have access to.

Identify Current System Usage and Role Definitions Next, determine the impact of role definition on proliferation and then attempt to define existing user roles. *Role definition* is the understanding of what access a user should have on a particular system. The general lack of clear and detailed role definition within an environment often prevents a straightforward proliferation procedure. Roles may be defined by job type or a group of users' responsibilities; however, you may have difficulty analyzing how these roles are translated into electronic system access.

Determine What Role Definitions Should Be Defining roles will be easier if you determine how granular you want to get with role definitions. For example, if there are 100 different job roles within your organization, you essentially need 100 different proliferation procedures to propagate identities and accesses based on how each one of those roles is defined. This can be a very time- and resource-intensive exercise that could ultimately end up being very fragile. For example, if all the roles are defined within your current environment, and those roles are mapped to their electronic equivalents of access, what will occur if your CEO decides to reorganize the entire organization, or even parts of the organization? Your entire mapping process could have to be completely redone. It is also worth noting that the role reassignments are only part of the issue; the other part is managing the exceptions to roles that personalize a user's digital identity.

To alleviate some of the issues associated with roles, it is worth investigating the potential of making multiple roles and assigning multiple roles to a single user. This approach may be better for your environment because it is more resilient to organizational changes and focuses on system access for users as opposed to user accesses to systems. Additionally, systems are generally more stationary within an environment than are users, because systems do not get promoted, demoted, or leave the organization. Another benefit of having multiple roles assigned to a user is that most network users have common accesses, such as e-mail, proxy server for web access, and the like. Examples of roles might be "e-mail users role," "proxy users role," etc. Essentially, once these roles are established, they can then be assigned to individual users.

NOTE When creating a strategy for how you will proceed with your proliferation efforts, you can create either single roles for multiple groups of users (create a role for Department A, Department B, Department C, etc.) or multiple roles for single users (e-mail role, proxy server role, intranet access role, etc.).

Choose the Order of Identity Proliferation by Role Implementing identity management takes time and effort. You should begin with areas where you will see the most benefit. There are certain resources that virtually every enterprise user needs access to (HR system, e-mail, intranet), and there are large subsets of users that can be adequately addressed (e.g., systems administrators, call center personnel) as a next step of proliferation; however, you have to determine what is the next best step to address roles within your environment.

For example, suppose that your organization has a call center in which the workers need access to ten different applications to adequately perform their jobs. Since call centers are normally profit centers for organizations, you can probably assume that the time and accuracy involved in setting up an identity for a new call center employee is well spent. Do it correctly and profits will increase. Do it wrong (for example, by providing incorrect access or preventing preexisting users from performing jobs) and there could be a negative dollar impact to your organization. Setting up the call-center identity is a high-visibility task that can make or break your identity management project.

Another aspect that is of concern with regard to the call center example is the fact that call center personnel normally are not technically trained and can determine only whether or not the product is working. If you elect to address user-focused applications such as call center applications, it is definitely worth your time to become very intimate with the call center business processes and how the call center applications work.

Another identity to consider as an initial proliferation process task is the IT administrator subset of users. Administrators have a number of systems that they administer, and identities for every administrator need to be established on every machine. As an example, suppose that a particular administrator needs access to 75 different machines. In some organizations, one of the first things that a new administrator has to do is have a unique identity established on each one of the machines that she is administrating. Even if this is automated by a script, the administrator must still log on to each machine and change her password. The ability to securely proliferate identities across these 75 machines not only can save time of the current administrator that needs to establish these accounts, but also can make the new administrator more productive in a quicker time frame.

If you select this task to accomplish, the added benefit is that systems administrators will be able to help troubleshoot any issues with the proliferation process and may even be able to provide input to do it more effectively. The drawback is that administrators are the only employees who really benefit from identities being set up in this situation, and quantifying the soft costs of an administrator's time is more difficult than quantifying the soft costs of a customer service center, which can show a dollar profit per man hour once their identity is established. From a corporate viewpoint, little notice is given to the fact that an administrator's job is now a little easier and they can become more productive in a shorter amount of time, because the bottom line does not reflect such information.

There is also the possibility that many systems within your organization are already centrally administered and thus the impact of developing the system administrator identity may have less impact on administrators than you imagine.

The examination of these two identity roles, the customer service center employee and the systems administrator, provide examples of the decision-making process and the types of strategic decisions that you have to ponder as your environment starts leveraging more elements of identity management systems. There is not a right or wrong way to proceed through the proliferation step. However, a significant amount of thought is required to understand what is best for your environment.

HEADS UP!

One of the inherent benefits of the proliferation process is that it reduces the number of passwords a user must remember. As identities are proliferated throughout the environment for a user or class of users, the credentials, or passwords for those identities, are also proliferated. This is beneficial because a user is given not just a single identity, but a single password for all the applications, platforms, and systems that the user needs to log into. Note, however, that if you use this technique, commonly referred to as single-sign on, you will be limited to the least stringent password policy of all the systems. For example, suppose that you have ten systems, nine of which allow passwords to be up to 100 characters in length and any combination of ASCII characters. The tenth system can only handle eight alphanumeric characters. Thus, your password standard for all ten systems is limited to eight alphanumeric characters if you elect to enforce a consistent password across all the systems.

Another approach is to choose to not centrally provide authentication for certain systems within your identity management infrastructure. For example, you may require some systems to have two-factor authentication (the use of passwords and biometrics, for example; see Chapter 4). Applications, platforms, and systems such as this may be selected to not have passwords propagated to them.

Control the Management Process

The management process consists of implementing the operational support required for an identity during its life cycle within an organization. Just as role definition must be defined (as outlined in the previous section) before proliferation can be accomplished, the identity life cycle must be defined before the management process can be controlled. There are many aspects of an identity life cycle. For example, what happens if an individual is promoted, demoted, transferred, or moved? The accesses associated with that identity will most likely need to be modified to compensate for the change in job role. As a result, your identity management solution needs be flexible.

Define Role-Based Access Controls

Managing role-based access controls (RBACs) can be difficult because users' roles may change. If a user is transferred from one department to the next, he will probably maintain his e-mail account; however, the shared drives and the applications to which he has access might be different. As a result, his identity needs to reflect these modifications.

NOTE Roles and the access controls necessary to define them are established during the proliferation process; however, actively and meaningfully managing RBACs is part of the management process. An example of RBAC management is the management of access controls as a part of account deletion.

Implement and Enforce Least Privilege

A best practice in developing RBACs is to implement the principal of *least privilege,* which states that any given identity can access only what they need in order to complete their job. Once your identity management solution is implemented, you should be able to isolate any given user within your environment and quickly and confidently state exactly what systems and rights that user has access to. This demonstrates that a formal, planned, managed, and auditable system of applying access controls is in place. In the past, decisions may have been made manually and perhaps left undocumented. Additionally, you should be able to determine which users have or have had access to what information at a given point in time. The inverse of this model should be true as well. You should be able to identify any application, platform, or system and quickly and confidently determine which identities have or have had access to what information.

The groundwork for least privilege is laid during the proliferation process. RBACs allow you to establish operational control over what users have access to after they have been established. Least privilege should be the guide for how users are established and what they have access to throughout the life cycle of their identity.

If agent-based technologies are deployed and a user is manually added to an application, platform, or system, the agent should be able to override the manual addition. Enabling this type of control ensures that the only users that have been established have gone through the identity management system within your environment. This will allow a level of audit and control with regard to the identities that are added.

HEADS UP!

Normally, cultural change within an organization is required in order to manage users on systems in this manner. In the past an administrator may have accepted ownership of specific systems. Administrators managed their users on "their" boxes in their own way and you will be replacing administrative control with an alien piece of software. The agent is going to overwrite the administrator's ability not only to set up users, but also to manage user access rights. Without education, administrators will not be comfortable with this new process. This is an example of one of the cruxes of identity management as a whole—you may be able to implement identity management improvements *technically*, but they won't be effective unless you also understand and address the ramifications the implementation will have on users and the political climate.

Implement and Enforce Separation of Duties

Identity management systems should also be able to flag and take actions on rights and permissions that do not conform to your organization's separation of duties policy. *Separation of duties* is the security principal that requires a process to be broken into tasks and the tasks to be assigned to different individuals in order to prevent fraud. An example of a separation of duties policy violation might be a developer having access to both a development system and a production system. Even though the identities for both systems may have gone through all the appropriate approval processes, the identity management system should be configured to the point that it not only understands the business rules of the environment (that a developer should not have access to both a development system and a production system) but also can make intelligent decisions if a contradictory access request is submitted.

Based on your environment, you may wish to have the identity management system eliminate the developer's access on the development machine prior to granting the developer access to the production machine, and also document that action in a log. Or you may have the identity management system prevent access to the production machine until another request is matched up with the production request that eliminates access for the same identity to the development machine. Or you could make a rule that states that under no circumstances will someone that is in a development RBAC have access to production machines. One of the more challenging aspects of incorporating RBACs is determining what could be allowed under certain circumstances versus what hard rules your environment requires.

User RBACs as Business Drivers

RBACs can also be used as business drivers. For example, suppose that your business offers outsourced call center services and that these services rely on different access rights for different customers on the same applications. In other words, for various reasons, including ones of a contractual nature, call center personnel cannot access company B's information while they are servicing company A's customers. One of your primary assets is the ability to leverage your call center operators across multiple accounts for overflow calls. A properly implemented identity management solution will be able to re-provision call center operators quickly to different customers based on where the need is. If RBACs are set up for each of the customer profiles, and the business logic is constructed in such a way that having access to one customer's information inherently disables the ability to access any other customer's information, you can rapidly use operator resources in different roles and provide assurance to your customers that you are not violating any contractual obligations. This is far easier to implement in automated identity management solution systems than in manual ones. This example is defined simply here; actual implementation may require a considerable amount of thought and logic. Additionally, it is strongly suggested that you review and have a grasp of the inception and proliferation management details before you move forward with defining RBACs.

ONE STEP FURTHER

Most users actually use applications, platforms, and systems for 8 hours a day, yet their accounts are active for 24 hours a day (plus weekends and holidays). If a user is not at their desk, there are probably not too many good reasons why the accounts should be active. Therefore, disabling users' accounts while they are not at their desks or on duty could have some unique security benefits. But how could this be done? Considering that most building access in corporate America today is done through electronically controlled badge systems, it is not unreasonable to assume that an identity management system could tie the identity of a user's badge to their identity on applications, platforms, and systems across the enterprise. If users were forced to "badge out" of the facilities that they were in when they leave for the evening, in theory, all of their accounts across the enterprise could be disabled. When they return in the morning and "badge in," the identity management system could re-enable all of their accounts before they arrive at their desks. Taking this thought another step further, when a user badges out at night and their accounts are disabled, their profile for VPN could be enabled. Once they return to the office the next morning, by badging in, they would disable their VPN profile. While this solution would have to be tailored to a specific environment to accommodate performance and failure processes, you can already see that a number of very interesting things could be accomplished with a properly implemented identity management system.

Control the Termination Process

Deleting orphan accounts is an ongoing process within any organization. *Orphan accounts* are accounts that do not have users associated with them anymore. Generally, orphan accounts are left behind as a result of setups that occur without a formal process and where termination processes are not clearly defined and enforced either. If inception of an identity within an organization is managed by a simple phone call, e-mail, or a conversation by the water cooler, termination is rarely initiated from the same source. The danger, of course, is that a terminated user's access to system resources is not removed and may provide an avenue for successful attack.

One of the first steps that you need to complete when creating a termination procedure for identities is to develop a timeframe in which to perform the termination and eliminate their access across the environment. You need to consider a number of factors, including your security policy, the conditions under which the user parted the organization, the class of employee that the user was, etc. The amount of time generally recognized as appropriate may vary by industry, by agreements that you have made with your customers, and even by department within your organization. Determining the right timeframe in which to terminate identities requires research and should be established prior to implementing a technology that facilitates the termination of identities.

Identity management systems can also be configured to work off a general trigger within the organization. For example, the point at which someone goes through an exit interview and is being removed from the payroll system could serve as the start of a process to automatically eliminate the individual's identity across the enterprise. Alternatively, if a user has not logged onto the network for two weeks, this could send an alert to someone who can investigate the user's status. They may be on maternity leave, on a sabbatical, or maybe have just not showed up to work for a while. From there, a determination can be made by someone in a position of authority on whether or not to disable the account.

As identity management solutions are starting to reach further and further past the walls of a traditional enterprise, it is important to realize that you can use a number of events to cause an identity to be terminated. For example, if one of your partners files for bankruptcy, you may wish to use that event to terminate access of its users into your environment. Additionally, you may wish to make decisions, either manually or automatically, if there is suspicious activity associated with an account or if the account is past due. The point here is to look at the identities that you are servicing and become intimate with the reasons why an account should be terminated.

Manage Identities Through Workflow and Audit Processes

Workflow and audit processes are threads that tie identity management together. They are as much the supporting foundation of an identity management implementation as they are the interface through which most people actually work with identity management. Throughout the four parts of identity management outlined in the previous section, "Use Identity Management to Enforce Corporate Access Control Policies," there is a consistent theme of how this will work within your environment. Workflow processing will provide the routing of approvals for an identity to be established, the plumbing for how exceptions will be agreed upon, and the conduits between the business direction and how identities are technically set up.

Most identity management products come equipped with their own workflow applications. One major point to consider here is this: do you want to use an identity management vendor's workflow? While workflows that are designed and built by identity management vendors typically work very well within their relative suite of products, most organizations already have their own preexisting workflow applications. As a result, you need to determine with regard to workflow applications whether you want to introduce an additional workflow application within your environment. You also need to determine whether the vendor can divorce itself from its workflow application and effectively work with one of your preexisting workflow applications? Some products on the market today cannot effectively leverage third-party workflow applications.

The audit functions within an identity management system are the story of how identities were used within the environment. Audit trails establish which identities were active and what access they had at what time. This level of detail is becoming more of a requirement in a world where executive management is starting to be held accountable for what controls it has in place and how it knows that those controls are accurate.

An interesting question that you should ask when looking at the auditing capabilities of identity management vendors is, "How do I know that the audit logs that I am looking at are accurate?" Because identity management solutions capture users and rights for those users, it makes an ideal place to audit user profiles and what accesses an identity had access to during its life cycle. When looking at identity management solutions, investigate how the logs themselves are protected, especially if one of your goals is to effectively report on user accesses. First of all, you must determine who has access to view and modify the logs; and you'll want to be able to identify if the logs that you are viewing have been tampered with. Many identity management systems create audit logs as text files that normally are not tamper-resistant on their own. It is a good idea to investigate methods to digitally sign logs so that some level of assurance can be provided that they have not been tampered with. While there are homegrown methods to do this, the most effective approach is to hold the vendor you select responsible for providing tamper resistance.

Chapter 4

Hardening Cross-Platform Authentication

by Jason Zann

- Harden Passwords
- Choose the Most Secure Authentication Processes
- Use Strong Authentication to Protect Sensitive Resources
- Harden Your Authentication Sources
- Use Your Hardened Authentication Methods Cross Platform

Authentication is the process of proving that we are who we say we are. In many networks, authentication is one of the cornerstones of security. Access to resources and privileges on the network is assigned to a digital identity—for example, a user ID. To read the file, run the program, or configure the system, we must not only know which digital identity to use, but have some credentials to prove that we are the user represented by the digital ID. Conversely, should we lose or give away control of our credentials, we have given away our digital identity—he who has the credentials becomes us. Ensuring that only the true user is able to prove her identity is the goal of hardening authentication. Coordinating and ensuring this process in an organization that has multiple operating systems and other network devices is the goal of hardening cross-platform authentication. In order to do so, knowledge of common authentication algorithms, devices, and processes is necessary.

NOTE Authentication is not just the purview of human users of computers. Operating systems, specialized services, and applications may run under the context of an identity and therefore may also authenticate before accessing system, network, file, or other resources. Examples of the use of such identities are programs that monitor operating systems and applications that need access to databases. Many discussions of authentication use the term entity instead of "user."

The most common credential used to authenticate is a password. For each identity, a password must be presented. If the password matches the password stored for the identity, the identity is considered validated. Other examples of credentials, such as digital certificates, tokens, and biometrics, can be used to authenticate entities based on the possession of unique characteristics of the identity itself, such as a finger or voice print.

While some forms of authentication are considered more secure than others, it may be impossible to move to more secure forms of authentication, especially in a mixed environment. Some operating systems and network devices are not compatible with some devices, and even where homogeneity exists among systems and more secure authentication processes and/or devices can be implemented, the cost to do so may be prohibitive. Regardless of the authentication processes that must be used, there are numerous ways to harden authentication, and the desire to totally modify or move to more secure systems should not prevent actions that can make any authentication process more secure.

Harden Passwords

Passwords are the primary method of authentication for systems, but may also pose the largest risk of exposure to attacks. As a good rule of thumb, passwords should be complex. This means that they should be at least six characters long and comprise letters (upper- and lowercase), numbers, and at least one special character. Special characters are the SHIFT characters for numbers, -, _, +, =, :, ;, ", ', ?, /, ., comma, and so forth. Complex passwords should be a minimum requirement for every system.

Complex passwords are more important than people realize. Passwords that are six characters in length and use upper- and lowercase letters, numbers, and special characters (essentially, all printable ASCII possibilities) have approximately 670 billion possibilities (94 unique characters using a password length of six characters, or 94^6). To put this into perspective, if enough processor power were made available to attempt matching 100,000 random character combinations against the password per second (a standard desktop bought at a computer store in early 2004 would suffice), it would take a little over 2.5 months to attempt all the possible combinations. This type of attack is called a *brute-force attack*. While this may seem extreme, using simple probability, you can deduct that there is a 50 percent chance that a password could be determined in half the time (a little over 1.25 months), a 25 percent chance that a password could be discovered in about 2.5 weeks, a 12.5 percent chance in 1.25 weeks, and so on.

HEADS UP!

Modern password-cracking programs can and do increase the likelihood that passwords will be cracked in less time by using heuristics and by distributing the cracking load on several computers. For example, the creators of these programs surmise that most users will add numbers and/or capital letters at the beginning and end of their password, and so test those combinations before doing a brute force. They also know that many of the 670 billion or so possibilities are known words, and so use a dictionary attack (run the passwords against an encryption of a dictionary of words, looking for matches) to deduce the value of the password. This does not mean that complex passwords should not be used, but rather that users need training to reduce the possibility that they will create complex passwords that are easy to crack.

Table 4-1 compares the time taken to cycle through all combinations of a given password, when passwords are derived from either a 26- or 94-character set. These calculations assume that 100,000 computations per second are being processed.

Harden Users Passwords

Most organizations have two general categories of users: internal users (such as employees) and external users (such as customers). It is important to recognize this distinction, because you most likely need different password policies for each type of user.

Generally, you have more control over internal users than external users and thus can enforce a stricter password policy for internal users. Additionally, in most cases, internal users have access to more network resources than do external users, so usually a greater need exists to have more controls in place for your internal users.

Number of Characters	Total Time to Attempt Every Possibility of a Password Derived from a 26-Character Set	Total Time to Attempt Every Possibility of a Password Derived from 94-Character Set
3	0.18 second	8.3 seconds
4	4.57 seconds	13.0 minutes
5	1.98 minutes	20.4 hours
6	51.5 minutes	2.63 months
7	22.3 hours	20.6 years
8	24.2 days	1930 years
9	1.72 years	182,000 years
10	44.8 years	17,079,000 years
11	1160 years	1,605,461,000 years
12	30,300 years	150,913,342,000 years

Table 4-1. Password-Cracking Time Comparison

For external users, especially if they are customers, you have to consider a number of other factors with regard to the password policy. Generally, password policies for external users are a little more relaxed, normally for business reasons. For example, you want your customer password policy to be more relaxed so that customers can easily complete business transactions with your company. Depending on the environment that you are in, insisting on a strict password policy for customers could inhibit business.

Recommendations for Internal Users

The most important step toward hardening users' passwords is to create a culture in which secure passwords are the norm. As indicated previously in Table 4-1, the security of passwords increases with complexity and length. When creating a culture for secure passwords, you must do the following:

- *Alert users that they are responsible for following secure protocols with their passwords.* It is difficult to hold someone responsible for what occurs with their ID, because an attacker may gain access to a user's password through no fault of the user. For example, an attacker might be able to use a password-cracking program, or trick an administrator into changing the password. However, you can hold users personally responsible for following secure protocols with their passwords. For example, a user who places their password on a post-it note on the side of a monitor or uses it as a screen saver should be strongly reprimanded. In the banking industry, signature cards are used to validate an individual's signature. If the bank releases money to an individual without verifying the signature against the signature card, and the signature turns out to be fraudulent, the employee who allowed this to occur is generally punished up to, and possibly including, termination for violating the protocol. A similar model for users and password protocols may be warranted.

- *Give users a method with which to remember secure passwords.* Users generally have multiple passwords to remember. You don't want passwords to be so complex that users have to write them down, but you also don't want easy-to-remember passwords that are not very secure. Here are some suggestions for secure password construction to pass along to users:
  - *Condense a phrase into a set of letters.* It is generally best for the user to choose a phrase that they are familiar with. Suppose the user is a fan of Charles Dickens, whose book *A Tale of Two Cities* begins, "It was the best of times, it was the worst of times." For a password, the user could take the first letter of the first six words, keep the comma, and exchange the lowercase *o* with the number 0. So, the password would be Iwtb0t,. This password fulfills all the complexity requirements, and the user should be able to recall the password. For future passwords, suggest that the user continue this theme. For example, maybe this year the user could derive passwords from different quotes from *A Tale of Two Cities*, and next year could use another book by Dickens. Or, maybe this year the user could use quotes from Charles Dickens' books and next year use quotes from another favorite author's books. This method also works well with songs, poems, movies, and the like.
  - *Make a password stronger by inserting numbers and special characters toward the middle of a password.* Many password-cracking programs try to use special characters at the beginning and end of the password before trying them in the middle.
  - *Merge two mutually exclusive categories, using a special character in between.* For example, one category could be sports cars and the other could be sports teams. The goal here again is to use something that the user is familiar with. Suppose that the user has a mental list of their favorite sports cars, in alphabetical order starting with Corvette, and has a mental list of their favorite professional baseball teams, starting with the Detroit Tigers. For this example, they could merge the first syllables of Corvette and Tigers and use a number and special character combination to merge them, such as Cor2&Tig. When the password needs to be changed, the user can simply rotate one or both of the abbreviated words and keep the number and symbol the same.

CAUTION Users must come up with a way to create, sustain, and rotate passwords that are familiar to them and that are also secure. It is important to tell users not to reveal the logic behind their passwords to anyone.

- *Provide users a secure place to store their passwords.* While it is nice to think that all users will remember their passwords without having to jot them down, the reality is that it will never happen. Sometimes access is granted to a system that is used only a few times a year (for example, generally, users log into HR systems only when it is time to re-enroll for benefits, once a year). If a user has not logged into a system for a while, it is only natural that they may have forgotten their password. To address this, third-party applications are available that provide secure storage of passwords. Products like eWallet from Ilium Software (http://www.iliumsoft.com) enable users to store securely not only passwords but also credit card numbers, calling card numbers, and the like.

Recommendations for External Users

As for external users of your systems, such as customers, it is a little more difficult to educate them and to enforce the use of strong passwords. This may be due to technical limitations, such as the inability of their applications and systems to meet your standards, but if your controls are too strict, customers may simply be unwilling to use your system. If you make things too difficult to use, the result may be a reduction in your business. Conversely, if you make things too easy to use, it may be easy for an attacker to compromise the system and steal money and/or an identity. As a rule of thumb for external users, evaluate the risk and enforce a strict a password policy that is appropriate to the risk. Ensure that both you and your customers understand the risk when customers do not engage in a secure password protocol.

Additionally, it is a good idea to have in place countermeasures, such as checks and balances, to limit your exposure. For example, an online banking company might want to limit the total amount that can be cleared in one transaction (much as ATMs do in the physical world), or an online brokerage firm may not want to allow address changes and redemptions to be done within a short amount of time. Another very useful countermeasure is to monitor addresses changes on accounts. If an address changes, send snail mail informing of the change to both addresses and include a phone number for any questions. While there is exposure any time that you entrust a customer with something that could negatively impact your business (like their password protocols), it is important that you understand your exposure and how to address it.

Harden Non-User Passwords

Non-user passwords are passwords for accounts (digital IDs) that either are not tied to a person or cannot be restricted to use by only one person. Instead, they are used by computers or processes (such as services) or must be used by many people. It is important to minimize the number of these passwords, but they inevitably are necessary so you must be able to deal with them.

Harden Service Account Passwords

A common example of a non-user password is one that is used by a service account. A *service account* is an account that is set up by an administrator for an application or process to log into the machine. For example, service accounts would be set up for machine monitoring software and backup software. In both examples, administrator-level or otherwise-privileged accounts are set up at the time that the software is loaded. In many organizations, the passwords for these accounts are rarely, if ever, revised, making them easy targets for password-cracking programs.

Another issue with service account passwords occurs when administrators set the password for all service accounts to the same thing. If the password is cracked for one account, all the accounts are compromised. If service accounts have administrative privileges, an unauthorized user could gain local administrator privileges on every machine that has one of these accounts set on it. Where computers are joined in a Windows domain, if domain-level accounts are used, the unauthorized user might gain administrative privileges throughout the domain.

When you use service accounts, you should follow these hardening rules:

- Service accounts should be local accounts so that whatever privileges they have are applicable only to a specific computer.
- Service account passwords should be periodically changed. This could be done through a product like Microsoft Systems Management Server (SMS) for Win32 platforms.
- Service account passwords should be long and complex. Computers, not users, use the passwords, so you don't need to be concerned about the passwords being too long and complex; no legitimate user should ever log on using these accounts. However, because attackers might see them as good targets to attack, you need to make sure to use long, complex passwords.

Harden Passwords Used by Multiple People

Occasionally an administrative-level account cannot be restricted to use by one individual. This is not a good practice, and most computer operating systems now allow the creation of a number of user accounts so that every user can have a unique account. However, this is not true of some network devices such as routers and switches. For these network devices, you should use RADIUS or TACACS (as explained later in this section) to ensure user accountability. If RADIUS or TACACS is not available, a password is required to put the router or switch into "enable" mode. This password, even though it may rarely be used, is a single password that may be known by multiple people.

When multiple individuals must be able to manage such devices, they all must know the password. Not only does this make it more likely that an unauthorized individual will learn the password, but it also prevents strict accountability for any configuration changes made to the device. Instead of being able to hold one individual accountable, multiple people must share accountability. Nevertheless, you can make the situation more secure by frequently changing the password, by ensuring only authorized individuals are given access to the password, and by ensuring that those individuals understand and practice secure protocols for handling the password and understand that they cannot share the password with others, even those they believe are authorized.

Another secure practice is to implement centralized control of an authentication, authorization, and accounting (AAA) server, such as a TACACS server. This server can be used to provide individual accounts for administrators that then will provide them access to network devices.

NOTE For more information on RADIUS and TACACS implementations, please see the *Hardening Network Infrastructure* book in this series.

If direct access via modem or console is required for a specific network device, and the device cannot see the RADIUS or TACACS server, the local enable function can be used, which requires a static local password. The need for an enable password should be the exception rather than the rule; therefore, the enable console password could be stored until it is needed. One of the best ways of building in security to this practice is to have one individual who is responsible for creating and testing the password. Once the password is tested, it should be placed in a sealed, nontransparent envelope in a secure location (such as a locked file cabinet) that can be accessed by all parties that could potentially need the password. If the password is needed, an authorized individual can retrieve the envelope, open it, and use the password. Once the password has been used, the individual who created the password is notified. That person then resets the password, places it into an envelope, and puts the envelope back in the secured location.

This solution actually solves a number of issues with regard to shared passwords. It limits to one the number of people who know the password before it is used (the individual who created the password), it provides a level of tamper resistance (if the envelope is opened, it can be assumed that the password is known and should be changed), and it lends itself nicely to being audited (there are checks and balances that can validate whether or not the password is known).

Choose the Most Secure Authentication Processes

At its core, authentication is a binary decision—after an entity presents credentials, the authentication source returns a response of either pass or fail. There are a number of different ways to authenticate subjects to a system, and numerous technologies that can be used. Before you decide which method and technology to use, you must understand how and where to implement whichever type of authentication you choose. Many of these considerations vary based on the amount of time, money, and resources that you have to put into an authentication system, and on an evaluation of risk. You have to make these decisions based on your environment. This section covers the three types of authentication, listed next, and what you need to consider when implementing each of them:

- Authentication based on something that you know
- Authentication based on an immutable physical characteristic
- Authentication based on something that you have

Authentication Based on Something that You Know

As stated earlier in the chapter, the most common method of authentication is the use of a password. A password is something that an individual knows that allows them to gain access to a system. You must know the different parameters of passwords and understand how and why they must be implemented. Password length is only one of six common password parameters. All of them are listed in Table 4-2. These parameters may not be addressed in every existing password implementation in your environment; however, you need to be familiar with these parameters, because they may drive the decisions for how you implement a product that you select.

Parameter	Explanation	Recommendation
Password History	Indicates how many of a user's old passwords will be stored. When passwords are changed, neither the current password nor any of the stored passwords may be used. Users cannot, therefore, reset their password to the password that has just expired. If Password History is set to 6, for example, users cannot set their password to any of the past six passwords. Additionally, this forces users to engage in a password rotation scheme, at a minimum.	Require at least six unique passwords before allowing reuse.
Maximum Password Age	Indicates how long a password can be used before it must be changed.	Allow passwords to be used for 35 days for user accounts and 90 days for service accounts. These numbers may change in your environment based on the rules that you have in place for password length and complexity. Think of this setting as playing the odds. As Table 4-1 indicates, a direct correlation exists between the length and complexity of a password and how long it takes to crack.
Minimum Password Age	Indicates the minimum amount of time that a password must be used before it can be changed. Without this setting, users may be tempted to change their password multiple times in one day to fulfill the Password History requirement and get back to their original password.	Set it to 7 days. This timeframe generally forces users to adopt their new password, and they are less likely to change it every 7 days simply to get back to their original password.

Table 4-2. Password Parameters

Parameter	Explanation	Recommendation
Password Length	Indicates the minimum number of total characters that a password must be.	Password length should be at least six characters. While users generally gravitate toward the minimum, you should be sure to make them aware of the available password length that they can use and that longer passwords are more secure.
Password Complexity	Refers to the actual types of characters that should be used to create a password. In a Windows environment, passwords must meet three conditions: 1. Must include three out of four types: uppercase letters, lowercase letters, numbers, and special characters. 2. Cannot include usernames or IDs. 3. Must be at least six characters long.	In a Windows environment, choices are Enable or Disable. When enabled, users must meet the requirement. Provide users with instructions to use, at a minimum, at least one uppercase and one lowercase letter and one number or one symbol. *Caution:* Users are traditionally like electricity—they follow the path of least resistance. As a result, even if you have a password complexity scheme, users could potentially make weak passwords. For example, a password of June2004 or June2004! incorporates a special character and may follow your complexity standards, but it is not a secure password. Teach users to avoid using implementations such as capital letters at the beginning and numbers at the end that make passwords easier to crack.
Account Lockout	Can prevent account compromise by preventing endless attempts at "guessing" passwords. A maximum number of incorrect password entries may be made after which the account is locked out and even a correct password entry will not be processed. Can also prevent legitimate users from authenticating. If an attacker guesses the password before the account is locked out, or cracks the password offline, account lockout will not prevent account compromise. This feature has several parameters.	Set the parameters as follows: **Account Lockout Threshold** Set to 3. Three bad passwords, and the account is locked out. **Account Lockout Duration** Set to 30 minutes. The lockout will be terminated after 30 minutes. This parameter can also be set to require administrative reset. **Reset Account Lockout Counter After** Set to 30 minutes. If an incorrect attempt is entered and the account lockout threshold is not met, and if 30 minutes or more elapses before another attempt is made, the lockout counter (how many bad attempts have been made) is reset to 0.

Table 4-2. Password Parameters *(continued)*

The recommendation to set Account Lockout has become controversial, because doing so can result in forgetful, legitimate users being locked out. Doing so may also make it easy to mount denial of service (DoS) attacks against many accounts by simply running a password cracking attack against them. The attacker may not crack any passwords, but his attempts will result in many accounts being locked out and legitimate users denied access. To make the former issue less of a problem, many organizations increase the number of incorrect passwords that may be entered before an account is locked out. One possible solution for the latter problem is to make it difficult for an attacker to obtain or guess user IDs. In addition to preventing anonymous access (access that does not require an authorized account) to account lists, another technique is to not use an incremental naming convention.

Just as it is necessary to keep passwords private to provide for user security, it is equally important to keep user naming conventions (user IDs) as confidential as possible, to prevent an adversary from systematically locking out all of your accounts. For example, suppose that your user naming convention consists of an incremental user ID (User1, User2, User3, etc.), adopted to facilitate the setup of numerous users. The logic is that an account can be set up, and then assigned to a user at a later time. The potential issue with this approach is that if an adversary is aware that you are using it and also knows your password parameters (three bad attempts and the account gets locked out), they could write a very short program that would go in a loop (User1 and password *XXX* three times) and systematically lock out every account that is using this convention. Because the naming convention is constant and incremental and the adversary knows the password limitations, the attack could be an automated attack that happens very quickly and causes a tremendous amount of problems. Imagine for example a DoS on a Web-facing application. As a countermeasure, prepare a counterscript to unlock all the accounts.

CAUTION A counterscript created to re-enable all the locked accounts could actually re-enable legitimately locked accounts.

A possible workaround that prevents enablement of legitimately disabled accounts is to create a script that ties the account login attempts to a timestamp. The timestamp would reveal the time that the lockout occurred. If a mass lockout occurred, you could query all the lockouts that occurred within a limited amount of time (say, 15 minutes) and then write a counterscript to re-enable just the accounts that were locked during that particular period of time. While this may not re-enable every account that was locked by the attack, it prevents you from unlocking legitimate accounts that were locked for security purposes before and after the attack.

However, you need to understand that the adversary could modify their program to lock out random accounts at random times, possibly masking that this is actually an attack. This type of attack could cause a number of issues even if it is only marginally successful. The best way to prevent this type of attack is to not use incremental user IDs and to protect the user account list. One method of creating nonincremental user IDs is to allow users to choose their own user IDs. If you must create a large number of accounts with a common structure, use some identifier that is specific to the user in addition to a sequence. For example, for user John Dean Doe, you could have a user ID of JDD001 instead of user00001. Jane Dora Doe would be JDD002, and so on. If an attacker were to lock out a system like this, they would need more information than just the sequence of numbers. They would need to know specifics about the accounts.

CAUTION The difficulty of using unstructured, nonsequenced accounts increases with the size of the environment.

Authentication Based on an Immutable Physical Characteristic

Immutable physical characteristics such as fingerprints, voiceprints, retinal scans, and the like can be used for authentication. This is also sometimes referred to as "something you are." The process of identifying an individual to a system based on a unique personal characteristic is called *biometrics.* With the implementation of biometric systems, instead of using a user ID and password to log into a system, you use something specific to you, like a fingerprint. Unlike passwords, users cannot forget fingerprints.

Biometrics also introduces a new paradigm. In addition to authentication—the process of proving that you are who you say you are—biometrics may be used for identification: who is the person that matches the biometric that has just been entered? In the case of authentication, the person enters or selects a user ID and then presents the biometric. If the biometric matches the biometric stored for the user ID, the user is authenticated. In the case of identification, no user ID is entered. The person presents the biometric, and the database is searched for a matching, stored biometric. If a match is found, the user is identified and authenticated. Unlike biometrics, passwords cannot be used for identification, since there is nothing in place that physically ties every password to a user.

While the use of biometrics does eliminate the need for users to remember passwords, you need to take into account the following critical considerations before you implement a biometric solution on a large scale:

- How is the enrollment accomplished?
- How are biometric readers secured?
- How are false accepts and false rejects addressed?

Create a Secure Enrollment Process

Biometrics is considered by many to be the most singularly secure authentication method available, because, in theory, you should be the only person capable of producing your biometric. One of the primary issues with biometrics is the enrollment process, in which a user's biometric is given a digital representation and bound to a user account. In the world of password authentication, if a user is being set up on a system, a user ID and password can be entered by an authorized administrator and distributed to the user via e-mail, postal mail, or over the phone. In the world of biometrics, this process is not available because the user must be physically present at the time of initial enrollment.

If done correctly, the enrollment process needs to be done only once per user. Before you begin the enrollment process, you should address the following questions:

- How do you know that the individual being enrolled is really who they say they are?
- What is being enrolled, and what if it is not available?
- What if the enrollment is compromised?

As an example of how you might address these questions, the preceding questions are addressed next using a scenario in which your organization would like to implement fingerprint biometrics as a manner of authentication to the network.

How do you know that the individual being enrolled is really who they say they are? Most corporate environments have a predefined way to verify that an individual is who they say they are. This type of verification could be done by matching a face on a badge with the individual who is enrolling. Additionally, there is usually a name on the badge that could be matched with some preexisting internal record of the individual. In smaller organizations, verification is generally done by personal recognition, because there is a higher probability that everyone knows everyone else. At the time of enrollment, that personal recognition would be done and the proper information would be associated with the individual's biometric.

Enrollment becomes more complicated when contractors, customers, and business partners need to go through the enrollment process. How do you validate that they are who they say they are? This is similar to the problem traditionally confronted by departments of motor vehicles across the country. In this scenario, two colluding individuals go to a DMV and one requests a new driver's license. When that individual is called to have his photo taken, the second individual stands up and has his photo taken. As a result, incorrect information is associated with a proper biometric. While this scam generally is intended to enable a younger person to authenticate as an older individual, it is a classic example of how a weakness in the enrollment process of a biometric can yield longer-term adverse effects.

With regard to enrolling third parties, normally your company does not have sufficient shared resources with a third-party company to validate an individual's identity. Therefore, despite the prior example, the common procedure is to request from the individual a common, government-issued ID (like a driver's license) to validate that individual. The point here is that these types of issues need to be considered, mapped out, and enforced through processes.

What is being enrolled, and what if it is not available? Assume that your company is using the right-hand index finger as the biometric. Your procedure must identify what to do if an enrolling user has no right index finger or has one but it is unavailable at the time of enrollment because, for example, it was cut or burned and is now bandaged. Obviously, someone whose index finger has been amputated will have to use a different finger. But for someone whose right index finger is bandaged at the time of enrollment, will you use a different finger or have them re-enroll when it's healed? This is not just an issue for fingerprints. Similar questions need to be addressed for retina scans, voice recognition, etc. The goal of enrollment should be to complete it at one time. So, when you are determining what is necessary to be enrolled, you need to think of all the issues that may occur that could make the enrollment invalid.

You also need to consider what will happen after enrollment if a person's enrollment biometric becomes unavailable. If only the right index finger is used, and it is later amputated or temporarily unavailable, what then? While this is an authentication problem, it should be considered when deciding what to choose as the biometric for enrollment. In this case, perhaps more than one finger can be enrolled. A damaged or missing finger would therefore not cause a problem since another enrolled and available finger could be used.

What if the enrollment is compromised? A biometric system stores credentials in a digital format. As a result, you need to consider the possibility of that biometric being compromised. If a password is compromised, it can be reissued, whereas that same luxury is not available for biometrics. A Japanese cryptographer by the name of Tsutomu Matsumoto wrote a paper in 2002 on how he could circumvent the top 11 fingerprint biometric companies' products with $10 worth of household goods (http://cryptome.org/gummy.htm). This is an example of an attack that could render a biometric implementation virtually useless, not because the product does not work but because there is a published method to defeat the strengths of a biometric implementation.

Secure Biometric Readers

Biometric readers come in two types: centralized and decentralized. As the name indicates, centralized biometric readers are generally centrally located and utilized. They are commonly used for access to physical facilities, like data centers. Thus, only a limited number of locations actually house a reader, but each reader is used to authenticate many users. Retinal scanners and hand-geometry devices are examples of centralized readers. Another good example of a centralized biometric reader is voice-recognition software, which could be accessed via phone and does voiceprint analysis of users that call in against a prerecorded voiceprint.

Centralized biometric implementations do have some drawbacks. For example, if the reader is down, multiple users are affected. However, as in most centralized environments, this type of implementation has a single place to build in redundancy and scalability. A backup device should be available.

NOTE Voiceprint biometric software is often a very good solution for self-help password resets. Generally, if a user forgets their password for a network login, they are locked out of the network until someone can reset their account. Implementing voiceprint biometrics enables users to be authenticated via their voice; once they are authenticated, the system can automatically reset their account. Using this software often saves costs, because password resets are statistically one of the top five reasons that users call the enterprise help desk.

Decentralized biometric readers are those in which there is usually a one-to-one relationship between the reader and a user, and these are the type of readers typically used for network authentication. Examples of decentralized readers are fingerprint readers and iris scanners at every desktop. Decentralized readers can work with a local database (available on the local computer) or be used to capture and forward credentials to a central server for verification. If you are building a decentralized biometric solution, you need to include backup procedures that assist users in dealing with malfunctioning or missing devices. Additionally, you need to address how users will log into machines if the authenticating server is unavailable (for example, connectivity to the server is down). It is important to remember that including biometrics in a decentralized manner, such as at the desktop, adds another layer of complexity with regard to users authenticating. While you may achieve additional security benefits, you must weigh them against the impact on the usability of the system.

Choose a System with Low False Accepts and False Rejects

Biometrics is not a perfect science. A *false accept,* someone other than you might be authenticated as you, or a *false reject,* you may not be able to authenticate as you, is possible. A continuing issue with the implementation of biometrics is how to deal with these types of biometric failures. Depending on how you plan to implement biometrics, these issues could have very adverse effects. For example, suppose that you were going to implement facial-recognition biometrics at a high-traffic location, like a sports venue or an airport, to identify criminals or individuals on a "watch list." Assuming that the issues of enrollment (as previously outlined) were adequately addressed, you would still have to concern yourself with the inherent failures of biometrics. To take this example a step further, suppose that the biometrics product that you selected has only a 1 percent failure rate (consisting of .5 percent false accept and .5 percent false negative). This means that for every 1 million people that are read by these facial-recognition devices, 5000 people that are on the watch list will not be detected (false rejects) and 5000 people that are not on the watch list will be identified as someone on the watch list (false accepts). These failures not only are unacceptable, but may cause more problems than they solve.

To look at another example, suppose that you wish to implement a biometric hand-geometry solution for people to access your computer-room floor. A total of 50 people require access to the computer-room floor and they pass through the biometric device four times daily. This means that there will be 200 authentications per day and 1000 total authentications for a standard workweek. Using the same failure rate of 1 percent, there would be an average of ten problems per week with this example's limited parameters.

The examples here use a 1 percent failure rate. This may be a little optimistic. While some vendors claim .01 percent failure rates, you can find varying rates from actual usage by browsing the Internet. A 99.7 True Accept Rate and 0.01 False Accept Rate was found in tests of the IDENT system used to authenticate U.S. visitors by using fingerprint biometrics (from the National Institute of Standards and Technology at http://www.itl.nist.gov/iad/894.03/fing/imbe04_clw.ppt). A 2 percent failure rate for fingerprint readers and a 40 percent failure rate for facial recognition when used for identification is reported in an article from SecurityFocus at http://www.securityfocus.com/news/566. Other widely quoted reports indicate failure rates of 4 and 5 percent, respectively. Caution should be used when reading all such reports. Failure rates will vary due to the quality of the hardware (the NIST report states that the equipment it tested was not the commonly available commercial products), how the systems are configured, whether they are used for identification or authentication, and how they are used.

The issue to understand is that biometric solutions are not perfect. If a vendor claims a suspiciously low failure rate, investigate what the conditions were when the rate was determined, such as how long the tests were run, what the weather conditions were like (were the sensors near warmer or cooler environments), what the location of the reader was (in a manufacturing facility or a clean room), what the users were like (did they have salt on their hands from French fries at lunch), and so forth. Failure rates should be considered, since failure rates have the ability to make or break a biometric solution.

NOTE When considering biometric error rates, consider error rates in other databases. The NIST report has the following to say, "Consolidation results on various datasets available to NIST demonstrate that the errors obtained for one-to-one matching is less than the clerical error rate in most government databases. Clerical errors will be more common than biometric errors for one-to-one matching."

Authentication Based on Something that You Have

Some authentication systems require users to use a physical object such as a key card or token. The object may be linked to your digital identity or may be shared devices. These are authentication systems based on something that you have.

One example of such a system is based on the use of key cards. Key cards are often used to provide access to buildings. In many key-card systems, anyone with the physical card can gain access to anywhere the card permits. Nothing actually ties the card to an individual, other than the fact that it was assigned to an individual. The goal of requiring a user to have a physical object with which to authenticate is twofold. First, it limits the number of people who can authenticate. Second, it makes the user responsible for the key card and thus requires the user to keep track of whether it's secure and, if it is not, to report its loss or theft immediately so that it can be disabled internally. If the user misplaces or loses the key card, they cannot get in the building and thus know that they do not possess it. Contrast this with the use of a password. A user really never knows for certain that their password has not been compromised.

One of the primary benefits to using something that the user possesses for authentication is that the user does not have to remember a password. If the user needs to authenticate, the physical device provides the authentication credentials for the user. Physical devices that are used for authentication to systems rely on three primary means to do so:

- Random seed value
- Challenge/response
- A key

Choose Authentication Systems with Random Seed Values

A *random seed value* is a random number produced by a process. Each time authentication is necessary, the authenticator can be viewed to determine what the current password is. The random numbers that are generated on the device are unique to the device, the user, and the time that the user is logging in. Probably the most popular example of a random seed device is RSA SecurID. Figure 4-1 is an image of the RSA SecurID Key Fob (SD600). RSA SecurID allows a new password to be displayed every 60 seconds, which is valid only for a short length of time.

ONE STEP FURTHER

Some problems can be solved rather creatively when you deploy physical devices like random seed value tokens. For example, if a user needs to be authenticated over the phone, the call center representative could simply ask the user to recite their user ID and the current password being displayed on their token. The information gathered can be used to authenticate the user on the other end of the phone. Because the password on the fob changes randomly over a period of time and each password can be used only once, it is okay for the user to verbalize the password.

To facilitate this process, a small, web-based application could be built to allow the representative to input the user ID and password that is given to them over the phone. The application does not have to authenticate the representative to any application, just generate a response that the user ID and password given from the token match the name that the person on the phone provides. This procedure can be much more reliable than asking users static information, such as the last four digits of their social security number.

Figure 4-1. RSA SecurID Key Fob (SD600)

Choose Systems that Use Challenge/Response

The second method of authentication that uses something that you have is challenge/response. In old spy movies, a spy would go up to whom they believed was their contact and make a statement. Based on the response the contact gave, the spy would know whether or not to trust the contact. This is a classic example of challenge/response. It is also used by some web sites when a user forgets their password. During their original enrollment, the user is asked for some specific information that could be used to identify them at a later date, for example their mother's maiden name. When the user requests a password reset, the system presents a challenge, "Enter your mother's maiden name." If the user can respond with a match for the entry they originally made, they are issued a new password.

Challenge/response is also used in password-based systems such as Microsoft Windows. In a challenge/response password-based system, the system issues a challenge, in response to which the client device does some manipulation or computation using some information known to the user and the system issuing the challenge, and then issues a response. The information known to both client and server might be the user password or it could be some number stored in a physical device. Since the challenge-issuing system knows the challenge, the client information, and the computation, it can create a response and compare it to the one issued by the client. If there is a match, the user is authenticated. The process of using a physical device in a challenge/response system works as follows:

1. The user is presented with a login screen for an application that is enabled with challenge/response authentication.
2. The user inputs their user ID and presses the ENTER key.
3. The back-end authentication server looks at the user ID that was presented, recognizes what token the user should have, and issues a challenge (usually numbers) to the user's screen.
4. The user inserts the challenge numbers into the authentication device that they have been issued, and the device returns a response.
5. The user types the response from the device into the application and presses the ENTER key again.
6. If the response that the user types in matches what the server calculated the response should be, the user is authenticated.

CAUTION If you are using only something physical, such as a token, to authenticate a user to a system, and the token is lost or stolen, the authentication system will fail to protect the system from the time that the device is lost or stolen until the account for the device is disabled. In this respect, this is like using a password. Anyone who possesses your device can masquerade as you. It is very important to communicate to users that if they have lost control of their physical authentication device, they should report it immediately.

Systems can also be programmed to use a challenge/response to authenticate. One solution would be to create a digital hash of an application (something the program on the system *is*) and load an encryption key on the system for the application (something that the system *has*). Every time that the system tries to authenticate, the system responsible for the authentication takes the hash and the key of the authenticating system and runs a calculation, like a question (the challenge). When the authenticating system gets this challenge, it takes its elements (which need to be the same as the system that it is trying to authenticate to), the hash of the program, and the key and runs the challenge computation to generate the answer (response) to the question asked by the system to which it is trying to authenticate. If the same hash value is not available on both systems (the program has been changed) or the key is not available, the correct response to a challenge cannot be completed. By using this process, the system never has to send password-based credentials over the network, because the system is simply asking a question based on known elements of both systems.

Choose Systems that Use Digital Certificates

The third method of authentication that uses something that you have is the use of digital certificates. Digital certificates can be issued to computers and users and used in various security protocols such as authentication, e-mail encryption, digital signing, and file encryption.

The previously described authentication systems use symmetric encryption, in which the same key is used to encrypt and decrypt. Asymmetric encryption uses a key pair. One of the keys, the public key, may be publicly available, but the other, the private key, must be known only to the entity that owns the key pair. When the public key is used to encrypt, the private key must be used to decrypt, and vice versa. Digital certificates are used to bind the key pair to an identity. Digital certificates contain information about the entity they are issued to, contain the public key of a public/private key pair, and are signed by the Certification Authority (CA) that issued them. A CA is a process running on a server that manages and issues certificates to authorized entities (computers and users). The private key of the key pair is not part of the certificate.

When asymmetric encryption is used in authentication, the client presents the certificate to the authenticating server as proof that they are who they say they are. The authenticating server accepts the certificate as this proof only if it is signed by a CA it trusts and it can confirm that the digital signature on the certificate is valid. The certificate was signed by the CA by first making a message digest (a process that creates a small, condensed version of some data) of the certificate and then encrypting the message digest with the CA's private key. If the authenticating server trusts the CA that signed the certificate, the authenticating server will use the CA's public key to decrypt the message digest. It then makes its own message digest of the client certificate. If the two hashes match, then the signature is valid and the certificate is accepted as proof of the user's identity.

Because digital certificates are electronic data, they are subject to the issues that can affect any electronic data, such as copying, corruption, and so forth. To counter these issues, the most effective implementations of digital certificates for authentication store them on a physical device such as a smart card or a USB authentication token.

If you're implementing smart cards, you need a smart card reader at the location where you wish to authenticate users. Similarly, if you are using a USB authentication token, users must have access to a machine with a USB port. This method of authentication may not be practical for mobile users who need to use public computers. For example, if users will be using cyber cafés to access corporate resources while traveling and the machines that they are using to connect do not have a smart card reader or access to a USB port, your users will not be able to authenticate.

HEADS UP!

One of the most common security issues with smart card implementations is that users sometimes accidentally leave the smart card in the reader. If they do so, the next user of the computer could use it and authenticate as the former user. One of the best ways to reduce this problem is to have multiple uses for smart cards, to motivate users to better manage and control their smart cards. For example, many deployments, including U.S. government implementations, use smart cards for authentication not only to a computer system but also to a facility. Thus, if a user leaves his secure working area, he needs to take the smart card so that he can re-enter the area. Other smart card implementations enable users to store cash balances on their smart cards, similar to a credit card, so that they can make purchases with the smart card in the company gift store or cafeteria. With actual money attached to their cards, users are more inclined to take better care of their smart cards.

Another valuable use of encryption for authentication is for entity-to-entity authentication, such as business-to-business (B2B) communications. In these scenarios, one system on the Internet needs to authenticate with another system on the Internet. Enabling systems to authenticate to other systems is becoming more of a necessity as organizations begin to rely on each other to provide more services to their clients, such as web-based retailers' reliance on commercial shipping companies to ship goods to clients. Thus, one of the issues that you need to overcome is how to properly authenticate other systems.

While computers can be programmed to store and use passwords, using asymmetric encryption provides a more secure way of managing computer-to-computer authentication. Passwords could be used in this situation; however, a password is an example of a shared secret. Both the authenticating system and the system that is doing the authentication know the secret. However, asymmetric cryptography can be used by each of the entities to determine accountability. For example, if a password is discovered, either one of the entities could be responsible for allowing the secret to be divulged. If asymmetric keys are used for authentication, each entity has a private key. If the private key is divulged and fraudulent transactions are made with that key, it would be clear which entity allowed its secret to be compromised (providing for accountability).

ONE STEP FURTHER

As mentioned, smart cards and USB tokens are generally used to store digital certificates that are used for authentication to a system. Another use for digital certificates assigned to users is to digitally sign a document. The process is the same as that used by the CA to sign the digital certificate. The entity uses its private key to encrypt a message digest of the document. To prove the origin of the document, the encrypted message digest is decrypted by using the entity's public key. If the message digest matches one created by the entity testing the signature, then it is highly likely that the entity bound to the key signed the document. The caveat is that this method assumes the owner of the private key was in possession of the key at the time of the signing. As an additional note, this same signing process can be used to sign other data elements.

Use Strong Authentication to Protect Sensitive Resources

Strong authentication refers to using any two or more of the forms of authentication previously described (something that you have, know, or are) to authenticate to a system. Traditionally, strong authentication (in the security community) requires something you have and something you know. A classic example is an ATM card: to get money out of an ATM, you must physically have a card and know the PIN for the card that you present. However, strong authentication could require something you are and something you know (for example, a biometric and a password) or something you are and something you have (a biometric and a smart card).

NOTE Strong authentication is also known as *two-factor authentication* in the information security community.

If you elect to use something physical to authenticate someone to an electronic resource, such as an application or network, you should plan to use two-factor authentication. In fact, most commercial products that require users to use something that they have for authentication already have built-in configurations that support also requiring users to use something that they know. For example, if you are using RSA SecurID, out of the box, you can require users to use a password and the value that is displayed on the token for authentication. In the world of smart cards, most solutions force a user to enter a PIN or password to "unlock" the key so that it can be used for authentication.

Strong authentication has two layers of security built into it:

- A physical device must be present at the time of authentication. Users know if their physical device is missing, and thus can call the help desk to disable the account until a replacement is furnished.
- Even if the physical device is stolen, the adversary still needs the PIN or password (something the user knows) to append to the password produced by the token.

NOTE Create and enforce policies that prevent the user from taping the password or PIN to the back of a token (or etching it into the device itself!).

Harden Your Authentication Sources

Your authentication sources are some of the most important aspects of your environment because they store a large amount of user password information. Hardening these authentication sources is becoming more important in today's world as more attacks are directed at the authentication source and as government regulations continue to broaden to specify how some of these sources must be protected.

Traditionally, if your organization did not want to secure an authentication source, that was its prerogative. However, government regulators, like the Federal Trade Commission (FTC), and various state agencies are starting to take these issues more seriously and administering consequences for authentication sources with poor security. They are often able to collect large fines from companies who do not adequately protect authentication sources. Many of these fines are over concerns for the security of the private information kept about customers on authentication sources. Over the past couple of years, multiple organizations such as DoubleClick, Eli Lilly, US Bancorp, and Ekard have been fined for having less than adequate security for their authentication sources (http://64.233.179.104/search?q=cache:3IQbipapjqcJ:www.ehcca.com/presentations/compcongress6/schiavoneH.pdf+FTC+fines+privacy+authentication&hl=en). Similarly, Microsoft avoided a fine for misrepresentation of the security level of its Passport online authentication system only by accepting 20 years of independent audits and by modifying statements describing its system (http://www.isp-planet.com/news/2002/ftc_020809.html).

In addition to hardening the OS used on authentication stores and patching the OS and authentication processes, periodically audit their compliance with your organization's authentication policy and harden systems based on the authentication process used. If password authentication systems are used, there are some specific requirements that should be met to harden password stores. Once a password has been created, converting it back to clear text should be impossible. This is typically implemented by using a cryptographic hash of passwords stored in the password database. A hash is a one-way process that cannot be reversed. Instead of decrypting the stored password so that it can be matched with the password entered by the user, the entered password is cryptographically hashed using the same process. It may then be compared to the stored password directly or used in a challenge/response authentication process.

CAUTION Do not encrypt passwords! Encrypting passwords involves using an encryption key, which means that an encryption key can be used to decrypt the passwords as well, leading to the possibility that encrypted passwords will end up in plain text. In addition, if passwords are encrypted, the process can suffer from all the key-management issues outlined in Chapter 7.

For the most part, third-party applications have their own method to store passwords. If you are using a third-party application that has its own password store, you should make the vendor explain to you how passwords are stored and use the criteria in this section to make a decision on how secure the password store is. When evaluating a password store for a third-party product, ask the vendor the following questions:

- *Can the passwords be converted back to plain text?* If the answer is yes, for any reason (including the password being stored in plain text), you should avoid implementing the solution.
- *Does the solution use a cryptographic hash?* As previously outlined, when a password is created, it is sent through the process of a cryptographic hash. A hash, by its very nature, is a one-way function that cannot be reversed. (Cryptographically hashed passwords are subject to dictionary and brute-force attacks, as described in Chapter 7.) If a hash is used, the question to ask is whether it is a well-known hashing algorithm, like SHA1 or MD5. Using a well-known cryptographic process is always preferable to using a proprietary or obscure one. This is because many cryptographers have studied the algorithms and the algorithms are more likely to be more secure.
- *Does the solution offer a salted cryptographic hash?* A unique element that is added to a hash to make it more resilient to attack is called a *salt*. For example, if a password was simply hashed with SHA1, anyone who has access to SHA1 (which is freely available on the Internet) could precompute a list of potential passwords to compare with the hashed passwords within your application. This is another reason that you should take additional steps to secure your authentication sources. A salt added to SHA1 could make the implementation of SHA1 specific to an application. This means that an adversary would need

not only the hashing algorithm but also the salt that was used for the specific implementation of the hashing algorithm. If you are using this process, you should use different salts for every application so that if a password is determined for one application, the authentication stores of the other applications will not be affected.

ONE STEP FURTHER

Secure Remote Password (SRP) offers a unique password authentication solution if you are looking for alternative solutions for your environment. SRP not only solves the issue of how passwords are stored in a back-end server, but also provides a method to securely transmit passwords from the client to the server. SRP was designed to work in environments in which a trusted third party is not available and adversaries have, among other things, a working knowledge of the protocols used for authentication, access to large dictionary files that can be used for dictionary attacks, and the ability to snoop communications. For more information about SRP, refer to http://srp.stanford.edu/.

Use Your Hardened Authentication Methods Cross Platform

This chapter has discussed how to harden your authentication methods. To add efficiencies to your authentication implementations, you must look at ways to leverage authentication implementations across your environment. Systems normally support two methods of authentication: native authentication and third-party authentication. *Native authentication* refers to an authentication store that is native to the system. *Third-party authentication* is the capability for a system to "skip over" its native source and present credentials for authentication to a third-party system for a response to the credentials that have been supplied.

The first thing to consider when leveraging an authentication system across your environment is what common systems the majority of your users log into. If you are using Microsoft operating systems and have implemented Active Directory, you might want to point the authentication for as many systems, applications, and programs as possible to Active Directory. This offers a level of consistency with regard to passwords that a user has to remember and gives a centralized location to enforce passwords and disable accounts. If multiple systems are using a single authentication source, you can disable a user at one location (the authentication source) and the user will be disabled on every system that the user has access to that is using that authentication source.

A common example of this is Microsoft Exchange 2000 and 2003. For these versions of Exchange, Active Directory is the account database. No separate account or password is necessary. This makes the user experience easier because they have one less password to remember. Many other applications (third-party as well as homegrown applications) also offer the ability to use Active Directory as an authentication source.

CAUTION If an authentication source that is used by multiple systems goes down or cannot be seen by the systems that rely on that authentication source, login access to those systems will not be available.

Another option for leveraging pre-existing authentication sources for strong authentication is to point multiple systems to a strong authentication source, like RSA Security's RSA ACE/Server. Many applications now include an option to integrate directly into RSA ACE/Server. This allows multiple applications to have two-factor authentication (even ones that do not natively support two-factor authentication). Additionally, homegrown applications can take advantage of an RSA ACE/Server implementation by simply making a call to the RSA ACE/Server as opposed to its native password store. While this does offer an increased level of security, sometimes the user experience can be quite painful if every application that they have to log into or re-log into requires an additional step of referencing a token. The more times and systems that the user has to log into, the more painful the experience becomes. However, the benefit of being able to disable an account in one location and have related accounts disabled for multiple systems is still available in this type of implementation.

Another effective way to implement cross-platform authentication is to use a password management application, such as TFS ApplicationControl from TFS Technology (http://www.tfstech.com/). TFS ApplicationControl allows passwords to applications to be stored on a user's desktop in a secure format. Once a user authenticates to the TFS ApplicationControl program, passwords are inserted into applications at the time that a user accesses the application. This enables users to authenticate once (through TFS ApplicationControl) and thereafter allow TFS ApplicationControl to manage application passwords without user involvement. Any time that a password needs to be changed, TFS ApplicationControl can facilitate this process so that users do not even have to create or remember passwords.

Additionally, TFS ApplicationControl can be used in combination with SecurID on the front end. In other words, users can be authenticated to the RSA ACE/Server using their SecurID via two-factor authentication, and then the TFS ApplicationControl application will manage all the passwords to the applications that users need to access across the environment.

Another solution that can be used across the environment for authentication is Kerberos, an authentication protocol that uses "tickets." After the user authenticates, an authentication ticket is provided, which is then used by the operating system to request access to resources such as files, printers, and applications. Then, another ticket is issued to the client, which the client presents in lieu of a password to the resource. Using tickets instead of passwords provides an increased level of security, because users do not need to remember passwords for all the systems that they access. The tickets are cryptographically based, which means that they are fundamentally more secure than passwords. If you wish to implement Kerberos within your environment, you have to make sure that all the applications on which you intend to use Kerberos support Kerberos. For more information on Kerberos, visit http://web.mit.edu/kerberos/www/.

Chapter 5

Hardening Web Services

by Mark O'Neill

- Harden Your Web Services Environment
- Understand Web Services
- Understand and Use Standards, Profiles, and Specifications Such as W3C, OASIS, and WS-I
- Implement Security Requirements for Your Web Services
- Block "Malicious XML" Attacks
- Implement a Policy to Secure Your Organization's Services-Oriented Architecture
- Review and Implement Products that Protect Web Services

Imagine the scene: a chief security officer (CSO) has found out that her colleagues in the IT department are going to be using web services for internal integration projects. In fact, there are *already* some pilot web services deployments and soon the company will be sending eXtensible Markup Language (XML) across the firewall to business partners. The CSO must bring these web services under the blanket of corporate security, the first step of which is to research exactly what are the specific security issues facing web services. After reading a few introductory web services security articles, the CSO starts to get a sinking feeling because she has learned that XML is sent over web ports, firewalls are oblivious to XML traffic, and business applications talk to each other by sending messages across the network, using text-based protocols. To the CSO, this sounds like a grand plot to bypass the company's carefully constructed security policies.

This scene has been played out in countless organizations since web services emerged. The security picture actually seemed darker in the early days of web services, back in 2001 and 2002, when many of the press descriptions of web services described a "giant directory in the sky" (using Universal Description, Discovery, and Integration [UDDI]) for businesses to connect to other businesses on an ad hoc basis to order goods and services. This early fixation on ambitious e-commerce scenarios came about because the early days of web services happened to overlap with the last days of the business-to-business (B2B) hype wave, when the promise of "e-marketplace hubs" was beginning to sour. The legacy of that period in some quarters is a deep suspicion of web services.

This suspicion has been shown to be misdirected. Instead of being an immediate silver-bullet solution for B2B, web services gradually found a niche in solving internal application-integration problems. Although less glamorous than B2B, application integration is an acknowledged problem familiar to anyone who has ever tried to roll out a new Customer Relationship Management (CRM) or Enterprise Resource Planning (ERP) system, or tried to access the information held inside such systems. This position inside the organization is where web services have found their niche, with the ambitious cross-firewall B2B scenarios being set aside until recently.

At the same time that web services were finding a niche on the internal network behind the firewall and progressing through the early proof-of-concept stage, a great deal of work was being done to develop standards for XML and web services (WS) security. These standards were needed to fulfill basic security requirements, such as confidentiality and integrity, and to deal with situations in which XML travels between systems that use differing security technologies. This chapter examines these standards, which include WS-Security, Security Assertion Markup Language (SAML), XML Signature, and XML Encryption. This chapter also examines new specifications that, although not yet standards, address important security requirements for web services, such as WS-Trust, WS-Policy, and WS-SecureConversation.

While vendors and standards bodies were developing new standards and specifications for web services security, parallel work by security researchers on both sides was underway to discover security vulnerabilities in XML and web services. It turns out that, like a Shakespearean tragic hero, some of the most powerful characteristics of a web service are also its chief vulnerabilities and can be used against it by an attacker.

However, applying sound security practices can protect your web services from known attacks and potentially protect them from attacks as yet unknown. In this chapter, you encounter some of the chief vulnerabilities of web services, including their susceptibility to XML denial of service (DoS) attacks, and learn how to defend your own web services against them.

A recent trend has been to link together isolated internal web services projects into a services-oriented architecture (SOA). An SOA allows you to apply management and co-ordination to web services traffic in a top-down view. An SOA also allows you to add and remove web services, or swap them for different implementations, without disruption to the system as a whole. The use of SOAs introduces security challenges, so this chapter also examines how you can map security to an SOA.

Finally, this chapter looks at practical examples of vendor products for web services security, one from each of the following established categories: a web application security product that also addresses web services security, an XML router, and an XML gateway/firewall product.

Harden Your Web Services Environment

Although web services are new technologies, they depend on an underlying stack of preexisting technologies, some of which have been around for ten years or more. A security professional who secures only their web services interface, and whose system is then brought down by an attack at the operating system level, hasn't done their job properly. An attacker always goes after the point of least resistance. Do not make the attacker's job easy by failing to apply patches or to follow other security-hardening best practices for the OS, the network environment, and the development process. If your web services are being deployed using a web server, then ensure that your web server patches are up to date and that the web server is fully secured according to best practices and according to your specific requirements. If you are reading that last sentence and wondering what "*If* your web services are...using a web server" means, then the next section is for you. It explains both what web services are and, along the way, why the name "web service" is so misleading.

Understand Web Services

You cannot secure an information system, application, or service that you know little to nothing about. Before you can harden web services, you need to understand what they are, where they are currently used, and how they are integrated into the rest of your information systems. The term *web services* implies a definition of "services on the World Wide Web." If this were the definition, then an airline-booking web site would count as a web service. However, the term *web service* refers to something specific. There are many definitions of web services available, mostly from vendors who add a spin in order to say "this is not all that different from what we've been doing all along." So, to get a more accurate, objective definition, here is the definition of web service from the World Wide Web Consortium (W3C):

> A Web service is a software system designed to support interoperable machine-to-machine interaction over a network. It has an interface described in a machine-processable format (specifically WSDL). Other systems interact with the Web service in a manner prescribed by its description using SOAP messages, typically conveyed with HTTP using an XML serialization in conjunction with other XML-related standards.
>
> [Source: *W3C Web Services Glossary,* Sec. 3, "General Terms," http://www.w3.org/TR/ws-gloss/#defs]

This definition includes several key points, which are examined in the following sections.

Web Services Processing Is Between Machines, Not People and Machines

A web service is for *machine-to-machine* interaction. A human end user does not directly invoke a web service. The web service is accessed by a client, which the W3C defines as "A system entity making use of a Web service." Either no human end user is involved at all or the human end user accesses the web service indirectly. An example of the latter scenario is the National Basketball Association's web site, http://www.nba.com, which uses Amazon Web Services (AWS). An NBA.com customer does not access AWS directly. Instead, the customer browses to NBA.com, fills their shopping cart with basketball gear, and then pays for the purchase, all the time staying at NBA.com. In the background, XML passes between NBA.com and AWS, unknown to the end user. Prior to the existence of the Web, this system may have been implemented by giving the customer a specific application that orders basketball gear by communicating over the Internet with the NBA (client/server architecture). In a classic business-to-consumer (B2C) web system design, an n-tier architecture (a system where parts of an application reside on some number, or *n* computer systems) would be used. Web services can therefore be seen as a third evolution of system architecture, evolving from client/server and n-tier architecture. Figure 5-1 shows this evolution in context.

The difference between "client" and "end user" is very important in web services security. If a web service is to be locked down such that only certain end users (human beings) can access it, XML messages passed to that web service must contain information about the end user, such as where they were authenticated or what attributes they have (e.g., Manager). This is more complex than authenticating an end user at a web site, since the end user directly "touches" the web site. Standards such as SAML and WS-Security

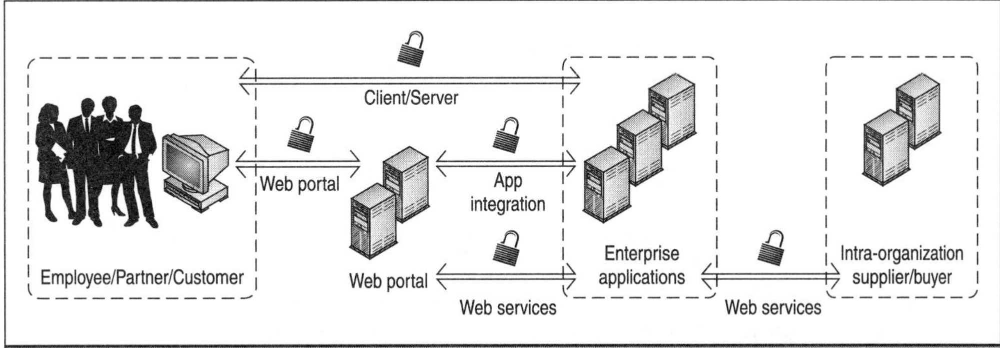

Figure 5-1. The arrows in the center of the diagram show an n-tier architecture, with multiple computer systems involved in processing the user requests.

are relevant for solving this architectural problem, as you will see in the sections "Use Principal Propagation to Permit Identification of Authenticated and Unauthenticated Messages" and "Understand and Use Standards, Profiles, and Specifications Such as W3C, OASIS, and WS-I" later in this chapter. Techniques such as credential propagation and credential mapping are also options to consider.

Web Services Definition Language

The second sentence of the W3C definition states that the interface of a web service can be described using WSDL. This is not the same as saying that a web service *must* advertise its interface using WSDL. Clearly, from a security point of view, it is not wise to give an attacker information about your web service. If you use WSDL to describe the web service interface for authorized users, you should protect it. If you have created a policy to protect your web service's SOAP interface, it makes sense to also bring the WSDL interface under the same cloak of protection.

As well as being the subject of security protection, WSDL itself can be used to express security policies. WS-PolicyAttachment is a specification that adds security policy information to WSDL files, including directives on what parts of SOAP messages must be signed, what parts must be encrypted, and which keys and token formats to use. This information is used by clients who must send secure messages.

REST and Plain-XML Web Services

The last sentence of the W3C definition ventures into somewhat controversial territory: "Other systems interact with the Web service in a manner prescribed by its description using SOAP messages, typically conveyed with HTTP using an XML serialization in conjunction with other XML-related standards." Many people would argue with the contention that using SOAP is a hard-and-fast requirement for a system to qualify as a "web service." Many early adopters of web services chose not to use SOAP, and instead sent XML messages without SOAP "envelopes." Proponents of REST (REpresentation State Transfer) would argue that a web service should be called by sending HTTP GETs and POSTs to a URI, which simply returns XML (not SOAP). From a security point of view, you should be aware that the choice to not use SOAP means that security standards that rely on SOAP, such as WS-Security, cannot be used.

RPC and Document-Based SOAP

A full name is not given for SOAP in the preceding section because SOAP is no longer an acronym. In the days when web services were synonymous with object orientation and remote procedure calls, and were seen as being "CORBA through firewalls" or "DCOM with angle brackets," SOAP stood for Simple Object Access Protocol. It was intended as a way for the methods of objects to be accessed in a simplified fashion, using XML to serialize the parameters passed to them. Some of the earliest SOAP applications would simply take an EJB or COM component and create a separate SOAP operation for each method of the object. They would then send and receive SOAP messages and "marshal" the data to and from the "web service enabled" object.

Early adopters using these first SOAP tools quickly realized the shortcomings in this map-SOAP-operations-directly-to-the-methods-of-an-object model. The first was interoperability. It was one thing to say "anyone can access my application because it talks XML, and you can make XML in Notepad," but it was quite another thing to create a SOAP message containing serialized Java objects as its parameters. Similarly, although web services were supposed to be "loosely coupled," early SOAP products placed a lot of demands on the web service requester, such as a requirement to be online at the same time as the service that they were accessing. It was not qualitatively better than using an API. Finally, creating a web service at the fine-grained method level was not optimal for message transfer, given the size of XML messages. It was a better option to create a higher-level web service that in turn called the lower-level methods directly. This use of high-level web services also makes web services more portable and less tied to a specific implementation.

Because of the preceding shortcomings in the model, a backlash caused movement away from "RPC-style" and "encoded" SOAP and toward "messaging-style" and "document-based" SOAP. *Document-based SOAP* means that an XML message is not an encoded object but rather is an XML document that is independent of the application used to create it and is generally definable by an XML Schema using simple XML elements such as strings and integers. *Messaging-style SOAP* means that the SOAP message can be sent in a store-and-forward manner, like e-mail, and can involve the kinds of asynchronous exchanges that are very difficult to implement in an RPC system. It is not unreasonable to now think of SOAP as a kind of e-mail between applications. Ensure that the people charged with developing web services for your organization see the value of loosely coupled architecture and are not just developing web services for the sake of using the latest technology.

Any system, including a system based on web services, must fulfill these basic requirements of security:

- **Authentication** Who is sending this message?
- **Authorization** Is the authenticated subject allowed access to this target?
- **Integrity** Was the message, or system, tampered with?
- **Confidentiality** Can the information be read while in transit or in storage?
- **Audit** Is a secure store of transactions recorded?
- **Administration** How straightforward is policy management?
- **Availability** Is this system vulnerable to a denial of service (DoS) attack?

It is important to keep these general requirements in mind and avoid fixating on specific standards. This means thinking of ways in which you can guarantee integrity of these messages rather than thinking of how you can build XML Signature into this system.

Implement Authentication for Your Web Services

If you reexamine Figure 5-1, you will see that two types of authentication are important for web services:

- **Client authentication** Authenticating the application that is sending the XML message to the web service
- **End-user authentication** Embedding information about the end user into the messages sent to the web service

When implementing you should choose between transport- or message-based client authentication, make sure you remove credentials after authentication, and create a system that allows the identification of authenticated and unauthenticated messages.

How to Choose Between Transport- and Message-Based Client Authentication

Client authentication may be performed using transport security technologies such as mutual SSL, SSL with HTTP-Authentication, or SSL with HTTP-DigestAuthentication. Client authentication may also be performed using message-level authentication, which is independent of the transport that is used. WS-Security is used for message-level authentication; in particular, the WS-Security X.509 Certificate Token profile for certificate-based authentication, the WS-Security Kerberos profile for Kerberos authentication, and the WS-Security UsernameToken profile for password-based authentication.

So, when should you use transport-based authentication and when should you use message-based authentication? The answer is that when your web services are point to point, with clients sending XML directly to web services, then transport-level authentication is sufficient. When SOAP intermediaries are involved, creating multiple hops between the client and web service, then message-level authentication should be used for end-to-end security.

TIP HTTP-Auth and HTTP-DigestAuth, which are challenge-response authentication systems, both involve two round trips to the target web server: the first to pick up the challenge, and the second to send back the response. Therefore, HTTP-Auth and HTTP-DigestAuth are not good choices for authenticating large XML messages, since the messages must be sent up to the web service twice.

Authentication is based on *credentials* that are used to establish identity. Examples of credentials include username/password combinations and X.509 certificates (when combined with a proof of possession of the corresponding private key). Following authentication, the *principle name* is proven. This is the identity of the authenticated party. Examples of principle names include a username, the distinguished name (DN) of an X.509 digital certificate, or a Windows logon name such as \\ServerI\JoeUser.

Remove Credentials After Authentication

A WS-Security UsernameToken structure that contains both a username and a password is a credential. If you do not trust the applications processing the message downstream, consider removing the credentials from the message following authentication. The following Extensible Stylesheet Language Transformations (XSLT) transform will remove the contents of a SOAP header, including the authentication credentials, from a SOAP message:

```
<?xml version="1.0"?>
<xsl:stylesheet exclude-result-prefixes="SOAP-ENV SOAP"
xmlns:SOAP-ENV="http://schemas.xmlsoap.org/soap/envelope/"
xmlns:xsl="http://www.w3.org/1999/XSL/Transform" version="1.0">
<xsl:output method="xml"/>
<xsl:strip-space elements="*"/>
<xsl:template match="/">
      <xsl:apply-templates select="//SOAP-ENV:Envelope"/>
</xsl:template>
<xsl:template match="*">
  <xsl:if test="not (name(.)='soapenv:Header')">
    <xsl:element name="{name(.)}" namespace="{namespace-uri(.)}">
      <xsl:apply-templates select="@*|*|text()"/>
    </xsl:element>
  </xsl:if>
</xsl:template>
<xsl:template match="@*">
  <xsl:copy/>
</xsl:template>
</xsl:stylesheet>
```

Use Principal Propagation to Permit Identification of Authenticated and Unauthenticated Messages

Following authentication, an SAML token may be issued to assert that the client was authenticated, is authorized for a particular service, or has a certain attribute (such as a credit limit). In this way, authentication information, such as the Principle name (the name of the client that was authenticated) can be propagated to the next web service that processes the XML message. Without this "principle propagation" functionality, information about the client may be lost following the authentication event. Other benefits of this principle propagation approach include

- An application can ensure that XML messages passed to it have come through an XML security gateway, by examining the message for a security token that was digitally signed by the XML security gateway. If this security token is not present, the message may be passed up to the XML security gateway for processing, may be quarantined, or may be dropped.
- An application may enforce a rule such as "only clients who authenticated with X.509 certificates are allowed to access this service," since information about the authentication method is included inside an SAML Authentication Statement.
- Messages may be correlated together, across multiple XML-processing applications, based on having identical security tokens inside

An example of a SOAP message that uses principle propagation, by embedding an SAML authentication token, is shown here:

```
<?xml version="1.0" encoding="utf-8"?>
<soap:Envelope xmlns:soap=
"http://schemas.xmlsoap.org/soap/envelope/"
xmlns:xsd="http://www.w3.org/2001/XMLSchema"
xmlns:xsi=
"http://www.w3.org/2001/XMLSchema-instance">
<soap:Header>
<wsse:Security soap:actor="current" xmlns:wsse="http://docs.oasis
-open.org/wss/2004/01/oasis-200401-wss-wssecurity-secext-1.0.xsd">
<saml:Assertion AssertionID=
"vordel-1087530254730" IssueInstant="2004-06-18T03:44:14Z"
Issuer="Corporate CA" MajorVersion="1" MinorVersion=
"1"xmlns:saml="urn:oasis:names:tc:SAML:1.0:assertion">
<saml:Conditions NotBefore="2004-06-18T12:00:00Z"
NotOnOrAfter="2004-06-18T12:10:00Z"/>
<saml:AuthenticationStatement
AuthenticationInstant="2004-06-18T03:44:14Z"
AuthenticationMethod="urn:ietf:rfc:2246">
<saml:SubjectLocality DNSAddress="client.com" IPAddress="192.168.0.1"/>
    <saml:Subject>
    <saml:NameIdentifier Format=
"urn:oasis:names:tc:SAML:1.1:nameid-format:X509SubjectName">
CN=Client Name, O=Client Organisation,
```

```
C=SE</saml:NameIdentifier>
    </saml:Subject>
    </saml:AuthenticationStatement>
</saml:Assertion>
</wsse:Security>
</soap:Header>
<soap:Body>
<StockQuoteRequest xmlns="http://www.mystockquoteexample.com">
<symbols>
<Symbol>BENO</Symbol>
<Symbol>KSTN</Symbol>
</symbols>
</StockQuoteRequest>
</soap:Body>
</soap:Envelope>
```

In the preceding code example, the "urn:ietf:rfc:2246" in the AuthenticationMethod attribute refers to SSL/TLS (Transport Layer Security) client authentication. The client's information is contained in the Subject/NameIdentifier element (CN=Client Name, O=Client Organization, C=SE). Applications that process this XML message know the identity of the authenticated party, how they were authenticated, and when they were authenticated (via the AuthenticationInstant attribute). It is recommended that SAML assertions be digitally signed, together with the SOAP messages to which they are bound, to detect a trivial copy-and-paste attack whereby an SAML assertion is hijacked for use in a different SOAP message.

Embed User Authentication Tokens

End-user authentication is achieved through a similar means to principle propagation. A token, embedded inside the SOAP message, conveys information about the end user. This technique is the basis of Project Liberty (a project defined by the Liberty Alliance, http://www.projectliberty.org/), whereby a user can log on once to an authentication provider, who then issues tokens that are passed to other services used by the same user. Therefore, the user does not have to be reauthenticated. This solution is safer than the cruder forms of single sign-on, such as credential propagation (passing the user's password with onbound requests, to log the user into the remote service) or the use of cookies (which are exclusive to the HTTP transport method and thus are unusable for SOAP messages, which do not use HTTP).

When security tokens must be converted from one format to another, for example to convert an incoming Kerberos ticket into a UsernameToken structure to place into outbound messages, WS-Trust may be used. WS-Trust includes a RequestSecurityToken message that may be used to request a certain security token, based on a different security token. WS-Trust is designed to enable trust relationships that span multiple security domains.

TIP To test a web service for compliance with SSL, HTTP-Auth, WS-Security, or SAML, or to generate example XML messages that use these standards, use the free SOAPbox tool from Vordel that is available at http://www.vordel.com.

Implement Web Services Authorization Using SAML and Link to Web Site Authorization

Once the sender or end user is authenticated, the next step is to decide if they allowed to access the resource that they are requesting. This step is called authorization. Authorization typically follows authentication—however, with role-based access control (RBAC), there is an intermediate step. In RBAC, the authorization isn't directly based on the user's identity; instead, it is based on an attribute of the user (e.g., their role) or on an attribute of the "environment" (e.g., whether or not the day is a public holiday). This is more scalable and manageable than the use of access control lists (ACLs).

You saw in the previous section, "Implement Authentication for Your Web Services," that SAML can be used to "assert" attributes of the user, which are used for authorization. SAML can also be used to request authorization. Many existing tools exist for web site authorization (such as Netegrity SiteMinder, Entrust GetAccess, RSA ClearTrust, and Oblix COREid). Some, such as the Entrust GetAccess product, include an SAML interface that may be used to request authorization.

The XML Access Control Markup Language (XACML) may be used to express authorization rules in XML format. XACML is a good example of an XML security specification that is not specifically designed to secure a web service; instead, it is an example of XML technology that is used to solve a security interoperability problem. Before XACML, there was no standard method of expressing access control information in a structured, vendor-neutral format. Now that XACML exists, it is an obvious choice for organizations that wish to submit their access control policies to third-party audit, or for organizations that wish to migrate access control rules from one system to another without the need for rekeying.

Ensure Message Integrity—XML Signature, PKCS#7 Signature, SSL/TLS, and IPSec

It is a common misconception that when cryptography is used, message integrity is a side benefit that is obtained "for free." This is not true—an encrypted message may be subtly changed without impacting its ability to be decrypted. Therefore, it is important to ensure that any messaging system, including web services, guarantees message integrity. SSL/TLS guarantees integrity at the transport layer. IP Security (IPSec) also guarantees integrity, at a lower level. Digital signatures may be used at the message level. PKCS#7 signature is the basis of digitally signed Secure/Multipurpose Internet Mail Extensions (S/MIME) e-mails and is sanctioned by the WS-I draft Basic Security Profile for use with SOAP messages.

XML Signature is a W3C and IETF signature standard that allows a digital signature to be expressed using XML. XML Signature does not invent any new signature algorithms and therefore cannot be said to be "stronger" or "weaker" than signature formats that preceded it, such as PKCS#7 signature. WS-Security describes how a SOAP message is signed. In particular, WS-Security specifies that the XML Signature structure is placed inside the Security element, which in turn is placed into the SOAP header (SOAP messages, like TCP packets, have headers and bodies).

XML Signature supports the signing of more than one "reference." This is very useful for digitally signing SOAP messages, since, as well as signing the message body, a timestamp must be signed in order to avoid a capture-replay attack. XML Signature provides "persistent" integrity for XML documents, meaning that the integrity is still enforced after the XML message has been received, processed, and stored.

Inform Clients of Security Requirements Using WS-Policy

If you have set up a web service that requires incoming message bodies and message timestamps to be digitally signed, how can you convey that information to clients? This is where WS-Policy comes into play. WS-Policy allows a web service to convey information about its security policy to clients. The following WS-Policy document describes a policy for a web service endpoint at the fictitious web site http://www.mycompany.com/StockService. The web service policy states that all messages sent to the web service must have their SOAP bodies digitally signed and must contain digitally signed timestamps.

```
<?xml version="1.0" encoding="utf-8"?>
<policyDocument xmlns="http://schemas.microsoft.com/wse/2003/06/Policy">
<mappings xmlns:wse="https://schemas.microsoft.com/wse/2003/06/Policy">
<endpoint uri=" http://www.mycompany.com/StockService ">
<defaultOperation>
<request policy="#Sign-X.509" />
<response policy="" />
<fault policy="" />
</defaultOperation>
</endpoint>
</mappings>
<policies xmlns:wsu=
"http://docs.oasis-open.org/wss/2004/01/oasis-200401-wss-wssecurity-utility-
1.0.xsd"
xmlns:wsp="http://schemas.xmlsoap.org/ws/2002/12/policy"
xmlns:wssp="http://schemas.xmlsoap.org/ws/2002/12/secext"
xmlns:wse="http://schemas.microsoft.com/wse/2003/06/Policy"
xmlns:wsse="http://docs.oasis-open.org
/wss/2004/01/oasis-200401-wss-wssecurity-secext-1.0.xsd"
xmlns:wsa="http://schemas.xmlsoap.org/ws/2004/03/addressing">
<wsp:Policy wsu:Id="Sign-X.509">
<!--MessagePredicate is used to require headers.
```

```
This assertion should be used along with the Integrity
assertion when the presence of the signed element is required. -->
<wsp:MessagePredicate wsp:Usage="wsp:Required" Dialect=
"http://schemas.xmlsoap.org/2002/12/wsse#part" >
wsp:Body() wsp:Header(wsa:MessageID) wse:Timestamp()
</wsp:MessagePredicate>
<!--The Integrity assertion is used to ensure that the message
 is signed with X.509. Many Web services will also use the token
for authorization, such as by using the <wse:Role> claim or
specific X.509 claims.-->
<wssp:Integrity wsp:Usage="wsp:Required">
<wssp:TokenInfo>
<wssp:SecurityToken wse:IdentityToken="true">
<wssp:TokenType>http://docs.oasis
-open.org/wss/2004/01/oasis-200401-wss-x509-token-profile-
1.0#X509v3</wssp:TokenType>
<wssp:Claims>
<wssp:SubjectName MatchType="wssp:Exact">
StockClient
</wssp:SubjectName>
<wssp:X509Extension OID="1.2.23.44"MatchType="wssp:Exact">
fpmjxsEad4rl2dms0d
</wssp:X509Extension>
</wssp:Claims>
</wssp:SecurityToken>
</wssp:TokenInfo>
<wssp:MessageParts Dialect=
"http://schemas.xmlsoap.org/2002/12/wsse#part">
 wsp:Header(wsa:MessageID) wse:Timestamp()
</wssp:MessageParts>
</wssp:Integrity>
</wsp:Policy>
</policies>
</policyDocument>
```

In the preceding WS-Policy code listing, notice the stipulation that the SOAP body and the WS-Security timestamp are both signed. In addition, there is a stipulation that an X.509 certificate is the token format that is to be sent with the incoming messages to the web service. The Microsoft WSE 2.0 toolkit supports WS-Policy and allows you to automatically generate a WS-Policy document like the preceding example and attach it to web services that use the WSE.

Guarantee Integrity by Validating the Integrity of the System as a Whole

You can guarantee the "integrity" of the message only if you can guarantee the integrity of the system as a whole. This means you must provide intrusion detection safeguards, as well as tamper-control tools such as Tripwire.

TIP In addition to checking XML Signature over incoming XML messages, it is also a good policy to digitally sign outgoing messages. This ensures that no recipient can claim to have received a different XML message from your web service. Consider performing outbound signing (or response signing) as a matter of course, unless the processing overhead is too great (and in that case, consider using a cryptographic acceleration card from a vendor such as nCipher or SafeNet).

Implement Confidentiality: XML Encryption, SSL/TLS, and IPSec

Many people new to information security believe incorrectly that confidentiality is synonymous with security and that encryption is synonymous with confidentiality. In this view, a "secure" document means an encrypted document. Therefore, XML Encryption is often singled out as being the most important web services security standard. XML Encryption is certainly important, since it allows part of a SOAP message to be encrypted, while the rest may be in plain text. The reason for not encrypting an entire SOAP message is to allow SOAP intermediaries to read the message and discern the routing information that they require. Like XML Signature, XML Encryption is bound to SOAP using WS-Security. The "confidentiality" WS-Security element is where the XML Encryption structure is placed, and this in turn is placed inside the SOAP header. WS-Policy may also be used to convey a rule that a certain part, or parts, of a SOAP message must be signed. WS-Policy can also be used to convey a public key that is to be used to encrypt the SOAP Body parts of incoming SOAP messages.

XML Encryption operates at the message level and is independent of the underlying transport. Another message-level specification that is relevant here is WS-SecureConversation, which allows a security session to be set up between a web service requester and a web service. This session typically is initiated by negotiating a symmetric key, which is then used for encryption of all subsequent messages that are part of that session. This is directly analogous to how SSL works, and carries the same benefits as SSL in terms of speed of throughput.

IPSec and SSL/TLS also provide confidentiality, although they do so only on a per-hop basis. If you do not trust the intermediaries who are processing your XML messages, or if you require complete transport independence of your XML messages, then consider using XML Encryption for end-to-end security. One particular advantage of XML Encryption is that its confidentiality extends beyond the time when the message is transported, to the time when an XML document is stored. In this way, XML Encryption provides *persistent* encryption.

Privacy is sometimes confused with confidentiality. Privacy implies consideration of the context and semantics of the data to be protected. Typically this means that user preferences or a legal requirement specify that certain data must be kept confidential. Although privacy is different from confidentiality, it is often enforced using confidentiality. For example, a WS-Policy document may stipulate that the PatientRecord block of XML messages sent to a web service is always encrypted, and the WS-Policy document may contain the key used for this encryption. That is an example of privacy rules being enforced using web services security.

Provide Web Services Auditing Using XML Signature and XAdES

The ability to write an audit trail is important for any security system, including a web services security system. XML Signature is clearly useful for ensuring that audit trail information cannot be unknowingly tampered with. An audit trail must be long-running, however, and that is why the European Union Digital Signatures Directive was created. The European Telecommunications Standards Institute (ETSI) developed a standard named XML Advanced Electronic Signatures (XAdES), which is now ETSI standard TS 101 903. XAdES extends XML Signature by defining XML formats for advanced electronic signatures that remain valid over long periods of time (e.g., 30 years). This involves storage of the key and all key-validation information with the signature. If you wish to store web services audit logs over a long period of time, consider using XAdES.

Avoid Solutions that Require You to Configure Security Manually by Editing XML Files

Administrating a security policy for web services involves two broad activities: *provisioning*, the task of assigning new security policies and new client profiles to the system, and ongoing *policy management*, which involves changing policies, rolling back policies, and adding new policies. Policy management becomes an urgent task when a security policy must be changed in a hurry—for example, when a system is under attack. Therefore, the administration of your web services security policies must be as intuitive and straightforward as possible. It is strongly recommended that you do not rely on the direct use of XML files to configure your web services security policies. Although you have seen in this chapter that technologies such as WS-Policy and XACML can be used to express security policies, that does not mean that you must construct these XML files manually. XML, like web services, is designed for machine-to-machine communication, not for human consumption. Therefore, steer clear of solutions that require you to manually manipulate XML files to set security policies.

Ensure Web Services Availability

Availability involves protecting a web service by blocking unwanted message "storms." That is a job for a traditional network firewall. In addition, messages that are designed to cause XML processing problems must be blocked. These are called XML DoS attacks, but may also be unintentional. An XML DoS attack differs from a traditional DoS attack because it is asynchronous. A single XML message can do significant damage, as we will see in the following sections.

Block "Malicious XML" Attacks

The use of XML introduces new forms of attack. These attacks can bring an XML-processing system to a halt or provide unauthorized access to data. This section examines these attacks and shows what you can do to block them. Many XML firewall products block these attacks. The following sections describe what these attacks are, what the countermeasures are, and how you can ensure that your XML Firewall supports them.

Prevent Web Services SQL Injection

SQL Injection attacks involve the insertion of SQL statements into web forms in order to force a database to return inappropriate data or to produce an error that reveals database access information. A web services SQL Injection attack works on the same principle, except that it involves appending SQL data to parameters inside a SOAP message, in the hope that the SQL will be interpreted by a back-end database.

A successful SQL Injection attack requires two factors to be in place:

- Data received from a network connection is inserted directly into a SQL statement.
- The SQL statement is run in the context of a user with sufficient privileges to execute the attack.

The following is an example:

```
<SOAP-ENV:Envelope
xmlns:SOAP-ENV="http://schemas.xmlsoap.org/soap/envelope/">
<SOAP-ENV:Header></SOAP-ENV:Header>
<SOAP-ENV:Body
<BookLookup:searchByIBSN
xmlns:BookLookup="https://www.books.com/Lookup">
<BookLookup:IBSN>0072224711<BookLookup:IBSN>
</BookLookup:searchByIBSN>
</SOAP-ENV:Body></SOAP-ENV:Envelope>
```

This message is processed by the following VB.NET code, which inserts the content of the ISBN element into a SQL statement:

```
Set myRecordset = myConnection.execute("SELECT * FROM myBooksTable WHERE
ISBN ='" & ISBN_Element_Text & "'")
```

In the case of the preceding SOAP message, this becomes

```
SELECT * FROM myBooksTable WHERE IBSN = '0072224711'
```

Now consider what happens when the following SOAP message is received:

```
<SOAP-ENV:Envelope
xmlns:SOAP-ENV="http://schemas.xmlsoap.org/soap/envelope/">
<SOAP-ENV:Header></SOAP-ENV:Header>
<SOAP-ENV:Body
<BookLookup:searchByIBSN
xmlns:BookLookup="https://www.books.com/Lookup">
<BookLookup:IBSN>0072224711'; exec master..xp_cmdshell 'net user Joe
pass /ADD'; --<BookLookup:IBSN>
</BookLookup:searchByIBSN>
</SOAP-ENV:Body></SOAP-ENV:Envelope>
```

In this case, the SQL statement will read

```
SELECT * FROM myBooksTable WHERE IBSN = '0072224711'; exec
master..xp_cmdshell 'net user Joe pass /ADD'; --
```

The code after the SELECT statement attempts to create a user called Joe with password of *pass*. An attacker could then attempt to use this new user account to gain access to the target machine.

To block this attack, ensure that data received from untrusted users is not directly placed into SQL statements. You can achieve this by using stored procedures rather than SQL statements built on-the-fly. SQL Injection can also be blocked by enforcing content-validation rules over incoming content. In this case, an XML security gateway would enforce a Schema-based rule, containing a regular expression (RegEx), such as the following:

```
<simpleType name="ibsn"> <restriction base="string"> <pattern
value="[0–9]{10}"/> </restriction> </simpleType>
```

This Schema would be validated against data isolated by the following XPath expression:

```
/Body/BookLookup:searchByIBSN/BookLookup:IBSN
```

In this case, `0072224711` passes the regular expression in the Schema, whereas `0072224711'; exec master..xp_cmdshell 'net user Joe pass /ADD'; --` fails.

It is likely that XPath Injection, which is analogous to SQL Injection, can be used to "harvest" information from an XML database. XPath Injection can be blocked by ensuring that data passed into an XPath expression does not itself contain XPath.

The use of SQL stored procedures is another good solution to the problem of SQL Injection. As a security professional, ensure that the developers in your organization are familiar with SQL Injection and are not implementing web services that are vulnerable to this attack. If you are not 100 percent assured that SQL interfaces will be implemented securely in your organization, then ensure that your XML firewall solution blocks SQL Injection by detecting SQL statements inside incoming XML messages.

Protect Web Services from Capture-Replay Attacks

Imagine this scenario: a web service is being protected by an XML gateway that scans incoming requests for X.509 certificates contained within SOAP messages and makes sure the messages are encrypted and signed. This system is vulnerable to a capture-replay attack, which captures a valid message and then submits it to gain unauthorized access.

TIP Do not confuse capture-replay attacks with "flooding" DoS attacks. Although both involve a message being replayed, the DoS attack is a brute-force attack designed to disable the target system, whereas the capture-replay attack is (arguably) a more clever attack that exploits a flaw in the target system's authentication scheme.

The solution to this problem involves the use of timestamps. WS-Security includes support for timestamps and, as you have seen in the WS-Policy example earlier in this chapter, the protected web service can mandate that a signed timestamp be present in incoming messages. A replayed message will include the same timestamp as the original message. If the message arrives a short time after the first message, both messages must be discarded, because it cannot be established which message is the original and which is the copy. This is why you must carefully decide the timestamp trust interval. It must be short enough that an attacker does not have time to capture, decrypt, and replay a valid message yet it must be long enough that slight discrepancies between the system clocks of the web service and the web service requester do not result in valid messages being blocked.

TIP Beware of any solution that claims "this is secure because all incoming messages are signed." Such a solution is a prime candidate for a capture-replay attack.

Ensure that Your Application Server Is Not Processing DTDs

The XML External Entity (XXE) attack takes advantage of the fact that outside data can be embedded into an XML document via a document type definition (DTD) entry. The following is an example of this type of DTD entry:

```
<!ENTITY name SYSTEM "URI">.
```

By specifying a URI that points to a local file, some XML engines could be made to access unauthorized information or to cause a denial of service by spending cycles "slurping up" large files from the local file system. Ensure that the XML platform used for your web services is not vulnerable to this attack. SOAP is not allowed to use DTDs, so a fully SOAP-complaint web services product *should* not be vulnerable to this attack. However, some SOAP-compliant web services products are vulnerable. Therefore, ensure that the SOAP stack used by your company's web services is not processing DTDs.

HEADS UP!

The XDoS attack, described next, proved that many vendors (including IBM and Microsoft) overlooked the facts of the SOAP requirement and processed DTDs anyway. In addition to ensuring that your web services do not process DTDs, you should not simply rely on a standard to ensure the security of an implementation. Although a standard may promote sound security practices, the *implementation* of the standard may, for whatever reason, produce a product that does not exactly follow the standard and thus may fall victim to attacks that exact implementation of the standard might have repulsed.

Apply Patches for XML Denial of Service Attacks

The XDoS attack is like the XXE attack because it also uses a feature of DTDs. However, the XDoS attack is based on the fact that entities defined in DTD can be pulled in. For example, HTML developers who display HTML source code in a web page are familiar with the requirement to use `<` and `>` instead of angle brackets so that the web browser does not parse the HTML source code. The use of the ampersand instructs the browser to look up `lt` and `gt` in the HTML DTD and replace them with whatever it finds. A similar technique is used for `£` to display the British pound sign.

Now, think about what happens if an entity is defined recursively. Suppose `&x100` is looked up in a DTD and it is found to be `&x99;&x99;` (i.e., the entity called `&x99;` appended to itself). The DTD parser must then look up `&x99;`. Suppose that it finds that it is `&x98;&x98;`. You can imagine the rest—the XML message explodes in memory (hence the term "XML bomb") and causes a denial of service. The entire XML bomb DTD is shown in the following code listing:

```
<!DOCTYPE foobar [
       <!ENTITY x0 "hello">
       <!ENTITY x1 "&x0;&x0;">
       <!ENTITY x2 "&x1;&x1;">
       <!ENTITY x3 "&x2;&x2;">
       <!ENTITY x4 "&x3;&x3;">
        ...
       <!ENTITY x98 "&x97;&x97;">
       <!ENTITY x99 "&x98;&x98;">
       <!ENTITY x100 "&x99;&x99;">
   ]>
   <foobar>&x100;</foobar>
```

As in the XXE attack, the fact that SOAP implementations are required by the SOAP specification *not* to process DTDs did not deter many SOAP vendors from including DTD processing in their products anyway, making them vulnerable to XdoS attacks. Patches against the XDoS attack are available from Microsoft, IBM, Macromedia, Sybase, and others. Ensure that your company's SOAP implementation is patched against this attack, which can severely reduce the performance of a web services platform.

Do Not Blindly Process SOAP Attachments, Which May Harbor Viruses

SOAP messages may contain attachments, which may be threatening if they are very large and difficult to process (a "clogging attack") or if they harbor viruses. Attacks using SOAP attachments are somewhat mitigated by the fact that competition between two different specifications for SOAP attachments (one using Multipurpose Internet Mail Extensions, MIME, and the other Direct Internet Message Encapsulation, DIME) means that many organizations are eschewing the usage of SOAP attachments entirely until the Message Transmission Optimization Mechanism (MTOM) becomes a W3C recommendation. However, even if an organization chooses not to use SOAP attachments, it must ensure that its web services platform does not process attachments that the company unwittingly receives.

The solution to the security problem of SOAP attachments is to ensure that SOAP attachments are blocked entirely, filtered based on their MIME type, or passed through a virus scanner from a vendor such as McAfee or Symantec.

Ensure that You Are Not Vulnerable to an XML Signature Redirection Attack

An XML Signature includes a Reference element that points to the data that has been signed. To validate the XML Signature, the parsing application must "dereference" (i.e., pull down the content at) the reference URI. Consider what happens if the Reference element contains the following:

```
<dsig:Reference URI =
"http://ardownload.adobe.com
/pub/adobe/acrobatreader/win/5.x/5.1/AcroReader51_ENU_full.exe">
```

The XML Signature recommendation states that "XML signature applications MUST be able to parse URI syntax. We RECOMMEND they be able to dereference URIs in the HTTP scheme." (*XML-Signature Syntax and Processing,* W3C Recommendation 12 February 2002 [emphasis in the original text].) So, if an XML Signature processor follows the preceding URI reference, it must download a 20MB file and then compute the signature over it. This uses up the bandwidth of the target application and locks threads in a long wait for the 20MB file to download. An XML Signature dereference attack takes advantage of a web service that naively implements URI dereferencing. But an XML Signature engine for a SOAP application does not have to blindly download data from any URI in a Reference element, because the *XML-Signature Syntax and Processing* specification states the following:

> Note, there may be valid signatures that some signature applications are unable to validate. Reasons for this include failure to implement optional parts of this specification, inability or unwillingness to execute specified algorithms, or inability or unwillingness to dereference specified URIs (some URI schemes may cause undesirable side effects), etc.

So, vulnerability to this bandwidth-clogging attack is unnecessary. Ensure that the XML Signature protecting your web services is not vulnerable to this attack.

Implement a Policy to Secure Your Organization's Services-Oriented Architecture

Service-oriented architecture (SOA) and "software as services" are widely regarded as opportunities to ease integration problems and to improve business productivity. Although definitions vary, an SOA is basically a distributed-computing model that uses services as fundamental elements for developing applications. Services become the basic building blocks with which new applications are created. Web services are a prime example of such services. Although arguably SOA principles predated web services and could be implemented using CORBA, the invention of XML and web services has meant that SOA is within reach of many more organizations than before. Services implemented as web services in an SOA support composition into distributed applications. The services interoperate at run time to achieve the system's objectives.

Figure 5-2 shows the location of an SOA in an organization's IT infrastructure. An SOA places a services layer in front of back-office systems and is often implemented using an application server or a message bus. This services layer protects the developer from the complexity at lower layers and allows applications to be developed rapidly. SOAs are particularly suited to "dashboard" applications, which allow access to information that was previously "locked up" inside back-office systems. At the top left of Figure 5-2, you see such a "dashboard" for employees to access information through a portal.

Applying a security policy to the SOA in Figure 5-2 involves the following challenges:

- Persisting a "security context" from the end user or client to the business systems (i.e., from the top of the diagram to the bottom), so that you can control who accesses the web services
- Ensuring that an attacker sending malicious XML (such as an XDoS attack) is blocked at the services layer
- Blocking rogue XML messages that bypass the XML gateway

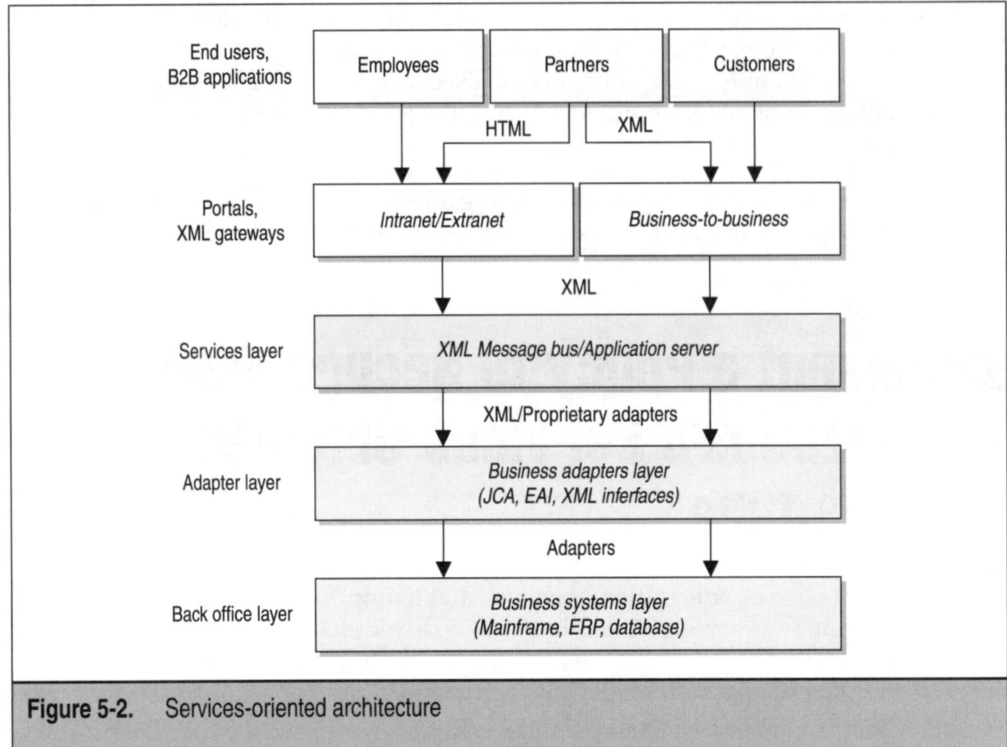

Figure 5-2. Services-oriented architecture

Use Security Tokens to Pass the Security Context to the Services Layer

At the systems layer, business applications may have security profiles that must be mapped to the end users or web service client applications. To avoid losing the client/user security context between the access layer (where the identity of the client or user is authenticated) and the services layer (where applications authorize and tailor responses to the end user or client), security tokens (such as an SAML assertion or WS-Security UsernameToken) should be "injected" into XML messages that pass to the services layer.

Deperimeterize Security

Wireless LANs, open VPNs, and other remote access options have produced a general breakdown in perimeter security models. A widespread use of malicious code, such as Trojan horses, contributes to the need for a new approach to security. The arrival of XML traffic at the services layer through an XML gateway cannot always be guaranteed. Therefore, you must "deperimeterize" security by enforcing security rules at the services layer, close to the web service endpoint. You can achieve this by inserting a "security agent" into the web services containers, to run in-process at the web service itself. Messages that have not arrived through the XML gateway may be routed back to the XML gateway for processing, or they may simply be dropped. This caters to "deperimeterization" attacks where the attacker has bypassed the firewall.

When security is being enforced in mulitple places, it is important not to create duplicate stores of security policies and credentials. This duplication can be avoided by using a central XML Security Server to provide security services to all the applications that are applying security to XML documents. This is actually the web services model; rather than duplicate functionality in multiple applications, deploy it as a service and reuse it.

Ensure SOA Availability

Remember that availability and administration are aspects of security, too. Existing network management tools can be reused to aggregate alerts and quality-of-service (QoS) indicators generated at the services layer. Some existing network management tools now support the option to enforce QoS rules over web services. This is often called "web services management."

Review and Implement Products that Protect Web Services

Although web services are new technologies, a number of vendor products exist to protect them. This section examines three of them, each of which attacks the problem from a different angle.

Vordel—XML Gateway/Firewall and XML Security Server

Vordel's products perform both access control and content filtering for XML traffic. Access control is performed by using SSL, HTTP-Auth, WS-Security, SAML, and WS-Trust, as well as through adapters to the identity management infrastructure such as directories and web access control tools. XML content filtering is implemented by scanning XML messages for content-based threats such as executable attachments, malformed or invalid XML, unexpected MIME types in SOAP attachments, SQL Injection, or buffer-overflow attempts. Service scanning and brute-force "flooding" DoS attacks are also blocked. Blacklisting is performed by alerting upstream network firewalls and load balancers of the IP addresses of senders of malicious XML.

Vordel has two products. VordelSecure is an XML gateway/firewall, while VordelDirector is an XML security server that is designed to secure an SOA. Figures 5-3 and 5-4 show the Vordel Management Console.

In Figure 5-4, we see the pipeline of available security filters on the left-hand side of the screen. This is where the administrator configures the rules for XML messages that are being used by their organization. The rules are enforced either at the VordelSecure XML Gateway, or in software agents that are embedded into Web Services containers.

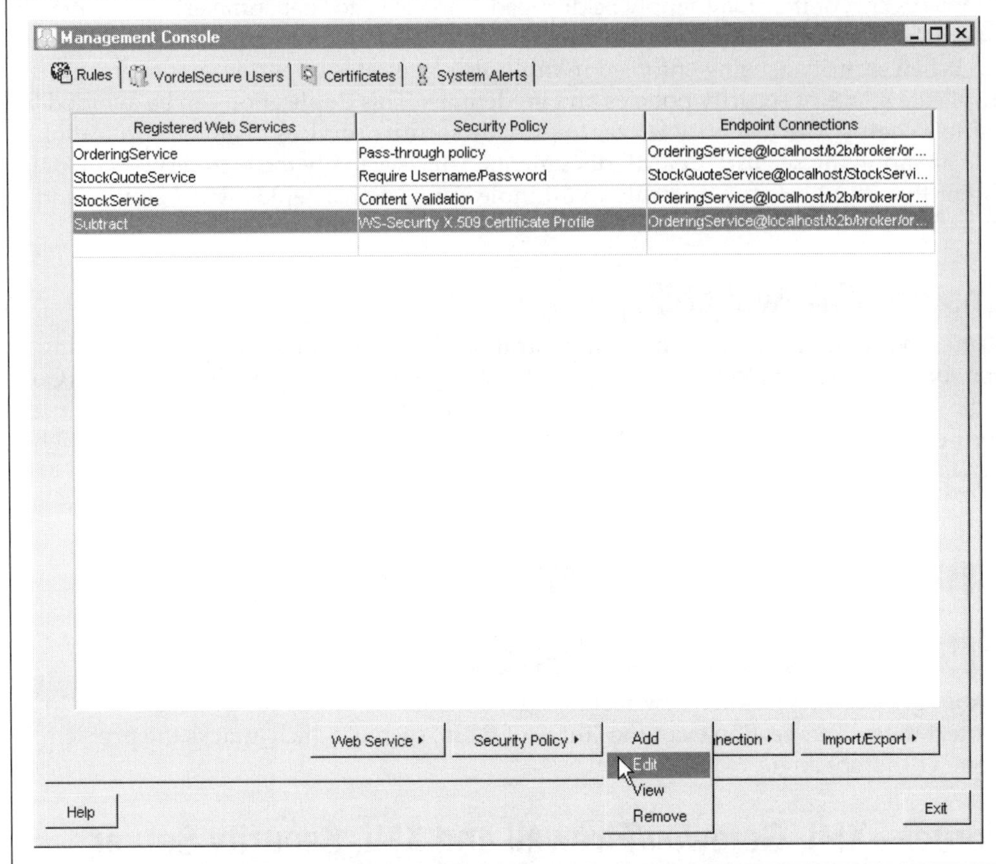

Figure 5-3. Viewing policies for web services protected by rules in the Vordel Management Console

Teros—Web Application Security

In the SQL Injection example in this chapter, you saw that web services security inherits a number of characteristics from web application security. In fact, when deployed on a web server, a web service may be seen as an example of a web application. Web application security products ensure that carelessly written web applications are not vulnerable to attack. Arguably, it would be better to simply educate developers to not develop web applications that expose vulnerabilities, but this is easier said than done. Only recently have books been published that educate developers about writing secure code.

Web application security products provide a "shield" in front of insecure web applications. One such application is the Teros Secure Application Gateway, a hardened security appliance that is deployed directly in the data path of application traffic and

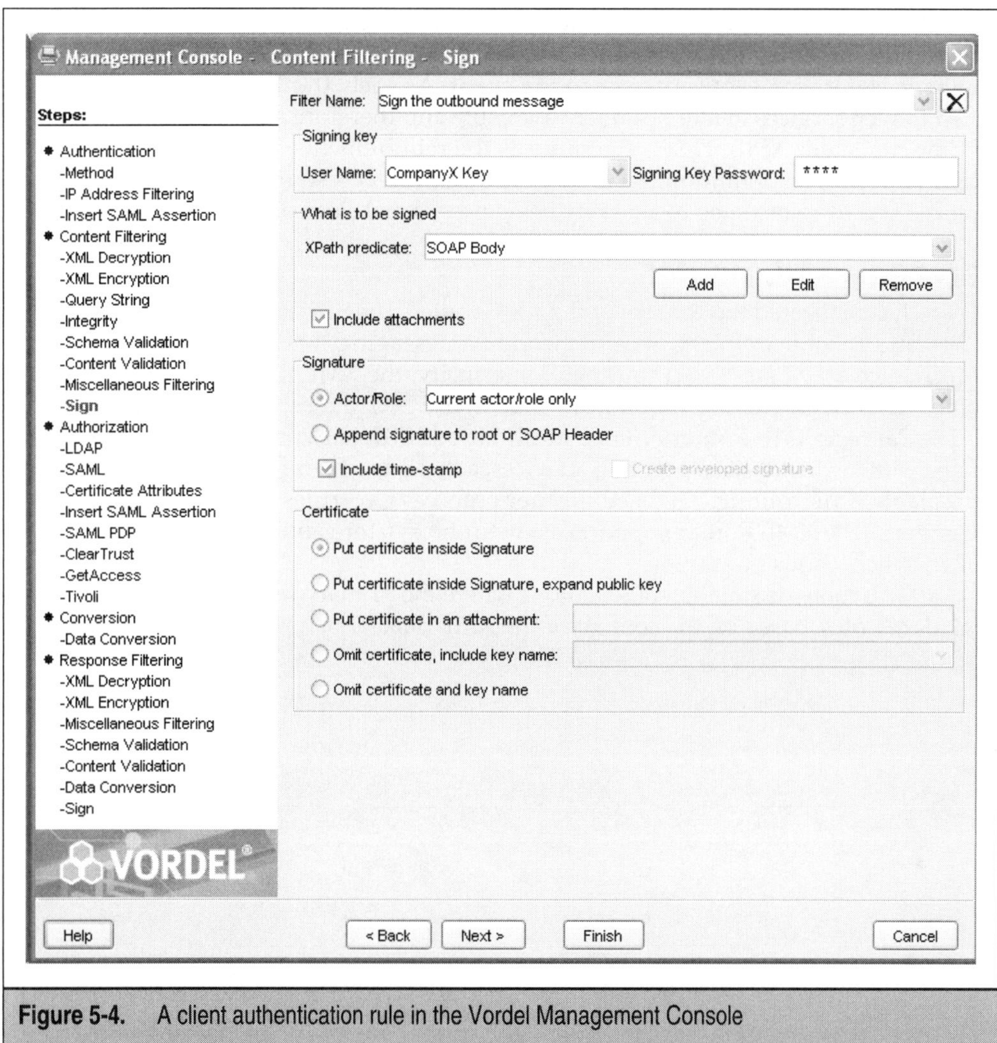

Figure 5-4. A client authentication rule in the Vordel Management Console

blocks application layer attacks that are not detected by network-based firewalls or intrusion detection systems. The Teros Secure Application Gateway permits only correct application behavior and blocks anomalous behavior, without the use of attack signatures. It includes support for the configuration of regular expressions over incoming XML traffic. In this chapter, you saw a regular expression in an XML schema definition being used to block a SQL Injection attack.

The Teros product works by ensuring that the content of incoming XML messages is appropriate. As such, it is analogous to a traditional firewall or application-level gateway, which knows what valid traffic looks like and therefore can block invalid traffic. The product also includes a safeguard to ensure that sensitive data, such as credit card numbers, is not sent as output back to the client. As such, the Teros product is most suited to web services that are publicly available and therefore susceptible to attackers sending malicious XML. This is the same as the requirements for web application security, where, by definition, security products protect resources that are publicly available and therefore open to attack by being passed malicious data.

Sarvega—XML Router

Sarvega has pioneered the concept of the XML router. The Sarvega XML Router supports end-to-end reliable delivery of asynchronous messaging, with Gigabit Ethernet performance for XPath-based routing. For security, the XML Router performs fine-grained inspection, filtering, and transformation of SOAP message headers and content.

The Sarvega XML Router offers a mesh-based XML network topology with XML context routers deployed as peer edge devices, as well as a hierarchical network topology for scalable XML routing. The XML Router enforces QoS rules and supports delivery guarantees. The XML Router supports asynchronous (store and forward) messaging as well as synchronous messaging.

An XML router is suitable for situations where the primary requirement is to control XML data flows, based on the content of the XML data.

Chapter 6

Hardening Mobile Environments

by Jason Zann

- Defend Yourself from the Risks of Mobile Devices in Your Environment
- Defend Your Environment from Mobile-Connectivity Risks

The mobile environments of today are becoming more populated, more widely used, and more difficult to control. Multiple factors explain these trends, ranging from increased device functionality and storage capacity, to expanded connectivity requirements and relatively inexpensive device prices (e.g., most PDAs today range from $200–$700). These issues, when factored in with loose central administrative controls, make mobile devices difficult to govern. Additionally, because these devices rest on the outskirts of corporate control, it is difficult to impose policy on them. Furthermore, in their eagerness to obtain information, be an "early adopter," or just have something new, users tend to disregard commonsense security procedures.

Defend Yourself from the Risks of Mobile Devices in Your Environment

Microsoft Pocket PC, Microsoft Mobile, Palm, and Symbian-based devices and even laptops are a few examples of mobile computing platforms. Generally, a mobile device is any untethered computing platform. New generations of these devices continue to increase in power and functionality. Spreadsheets, documents, and data that could barely be loaded on earlier versions of mobile devices are now becoming requirements for average corporate users. With that increased power and functionality comes increased risk.

NOTE Although laptops are larger and more powerful than what is traditionally considered a mobile device, laptops are by design mobile devices and thus are covered in multiple places in this book.

Establish a Mobile-Device Security Policy

Creating a mobile-device security policy should be the first thing you do. The following are some general guidelines to follow when you are establishing a mobile-device security policy:

1. *Determine whether mobile devices will be authorized.* Does your environment even require the use of mobile technologies? With the proliferation and advances that are occurring in the mobile arena, banning mobile devices in your organization may seem like a radical concept; however, considering the potential for vast amounts of corporate information to be loaded on devices that are difficult to track and detect and the ability to access corporate resources from anywhere with phone service, security considerations could warrant banning mobile devices in the enterprise. If your policy becomes "no mobile devices allowed" (as you would see in security-conscious government facilities), you'll need a way to enforce it. While there are no formal solutions that can stop users from

syncing corporate data onto mobile devices, you can scan PCs (by using, for example, Microsoft Systems Management Service, or SMS) for ActiveSync (Microsoft) or HotSync (Palm) executables and remove them. Disabling USB and serial ports is another option, depending on whether they are used for other purposes in your environment.

2. *Document and provide information on risk.* If your organization determines that there is a business requirement to sync mobile devices, it is important that you inform your executive staff of the potential risks associated with the requirement. Many times, mobile initiatives are driven by availability rather than security, so security is often lower on the priority list when evaluating mobile solutions. Remember, just because a device or service has the capability to do something does not mean that you have to do it.
3. *Define the mobile-device policy.* If your executive management is willing to accept the potential risks to the organization of allowing mobile devices, your next step is to define a policy that specifies the parameters regarding what can be synchronized with a mobile device. Your policy most likely will permit the synchronization of PIM (personal information manager) software—to manage contacts, a calendar, and the like—and data such as notes, contacts, to do lists, calendars, and e-mail. You should be cautious about permitting anything else to be synchronized, such as spreadsheets, documents, PDFs, and corporate applications, especially if the data contains information that is sensitive to the company.

Secure Mobile Authentication

One of the things that make mobile devices so attractive is their "always on, always available—anytime, anywhere" functionality. In the past, to take advantage of the proliferation of new applications and messaging technologies, users had to be physically connected to a network or computer. This is a hindrance when users need to be mobile. The introduction of laptops did a lot to free up mobile users, but mobile devices are even less cumbersome than laptops and can relay information quickly and efficiently. Today, anything that hinders the quick and efficient delivery of information is seen as an inhibitor of what the device primarily provides. Authentication is often viewed as one of those inhibitors.

TIP Good authentication is the first line of defense if a mobile device is lost or stolen.

Chapter 4 defines the three bases of authentication: something that you know, something that you are, and something that you have. The same principles apply to the authentication of mobile devices.

Authenticate Mobile Devices Based on Something that You Have

To determine what can be used to authenticate a user to a mobile device, look at these common interfaces that are available to mobile devices:

- Most devices have the ability to accept external cards, in the form of an SD card, CF card, or PCMCIA card.
- Most devices have a native touch-screen interface and a microphone interface.
- Some devices have an external sleeve that can be attached. Sleeves are normally used for expansion and provide functions like GPS receivers.
- Some devices support attachments through cradle interfaces, like QWERTY keyboards. (QWERTY keyboards are "thumb-driven" keyboards and come as an integrated part of a mobile device that may or may not have the ability to use a stylus as well.)
- Some devices support mini-USB connections to be plugged into them. This is generally done to allow for syncing and the attachment of power cables.

Notice that this list does not include any common interfaces. In other words, there is no way to use something that you have to authenticate to every mobile device. This lack of a common interface means that few products actually offer user authentication via something that you have. Some exceptions are OMINKEY's CardMan Mobile (http://www.omnikey.de/en/produkt_details.php?produkt=5) and Axcess Mobile Communications' Blue Jacket (http://www.axcess-mobile.com/bluejacket.shtml) for the Pocket PC, Pro-Active's SpringCard for the Handspring Visor (http://www.pro-active.fr/products/sc-vs/index.php), and APRIVA's Smart Card Reader for the BlackBerry (http://www.apriva.com/solutions/government.cfm#). Any authentication mechanism that has to be physically present on a mobile device to authenticate, including smart cards, often remains plugged into the device at all times. Users do this for ease of use. Remember, one of the incentives for using mobile devices is the capability to get quick and efficient access to relevant information. If an authenticator needs to be presented every time that an authentication occurs, it will impede this process and users will be tempted to find ways around it.

Unless your enterprise has unique requirements, you should avoid methods of authenticating mobile devices that rely on something the user has. The one exception to this rule is the use of a native BlackBerry implementation with a corporate BlackBerry Enterprise Server (BES) to access corporate resources. In this solution, the BlackBerry device has a randomly generated encryption key that is created at the time of installation. This key is loaded on the device itself and shared with the server. This type of implementation not only enables encrypted data to be transferred over the network, but also enables users to authenticate, because the BES associates the key with a specific user profile. This solution is transparent to the user, and can be used in combination with a password on the device to properly authenticate a user. While there is an additional layer of security in the fact that the user must possess something to authenticate, it is still very important to train users to report immediately a lost or stolen BlackBerry device, so that it can be remotely formatted.

NOTE If you are in a wireless mobile environment, you may elect to use an RSA SecurID token (as described in Chapter 4) to authenticate users. While technically this type of implementation works, from a functionality standpoint, trying to juggle the token and the mobile device at the time of authentication is a drawback.

Authenticate Mobile Devices Based on Something that You Are

One of the primary benefits of using biometrics (something that you are) to authenticate is that it is one of the fastest and easiest methods for users to authenticate to their devices. Users don't even have to remember a password. The primary difference between using biometrics to authenticate users to a corporate application (as discussed in Chapter 4) and using biometrics to authenticate users to a mobile device is the enrollment process. With mobile devices, users are enrolled locally on the device. This means that fingerprints, for example, are authenticated directly to the mobile device rather than to a central repository or a server.

If you are considering the use of biometrics for mobile-device authentication in a corporate environment, you should review signature-based authentication. Companies like CIC (http://www.cic.com) specialize in these solutions. Signature-based authentication solutions not only offer the ability to verify the signature of a user prior to granting the user access to the mobile device, but also offer signature dynamics such as how a *t* was crossed or what speed and acceleration were used when the signature was signed.

Some of the drawbacks to using biometrics as an authentication method for mobile devices are the availability and cost of the biometric readers themselves. Very few mobile devices have integrated biometric readers. One of the exceptions is the high-end HP 5400 series Pocket PC, shown in Figure 6-1. (Its only real drawback is that users have the option of not using the reader.) As another note, the price points of technologies with integrated biometric support are continually dropping.

If a mobile device does not have an integrated biometric reader, some alternative solutions are available, depending on the type of device that needs to be authenticated to. For example, Veridt (http://www.biocentricsolutions.com/mobile.html) offers biometric fingerprint solutions that fit into a CF card slot on a Pocket PC or Windows CE mobile device or that come via a sleeve (hardware that a PDA can slip into). Some PDA biometric sleeves have finger print readers located on the sleeve itself and can turn a normal PDA into a PDA with biometric authentication.

As outlined earlier in this chapter, there are limitations with regard to input methods to mobile devices. Standardization of mobile-device authentication should be a direction within your environment, because a common authentication method allows for easier support and policy enforcement. Standardization should apply to both method and technology. Having multiple biometric implementations not only hinders a consistent corporate solution across device and OS, but makes supporting the devices difficult as well because of all the potential variations of hardware and software that need to be supported. Consistency of devices should be a goal. However, this is a very difficult goal to achieve if device acquisition is not corporately controlled.

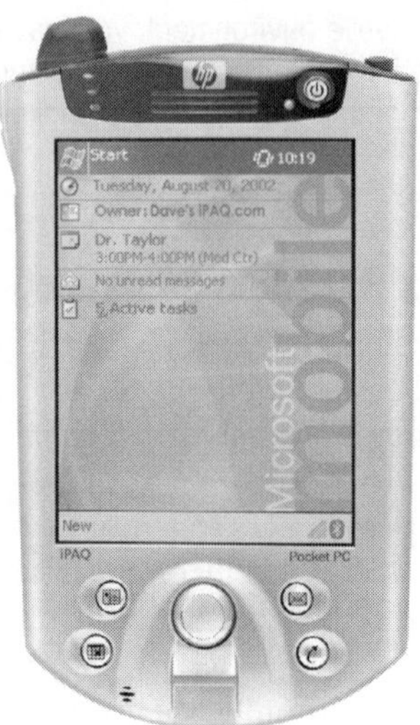

Figure 6-1. HP 5400 iPAQ Pocket PC

Authenticate Mobile Devices Based on Something that You Know

Using passwords is the most common method of authenticating based on something that you know. Mobile devices traditionally offer basic password authentication. Usually, this password authentication requires the user to enter an alphanumeric password on a keyboard or a numeric password on a number pad. These solutions are normally integrated into the mobile devices themselves and offer the capability to create a secure authentication (at least as secure as a password or numeric combination can be). Using passwords on a mobile device is a little clumsy and not very natural for the user, which often leads the user to look for a way to circumvent the process. This makes the device even less secure. (The last point refers more to stylus-driven mobile devices and not as much to QWERTY-driven devices.)

Another method of authentication to mobile devices based on something that a user knows is to require the use of a stylus to select an image or image sequence. This enables you to leverage the graphical characteristics of the mobile device's screen in concert with visual recognition to authenticate. The concept here is that human memory is better suited to identify and correlate images (that would have equal, if not better, strength than traditional passwords) than to memorize and enter an alphanumeric password. Also, using a stylus or touch screen to make a selection usually is physically easier than inputting an alphanumeric string.

When using image-based passwords, a picture is displayed when the mobile device is turned on or needs to be authenticated to. The picture itself is manipulated by the user either by tapping certain images or parts of images in a certain order or constructing an image based on a predefined user sequence. For a more detailed explanation of image-based password authentication alternatives, refer to the NIST publication *Picture Password: A Visual Login Technique for Mobile Devices* at http://csrc.nist.gov/publications/nistir/nistir-7030.pdf.

A product that can incorporate an image as a password is visKey by sfr (http://www.viskey.com). One of sfr's solutions allows a user to select an image and determine the locations and sequence of locations that need to be tapped to authenticate. While the picture itself may be common, the manner in which the picture is manipulated through the tapping process may be completely unique per user. This process is easy for a user to master, especially if they are familiar with the picture being used. For example, a user could use a picture of their family at the Grand Canyon. They could say to themselves, "we went from the top of the canyon to the bottom of the canyon, and here we stand." During the enrollment process, they could turn this statement into a password by tapping one of the tops of the Grand Canyon walls (the top of the canyon), then tapping a part of the image that is close to the Grand Canyon floor (the bottom of the canyon), and then tapping the faces of the family members in the picture (and here we stand). An adversary would have difficulty reproducing this login.

Some implementations of technologies such as this allow the user to simply tap an image or tap and hold (for two seconds, for example) an image in a particular order. As a result, there are many sequences that can be used to authenticate a user. This allows the total available inputs to far surpass the total 94 ASCII combinations, as outlined in Chapter 4, allowing for an even more secure password to be created by the user with less effort.

Another solution that can be used to manipulate authentication based on images is from a company called Real User (http://www.realuser.com). In this solution, called Passfaces, users are shown a grid of nine different faces on their screen at the time of authentication. One of the faces is legitimate and the other eight are decoys. The real strength of this solution is that you can specify how many challenge grids must be passed successfully before authentication is granted. For example, a grid of nine faces is displayed. If the user selects the right face, they are presented with another nine faces. If they select the right face, they are challenged by a third grid. For a user who knows the authentication scheme, this is a simple and quick authentication process. For an adversary, this can be a very long and tedious process with no guarantee of success. To make this implementation more secure, the adversary could be forwarded to the next set of challenges even if they select the wrong picture. After the adversary completed the set of challenges, they would not know which image they failed on.

CAUTION Any solution, including those just described, that gives the local mobile user the option to enroll in and configure an authentication scheme can also be disabled by the user. It is very difficult to enforce authentication requirements on disbursed mobile devices, which is why the use of mobile devices within an organization can be very dangerous.

Secure Mobile Devices from Malicious Code

Mobile devices have not had the power, access, and capability to be affected by wide-scale malicious code. Those dynamics are changing as mobile devices become more like PCs in terms of capabilities and connectivity. Solutions such as Trend Micro's PC-cillin for Wireless 2.0 (http://www.trendmicro.com/en/products/desktop/pcc-wireless/evaluate/overview.htm) can scan for viruses that may infect a mobile device via synchronization, beaming, or the Internet. While this is currently a niche market, it will grow as mobile devices become more powerful and start being used more pervasively by corporate applications. The major threats to mobile devices at this time are theft, the manipulation of file integrity, and the changing of device configurations. These modifications are done by individuals with physical access to the device, which is why device authentication should be required on mobile devices.

Protect Stored Data on Mobile Devices

Larger memory storage capacities on mobile devices may lead to a larger amount of corporate data being stored on mobile devices. The first approach to eliminating this risk is to create a policy that states that sensitive data should not be transferred to or loaded on mobile devices. If loading sensitive data on mobile devices is a business requirement, you should consider using some form of encryption for sensitive data.

The most important point here is that if you are going to encrypt data, the method used to authenticate the data should be separate from the mechanism used to authenticate to the device. Because connectivity cannot be guaranteed for a mobile device, you must have the capability to decrypt the data while the device is in stand-alone mode. This can be accomplished through the use of Tricryption Engine from a company called ERUCES (http://eruces.com/). Keys for encrypted data can be used in a mobile environment in stand-alone mode through the key-checkout process. In this solution, separate authentication can be used to access sensitive documents that have been encrypted, with the caveat that the document can be accessed only a specific number of times before the device needs to connect to the corporate LAN to refresh the number of times that the encrypted data can be viewed.

Defend Your Environment from Mobile-Connectivity Risks

In the past, the only way to get data to or from a mobile device was through the synchronization process with a desktop. Today, devices can also be synchronized through a server, even without having to be physically connected to the corporate LAN. There are numerous other connectivity possibilities for today's mobile devices. Figure 6-2 shows an overview of some of the connectivity options. This section describes the risks and the areas that you should consider for selected connectivity technologies.

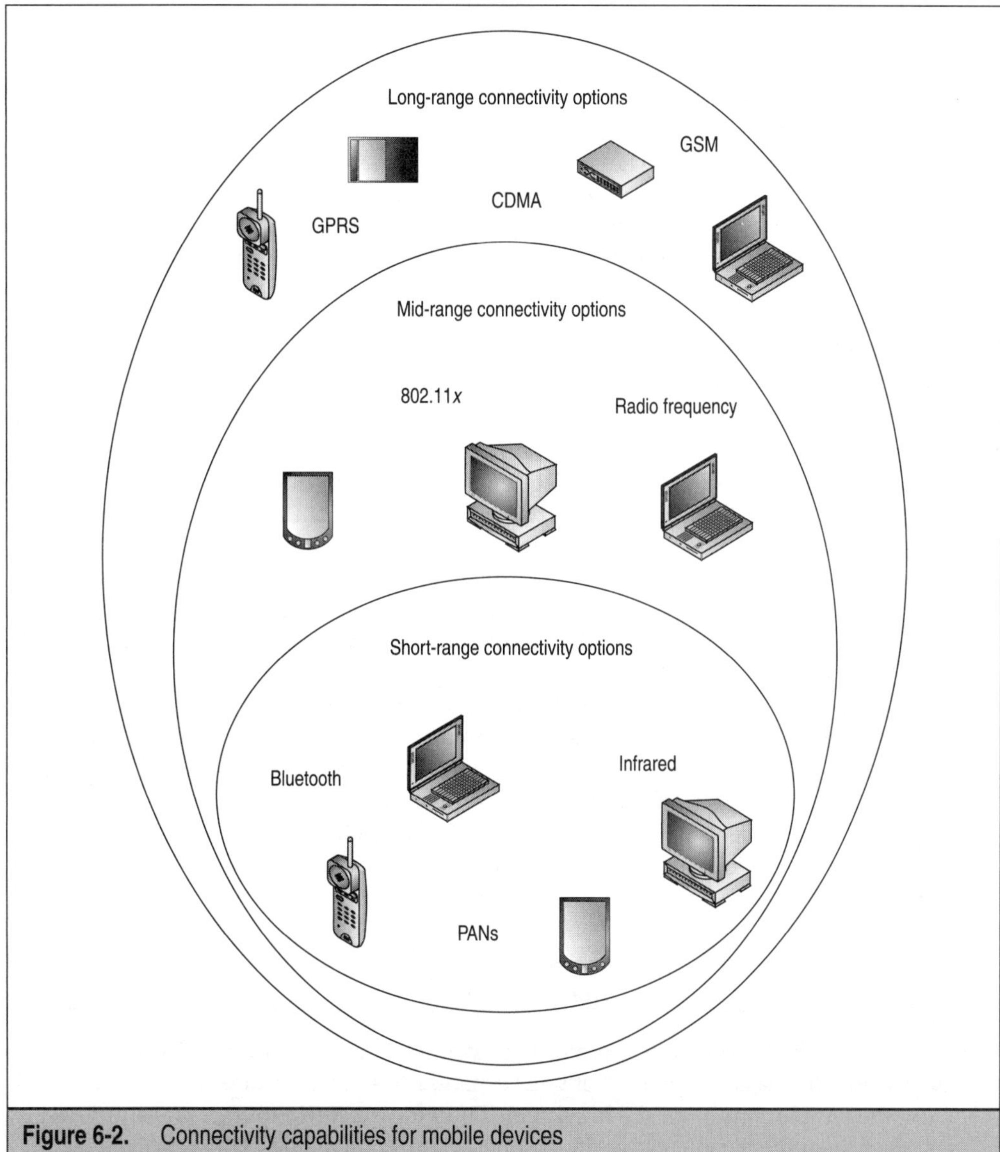

Figure 6-2. Connectivity capabilities for mobile devices

As you can see in Figure 6-2, there are a number of different connection possibilities with mobile devices. Because each of these categories of connection options can be used to fulfill different requirements, the threats to each of these categories are analyzed separately in the sections that follow.

Defend Your Environment from Short-Range Connectivity Threats

Short-range connectivity solutions are used to provide communications between devices in close proximity to each other. These solutions satisfy tasks ranging from synchronization of PIM to transferring files. While these implementations normally are not considered production connectivity solutions (they are not the most pervasive form of data transfer), we will examine which security threats to organizations they pose and what to do about those threats.

Protect Yourself from IR Threats

Infrared (IR) is a short-range communication method that is present on many PDAs, phones, and laptops today. It is useful because it is wireless, ubiquitous, and allows for synchronization of mobile devices and the transfer of data between devices. One of the functional limitations of IR is that it must be within close proximity and line of sight in order to work. Ironically, this is one of the security benefits of IR. If something is being transferred via IR, both devices need to be in a certain position and within a short distance, making rogue transfers more difficult. For this reason, IR is a relatively low security risk. Transferring contacts from one mobile device to another and synchronizing with a desktop via IR do not have a high degree of exposure for the devices. To transfer data from one mobile device to another, the receiving party has to accept the transfer in order for it to complete, adding another step in the security process.

IR has one major threat: if a program or application is transferred and the recipient accepts it, rogue code could be loaded on the mobile device. The easiest way to address this threat is to not accept anything that you receive unless you have a high degree of confidence in the source. It is very important that you include this guideline in your security awareness policy. Additionally, you should disable the capability for laptops to accept file transfers by default in the build process.

HEADS UP!

IR on mobile devices may affect not only computers and other IR-enabled mobile devices, but other security aspects of your organization as well. For example, in many hotels, the remote control for the big-screen TV in the executive lounge is a simplified version of the remote control used in the guest rooms. The biggest difference is that the remote control in the lounge has no Pay button for movies. Today, getting codes for remotes (codes that allow a mobile device with IR functionality to act as a remote control) or learning remote control codes on a mobile device is rather easy and the cost impact to a hotel is usually pretty straightforward—the hotel loses money if guests are able to watch movies without paying. This risk is usually mitigated through the use of other controls (like a static lock placed on the TVs in the lounge, preventing guests from purchasing movies); however, these mitigating controls are usually configuration options, which are subject to human error.

Protect Yourself from Bluetooth Threats

Bluetooth was designed by the Bluetooth Special Interest Group in 1998 as a short-range, inexpensive method to connect mobile products. Since then, the uses and ideas for Bluetooth implementations have expanded well beyond its original purpose. Currently, Bluetooth is being used as a short-range communication mechanism for products ranging from mobile phones, PDAs, printers, and monitors, to washers and dryers, cars, and beyond.

Because of the numerous and disbursed deployments of Bluetooth, the threat models and potential integration points have increased exponentially. This is because Bluetooth is not just limited to mobile devices (when was the last time you walked by a washing machine that had the ability to connect to your PDA?). As a good rule of thumb, *if you are not using the Bluetooth functionality of your device, turn it off!* This is the best way to eliminate any threats caused by Bluetooth.

One of the primary benefits of Bluetooth is its capability to create personal area networks (PANs) and wireless personal area networks (WPANs). For example, if you have a Bluetooth-enabled PDA and a Bluetooth-enabled phone, you can use the PDA to wirelessly connect to your phone to get an Internet connection on your phone. The same is true for using a laptop to connect wirelessly to your phone to gain Internet access (which has benefits in places like airports if you do not want to juggle a phone that is tethered or cabled to your laptop). If you have a Bluetooth-enabled phone and a Bluetooth-enabled headset, you can talk on your phone without having wires limiting your range of motion. In other implementations, you could move your printer to the other side of your home office without having to run cables across your office.

The bottom line is that the uses for Bluetooth will continue to expand as Bluetooth is integrated into new devices. As a security administrator, you must realize that each one of these uses represents one more point of entry or security risk that could be enabled as a result of this functionality. Unfortunately (for security's sake anyway) Bluetooth will continue to proliferate in devices and be used in ways that we have not even thought of yet. If Bluetooth is starting to arrive in your environment (or, better yet, if Bluetooth has not yet arrived in your environment), take the time to investigate how Bluetooth could be used in different scenarios within your environment. Then, create a security strategy to properly manage and contain Bluetooth, before its use leads to a significant growth in security risks to your environment.

When doing security testing on Bluetooth, familiarize yourself with how Bluetooth is supposed to work and what versions you will need to deal with. Currently (May of 2004), version 1.2 of Bluetooth is being implemented into devices. This means that you have to look at backward compatibility (security compatibility) with version 1.1 and look ahead at new features and potential exposures with version 2.0, such as the proposed ability to transmit unencrypted information between devices passing each other at high speeds. For the best information on Bluetooth developments and how the standard is evolving, get a subscription to palowireless (http://www.palowireless.com), monitor http://bluetooth.com, and use the NIST recommendations for wireless devices, located at its Computer Security Resource Center (CSRC), http://www.csrc.nist.gov/publications/nistpubs/800-48/NIST_SP_800-48.pdf. Be sure to look at the Bluetooth Security Checklist section in this document.

There are also a number of known attacks against Bluetooth. It is important to understand these attacks as they may affect how you wish to deploy Bluetooth within your enterprise. The first thing to take into account is the positioning for an attack. While there are Bluetooth specifications (based on Class 1: 10m range; Class 2: 50m range; and Class 3: 100m range) that can affect the range of Bluetooth devices, a majority of the Bluetooth implementations in mobile devices are within the 10m class. As a result, the proximity in which an attack on these types of devices can occur is limited to 10 meters.

In the prior rogue connectivity seeking models (methods of seeking connectivity entry points into an environment), the attackers, using methods such as war dialing and war driving, had discrete methods of surveillance. These surveillance models do not promote needing the attacker to be physically exposed; in other words, the attacker can gather this information from a distance. On the other hand, in the case of seeking out Bluetooth connections, the adversary needs to be within a relatively close proximity to the target that they are after. As a result, instead of driving around, looking for 802.11 access points, the adversary needs to find a congested area of Bluetooth-enabled devices (like a train station, airport, or lobby) and remain stationary. This is why, for security purposes, you should heavily discourage the use of Bluetooth devices in highly congested areas.

The types of attacks that can be executed against Bluetooth devices range from simple annoyances, to privacy violations, to some potentially major security concerns. The following are two common Bluetooth attacks:

- **Bluesnarfing** Connecting to various types of Bluetooth devices without the owner being aware. This type of attack can yield restricted information from the Bluetooth mobile device, like contacts, calendar information, and the like.
- **Bluejacking** Misusing a Bluetooth device's "pairing" protocol, allowing messages to be sent to the device during the initial handshake. This attack can be used to anonymously contact people in public places for advertising or solicitation purposes. It can also lead to sensitive information being attained from the Bluetooth device.

Although these attacks are known, there are still devices being sold that are natively susceptible to these attacks, including devices from major phone manufacturers. While this is expected, as new features often lead to new security vulnerabilities, you now have a new vulnerability profile of concern. This means that in addition to monitoring new vulnerabilities associated with OSs and applications in your environment, you now have to stay abreast of the vulnerabilities in mobile devices that users may purchase outside of the corporate channels and load data on. This is a very difficult issue to contend with. To help you address these new issues, Bluetooth security applications are available that can help identify Bluetooth security vulnerabilities in your environment. The following table lists and describes four such applications.

Application	URL	Use
@stake's Redfang	http://www.atstake.com/research/tools/info_gathering/	This tool assists in finding Bluetooth nondiscoverable devices by brute-forcing the last 6 bytes of the device's Bluetooth address and doing a read_remote_name() (determining the name of the remote device).
Shmoo.com's Bluesniff	http://bluesniff.shmoo.com/	A user-friendly front end to Redfang that is integrated with Airsnort.
Frontline Test Equipment's FTS for Bluetooth	http://www.fte.com/blu01.asp	A PC-based Bluetooth analyzer that can capture and decode encrypted Bluetooth data in real time.
Bluefire Security Technologies'Bluefire Mobile Firewall	http://www.bluefiresecurity.com/mobile_firewall_plus.php#top	A protection tool that can be placed on mobile devices to actually defend against Bluetooth connections.

Another valuable tool in this space is developed by IVT (http://www.ivtcorporation.com/). IVT has a whole suite of products that allow you to securely enable Bluetooth within your environment. Managing Bluetooth uses and implementations within your environment will be difficult, regardless of the tools and expertise that you have. Again, the best way to protect your environment is to follow this rule: If you are not using or do not need Bluetooth, turn it off!

Protect Your Environment from Medium-Range Connectivity Threats

Chapter 12 deals with IEEE 802.11*x* security requirements, so be sure to refer to it if your organization has or plans to implement a wireless LAN. The primary point that needs to be addressed here regarding medium-range connectivity threats is that although mobile devices are viewed as being in a different category than PCs or laptops that are using wireless, they still have the same security concerns. Mobile devices can be used as soft APs (access points)—or APs that serve up wireless connections from a computer, like a laptop—for peer-to-peer networking and can serve as a vulnerable access point into the corporate environment. Because mobile devices are managed by the local user (as opposed to a laptop, which can be centrally managed by SMS), there is the potential for more security vulnerabilities in terms of configuration. Mobile devices cannot be supported by a central management system, so their control in this arena is difficult. You cannot let your guard down with regard to mobile devices that connect into your environment, because mobile devices are starting to ship with 802.11*x* technologies imbedded in them.

Protect Your Environment from Long-Range Connectivity Threats

One of the primary reasons that mobile technology started and continues to gain momentum is its capability for content delivery and messaging. This hunger was first addressed when mobile devices had the capability to sync with and download content from the desktop, enabling users to complete work while away from the desktop. Today, this feature is barely considered an appetizer. As functionality, services, and features that were once limited to LAN desktops are pushed further and further past the corporate perimeter, a vast new host of security concerns need to be addressed.

The first option to secure messaging and mobile content delivery is to use preexisting connections, such as current web-based e-mail configurations. If your corporate information is available via the Web from a browser on your home ISP, it may also be available in a simplified format on a mobile device that is connected to a mobile data service provider. This offers a consolidated access point that is presumably tested and in production for mobile devices. All that is needed is a browser and an Internet connection.

The second option is to use the mobile device to RAS (remotely dial) into your corporate environment through a preexisting dial-in solution for your organization, and then use a browser to access your organization's content.

While it would be nice to draw the line at the preceding two options and force mobile users to engage in these practices, in reality these options are usually nothing more than alternatives because these solutions were not initially designed for mobile technologies. From a security perspective, if you are using a preexisting solution, like the solutions outlined in the previous paragraphs, through another method, your risk is limited to what you have in place today.

Most mobile devices have integrated messaging solutions that users have learned to use over the years while synchronizing. These messaging solutions transfer content to the device so that work can be done while not connected to any network. They have nice integration with the contact lists and other functionalities on the device, and are very user friendly (with regard to buttons and layout) compared to making a connection, opening a browser, waiting for a response, entering login credentials, then looking at a screen that is a shaved-down version of what users see on their laptops. As a security administrator, you have to find a secure way to allow users to access messaging and content features on mobile devices, because that is where user demand is going to force you. This is going to most likely force another point of entry into your environment.

Protect Your Long-Range Connectivity Solutions with BlackBerry

If the use of preexisting access connections is not viable or sufficient for your environment, your next step should be to attempt to standardize on one type of mobile solution. Having a single mobile solution in your environment will allow for easier security, support, and administrative functionality. This generally means that there will be an additional up-front cost to your mobile environment.

Research in Motion (RIM; http://www.rim.com) offers BlackBerry as a unique and time-tested solution for mobile messaging and content delivery. This solution offers both the server and the devices for users to access corporate content. From a security perspective, a number of unique benefits make this solution stand apart. These security benefits are listed next for both the device and the server. These points should be

HEADS UP!

Just because a device is a mobile device does not mean you should treat it any differently than you would treat any other connection into your corporate environment. This means *do not* do something like open POP (Post Office Protocol, a method to deliver e-mail to mobile devices) to your mobile devices to receive e-mail if you do not currently do this for your corporate users. Mobile devices are often looked at differently by many administrators because they are small and usually outside the control and influence of the corporate IT functions. Additionally, user demands will push you toward the anytime, anywhere mindset that data *needs* to be accessed or work will not get done. In some cases, addressing demands like this will be very difficult; however, it is important not to seriously degrade your perimeter defenses because of user demands. Finally, all of us have had solutions that were being tested or were left temporarily exposed that became production implementations over time. Do not let this happen with anytime, anywhere access on mobile devices, because once users get a taste of this access they will be very unwilling to give it up.

considered for any corporate-sponsored mobile-device deployment. The asterisk (*) indicates features that have to be enabled in the policy that you create for BlackBerry in your environment.

- *BlackBerry devices are configured on a per-user basis.* This means that one device is provisioned and users are accountable for the device that they use.
- *BlackBerry devices have relatively few third-party software and hardware add-ons.* This may be a drawback if you are looking for a multipurpose, multifunctioning device. From a security perspective, however, it is actually positive, because there are fewer complexities and user modifications to manage. Ensure that you have the capability to control as many of the add-ons, both software and hardware, as possible.
- **Devices can be configured to enforce password policies.* Find a way to enforce a sufficient level of user authentication for mobile devices. To do this, use this setting in the configuration for user authentication. The benefit in this is accountability for the primary user. To configure BlackBerry to enforce a password policy, use the following configuration:

```
; Determine if the password is required on device
PasswordRequired {policy}= TRUE

; Determine if the user can disable the password
```

```
UserCanDisablePassword {policy}= FALSE

; Minimum length of the password.
; Valid range is 1 to 12 characters, inclusive.
;
; This value indicates the minimum length of an acceptable device
; security password.
MinPasswordLength {policy} = 6

; Password Pattern Checks
; Valid range is 0 or 1 at this time
;   0 -> no checks
;   1 -> ensure password has at least one letter and one digit
PasswordPatternChecks {policy} = 1
```

- **Devices can be configured to enforce account variables.* This includes aging, lockout parameters, and the like. To properly secure a mobile device, be certain that you can enforce account variables. To enforce account variables on BlackBerry, use the following policy configuration:

```
; Maximum device security timeout.
; Valid range is 1 to 60 minutes, inclusive.
;
; The handheld user is permitted to select any security timeout value
; less than this value.
MaxSecurityTimeout {policy}= 10

; Determine if the user can change the timeout
UserCanChangeTimeout {policy}= TRUE

; Password aging.
; Valid range is 0 to 365.
;
; Specifying a value of 0 indicates password aging is disabled. Other
; values specify the maximum age of the password before the handheld
; user is prompted to change it.
MaxPasswordAgeInDays {policy}= 30

; Indicate if Long Term Security Timeout is enabled/disabled
;
; If true, handheld long term timeout is enabled
; If false, handheld long term timeout is disabled.
LongTermTimeoutEnable {policy} = true
```

- *Consistent owner information can be set that reflects the organization rather than the individual.* This enables you to implement a standard method for dealing with lost or stolen devices. To reflect this, use this setting in the configuration policy:

```
; Owner Name - if value = '*' use the registry setting
OwnerName {default} = My Company.

; Owner Info - if value = '*' use the registry setting
OwnerInfo {default} = Please return to My Company\
Phone # (800) 555-1212\
1234 Any Street Address\
Anytown, State\
Zip
```

- *The device should be configured to reformat if an incorrect password is entered a certain number of times.* This is a useful feature if the device is lost or stolen, because whoever steals or finds the device has a limited number of attempts to guess the password (which enforces authentication, as discussed earlier in this chapter) before the device is reformatted. If an adversary is the one who locks out the device, they possess only the hardware, not the data. If a legitimate user is locked out, they just have to restore the information from their desktop while connected to the corporate network. For the sake of security, you should make every effort to ensure that the device formats itself after several unsuccessful attempts at authentication.
- *You can make the device specific to the user.* At the time of installation, the user is required to randomly move their mouse across their desktop. This random motion is used as the seed value for a key that is shared between the device and the server. This key is used both to encrypt the data between the mobile device and the server and as a form of authentication of the device to the server. With regard to authentication, the user can be authenticated to the device via a password (or via a smart card, by using a third-party product like APRIVA's Smart Card Reader, mentioned earlier in this chapter) and the device is authenticated to the account that it is servicing via the encryption key.
- *You can make the policy parameters for mobile devices centrally enforced.* From the server, an administrator can make a global policy setting and enforce it on all the devices that are connecting to the corporate BlackBerry server. This is beneficial in maintaining a level of consistency on the devices in the field.
- *The RIM solution is carrier independent.* This means that you do not have to support multiple device types. If you have users who are using different telephone technologies—some are using CDMA and others are using GSM—and everyone has a different provider, you can still reap all the benefits outlined above.

Protect Your Long-Range Connectivity Solutions with Other Devices

Some environments are not willing to purchase devices for all of their mobile employees. As a result, users may purchase their own devices independently of the organization and want to use those devices to connect to a corporate messaging solution. While these types of employee-purchased solutions are currently not as elegant as a solution that controls every aspect of the connection, there are steps that you can take to make these implementations secure.

HEADS UP!

Numerous solutions from various manufactures and providers address the issue of how to safely transmit real-time content and messaging to mobile devices. Some solutions require desktop software to be loaded on a logged-in workstation and messages to be forwarded to the mobile device at the time that they arrive on the workstation. These solutions are the mobile equivalent of GoToMyPC.com and carry most of the security risks as well. These solutions, like GoToMyPC.com, should be vigorously discouraged, because they decentralize the security control of interactions between corporate content/messages and the mobile device and potentially bypass the layered perimeter security that you have in place.

Similarly, you should refrain from using any carrier proxying solutions, which are solutions that establish a VPN from your corporate environment to the carrier's environment to forward corporate messages and content. When the connection reaches the carrier's environment, the VPN connection is terminated and the messages and content are transferred to clear text and then sent over the CDMA or GSM network to the mobile device, using the inherent security of the carrier's transmission services. Although your data is encrypted from your environment to the carrier and from the carrier to the mobile device, there is a point in time that your corporate information is in clear text. Carriers will admit that "theoretically" they have the ability to view transmitted corporate information in clear text, but they typically claim that the risk is mitigated by the fact that all of their employees are trustworthy.

Bottom line, this is not a risk that you need to take. There are plenty of methods available to provide secure transmissions from your corporate environment to a mobile device. Data does not need to be converted to clear text at all during the transmission. For example, you could use SyncML over transport layer security (TLS) to accomplish this. SyncML is a method for remote message delivery to connected mobile devices. TLS can provide a layer of encryption from the server in your environment to the mobile device across any carrier without allowing the carrier to see the actual message.

IBM's pervasive computing initiative (http://www-306.ibm.com/software/pervasive/enterprise/) and Nokia's One Business Server (http://www.nokia.com/nokia/0,8764,43106,00.html) are both making big strides to offer security, control, and functionality to disbursed mobile devices from the enterprise. These types of solutions enable devices to use their native mail features in combination with secure delivery of messages and content from the enterprise, across multiple carriers, and to the mobile devices. Because these solutions are designed to work across multiple devices, the feature sets for control of the remote devices are not as mature as RIM's. There are a number of security features available today from companies such as Nokia and IBM. First, end-to-end security for content delivery (via SyncML) can be done via a secure medium, like TLS. Second, users can be forced to authenticate (even strongly authenticate) prior to receiving messages or content.

One deficiency in these solutions is their inability to secure a device if it is lost or stolen. As previously discussed, in the BlackBerry solution, a device can be programmed to be formatted if the wrong password is entered a number of times. If your environment supports many different devices from many different manufacturers for the purposes of remote messaging, it is very difficult to achieve a level of granular security control on the devices themselves. Companies such as CREDANT Technologies (http://www.credant.com/products/onDeviceSecurity.php) provide third-party solutions that have the ability to lock up or wipe out applications if a device is lost or stolen. In today's environment, this type of functionality should be considered imperative. These types of solutions are not available on every device at this time because of the multiple types of devices and device OSs that potentially need to be supported. As the market matures for disbursed mobile devices, this functionality will become more of a standard feature.

Another security issue with long-range connectivity is the use of connection cards. Connection cards are PCMCIA devices that connect to a laptop or handheld PC device to give it connectivity on a mobile-phone network. For the most part, these connections pose the same risks as a user that connects their laptop or handheld device to a public Internet connection. Personal firewall settings, patched machines, and updated antivirus software should be standard on devices using these cards. If a connection is being made to the corporate network, a VPN solution should be used.

The major point that you need to take away regarding connection cards is that you do not need a carrier to terminate the connections for you. Once again, plenty of solutions are available that can provide secure connectivity between a remote device and your corporate infrastructure. The addition or use of a carrier to terminate the connection and then forward the data to your environment is a less-than-desirable implementation from a security perspective. If your organization has a VPN solution, you do not need to rely on a carrier to decrypt and forward data bound for your corporate environment. Even if your organization does not currently have a VPN solution, using SSL or SSH back to your corporate environment will eliminate the need to utilize a proxy-based solution from the carrier.

Chapter 7

Beyond Access Controls: Protecting Stored Data

by Jason Zann

- Use Encryption as a Layer of Security
- Make an Informed Choice of a Cryptosystem
- Understand Who You Are Protecting Your Data From
- Determine What to Encrypt and Why
- Encrypt Sensitive Data in Databases
- Provide for "Un"real-Time Encryption
- Where Encryption Takes Place
- Authentication
- Make Encryption Work for You in Your Environment

Data stored in files and databases on physical media is traditionally protected by access controls. Using access controls, however, is only one element of a comprehensive data protection plan. Using encryption can provide additional protection. Cryptography and encrypting data traditionally has been considered to be within the exclusive realm of Ph.D.s in mathematics. While this may still hold partially true as far as the creation of encryption algorithms, the use of encryption algorithms in computer networks is now considered best practice to increase the security of an environment. This chapter does not cover the intricacies of creating a solid cryptosystem, which is beyond the scope of this book, but it does cover how to properly select an encryption system and implement it within your environment.

Some general rules apply when using encryption to harden your stored data. This list provides a quick reference to use when considering the use of encryption within your environment:

- Do not use proprietary encryption algorithms; use tested, industry recognized algorithms.
- Layer your defenses; encryption is only one part of the picture.
- Do not "self-bake" a solution without extreme caution.
- Do not encrypt all data with the same key.
- Do not store the encryption keys with the encrypted data.
- Prioritize good key management.
- Identify the weaknesses of any implementation and harden it.
- Train users in proper use of encryption.

This chapter discusses these guidelines in more depth and provides direction for the practical and secure implementation of encryption.

Definitions

The following are important terms to know for purposes of this chapter, as defined at Dictionary.com:

- **Encryption** Any procedure used in cryptography to convert plain text into cipher text (encrypted message) in order to prevent any but the intended recipient from reading that data.
- **Cryptography** The practice and study of encryption and decryption—encoding data so that it can only be decoded by specific individuals.
- **Cryptosystem** A system for encrypting and decrypting data.

Source: http://www.dictionary.com

Use Encryption as a Layer of Security

Cryptography by itself is not a security solution; it is simply one part of a layered security approach. Specifically, it is the layer that focuses on the state of the data. For the purposes of this chapter, data can be in either of two states: encrypted or unencrypted.

Encrypting data provides an additional defense against an attack. If an attacker can gain access to the network, the host, and ultimately data, encryption that is properly implemented can serve as an additional layer of defense. This additional layer of encryption, as long as it is done correctly, can deter the attacker from being able to compromise sensitive data. Because encryption is just one layer of security, however, if the other layers of defense are weak, or not present, encryption alone will not be as effective in protecting data.

Make an Informed Choice of a Cryptosystem

There is no single way to implement encryption for every environment because every environment is different—different applicable laws and regulations, different client requirements, different internal requirements, and so forth. However, the considerations that you need to make are generally the same regardless of your environment. These considerations generally revolve around algorithm selection and length, key usage, key management, and the like. It is important that you understand the motivation to use encryption before you begin to study how to implement encryption.

Do Not Trust Proprietary Cryptosystems

As an overriding theme of this chapter, and a useful note to always keep in mind: *never trust a proprietary encryption algorithm.* A proprietary encryption algorithm refers to an algorithm that has not been reviewed publicly by qualified professionals. Companies that sell products with "secret algorithms" often inspire the use of a proprietary cryptosystem. From a security perspective this should raise caution—it is important to only use an algorithm that has been reviewed by as many professional cryptographers as possible in an open forum.

A good resource for finding algorithms that have stood up to enough professional review to be considered for implementation is the National Institute of Standards and Technology (NIST) web site: http://csrc.nist.gov/.

Advanced Encryption Standard (AES)

AES is an example of an algorithm that has been sufficiently reviewed publicly by qualified professionals. In January 1997, NIST announced plans to implement a system of information-processing standards within the U.S. federal government, called AES, and invited proposals for this system from the public. All of the proposals submitted were narrowed down to 15 candidates by August of 1998, and then down to 5 finalists a year later. In October of 2000, NIST chose the Rijndael data encryption formula for AES as its new standard. The strength (among other qualities) of AES withstood public scrutiny, including by quite arguably some of the world's best cryptographers. AES is an example of what is *not* a proprietary encryption algorythm. For more informaiton on the steps that AES went through and, ultimately, what a good public review for an encrytion algorythm is, review the NIST press release at http://www.nist.gov/public_affairs/releases/g00-176.htm#release.

Understand Different Key Algorithms

After you have made sure that a particular algorithm has withstood sufficient public review, you have to select the appropriate key algorithm. Cryptography is all about keys. A key is used to change plain text into cipher text and vice versa. While this may seem like an oversimplification, cryptography has been around for thousands of years and these basic mechanics have not changed. In fact, the only major change has been the method, or *algorithm,* used to apply a key to plain text to create cipher text and vice versa.

ONE STEP FURTHER

Cryptography involves the use of algorithms. A discussion of algorithms is beyond the scope of this book and is unnecessary if you heed the advice to only use algorithms that have been subjected to organized public review by professionals. If you wish to gain a better grasp on the fundamentals of cryptography, I suggest getting a copy of *Applied Cryptography,* Second Edition, by Bruce Schneier (John Wiley & Sons, 1996).

Two common methods of key cryptology are in use today: symmetric key cryptography and asymmetric key cryptography. While both of these methods are mentioned here, this chapter will focus on hardening symmetric key cryptography.

- **Symmetric key cryptography** The same key that is used to encrypt data is used to decrypt it (see Figure 7-1). When properly implemented, it is known to be fast and secure; however, the problem has always been how to securely manage the key, especially if the key is required by a second party to complete a secure transaction. Common examples are 3DES and AES.
- **Asymmetric or public key cryptography** Requires one key to encrypt data and a different key to decrypt data, as shown in Figure 7-2. It has more of a performance overhead than symmetric key cryptography, but it solves the biggest problem with symmetric key cryptography in that it enables encrypted data to be exchanged without requiring secret keys to be divulged. The best example of public key cryptography is RSA.

Harden Your Implementation of Symmetric Key Cryptography

In the world of symmetric key cryptography, the biggest challenge for implementation is to figure out where and how to store the key that is used to encrypt data. To address this issue more thoroughly, the sections that follow present an example process of how keys can be managed.

This example assumes that an industry-recognized encryption algorithm is being used: specifically, AES. The data that needs to be protected in this example is a series of text fields in a database. You will learn more about database encryption later in this chapter, in the section "Encrypt Sensitive Data in Databases," but you do not need to read that section to understand this example.

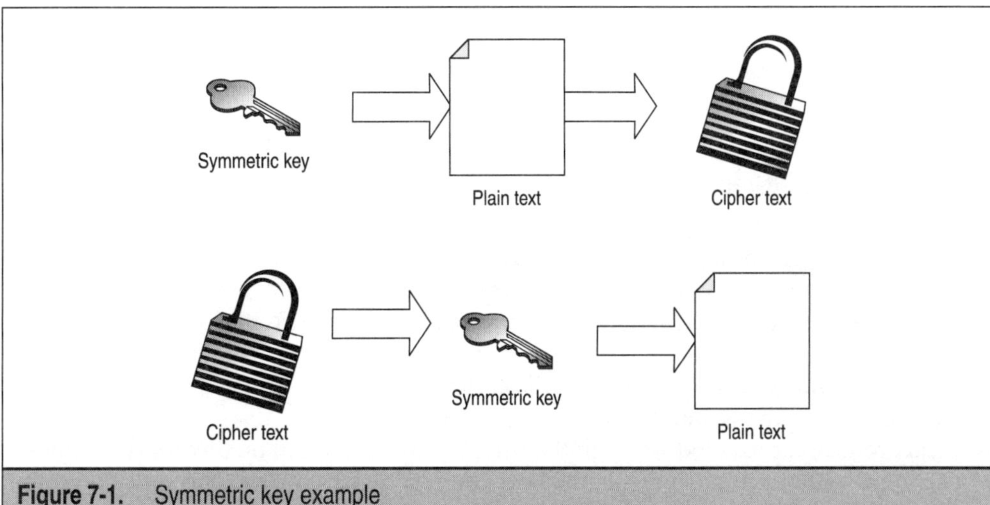

Figure 7-1. Symmetric key example

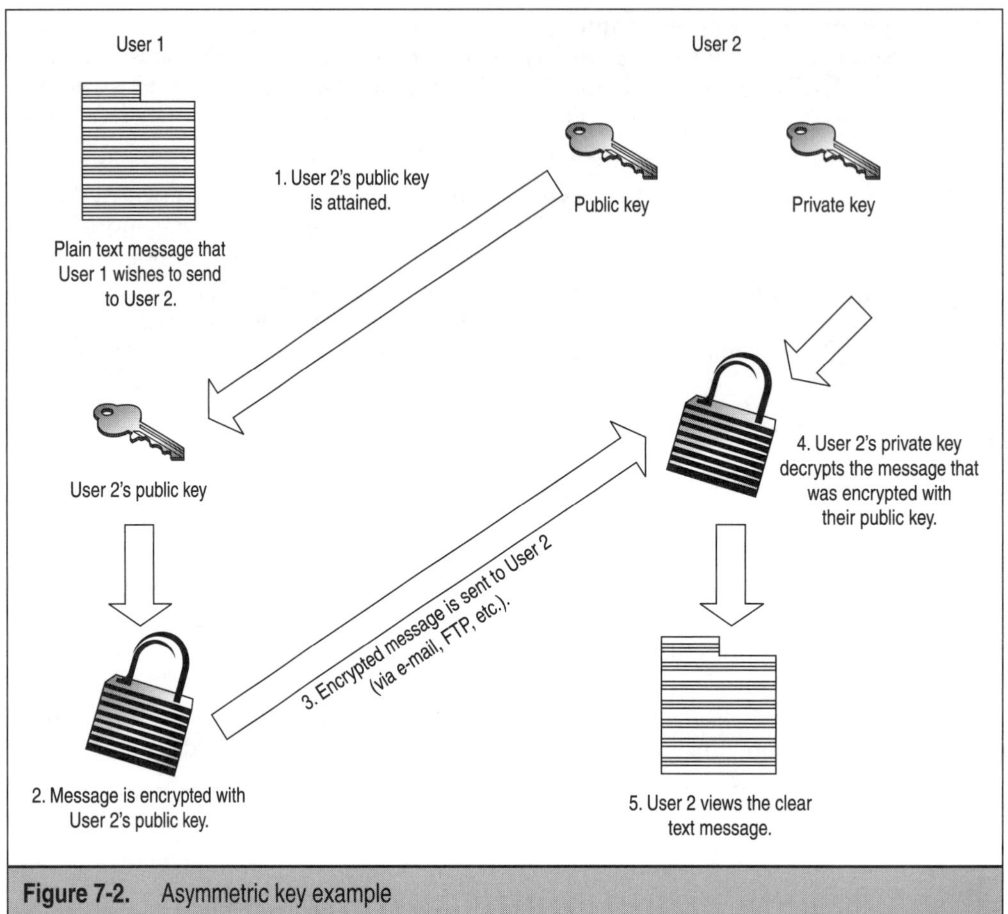

Figure 7-2. Asymmetric key example

Use More than One Key

When symmetric key algorithms are used to encrypt data, all the data can be protected with a single key, or different parts of the data can be secured using different keys. If you are using a single key to protect data, you must address how you will protect the key. If that key is compromised, all the data that is protected with that single key is compromised as well, because the key is combined with every piece of data. And although the data is encrypted, it is not necessarily protected. This section explains and demonstrates through examples the weaknesses of using one key.

The protection provided through the use of a single key can be thwarted in either of two ways without compromising the key. The first of these methods is called a brute-force attack and the second is what is referred to as a replacement attack.

A brute-force attack creates every possible combination of what a key could be until plaintext data is revealed. The second form of attack bypasses the encryption process altogether. Remember: it is a mathematical fact that the more data that is encrypted with a single key, the higher the probability of an attacker being able to ascertain the plaintext value of data protected with that key.

Definitions

- **Brute-force attack** Trying every relevant combination of an element (code, PIN, password, key, etc.) until a success can be measured.
- **Dictionary attack** Taking every word in a dictionary and running it through a process to determine a result. With regard to encryption, this attack could run every known word through an encryption process so that like-encrypted values could be matched up. Dictionary attacks (if the system or implementation is susceptible to them) are generally faster and more efficient than brute-force attacks because they have a much smaller keyspace.

A brute-force attack involves running every combination of data through the encryption process. As an example, suppose that you are looking at a list of social security numbers (SSNs) in a column of a database as the target data. If the SSNs are currently encrypted, they look like jumbled text; however, suppose that you know that only one key is used to protect the data. If you were to create a list of all known SSNs (000-00-0000 through 999-99-9999) and run it through the same process (encrypt all of them with the same key) as the column of currently encrypted SSNs, you would know both the plaintext value and the encrypted value of the encrypted SSNs.

From this point, you could simply match your known values for SSNs with the encrypted values of the SSNs and cross reference your encrypted values with the values of the originally protected SSNs. Since the two encrypted values (the original encrypted SSNs and the SSNs that you injected into the encryption process) will have matches and you can translate the encrypted values to plain text (the original list of known SSNs that you created), you can essentially extrapolate the plaintext value of the originally encrypted SSNs.

A simpler version of the SSN example assumes that the column that you are encrypting with one key is a gender column. You know that only two results could appear in the gender column, male and female. Suppose that you make one entry into the database, Male. You now know that you entered Male in the database, and you can ascertain what the encrypted value for Male is by looking at its encrypted value. You can further infer that all the encrypted values that are the same also have the value of Male. By process of logical deduction, you then know that every entry that differs from Male is Female.

The second way to hack a single key encryption method is to perform a replacement attack. For example, suppose that a DBA in a company's HR department is looking at the personnel database. The values in the Name, Title, Phone Number, and other columns are in plain text, because this information is available in the corporate phone directory; however, the Salary column is encrypted. Suppose that the DBA does not know much about the mechanics of encryption but really feels that he deserves a raise. The DBA knows that his salary is far lower than that of an executive vice president, so he simply copies the cell of the EVP's encrypted salary and pastes it into the cell that his encrypted salary value is currently in. In theory, the DBA just got a raise, even though he won't know how much it is until the next pay period (unless security shows up at his desk before then!).

The three examples given in this section were a little oversimplified, but they are intended only to prove the point that using a single key to encrypt all data can pose a very real security risk.

Use Transactional-Based Keys

If you use multiple keys to encrypt data, you must decide when the keys should change. Should you select some fixed number, or create a new key for every transaction that occurs? This question is among many related to key management.

If you are using a single key, key management is somewhat simplistic, because there is only one key to back up, guard, and so on. When you are using multiple keys, the problem becomes exponentially more difficult. Whether you choose to use a fixed number of keys or transactional keys, using multiple keys is arguably more secure than using a single key from a protection standpoint. However, the functional and operational controls to support multiple keys can potentially become very cumbersome and do not necessarily guarantee a more robust level of security.

In the hierarchy of security, whereas using a pool of keys is more secure than a single key, using a different key for every transaction is more secure than using a pool of keys. But without proper planning, attempting to use a new key for every transaction and indexing every new key for every transaction can lead to a very stressful key-management environment. In fact, this is a process that would be nearly impossible to do manually, especially in high-volume environments. The only way to effectively accomplish using transactional-based keys is to have an automated process that can support an initiative such as this.

Store the Key Separate from the Data

If you use a symmetric key to encrypt data, you need that same key to decrypt the data. But you need to store the key in a separate place from the data that it is protecting; otherwise, if someone steals your computer, then they also have the keys to decrypt the data. The following two sections examine this issue in the context of two different solutions.

Encrypted File System A good analogy to explain why you need to store the key and the data it protects in separate places is the problem of bank robberies in the Old West.

Bank robbers would break into a bank, blow the hinges off a safe, take the valuables in the safe, and ride to a safe location to divide the loot. One engineer noticed this strategy and decided to construct a safe with hinges on the inside of the safe. Additionally, the safe was constructed in a round, tubular manor, to better resist having the door blown off. Bank robbers, upon seeing this safe, realized that their traditional tactics would not work, so they simply stole the entire safe, took it to their secret location, and spent as long as needed to figure out how to get inside.

The same concept exists for storing the key that is used to protect data with the data itself. In the preceding example, the safe (encryption key) and the money in the safe (data) were stored together. If the data and the key are stored together and are stolen together, it is only a matter of time before the thief determines from the key and the data itself how to decrypt the data.

Encrypted data may not be as secure as you believe. Consider a few examples. For the first example, suppose that you have a laptop that stores sensitive data and you need to protect that data. You decide to use Encrypted File System (EFS), a new feature that Microsoft introduced in Windows 2000. To access this feature, you simply right-click a file or folder, select Properties, click the Advanced button on the General tab, and then check Encrypt Contents To Secure Data, as shown in Figure 7-3. Figures 7-4 and 7-5 indicate how this would be done logically.

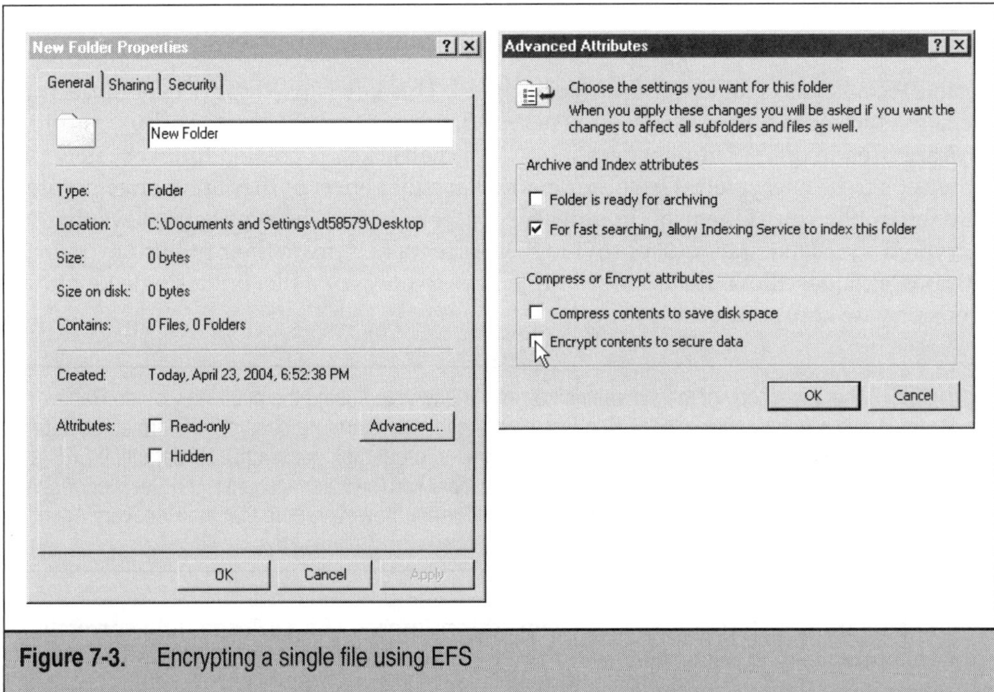

Figure 7-3. Encrypting a single file using EFS

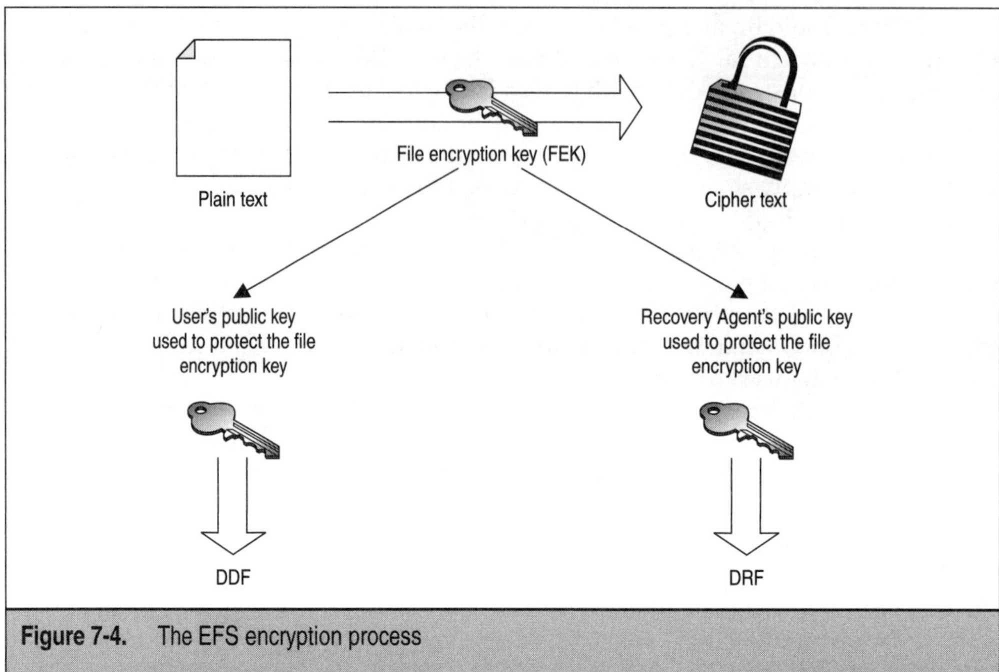

Figure 7-4. The EFS encryption process

In EFS, a key is created per user (public key). This key is used to encrypt or decrypt the keys (symmetric) that are used to encrypt data for the user's profile. Thus, multiple keys are used in an EFS implementation. A symmetric key is created for every new file that needs to be encrypted. Those symmetric keys that encrypt files are then encrypted with the public key of the user. In order for a user to access the symmetric keys that encrypted the file(s), they must provide their private key (from their public key pair). This process does allow the use of multiple keys to encrypt a file, but a single key (the user's private key) secures this process.

NOTE There is a copy of the symmetric key that is encrypted using the public key of the Recovery Agent, a role within Windows 2000. The Recovery Agent can therefore decrypt EFS-protected data if a user is unable to (either because they lost their key or forgot their password). By default, if EFS is used on a stand-alone Windows 2000 computer, the local Administrator account is the Recovery Agent. This example does not discuss the Recovery Agent further; however, note that the Recovery Agent could also be a point of vulnerability because it has access to multiple keys.

Implementing EFS requires you to consider numerous variables to do it correctly, for deployments of any size. You are strongly recommended to turn off EFS until you can commit the time to implement it correctly. If you are looking for more information on how to correctly implement EFS, refer to *Hardening Windows Systems* by Roberta Bragg (McGraw-Hill/Osborne, 2004).

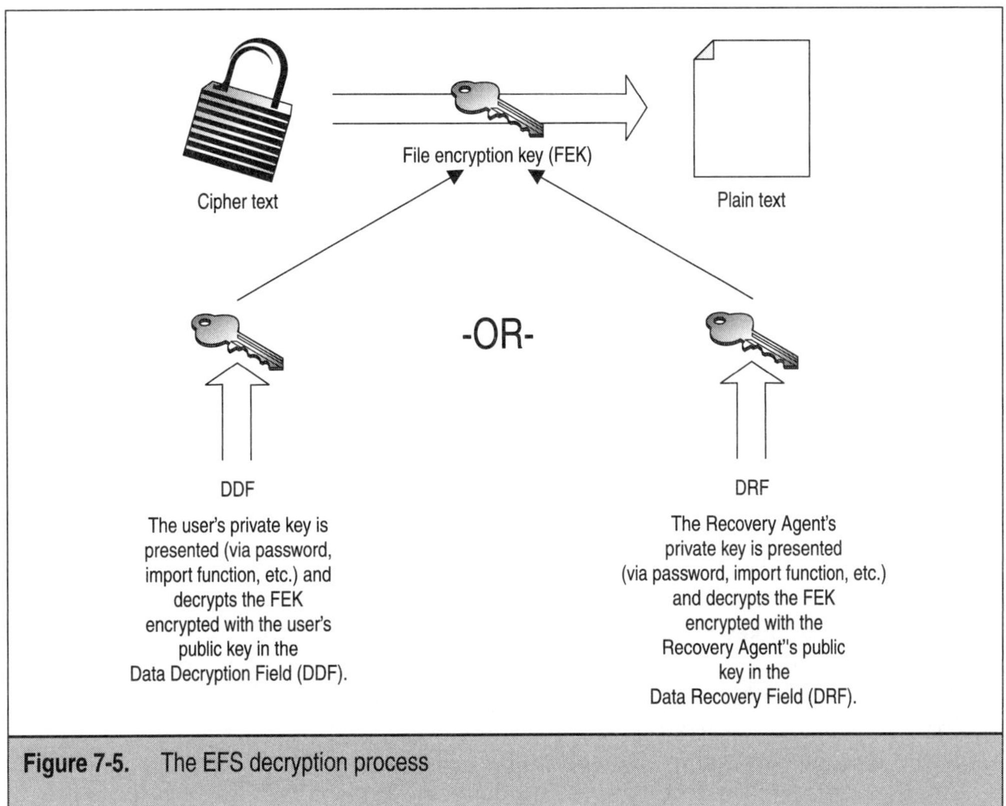

Figure 7-5. The EFS decryption process

The key that is used to encrypt the keys that are used to encrypt the data in EFS is tied to the user account. Anyone who logs into the laptop with the credentials of the user that is using EFS can view all data that the user encrypted with EFS. As you may know, if you have physical access to a Windows 2000 machine and enough time, you can log in as any user. (There are many tools and methods capable of doing this for password recovery.) If you can obtain the password for the user who has protected data using EFS, you can view any of that data. In Windows 2000, you might also log on as the local administrator and change the local user password, then use that password to log on as the user and read the user's EFS-encrypted files. This is not possible with XP. If you log on as the local administrator, change the local XP user's password, and then use the new password to log on as the user, you will not be able to decrypt the XP user's EFS-encrypted files.

If you were to take a laptop that has encrypted data, and the key that is used to encrypt the data is also on the laptop, you have all the elements required to retrieve protected data. The problem here is that the key is being stored with the data that it is protecting.

The second example of why encrypted data may not be as secure as you think starts with the example of using EFS on a laptop and takes it one step further. In the first example, EFS provided only a limited increase in security because even though the data was protected by an industry-standard algorithm, the key that was protecting the data was in very close proximity to the data that it was protecting. To address this issue, Microsoft enables you to export the key pair that was used to protect the key used to protect the data. The exported key pair is protected by a password chosen at the time of export and is required before import. In addition to choosing a complex password and not making it available to others, you should choose media that is protected to store the keys.

To keep this example simple, assume that there is sensitive data on the laptop and EFS is used to protect the data. Now you want to separate the protected data from the key that was used to protect the data. To accomplish this, you export the private EFS key to removable media (floppy disk, USB drive, etc.), protect that media, and store it in a safe location. In this example, if the laptop is stolen, you get the full benefit of having encrypted the data because the key used to decrypt the data is not with the laptop.

By separating the data and keys, it might seem that you have a foolproof method to secure your data. But what if the key is stolen instead of the laptop? Without the key, even the legitimate user will not be able to decrypt the data they protected, which likely is important, sensitive data because it was worth protecting. Thus, you have to consider a few other items about your security solution. For example, if a single USB device that is housing an exported key for important protected data is misplaced or stolen, you need to have a path for recovery, such as yet another copy of the key in a different safe location. But that presents another issue: if you have an additional place where the key is stored, you have to consider the security of that location also. There is the possibility that the key could be compromised from that location without your knowledge.

Another aspect of separating keys and data, and especially if the user takes the responsibility of managing the keys into their own hands, is what happens if the user leaves the organization. They will most likely turn in their laptop, but you must also consider the keys that are used to protect the data on the laptop and recover those as well. If they do turn over all of the keys for the laptop, who will they be assigned to next? Will all of the data be decrypted and will new users be responsible for re-encrypting the data with their keys? These are questions that must be resolved through policies and procedures, the specifics of which you must determine based on the requirements and risks of your environment.

Thus far, you have looked at a very micro example of separating keys and data when protecting data on a laptop. Now consider a larger example, in which you are responsible for protecting data on 10, 100, or even 1,000 laptops. The point is that the added protection of separating keys and data can sometimes come with an extremely heavy management burden. When you consider deploying a solution that separates keys and data for users, you must not forget about how the users will manage the solution, because the management may be the most time-, money-, and resource-consuming aspect of the operation—and potentially the biggest security hole if not done properly.

Hardware Security Modules The use of hardware security modules (HSMs) is another good example of a method to separate keys and data. HSMs are stand-alone devices that are separate from the data they protect and provide for the cryptographic functionality for data sent to the HSM (encrypts and decrypts). This solution offers some performance benefits, because all of the cryptography procedures are offloaded from the processor of the machine that is housing the data, but the focus of this discussion is the security aspects of this solution.

HSM devices can be placed inside the physical machine (SCSI connected) that they are providing protection for or they can be completely separate devices that sit outside of the machine where data is being protected. HSM devices are designed to take an encryption key, provide an increased level of security for the key, and then allow outside applications, OSs, processes, etc., to make calls to the HSM. The level of compliance for HSMs is usually validated by having FIPS certification; however, this level of compliance focuses on the protection standards of the key that is used to encrypt and decrypt data, not necessarily on how the solution is implemented in an enterprise. The following are some of the issues regarding the protection of the key with this solution:

- How to store the key
- What happens if someone tries to remove the key
- How to prove that the key cannot be tampered with

Some common examples of HSM products are Sentinel (now owned by SafeNet, http://www.safenet-inc.com/index.asp, after its merger with Rainbow Technologies) and nCipher (http://www.ncipher.com/). Figure 7-6 shows a common example of how an HSM product is used.

If an adversary were to steal an entire backup tape of data that has been encrypted with an HSM, the adversary would not have the key(s) needed to change that data into plain text. Additionally, if an adversary were to attempt to tamper with an HSM, the key(s) in the HSM would be rendered useless before it could be compromised.

With an HSM, you can also implement another security principle: separation of duties. Separation of duties implies that a single individual does not control all of the aspects of the HSM. In other words, there has to be collusion of at least two separate individuals in order to purposely affect the security of an HSM from an administrative standpoint. An HSM separates key usage by an application (based on a decision made by the application owner) and protection of the keys (individuals other than the application owner/user). Separation of duties is important because it will force a requirement of having multiple parties involved in order to thwart a piece of security.

The principle of separation of duties has been around for a long time: to provide accountability in accounting, checks and balances between the three branches of U.S. federal government, and even safeguards against premature nuclear missile launches. The premise is that one person (or department) cannot foil an entire process that was set up.

If a department outside of the application development department owns the keys, in theory, the only way that the security of the keys will be compromised is through collusion between the two departments, and not someone acting alone. While there is

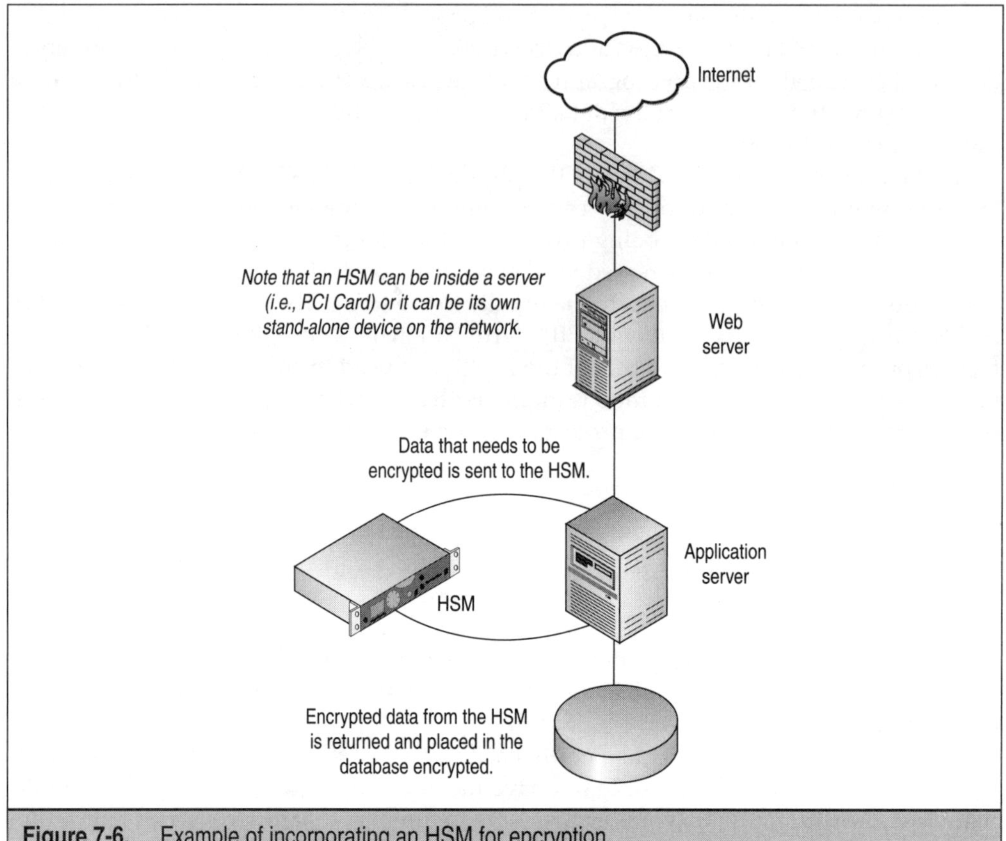
Internet
Note that an HSM can be inside a server (i.e., PCI Card) or it can be its own stand-alone device on the network.
Web server
Data that needs to be encrypted is sent to the HSM.
Application server
HSM
Encrypted data from the HSM is returned and placed in the database encrypted.

Figure 7-6. Example of incorporating an HSM for encryption

strong protection through separation of duties for the keys that will be used in HSMs, the threats associated with using a limited number of keys still exist, as discussed previously in this chapter in the section "Use More than One Key."

Protect the Association Between Keys and the Data They Protect

The previous sections have established why you must separate keys from the data that they are protecting; however, if the keys are separated from the data, you have to determine how to match up the right key with the right piece of data. Thus, this section discusses the methods of associating an encrypted piece of data with the key that was used to encrypt that piece of data.

At a basic level, if only one key is used to protect a single piece of data, and that key is separated from the data, the indexing is straightforward. A few examples earlier in the chapter demonstrate this. The laptop user who was using EFS and loaded the key onto a USB fob had a very simple indexing technique: anything that was encrypted with EFS needed the key, and if the key was exported to a fob, every time that the data needed to be accessed the fob was presented to re-import the key that was used to encrypt the data. In the example of HSMs, if a single key is on the HSM, and every application that encrypts/decrypts data points to that HSM, the indexing is done by pointing to the HSM for encrypts and decrypts.

Aspects of Key Management

Key association is only one aspect of key management. Key management in its entirety accommodates all aspects of the health of the keys that are used to protect data. Key association generally refers to the operational controls that are placed on keys for day-to-day use to encrypt and decrypt data. Other aspects of key management are the following:

- **Key backup and recovery** Provides backup keys in case the original keys that are used day-to-day are destroyed or corrupted.
- **Key availability** ensures that keys are readily available. If this is not managed properly, a key may be unavailable for use when the data needs to be decrypted. For example, if too many requests for encrypts and decrypts occur on an HSM and the resources on the HSM cannot fulfill the requests, the key may not be available for some requests (it is not corrupted or destroyed, just unavailable).
- **Key protection** Protects keys and provides levels of assurance that keys have not been compromised. Some products offer tamper-proof or tamper-resistant solutions that provide levels of assurance that keys have not been compromised.

Since using multiple, transaction-based keys is more secure than using a single key, that is likely the situation that you are going to confront. Thus, the issues related to associating an encrypted piece of data with its proper key multiply exponentially from the straightforward one-to-one association in the previous examples. In fact, you run into some of the same issues associated with key management when using multiple transactional keys, as discussed earlier. In both issues, inadequate key management and selecting a poor algorithm, the chances of encrypted data being compromised by the use of a key by an adversary increase significantly.

So, on one side of the network you have multiple pieces of data that are encrypted with different keys, and on the other side you have all the keys that were used to encrypt the data. How do you associate the two? A common solution is to place an identifier on both the key and the data. For example, encrypted data with identifier 1234 matches the encryption key with identifier 1234.

Example: encrypted data (ID 1234) Network encryption key (ID 1234)

This seems simple enough; however, if an adversary knows or guesses that this indexing scheme is being used, they know they simply need to steal two databases (or backups of those databases) to reconstruct the plaintext data. Of course, stealing two databases should be harder than stealing a single database, but as a precaution, you can encrypt one of the identifiers. Using the preceding example of both the data and the encryption key being given the identifier 1234, if you encrypt one of the identifiers, you have solved the problem.

To encrypt one of the identifiers, you need a key. That key would need to sit logically (if not physically as well) between the data that was encrypted and the keys that were used to encrypt the data. While this does take you full circle (still needing to manually manage a key), the key could be tied to a department or function rather than to an individual. The key itself could be exported to a secure device, like a smart card, and a department could manage the smart card. This would provide a unique separation of duties. First of all, if the database with the protected data were compromised (even by a DBA), the unique keys that were used to protect the data would make it nearly impossible to determine the encrypted value of the data without the key. If both the database with the encrypted data and the database with the keys were compromised, there would be no way to associate the keys with the pieces of data (because the identifiers are encrypted). Thus, to foil this model, the key that protects the identifiers would also have to be compromised.

Additionally, the keys themselves will be in an encrypted form in the database with the hidden identifiers, and a completely different key could be used to encrypt all of the encryption keys. So, there could be an additional separation of keys within the security department—one person could be responsible for the key that protects the identifier, and the other person could be responsible for the key that protects the keys. In this model, there would actually need to be collusion among at least three (or more) parties to foil the security process. As an example, on one side of the network is encrypted data with ABCD as the identifier (the encrypted value of 1234) and the other side of the network is the encryption key with the identifier 1234.

Example: encrypted data (ID ABCD) Network encryption key (ID 1234)

Use a Decision Tree

You now understand the various options that you have if you elect to use symmetric cryptography to protect data at rest. ("Data at rest" is an industry term that refers to data that is on disk rather then being in transit to a destination.) You learned that the trade-off for simplicity is less protection, and the trade-off for more protection is greater complexity. To summarize the options presented in this entire discussion, Figure 7-7 presents a decision tree. Each step of the tree requires you to make decisions about trade-offs and to consider which solution is best for your network.

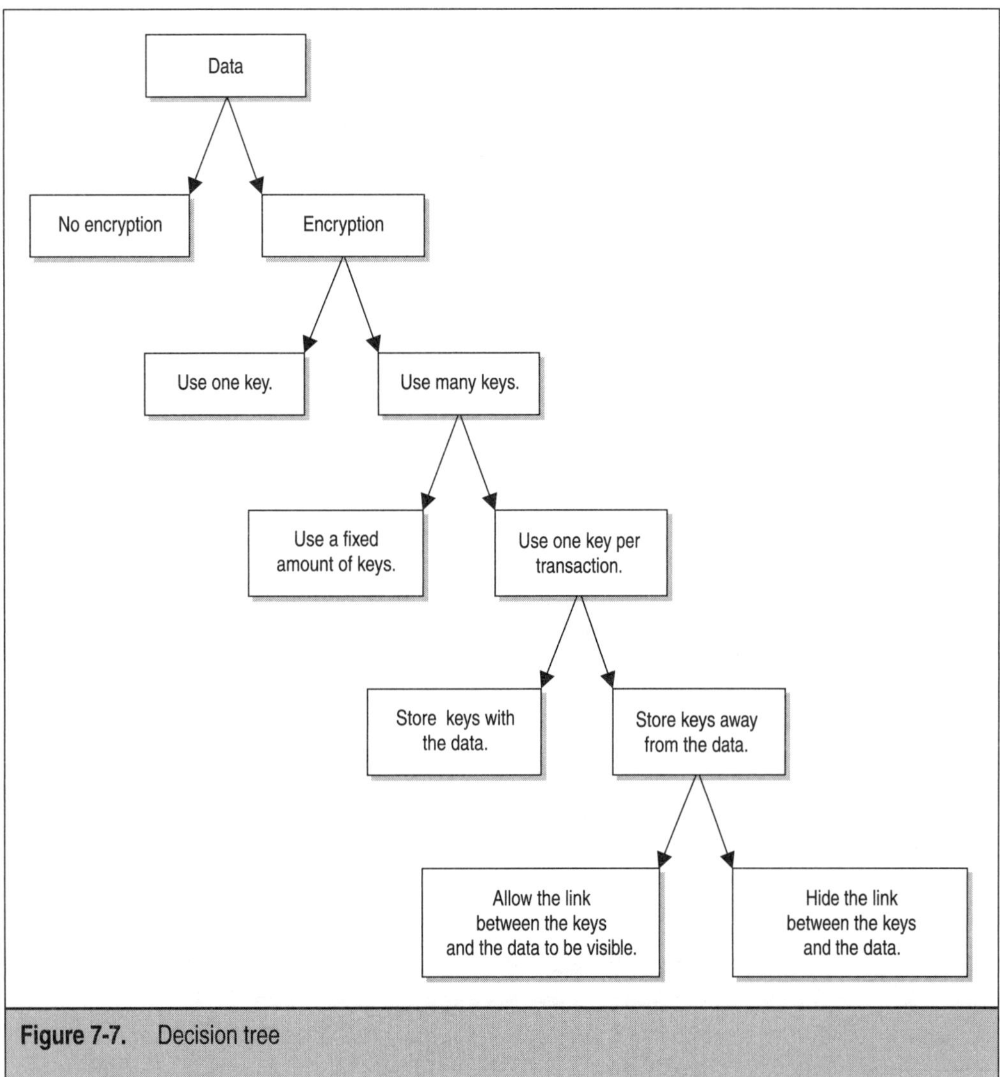

Figure 7-7. Decision tree

This reference could be used for the following:

- Understanding vendor products and knowing what questions to ask and where potential issues with their cryptography implementations may be
- Questioning internal custom development implementations of cryptography and considerations that should be made in the design stage
- Determining a starting place to investigate how an organization that you outsource to is actually protecting your data at rest (to see if they are just meeting the letter of the law rather than the spirit of the law)

Understand Who You Are Protecting Your Data From

To properly use cryptography, make sure you understand who you are protecting your data from, and then determine how you can achieve that result. Otherwise, you may simply be adding a layer of complexity without adding any security.

For example, if you are encrypting data on a server, make sure that there is at least someone (or some identity) on the server that will not be able to view the data once it is encrypted. If the encryption key is maintained by an administrator account on the server, it would stand to reason that anyone with those administrator privileges would be able to get the key and view the data. Additionally, if there are users on the server who need to use the data, they will be able to decrypt data as well. In short, encrypting data in this situation would add another layer of complexity (encrypting the data) without adding a layer of security (each of the user classes, both administrator and user will still be able to decrypt the data).

Conversely, if there was an additional person or identity that was responsible for maintaining the key, like a security administrator, there could be a security value to encrypting data. In this example, the key could be managed by the security administrator. This would mean that the users could still interact with the encrypted data and the server administrator could still do their normal function; however, since the server administrator does not administer the key, data is shielded from their view.

This simple model could be broken by the server administrator changing the security administrator's password and logging in as the security administrator to get the key and view the data. This is why decisions are made as to the proximity and control of the key in relation to the data that it is protecting.

Determine What to Encrypt and Why

Determining what to encrypt and why can sometimes be more cumbersome than determining what risks are associated with the methods that are used to encrypt data. However, with a good corporate security policy in place, the decisions should be less burdensome. Therefore, your primary goal should be to establish a good corporate security policy. It should address, at a minimum, the following areas with regard to what should or must be encrypted while the data is at rest:

- Legal requirements
- External business requirements
- Internal business requirements
- Sound business practices

While there may be other reasons that data gets encrypted that fall outside of these areas, these are the areas of concern for anyone who is performing hardening procedures across the enterprise. Other, more traditional methods are available for classifying data and determining how it should be treated while at rest; however, this can be a very time-consuming process and it can change frequently. The focus of this section is to give you a practical method that can be used in day-to-day work to analyze what data should be considered for encryption.

Determine Legal Requirements for Encryption

You need to determine what legislation and regulations exist regarding encryption that cover your particular industry. (Ideally, you have a legal department to help you out.) It is important to realize that very few pieces of legislation actually mandate that certain data must be encrypted. For the most part, the legislation will mandate that organizations in a particular industry are responsible for the implementation of secure controls to protect the data of a patient, customer, etc., as described in the legislation. Some examples are HIPAA (Health Insurance Portability and Accountability Act), GLBA (Gramm-Leach-Bliley Act), and SOX (Sarbanes-Oxley Act), all of which were discussed in Chapter 2. Encryption may be one piece of your overall corporate strategy to comply with legislation and regulations, but it should never be the only thing that you do in an attempt to comply.

One minor exception that does encourage specifically the use of encryption is California Senate Bill 1386 (CA SB1386). In short, and among other things, CA SB1386 states

> Any agency that owns or licenses computerized data that includes personal information shall disclose any breach of the security of the system following discovery or notification of the breach in the security of the data to any resident of California whose *unencrypted personal information* [emphasis added] was, or is reasonably believed to have been, acquired by an unauthorized person.

With regard to CA SB1386, "personal information" is defined as

> …an individual's first name or first initial and last name in combination with any one or more of the following data elements, when either the name or the data elements *are not encrypted* [emphasis added]:
>
> (1) Social security number.
>
> (2) Driver's license number or California Identification Card number.
>
> (3) Account number, credit or debit card number, in combination with any required security code, access code, or password that would permit access to an individual's financial account.

Although this bill indicates that disclosure is mandatory only for *unencrypted personal information* after a security breach, there are no further provisions for the type of cryptography that is required, the strength of key, or how and where the key will be stored. The issue here is that the "letter of the law" can be met even with a sloppy implementation of encryption; however, the first part of this chapter provides guidelines that enable you, as an IT professional, to adhere to the "spirit of the law."

Determine External Business Requirements for Encryption

If you are in a business that requires that data be left in a DMZ for a client to pick up, the client may require (per its security policy) that the data that is left for it must be in an encrypted state in the DMZ until it is retrieved. Often, these client requirements translate into contractual obligations.

NOTE As part of your own security policy, you may want to specify that organizations that you do business with store data that you pick up or drop off in an encrypted format. Placing such language in contracts is an effective way to ensure adaptation.

With the increasing awareness of the importance of security and privacy in an electronic world, there is increasing pressure for organizations to undergo third-party audits and assessments to demonstrate to potential business partners and clients that its security is implemented in a commercially reasonable manner and to provide for a level of due diligence.

Some of these audits and assessments will be based on proprietary scales of a level of security. In other words, the firm doing the audit will leverage its experiences in what it has seen across a particular industry to encourage the implementation of certain security controls. (Beware: these motivations could also be based on what products they have to sell as well.) Other assessments will be based on what is considered to be "commercially reasonable" for the industry that you are in. While the term "commercially reasonable" is pretty nebulous and may mean a number of different things, the general assumption is that some industry best practices exist that govern what the auditor reviews and what it includes in its assessment.

Probably the most influential standard regarding industry best practices for security is the ISO 17799 standard, which has provisions for how cryptography and key management should be done. Your organization must implement these cryptography and key management best practices to become ISO 17799 compliant, which is held in high regard in many industries.

Determine Internal Business Requirements for Encryption

Internal business requirements for encryption are those that are not dictated by external forces but are necessary to ensure that the business remains healthy and competitive. Probably the most common example of an internal business requirement is the need to protect internal confidential information beyond the protection available with access controls. For example, suppose that your organization has created some competitive intelligence documents. These documents may not contain any customer-specific information or any information considered confidential per existing legislation, but they are sensitive to your organization and their loss could be very damaging to it. Taking additional steps to encrypt these documents while they are at rest could provide value.

Another internal business requirement for encryption is to protect mobile data within the organization. Mobile data refers to data that is not always in a single specific location, such as a server, where it can be protected. For example, in most consulting organizations, data (like proposals) that would traditionally only be on and accessed from a file server is downloaded to laptops and transported from client site network to client site network as they are being worked on. If this data were accessible only on the server, it would be easier to protect; however, because the same data might be copied onto multiple laptops, it needs to have another level of security such as encryption.

Other forms of data at rest that should probably be encrypted are small pieces of data that can be used as a reference to much larger amounts of data. A good example is web applications. While it is common to be concerned about SSL for encryption in web applications and encryption for databases that those web applications access, often overlooked is the security of cookies. Cookies can contain all types of information, including personal information, session information, etc.; however, cookies are normally housed on the client's machine (browser) and not on systems that you control. The client should not need to see any of the information in a cookie. In this example, you would want to consider the use of encryption to protect that cookie at rest on the client's machine.

As covered earlier in this chapter, a key is needed to encrypt and to decrypt. If you encrypt a cookie before you send it back to the client, you not only have separated the key from the data, but have also protected an unsuspecting client of yours from potentially having personal data compromised.

NOTE The mechanics of the cookie problem and how to code against it are much more complex. It was mentioned here because it is a development issue that administrators need to be aware of.

Passwords are another, more simplistic, example of small pieces of data that can expose much larger amounts of data. Most computer users have a number of user IDs and passwords to remember, leading naturally to the temptation to write them down. You know that it is going to happen despite policies admonishing the practice, so you need to provide an easy way for users to securely store their passwords. A product that might help is PasswordSafe, a free password-management utility from SourceForge that organizes and encrypts user credentials. Figure 7-8 shows the information gathered when a user is adding a new record.

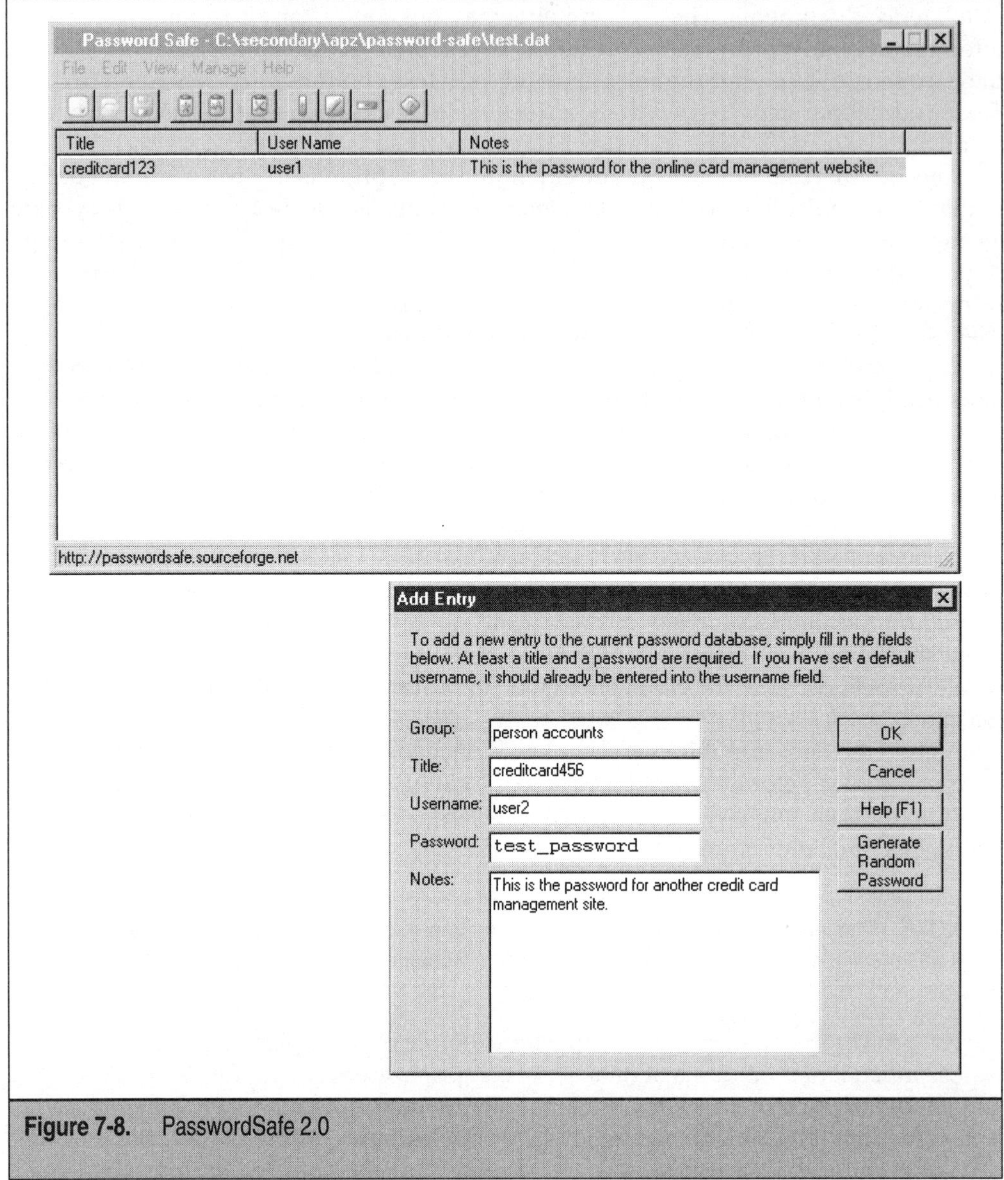

Figure 7-8. PasswordSafe 2.0

Determine Sound Business Practices that Support Encryption

The category of sound business practices is a hybrid of the external business requirements and internal business requirements for encryption. It considers the potential negative impact on the company's good will with clients and customers if it fails to encrypt their private data and that data is later made public, either accidentally or through malfeasance. This category refers only to information that is not required by law to be secure. Because this category varies widely depending on the nature of each individual business, it is best described through an example. Use this example to consider scenarios that could occur in your organization if client information is left unencrypted.

In early 2004, an online bookstore accidentally posted on its web site the names associated with anonymous book reviews. While there was not a great loss of privacy with regard to personal information such as SSNs or account information, there was a loss of anonymity. The incident ended up revealing that family and friends of authors were giving positive reviews of their books, and that the same family and friends of authors were giving negative reviews to competitive works. There is no indication that the online bookstore meant to do this, and no law required the bookstore to encrypt user IDs of reviewers, but the incident damaged reputations, including the bookstore's, and caused a controversy. If the user IDs had been encrypted, it is unlikely that the personal information and comments of the reviewers would have been posted on the Web.

As is true for all online consumer-oriented businesses, the bookstore had external pressure from customers and reviewers to keep user IDs private, and it should have had internal requirements that would have avoided such a scenario, for the sake of the bookstore's reputation. If an online company is perceived to be careless about customer information, it likely will not do well.

Encrypt Sensitive Data in Databases

Databases are the largest repositories of organized data in the world. Financial, healthcare, insurance, communications, and many other industries have been collecting electronic data on people for many years now. Law enforcement, government, e-tailers, and many others are starting to share databases with each other to cross reference personal data. And in many organizations, databases and other back-end data repositories are becoming the most critical piece of infrastructure that ensures an organization's worth or survival. With all of this in mind, the protection of databases is one of the most critical requirements of any organization, as described in the following sections.

Understand Common Reasons for Not Using Database Encryption

There are three primary reasons that data is not always encrypted in databases:

- **Performance** Encrypting and decrypting data involves another step that data must go through prior to being used. This additional step could affect the overall transaction time of a request and ultimately the performance of the system as a whole.

- **Usability of the data** Once data is encrypted there are certain functions that will be limited, unavailable, or have to be worked around, like reporting and searches.
- **Sizing** Encrypted data is larger than plaintext data; as a result more disk space is needed to accommodate encrypted data.

Performance is always a concern in database deployments. Encryption involves one additional step for the data to go through before it can be used (encryption for storage and decryption for use). This additional step becomes more critical as performance resources become scarcer in a database. There are many ways to analyze the performance impacts of encrypting data in a database. The amount of data that is encrypted per average transaction, the size of the key that is used, and the location in which the encrypts and decrypts take place (in the database versus outside the database, such as on an HSM) are just a few of the variables that can affect performance.

NOTE While offloading data encryption and decryption to an HSM improves performance, it does not totally address the degradation in performance. Totally fulfilling a transaction still takes more time because of the encryption. As a rule of thumb, assuming that you are encrypting only 10 percent of the total database and not every transaction that the database is fulfilling requires the use of all the encrypted data, a safe estimate is that there will be approximately a 10-percent increase in total transaction time (performance hit). While a 10-percent increase will not cripple most systems, it is large enough to consider when trying to decide whether or not to encrypt data.

The second issue regarding database encryption is usability. In a database in which everything is stored in clear text, it is relatively easy for a DBA to run spot checks to see if data is ordered or is presented properly. Additionally, ad hoc reports often are created to fulfill business requests or to test data outputs. If the data is encrypted, these reports become very difficult to complete—or at least should be very difficult to complete, as you will see later in the section "Examine 'Transparent' Solutions for Correct Implementation," which discusses the security value of encrypting data in a database. Depending on the importance of ad hoc reporting, this might be a reason unto itself not to encrypt data in a database.

The third issue that you need to consider is database sizing. Sizing affects the database in two primary ways, the first of which is column sizing. If a database column is currently being used to store unencrypted SSNs, you know that it requires a maximum width of only nine characters. However, if you encrypt that column, depending on the type and strength of the key that is used, that column might need to be stretched to 15, 20, or more characters in width. This is not a major undertaking for a DBA, but you must take it into account. The second sizing issue that you need to take into account is the total increased size of the database in terms of disk space. As a rule of thumb, once again depending on the algorithm, key size, etc., if you want to encrypt 10 percent of the database, the total size of the database itself will increase by approximately 12 to 14 percent.

This is generally not very much of a concern, as disk capacity is not very expensive these days; however, you must account for it when you consider encrypting data on a database.

Select a Sound Encryption Process for Databases

One of the largest issues that you need to consider when encrypting data in a database is the security value. The security value is determined by understanding what security problem is being solved and how well the solution is actually solving the problem. Two major points that you will need to review to realize this value are

- Using "transparent" solutions for correct implementation
- Requirements for a sound key-management processes

Both of the issues are discussed in the following sections.

Examine "Transparent" Solutions for Correct Implementation

When you are looking at the security of encrypting data in the database, you must first look at how that protection is provided. One of the biggest red flags to look for when evaluating solutions is if the solution is marketed as being "transparent to everyone using the data." This type of statement is included in a lot of marketing literature for vendors and solutions providers alike. The reason this should raise a flag is that if the encryption process is transparent to everyone, who is the data being protected from? In general, most "transparent solutions" use one key to encrypt all the data in a column of a database.

The key will usually be protected by a password to restrict who can use it. This is a rather easy solution; however, the first question then becomes, who knows the password to the key? In this type of implementation, the DBA is responsible for the password. Not to imply that a DBA cannot be trusted, but DBAs have a tremendous amount of power and control with regard to the data in the database, and their ID and password could yield anyone that power. To really offer a security value here, someone other than the DBA should control that password. That way, even if the DBA's password is compromised, all the data in the database is not compromised as well.

A big red flag is if a product or solution provider states that they can do * or <> searches on protected data. Consider the example of encrypted SSNs in a database. An example of a * search would be 123*, the result of which would be any SSN that starts with the characters 123. An example of a <> search would be 123<, the result of which would be any SSN in the column that starts with a number greater than 123. Doing * or <> searches is generally very bad from a security perspective because the only way that this function could be done is to decrypt all of the SSNs. If all the SSNs are decrypted every time a search like this is executed, it creates a location where an adversary can hijack the numbers.

There are some "less-threatening" ways to do these searches by decrypting data elements one by one in memory to see if there is a match and then deleting the element before moving on to the next. There is generally more of a performance hit in these types of models. Besides, the whole reason for encrypting an entire column is generally to prevent all of the values from being exposed in cleartext. As a final note, if this option is implemented, the rule-of-thumb 10-percent performance hit discussed earlier would be an extremely low estimate.

There are other methods to accomplish searches on encrypted data; however, the focal point in any analysis of this nature should be on the process that the search value is put through to find its associated results. If that process can successfully pull back the requested search data, you need to determine whether an adversary could use that same process to reveal protected data.

Require Sound Key-Management Processes

In order to effectively and efficiently implement encryption in a database, a sound key management process must be in place. Without a sound key management process, not only will encryption give you little or no value, but you could run the risk of not being able to access your encrypted data if the key is not available.

To further the previous example from, suppose that someone outside of the DBA's group, such as a security administrator, is responsible for the password that protects the key that encrypts the data in the selected column in the database. Even with this contingency in place, you should still question the security of this solution. As discussed earlier in the section "Use a Decision Tree", this implementation is susceptible to a brute-force or dictionary attack.

In other words, every possible combination of an encrypted value could be calculated using that single key to reveal the plaintext value of the encrypted data. Additionally, this type of implementation could be subject to a replacement attack, in which an encrypted value is copied and pasted in place of another encrypted value without the security administrator ever knowing.

The following are other considerations that have to be made for this implementation:

- What if the security administrator forgets the password to the key?
- How will the password for the key be recovered?
- What happens if the administrator is unavailable?
- Will the security administrator have a backup that also knows the password?
- If two people know a single password, how is accountability assigned?

These are just a few of the types of questions that need to be considered and are examples of the roots of key-management issues.

Another point covered earlier in the chapter is the fact that the more data that is encrypted with a key, the higher the probability of being able to determine the plain-text values of the encrypted text. Because of this issue, key rotation is a good security practice. *Key rotation* refers to using a new key to encrypt data from time to time (monthly, quarterly, yearly, etc.) based on your security policy. There are two ways that this can be done.

The first option is to decrypt all the data with the old key, then re-encrypt all the data with a new key. Decrypting all encrypted data in a column of a database is generally a bad idea, because it means that the data that you have spent time going through the steps of protecting is now exposed. In other words, you need to weigh the risk of your data being exposed for a brief time during this process against how long you are willing to use the same key.

The second option is to start encrypting new data every so often with a new key; however, this becomes exponentially more complex with every new key that is added, because you not only have to add a key, you also have to index which key was used to encrypt which piece of data in what part of the column.

The second option, even though it does offer a little more security because the data is never decrypted and exposed, should be strongly cautioned against because of the complexities that are involved unless you have an automated process in place to address this.

There is a third option, which involves changing the key that is used to encrypt the key that encrypts the data. This option generally involves using a password to protect a key, someone knowing that password, someone providing a strong password, someone rotating that password, some way of being able to retrieve that password if the owner of the password is not available, and the list goes on. While this is still key management, it is key management of the keys that are used to protect the keys that protect the data, instead of the keys that protect the data directly.

To build on this example another step further, assume that three columns in the database need to be encrypted. This is a pretty common security and performance requirement, because you may not want to encrypt all the data in the database, but just enough to de-identify or obscure the record so major identifiers like SSNs and last names are encrypted, but the state, or city is not. In this example, three columns are enough to de-identify the records in the database. From a security perspective, you have to consider who will own the passwords for each of these three columns. Ideally, you would have three different security administrators to protect one key each; however, who would be their backups? You probably do not want the security administrators backing each other up, because then one single individual could potentially compromise multiple columns. What you now confront is the fact that all of the problems and questions that you have with one key and one administrator are multiplied by the power of three, and to top it all off, there are still looming security issues of using a single key for an entire column.

Taking this example to the next level, suppose that you are going to use a different key to encrypt each individual piece of data in each column. You can see how this would be more secure from the standpoint that dictionary attacks would not work. Additionally, a replacement attack would not work either. Because a different and unique key is used to encrypt every piece of data, there will be no consistencies if sequential data is entered to actually create the attack. Additionally, if the data is switched (replacement attack) from one cell to another, the correct key would not be used to decrypt the data. As you may have guessed, the issue with this type of implementation is that it could lead to a key-management nightmare. The only way to effectively manage this number of keys is in an automated fashion. This type of implementation would traditionally be done as follows:

- A new piece of data that needs to be encrypted is presented to the database (e.g., via application).
- A process is invoked that dynamically creates a key and an arbitrary identifier for the key (this could be a randomly generated value).
- The data is encrypted with the key and placed into the database with a receipt (the arbitrary identifier for the key that was used to encrypt the data). Note that the receipt or arbitrary identifier needs an additional column in the database. In other words, there will be the column with encrypted data and an additional column for the receipt of the key that was used to encrypt the data.
- A second database is used to store the key (in an encrypted form) and the arbitrary identifier (or receipt) that was used to index the key.

A solution to address key management has been identified; however, there is still the issue of keeping track of what key was used to encrypt what piece of data. Decryption is not done through the use of knowing the password to the key, but by being able to determine what pieces of encrypted data match up with which keys by matching the receipts on both sides of the equation (in the database that has the encrypted data and the receipt and the database with the keys and the matching receipt). In most organizations, all of the database maintenance, control, etc., are handled by one group. If the same DBA (or anyone else for that matter) has access to both databases, the security of this model is broken.

HEADS UP!

As mentioned in this section, a replacement attack model would not work in this situation. The reason is that if a unique key is used to encrypt every piece of data, and the receipt for the key that was used to encrypt every piece of data was placed in the same database, an adversary would simply have to replace the receipt at the same time that they replace the data. An easy way to prevent this would be to use a unique key for every row of data rather than every element of data. For example, if there were ten total columns of data in a database, only three of which needed to be encrypted, you would use one key to encrypt every row (encrypt three elements of data, one per row, with one unique key) instead of using one key for each one of the three data elements that needed to be protected. If you were to use one key for each of the elements, there would be three receipts presented; however, if the same key were used per each row encrypting the three elements, there would only be one receipt presented. If an adversary tried to replace one of the three data elements, the process would break because the correct key for the decryption process would not be indexed.

The final addendum to this example would be if the receipts in one database were to be encrypted. In this example, on one side of the equation would be the actual database with encrypted data and a plaintext receipt, and on the other, in the database with the keys, there would be the keys and an encrypted form of the receipt.

In this scenario, even if the DBA has control over both databases, they cannot determine what piece of data is associated with which key. Even though this implementation has solved a number of security issues, such as the elimination of a number of attacks, effective and efficient key management for the data that has been encrypted, and so forth, the receipt for the key was encrypted in the database that housed the keys. While the questions for how that key will be managed need to be addressed, you are back to managing a single key for the protection of data in a database, but now you have a noticeable increase in the security through the use of encryption in a database.

ONE STEP FURTHER

Some "transparent" solutions offer searching as an option. Searching on encrypted data is a mathematical impossibility without creating a security weakness! (While this statement is true as of this writing in late 2004, some significant progress is being made on the issue of securely searching on encrypted data. If you are interested in learning more about this topic and checking the latest developments, go to http://crypto.stanford.edu/~eujin/papers/secureindex/2003nov-encsearch.pdf.) Consider how a search works from the client's perspective: enter a value into a text box, click a button, and wait for the results to be returned. Now consider the mechanics of how that search is completed by most solutions: take the value entered in the text box, encrypt it, match it with the encrypted value of the data in the selected column of the database, select the matched encrypted data, decrypt it, and present it to the client in plain text. Essentially, this a variation of the dictionary attack described in the "Use More than One Key" section earlier in the chapter.

Use a Secure Method to Decrypt Data from a Database

The discussion thus far has focused on the use of encryption in a database and the true security value that is added. Looking at this value in the light of how a database operates, you need to consider an additional issue: How is data actually going to be permitted to be decrypted securely? There has to be a legitimate business reason to decrypt data; however, what prevents that reason from being exploited to carry out illegitimate activities? Viewing the situation from a traditional three-tier architecture clarifies how these issues are resolved. In three-tier architecture, you have a web server, an application server, and a database server. The web server handles presentation, so it is not really relevant to this example. The application server determines which data to use based on business logic. In other words, the application server has a legitimate need to access data in the database. Even if you employ the earlier example of protecting data in a database, you cannot prevent the application from using data. In this scenario, imagine that the adversary is an application developer (or someone impersonating an application developer). The attack would look like this: The application developer creates rogue code and makes a properly formatted request from the application server to the database, and requests are then fulfilled by the database, thus defeating the elaborate data-protection structure in the database. To correct this, you need to find a way to authenticate only the legitimate application that is making the request and no others.

As mentioned in Chapter 4, there are three bases on which to authenticate: something that you have, something that you know, and something that you are. Something that the application has could be a unique key that is known only by the application and the database that is authenticating the application. Because this would have limitations—primarily, how the key is managed, and the fact that the key could be copied and used by an adversary—using a key by itself would not be sufficient.

The next possibility is to use what the application *is* as the basis for authentication. This could be accomplished by taking a hash of the application that actually needs to communicate with the database. While this would provide an initial indication of what the application "is," the application could be subsequently modified by an adversary and sensitive data could be leaked. To confirm the application is still legitimate, something known to both the application and the database fulfilling the requests would have to be used. For this, you bring all of these aspects together: the key (what both the application server and the database server have), the hash (this will be created for the application running on the application server and be shared with the database server), and finally, what both the application server and database server know, or a combination of the key and the hash to create a challenge response. This implementation will lock (on a real-time basis) what application can actually make requests to decrypt what pieces of data, and a rogue application developer or DBA will not be able to circumvent this process to recover protected data. The part that makes this all come together is, once again, the key that could be loaded at run time (from a smart card for example) and stored in RAM; the security administrator could posses the key (smart card). In this situation, the only way to foil this process would be for the application developer, the DBA, and the security administrator to all be in collusion. As stated in the first part of this chapter, after you fully review a cryptography solution for your data at rest and determine that it does not impede business operations, you should implement it only if you can conclude that the individuals against whom the data is being protected would have to be in collusion with another individual outside of their department to be able to view the data. This solution ultimately fulfills that objective.

Provide for "Un"real-Time Encryption

If you analyze how your network environment is secured, you should see a layered approach. These layers usually exist in the form of network devices (such as firewalls and IDSs), access controls (NOS and application logins), and many other security tools (most of which are described in this book). The point is that a lot of attention is given to our real-time environments. While that is a worthwhile cause, you are ultimately in the business of protecting data, and if that data is backed up to a tape and stored at an offsite location, you have to look at how it is protected there as well. The question here is this: how is data that is not in real time protected? As security professionals, we must contemplate on a regular basis how attackers can foil our security models: what systems they could gain access to, how they could use our systems against us, and the like. We must also profile who our attackers could be: external attackers that are looking for fame, insiders looking to tamper with or steal information, etc. But have you considered an attacker being a delivery truck driver, or a security guard at your offsite storage facility, or the person that is responsible for cataloging your tapes inside of a large cave?

Imagine this scenario: An adversary wishes to steal data from your organization. The adversary realizes that you have a hardened environment, and realizes that a lot of time and resources would be involved in successfully penetrating your environment. Thus, as an alternative, the adversary decides to make an offer to a cataloger at the facility where your backups are kept: "I will give you $1000 if you let me see a particular tape for a little bit (long enough to make a copy) and I will give the tape back in the exact same form that you gave it to me." If successful, the attacker could steal the data from your organization without making one log in a firewall, leaving one bit of an audit trail behind, speaking with one of your employees, or even having to come on site. This scary scenario is where encryption could play a valuable role in delaying the theft of data.

As covered earlier in this chapter, the true value of encryption is realized when the keys and the data are separated. Imagine the same scenario but this time the data that is actually transferred from real time to backup (whether that backup is done over a storage area network [SAN], straight to tape, etc.) is encrypted. You know from the principles of encryption discussed earlier that even if the data that is stolen is in an encrypted form, if you still maintain the key, the privacy and integrity of the data can still remain intact. In other words, if data is encrypted before it is put on the backup media (tape, disk, etc.), anyone who is involved in the backup process (such as the cataloger) will not be able to compromise the data without breaking the encryption.

While there is a distinct value proposition here—protecting data in non-real-time, offsite environments—you must also consider how the key that protects the data will be stored. Some questions that you should reflect on are the following:

- Will all data that is stored offsite be encrypted?
- Assuming the keys that are used to protect the data will be backed up offsite, where will they be in relation to the data that they are protecting?
- If I elect to rotate keys from time to time, how will I catalog which keys were used to encrypt which pieces of data?
- Who will be responsible for what keys?
- What happens if the persons responsible for the keys leave the organization?
- If passwords are used to protect the keys that are used, what if the person responsible for the password forgets the password?

In short, prudent security practice dictates that you must consider offline data security as well as real-time data security.

NOTE There are a number of products that provide for the encryption of offline data; however, I do not think that it is that large of a security hole. It might be an issue if you were backing up your personal PC to a USB disk drive and storing that drive offsite; however, most enterprise backup products have their own methods used to back up and restore data. This commonly requires gathering together a certain sequence of tapes simultaneously to re-create a portion of data. Additionally, there are many specific requirements within an organization and the logic in which data is backed up that serve as preventative measures for data protection. Bottom line: determine what is involved in being able to re-create sensitive data within your infrastructure and then analyze the threats around it and determine whether encryption really solves a legitimate business problem for you.

Where Encryption Takes Place

Much of this chapter has discussed the different aspects of key management and places that data could be encrypted. This section focuses more on where the actual data encryption takes place. Aspects of this issue have been touched upon throughout the chapter, but this section addresses it directly. Data can be encrypted in the following places:

- At the client
- At the server
- At the application server
- In the network
- At the database server
- Behind the enterprise

At the Client

Encryption at the client should be an option reserved for only those users who are security savvy (or, more specifically, encryption savvy). Encrypting data at the client is useful and offers an incredible value from a security perspective if the user is security savvy. The security savvy user entrusted with encryption normally is given responsibility for making intelligent decisions regarding which data needs to be protected. In addition to selectively encrypting data, they will be responsible for properly managing the keys that are used to protect the data. Additionally, because the actual cryptography process is done selectively and locally, there will not be a large performance hit on any device outside of the local machine.

If this is an enterprise strategy, a client-side encryption strategy can be very complex. First of all, users must be trained regarding how and what to encrypt. This is particularly difficult and complex (increasingly so the larger and more dispersed the environment) because data that may seem sensitive to one individual may not be considered sensitive by another; thus, standardization of what must be encrypted is sometimes difficult. Standardization of what should be encrypted and how it should be encrypted is normally and most effectively done by policy.

The second reason that a client-side encryption strategy can be very complex is that if copies of the keys are going to be stored centrally or backed up somewhere, the issues of managing those keys arise, as discussed earlier: how the keys are stored, who has access to those keys, how the correct keys are redistributed to the correct parties, what course of action will be taken if the keys are stolen or need to be replaced, and so forth.

At the Server

Encrypting data on the server is generally a difficult value proposition. There are a number of reasons for this; however, the primary one is usually answered in response to the question, Who am I protecting data from? As an example, consider encrypting data on a file server. First of all, access control determines who has access to what folders on a file server; if you do not have access to the folder, you cannot view the data (or the encrypted data) in the folder. Second, the system administrators not only have access to the entire machine (so if the key is stored on the machine, they can easily retrieve it) but also have the ability to change the password on any user's account and log in with the access of the user.

If you are going to encrypt data on a server, it is best to have a method to prevent the administrative account from being responsible for the encryption processes as well. While you may ultimately trust an administrator as a person, you can't always trust their identity. For example, what if an administrator has their credentials compromised? The point is that by separating the administrative and encryption management roles, you can provide a higher level of security by ensuring that if one account is compromised, the data is not immediately compromised.

In the Application Server

Encrypting data in the application server is quite arguably one of the most secure methods in which to encrypt data in an infrastructure. While there is a limitation in the fact that data must pass through the application server (so this would not work with off-network assets like mobile laptops), the benefits of being able to control the data and how it is protected far outweigh this limitation. The business logic for an application server can be configured to selectively encrypt specific pieces of data based on a corporate policy. This also enables you to control the performance impact to the application server. And if the performance hit is unacceptable, you can always offload the cryptographic process to an HSM. Additionally, the data would be encrypted and decrypted outside of the database, so the data is protected from access by the DBA. Because the DBA should not have any direct control in the encryption process in this model, if properly implemented, the DBA cannot compromise data. Finally, if properly implemented, only the application that is responsible for the inputs and outputs of the data will be able to use the data.

If you elect to use encryption in the application server, you have a couple of additional items to take into account, primarily, how the application will use encryption. First of all, the application must be made aware of the use of encryption. Normally, this involves developers attaining an encryption toolkit, analyzing and understanding corporate encryption procedures, and implementing an encryption strategy. This is not necessarily an impossible task; however, there is a learning curve that is involved with effectively implementing encryption.

Another caution that needs to be addressed here is commercial *off-the shelf* software (COTS). To effectively implement encryption in an application, changes have to be made to the application itself to make it aware of the encryption. There are no guarantees that a third-party application will adapt to your corporate standards for protecting data or that your warranty with the software vendor will be valid after your modifications. If that is the case, data that is encrypted by one of your home-grown applications will not necessarily be able to be decrypted by your third-party application that is accessing the same data.

In the Network

There are tools and methods (generally through the use of an appliance, like an HSM) available that enable you to encrypt data in the network so that data at rest remains encrypted. Essentially, these solutions sit inline between the sources where the data comes from and the place where the data will ultimately rest. These solutions are relatively easy to employ; normally, you can simply redirect the connection between the server and the source so that it goes through the network encryption appliance (for example, in an ODBC or JDBC stream between an application server and a database server). Because the crypto processing is handled off of the application server and database, there is generally not a large performance impact.

One of the major differences in this type of implementation is the fact that neither the application server nor the database has knowledge of the crypto procedures. Thus, you sacrifice quite a bit of security in the implementation of a solution like this, such as the ability to efficiently enforce a corporate encryption policy, manage keys, and tie accountability to access of protected data.

In the Database Server

As mentioned earlier in this chapter, there are some benefits to encrypting data in the database directly. One of the primary benefits is that it can be implemented by the individuals who know the database best, the DBAs. DBAs are generally aware of the encryption options that are available within their databases (at least encryption features provided by database organizations like Oracle and DB2). The issue that must be considered is whether the DBA understands security sufficiently to implement an encryption scheme correctly.

An additional benefit of encrypting data in the database server is that there are methods available to farm out the control of the keys to departments outside of the group that is responsible for the databases (like the information security department). Another benefit is that you will be able to index or search on protected data, because the database "understands" how data is protected.

As indicated earlier in this chapter, there are some serious security and nonsecurity considerations that you need to take into account if you plan to encrypt data in a database. You would need to look at performance, sizing, and logistic impacts, as well as take a close look at and understand what security value is really added if data is being encrypted in the database.

Behind the Enterprise

Protecting data behind the enterprise refers to protecting data as it goes into storage. A basic benefit to this includes the peace of mind of knowing that everything outside of your real-time environment is encrypted. Most of these solutions come in the form of SAN encryption products. These solutions plug into your current SAN and, for the most part, are transparent to the environment.

A key concept to take into account here is the fact that if data is encrypted before it gets into a database, it will be encrypted however it is backed up, stored, etc.

Authentication

Other parts of this book are dedicated to authentication, so this section does not focus on all the intricacies of authentication; however, some important points need to be made with regard to authentication and encryption. First of all, authentication must tie directly into encryption in order for encryption to really be effective. In many of the examples given in this chapter, there have been references to key management, and at the heart of key management is the question of who is authenticated to the key. One of the questions that you can ask yourself to determine whether encryption offers any value is, does the user have to be in collusion with another individual outside of their department to foil the encryption process? (This was discussed earlier in the context of separation of duties.) The second question should be, how are people authenticated to use or access the key?

In many cases, authentication may be driven by a process for server-side solutions. As an example of process-driven authentication, the keys may be stored on a separate network machine that requires a smart card to access, or they may be stored in a safety deposit box that cannot be accessed unless two individuals from the organization sign and present ID.

But for client-based authentication to keys, process-driven authentication is normally not the best approach because of the steps involved. However, a mechanism must still be put in place to authenticate a user to the keys that they use. The primary method of authentication in a user community is the use of passwords. If you use this method, you have to make some decisions. Do you want to use a preexisting authentication structure or create a new authentication structure to support authentication to keys? If you use an existing authentication structure (such as NOS authentication or an LDAP, Lightweight Directory Access Protocol, authentication server that everyone already accesses, like an HR application), you can piggyback on a number of preexisting processes, including user setups and teardowns. The logic here is that if the authentication for keys is handled in this manner, if a user is terminated or denied access to the authentication source, they cannot access the network or their keys.

Alternatively, if a separate authentication source is created, an additional piece of user management is required; however, if one of the authentication sources is foiled (e.g., the NOS), the keys that the user is authenticated to will necessarily be foiled as well. Bottom line: the weakest link for clients (end users) that need to use keys is generally the authentication that is required to access the keys. As an individual that is implementing a solution for user authentication for keys, you need to determine which method is better based on your knowledge of your environment.

Make Encryption Work for You in Your Environment

One of the largest issues in today's environments is complexity. Generally, the core of what you are trying to protect is data, and there may be multiple interfaces to that data, some of which you may not even know about. By encrypting data with a standardized encryption abstraction layer, you can better control, or at least be aware of, the paths to access encrypted data.

If you decide to harden your environment by using encryption, your number one priority should be to *manage the encryption process.* Circumstances, skill sets, and other factors will determine your operational role with regard to encryption in your environment. However, if you can effectively manage the process, you can make the implementation easier and greatly affect the level of security introduced through the use of encryption. In managing the encryption process, you should concentrate on the following four points:

- **Automate** Automation of the encryption process and key management will greatly reduce overhead work involved in sustaining a consistent theme in your environment. Additionally, automation reduces the number of facets of the encryption process across the environment that needs to be controlled to do it securely.
- **Secure** This chapter has covered items like the decision tree that illuminate the issues behind key management and the issues with key associations and data. You have discovered what makes some implementations more secure than others and where encryption simply adds a layer of complexity without a corresponding layer of security.
- **Standardize** Lack of standardization is one of the primary issues that contribute to the lack of value in encryption implementations. Users, administrators, DBAs, developers, and an entire host of technical individuals across the environment will implement cryptography differently based on their perception of requirements,

their personal knowledge and experiences, and how they see fit. This may work in isolated pockets of your environment for short periods of time, but the minute that these different encryption processes need to work together or encrypted data needs to be shared by multiple organizations, people, applications, and so on, you will have significant difficulties. Standardizing an encryption process across your environment enables you to manage when and how encrypted data is used and by what processes, applications, developers, users, etc. Another aspect of standardization is the notion of centralization versus decentralization, or where the keys will be managed. In a centralized model, all the keys within your environment could be managed in one location, allowing for pooling of resources, support, etc. A decentralized environment allows the encryption, decryption, and key management to be done locally to the source that is using the key. This can help from a performance perspective as well as offer some resilience in case of failure; however, the underlying point is that the different implementations should be able to work together.

- **Scale** You can scale up or out. *Up* generally refers to improving performance characteristics, such as being able to exchange a smaller processor or device with a larger processor or device to a specific encryption implementation to support higher performance requirements. *Out* generally refers to adding devices or processors of the same size to accommodate higher performance requirements. With the out option, you also gain the ability to load balance, fail over, and the like.

In the Development Arena

Applications and, more specifically, developers can have a wide range of requirements when it comes to encrypting data. This data could be anything from session data for an application to data that will ultimately end up in a database. As a result, from a security perspective, you may end up with a number of implementations of encryption. With all of these implementations, you confront not only the business concerns as to why the encryption processes will be implemented but also how the key-management process will be addressed and what real value is brought forth by encrypting data. Additionally, you have to predict whether the data from different applications and back-end data sources will ever be merged or need to work in concert with each other. This is very difficult, if not impossible, to predict accurately because of the vast changes that frequently occur in organizations, such as changes in business direction or mergers, acquisitions, etc., that require merging your data with another organization. Having a nonautomated, nonstandardized, and nonscaleable solution could lead to situations in which the method of encryption that is used will not work effectively in the future. As a result, it may be very time and resource intensive, if not all together cost prohibitive, to change your encryption environment to a solution that is automated, standardized, and scaleable. These are all very large drivers to use an encryption abstraction layer.

An abstraction layer provides a centralized way to manage the encryption process and enables any application that needs to utilize encryption to simply interface with that layer. These interfaces normally may be APIs that are developed for your environment based on your programming languages. As a security administrator, you can manage the encryption process and the interfaces to that encryption process. This is significantly different than trying to manage multiple encryption implementations that you may or may not be familiar with. Additionally, you should consider the intricacies of the toolkits that developers are using and the associated weaknesses or issues with those toolkits.

As mentioned earlier, the number of implementations of corporate applications exposing web services continues to increase. A very relevant example of this would be the data that is transferred back and forth between organizations for web services requests. By standardizing on an encryption framework, data being exchanged in XML messages could be protected so that only relevant applications are able to decrypt and use the data.

NOTE While there are a number of crypto toolkits available (both free and commercial), none of them comes with an integrated standardized or scaleable key-management system. Building a key-management infrastructure is still required if you want to effectively scale and standardize how keys will be handled within your organization. The cost of effectively building a mechanism to manage keys is much more expensive than acquiring a product that will do it for you. An example of an encryption key management system is the Tricryption Engine from ERUCES (http://www.eruces.com).

While most of the examples that have been given revolve around enterprise-class applications that could be driven by thin or fat clients, it is equally important to address mobile and wireless applications and data. More and more, enterprise applications and data are migrating from desktops and laptops to smart devices like PDAs and smart phones. Encryption requirements still exist; however, there is an entire new class of interface devices that need to be addressed. These devices are becoming increasingly more "always-on, anytime, anywhere" than we have ever seen before. Consequently, you need to address the following considerations:

- If there is a back-end key-management system that can always be accessed by these devices, the need to check out keys or even store keys locally on the smart device could potentially be eliminated.
- These devices are generally very lightweight with regard to their computing capabilities and this plays very nicely into a back-end key-management system. If a file is encrypted locally, when there is a request to view data, there is only the remote call to retrieve the key used to encrypt the data; the entire file does not have to be transmitted.
- If the smart device is lost or stolen, as a security administrator, you have to remove the ability for the device to retrieve the keys used to protect the data on the device. As a result, even though you may not control the device, you have the ability to access the protected data on the device.

Chapter 8

Hardening Database Access from the Web

by Rob Kraft

- Protect the DBMS During Install
- Use Permissions to Secure Data
- Use Application Partitioning and Network Technologies to Secure Access to the DBMS
- Use Sound Practices to Secure Applications
- Monitor and Audit
- Secure Backups and Archives

Databases are often at the heart of security efforts. These repositories of information are the most likely place that a business will store sensitive information about itself and its customers. Protecting this data is the role of database management system (DBMS) security, operating system (OS) security, network security, and business practices. Failure to protect the information can result in theft, loss of business, loss of reputation, embarrassment, and legal discipline. The DBMS is the last line of defense in the array of barriers protecting data from misuse and abuse. In today's business network environments, hackers and thieves must go a long way before even attempting to compromise the contents of a database, but that does not mean the security features of a DBMS have little or no value. Some of the features provide the most reliable data protection available for a company-wide data security plan; and many of the features are easy to implement.

All major DBMSs offer security tools to protect data. By market share, the leading DBMS products are IBM DB/2, Oracle Database, and Microsoft SQL Server. These three will be used for examples throughout this chapter. All three, along with many other DBMS products, continually improve and patch their software to protect against the latest threats and vulnerabilities. These are the actions you should take to secure a DBMS:

- Protect the DBMS during install.
- Use permissions to secure data.
- Use application partitioning and network technologies to secure access to the DBMS.
- Use sound practices to secure applications.
- Monitor and audit.
- Secure backups and archives.

Protect the DBMS During Install

Best practices for securing your databases actually begin prior to installing the DBMS software. Before you consider securing the DBMS, you need to secure the environment the DBMS runs in. This includes both the operating system and the network connections.

Secure the Operating System for the DBMS

Most DBMSs in use today operate on one of three OSs: Windows, Unix, or Linux. Each OS has minor security advantages and disadvantages relevant to databases, but all are capable of providing a secure environment for your DBMS when properly configured and maintained. Unless your DBMS of choice is Microsoft SQL Server, which only runs on Microsoft Windows, your choice of OS will probably be made on factors other than those related to the DBMS. In any case, it is important to keep the OS as secure as possible by installing the latest version updates, service packs, and patches. If you have a choice between installing a DBMS on a server in use running Windows 2000 or a server in use running Windows 2003, all other things being equal (such as hard drive speed, RAM, CPU speed, etc.), choosing to install on the server running Windows 2003 is generally preferable because the security features of the OS itself are more robust.

NOTE Chapter 20 provides more information and guidance for keeping your operating system up to date.

Install the DBMS on a Server with Few Other Processes

Every service (or daemon) on a server represents a possible source of a security breach. Services listening for input from other devices on a network pose a greater risk because a hacker may be able to access a machine remotely by compromising one of them. When the security of one service is compromised, it may lead to a breach of the other services on the computer as well. For example, if DBMS and e-mail servers are installed on the same computer, a breach in one can lead to the compromise, or destruction, of data in the other. If a single service is taken over by a hacker, the hacker's ability to take over other services depends greatly on the privileges assigned to the compromised service—and a compromised service running with local system or administrative privileges probably provides sufficient permission to do most anything.

HEADS UP!

In particular, you should avoid installing a DBMS on a Windows domain controller. An attacker that can breach the database security may be able to interact with the host OS using the permissions of the account assigned to the DBMS. If that account is the local system account, a skilled hacker may be able to create a Windows administrative account and, from there, control the entire domain.

Isolate the Computer or the Default Ports Used by the DBMS

The DBMS begins listening for requests during the install process of most DBMS applications. This may occur before the person installing the DBMS has a chance to change administrative passwords or the TCP/IP ports the DBMS listens on. For this reason, the DBMS should be installed on a computer that is not on the network. This eliminates the risk that elsewhere on the network a virus-infected computer that is running a program that continually looks for known default DBMS ports will be able to infect the new DBMS server as soon as the DBMS begins listening for requests. If the server requires a network connection during the install or application of a service pack, you should find the nearest upstream router or firewall and block the ports that the DBMS will, by default, be listening on.

Hacking Attempts Can Occur Very Quickly

A friend of mine recently installed cable-modem service to his home computer. Within 30 seconds of the service activation, and while the service installer was still sitting at the computer, the computer became infected with a virus from the Internet that overtook his OS and required hours to clean up. This could have been prevented with a firewall or port-blocking router in place. Likewise, in the case of a DBMS, a worm like SQL Slammer could quickly corrupt a fresh SQL Server install by using the default ports and passwords.

Assign Separate Accounts to Each DBMS Service

To interact with the OS, DBMS services (or daemons) generally provide an account and password to the OS to establish the service credentials and identify the permissions available to the DBMS service. In some cases, the DBMS service can run with a special local system account that allows access to just the local server, but in many situations, the DBMS services are assigned specific domain-level accounts with privileges that allow them to access resources on the network. Assigning to each DBMS service a different OS account with restricted privileges helps to protect the other services if a hacker is able to compromise a single service. To assign a Windows account to the Microsoft SQL Server service:

1. Open SQL Enterprise Manager.
2. Open the SQL Server Properties window by right-clicking the registered SQL Server name and clicking Properties.
3. On the Security tab, select the This Account option and type in the account name and password.

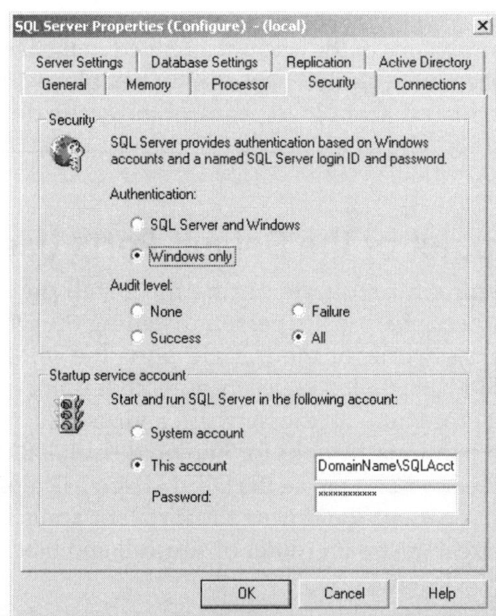

CAUTION Do not use the Services applet in Control Panel to assign OS accounts to Microsoft SQL Server services. Instead, use SQL Server Enterprise Manager (SEM), because SEM also sets permissions on files and registry keys used by SQL Server.

To assign a Windows account to the Oracle DBMS listener service of a database:

1. Open the Services applet in Control Panel.
2. Open the desired Oracle service and select the Log On tab.
3. Type in, or navigate to, the account name and password and click Apply.

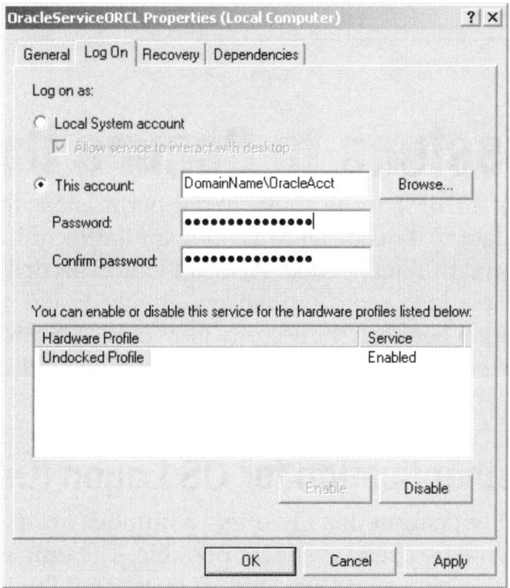

Remove Sample Databases and Code

Many DBMS installations provide sample databases and sample applications with source code to aid developers. This is very nice on the developers' computers, but unnecessary and potentially dangerous on production servers. You should drop sample databases and delete sample code and sample code directories. With Microsoft SQL Server, for example, you should delete the two sample databases, Northwind and Pubs; delete the sample code and template directories named DevTools, Scripts, and Templates; and delete or archive the sqlstp.log, sqlsp.log, and setup.iss files created by the installation in the install directory. These items pose at least two risks. The first risk is that the items will be overlooked and not secured when security is implemented for other components. The second risk is that hackers may have good knowledge of the sample databases and scripts and may be able to use that knowledge to help them exploit vulnerabilities.

HEADS UP!

A security risk exists when installing a version of SQL Server prior to SQL Server 2000 SP4. The sa password may be stored in cleartext in the install log files. Microsoft provides a utility to clean up the install environment on its web site. Knowledge Base Article 263968 (http://support.microsoft.com/default.aspx?scid=kb;en-us;263968) provides more information and a link to download this utility. If you have installed SQL Server 2000 at SP0, SP1, SP2, or SP3 and then applied SP4, your DBMS may still be exposed to this risk and you should use the utility. Also, if you have doubts or concerns about legacy installs, you should use this utility to eliminate the risks.

Use Permissions to Secure Data

An important feature of a DBMS is the ability to use permissions to control which people can view and modify data. All major DBMSs offer similar techniques for limiting user access to the least amount of data needed. Also, all DBMS security implementation schemes should be well planned and coordinated with the OS and network administrators.

The level of integration between the security tools of the OS and the security tools of the DBMS affects the overall security, ease of administration, and development efforts of programmers.

Avoid DBMS Authentication for OS Logon IDs

Operating system authentication usually offers a number of advantages over DBMS authentication and should be used whenever possible. The only exceptions are when a low-security OS such as Microsoft Windows 95 is used for the DBMS server, or when the OS is not configured to enforce good security principles.

Although DBMSs provide extensive granularity for assigning permissions to user accounts, they generally do not offer authentication features comparable to those of the host OS. DBMS vendors are not looking to improve their products' authentication mechanisms. Most everyone acknowledges that authentication is best handled by the OS, because the OS supports password expirations, strong password guidelines, and nonpassword authentication techniques based on biometrics or secure ID cards. Another complication of DBMS authentication is that each user must learn and provide a logon ID and password in addition to their network logon ID and password, which in turn means more work for database administrators (DBAs). A final reason for using OS authentication is that the tools and capabilities to integrate and accept the OS authentication are steadily improving; thus, adopting this approach now will situate your application best for the future.

Use Operating System Authentication

Often, the biggest question regarding authentication is whether to let the application perform its own user authentication or to trust the DBMS, OS, or network to handle the authentication. Historically, an application or the DBMS had to perform its own authentication, because integration with other authenticating mechanisms was not an option. Today, there are few cases where application or DBMS authentication is appropriate; in most cases, developers should use OS authentication. Technologies such as Microsoft .NET and Active Directory now make it possible to achieve this goal.

Use Impersonation to Establish an OS-Authenticated Connection to the DBMS

Many applications require permission designs that do not map directly to structures in the database. Therefore, as part of the application, developers create permissions such as "Allowed to approve claims over $500" and store the permissions in the database to be assigned to the correct users. Because the application determines which users can perform specific actions, the account used by the application to connect to the database does not matter to the application, as long as that account has all the privileges needed by any user of the application. Several techniques exist for connecting to the database, such as using a single DBMS account for all users, using an application role account in the DBMS, or mapping all permissions to each user and trusting the application and other security measures to protect the data from the users accessing it with other tools.

A better solution is to use the ability of an OS account to impersonate another OS account. For example, an OS account named MyAppDBLogon could be created and given permissions to all objects in the DBMS that are needed by any user of the application. When an OS-authenticated user runs the application, the application could impersonate the MyAppDBLogon account in the code that accesses the DBMS. The MyAppDBLogon account provides a safe mechanism because it is never used to log on to the OS, has minimal privileges in the OS, and is used only by users that have already been authenticated.

Operating system account impersonation makes a number of security challenges simpler to resolve. For example, a user who needs to access the DBMS outside the application with an ad hoc query tool can be granted (to their logon ID) only the DBMS permissions that are needed for use with that tool. This will not affect the user's permissions when accessing the database through the application with an impersonated account.

Some cases still exist where using OS authentication or storing permissions in the OS security database will not meet the user's needs. Here are some examples:

- The application is developed to work on multiple OSs and the OSs do not share a common standard interface for such user administration. The application would have to be customized for each OS.
- The users of the system want to be able to add users and reset passwords but do not want the OS administrators to be capable of doing the same. This could be supported only by an OS that allows creation of users and permissions that the system administrator cannot access.

In cases where the OS is not used to authenticate, it is often the application that performs the authentication. Users connecting to the application must provide a logon ID and password that the application uses to determine whether the user can connect and what actions the user is allowed to perform. Behind the scenes, when application authentication is used, the program must connect to the DBMS to see whether the user-entered logon ID and password combination has a match in the database. To make this initial connection, the program must use either OS or DBMS authentication. If OS authentication is used, then every application user must have an OS logon ID (something undesirable in some cases), or every person with an OS logon ID must be mapped to an application logon ID to use the application.

OS and DBMS Administration Is Often Performed by the Same Person

As both the network administrator and DBA for a former employer, I grew tired of creating and deleting accounts on SQL Server every time an employee was hired or left and was added to or deleted from the Windows NT domain. To simplify my workload, I created a stored procedure in SQL Server to create and delete accounts automatically and scheduled it to run every four hours. Six months after I left the company, I received a call from a friend at the company, seeking my help in determining why new employees hired after the company had installed a new server were not able to access internal database applications. Whoops! Luckily, they had the script and we were easily able to re-create that piece of automation.

CAUTION When using integrated security, you need to consider the administrators themselves. In a payroll application, for example, the application owners may desire to restrict payroll data access to employees in the human resources department. However, a user that is a member of an administrative group may automatically receive database owner privileges when connecting to databases, and therefore access to the payroll data. One practice to alleviate this problem is to provide administrators two logon accounts, one to be used only for administrative work, and the other to be used for all other purposes.

Secure Program Access with Application Roles

In scenarios like those mentioned previously where use of a single logon ID seems to be easier to implement, you should consider using an application role instead. Many DBMS systems provide the ability to create a DBMS logon ID tied to an application. Only the application can use the logon ID. Although an application-level logon seems similar to a user logon that is used only by a specific program, it offers four advantages:

- The OS logon ID of the connected user will still be available to the DBMS. If a single DBMS logon ID and password combination is used to connect to the DBMS, then some DBMS auditing tools become less valuable because auditing cannot be filtered by user (because, to the DBMS, only one user ever logs on).
- A user who needs permissions to various database objects for ad hoc queries can be granted such permissions, tied to their OS logon ID, but those permissions will not apply when the user runs the application that uses the application role.
- The permissions available to the application are only those explicitly granted to the application logon ID. The permissions granted to the OS logon ID, even if the user is an administrator, are ignored.

If you have an application that cannot use permissions assigned to the user's operating system logon ID, then you should consider using an application role logon ID.

NOTE On both SQL Server and Oracle Database, the user's OS logon ID must exist within the DBMS. On SQL Server, the application role replaces the user's assigned permissions after the user successfully connects, but on Oracle, application roles are assigned to user roles. Therefore, on Oracle, no application logon ID and password need to be passed from the application to the DBMS.

Protect the Logon in Application-Level Security Programs

For applications that do use the DBMS to authenticate the user, or for SQL Server applications using application roles, a logon ID and password must be passed from the application to the DBMS. This introduces a dangerous security vulnerability. You should not send cleartext passwords from the program to the DBMS, nor should you store cleartext passwords in the application code. You should store the encrypted connection string in the registry, use the program to decrypt it, and use an encrypted connection to pass it securely to the DBMS (as described in the section "Encrypt Communications Between Clients and the Server," later in this chapter). In the registry, the encrypted password should be stored under the current user key, or under the local machine key after that section of the local machine has been set to read-only permission for all users except OS administrators.

Restrict Account Access

Regardless of the authentication method chosen, the accounts that have database access should obviously be restricted to the fewest permissions necessary. Some applications' users may need to be able to read and modify the data in every table, but that does not mean they should be configured as database object owners with the ability to alter or drop tables. Likewise, even if users do need to drop and create tables, it is not likely that they need this permission for all the databases in the DBMS. Other considerations for configuring DBMS permissions follow.

HEADS UP!

It may seem obvious to seasoned security administrators, but DBMS system accounts such as SQL Server's sa or DB2's db2admin should not be used by applications. Unfortunately, in many cases these accounts are used. Developers who are unfamiliar with DBMS security and practices are primarily responsible for this when they use the only DBMS account they know in the development environment, and then the application is pushed into production without correcting the issue. If you discover applications using the DBMS admin accounts, you should take steps immediately to get the applications switched to a nonadministrative account and close that security threat. Specific instructions for securing SQL Server can be found at http://www.microsoft.com/sql/techinfo/administration/2000/security/default.asp; for securing Oracle at http://www.oracle.com/technology/deploy/security/index.html; and for securing DB2 at http://www-306.ibm.com/software/data/db2/udb.

Assign Permissions to Groups Instead of Individuals

DBMSs offer the ability to assign permissions to individual users or to groups, very similar to most operating systems. You should always strive to assign permissions at the group level, just as you would for operating systems. Assigning permissions to a group of one gives you much more flexibility for the future than does assigning individual permissions.

Understand and Limit Use of Default Groups in the DBMS

A DBMS may provide default groups or roles in addition to the default administrative and guest user accounts. If you do not intend to use the groups and can delete them, you should do so. If you do intend to use the groups, or are unable to delete the groups, you should understand how the group permissions work in the databases. SQL Server, for example, offers a default role called public. All accounts always inherit permissions assigned to public, even if they are not specifically assigned that role. Therefore, permissions granted to the public role are given to all DBMS users.

Use Views to Restrict Permissions at the Column Level

Some DBMSs allow permissions to be set at the column level. Although an option, best practices recommend that you not implement column-level permissions, because a better alternative is available. Create a view of the columns that a group of users should have permission to, and then assign permissions to the view rather than to the underlying table. The performance impact on the DBMS of implementing column-level permissions is best avoided.

Use Stored Procedures and Views Instead of Tables

A best practice for both DBMS performance and security is to make use of views and stored procedures. Aside from the numerous software development productivity and performance benefits, views and stored procedures provide substantial security benefits. Calling stored procedures and views from programs is more secure than SQL written against tables because

- Permissions need to be granted only on the stored procedures and views, not on the underlying tables. This makes it impossible for users to execute queries directly on the tables.
- The names of the underlying tables can be hidden from the developers, making it more difficult for them to write unauthorized queries against the data.
- Only a subset of the actual data needs to be revealed through the stored procedures and views, or made modifiable through them, additionally limiting what could be achieved through ad hoc queries.

As shown in Figure 8-1, permissions do not need to be granted to the tables that actually contain the data. Permissions can be limited to just the views and stored procedures, but all the desired functionality is still available.

Do Not Allow Database Users to Own Database Objects

Cases certainly exist where creating tables "on the fly" is useful in an application. However, if the application user is designated as the table owner in the DBMS, it can lead to problems in the future. As the database evolves, stored procedures, views, and other constructs may be added to the user-owned table. Eventually, that user may leave the company and the user's logon ID will be destroyed. This causes problems for the DBMS. In the best case, the DBMS will prevent the deletion of the logon ID until a DBA manually changes the owner of all the tables and derived objects to a different owner in the database. In the worst case, deleting the logon ID will cause a cascade delete of all the objects owned by that logon ID, including tables that the company may prefer to keep. Strive to develop applications where a generic DBMS account owns the database objects, rather than individuals.

Secure Built-In Accounts and Passwords

Every DBMS provides at least one built-in account for accessing the DBMS. Many DBMSs provide multiple accounts, some with administrative privileges, and some with guest account minimal privileges. You should take appropriate steps to restrict the permissions of all built-in accounts as described in the following sections.

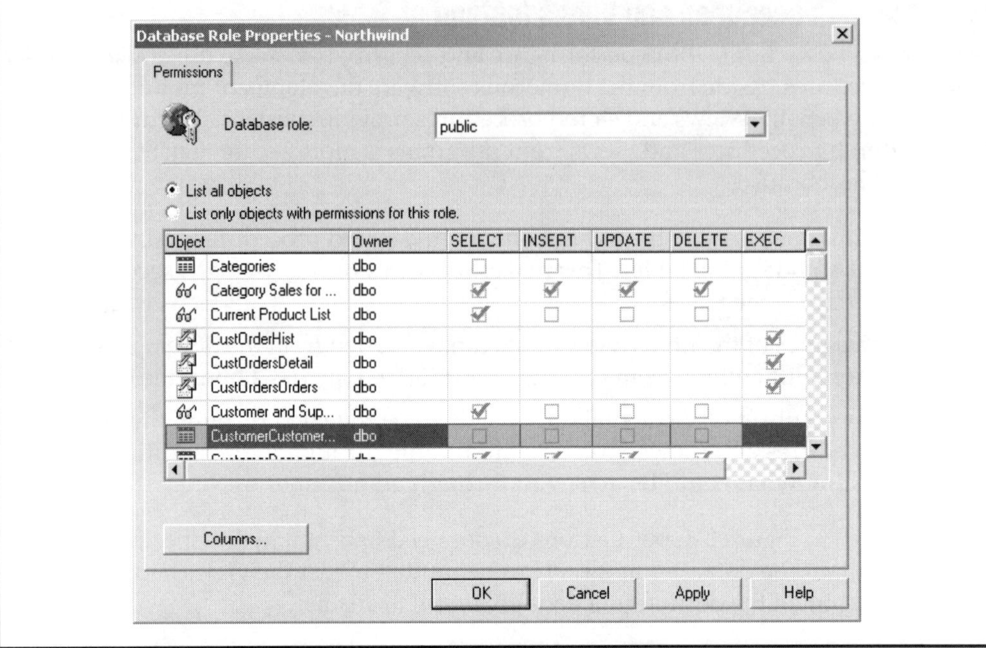

Figure 8-1. Granting permissions to views and stored procedures instead of tables hardens security.

Secure Built-In Administrative Accounts

If you are familiar with DBMSs, then you know you should change the default administrative passwords very soon after the installation. On Microsoft SQL Server 2000, there is a single account name, sa. On an Oracle DBMS, you will discover multiple accounts such as system, sys, appl, and applsys. All accounts should have the passwords changed to appropriately strong values. To set the password for the sa account in SQL Server:

1. Open SQL Enterprise Manager.
2. Open the sa account Properties window by right-clicking the sa logon in the Logins folder within the Security folder of the registered SQL Server.
3. Enter a secure password. You will be prompted to enter it a second time.

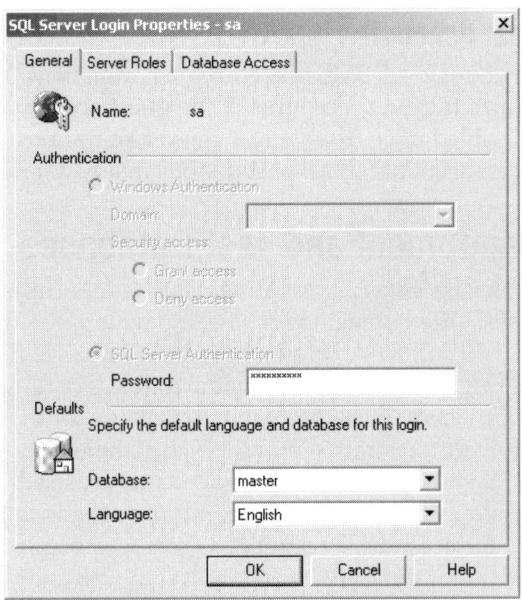

CAUTION The default sa password in Microsoft SQL Server should be changed even if Windows only authentication is used. This ensures that a hacker cannot access the DBMS through the sa account if the hacker manages to change the SQL Server authentication mode from Windows only to SQL Server and Windows Authentication.

IBM's DB2 database uses OS integrated security by default. Therefore, you can change the password for the db2admin account using the account management tools of the OS.

To set the password on an Oracle account:

1. Open SQL*Plus.
2. Enter the **alter user** command for each system account, particularly for sys and system:

```
ALTER USER sys IDENTIFIED BY <new password>
ALTER USER system IDENTIFIED BY <new password>
```

NOTE The default logon ID and password for many products are easily found on the Internet. If you don't know the default password for your DBMS, you can click the Default Logins and Passwords link at http://www.governmentsecurity.org for a listing for many major networked devices.

Secure Built-In Guest Accounts

By default, the guest account in a DBMS has few or no permissions. You should take every step possible to minimize the guest accounts. If the guest account can be deleted, then delete it. If it can be disabled, then disable it. If those two options are not available, then make sure that the guest account has no permissions in any databases.

Secure the Development and Test Databases

Database administrators are generally more lenient with permissions on test and development databases. Often, developers have a development DBMS installed on their own computer, with full DBA privileges to help improve their development speed. However, this can lead to problems as the date for cutting the application over to production approaches. Everything may work fine for the developer running the application with full administrative privileges, but then testers may find that the application fails when their nonadministrative accounts are used. If the developers cannot resolve the problems quickly, management may decide to push the application into production using administrative accounts. Of course, the plan is to correct this very quickly afterward, but if the application is working well and there are other tasks to be done, changing the application to run with less-privileged accounts may not receive a high priority.

To reduce the chance of this happening, DBAs should encourage developers and management to get the development and test environments configured using logon IDs (instead of administrative accounts such as sa) as soon as possible.

Secure the DBMS with OS File Permissions

File permissions may not be your first thought when considering database permissions, but they should be given due consideration. Only the OS administrative accounts, local system accounts, and the accounts used by the DBMS services should be allowed Full Control of the program files and the files containing database data and logs. User accounts and user groups should have no permissions for these files.

When a DBMS is installed on a Windows OS, the DBMS may place some configuration information in the Windows registry. Changes to these configurations may aid a hacker's ability to compromise the DBMS; therefore, keys relevant to the DBMS should be secured with restrictions similar to those of files. To restrict permissions to the registry keys, find the relevant DBMS keys by using Regedit (HKEY_LOCAL_MACHINE\Software\Oracle, HKEY_LOCAL_MACHINE\Software\Microsoft\MSSQLServer, or HKEY_LOCAL_MACHINE\Software\IBM\DB2), right-click, and select Permissions. Figure 8-2 shows an example of restricting permissions on registry keys.

NOTE Microsoft SQL Server restricts these permissions for you, if you use SQL SEM to specify the accounts.

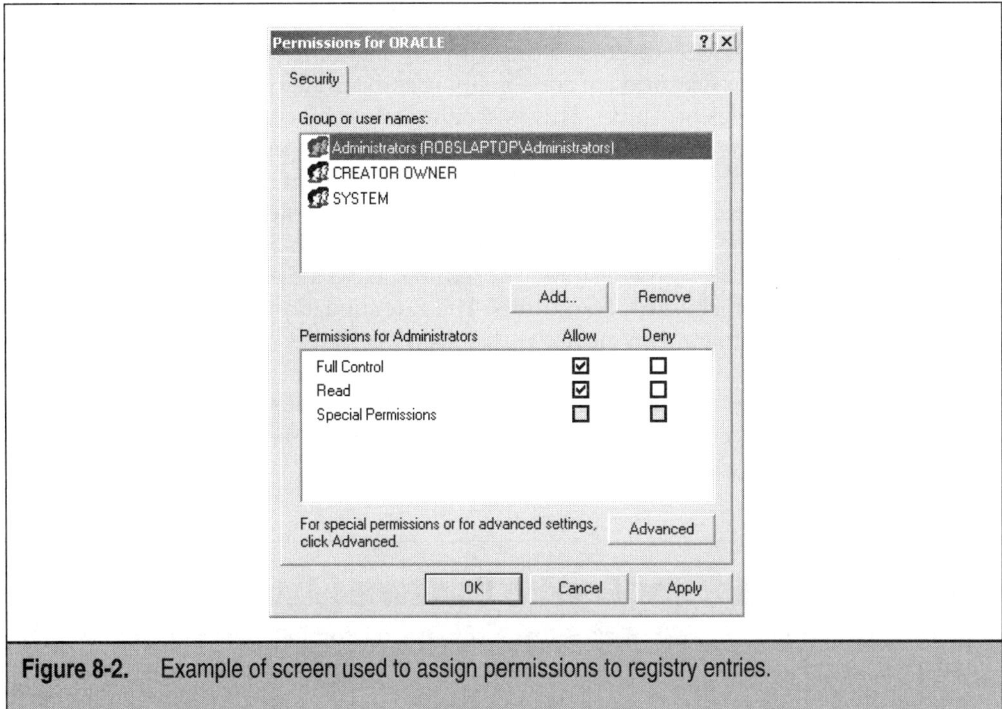

Figure 8-2. Example of screen used to assign permissions to registry entries.

Protect the OS from Programs Launched by the DBMS

Launching programs external to the DBMS is a feature sure to grow in popularity over the years to come. For myriad reasons, including encryption subroutines, advanced auditing and troubleshooting, and automated processing, the desire for developers to be able to execute programs written in C, Java, and .NET in response to data modifications in the database is increasing. Given the promise of the next generation of tools, particularly of the .NET embedding in SQL Server 2005, this technique is sure to proliferate. What does that mean for the DBMS and security? It means that these processes launched from within the DBMS will probably run on the OS with the same permissions that the DBMS service used to connect to the OS. If the DBMS service connects with the local system account, then a process launched from within the DBMS may also be running with local system privileges. This not only requires a level of trust for the developers of programs launched by the DBMS, it also opens a potential hole in the security net. For example, as a smart DBA, you may write your own external program named xyz.exe and launch it from the DBMS knowing exactly what it is doing. The security hole is that a hacker could replace your xyz.exe with his own xyz.exe. The new xyz.exe probably is not doing what you want it to, and its permission level could be much greater than you would like for that program to have.

This is not just a problem waiting to happen to SQL Server 2005 administrators; it is already a concern for DBMS administrators with external libraries called from within the DBMS. Oracle allows execution of code in libraries external to the DBMS (read DLLs on Windows and SO files on Unix). This is accomplished by connecting to a special Oracle process called the External Procedure Listener. A DBA must be aware not only of the code called through the DBMS to this Listener, but also that a hacker could emulate an Oracle process and call the Listener directly, allowing the executed code to run with the same privilege as the External Procedure Listener. On SQL Server, special stored procedures, referred to as extended stored procedures, have the ability to read and write to the registry and interact with OS accounts. The extended stored procedures also may be used to launch any program on the network if the account used to start the SQL Server has that permission.

With these warnings in mind, the prudent DBA should not run the DBMS processes with the local system account on Windows. Rather, a less-privileged Windows account should be created and assigned to the processes.

Access to a DBMS May Provide Unintended Access to the OS

In my role of providing SQL Server support to my customers, I am allowed to establish a VPN connection to their sites and use SQL Server tools to investigate and resolve DBMS problems. On some occasions, I have needed to view and edit non–SQL Server files such as application logs and INI files, and to get directory information about application files. I've learned to execute DOS commands and OS programs through the single xp_cmdshell stored procedure in SQL Server to provide me this information. Motivated hackers could learn just as well if they found they had access to that tool.

Use Application Partitioning and Network Technologies to Secure Access to the DBMS

The previous section covered the tools most DBMSs provide for the purpose of securing the data. This section covers additional tools and practices that, although not designed to secure data, do contribute to the overall security of the data.

Use Firewalls to Close Ports

Most DBMSs communicate over the TCP/IP protocol. For an application to connect to the DBMS, the application must know the port or ports the DBMS is listening on.

Therefore, another important and powerful technique to block hacking attempts is to block the ports on the nearest upstream router. Web applications running on a web server need to be able to connect to the DBMS through the port, but the Internet or intranet users of the web application do not need access to the DBMS through the port. In general, DBMS ports should not be exposed across network segments where access to the database is not required. Where access is required, access should be restricted to the services that need them, such as the web application. Routers and firewalls can be used to manage such access. You should make sure that the ports used by your DBMS are not exposed to the Internet.

NOTE The default UDP and TCP ports for Microsoft SQL Server 7.0 and 2000 are 1433 and 1434. The default ports for IBM DB2 5.*x*, 6.*x*, 7.*x*, and 8.*x* are 523 and 6789. Some DB2 services often use ports that start numbering at 50000. The default port for Oracle is 1521. Oracle Enterprise Manager commonly uses ports 1810 and 1811, and other Oracle services use separate ports as well. Consult the documentation for the Oracle services you are using to identify other default ports.

Port Blocking Firewalls Provide a Great First Line of Defense

In 2003 the SQL Slammer worm wreaked havoc on many Microsoft SQL Server installations. Despite the prevalence of the worm, I was never the least bit concerned for my SQL Servers because I knew they were all safely behind a firewall that was blocking ports 1433 and 1434. My company also had no employees or consultants bringing laptops in to connect to our network. This was not the case for many companies that had secured ports 1433 and 1434 from the Internet, but were infected when employees or consultants brought in a computer running a version of SQL Server that was already infected and placed it on the internal network.

Isolate Application Components

You should isolate application components at every security level possible. Don't make anything potentially available to users who do not need it. Both programs and data should be placed on separate computers and on isolated networks. If your company has data that should never be accessed from outside the internal network, then you should place a firewall between that data and any data that is accessible from the Internet.

Run the DBMS on a Different Computer than the Web Server

Your DBMS should not run on the same computer as your web server. The computer running the web server (likely Apache or Microsoft Internet Information Server) is the computer most likely to be attacked and compromised, and therefore the last place you want any data, especially sensitive data. Therefore, you should place the DBMS providing data to the web on a separate computer from the one running the web server.

Run Privileged Sections of a Web Site on a Different Web Server

A company's web site is generally open to the public. The company web site may also contain a section for privileged users to log in and obtain additional information. The privileged web site could be hosted on a separate server with a different IP address. At a minimum, any pages and documents that are intended just for the authenticated audience should reside in separate folders on the web server, where additional security by the OS can be implemented on those folders.

Run Web Applications on a Different Server than the Web Server

In web farms and robust web applications based on J2EE, .NET, or other web server technologies, another level of separation is often implemented for performance reasons, but it provides security advantages also. Web applications often run on a separate computer than the web server. Separating the web application from the web server allows tighter security to be implemented via code identity permissions within the web application objects. The DBMS on yet another server can require that the programs calling it be fully trusted and that web applications using it meet this level of security.

Make Data Available Only Where It Is Needed

A final level of separation is between data and data. The web applications will be connecting to a DBMS to provide data back to the web site, but that DBMS does not need to be the primary DBMS in the company. In fact, it would be safer to place your web server and the DBMS serving it behind one firewall, and place another firewall between your web DBMS and the corporate DBMS. You will need to provide techniques such as replication to keep the two in sync, but the security advantages could be well worth the effort.

Mask Error Messages

It is important that your application developers not allow error messages generated in the program to provide revealing information on a web page. It is very likely that an untrapped failure attempting to connect to the database will reveal to the web browser the error message along with the database connection string that failed. It is simple to prevent this from happening. For ASP.NET applications, just specifying a default error page, as shown here, will prevent the error from propagating back to the web user:

```
<customErrors mode="On" defaultRedirect="MyCustomErrPage.htm" />
```

NOTE Error messages describing failures to execute database commands provide the first indication to a hacker that the site may be susceptible to SQL Injection attacks.

Use Sound Practices to Secure Applications

Even after you take appropriate measures to secure your DBMS, new vulnerabilities may be introduced by the applications developed that use the DBMS. In particular, to prevent loopholes in security being opened, you should proactively implement the measures presented in this section.

Protect Database Connection Strings

DBMSs have been around as long as networks themselves. In the early years, networks and databases could not share information such as logon IDs and permissions, so DBMSs had to develop their own logon authentication mechanisms. As both OSs and DBMSs have evolved, the two groups of products have learned to communicate and to share information, particularly logon IDs, securely.

However, most DBMSs still retain their authentication features. In fact, in some applications, the DBMS authentication offers advantages over the OS authentication. Therefore, some applications use the DBMS authentication. This introduces a security problem. The logon ID and password to the DBMS must be stored and passed from the client application to the DBMS. To avoid this security risk, you should develop applications to use integrated security (DBMS security is integrated with the OS security). This eliminates the need to pass a logon ID and password across the network.

For those applications that do not use integrated security, application developers should take appropriate steps to secure the logon ID and password. Appropriate steps include the following:

- Encrypt the database connection string (which includes the logon ID and password) before it is sent across the network (this also requires that a certificate be installed on the server).
- For applications that create a single logon ID and password for all users, you should store these values in a secure registry key, in encrypted form. Storing them in the program runs the risk that they will be exposed programmatically through an object model, or by a deconstruction or de-obfuscation of the code.

Hash or Encrypt Sensitive Data

The last safeguard in the chain of security measures protecting your data is to encrypt the stored information. You should encrypt data that you don't want anyone to discover even if they manage to steal a hard drive from your company and take the database to their own home hacking laboratory. You also may need to encrypt data to help keep employees out of it. There are two schemes for jumbling up the data stored in the database. The first scheme is often called *hashing* and is usually used for passwords. Hashed data is never decrypted, so hashing is useful only for data for which you don't need to retrieve the stored value. You don't need to retrieve a stored password because the next time the user logs on, they will type in the password, and the program will hash the password again to see if the newly hashed value matches the stored hashed value. This is quicker to execute than decrypting, and easier to implement.

The second scheme is encryption, of which many techniques abound. Generally, the more secure an encryption technology is, the longer it will take to encrypt and decrypt the data (certainly an issue of concern for large volumes of data). An example of data to encrypt would be credit card numbers. A database full of encrypted credit card numbers is much less useful to a hacker than a database full of unencrypted numbers. However, implementing encryption means that the data also has to be decrypted when needed. The need to decrypt the data reduces the usefulness of many reporting tools and the usefulness of writing raw SQL to get the data. Only the decryption code can get the data back out. Microsoft SQL Server 2005 promises to have encryption and decryption built in that should make retrieval of encrypted data much easier.

Encrypt Communications Between Clients and the Server

In addition to storing data in encrypted format, you can also configure many DBMSs to require that data be transmitted to the DBMS in an encrypted format. In SQL Server, setting up a Secure Sockets Layer (SSL)–encrypted connection is very easy. After you acquire a certificate for the server, all login-related packets sent to the server will be SSL encrypted automatically. To configure all data transmission to a SQL Server to be SSL encrypted, open the SQL Server Network Utility and select the Force Protocol Encryption option, as shown in Figure 8-3.

After you reboot the server and make a similar change on all clients to Force Protocol Encryption, all data to and from the SQL Server will be encrypted. If both the server and the clients are not configured the same, clients will not be able to connect to the server. Chapter 10 provides more information about encryption protocols and certificates.

Protect Against SQL Injection

DBMS-savvy hackers years ago discovered a technique now known as SQL Injection. Hackers noticed that when entering certain values, often a single quote, in a field on a web page, the server returned an error because the SQL statement to save the data failed. With diligence and practice, hackers discovered how to pass a single quote to end a statement, followed by various other characters to initiate a new statement, and eventually could send custom SQL commands to the server. If the web server used a DBMS logon account with sufficient privileges, hackers could drop databases, or even create OS administrative accounts, through clever SQL commands.

An example of code vulnerable to SQL Injection follows:

```
SELECT FNAME, LNAME FROM CUSTOMERINFO WHERE ID='" + strInput + "'"
```

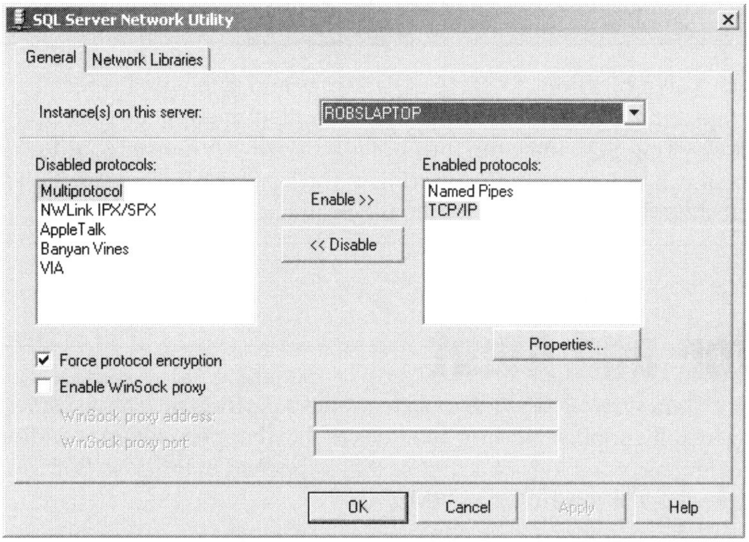

Figure 8-3. Configuring encrypted data transmission for SQL Server

You expect the web page user to enter a value like **888-44-1234**:

```
SELECT FNAME, LNAME FROM CUSTOMERINFO WHERE ID='888-44-1234'
```

But a hacker may enter **' ; shutdown**. The DBMS will receive this as

```
SELECT FNAME, LNAME FROM CUSTOMERINFO WHERE ID='' ; shutdown
```

To the DBMS, this looks like two commands and, if the account connected to the DBMS has sufficient privileges, it will execute both commands successfully. In this example, the second command would shut down a SQL Server—not a good thing to happen in the middle of the day when every minute of downtime equates to loss of money. For most programmers, the steps to take to prevent SQL Injection are simple and just a matter of discipline:

- *Constrain input.* Restrict the data entered by type, length, and format before it is sent to the database. If a field expects only numbers, then disallow anything else.
- *Use the features of data access technologies to prevent SQL Injection.* Through strict use of stored procedures and parameters in Microsoft's ADO.NET framework, all parameter values are treated as literals and cannot be executed as database commands.

HEADS UP!

Writing your own functions to parse SQL strings and safely treat special characters (such as replacing a single quote with two single quotes) goes part of the way toward preventing SQL Injection, but not all the way. A hacker could use ASCII hexadecimal values to bypass the filtering in the function. Such a function is a good step, but it should not be relied upon to block all hacking attempts.

Monitor and Audit

All the major DBMS systems provide tools to monitor performance and suspicious activity. Monitoring generally implies viewing activities as they happen, whereas auditing usually implies reviewing recorded logs of activities that happened in the past. Both features offer value for improving the security of a DBMS.

DBMS Monitoring Tools

Monitoring tools are generally used when a problem is occurring and the DBA or network administrator wants to track down what is going on immediately. Monitoring can be done with network packet-sniffing tools such as SNORT, but when you are working with network traffic to and from a database, you may want to consider monitoring tools provided with the DBMS. These tools ignore most of the non-DBMS network traffic and present the information gathered in a format more understandable to a DBA. However, monitoring even a small portion of this network traffic on an active DBMS can easily yield hundreds or thousands of SQL statements in the span of a few minutes. This leads many DBAs to a process of collecting data for a minute, then stopping the monitor to analyze what they have, then starting the monitor again later if they are unable to find anything relevant.

A better approach, when available, is to filter what is being monitored. Tools such as SQL Profiler, a component of the Microsoft SQL Server DBMS, offer the ability to filter on user, database, source computer, and much more. Figures 8-4 and 8-5 show some of the filtering options available for monitoring the traffic coming into the database.

Audit Logon Failures and Successes

Auditing provides a record of events. This record of activity allows database or security administrators to identify possible holes in the security framework, and to identify individuals who made unapproved changes. Auditing is often the only tool available to track the actions of privileged users such as DBAs. Although auditing does not use technology to prevent actions, the knowledge that actions are monitored through auditing serves as a deterrent to internal users.

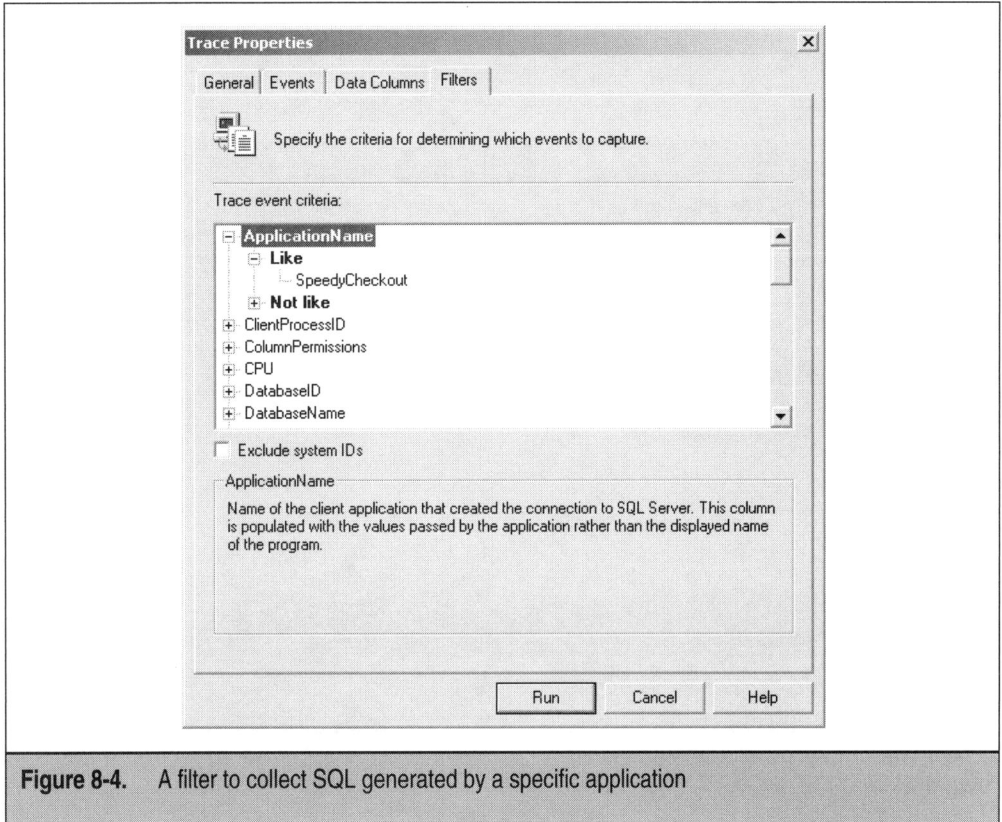

Figure 8-4. A filter to collect SQL generated by a specific application

From the perspective of security administration, auditing everything relevant is desirable to enable company auditors to review changes. From a practical perspective, however, you must realize that enabling audit tracking will have a performance impact on the system; and the more auditing that is enabled, the greater that impact will be.

You should consider auditing failed logon attempts for regular review to identify possible hacking attempts. If you discover a large number of failed logon attempts that used a systematic approach, or that occurred in a short time frame, this may indicate that a hole is open in your external firewalls that has allowed an outside hacker the opportunity to attempt to hack a database. It could also indicate that an internal user is inappropriately attempting to access a database. Monitoring successful logons can also be valuable to identify logons that occur at unexpected times and thus may indicate a successful breach of system security.

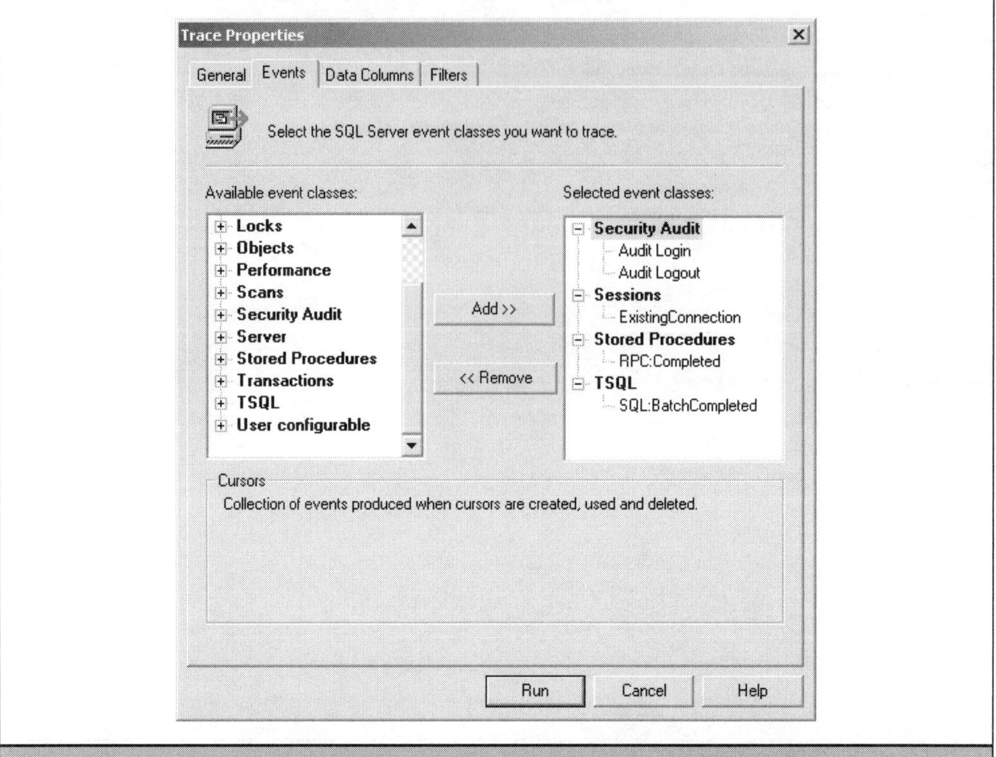

Figure 8-5. A filter to specify which SQL command types to collect information about

To monitor logon failures and successes in Microsoft SQL Server:

1. Open SQL Enterprise Manager.
2. Open the SQL Server Properties window by right-clicking the registered SQL Server name and clicking Properties.
3. On the Security tab, select All under the Audit Level section and click Apply. Choosing the All option will begin logging all login attempts, successful or unsuccessful, once SQL Server is restarted.

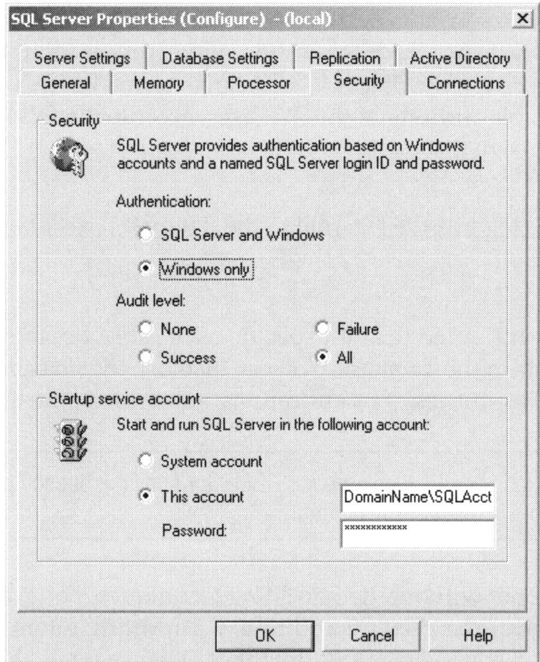

To view the results of the logging efforts, use the Security log of the Windows Event Viewer.

Auditing Everything Else

Auditing logon attempts is very basic; a more advanced form of auditing is to audit user activity. Although permissions are designed to prevent unauthorized access and modifications of data, there are cases where permissions are not sufficient. One such case is the ability of the HR director to change salaries. The HR director may have the permission to change salaries, but you want to know when the HR director changes his or her own salary. One way to restrict this is to audit the salary changes and make sure the HR director knows the changes are audited. To enable such an audit, programmers often use stored procedures or triggers built into the DBMS.

It is also often important to audit the activity of system administrators and DBAs. At first glance, the approach used for the HR director may appear to work for these other groups, but then you realize that the DBA could disable the trigger, make salary changes, and then re-enable the trigger. In that case, you need to be able to audit changes to structures within the database, and that audit trail needs to be stored in a location the DBA cannot alter. To implement this level of auditing, you need cutting-edge auditing tools, and Oracle has the most cutting-edge and configurable auditing tools. Audit trails can be stored in the database, or in an external file that a DBA does not have access to. To enable auditing of the SYS user, execute the following command:

```
AUDIT_SYS_OPERATIONS = TRUE
```

To place the audit log in a file external to the database, execute this command:

```
Alter System set AUDIT_FILE_DEST = <dir> DEFERRED
```

Auditing can be configured to audit specific users, specific statements, or actions against specific objects in the database. You can also use the Flashback Query feature to view before and after images of modifications, subject to some limitations.

NOTE Oracle has long been a leading-edge DBMS for auditing, but some features mentioned here are only available in release 10*g* or later.

Other DBMSs are not without their auditing techniques. For example, Microsoft SQL Server offers a feature called C2 auditing. C2 auditing refers to the C2-level designation developed by the U.S. Department of Defense for evaluating the security level of a computer system. C2 auditing also allows you to record all activity by users and DBAs in a file external to the server. To turn on C2 logging, run the following configuration command, then restart the DBMS:

```
sp_configure 'show advanced', 1
go
sp_configure 'c2 audit mode', 1
```

CAUTION Having an audit trail to review everything that happened is very nice, but running an audit for a long period of time can cause serious performance problems and quickly consume disk space. When possible, you should configure auditing to collect only the information you are truly interested in, and you should turn it off when it is not needed. Unfortunately, turning auditing on and off often requires restarting the DBMS.

Audit Reviews

Monitoring database growth and performance was a core task for DBAs early in the evolution of the DBA role. Improved features with many DBMSs and from third-party vendors have eased the burden of space and performance management, but the automation of security monitoring and management is just beginning. This means that while you can rely on an automated process to manage your database space and let you know when your assistance is needed, tools for managing security issues in an automated way are not generally part of your DBMS. You should create a list of items to be reviewed periodically. Then you should determine the schedule (for example, monthly) to perform your review. Some items may need different review schedules, but it is best to have a single schedule for all items and get them all done at once. Things to review include the following:

- **Failed logon attempts** Are there numerous failed logon attempts in a brief timeframe such as may be generated by a program attempting to guess the password? Are there failed logon attempts for accounts that don't exist? Are there failed logon attempts for built-in account names that you don't think are in use?
- **Successful logon attempts** Are there logon attempts at suspicious times? Are restricted logon accounts like DBA accounts being overly used to log on? Was a long string of failed logon attempts for account A followed by a successful login for account A, indicating the attacker managed to hack in?

Logging Activity Information Can Help Solve Problems

I had a SQL Server shutdown at 2:15 A.M. recently and no employee had been on the network for hours. Fortunately, it was a test server; unfortunately, I was not logging SQL Server connections or network connections to the computer, so I will probably never know whether someone managed to hack our network and take this action or some unrecorded failure on the server caused it to shut down. I used antivirus tools and manually examined the drive for file changes, but never could identify the cause of the shutdown.

- **Other security measures** For example, ensure that closed ports are still closed.
- **File permissions** Is access to the files at the OS level still restricted?
- **Assigned permissions** Do any database logon accounts or groups seem to have permissions beyond what would be expected?
- **Service packs and updates** Does the DBMS Server computer have the latest OS updates? Does the DBMS have the latest DBMS service packs and updates?
- **New vulnerabilities** Have new vulnerabilities been identified and have you taken appropriate steps to protect your system if needed?

Proactive Auditing

As DBMSs evolve, reviews will surely become more automated. In some cases, you may want to receive notification as soon as a violation occurs. Most DBMSs already support generating alerts in response to activity recorded in an event log, to activity in a database table, or to customizable trigger based action. Through a combination of features available in OSs, e-mail systems, and DBMSs, you can configure e-mail and SMTP notifications to be sent when login attempts fail, queries fail due to security violations, or for other reasons. Review the features of your particular DBMS for instructions on how to configure automation alerts.

Policy Reviews

The audit review in the preceding section listed some items you should consider reviewing on a periodic basis. Unfortunately, providing an exhaustive list is not practical, and as your business grows and changes, you may discover other items that should be monitored and reviewed. We often discover new things to review the hard way—after getting hacked or losing some data. Thus, it is wise to schedule an annual or more frequent review of the audit review you have created based on the preceding section. Questions to consider for the policy review are the following:

- Are there any items that we should add to the periodic audit review?
- Are there any items on the periodic audit review that we could automate?
- Can we remove any items from the periodic audit review?
- Should we change the schedule for which we perform this periodic review of audits?
- When should we hold the next policy review?

Secure Backups and Archives

Database administrators generally put a lot of thought into securing data and making it available only where appropriate. However, an area that sometimes is given less attention is the data in backup locations and test environments. Generally, a backup copy of a database is as good as the live data itself. In some cases, a backup copy may be more accessible due to the security design of the DBMS. Data is backed up not only for recovery purposes, but also for creating test environments. The following sections cover things to keep in mind related to these backups.

Secure Backup Copies of Data

Use directory permissions to restrict access to file backups on disk. This should also be done for database logs. Place permissions or passwords on files on tapes and digital media such as CDs and DVDs. Unfortunately, the password strength and controls of many backup devices are not complicated and are easily bypassed. Therefore, you should keep backups in a physically locked location (that is hopefully fireproof as well). When backup files are written to another server, make sure the server storing the backups is just as secure as any other server in your company.

Verify the Security of Remote Backups

One of the goals of data backups is to get the data to a remote location in case the primary location is completely destroyed by natural disaster, fire, etc. The traditional approach was to place the data on backup tapes to be physically carried offsite by staff in data center operations. But, with the advent of inexpensive high-speed data connections, more businesses are copying backups over networks to geographically distant locations. This introduces new areas of concern for security administrators. Should the data be encrypted before it is transmitted to the backup site? Is the data secured at the backup location? Can I back up to a remote location within my company, or should I contract an ISP to provide this service? The answers to these questions vary for each organization, but a few rules should be followed in any case:

- Make sure the environment and the operating system hosting the backup are secure.
- Make sure the site hosting the backup follows good practices to keep its site secure and its OSs patched and up to date.
- When using an ISP for backups, ensure that the appropriate level of encryption is used for the data in transmission, and that it is appropriately secured or encrypted at the host backup site.

Secure or Obfuscate Test Data

A wonderful feature of DBMSs today is the ease with which we can back up data, copy it to a development environment, and use actual production data to re-create software bugs and simulate performance in a production environment. When doing this, a major issue for many clients is preventing the developers from viewing sensitive data such as credit card numbers and medical histories. As a DBA, one of your tasks in securing data may include taking steps to alter the data before it is given to developers so that sensitive information is unavailable yet simulates the actual data well enough to re-create problems and simulate volume. This usually requires a data analyst to identify what data needs to be obfuscated, and what data does not. Note that you cannot use encryption or hashing of the data to secure it because the data needs to retain the form of the original information. In principle, most data-obfuscation techniques are simple, and most data does not require obfuscation. In practice, setting up an automated process to obfuscate the data can be tedious. Here is an outline of steps for obfuscating data for use in a development environment:

1. Identify what data elements need to be obfuscated.
2. Write SQL scripts or programs to obfuscate the data. In the case of encrypted credit card data, a script may simply encrypt 4444 4444 4444 4448 and store the encrypted value in every record where a different credit card number currently resides. In the case of medical notes about a patient, information may be deleted

or may be replaced by gibberish. The actual method of alteration will depend on the needs of the developers. In many cases, it is a very difficult task to produce data that mirrors production systems and is sufficient for adequate quality testing.

3. Create a process to do the following:
   - Back up the database.
   - Restore the backup to an interim DBMS.
   - Run the programs or scripts to obfuscate the data.
   - Back up the obfuscated database.
   - Destroy the online interim database.
   - Make the backup of the obfuscated database available to the development environment.

Data Obfuscation Requirements May Be Very Complex

You may wonder why I picked 4444 4444 4444 4448 in my obfuscating data example. I picked this from years of experience working with credit card number applications. The first digit is a general indicator of the major credit card provider (4 for VISA, 5 for MasterCard, 3 for American Express, and 6 for Discover). The rest of the digits vary, but the last digit is a check digit and can be calculated with an algorithm known as the LUHN calculation. In the case of a credit card number with fifteen 4s, the check digit would be an 8. Having the data generated for the developers conform to the LUHN algorithm may be a requirement for my obfuscation technique.

Chapter 9

Hardening Cross-Platform Access Controls

by Paul Love and Roberta Bragg

- Understand Operating System Access Controls
- Determine Permissions Required for Resources
- Understand Role-Based Access Control
- Harden Cross-Platform Tools for Secure, Seamless Access Control
- Avoid Data Integrity Problems

Access to computing resources is a fundamental requirement in the networked enterprise. Consumers of network resources expect the resources that they need to be available with minimal hassle and restrictions. As someone responsible for information security, you will find that you have to strike a balance between providing unrestricted access to resources and securing access to resources. Business needs will dictate access requirements to resources, and you need to consider those needs before you embark on a cross-platform, access control program. A common mistake is to implement too much security, to the detriment of the business goals, or to allow the requirements of a selected interoperability path to dictate less security than is actually required.

Access control within a homogeneous operating system environment is difficult, but the challenges and difficulties of access control within a heterogeneous environment are even more complex. The two major network operating systems in use in most corporate environments are Microsoft Windows and one of the variations of the Unix operating system (Sun's Solaris, IBM's AIX, HP's HP-UX, Linux, BSD, etc.), so this chapter focuses on using access controls in an environment that is using both Windows and Unix. If your environment incorporates additional operating systems, you can use the principals presented here to examine proposed interoperability paths, or to consider hardening techniques that are appropriate.

Understand Operating System Access Controls

Unix and Windows both include native access control mechanisms that allow for a very granular level of control of resources. The access control concepts for Unix and Windows are similar, yet the implementations are different enough to warrant a discussion on their respective inner workings. Keep these discussions in mind when evaluating the security mechanisms of cross-platform tools.

Understand Access Controls on Unix

Unix at its most basic level uses resource permissions to determine the access to files. In Unix, everything is considered a file (including devices, directories, etc.), and permissions are primarily based on file ownership. Most Unix versions are based on the discretionary access control (DAC) methodology, which means that the resource (file) owner sets the access control to the file for all other users. This is opposed to mandatory access control (MAC), which forces the level of access control based on the information label provided by the system or originator of information. This means that a user couldn't give access to a file that had a label of private if the user didn't have that level of access, regardless of the permissions set on the file because it is not up to the owner of the file—it is set by the label associated with the file/resource.

Some Unix versions have the capability to utilize MAC, either because they are specially modified variations of Unix or because modules or add-in programs are being used that support MAC capability.

There are three basic permissions you can use when allocating access to files in Unix: Read, Write, and Execute. In a file listing, these permissions are represented by **r**, **w**, and **x**, respectively. Each file contains three sets of permissions: one for the user (or owner), one for group members, and one for others (often referred to as the *world*, meaning anyone else). The following is an example of these three permission sets for the example file /home/jdoe/example_file; the command **ls –l** is used to produce the output:

```
linux1: # ls -l
-rwxr-xr-x    1  jdoe   users      11  Sep  9 06:30 example_file
```

The file permission string can be divided into several fields. The first field, or first character in the string, identifies the type of file that is being shown; in this case it is a dash (–), which represents a regular file with a hard link (synonymous with a shortcut in other operating systems). The other possible first characters and the types of files that they identify are outlined in Table 9-1 (you can also refer to the man page for **ls** by typing **man ls**).

The next nine characters of the previous listing of the example_file represent the accesses that are available on the file. Read, Write, and Execute are the most common access types found on all files. Table 9-2 lists and defines the symbolic letters that can be used to identify access types.

Character	File Type	Definition
–	Hard-linked regular file	A regular file (such as text file).
b	Block special file	A file for device input/output in block format, which allows communications to a device in blocks of characters.
c	Character special file	A file for device input/output in character format, which allows for communications to a device by characters.
d	Directory	A file that contains another set of files.
l	Link	A file that points to another file within the file system (symbolic link) or to the same inode (hard link). An inode is a numerical representation of a file that the system uses to reference the file (rather than using the filename).
p	Named pipe	A file that is used for interprocess communications (allows for communications between two programs).
s	Socket	A file used for interprocess communications in which both a source and destination IP address and port are identified.

Table 9-1. File Types

Symbolic Letter	Access	Description
r	Read	Gives the ability to view a file or list contents for a directory.
w	Write	The file can be modified or the ability to delete or add files on a directory.
x	Execute	The file can be run, or the ability to **cd** to a directory.
t	Sticky bit (keep executable in memory)	On a directory, this prevents a user from deleting files that they do not own in that directory.
s	suid/sgid	In the user set of permissions this represents "set user id"; in the group set of permissions it represents the "set group id," which means the file will be run with the privileges on the file's user or group designation.
l	File locking	Sets mandatory file locking, which can be set to prevent reading or writing to a file while it is in use.

Table 9-2. Access Types

With this information in mind, re-examine the previous file listing (shown again here for convenience) and identify its meaning. The output is described in Table 9-3.

```
linux1: # ls -l
-rwxr-xr-x    1  jdoe   users      11  Sep  9 06:30 example_file
```

Field/Part	This File	Meaning	Meaning for this File
First character	–	Type of file	Hard-linked regular file
Characters 2–4	rwx	File owner permissions	Read, Write, Execute
Characters 5–7	r–x	Group permissions	Read, Execute
Characters 8–10	r–x	Other permissions	Read, Execute
Field 2	1	Number of links	One
Field 3	jdoe	File owner	jdoe
Field 4	users	Group owner	users
Field 5	11	File size	11Kb
Fields 6, 7, 8	Sep 9 06:30	Creation time	Sept. 9, 06:30
Field 9	example_file	Filename	example_file

Table 9-3. Listing Fields

So for the file named example_file, based on the permission set described in Table 9-3, the user jdoe, who is the owner of the file, can read, write, and execute the file. Anyone in the users group, as well as anyone else with access to the file, can read and execute the file.

There is another way to represent permissions that is known as *absolute mode.* This means that you can represent permissions numerically rather than with the **r**, **w**, and **x** characters. The numerical representation is described using the Octal number system and is listed in Table 9-4.

To obtain the numeric representation, the numbers for each permission listed are added and the result is a three-digit number. The numeric representation of the permissions on example_file is 755 because **r** (4) + **w** (2) + **e** (1) = 7 for the user, and **r** (4) + **e** (1) = 5 for both the group and other users.

Defining permissions on a Unix-centric network is of critical importance. When there is only one type of OS on the network, defining permissions is more difficult, although in heterogeneous networks this problem becomes more of an issue. For a more in-depth discussion of Unix/Linux-specific issues with file permissions, refer to one of the many books on Unix/Linux security available, such as *Hardening Linux* (McGraw-Hill/Osborne, 2004) or *UNIX System Administration Handbook* (Pearson Education, 2000).

As an example of some permission sets, consider the imaginary file /etc/unix_file. User jdoe is part of the fake group (as shown by the **groups jdoe** command). As part of the default permission sets provided the user (which can be modified by the **umask** command), there is **rwx** for the owner and **r** for the group and others.

To determine who has access to a group, simply type

```
groups <group name>
```

If you want to give a group of people access to your files, but don't want to open the file up for everyone in the world, you could modify the files' permissions to allow the group write and execute permission. To do this, you would use the following command to grant that permission:

```
chmod g+rwx /etc/unix_file
```

Permission	Meaning
4	Read
2	Write
1	Execute

Table 9-4. Octal Permissions

To minimize access to files and directories, you must understand what you are doing or else you may inadvertently create issues for users. For instance, you can set a directory permission to Execute without Read or Write permission for everyone (`d--x--x--x` or `111`), which enables anyone who knows the exact name of a file in the directory to execute the file, but does not allow anyone to execute a directory listing. This is useful if you want to obfuscate the contents of a directory while allowing people in the know to execute commands (security through obscurity is never a good idea, but it does have its uses sometimes; while it doesn't guarantee security, it makes it harder for the casual observer to see the contents of the directory). Understand the reasons for modifying directory permissions and then test before implementing permission changes in a production environment.

Using access control lists (ACLs) is a more finely tuned method for implementing access control on files and directories. ACLs allow you to break down permissions to a file on a user-by-user basis. You can take the standard set of Unix permissions to the next level because, for example, you can give one user (user1) Read and Write access to the file and then give another user (user2) only Read access to the file. ACLs are implemented differently on the various Unix versions, so refer to your system documentation for specific information on the implementation. Using ACLs makes the method of assigning Unix permissions closer to the method of assigning Windows permissions, but not all Unix versions support the use of ACLs (check with your vendor or distribution to determine availability).

As with all things Unix, there are many ways to do the same thing when using ACLs, so refer to the man pages for further options by typing the command **man** followed by whatever commands you want information for. So, if you want information on the **ls** command, typing

```
man ls
```

would enable you to see the manual pages for the **ls** command, including usage statements.

Now that you understand the basics of file permissions, you should try to find any vulnerable or suspicious files on your system. The first step is to find suid/sgid files. These files are potentially dangerous because they can allow an attacker to run programs or scripts with elevated privileges. If a suid or sgid program is not correctly written, it can be exploited using trivial mechanisms.

Run the following command to find your suid/sgid files:

```
find / -type f \( -perm 04000 -o -perm -02000\) -exec ls -la {} \
```

This command runs the **find** command from the root file system (`/`) and finds all files that are actually files (type –f) and then looks for files with permissions of 04000 or 02000 (–perm 04000 –o –perm –02000) for setuid and setgid, respectively. When any files matching those permissions are found, you can run the ls –la command to show extended information about the file.

Another thing to search for in your systems are any .rhosts files, because such files can allow malicious users or outsiders to gain access to your systems using this legacy authentication mechanism, which provides for access according to machine name address. Another potential problem is the presence of .netrc files, which indicate that a user may have their password hard coded for FTP transfers. To find any .rhosts or .netrc files, run the following command:

```
find / -name .rhosts -name .netrc
```

If you find any, you should investigate and validate the purpose and need for the files. As mentioned, these pose serious security concerns, as attackers could discover user passwords or authenticate to a user's account. To validate the file contents, you need to contact your system administrator or refer to specific documentation regarding your environment, because the entries may be needed.

Understand Access Controls on Windows

The access controls available on Windows systems vary depending on the operating system version and the type of object protected. Windows 95/98 and Windows Me systems do not provide any local file system or registry access controls.

Remote access is controlled via passwords on shared directories. User accounts on these systems are used only to provide local profile configuration; they are not required for local system access. Windows XP Home Edition also does not provide file-level access controls. It does, however, require logon using a user ID and password and, by default, is not remotely accessible via accounts that do not have a password. Windows NT 4.0, Windows 2000, Windows XP Professional, and Windows Server 2003 utilize discretionary access controls for files, directories, shares, and registry keys. In addition, discretionary access controls are used on objects in Active Directory on Windows 2000 and Windows Server 2003 domain controllers.

Folder- and file-level access controls may be assigned to local Windows user accounts and/or local groups. Local accounts and local groups exist in a database on a single computer. When Windows computers are joined in a Windows domain, the user database is centralized and access to files and folders on any machine in the domain can be assigned to these accounts.

If a user is a member of multiple groups, she will be assigned permissions granted to each group she is a member of in addition to those permissions assigned specifically to her account.

The file system, registry, and Active Directory database are hierarchical structures, and permissions can be inherited. *Inheritance* is the process of transferring assigned permissions from parent objects to child objects. Inheritance, and the possibility that both permissions that Allow and permissions that Deny access can be assigned makes the problem of determining the effective permissions (those permissions that affect the user's ability to access the object) difficult.

Understand Inheritance

Windows NT 4.0 files and folders always inherit the permissions assigned to their parent folders. As an example, consider the folder structure in Figure 9-1. If Read permission is given to the Accountants group to the top level, the Midwest folder, then members of the Accountants group will also be able to read files in the Branch 1 and Branch 2 folders. While inheritance makes assigning file permissions easy, inheritance also makes file permissions easily subject to misconfiguration or attack. If, for example, file and folder permissions are carefully planned and implemented to give just the right level of access throughout some portions of the file system, these permissions can be quickly modified by changing permission on a top-level folder. The system32 folder, for example, which contains Windows system files, is protected by default by reduced access permissions on sensitive folders and files.

Stricter regulation is often advised and implemented to harden Windows NT. However, an administrator may change permissions on the root of the drive within which the system32 folder exists, and this new permission set will propagate to the system32 folder and all of its subfolders. This could mean that sensitive files are unprotected (if, for example, the group Users, which contains all accounts on the system, is granted Full Control on the root of the drive) or could result in system failure (if, for example, the group Everyone, which contains every account that is logged on, is granted the Deny permission). Windows 2000, Windows XP Professional, and Windows Server 2003 folders and files can be marked to *not* inherit permissions from parent objects. This option allows you to craft the exact permissions required for sensitive files and folders, eliminating the worry that they will inadvertently be changed. An example of default settings to this effect is shown in Figure 9-2. Note that several

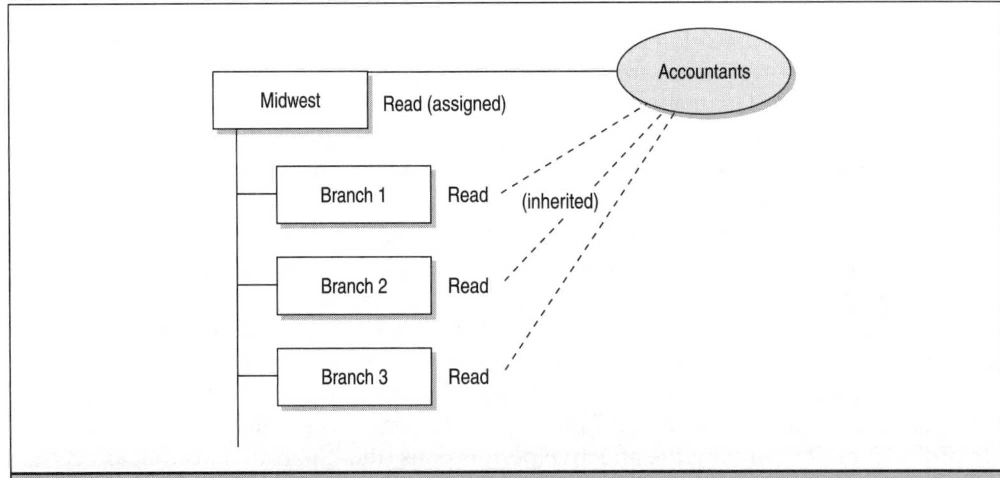

Figure 9-1. Inheritance makes it possible to assign permission at a higher level and have them propagate downward.

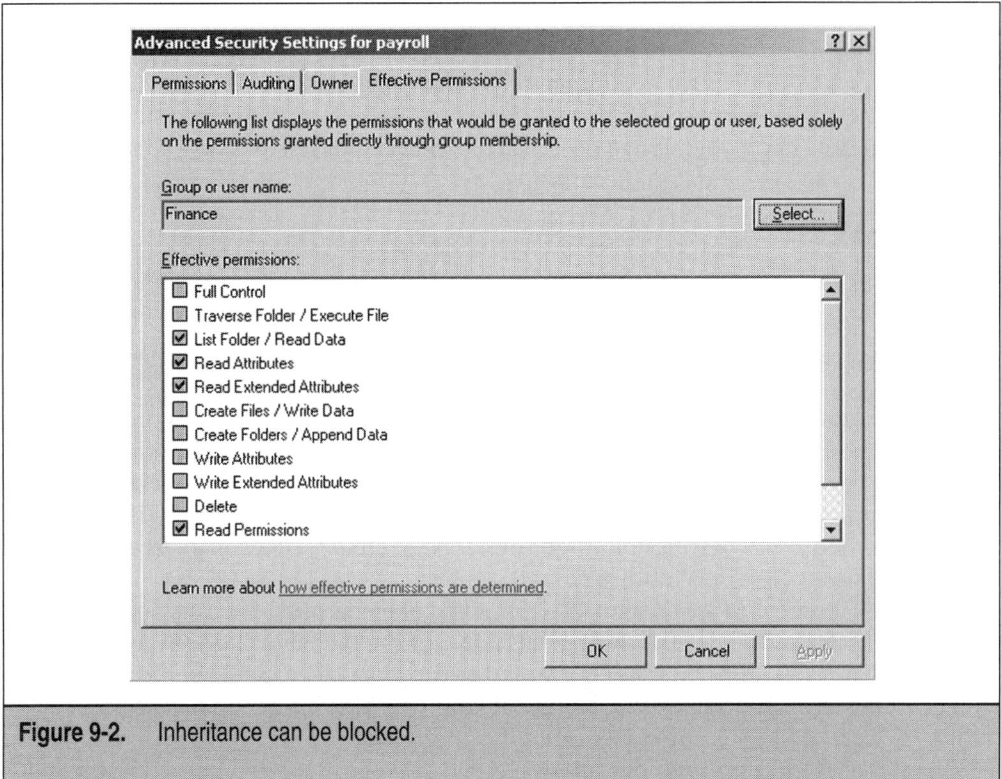

Figure 9-2. Inheritance can be blocked.

groups are assigned permissions. When the top check box, "Allow inheritable permissions from the parent to propagate to this object...," is checked, permissions are inherited from the parents of this folder.

Understand Effective Permissions

In general, the following rule can be used to determine the effective permissions (the combination of permissions that will be applied, both inherited and explicit) for any user or group on Windows systems: Permissions are cumulative unless a Deny permission is reviewed first.

Windows NT 4.0 systems automatically place any assigned Deny permissions at the top of the Access Control List. The access control list (ACL) is a structure that stores access control entries (ACEs), which are structures that list permissions and identify the group or user who has that permission. When a user requests access to a file or folder, the list is evaluated; if the user, or a group that they are a member of, is denied access, then no additional entries are evaluated. If no permissions that deny access (deny permissions) are applied to the user, then each additional ACE is evaluated to see if it supplies the permission requested. If so, then the user is granted access; if not, the user is denied access. (Access must be explicitly granted, otherwise it is implicitly denied.)

Windows 2000 and above evaluate effective permissions in a slightly different manner. Whereas Windows NT 4.0 treats inherited and directly applied permissions equally, Windows 2000 and above do not. This means that it is possible for a Deny permission not to be evaluated. Permissions are evaluated in the following order:

- Local Deny
- Local Allow
- Inherited Deny
- Inherited Allow

Like Windows NT 4.0, if a Deny permission is evaluated, then it takes precedence over Allow permissions. However, since the Deny permission can be granular, a Deny Write permission has no effect if the permission requested is Read. Explicit Allow permissions are evaluated before inherited Deny permissions. Therefore, it is possible that an inherited Deny permission might never be evaluated. This is different from how permissions work in Windows NT 4.0.

Examine Figure 9-3 to see the impact of inherited deny permissions. This figure shows the result of calculating the effective permissions for the file payroll.doc in the Urchin folder. The Allow Read permission is granted to the Finance group for folder Urchin. However, the Deny Read permission is applied for the Finance group on the parent folder, folder Sea. Mary is a member of the Finance group.

When the effective permissions are calculated, the permissions assigned to the file are Finance—Allow Read. When Mary tries to read the payroll file in the Urchin folder, she can read the file even though there is a Deny Read permission inherited as shown in Figure 9-3. Windows XP Professional and Windows Server 2003 provide an Effective Permissions tab to assist you in determining effective permissions.

Understand File and Directory Permissions

Windows file and directory permissions are more granular than those provided on most Unix systems. Seven broad categories may be assigned, each of which may consist of multiple tasks. Table 9-5 lists these broad categories along with the access they grant on files and folders. Table 9-6 details the tasks included in each category. Instead of selecting one of the categories, you can assign individual task permissions. For example, a group could be assigned the Delete task. A collection of these individual task permissions is sometimes called *Special Permissions.* On Windows NT 4.0 computers, access permissions either allow a specific type of access or deny all access. When assigned to a user or group, the Deny permission denies access to the file or folder by that group. Windows 2000, Windows XP Professional, and Window Server 2003 computers do not have the Deny permission; instead, any of the other permissions can be assigned either as Allow or Deny.

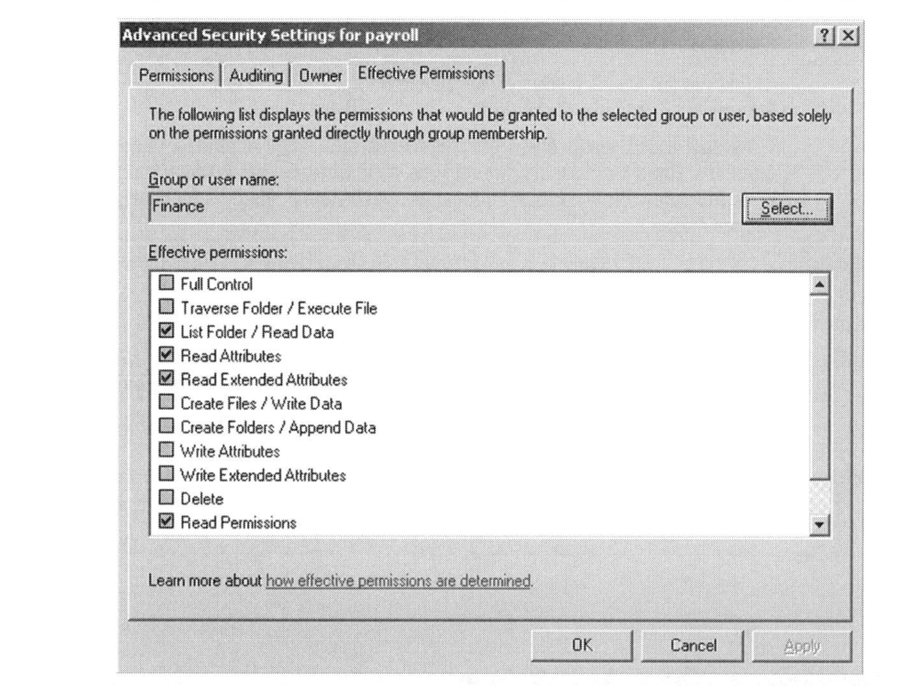

Figure 9-3. Consider effective permissions when evaluating access controls.

Broad Category	File Access	Folder Access
Full Control	Apply all permissions.	Apply all permissions.
Modify	Read, delete, change, and execute files and file attributes.	List the folder, read and modify folder permissions and attributes. Delete folder. Add files to the folder.
Read and Execute	Read and execute the file. Read file permissions and attributes.	List folder contents, read folder permissions and attributes.
List Folder Contents	N/A	Traverse folder (view folder and its contents). Execute files in the folder. Read attributes. Read data. List files in the folder.
Read	Read file and its attributes.	List folders. Read attributes and permissions.
Write	Write data to the file. Append data to the file. Write file permissions and attributes.	Create files. Create folders. Write attributes and permissions.
Special Permissions	Granular selection.	Granular selection.

Table 9-5. File and Folder Permission Categories

Category	Contains
Full Control	All tasks in the Modify category, plus Delete Subfolders and Files, Change Permissions, and Take Ownership
Modify	Traverse Folder/Execute File, List Folder/Read Data, Read Attributes, Read Extended Attributes, Read Permissions, Create Files/Write Data, Create Folders/Append Data, Write Attributes, Write Extended Attributes, and Delete Folder/File (but not subfolders and their files)
Read and Execute	Traverse Folder/Execute File, List Folder/Read Data, Read Attributes, Read Extended Attributes, and Read Permissions
List Folder Contents	Traverse Folder, Execute Files In The Folder, Read Attributes, Read Data, and List Files In The Folder
Read	List folder/ read data. Read attributes. Read Extended attributes. Read Permissions.
Write	Create files/ write data. Create folders/ Append data. Write attributes. Write Extended attributes.

Table 9-6. Permission Categories Defined by Their Tasks

Understand Windows Share Permissions

Windows shares are remote access points to folders and files. Windows 95/98 has two levels of sharing:

- **Share level** Folder shares are protected by a password. Share-level passwords are associated with the share object, not with specific user accounts. Any user with knowledge of the share-level password can access the share. Since the underlying data itself cannot be protected by file or folder permissions, the share-level password is the only thing protecting the files from network access.
- **User level** Folder shares can be protected by granting access to groups and/or users if a Windows domain is present to authenticate the user. Users must use a Windows domain user account and password in order to access the share.

Windows XP has five levels of sharing and two sharing types, advanced and simple. Whereas Windows 98 files are always available to any user who can physically access the computer, Windows XP requires users to log on using an account and password, and local files can be protected from other user accounts. Table 9-7 lists and describes the five file-sharing levels. In all cases the operating system has Full Control access permission to the folders. These are default settings. Simple file sharing provides the five share levels described in Table 9-7. If the NTFS file system is used, permissions can be set as desired. If advanced file sharing is used, share permissions can be set as desired.

Level	Location	Remotely Available?	File Owner Access Permissions	Others
1	My Documents folder (private)	Remote Desktop only	Full Control	No
2.	My Documents folder	Remote Desktop only	Full Control	Administrators only—Full Control
3	Shared Documents folder	Remote Desktop only	Full Control	Administrators—Read, Write, and Delete; Power Users—Change; Restricted Users—Read
4	Shared folders on the network (Read only)	Yes	Full Control locally	Administrators—Full Control locally; Everyone—Read network access
5	Shared folders on the network	Yes	Full Control locally	Administrators—Full Control locally; Everyone—Change network access

Table 9-7. Share Level Controls Windows XP

Windows XP Home Edition can use only simple file sharing. When simple file sharing is used, permissions can affect both local users and remote users. Simple file sharing can permit sharing with users who can log on to the computer, or restrict them only to the owner of the folder. If folders are made available to network users, they can be restricted to just Read access or to Change (Read and Write) access. Some other unique features of simple file sharing are the following:

- All remote users authenticate as guest. This means that even those with administrator-level accounts do not have elevated privileges when accessing files remotely or attempting to remotely administer the computer.
- The file sharing user interface is used to configure permissions for both local and remotely accessed folders and their files.
- When files are moved from one NTFS partition to another, the permissions are not retained. Permissions are inherited from the new folder. This is not expected NTFS behavior. (Files moved from one NTFS partition to another typically retain their permissions until folder permissions are changed at the new location.)

Windows XP Professional can provide simple file sharing or advanced file sharing. Simple file sharing is turned on by default when Windows XP Professional is a member of a workgroup (a logical collection of computers without any native Windows centralized management controls.) Advanced file sharing can be turned on. It is always turned on when a Windows XP Professional computer is joined in a Windows domain (Windows XP Home Edition cannot be joined in a domain). Windows XP advanced file sharing is comparable to network shares on Windows NT 4.0, Windows 2000, and Windows Server 2003.

Advanced file sharing allows an administrator to set permissions for access to groups or individual user accounts. Table 9-8 lists the types of permissions that can be used. By default, share permissions are Everyone Read.

Windows NT 4.0, Windows 2000, and Windows Server 2003 shares are permissioned in the same manner as Windows XP Professional advanced file sharing. However, Windows NT 4.0 and Windows 2000 shares are, by default, set to Everyone Full Control.

To determine the actual access granted to specific users and groups accessing folders via network shares on Windows XP (in advanced file sharing mode) and shares on Windows NT 4.0, Windows 2000, and Windows Server 2003, you must consider both the share permissions and the underlying NTFS folder and file permissions. The result is determined by determining the access potentially available according to each permission set (share and file/folder) and then using the most restrictive result. For example, if Jan is a member of both the Accountants and Users groups and the permissions granted to these groups and to her are as listed in Table 9-9, the following steps should be used to calculate her access permissions on the files in the folder that is shared:

1. Calculate Jan's share access. Determine the permission she has by adding them together. Jan therefore has Change permission on the share.
2. Calculate Jan's local file access permission. Determine the permission she has by adding them together. Jan therefore has Full Control of the file.
3. Compare the permissions Full Control and Change. Select the most restrictive. The most restrictive is Change. Therefore, using a remote connection to the share, Jan has Change permission. (If she is logged on locally, she will have Full Control. Share permissions have no impact when the user is locally logged on.)

Permission	Description
Read	Users may read files in the folder unless file-level permissions are more restrictive.
Change	Users may read or change (write) files in the folder unless file-level permissions are more restrictive.
Full Control	Users have full control over files in the folder unless file-level permissions are more restrictive.

Table 9-8. Share Permissions

Account	Share/File	Permission
Accountants	Share	Change
Users	Share	Read
Jan	Share	N/A
Accountants	File	Change
Users	File	Read
Jan	File	Full Control

Table 9-9. Permissions Exercise

Understand Registry Permissions

The registry is the storage database for many application, system, and user properties of the computer. The registry is organized into major divisions, or *hives,* which are in turn made up of registry keys, subkeys, and values. Permissions are set on all registry keys for Windows systems based on Windows NT technologies. Table 9-10 lists and describes the registry key permissions. Registry permissions can be inherited. Windows 2000, Windows XP, and Windows Server 2003 registry keys can block permission inheritance.

Permission	Is a Collection of Permissions?	Access Granted
Full Control	Yes, all permissions	Full control of registry key
Read	Yes, Query Value, Enumerate Subkeys, Notify, and Read Control	Read key information including value and permissions
Query Value	No	Read value
Set Value	No	Write value
Create Subkey	No	Create a new key under this key
Enumerate Subkeys	No	List subkeys under this key
Notify	No	Read audit information about the key
Create Link	No	Link to another section of the registry. HKEY_CLASSES_ROOT, for example, is linked to HKEY_LOCAL_MACHINE\Software\Classes
Delete	No	Delete key
Write DAC	No	Write permissions
Write Owner	No	Change the owner of the key
Read Control	No	Read the key's security permissions

Table 9-10. Windows Registry Permissions

Understand Printer Permissions

When printers are connected to Windows systems and shared on the network, permissions can be applied to restrict access. This is another way in which data access can be protected. Printed data can be shared, and some documents, such as checks, have direct monetary value when printed. Restricting access to printers and printing is a necessary part of access control. Printer permissions are detailed in Table 9-11.

Understand Active Directory Permissions

Active Directory object permissions are the most unique of all access controls in Windows. Like other objects, simple object access such as read, write, and more granular permission settings can be assigned to groups and users. However, in addition, multiple new permission types can be assigned. The number and kinds of permissions that can be set depends on the type of object. For example, user objects have permissions such as Change Password (all users have the default right to change their own passwords) and Reset Password (by default, administrators can reset passwords on all user accounts; this permission can also be delegated to other groups or user accounts).

Permission	Description	Special Permissions Included	Default Assignment
Print	Print documents	Print and Read Permissions	Everyone
Manage Printers	Install printer drivers and manage document printing for all documents	Print, Manage Printers, Read Permissions, Change Permission, Take Ownership	Administrators, Power Users
Manage Documents	Manage documents that the user has sent to the printer	Manage Documents, Read Permissions, Change Permissions, Take Ownership	Creator Owner (the user who sent the document to the printer), Administrators, Power Users
Print	Print	N/A	N/A
Manage Printers	Install printer drivers and manage document printing for all documents	N/A	N/A
Manage Documents	Manage documents that the user has sent to the printer	N/A	N/A
Read Permissions	Read printer permissions	N/A	N/A
Change Permissions	Change printer permissions	N/A	N/A
Take Ownership	Take ownership	N/A	N/A

Table 9-11. Printer Permissions

It is not practical to list and describe all Active Directory permissions here; there are too many of them. However, there are some basic facts that apply to all of them:

- Permissions are inherited by objects of the same type unless they are restricted. Inheritance rules are similar to those described for files and folders.
- Permissions have default assignments.
- Permissions can be delegated—that is, assigned to other than the default group or accounts. Delegation is used to provide users and/or groups elevated control over Active Directory objects. A common practice is to delegate control over computer and/or user objects within a specific organizational unit (OU) to a group of users. For example, the help desk may be given the ability to reset passwords and reset disabled accounts, or a specific group may be given the ability to add and manage users and/or computers within a specific OU.

Determine Permissions Required for Resources

This is a nontechnical issue that doesn't have the same interesting edge of the technical topics, but it is one that must be considered prior to embarking on or evaluating a cross-platform access control program, because this is the foundation upon which your resource access permission will be based. Even if you are inheriting a heterogeneous operating system environment with access controls set up, you should still consider classifying what access exists to resources under your control.

The first step is to determine the resource risk rating, or what level of loss would be incurred by inappropriate access to the system resources in question. For instance, the internal phone list of department members might be sensitive information, but not as sensitive as the payroll information for all the staff. Using an established classification policy (such as the ones available at http://www.sans.org/resources/policies/) in conjunction with determining resource risk rating can allow you to understand the risks associated with access to the resources.

After creating an inventory of your assets and their associated risk rating/classification, you can begin the next step in determining the security of your access controls: identifying who has access to what resources. The way to determine who has access to resources is different for every type of implementation, but there are methods for extracting resource permissions. This is the most tedious step, but it can pay back big dividends in the future, especially when someone needs access to new resources (allowing for modeling of another similar resource consumer) or no longer needs access to resources (allowing for revocation of privileges quickly).

Understand Role-Based Access Control

Role-based access control (RBAC) as a concept for access control has gained more popularity as of late due to more emphasis on information security in the corporate world. RBAC refers to provisioning access based on a user's group or role. Members of a role (group) are given a set of permissions based on the business needs for that user. This reduces administration overhead because a user is set up based on a standard framework, which means that adding and removing permissions can occur for a large group rather than based on each individual account. For instance, if a user is part of the marketing group, instead of provisioning access for each individual system, you could place that account into a standard role where all the roles are predefined, and then provide exceptions to the role as required on an individual basis. This concept is important to understand because many cross-platform products utilize roles when determining what access a person is given to a system.

There are many software packages available to accomplish RBAC and each has its own capabilities and configuration options. Here are some of the more common packages:

- **RBAC** Included with Sun Solaris (http://www.sun.com/blueprints/0603/817-3062.pdf).
- **RBAC/Web Release 1.1** RBAC for Portable Operating System Interface for Unix (POSIX)–based systems, which include Linux and most Unix versions. POSIX is a guide for the standardization of applications (http://hissa.nist.gov/rbac/RBACdist/README.html).
- **Sudo** (Most versions of Unix.) This allows for a high-level, role-based implementation (http://www.courtesan.com/sudo/). This package will allow the administrator to give access to privileged commands in a controlled manner.

There are also many commercial implementations available for the different Unix versions, which you can find via your favorite search engine.

Windows systems based on NT technologies do not natively support RBAC; that is, there is not a native way to use a default, or create a role and tie it to specific permissions and rights. However, a simple RBAC can be implemented by creating user groups and assigning them access and permissions required to fulfill a defined role. User groups do not have to be implemented in this way, and even when they are, individual users can still be granted rights and permissions outside of roles. Applications such as Microsoft SQL Server implement roles and provide the ability to define additional roles based on the requirements of the application. The Windows Server 2003 Authorization Manager utility can be used to assign roles defined in .NET Framework–based applications.

Harden Cross-Platform Tools for Secure, Seamless Access Control

There are many tools available for administrators in regard to cross-platform access control. In the past, resources were limited and administrators often were required to use combinations of default standard services such as FTP, a few commercial utilities, and/or make their own controls. As more heterogeneous networks required more advanced, secured interoperability, more third-party tools were developed for this task. However, not all tools that provide access have acceptable levels of access control.

Harden Simple or Traditional File Sharing/Transfer Services

Widely available tools exist for transferring or sharing files. Good examples are the network share options provided by Windows systems and the ability to mount remote Unix system drives. In addition, traditional FTP services and other file-sharing protocols are available.

Harden FTP Services

FTP services are not, by tradition or definition, very secure or easy to secure due to the nature of the protocol. Access to the server is secured via accounts and passwords, but passwords traditionally traverse the network in plain text when using protocols with no encryption. Permissions can also be set at the folder level, to restrict access after the connection has been made. It is difficult to secure FTP because of its traditional open-access history. Access can be secured by requiring the use of an encrypted channel such as a VPN or **ssh** in addition to any set at the FTP server level.

Alternatively, a secure form of FTP, FTP/S, uses an SSL wrapper to secure the FTP session. As is true of any transport-specific security control, all of these methods do nothing to secure the data before it is transferred across the network. Take time to provide a secure repository for data while it is at rest.

Block Instant Messaging File Transfers

Instant messaging (IM) products allow users to transfer files. Control over file access is provided only by the user offering the file for transfer. Virus and worm attacks can be initialized and propagated through this mechanism. Just as users may inadvertently spread an infection by opening an attachment, IM file transfers can also be a vector for infection. The only way to prevent such infection is to block all IM file transfers between users on opposite sides of a firewall. (Since this method of control can only be set at a firewall, users on the same side of a firewall cannot be prevented from sharing files by this method.) To block file transfers, the IM program must use a specific port. Windows Messaging and MSN IM both use ports 6891–6900 for file transfer.

Blocking these ports at the firewall will prevent file transfers. You should be aware, however, that IM programs exist that use port 80 for file transfer. If you must allow the use of such products, and thus allow port 80 access across the firewall to the machines participating in IM, then you will not be able to block file transfer by blocking ports alone.

Manage Peer-to-Peer File Sharing

Instant messaging provides a type of peer-to-peer file sharing. That is, files are not maintained on a single file server. Instead, any computer can transfer files to and from any other computer. In most cases, this means that some specialized software must be running on both computers. It is difficult to secure files shared using these utilities unless additional software, such as IP Security (IPSec), is used. On many Windows systems, for example, IPSec policies can be configured that require machine authentication before communication between computers takes place. So, for example, before the peer-to-peer file transfer can take place, each computer would have to authenticate to the other using Kerberos, or certificates or a shared key. This can prevent file transfers between an approved Windows computer and a rogue computer or a computer on the Internet that is not managed, does not have the wherewithal to authenticate, and is not approved for file transfer.

However, there are benefits to peer-to-peer file sharing. Many of these applications can provide interoperability for Windows, Unix/Linux, and Macintosh systems. The MacWindows Network Solutions web site (http://www.macwindows.com/Network.html) lists dozens of programs for integrating Macintosh, Windows, and Linux/Unix computers in a small network. Before adopting the use of any interoperability mechanism, research the access controls it may provide and test them or block the ports they generally use via the firewall.

Understand and Harden Microsoft Services for UNIX

Microsoft Windows Services for UNIX (SFU) (http://www.microsoft.com/windows/sfu/productinfo/overview/default.asp) consists of the Interix subsystem, tools, and utilities designed to support Unix interoperability with Microsoft Windows 2000 and Windows Server 2003. SFU uses the Network File System (NFS) to share folders to any Unix/Linux system that supports NFS. The default share permission is Read and can be set per client machine or group of machines. Shares do not provide root access or anonymous access. The underlying default file permissions are Read, Write, and Execute to the file owner, Read and Execute for the group that can access the file, and Execute for all others (`rwxr-x-x`). Windows DACLs are used to simulate Unix file controls.

An additional service, Gateway for NFS, when installed and enabled on a Windows 2000 or Windows Server 2003 server, can provide access from Windows machines to a Unix NFS file system resource. In essence, the gateway machine mounts the NFS resource and shares it with Windows systems by using the Windows Server Message Block (SMB) file-sharing protocol. To the Windows clients, it's as if the data resides on the gateway machine.

Authentication for NFS can be provided by NFS authentication methods using the NFS server for NFS authentication. The service must run on the server sharing files and on all domain controllers (DCs). To the Unix/Linux clients, it appears as if a Network Information Service (NIS) centralized user database has been provided.

Alternatively, SFU can provide PCNFS (NFS for PCs) if required by Unix systems. PCNFS is often required when the Unix systems are using shadow password files. PCNFS is used to create the files that map password/group files with the encrypted password in the shadow password file. To map Unix names to Windows user IDs, the User Name Mapping service is used to map Windows user to Unix or Unix user to Windows user. When a Unix user requests access to a file share:

1. A check is made to ensure that the machine the Unix user is locally logged on to is authorized to request access. Computer names are kept in the .maphosts file in the Mapper subdirectory of the SFUv3 installation directory. By default, the only access allowed is to the local machine. As administrator, you must add other machines. Adding a + sign in the bottom of the file on any empty line will allow access via any machine.
2. The User Name Mapping service looks up the Unix user in the Windows database and maps the username to the Windows SID.
3. A request for access authentication is made using this SID.
4. If the Windows user has the access permissions requested, then the Unix user is granted access.
5. If no name mapping or no user access permissions are available, then the access granted to an anonymous user is used.

If the Name Mapping Service is used to support the gateway, the Windows user account is mapped to the Unix UID/GID pair.

HEADS UP!

Unix administrators should make sure that the same user has the same UID/GID pair on all machines that will be accessed through the gateway service. If they are different, the risk is high of no mapping being made or, worse, of the mapping being incorrect. This could result in unauthorized access to resources.

Unix-like remote access services are installed when SFU is installed. The Windows remote shell service (WinRSH) is disabled by default in the basic, default installation, although a custom installation may enable the service. The ability to use remote services to connect carries great risk, and many traditional Unix remote access facilities have weak or nonexistent controls. WinRSH (its filename is rshsvc.exe) is not much better.

WinRSH uses an .rhosts file to determine which hosts can connect and does not use domain logon. There is always a danger in authenticating access via host name only. However, the risk of unauthorized access using WinRSH is somewhat reduced because host names in the .rhosts file must be of the form *machinename username1, username2....* In other words, the users who may remotely access the machine from an approved remote host must be identified. No machine names without usernames will be processed. On the other hand, WinRSH cannot distinguish between localhost\joe and domainb\joe. The Name Mapping Service is used to map Unix usernames to Windows names.

Inter-Unix remote services such as **rsh**, **rstat**, and **rdist** as well as the Inter-Unix **rshd** (remote shell daemon) for the client and server and **rcp** and **rlogin** are available but are disabled by default. They should stay that way, because they are easily exploited. Remote access should be protected.

Hardening steps for SFU should include practices established for NFS. This includes requiring appropriate file and share permissions are established that provide access only to those users who require it. When setting the access, you should restrict it to the least possible access that will allow users to get their assigned work done.

Understand and Harden Samba

Samba is an open-source project that provides file and print services and access services between Windows and Unix servers. Samba uses a very common protocol for sharing resources called Service Message Block (SMB) or Common Internet File System (CIFS), which is natively used by Microsoft Windows for file sharing. With Samba, Unix/Linux and Windows users can share resources as though they were Windows native resources. Many corporations are using Samba, and their users probably don't even realize it. There is no difference discernable to the common user.

As with any program, Samba has issues that you need to be concerned about, especially since this is a cross-platform application. You should take the following steps to harden Samba:

- *Locate the smb.conf file in a secure location and run some type of integrity checker against it periodically.* (An example of an integrity checker is Tripwire, http://www.tripwire.com.) This file controls SMB and can be used for nefarious means, such as the inclusion of configuration directives, if not properly protected.
- *Ensure that all externally called programs in the parameter file are absolutely needed, and remove them otherwise.* These programs may run with escalated privileges (such as root) when called, which could be an avenue through which someone could install a Trojan program and wreak havoc on your systems.
- *Configure Samba to prevent Windows user accounts from changing or viewing file permissions on the Samba machine.* When a Windows client connects, the Unix permissions are mapped to Windows permissions. Table 9-12 shows a typical translation. If the Unix version that is used supports POSIX 1, better correlation is available than if it does not; however, it still can be confusing and misleading when viewed or configured from the Windows side.

Windows	Samba
Full Control	rwx
Modify	rwx
Read & Execute	r–x
List Folder Contents	––x
Read	r––
Write	–w–

Table 9-12. Windows-to-Samba Permission Mapping

NOTE Windows permissions are the more granular and cannot be directly mapped to Unix permission. It might be possible to set permissions to something that cannot be mapped, or to assume an incorrect permission is set because of the way some permission mapping may be represented in Samba when viewed through the Windows user interface. For example, some implementations show untranslatable Windows permissions as the Windows permission Take Ownership. This permission is not really available to the assigned users on the Unix system; from a Windows client, however, it looks like it is. Another false reading can be Everyone Full Control (any user has any access they want).

- *Do not use Samba Invalid User options.* This option is used in Samba to allow or deny users access to a share. Windows shares can be configured to allow or deny access via user or group accounts. However, these permissions are not exactly the same and may not translate well. When configuring permissions, always test to determine if the anticipated result is actually returned.
- *Do not use the Admin Users option.* This option names a group whose members can manage access to the share. They can modify or destroy other users' files regardless of permissions set on the files. While Windows Administrators or other groups can be provided the Full Control permission on shares, it is possible to prevent their access to underlying files by using permissions. Administrators can modify these permissions to obtain access, but cannot access or delete files until they have done so.
- *Create consistent user-naming conventions.* Client names in Windows are not case sensitive. Samba names are case sensitive. Thus, in Samba, ANDY is a different user than both aNdy and ANdy. If required, Samba tries to map names by trying permutations of the name given. For example, if ANDY is sent, Samba will map it to ANdy, ANDY, and aNdy. The problem remains: What if both ANdy and aNdy accounts exist and have different access permissions to files? Which files will the user ANDY be able to access? Most likely all of them, which is not a good thing.

- *Understand and manage Samba levels of authentication.* Unless Samba will be used in a Windows workgroup (Samba servers can participate in a Windows NT 4.0 domain as a backup DC, and in a Windows 2000 domain as a member server), configure Samba to use user-level authentication. Samba has three share levels of authentication:
  - **Share-level authentication** Uses share passwords (not user passwords). Windows share-level authentication is similar to Samba share-level authentication in that access is granted to any user who knows the password.
  - **User-level authentication** Requires the user account to have permissions on the share.
  - **Server-level authentication** Similar to user-level access, but a different server is used to grant the access. This server can be another Samba server or a Windows NT DC. More than one authorized server can be designated.
- *Do not allow the use of plain-text passwords.* Samba can be configured to use plain-text passwords. When plain-text passwords are sent across the network, they can be captured and read, then used by unauthorized individuals to access and potentially control computers on your network
- *Configure the smbpasswd file in the /usr/local/samba/private directory to allow only root Read and Write access to the private directory and Deny access to all others.* According to the article available from the University of Bath Department of Mechanical Engineering, "Windows-Unix Permissions for Files Accessed by WinXP via Samba/Unix Shares" (http://www.bath.ac.uk/mech-eng/mecs/Updates/XP-Unix_Permissions.pdf), a listing of the directory should show the following permissions:

```
# ls -ld /usr/local/samba/private
drwx------   2 root   root   4096 Nov 26 01:11 /usr/local/samba/private

# ls -l /usr/local/samba/private/smbpasswd
-rw-------   1 root   root    204 Nov 26 01:11
/usr/local/samba/private/smbpasswd
```

Due to the complex nature of Samba configuration and the wide range of implementations, you should consult the Samba home page (http://www.samba.org) for the latest and in-depth information on securing Samba.

Harden SMB

SMB is the native Windows file-sharing protocol and is also used by Samba to allow Windows clients to access files on a Samba file server. However, many hardening techniques for SMB cannot be done when Samba is being used. Primary SMB hardening advice consists of doing the following:

- *Block access to the SMB ports at the firewall.* This will prevent access to Samba shares on the internal network from the external network as well.
- *Use the principle of least privilege.* Assign share and underlying folder/file permissions to only give the access that is absolutely required. This is more difficult when Samba is being used since Windows permissions do not easily translate to Unix permissions.
- *Implement SMB signing.* SMB signing is a technique available in Windows 2000, Windows XP, and Windows Server 2003. SMB packets are signed by the sending computer. The receiving computer can evaluate the signature and therefore know that the packets were sent by the computer from which an authenticated, authorized file transfer is established. Since packets are signed, the integrity of the data transferred is also guaranteed. If the data is changed, the signature cannot be matched. Samba is not able to do SMB signing, so this improved security technique is not available.

Harden SANS

Storage area networks (SANs) provide another way in which both Windows and Unix/Linux users can access data on a network. Many SANs can be configured to provide both Windows-style NTFS protection and NFS file access. To secure SAN file access, the Storage Networking Industry Association (SNIA) Storage Security Industry Forum (http://www.snia.org/ssif/home) provides the following suggestions:

- Identify all SAN interfaces.
- Use a separate management network for out-of-band access to the SAN. Use a VPN and/or use a firewall if necessary to access the SAN over the LAN.
- Use dedicated user IDs for access and different IDs for management tasks.
- Enforce strong passwords.
- Define small SAN zones for management and access.
- Disable unused SAN ports. Require them to be specifically enabled. Attaching a new device should *not* enable the port and add the device to the SAN.
- Change default passwords before connecting devices.
- Educate users and administrators of the necessity for strong passwords.
- Monitor access.
- Protect data from viruses and worms.
- Protect IP storage connections.
- Harden ports. Can they withstand the introduction of malformed packets? Is access control implemented? Is authentication implemented?

- Harden the underlying OS application layers such as FTP, Telnet, time services such as NTP, DHCP/boot, etc.
- Back up data.
- Require requests for quotes (RFQ) to specify how systems can be hardened and how they are or will be hardened against threats when delivered.
- Seek fabric security features such as virtual SAN (VSAN) technology, hardware-based zoning, port security, strong authentication, and IPSec. (Cisco MDS 9000 is an example of a system that provides these services.)
- Evaluate security appliances for SANS. For example, the Decru DataFort data security appliance (http://www.decru.com) provides AES encryption, authentication, and key management, while the Vormetric CoreGuard Information Protection System (http://www.vormetric.com) provides host protection, data encryption, and access control.

Harden NFS

NFS (Network File System) is a protocol created by Sun Microsystems in the early '80s, to share system resources over the network. It makes remote file systems appear local to the end user. Almost all versions of Unix support NFS, as do many non-Unix systems. If not properly configured, NFS can be a security vulnerability waiting to be exploited. Some basic steps you should take to harden NFS follow:

- *Install NFS on a separate partition on the file server.* If a malicious user attempts to crash the system by filling up the disk with large files, he will be unsuccessful since the system will still have space on its own partition.
- *Mount the NFS shares as Read only where possible.* This prevents unwanted modification or malicious use of the files. You can do this by editing your /etc/exports file by adding the **ro** parameter, such as

  ```
  /opt/shared <client machine name> -o ro
  ```

- *Use the nosuid/nosgid option, if possible, to prevent any suid/sgid programs from running from the mount.* This can prevent Trojans from running on the client.
- *Use the **root_squash** parameter to map any root requests (user id (UID) or group id (GID) 0) to the far less privileged anonymous or nobody UID.* This prevents the root on a client from elevating to root on server.
- *Set the **anon** parameter to accommodate any requests from systems that do not provide a user id (UID), such as some non-Unix systems.* If you set a UID of –1, this typically prevents access to the resource, and –2 will set it to nobody. The default is nobody, which allows you to set the permissions on the systems to prevent access. If, in addition to setting the **anon** parameter you set your exported files to 755 or 744 permissions to limit access, access to the files is very limited.
- *Make sure the implementation of NFS and the portmapper service are up to date on patches.* This has been a high vulnerability area in the past.

- *Use the ssh client and server to encrypt traffic and secure access.* This is so that sensitive information and or passwords and login IDs are not passed in clear text, which can be sniffed off the network.
- *Block traffic to portmapper (port 111).* Portmapper identifies which ports the NFS RPC service is using such as NFS (typically port 2049) as well as mountd (usually port 2219) (if mountd is used by your implementation), on routers and firewalls. In some versions of NFS, all three services must be running and accessible for NFS to work. mountd reads the /etc/exportfs file and creates a list of what hosts and networks the system can be exported to.
- *Use fully qualified domain names in the authorized .hosts file to minimize the risk of spoofing.* This reduces the likelihood of malicious activity.
- *Use NFS version 4.* Version 4 has ACL support using a Window NT model. Prior implementations had no ACL support attribute, although some implementations used the POSIX model and did provide it.

  Version 4 requires LIPKEY, a simple public key mechanism similar to SSL in which only the server needs to have a public key/private key pair and the client can use a secret key.

  Version 4 also removes the requirement to use the mountd protocol. The NFS server must listen on port 2049. There is no need to obtain the used port by contacting the portmapper. Prior to version 4, a connection to portmapper was required to obtain the port used by mountd. The initial file handle was also obtained from the mountd server, then a connection to portmapper was used to obtain the port for NFS. This simpler model eliminates possible portmapper or mountd vulnerabilities, and if access across a firewall is necessary, less ports must be opened on the firewall.
- *Watch permissions on NFS exported directory paths.* If two NFS exported directory paths exist inside another NFS export, and one is properly permissioned but the other isn't, NFS version 2 and 3 may allow unauthorized access.
- *Monitor NFS.* Use a product such as NFSWATCH, available at ftp://ftp.cerias.purdue.edu/pub/tools/unix/netutils/nfswatch/. The logs can be used to spot or potentially trace back malicious activity to find its source.
- *If using AIX, investigate IBM's secure NFS.* Secure NFS has the client and server compute a shared session key using public key cryptography. The client and server mutually authenticate by encrypting the timestamp with their keys and exchanging them. Since the client and server both have the same key, they can decrypt the timestamp and should note a time close to the current one. For more information, see documentation at http://publib16.boulder.ibm.com/pseries/en_US/aixbman/security/secure_nfs.htm.

For further options and security advice on hardening NFS, refer to your vendor's documentation.

Avoid Data Integrity Problems

Windows and Unix use different file-locking mechanisms. When a file is accessed by a user for changes, the file is typically locked so that another user cannot access and change the same file at the same time. If this simultaneous access were allowed, data corruption could result. Because locking mechanisms are different, it is possible that a user on a Windows system and a user on a Unix system might be accessing the same file at the same time, resulting in data corruption. Many systems designed to promote joint Unix and Windows interoperability add some facility to protect against data corruption. Samba, for example, handles the problem by allowing you to set locking options.

NOTE *Using Samba,* Second Edition, by Jay Ts, Robert Eckstein, and David Collier-Brown (O'Reilly & Associates, 2003), provides information on file locking, in Chapter 8. This chapter can also be read online at http://us1.samba.org/samba/docs/using_samba/ch08.html#samba2-CHP-8-SECT-3.

Chapter 10

Hardening Data Transport Using Encryption

by Wes Noonan

- Use Encryption to Harden Your Data Transport
- Determine Whether Encryption Should Be Used
- Determine Where to Use Encryption

One of the circumstances in which your data is most vulnerable is when it is in transit between systems. Whereas users must authenticate to access data that resides on servers, and access control lists further narrow access, rarely is consideration given to how to protect data while it is being transmitted across the network. The most effective method of protecting data while it is in transit is to use encryption. Traditionally encryption has been implemented for Virtual Private Networks (VPNs). However, as more attacks are targeting data on the LAN and data traversing public networks like the Internet, more attention must be paid to hardening data in transit, beyond the traditional VPN scenario. This chapter looks at when, where, and how you should implement encryption to harden your data transport.

Use Encryption to Harden Your Data Transport

Most data transported through the network is done so either in clear text or, at best, in a format that simply requires that it be decoded to be viewed. HTTP, e-mail, Telnet, FTP, and Microsoft Windows file-sharing traffic can be viewed with relative ease by someone with a network sniffer. Indeed, an attacker who seeks access to critical and sensitive information often will find that simply eavesdropping on network traffic is easier than breaking into the systems that store it.

The only effective method to protect against eavesdropping is to implement some form of encryption to protect the data while it is in transit. There are a number of encryption technologies that can be used. Before you implement encryption to protect the data in transit on your network, you need to make three decisions to identify the appropriate encryption solution:

1. Choose an encryption standard
2. Choose an encryption protocol
3. Choose an authentication method

Choose an Encryption Standard

Although numerous different approaches to encryption exist, most implementations support one or more of three encryption standards: Data Encryption Standard (DES), Triple DES (3DES), and the most recent, Advanced Encryption Standard (AES). The encryption standard that you select, in conjunction with several other variables, defines how well protected the data will be once it has been encrypted.

Don't Use Data Encryption Standard

DES, the oldest of the encryption standards, uses a 56-bit key. The key is applied to every 64 bits of data to provide encryption. This 56-bit key provides 72 quadrillion possible encryption keys (2^{56}), which sounds really good until you realize that 56-bit DES was cracked in a mere 22 hours and 15 minutes in 1999 at the AES conference as part of an industry challenge to see how easily it could be compromised. Since then, DES has been cracked within similar times using relatively inexpensive equipment.

While this means that only one key is cracked, and if the key changes, the new key must be cracked, it is now a relatively trivial task to crack the key. Therefore, if you place any real value on the data that is being transported, you should not use DES encryption. In fact, DES has been put out of use by the National Institute of Standards and Technology (NIST). Perhaps the only real benefit of DES encryption is that it can be exported from the United States with no special requirements. Even with this consideration, however, you should not use DES encryption unless 3DES or AES is not an option.

Use 3DES When AES Is Not Available

3DES is a more robust method of DES, performing three 56-bit encryption operations on the data (hence the name 3DES). This creates an aggregate 168-bit key length, which provides much stronger data encryption, although in actuality it is a 112-bit key because two of the keys (the first and third, or K1 and K3) are identical. 3DES has not been cracked…yet. Some estimates say that it would take trillions of years using today's technology to crack it, but then again, people made similar claims about DES cracking, and we know what the results were. Keep this in mind any time someone tells you that something is "impossible to crack."

3DES is generally exportable to most non–terrorist-friendly countries; however, you should verify with your vendor what the export status of its product is if your use of it will be international. Unless you run into export restrictions, you should at a minimum use 3DES for your data encryption.

Select AES as the Encryption Protocol of Choice

NIST always considered 3DES as an interim solution to address the insecurities of DES. NIST published AES in 2001 as a replacement for DES and 3DES and as a long-term (10 to 20 years) encryption standard. AES uses three key sizes—128, 192, and 256 bits—providing the following key possibilities:

3.4×10^{38} possible 128-bit keys
6.2×10^{57} possible 192-bit keys
1.1×10^{77} possible 256-bit keys

If you use AES, your encrypted data will be extremely difficult if not, with current technologies, impossible to crack within a meaningful time frame. According to the NIST web site (http://www.nist.gov/public_affairs/releases/aesq&a.htm):

> Assuming that one could build a machine that could recover a DES key in a *second* (i.e., try 2^{55} keys per second), then it would take that machine approximately 149 thousand-billion (149 trillion) years to crack a 128-bit AES key. To put that into perspective, the universe is believed to be less than 20 billion years old.

If you need the strongest level of data encryption and you are not restricted by export restrictions, you should select AES as your encryption standard.

Choose an Encryption Protocol

A protocol is a set of rules that defines how something works. An encryption protocol defines the rules for encryption that will be implemented. Some encryption protocols, such as IPSec, use one of the encryption standards described in the previous section, while other protocols may use encryption methods that are defined by the protocol itself.

The best indicator of which encryption protocol to implement is to consider the type of data that needs to be protected and how that data is transmitted across the network. This section describes the most common encryption protocols in use today:

- IP Security (IPSec)
- Point-to-Point Tunneling Protocol (PPTP)
- Layer 2 Tunneling Protocol (L2TP)
- Secure Sockets Layer (SSL)
- Transport Layer Security (TLS)
- Secure Shell (SSH)

NOTE PPTP and L2TP are not technically encryption protocols, but many vendors market and present them as such, so they are addressed here with the true encryption protocols.

When in Doubt, Use IPSec

IPSec is the de facto standard method of providing encryption for IP-based traffic. One of the biggest reasons this section recommends "when in doubt, use IPSec" is that IPSec is implemented at layer 3 of the Open Systems Interconnection (OSI) model, which means that it can protect virtually any application's IP data. IPSec does this by encrypting the data that is transported between two hosts at the network layer, thereby making the actual application that the data belongs to irrelevant with regard to the encryption process. Through the use of Transmission Control Protocol (TCP) and User Datagram Protocol (UDP) ports, for example, certain types of application data can be encrypted without the application necessarily being configured in any special way or even aware that the encryption is occurring. Because IPSec encrypts at the network layer, IPSec is referred to as network layer encryption.

IPSec has two subprotocols, Authentication Header (AH) and Encapsulating Security Payload (ESP). AH is defined in RFCs 1826 and 2402 and provides the following:

- **Message integrity** Ensures that the data has not been tampered with once it has been transmitted over the network
- **Antireplay functionality** Ensures that someone cannot resend the data and that the destination accepts the data
- **Authentication** Ensures that the transmitting host is who it claims to be

These are critical components to hardening your data transport. Figure 10-1 shows the format of an AH-formatted packet.

Notice that AH simply splits the original IP header and original transport header and inserts the AH information between them. A major drawback of AH, however, is that it does not encrypt the data contents and therefore provides no data confidentiality.

AH also does not support functioning in a Network Address Translation (NAT) environment, because when NAT changes the IP header, it invalidates the AH signature checksum. While AH can be used to authenticate hosts without the overhead of encrypting the data, if you require encryption, you should not use AH.

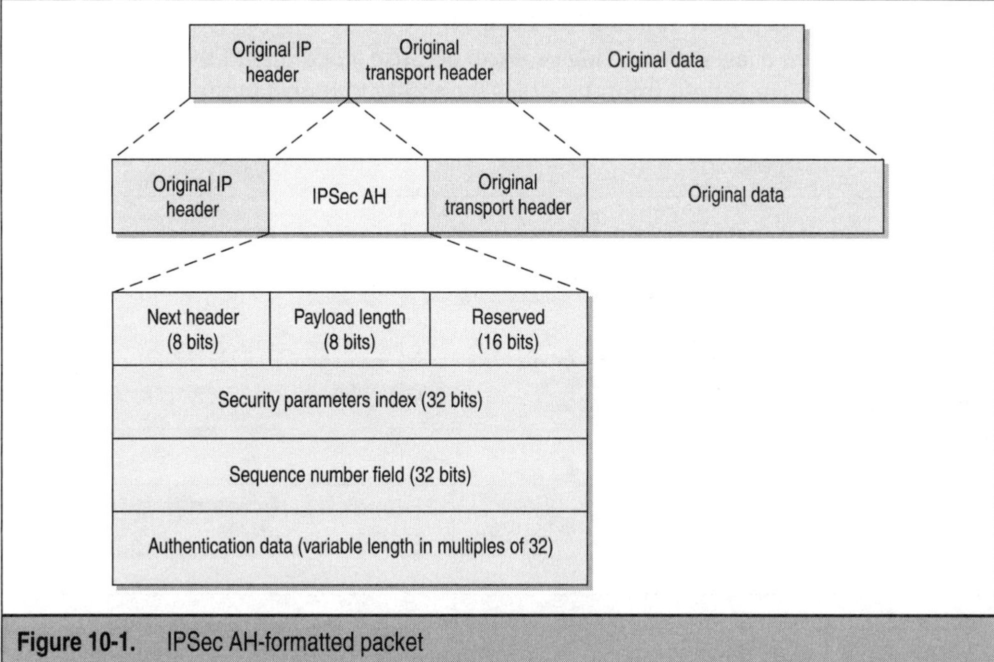

Figure 10-1. IPSec AH-formatted packet

The second IPSec subprotocol, ESP, provides not only authentication, integrity, and antireplay functionality, as does AH, but also data confidentiality, by encrypting the original packet's data contents. As you can see in Figure 10-2, ESP actually encapsulates the original transport header and data between an ESP header and trailer. This causes the original data to be encrypted as an encapsulated payload within the ESP header and trailer.

ESP also can function within a NAT environment through the use of NAT Transparency (sometimes referred to as *NAT Traversal*) on the source and destination systems.

NOTE Cisco Systems has an excellent white paper on NAT Traversal and how it works, located at http://www.cisco.com/univercd/cc/td/doc/product/software/ios122/122newft/122t/122t13/ftipsnat.htm.

IPSec supports multiple authentication and key protocols, although the most commonly used key protocol is the ISAKMP/Oakley protocol. IPSec also supports much more secure encryption methods, including 160-bit 3DES and 256-bit AES encryption.

IPSec is most commonly implemented for VPN connections, but can and should be used any time you want to protect data between hosts that the application is unable to protect—for example, to secure Telnet, TFTP, Syslog, and similar unencrypted application protocols.

Don't Use Point-to-Point Tunneling Protocol

PPTP is considered a layer 2 tunneling protocol because it operates at the data link layer of the OSI model. The benefit this provides is the ability to tunnel multiple protocols such as IPX/SPX and TCP/IP within the same PPTP tunnel.

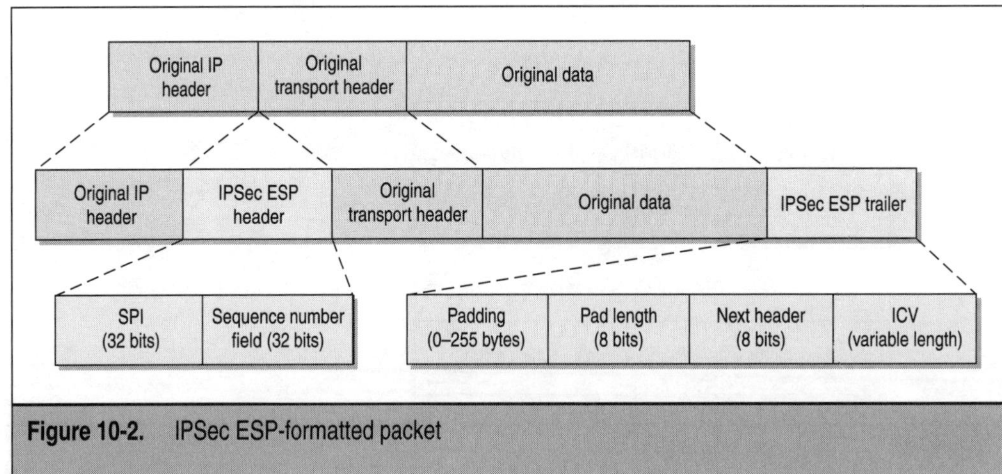

Figure 10-2. IPSec ESP-formatted packet

PPTP has some drawbacks, however:

- PPTP is not based on an open standard but rather is a proprietary system developed in large part by Microsoft, although other vendors can implement it.
- PPTP does not provide data encryption itself, although later versions of PPTP provide some rudimentary data-encryption methods through the use of Microsoft Point-to-Point Encryption (MPPE), which uses an encryption algorithm that is not as strong as the algorithm used by other encryption methods.
- PPTP historically has had security problems and has been exposed to significant security vulnerabilities. PPTPv1 was cracked in 1998 and thus should not be used under any circumstances. Although PPTPv2 is much more secure than PPTPv1 and addresses many of the security flaws of PPTPv1, it is still susceptible to password crackers such as L0phtcrack because key values in PPTP are a function of the user password. This allows a malicious user to gain access to the key values used to protect the data, and thus the data itself, by simply monitoring the network and then executing a dictionary hack using L0phtcrack against the challenge and response data.

PPTP is typically implemented as a VPN solution. Although PPTP is generally easier to deploy than other technologies, primarily because it is built into many Microsoft operating systems, implementing it is not recommended. Instead, to harden PPTP, you should use L2TP or IPSec.

Use Layer 2 Tunneling Protocol with IPSec for VPNs

L2TP is also considered a layer 2 tunneling protocol and, in fact, is based on the Microsoft PPTP and Cisco Layer 2 Forwarding (L2F) protocols. It combines the best of both and corrects the weaknesses of PPTP. L2TP provides for multiprotocol L2TP tunnels, much like PPTP does, and is based on Internet Engineering Task Force (IETF) open standards. Where L2TP differs, and is thus a better solution than PPTP, is that it uses IPSec ESP for data encryption and supports more robust authentication methods. Like PPTP, L2TP is commonly implemented for VPN solutions, and if you have to provide a multiprotocol VPN solution, you should use L2TP instead of PPTP.

Use SSL or TLS to Secure Application-Specific Traffic and for VPNs

While the previously mentioned encryption protocols function at layer 2 (PPTP and L2TP) or layer 3 (IPSec) of the OSI model and thus are effective solutions for encrypting all the data that is being transmitted and received by a system, SSL functions at layer 4 (the transport layer) of the OSI model in a client/server methodology. A benefit of this approach is that SSL can be used to secure an individual application's data, typically with much less overhead than the alternatives, provided the application has been coded to use SSL or TLS or you have configured an appropriate proxy service.

SSL uses the public-and-private key encryption system from RSA Security to encrypt the data that is transferred over the SSL connection. SSL typically uses certificates for server authentication and, if configured, for client authentication as well. SSL is most commonly implemented to encrypt Hypertext Transfer Protocol Secure (HTTPS) traffic. When implementing in this fashion, the HTTPS traffic uses TCP and UDP port 443 (though it is typically just TCP) rather than HTTP, which uses TCP and UDP port 80 (again, typically it only uses TCP). SSL is also gaining traction, however, as a general-purpose, application-specific encryption method and can be used to secure Post Office Protocol 3 (POP3) and Simple Mail Transfer Protocol (SMTP) traffic, among others. For Microsoft Outlook 2003 clients, you can implement POP3 and SMTP over SSL by checking the This Server Requires an Encrypted Connection (SSL) check boxes on the Advanced tab of the Internet E-mail Settings dialog box, as shown in Figure 10-3.

In addition to using SSL to encrypt application-specific data, a relatively new VPN concept known as an SSL VPN is being pushed by numerous vendors as an alternative to the traditional IPSec-, PPTP-, or L2TP-based VPN. An SSL VPN generally functions by tunneling application traffic, for instance Citrix traffic, over SSL using HTTPS. This has a lot of allure, for two reasons: the remote client does not need a traditional PPTP/L2TP/IPSec VPN client to be installed, and, because SSL functions at the transport layer, the traffic usually is not blocked by firewalls and does not run into problems with NAT, as does IPSec. As a result, SSL VPNs are often referred to as "clientless" since they generally use a client web browser and either Java or ActiveX plug-ins to function.

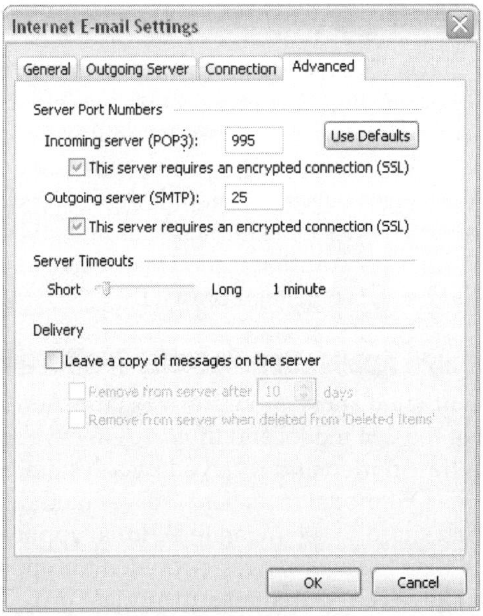

Figure 10-3. Securing e-mail client communications

While SSL is recommended for use in securing all web-based transactions and most application-specific encryption scenarios, it has been superseded, in theory at least, by Transport Layer Security (TLS) as a protocol. Regardless, you should consider SSL any time that you need to secure the traffic for a specific application, in particular web-based applications. You should also consider SSL VPNs if you want to implement a VPN structure that can be accessed from kiosks and other systems that you, as the administrator, may not be able to manage or control.

Although TLS is the successor to SSL and, in fact, is based upon the SSL 3.0 specification, TLS and SSL are not interoperable, which means that you can't use an SSL client to connect to a TLS server and vice versa. SSL is still the de facto standard, however, and many applications and systems continue to use SSL instead of TLS.

Use Secure Shell for Remote Administration

SSH differs from the previously mentioned protocols in that it is a combination of an encryption protocol and a command-line interface. SSH has a very specific purpose, namely to provide a secure and encrypted method of remote, command-line access to systems.

SSH is commonly implemented in Unix environments to replace Telnet. In addition, many network equipment vendors that support Telnet also support the use of SSH. SSH is also very similar in implementation to SSL, using RSA public key cryptography for both connection and authentication. SSH supports multiple encryption algorithms, including Blowfish, DES, 3DES, and International Data Encryption Algorithm (IDEA), with each vendor generally defining which encryption algorithm it will implement.

If SSH is supported by your systems, you should use SSH in every circumstance that you would have used Telnet.

Choose an Authentication Method

The final decision that you must make is what type of authentication method you will implement as part of your encryption solution. Whereas encryption is primarily responsible for ensuring the integrity, privacy, and validity of the data, authentication is responsible for ensuring that only authenticated users are able to access the data.

There are a number of authentication methods that you should consider, including preshared keys, certificates, one-time passwords, and user-based authentication such as Xauth. Another consideration in choosing an authentication method is whether you want to implement single-factor or two-factor authentication. Two-factor authentication is more secure and is recommended since it requires two means of authentication, such as a physical token and a security code. As a result, two-factor authentication is often referred to as "something you have and something you know." Three-factor authentication is also viable in high-security environments and combines the aspects of two-factor authentication with biometric data, such as a fingerprint collected by a finger scanner, or a voiceprint. This biometric data is sometimes referred to as "something you are." While single-factor authentication is adequate in many environments, you should implement two-factor authentication where possible and implement three-factor authentication when highly sensitive data will be transmitted.

User and System Authentication

Generally, an authentication solution authenticates the user, the system, or both. Often, the solution that you implement dictates the type of authentication that is performed. For example, solutions that offer SSL typically perform system authentication; solutions that offer IPSec typically perform either user or system authentication; and solutions that offer VPN connections using PPTP, L2TP, and IPSec frequently perform both system and user authentication.

Don't Use Preshared Keys

Preshared keys are perhaps the most commonly implemented authentication method for authenticating encrypted data. Preshared keys usually are used for system authentication. One of the biggest reasons for this is the simplicity of preshared keys. With preshared keys, the parties involved in communicating simply determine a shared, secret key that is used to authenticate the user.

While the ease of implementing preshared authentication makes it very appealing, it is a relatively weak authentication method because the master key that it creates is generally weaker than the master key produced by using certificates for authentication. Certificates typically generate a much longer master key, which makes it more difficult to crack. In addition, preshared keys are often stored in clear text on the system, leaving them vulnerable to viewing by attackers. Consequently, you should not use preshared keys in a production environment or in any circumstances where the security of the data in transport is critical.

Use Digital Certificates for Normal Data Communication Authentication

Using digital certificates is another effective method of providing authentication for your encryption solution. Digital certificates can be used for system and user authentication, depending on the type of certificate that is being used. Digital certificates are typically either obtained as a component of an internal public key infrastructure (PKI) implementation or are purchased from public companies such as VeriSign or Thawte. Digital certificates provide verification that a user or system is who he or she claims to be. Digital certificates also provide the receiving system with the mechanism necessary to encode and decode the data that is being transmitted.

The backbone of a PKI is a system known as a Certification Authority (CA), which is a server or host that has been authorized to issue and manage security credentials and public keys for encryption and authentication. CAs can be either external (for example, VeriSign or Thawte) or internal (for example, Microsoft Certificate Services). The devices that utilize the information obtained from the CA are known as applicants and clients. The *applicant* is the system that is obtaining a digital certificate, such as the web server that will be accessed. The *client* is the system that is connecting to and/or validating the applicant identity, such as the user using their web browser to navigate to the web server.

The CA is responsible for issuing the digital certificate that contains the applicant's public key and the appropriate information to identify the applicant (for example, a system or user). For example, if you had a web site with a fully qualified domain name (FQDN) of www.yourco.com and you wanted to ensure the identity of the web site, you would obtain and install a digital certificate from a CA for the name www.yourco.com (see your relevant web server software documentation for instructions for this process). If a client then attempted to access the web site, they could be assured that the site is indeed who and what it claims to be by checking to see that the FQDN they are accessing and the name contained in the certificate match. If they attempted to access internal.yourco.com and that same certificate was assigned to that web site, an error would be generated by the client since the identity of internal.yourco.com and the certificate do not match. This is an effective method of ensuring that a computer, user, e-mail message, or web site is or comes from who it claims.

Obtaining a digital certificate is a relatively straightforward process, entailing two major steps. First, you must configure both the client and server system with the CA certificate so that the system knows that the CA is a trusted CA. This is also known as a root CA certificate. Without this, the system either will require a user prompt before the certificate will be used (as one might see when using Internet Explorer to connect to a site that isn't using a certificate from a trusted CA) or won't allow the connection at all. If you are using public CAs, this step may not be necessary, because many systems have a list of trusted public CAs built into them. If you are implementing your own PKI, however, you need to complete this step to eliminate any potential problems with systems not trusting the CA. The second major step is to obtain a certificate from a CA. Figure 10-4 illustrates this process, the corresponding steps to which are described here:

1. The web site requests, obtains, and installs a digital certificate to identify itself.
2. The client requests, obtains, and installs a root CA certificate to identify that the CA is a trusted CA (certificates issued by it can be trusted to be accurate).
3. The client attempts to connect to the web site, typically using a secured URL such as https://www.yourco.com.
4. The web server responds by sending the web site certificate information to the client.
5. The client, either by using local root certificates or by accessing the issuing CA over the Internet, obtains the CA public key to decode the certificate.
6. The certificate is read by the client and the identity of the web site is verified.

   At this point, the identity of the web site has been verified. If the data should be encrypted, the following steps take place.

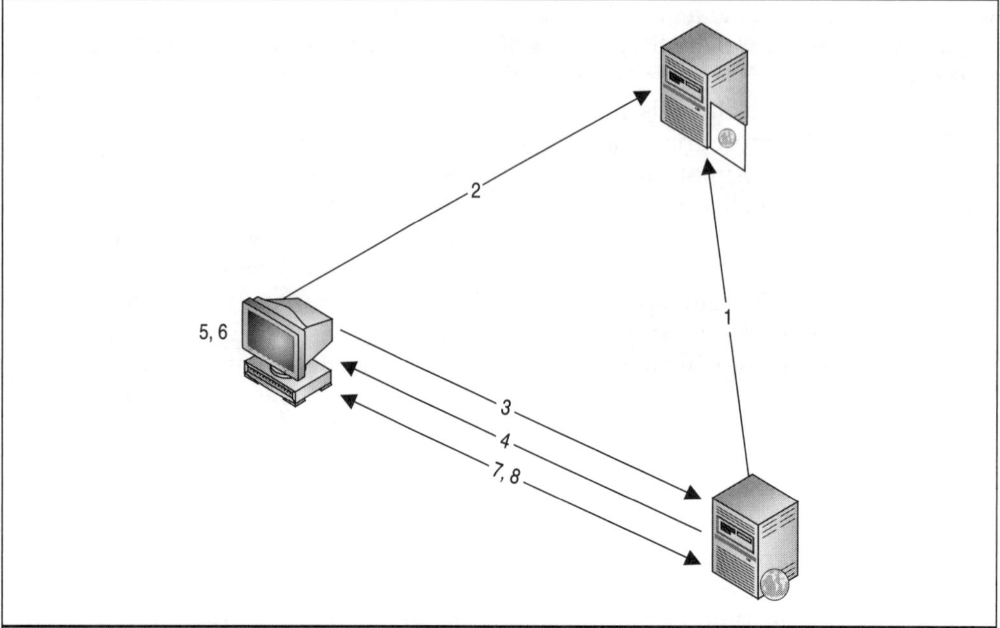

Figure 10-4. Example of PKI communications between a client and a server

7. The client web browser generates a unique "session key" to encrypt all communications with the web site. This is done by encrypting the session key itself with the web site's public key so that only the web site can read the session key.
8. A secure session is now established, taking only seconds and requiring no action by the user. The client web browser may see a key icon becoming whole or a padlock closing, indicating that the session is secure.

Table 10-1 helps identify the steps required to obtain a certificate depending on whether you are using a public or private CA.

For example, if you wanted to add a certificate for use in IPSec to a Microsoft Windows XP client from a Microsoft Certificate Services system, you would perform the following steps:

1. Connect to the Microsoft Certificate Services server (i.e., https://*servername*/certsrv), select Retrieve The CA Certificate Or Certificate Revocation List, and click Next.
2. In the Retrieve The CA Certificate Or Certificate Revocation List window, select the CA Certificate to download and click the Base 64 Encoded radio button. Click the Download CA Certificate link.

3. Select Open This File From Its Current Location and click OK.
4. In the Certificates dialog box, review the certificate details and click the Install Certificate button.
5. When the Certificate Import Wizard opens, click Next.
6. When the wizard prompts you to select the new stores for the certificate, select the Automatically Select The Certificate Store Based On The Type Of Certificate option and then click Next.

Using a Public CA Such as VeriSign	Using a Private CA Such as Microsoft Certificate Services
1. Ensure that the public CA is a trusted CA. If it is not, obtain the CA certificate and add it as a trusted CA.	1. Obtain the CA certificate and add it as a trusted CA.
2. Contact the CA vendor and purchase the appropriate certificate for your use.	2. Obtain the appropriate certificate for your use.
3. Install the certificate on the system.	3. Install the certificate on the system.

Table 10-1. Steps for Obtaining a Certificate

7. The wizard indicates where it is storing the certificate. A CA root certificate should be stored in the root store and a subordinate CA certificate should be stored in the intermediate CA store. Click Finish.
8. At the Add The Root Certificate Store prompt, click Yes.
9. If the import operation completes successfully, a message box displays the message The Import Was Successful. Click OK. Click OK to close the Certificates window. The next step is to request a certificate.
10. Connect to the Microsoft Certificate Services server (i.e., https://*servername*/certsrv), select Request A Certificate, and click Next.
11. In the Choose Request Type window, select User Certificate Request and click Next.
12. In the User Certificate – Identifying Information window, click Submit.
13. You may be cautioned about a potential scripting violation, depending on your Internet Explorer security settings. Click Yes.
14. In the Certificate Issued window, click Install This Certificate.

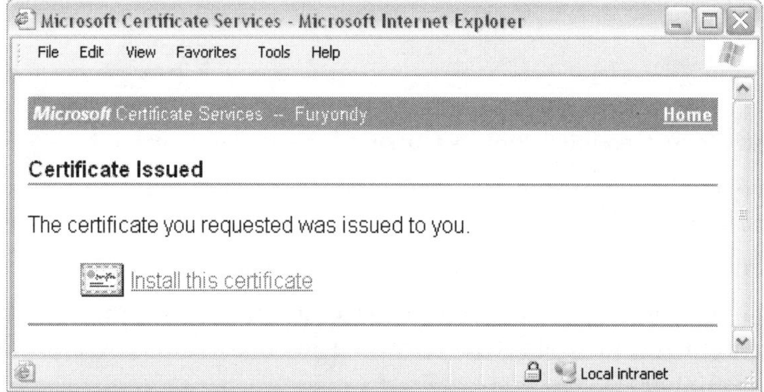

15. You may be cautioned about a potential scripting violation, depending on your Internet Explorer security settings. Click Yes.
16. You will be instructed that the certificate has been installed.

NOTE Obtaining different types of certificates is a similar process; you simply need to designate the type of certificate that is required. For example, you would designate a web server certificate for use in obtaining a certificate to protect a web site using SSL.

For digital certificates to function properly, all the hosts that are going to use certificates must trust the CA. For external CAs, the list of trusted CAs is generally handled by the OS vendor and is installed and updated periodically through Windows Update or similar functions. For internal CAs, you need to manually configure your hosts to recognize the CAs. The minimum method of authentication that you should implement in most environments is certificate-based authentication. Compared to preshared keys, certificate-based authentication requires a larger initial investment to get functioning properly, but it is much more secure and a much more scalable solution than preshared keys because, by design, each certificate is unique and easily validated and maintained.

Use One-Time Passwords to Protect Highly Sensitive Data

One-time passwords take authentication security one step further by using a constantly changing password that is usable once. One-time passwords are typically implemented for user authentication. The benefit of one-time passwords is that even if the username and/or password are sniffed, they are usable only once. Of course, the down side is that the user must know what the password is at any given time. To address this issue, a common method of implementing one-time passwords is to use a two-factor authentication system, such as RSA Security's SecurID. With SecurID the user *knows* a pin and they *have* a SecurID authenticator that has been configured to be synchronized with an RSA ACE/Server. The user simply enters their PIN and the authenticator generates a one-time password that is valid for 0 to 60 seconds depending on when the password was generated. The user can then use that password to authenticate the session, gaining access to the data or resources.

One-time passwords should be implemented any time security of the data is critical and can sometimes be implemented in conjunction with digital certificates. An advantage that one-time passwords have over digital certificates is that a digital certificate must be installed on the system that is being used for authentication, whereas one-time passwords typically do not.

Don't Use Single-Factor/User-Based Authentication

User-based authentication is the traditional username-and-password authentication method familiar to most Microsoft Windows users. User-based authentication includes using RADIUS and TACACS+ authentication, which is commonly tied back to a directory service (NDS, LDAP, or Active Directory) to provide provisioning functionality.

In the context of securing the data while in transit, relying on user-based authentication as the sole authentication method is not recommended. If you are going to implement user-based authentication, it should be implemented in addition to one of the previously mentioned methods of authentication to provide a two-factor authentication system. This helps to ensure that even if someone happens to know a preshared key, for example, they must also have a valid username and password before they will be permitted to connect.

Determine Whether Encryption Should Be Used

The knee-jerk reaction in security is that encryption should be used everywhere. Unfortunately, doing so is probably cost prohibitive in a lot of circumstances. Security will forever be a balance between being more secure and being more functional, and sometimes security is going to win ... and sometimes functionality is going to win.

As a result of the balancing act between security and functionality, it is important to identify not only when it makes sense to implement encryption, but also when encryption is not needed at all. The following are four situations in which you should always consider the use of encryption:

- To protect WAN traffic
- To protect traffic across the Internet
- To protect wireless connections
- To secure LAN-based host traffic

HEADS UP!

The implementation of encryption can often lead to a false sense of security that the network is protected. Make sure that you avoid falling prey to this fallacy. While the data itself is protected while in transit, encryption does not protect your network from all threats. For example, if a remote system has a virus or worm and establishes a VPN connection, your network is not protected from the virus or worm. Indeed, it simply means that the data the virus or worm transmits will be encrypted as it is passed from the client to the network. Make sure that you understand that encryption doesn't necessarily stop the transmission of "bad" traffic, it merely encrypts it.

Use Encryption to Protect WAN Traffic

Protecting WAN traffic is an often-overlooked hardening step. WAN connections are such a traditional component of a network, and people have been conditioned to think of a WAN connection as being secure since it is a point-to-point connection (in the case of a T1 for example), a dial-up connection, or is being segregated from other traffic in a packet-switched cloud (in the case of Frame Relay). In other cases, such as managed VPN services, network administrators trust the vendor to provide the necessary encryption within its network.

Unfortunately, in every one of these circumstances there is a security hole that, depending on the sensitivity of the data, is an unacceptable risk. In the case of traditional WAN service offerings like T1, T3, Frame Relay, and ATM service, the security hole is that anyone can implement a tap on the line and instantly gain full access to all of the data that is being transmitted. In the case of managed VPN service, one of the security holes is that, although the traffic may be secured within the service provider network by a VPN (you are relying on the service provider to ensure this), the corporate connection to the provider network may be a simple point-to-point or otherwise-unencrypted circuit.

HEADS UP!

Managed service providers legally are not prevented from viewing the data on their networks. In fact, in many cases service providers can explicitly view the data that is being passed on their networks with relative ease and impunity. Consequently, you should be very careful when deciding to implement something like Multiprotocol Label Switching (MPLS) or a managed VPN to protect your data. If the data is particularly sensitive, you may need to choose to implement your own encryption instead of relying on a service provider for that security.

You need to consider implementing encryption for all data that traverses any of your WAN connections. The section "Implement Encryption Between WAN Routers," later in the chapter, looks at how to configure a Cisco router to encrypt the traffic it is sending to a remote destination.

Use Encryption to Protect Traffic Across the Internet

It is rare to find a company that does not have an Internet connection. The Internet has rapidly become an instant WAN connection for many companies who have leveraged their Internet access to provide connections between different sites at less cost and sometimes with better uptime and service levels than traditional WAN offerings can provide. Using the Internet as the corporate WAN means more sensitive data is sent across the Internet. While there are no guarantees, you can usually be reasonably certain that the service provider network is relatively secure and protected. The same is not true of the Internet, and therein lies the biggest difference between transporting data across a service provider network and doing so across the Internet. The Internet is and always will be the Wild West. As a result, whereas you *may* want to consider using encryption for data that is being passed across a WAN link, you *always* want to consider using encryption for data that is being transmitted across the Internet.

Does this then mean that you should be using encryption to surf the Web? No. What you should do, however, is implement any of the differing encryption methods as appropriate, to ensure that all sensitive data is protected by encryption. Some of the circumstances in which to use encryption across the Internet are when using

- **The Internet as a WAN connection** Always implement a VPN solution, preferably using IPSec and AES encryption with certificates.
- **The Internet to provide remote access to internal resources** Implement a VPN solution, either traditional or SSL based, to ensure that the data being passed to and from the client is secured. An example of this would be ensuring that if you have implemented Microsoft Outlook Web Access (OWA) that the OWA server only accepts HTTPS connections, or requiring all remote clients to connect via a VPN client using IPSec, AES, certificates, and/or one-time passwords and user-based authentication.
- **E-mail across the Internet** If employees are going to be accessing their e-mail over the Internet using POP3, you should consider implementing POP3 over SSL to secure the content of the e-mail messages that are downloaded. This does not help secure e-mail traffic that is sent via SMTP, however. For this you need to implement an application-specific encryption solution such as PGP (http://www.pgp.com) to secure and encrypt the content of all e-mail messages. PGP functions by encrypting the content of an e-mail message, allowing the e-mail message itself to be transmitted using an unencrypted communications method such as SMTP.
- **Instant messaging (IM) software to communicate with external hosts** Similar to securing e-mail, if sensitive data is going to be transmitted across the Internet using IM software, you need to secure the IM data with encryption. This can be achieved by implementing the corporate versions of popular messaging clients such as Microsoft Office Live Communications Server for Microsoft Messenger and AIM@Work (www.aimatwork.com) for AOL Instant Messenger (AIM) or implementing third-party encryption plug-ins such as Secway SimpPro (http://www.secway.fr/home/home.php?PARAM=us,ie) or AIM Encrypt (http://www.aimencrypt.com/).

Use Encryption to Protect Wireless Connections

A wireless network connection is one of the most insecure network mediums. Unless wireless communications are properly secured, anyone within range can connect to any wireless LAN (WLAN) and view all the data that every host is transmitting and receiving. Fortunately, all WLANs have the ability to implement some form of encryption to protect the data that is being transmitted. There are two mainstream encryption technologies that you can use to protect the integrity of the data in transit over a WLAN:

- Wired Equivalent Privacy (WEP)
- WiFi Protected Access (WPA)

Use Wired Equivalent Privacy to Secure WLANs

As the name implies, WEP was designed to provide privacy to wireless connections on par with the privacy provided on a wired connection. WEP is designed to prevent eavesdropping, data tampering, and unauthorized access to the wireless network. WEP functions by using the RC4 cipher stream and combining a 40- or 104-bit WEP key with a 24-bit random number known as the *initialization vector (IV)*. This results in either a 64- or 128-bit encryption key. Because the IV changes with every message, a new encryption key is generated for each message. WEP functions by combining the encrypted data packet (known as *cipher text*) with the cleartext IV before transmitting. The IV is sent in clear text because the destination needs to know the IV used to generate the encryption key. The receiver then uses the WEP key and attached IV to decrypt the packet.

Unfortunately, for all this effort, WEP has some significant security flaws that make it a very ineffective protocol. Although WEP is better than nothing, a hacker using readily available tools on the Internet can crack WEP in 15 minutes or less, depending on the amount of traffic they can sniff. The more traffic that is transmitted, the faster WEP can be cracked. This is attributed to the following flaws:

- **WEP key recovery** WEP uses the same WEP key and a different IV to encrypt data. The IV has a limited range of values (from 0 to 16777215) to choose from and eventually it uses the same IV over and over. By sniffing the wireless network with a tool such as AirSnort and picking the same IVs out of the data stream, a hacker can gain enough information to figure out what the WEP key is.

ONE STEP FURTHER

RSA Security has developed a solution called Fast Packet Keying Solution that addresses the weak WEP key methods. It uses a hashing mechanism to dynamically generate unique WEP keys for each packet, thus preventing a hacker from being able to determine the WEP key. You can find more information about this product in the RSA Tech Note "WEP Fix Using RC4 Fast Packet Keying" at http://security.ece.orst.edu/koc/ece575/rsalabs/wep.pdf.

- **Unauthorized data decryption** Once the WEP key is known, a hacker can decrypt the data.
- **Violation of data integrity** Once the original data has been decrypted, a hacker could potentially use the hacked WEP key to change the cipher text and forward the changed message to the destination.
- **Poor key management** WEP keys are typically static keys that, once configured on a device, remain the same from that point forward. The problem is exacerbated

when an employee leaves the company, because the WEP key really needs to be changed to ensure security. Unfortunately, this is not a practical solution if your company has hundreds or thousands of wireless devices, because they would all need to be configured with the new WEP key.

NOTE Some vendors address the key-management issue through the use of proprietary "dynamic WEP" mechanisms, which cause the systems to dynamically generate WEP keys that devices will use in conjunction with 802.1*x* authentication. Essentially, a new secret key is generated for each client that is authenticated. Although this can increase the security of WEP, because these are proprietary implementations, they are only practical if you use wireless devices that support the mechanism.

- **No access point authentication** WEP functions by allowing the wireless clients to authenticate the wireless access point (WAP); however, the WAP has no means of authenticating the client. Consequently, a hacker can reroute the data to access points through an alternate and unauthorized path.

Although these flaws may seem to imply that you should not use WEP, this is not correct. If you can use a better protection mechanism, such as WPA or 802.11i, do so. If you can't, though, WEP is still better than nothing—even with the flaws.

Use WiFi Protected Access to Secure WLANs

WPA is a subset of the 802.11i standard and was created to address the vulnerabilities of WEP. In fact, the hardening procedure for WEP is simply to use WPA instead, and if you have the option, WPA is the preferred encryption mechanism for hardening WLANs. WPA is actually a combination of the following different techniques that mitigate the problems that WEP exposes:

- **802.1*x* authentication** Addresses authentication issues
- **Temporal Key Integrity Protocol (TKIP)** Addresses encryption issues
- **Michael Message Integrity Check (MMIC)** Addresses message integrity

802.1*x* Authentication The 802.1*x* specification was originally defined for wired networks and provides a mechanism that allows a client to be authenticated by a network device such as a WAP through the use of a RADIUS server. It is important to understand that the WAP does not perform the authentication; rather, it acts as a middleman by passing the client's credentials to the RADIUS server and letting it handle the actual authentication of the client.

802.1*x* uses a combination of the Extensible Authentication Protocol (EAP) and RADIUS to authenticate clients and distribute keys. RADIUS is used primarily to carry the authentication and configuration information between the authenticator and the RADIUS server. RADIUS does not have a mechanism for using anything other than password-based authentication. To address this, EAP is used to provide the means to support authentication, such as preshared key–based authentication (also known as

The Future of WLAN Security: 802.11i

WPA is forward compatible with 802.11i, an emerging technology that is designed to address all the security flaws related to WEP and is the direction that wireless security is heading. 802.11i incorporates all the aspects of WPA, including 802.1*x* authentication, TKIP, and MMIC. In addition, 802.11i addresses a number of issues that WPA does not. 802.11i uses stronger encryption than WPA through the implementation of AES. This presents one of the biggest hindrances to 802.11i, however, because the processing overhead of AES is significant enough to require hardware upgrades to support it in many cases. 802.11i will also support roaming, which allows users to move between WAPs without losing their connection when they switch from the old WAP to the new WAP.

If you do not need wireless now, wait for 802.11i to be finalized and for 802.11i products to come out.

shared secret authentication). Essentially, the WAP uses EAP to communicate with the client and uses RADIUS to communicate with the RADIUS server, encapsulating the data as required. EAP utilizes three common authentication means: EAP-MD5, EAP-TLS, and EAP-TTLS.

In addition, Cisco has a proprietary implementation known as Lightweight EAP (LEAP). However, LEAP uses a weaker authentication algorithm. LEAP is not recommended because of its proprietary nature and its use of a weaker authentication algorithm. Finally, Microsoft has implemented Protected EAP (PEAP), which was designed to overcome some of the limitations and vulnerabilities of the other EAP methods. PEAP can use MS-CHAP-v2 authentication within the EAP-TTLS tunnel to actually authenticate the user based on Active Directory. Many vendors support PEAP—in fact, so many vendors support PEAP that it is currently undergoing evaluation by the IETF to become a standard.

Temporal Key Integrity Protocol Although 802.1*x* addresses authentication problems with WEP, it does not address the security problems related to the weak encryption keys used by WEP and hackers' ability to determine what the WEP key is. TKIP fixes this. TKIP uses 256-bit encryption keys that are generated through a more sophisticated procedure to provide a much stronger encryption key. TKIP functions by adding the client MAC address and a 48-bit IV to a 128-bit temporal key (which is shared among clients) to guarantee that the encryption key is unique. The temporal key is changed every 10,000 packets to further ensure that hackers cannot begin decoding all packets if they are able to determine the encryption key, thus strengthening the security of the network.

Michael Message Integrity Check WPA also uses a MIC, known as the Michael MIC, to verify message integrity. A 64-bit message is calculated using the Michael algorithm, which can be used to detect potential tampering of the message or data.

Use Encryption to Secure LAN-Based Host Traffic

It is easy to recognize the need to encrypt traffic going across the Internet, a wireless network, or a WAN link, but the need to encrypt traffic that is being transmitted over the LAN is often overlooked. This is largely due to the false impression that the LAN is a relatively secure medium. In fact, the vast majority of security incidents occur from internal sources. To address this vulnerability, it is critical to protect the traffic that is being transmitted between hosts over your LAN.

The most effective method of securing LAN-based host traffic is to use IPSec. IPSec is probably not something that needs to be implemented everywhere on your network, however. Along with the benefits that IPSec provides, it also introduces a number of drawbacks. First, IPSec decreases your overall network performance due to the increased latency required to encrypt and decrypt the IPSec packets. Second, IPSec can make troubleshooting network connectivity problems very difficult since, by design, you will not be able to sniff the packets and view any of the data.

The key to successfully implementing IPSec on your LAN is to identify the circumstance where IPSec is required. Some scenarios where IPSec may make sense are to secure the following:

- Network management traffic
- Sensitive or critical client/server traffic

Secure Network Management Traffic

Virtually all network management traffic is unencrypted. Syslog, TFTP, FTP, HTTP, and NTP all potentially contain critical information that can be easily obtained by a network sniffer, or they can be used by a malicious user to manipulate the environment and potentially gain access to data. Because many of these protocols cannot be encrypted natively, you should use IPSec between the network management workstations and the network devices to protect the integrity and confidentiality of the data that is being transmitted.

Secure Sensitive or Critical Client/Server Traffic

While it is not practical to implement IPSec on every system in your network, there are situations where you need to ensure that the communication between hosts on the LAN is secure. For example, certain financial and medical data may need to be encrypted at all times—while on the systems as well as while in transit on the network. In these cases, you should implement IPSec to protect the data that is in transit.

ONE STEP FURTHER

IPSec can introduce a significant processor load on the systems for which it is configured. If you are going to implement IPSec on servers and workstations, you should use NICs that offload the processing of the encryption and decryption from the computer CPU. An example of such NICs are the "S" series of Intel NICs (http://www.intel.com/network/connectivity/solutions/security.htm?iid=connect_nav2+secsol&).

Determine Where to Use Encryption

Once you have identified the circumstances in which you need to use encryption, you need to identify the best situations and locations in which to implement encryption. This section describes where to implement encryption to protect various types of traffic:

- To protect your WAN traffic, implement encryption between your WAN routers.
- To protect your Internet traffic, implement encryption for VPN solutions for your Internet-based communications.
- To protect your LAN traffic, implement encryption between hosts.

Implement Encryption Between WAN Routers

To secure traffic across the WAN, you need to implement IPSec encryption between the WAN routers, such as by using Cisco IOS–based routers. This is a three step process:

1. Configure common IKE authentication.
2. Configure the IKE security policy.
3. Configure the IPSec protection parameters.

Configure Common IKE Authentication

The first step is to configure the preshared keys that will be used by both routers. For example, assume that you have two routers connected via a serial line and you want all traffic traversing that serial line to be encrypted. The local router is named local-rtr, and the remote router is named remote-rtr. You would run the following command on local-rtr:

```
local-rtr(config)#crypto isakmp key 12345abcde address 192.168.254.1
```

You would run the corresponding command on the remote-rtr:

```
remote-rtr(config)#crypto isakmp key 12345abcde address 192.168.254.2
```

Configure the IKE Security Policy

The next phase is to configure a common IKE security policy on both routers. It is critical that you run the exact same commands on both routers because IPSec is a temperamental feature, and any difference between the two policies can cause the IPSec tunnel to fail. You want to run the following commands from the global configuration mode on both routers (only one router example is shown):

```
!-- You can assign any policy number
remote-rtr(config)#crypto isakmp policy 1
!-- 3DES is the most secure encryption, though you could use DES
remote-rtr(config-isakmp)#encryption 3des
!-- SHA is a more secure HASH method than MD5
remote-rtr(config-isakmp)#hash sha
remote-rtr(config-isakmp)#authentication pre-share
!-- Diffie-Hellman group 2 is more secure than group 1
remote-rtr(config-isakmp)#group 2
remote-rtr(config-isakmp)#lifetime 86400
```

Configure the IPSec Protection Parameters

The final step is to configure the IPSec tunnel characteristics. You build the characteristics in three steps:

1. Configure the ACLs to define what traffic should be encrypted.
2. Configure the appropriate transform set.
3. Create the necessary crypto map.

Configure the ACLs to Define What Traffic Should Be Encrypted In this case, you want all traffic to be encrypted by IPSec, so you will create an ACL on both routers that causes this to occur:

```
remote-rtr(config)#access-list 175 remark ACL for IPsec
remote-rtr(config)#access-list 175 permit ip any any
```

Configure the Appropriate Transform Set Next, you want to configure the transform set with the appropriate encryption and authentication mechanism, and you want to set the tunnel mode on both routers:

```
remote-rtr(config)#crypto ipsec transform-set set1 esp-3des
esp-sha-hmac
remote-rtr(cfg-crypto-trans)#mode tunnel
```

Create the Necessary Crypto Map The final step is to create the crypto map that brings all the ISAKMP and IPSec information together to build the IPSec tunnel. Like the IKE security policy, both routers need to have exact matches of each other, with the exception of the peer value, which is configured with the neighbor router IP address:

```
remote-rtr(config)#crypto map pipe-1 1 ipsec-isakmp
% NOTE: This new crypto map will remain disabled until a peer
        and a valid access list have been configured.
remote-rtr(config-crypto-map)#match address 175
!-- Ensure that you specify the remote peer IP address, in this case
!-- the IP address of the local router
remote-rtr(config-crypto-map)#set peer 192.168.254.2
remote-rtr(config-crypto-map)#set transform-set set1
remote-rtr(config-crypto-map)#set security-assoc lifetime kilo 80000
remote-rtr(config-crypto-map)#set security-assoc lifetime sec 26400
```

Once you have performed the IPSec configuration steps, you need to turn on IPSec for the appropriate interface. The best way to do this is to configure the remote side first, because as soon as you configure one side, you will not be able to communicate with the other router until IPSec is functioning. By configuring the remote side first, when you lose connectivity (and you will), the connection will automatically fix itself when you finish the configuration on the local router.

First turn on IPSec on the serial interface of the remote router:

```
remote-rtr(config-if)#crypto map pipe-1
```

The link will not pass traffic until you turn on IPSec on the serial interface of the local router:

```
local-rtr(config-if)#crypto map pipe-1
```

At this point, all traffic passing across the serial interface should be encrypted by IPSec, as shown by the following command:

```
local-rtr#sh crypto isakmp sa
    dst            src            state        conn-id   slot
192.168.254.1  192.168.254.2  QM_IDLE            1        0
```

Implement Encryption for VPN Connections

Implement data encryption to protect communications between a remote client and the local network across the Internet or the public telephone system. The most practical method of doing this is to implement a VPN connection between the client and a VPN concentrator. As previously mentioned, there are two predominant VPN technologies, IPSec and SSL. You are recommended to choose either an IPSec or SSL VPN because both provide increased security. If you require the ability to tunnel multiple protocols, then you should implement L2TP, preferably over IPSec. Under no circumstances should you choose PPTP, because it simply is not as secure as the alternatives.

Using Certificates for IPsec

These instructions for using certificates for IPSec are based on using a Microsoft Certificate Services (CertSrv) server as the CA and assumes that you have properly installed and configured CertSrv for your environment based on Microsoft instructions and recommendations. In addition, to auto-enroll your routers, you must apply the Simple Certificate Enrollment Protocol (SCEP) patch from the Microsoft Resource Kit for the operating system you are running (you cannot use the Windows 2003 Resource Kit to patch Windows 2000 Server). You will need to install the program cepsetup.exe. You can find more information about this at http://support.microsoft.com/?kbid=249125. Make sure that you read the MSCEP help file that will be installed at http://*certservername*/certsrv/mscep/mscephlp.htm for more information about how to obtain the CA password used during enrollment, as well as miscellaneous troubleshooting instructions.

Using certificates for IPSec is actually very similar to using preshared keys in terms of how you configure the device; however, you must have a functional PKI to begin. The following is the procedure to use certificates for IPSec:

1. Ensure that you have configured the hostname and domain name for the device.
2. Generate an RSA public key by running the following command from the global configuration mode of execution (a minimum 1024-bit key size is recommended):

   ```
   remote-rtr(config)#crypto key generate rsa
   ```

3. Configure the router with the information required to communicate with the CA. This can be done by running the following commands from the global configuration mode of execution:

   ```
   local-rtr(config)#crypto ca identity ca1
   local-rtr(ca-identity)#enrollment mode ra
   local-rtr(ca-identity)#$url http://192.168.173.100/certsrv/mscep/mscep.dll
   local-rtr(ca-identity)#crl optional
   ```

4. Authenticate with the CA by running the following command at the global configuration mode of execution:

   ```
   remote-rtr(config)#cr ca authenticate ca1
   Certificate has the following attributes:
   Fingerprint: 96D2F4FA DFADAA55 DAEB4EC7 5C3F5FD0
   % Do you accept this certificate? [yes/no]: yes
   ```

5. You are now ready for the router to obtain its certificate. Run the following command from the global configuration mode of execution and answer the questions as indicated in bold:

```
remote-rtr(config)#crypto ca enroll furyondy
% Start certificate enrollment ..
% Create a challenge password. You will need to verbally provide
this
   password to the CA Administrator in order to revoke your
certificate.
   For security reasons your password will not be saved in the configuration.
   Please make a note of it.
Password:
Re-enter password:
% The subject name in the certificate will be: remote-rtr.wjnconsulting.com
% Include the router serial number in the subject name? [yes/no]: no
% Include an IP address in the subject name? [yes/no]: no
Request certificate from CA? [yes/no]: yes
% Certificate request sent to Certificate Authority
% The certificate request fingerprint will be displayed.
% The 'show crypto ca certificate' command will also show the fingerprint.
```

Your router is now ready to use certificates rather than preshared keys for authentication. Instead of running the command

```
remote-rtr(config)#crypto isakmp key <keyvalue> address <destip>
```

you would run

```
remote-rtr(config)#crypto isakmp identity hostname
```

Although the actual details involved in implementing an IPSec VPN depend largely on the vendor that you have selected, there are common steps that you need to perform regardless of your selection:

1. Implement a PKI to support the use of certificates. While preshared keys are generally easier to implement, they are less secure than certificates and thus should not be implemented as a production solution.
2. Define the encryption algorithms that should be used, either AES or 3DES.
3. Configure the IKE authentication and security associations.
4. Configure either user-based or one-time passwords for the second component of a two-factor authentication system (the first component being the certificates).
5. Install and configure the VPN client to connect to the VPN concentrator. (For detailed information about configuring VPN connections, see *Hardening Network Infrastructure* by Wes Noonan, McGraw-Hill, 2004.)

HEADS UP!

Split tunneling is a condition in which VPN clients can also access a local network while it is connected to the corporate network via a VPN. Preventing split tunneling ensures that the client cannot be inadvertently used as a router, permitting unauthorized traffic to enter your network via the client. For details on how to prevent split tunneling, please refer to your VPN vendor for the configuration commands.

SSL VPNs are generally much easier to implement. Simply configure the SSL VPN concentrator with the appropriate certificate and security settings and use the client web browser to connect.

Implement Encryption Between Hosts

Protect the data being transmitted between two host systems by implementing IPSec for the two hosts. The following steps detail how to configure IPSec on a Microsoft Windows XP/2000/2003 system that is acting as a network management system and how to configure IPSec on the network devices that need to be managed.

The first step is to create the IPSec policy:

1. Open the Local Security Policy administrative tool.
2. Right-click IP Security Policies on Local Computer and select Create IP Security Policy. This starts the IP Security Policy Wizard. In the Introduction window, click Next.
3. In the IP Security Policy Name dialog box, enter the appropriate name and description. When you are finished, click Next.
4. In the Requests For Secure Communication dialog box, uncheck Activate The Default Response Rule and click Next.
5. In the Finish dialog box, leave the Edit Properties box checked and click Finish.

The next step is to configure the filter list from the Microsoft Windows 2000 host to the device that will be managed:

1. In the NMS Security Policy Properties dialog box, clear the Use Add Wizard check box on the Rules tab and click Add.

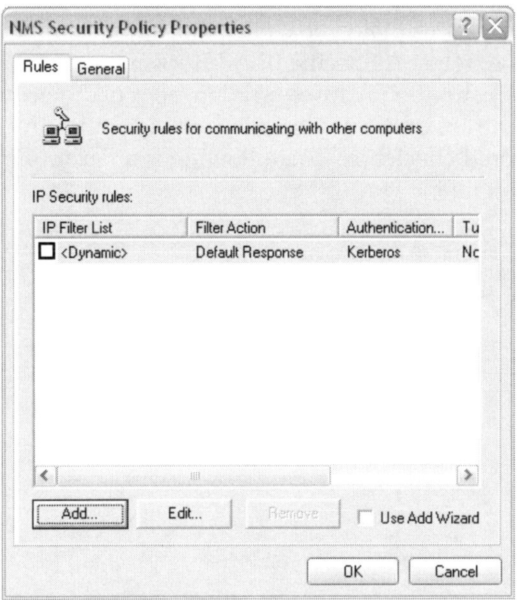

2. On the IP Filter List tab, click Add.
3. In the IP Filter List dialog box, enter the appropriate filter list name and description, as shown next. Clear the Use Add Wizard check box and click Add.

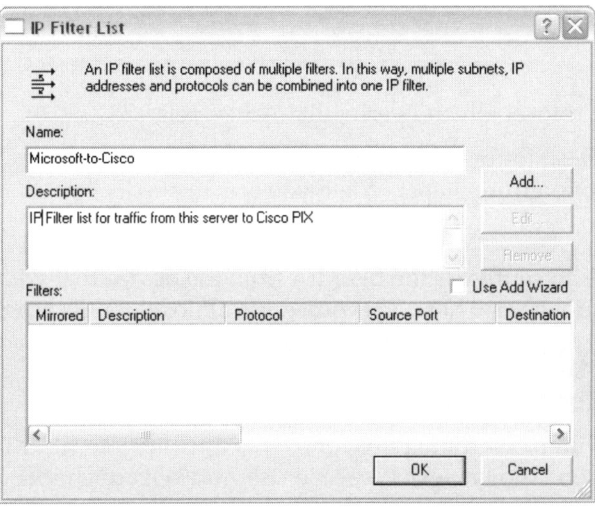

4. In the Filter Properties dialog box, click the Addressing tab. In the Source Address section, select A Specific IP Address and enter the IP address of the server. In the Destination Address section, select A Specific IP Address and enter the IP address of the device you want to communicate with. Finally, clear the Mirrored check box. The following is an example of what the dialog box should look like:

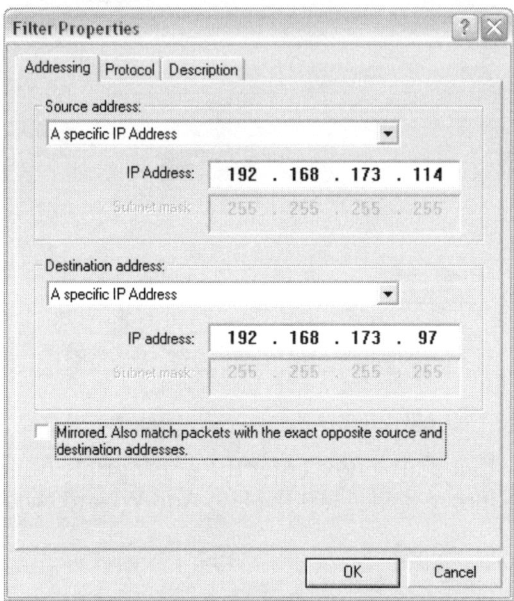

5. Click the Protocol tab and verify that Any is selected.
6. Click the Description tab and enter an appropriate description. You can copy the description from Step 3. When you are finished, click OK and then click OK again.

The next step is to configure the filter list from the device that will be managed to the Microsoft Windows 2000 host. This process is almost identical to the preceding process, with the exception of switching the source and destination addresses:

1. Click Add on the IP Filter List tab.
2. In the IP Filter List dialog box, enter the appropriate filter list name and description, as shown next. Clear the Use Add Wizard check box and click Add.

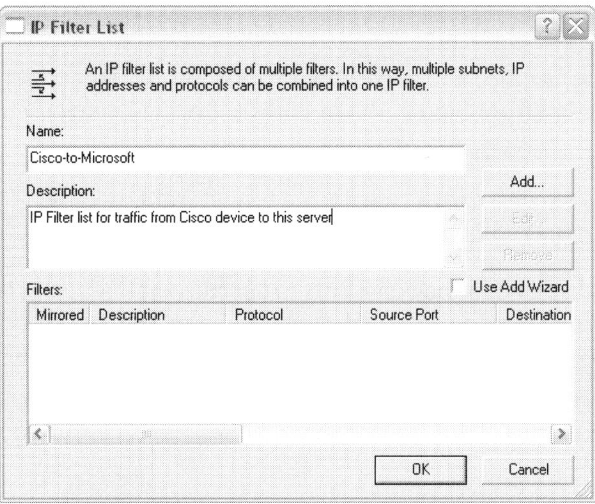

3. In the Filter Properties dialog box, click the Addressing tab. In the Source Address section, select A Specific IP Address and enter the IP address of the device you want to communicate with. In the Destination Address section, select A Specific IP Address and enter the IP address of the server. Finally, clear the Mirrored check box. The following is an example of what the screen should look like:

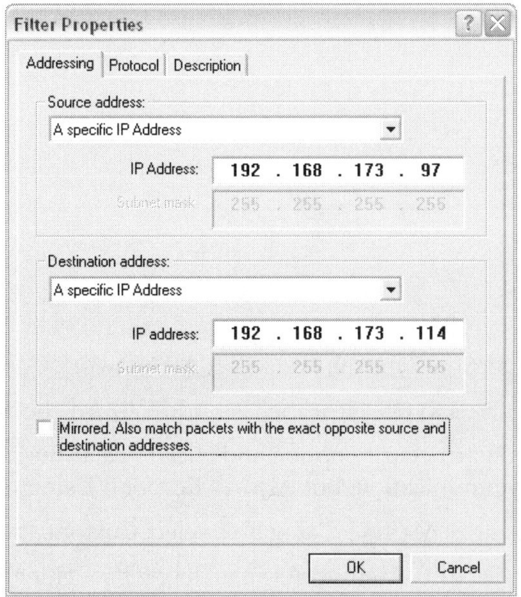

4. Click the Protocol tab and verify that Any is selected.
5. Click the Description tab and enter an appropriate description. You can copy the description from Step 2. When you are finished, click OK and then click OK again.

The next step is to configure a rule for the tunnel from the Microsoft Windows 2000 server to the device that will be managed:

1. You should still be in the New Rule Properties dialog box, with the two new IP filter lists you created displayed on the IP Filter List tab. Select the first filter list that you created (that is, Microsoft-to-Cisco) and click the Tunnel Setting tab.
2. Select the The Tunnel Endpoint Is Specified By This IP Address radio button and then enter the IP address of the remote device, as shown here:

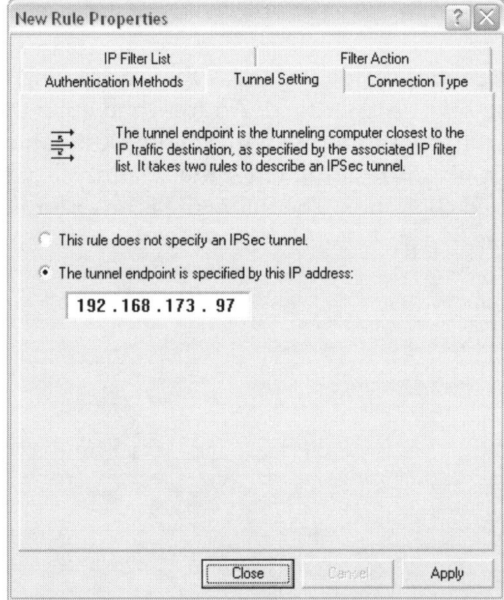

3. Click the Connection Type tab and select All Network Connections.
4. Click the Filter Action tab, clear the Use Add Wizard check box, and click Add.
5. Click the Negotiate Security option and click to clear the setting Accept Unsecured Communication, But Always Respond Using IPSec. Click Add.
6. In the New Security Method dialog box, select Custom and then click Settings.
7. In the Custom Security Method Settings dialog box, enter the appropriate settings under the Data Integrity and Encryption (ESP) section. To achieve the highest level of security, using SHA-1 and 3DES is recommended, since

Microsoft does not support AES at this time. If the remote device will be configured with session key settings, enter them here, as shown next. When you are finished, click OK and then click OK again.

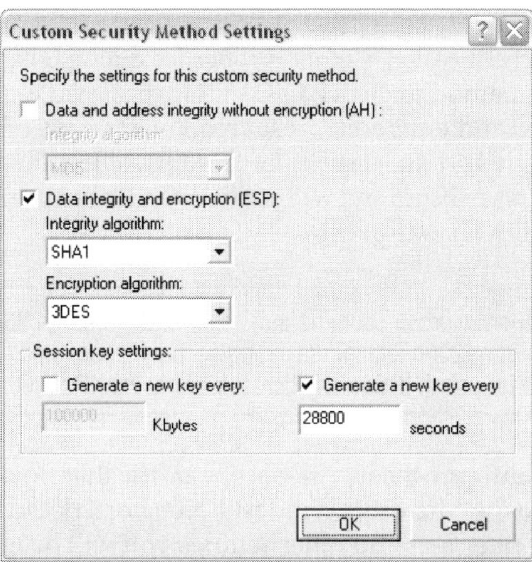

8. In the New Filter Action Properties dialog box, click the General tab and enter the appropriate name and description, as shown next. When you are finished, click OK.

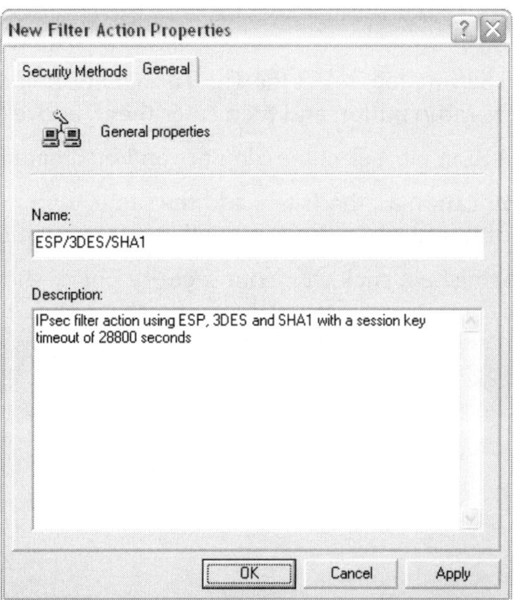

9. On the Filter Action tab of the New Rule Properties dialog box, select the filter action you created.
10. Click the Authentication Methods tab and click Add to add a new authentication method.
11. In the New Authentication Method Properties dialog box, select the appropriate authentication method and click OK. In this case, you would click Add, select preshared keys, and entered a preshared key for ease of implementation. However, you should use certificates in your environment if possible, because certificates are more secure and will scale better. Remove any other authentication methods and click Close.

NOTE See http://support.microsoft.com/default.aspx?scid=kb;en-us;253498 and http://www.microsoft.com/windows2000/techinfo/planning/security/ipsecsteps.asp for information about how to add a certificate for use in IPSec on Microsoft Windows XP, 2000, and 2003 systems.

The last step is to configure a new rule for the traffic that flows from the device that will be managed to the Microsoft Windows 2000 host. Because you have already configured most of the filter lists and other settings you will be using, the process is much shorter:

1. In the Security Policy Properties dialog box, click Add to create a new rule.
2. On the IP Filter List tab of the New Rule Properties dialog box, select the filter list for the traffic from the device that will be managed to the Microsoft Windows 2000 host.
3. On the Tunnel Setting tab, select the The Tunnel Endpoint Is Specified By This IP Address radio button and then enter the IP address of the server.
4. On the Filter Action tab, select the filter action you created.
5. On the Authentication Methods tab, add the same authentication method you previously configured and remove any other authentication methods.
6. When you are finished, click OK. Your security policy should look something like the screen shown next. Click Close to finish creating the new security policy.

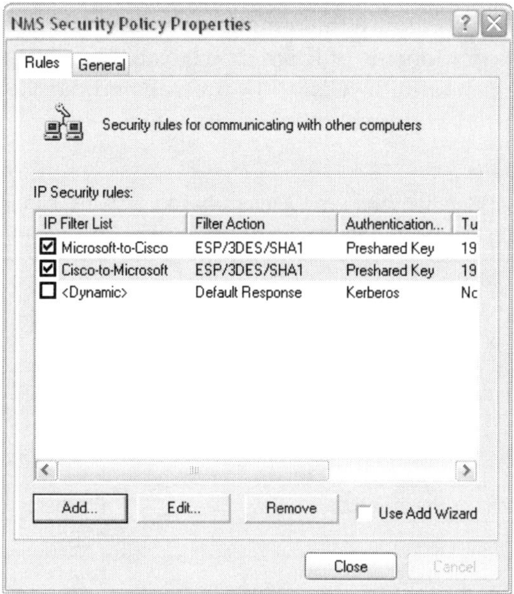

7. The final task is to assign the IPSec security policy that you created. Right-click the security policy and select Assign, as shown here:

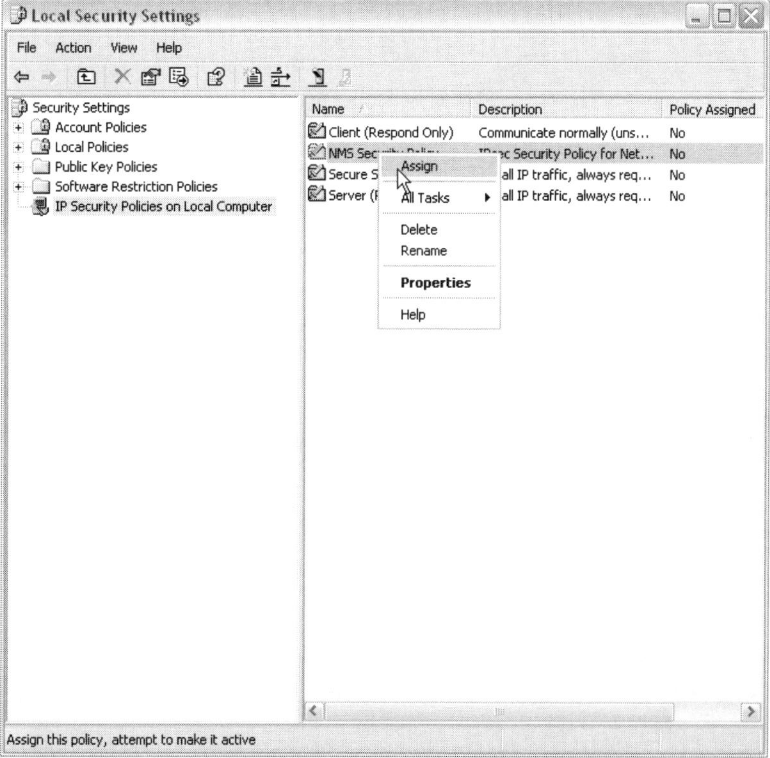

At this point, you can configure the remote host to use IPSec. It is important to make sure the various components of IPSec match exactly on both clients. Table 10-2 shows how the settings on both the Cisco PIX firewall and the Microsoft Windows XP host have been configured in this chapter.

NOTE To configure IPSec between two Windows-based systems, simply repeat these steps on both systems, changing the peer IP addresses accordingly.

	Cisco PIX Firewall	Microsoft Windows Client
Peer settings	192.168.173.114 (Microsoft server)	192.168.173.97 (Cisco PIX)
Transform set/filter action	ESP, 3DES, SHA	ESP, 3DES, SHA
IPSec authentication method	Preshared key	Preshared key
IPSec encryption method	3DES	3DES
IPSec integrity method	SHA1	SHA1
Key lifetime	28,800 seconds	28,800 seconds
Diffie-Hellman group	Group 2	Group 2
IKE encryption method	3DES	3DES
IKE integrity method	SHA1	SHA1

Table 10-2. Matching IPSec Settings

Chapter 11

Hardening Remote Clients

by Eric Seagren

- Select a Method of Remote Access
- Protect the Remote Client
- Protect the Remote Client Data
- Maintain Remote Client Security Policies

Remote clients are any clients used to access network assets from a location that is not controlled and administered by the organization that owns the network assets. The weakest link in an organization's security is often the remote client. This weakness is primarily due to lack of control, because access to the remote clients by technical staff is typically more limited than access to local resources. Additionally, there is the problem of "out of sight, out of mind," which simply means that the staff responsible for hardening the network is going to see the mobile user's laptop much less frequently than any of the systems that stay on the corporate network.

In an effort to ensure that the remote clients are not acting as a doorway for hackers or for other types of inappropriate access, this chapter looks at how to secure the remote clients as thoroughly as possible. At a high level, this means ensuring the confidentiality and integrity of data that the remote client is accessing, and ensuring the physical security of the remote client itself. While the focus of this chapter is to secure the remote client, it also touches upon some of the minimum steps that are needed on the network components, servers, and gateways. It is essential to secure the resources that the remote clients are accessing before they access them; otherwise, all of your efforts to secure the remote client will be in vain. This chapter covers how to physically secure the devices in various environments.

This chapter also describes the steps to ensure the integrity of the OS and other software on the remote client, including an in-depth description of the steps needed to secure the most important component of the remote client, the actual data. Finally, this chapter outlines some steps you can take to enforce all the policies that you have implemented in order to ensure that you keep the remote client secured.

Although the term *remote client* is most commonly used in a business environment to refer to laptop computers, a desktop computer used by an employee from home or from an office location in another city to access applications or data located at work is also a remote client. The real differentiating factor between a "client" and a "remote client" is that the medium used for connectivity is not governed by corporate security policy. While you can and should have policies regarding proper use of various mediums to gain access to corporate assets, you cannot *enforce* secure practices by your ISP, your telecom provider, or the systems that make up the Internet.

The principles behind most of the hardening steps outlined in this chapter apply equally to any type of remote client. This definition of remote client can encompass more than just PCs, though that is the focus of this chapter. Devices such as PDAs and cell phones have increasingly robust connectivity options. These technological breakthroughs make it increasingly difficult to maintain the confidentiality and integrity of data. The most secure option is to not allow access to corporate data from such hard-to-control devices. You will need to weigh factors such as the type of remote client, the data to be protected, your security policy, and your budget.

Select a Method of Remote Access

There are two main approaches to granting remote access. One approach is to use a remote access server to grant access, in which case the remote user has access to the remote access server on the corporate network. The remote access server acts as a *proxy* machine in that it does the actual accessing and processing on behalf of the remote client. The remote client in this case is really only getting screen updates and performing the basic keyboard and mouse input/output on the remote computer—all the real work is being done by the proxy. The second approach is to simply grant the needed access to the remote client directly, typically through some type of VPN software and VPN gateways. In this case, the VPN forms a communication path between the remote client and the corporate network. The real differentiating factor between the two approaches is where the processing takes place and programs are run.

Implement Proxy-Based Remote Access

Remote access via a remote access server is the preferred method of providing remote access. The two most popular examples of remote access servers are Microsoft Terminal Server and Citrix MetaFrame. Other choices are available, such as VNC (Virtual Network Computing) from RealVNC (http://www.realvnc.com/) or even Symantec pcAnywhere (http://www.pcanywhere.com/), both of which are single-user solutions. Citrix MetaFrame and Microsoft Terminal Server allow many users to simultaneously access virtual desktops hosted on a single computer, while pcAnywhere and VNC allow a single user to access and use a single computer remotely. The use of a solution that allows many users to use a single physical machine will usually be more cost effective. If you have a requirement for specialized hardware or software that is not compatible with Microsoft Terminal Server or Citrix MetaFrame, you should implement a VPN solution or, as a last resort, one of the single-user remote access solutions. As always, you should evaluate your specific business needs in order to choose an appropriate technology to implement.

NOTE The current implementation of pcAnywhere uses the crypto API to do symmetric (API V1) or public key (API V2) encryption. VNC encrypts the initial session password, but sends the session data unencrypted. VNC sessions must be encrypted via another means, such as secure shell (SSH). SSH is vulnerable to man-in-the-middle attacks if the attacker has the right connectivity, as are most protocols. The point here is that you must not blindly assume some component of your infrastructure is secure. You need to do your homework and research any piece of hardware or software you are considering using and make sure it really meets your requirements.

The primary advantage of using a remote access server is control. When you want to grant someone access to corporate resources via, say, Citrix MetaFrame, the server administrators will have direct access to the server that is doing all the work, such as accessing the data and running the applications. By contrast, if you grant direct access to resources, via an IPSec tunnel for example, support staff have far less administrative control over the computer being used to do the work—and sometimes no access at all unless the user brings the computer into the office for servicing.

A second advantage of a remote access server solution is simplicity. When you grant access through your Internet-facing firewalls to the remote access server in the DMZ, you can limit the number of ports you must open on the firewall. Citrix MetaFrame, for example, requires inbound access only on TCP port 1494. Depending on how your VPN solution has been implemented, your external firewall could require several ports and protocols to be opened for access. In some cases, using a remote access server solution will be a requirement because an application might require some insecure protocol that is not compatible with your particular VPN solution. By using the remote access server, you generally reduce to one the number of protocols and ports that you need to permit through your *external* firewall.

As you can see in Figures 11-1 and 11-2, a remote access server configuration can almost always be limited to only a single TCP port, while a typical IPSec VPN configuration is a little bit more complex. In any configuration, you only want to allow the *minimum* access through the firewalls that is required for things to work properly.

An additional advantage to using a remote access server is that it *can* entirely eliminate the need for a corporate VPN infrastructure. Your session with the remote access server should be encrypted and the remote access server is generally easily integrated into your current network authentication procedures. This means you can sometimes provide the users with the needed access to corporate resources without needing a separate VPN infrastructure to support it.

If the remote client machine is one that you have little administrative control over, like an employee's personally owned computer, a remote access server solution is

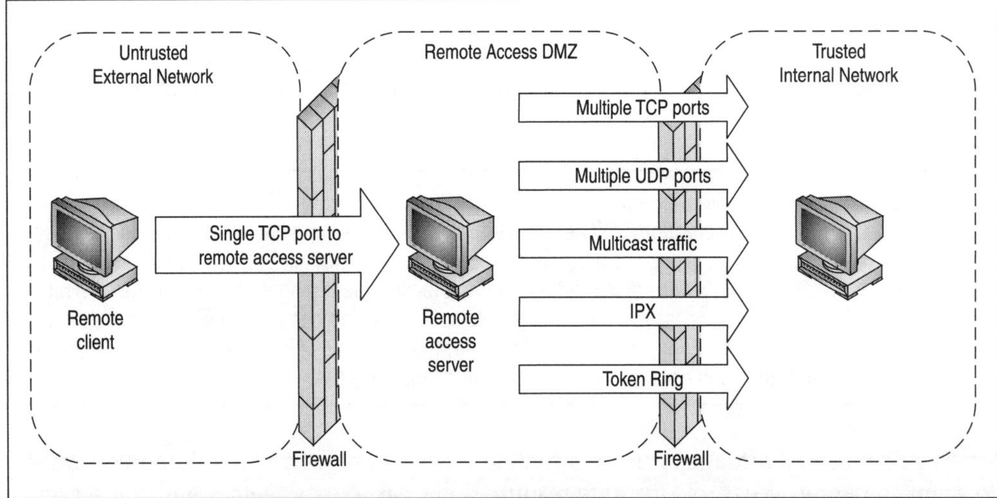

Figure 11-1. Firewall rules for remote access servers

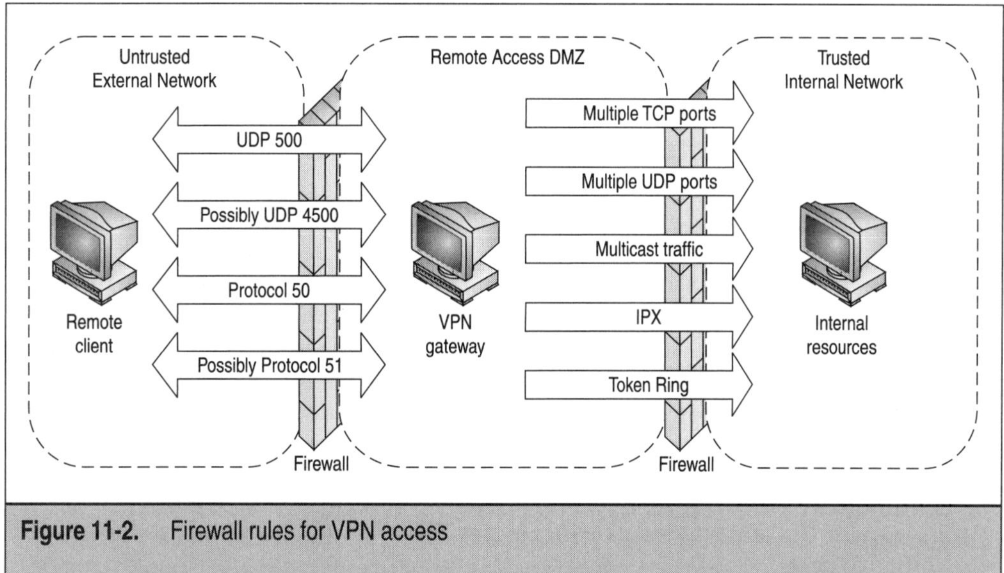

Figure 11-2. Firewall rules for VPN access

relatively easy to have up and running on the client machine. Truth be told, if you have no control over the computer being used to access the resources, the most secure option would be not to allow that computer any access at all to corporate resources. Under these circumstances, you have no way to know whether they are running the latest antivirus software, whether they have any Trojan software on their system, or whether there is a key logger or spyware installed. With many Trojan packages, the unauthorized user can view screen images, which could allow unauthorized access to data even if the client is using a remote access server. If you must provide access for remote clients you have no control over, a remote access server solution provides the least exposure to any malicious activity originating with the remote client. Restricting the traffic to a single port allowed from the remote client makes you more secure.

If a Trojan or virus infects the remote client, unless that malware uses the same port as your remote access server, the ports needed to spread the malware can be blocked at the corporate firewall. Restricting open ports helps insulate you from some viruses and Trojans. Using a remote access server solution keeps more control in the hands of technical support staff than performing the processing on the remote client itself does.

All that being said, a remote access server is not *always* the best answer. One common reason not to use a proxy solution is that it does not work well for all applications. In some cases, the application you want to access remotely does not work on a shared server solution due to the way the software is coded. The most common reason to not use the proxy solution, or at least not to use it exclusively, is that often times the remote user needs access to the data and applications while they are not connected to the corporate network. A good example of this would be so that the user can access an application while on a plane or someplace with no network connections available. You also need to weigh the cost of the hardware for a remote access server against the cost of a VPN infrastructure. Often, a combination of a remote access server and a VPN solution will need to be used, depending on your needs and circumstances.

Harden Proxy-Based Remote Access

If you decide to use a remote access proxy solution, there are many things that you should do to secure the server and, by extension, the clients. By hardening the remote access server, you may be able to alleviate some of the work that is needed to harden the client. For example, if the remote access server is running up-to-date antivirus software, you probably aren't as concerned with the remote client at the other end. This is *not* to say that the remote client should be overlooked, merely that the more you can do at your end, the less critical the far end will be. You can also use the remote access server to enforce remote client policies. For example, if you specify authentication and encryption selections for a connection, the client must meet these requirements before it is granted access:

- Configure your external gateways/firewalls to allow access only to the needed proxy ports.
- Implement IDS.
- Restrict the access privileges the user has to the remote access server.
- Disable mapping to local hard drives from the proxy.
- Keep antivirus signatures and software current on the proxy.
- Maintain patch levels on the proxy device.
- Implement two-factor authentication to the proxy device.
- Ensure that activity logs are being generated and monitored on the proxy device.
- Restrict logon hours based on business need.

Configure Firewalls

You should configure your firewalls to allow only the ports required by your remote access servers and to block all other ports. Allow inbound connections to the required ports to terminate only at the remote access server's IP address. Doing this restricts attackers to being able to target only the remote access servers and only on the appropriate port. As always, the more controlled the access, the better. The firewall rule sets for a remote access server typically are simpler and more straightforward than they would be for VPN access.

Implement a Intrusion Detection System

You need to implement some type of intrusion detection system (IDS). Placement of the IDS is critical. Figure 11-3 separates the different areas for IDS placement into zones. These zones are separated by firewalls. An IDS outside the firewall (zone 1 in the illustration) would be under an almost constant state of attack. An external IDS has no filtering between it and the public Internet. About the only value from having an external IDS is to generate reports for upper management of what attacks are *not* getting into the network.

An IDS on the remote access segment (zone 2) could be configured to show what was getting past the firewall and targeting the remote access servers. It could also show what hostile traffic was originating from the remote access server. Because the source IP address would be specific to the remote access servers, the IDS could differentiate between the two. The firewall between zone 1 and zone 2 would filter out all traffic, except traffic to or from the remote access server, and all ports, except those needed for the remote access server.

An IDS on the inside of the remote access DMZ (zone 3) would see only the malicious traffic that is actually entering your internal network. If any of the traffic seen here is identified as undesired, it should be investigated, because this is your internal network. You should place an IDS in both the remote access DMZ (zone 2) and on the internal network (zone 3) for maximum visibility. For a more in-depth discussion on IDS, refer to Chapter 14.

Restrict Access Privileges to the Remote Access Server

Restrict what the user can do on the remote access server. Remove access to any unneeded programs on the system. To prevent access, either delete the program files or use file-level permissions to remove read and execute access. Removing access via file system permissions is a simple and effective way to control access. You can limit the access on a group basis or on a per-user basis.

You should remove unneeded software from the remote access server. If the software is not needed for the remote clients or for support staff, there really is no reason to leave it sitting around. At best it's just taking up space on the system, and at worst it could

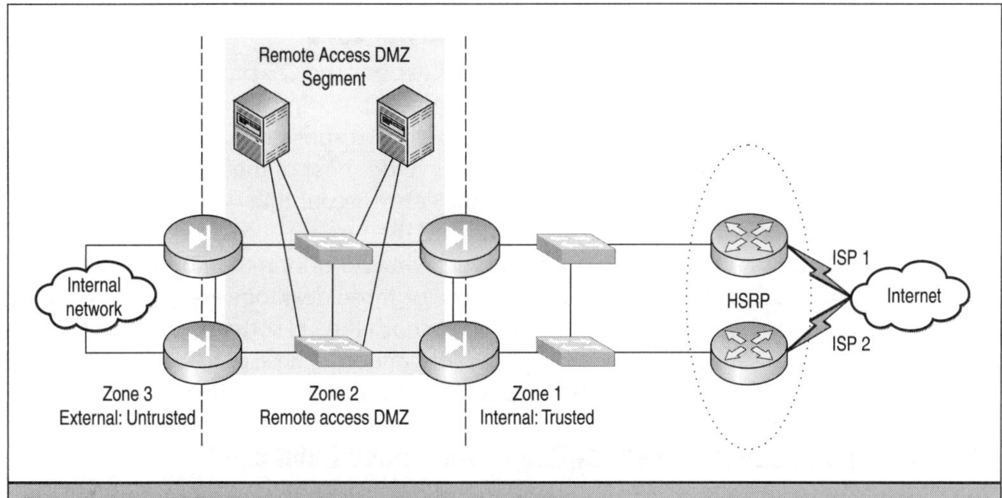

Figure 11-3. IDS placement for remote access servers

have some vulnerability now or in the future that allows privilege escalation or a denial of service (DoS) attack.

As a last option, you could use special program-execution software to limit what programs the user can run. You should allow only the minimum required access to directories on the remote access server as well. There simply is no need for a nonadministrative user to have access to some system directories. Do not allow nonadministrator remote access clients to reboot the server or install drivers for new hardware.

Disable Mapping to Local Hard Drives from the Remote Access Server

In most cases, the remote access server will allow the client's local hard drive to appear as a drive letter on the remote client's virtual desktop. This allows the user to use the remote access server's encrypted session to transfer files securely to the user's local computer. Unless the user needs this ability, it should not be implemented. Disabling drive mapping allows you to keep the data on the remote access server, where you have more control over it. Once you allow files to leave the remote access server, you lose virtually all the control over that data that you might have otherwise had.

Keep Antivirus Signatures and Software Current on the Proxy

Because the remote access server is going to be the doorway for users to come into your network, protect client computers by keeping the remote access server's antivirus software rigorously maintained. Also, because a lot of files will be accessed from the remote access server, that server constitutes a good focal point at which to ensure that the files the users are accessing are being inspected by antivirus software on a regular basis. Your remote access servers could be one of the first places to detect and control a virus infection.

Maintain Patch Levels on the Remote Access Servers

The remote access server simplifies the task of keeping the OS patched and current. From the perspective of the applications being accessed, patching a single machine keeps multiple users patched and current simultaneously. Suppose all members of your accounting department use a remote access server to do most of their work, remote or otherwise. If the new software package used by the entire accounting department requires the latest Internet Explorer service pack, updating the remote access server will let everyone use the new software. This can be a much simpler option than updating a large number of individual desktops, especially if some of those desktops are remote clients.

Be sure to monitor and maintain patch levels on both the OS software and the remote access software because they may be from different vendors. These patches and updates will address security issues as the vendors can analyze and address them.

Implement Two-Factor Authentication to the Proxy Device

You should generally implement two-factor authentication for the remote access servers. Which two factors you choose may be based on cost, convenience, and other factors, but you should always use two-factor authentication, such as an RSA SecureID token combined with a username/password. For more information, go to http://www.rsasecurity.com/node.asp?id=1157.

Ensure that Activity Logs Are Being Generated and Monitored on the Proxy Device

Log monitoring is one of the areas in which a shared remote access solution can shine. Having all the access funneled through a single remote access server, or a small number of them, allows you to more easily monitor all the log files. You should be monitoring and reviewing log files from the OS, any application-based log files, and the log files generated from any security software you are running on the remote access servers. With multiple users being serviced by a small number of servers that are generating the log files, the task of compiling the logs and correlating any events should be much easier. For example, if you see the same small range of ports scanned on all of your remote access servers, you have very strong evidence that someone is intentionally snooping around looking for vulnerabilities. The same trend might be harder to spot if the activity were spread across a large number of computers hosting many different services.

Restrict Logon Hours Based on Business Need

You can configure the user accounts to allow a logon only during business hours, or during the expected work hours of a given user. This prevents the machine from being broken into or used during off hours, even if an attacker obtained legitimate logon credentials. If you can implement restricted logon hours, this can greatly reduce the window of exposure for those accounts and the damage that compromising the remote client can do.

Secure Direct Remote Access

If a remote access server solution doesn't fit, you need to implement a direct method using a VPN. You should never allow remote clients to access internal resources directly without using a VPN to protect the traffic. Accessing resources via a VPN will likely involve a slightly more complex firewall rule set than what is required for a remote access server solution. Potential port/protocol considerations for an IPSec VPN are the base UDP port 500, protocol 50 (ESP) or protocol 51 (AH), and possibly UDP 4500 for Network Address Translation (NAT) traversal. The most common reason to implement a direct remote access solution is that the user needs access to resources while not connected to the corporate network. With a direct solution, the application runs on the remote client and the data is likely located on the remote client, allowing the user to work on their data while almost anywhere. This scenario is not limited to a mobile user and a laptop; it could easily include a small remote office that doesn't have local server resources or support staff. You could also have a tiered application, whereby a client application runs on the remote client and accesses data on a trusted network. Although a tiered application could be accessed via a remote access server, in some situations it could also be accessed via a VPN very cleanly and securely.

NOTE Most of the hardening steps discussed in this chapter will apply to a proxy-based solution or a VPN solution.

With a direct remote access solution, you are basically letting a remote client machine speak directly with internal hosts. The remote client might authenticate at a VPN gateway, but the point is that the remote client is doing the processing against data on the corporate network.

The client host will be running applications that need to be secured as well as processing and possibly storing data that needs to be secured. The considerations for hardening a client who is using a VPN for direct access will be different than the considerations for hardening a client who is using a remote access server.

If you elect to use a direct access method for remote access, you need to use encryption for all traffic between the remote client and the corporate network. You don't want to allow application usernames and passwords to travel unencrypted between the remote access client and the trusted resource. One approach is to choose a VPN solution, such as IPSec. Numerous VPN options are available, some of which are discussed in detail in Chapter 10. If you decide to implement a direct remote access solution, these are the minimum steps you should take before granting access:

- Configure your external gateways/firewalls to allow access only to the ports and protocols needed for the VPN.
- Ensure that activity logs are being generated and monitored on the VPN gateway.
- Require two-factor authentication to the VPN gateway where possible.
- Deploy an IDS on the inside of the VPN gateways to identify any suspicious activity from remote clients.
- Restrict the hours during which remote clients can access the corporate network, based on job responsibilities.

As you can see, the hardening steps are similar whether they are for a client using a direct VPN access method or for a client using a remote access server. These measures must be in place before you can tackle the task of hardening the remote client itself. If you do not take the basic steps just outlined, you should not allow any remote clients access to your network. The primary difference between a direct remote access method and a proxy-based method will be in the firewall configuration and decentralized application log monitoring. Logs may not be on just a single central remote access server. You should regularly monitor and report on the logs you have available.

Protect the Remote Client

Securing the server side of remote access and securing data communications are important parts of client security. However, you also need to do a lot of work to harden the client itself. There are several steps to be taken to harden the remote client:

- Harden physical security
- Control logical access
- Implement personal firewalls
- Control program execution
- Ensure software integrity

The OS is the foundation on which the system is built. It must be hardened against DoS attacks and privilege-escalation attacks. You want to ensure software integrity so that a malicious user cannot plant a Trojan or tamper with configuration files or log files. Finally, controlling program execution helps to make it harder for the system to be altered from the desired configuration, either intentionally or unintentionally.

Harden Physical Security

The primary consideration for physical security is preventing theft. A full-sized desktop computer used at an employee's home is typically at low risk of being stolen, whereas portable computers are generally favorite targets for theft. A portable computer's primary selling point is that it is portable; unfortunately, this is also its biggest hurdle when it comes to physical security.

Implement Locking Mechanisms

The laptop's small size makes it a prime candidate for being stolen or even just lost. The simplest protection against this risk is to implement one of the various forms of locking mechanisms. These most often work similarly to a bicycle lock, with a mechanism that can be cabled to something immobile and inserted into a hole in the laptop case and secured. While not as strong as most bicycle locks, they at least make stealing the laptop quickly or quietly more difficult. These locks should be used in the office, on the road, and even at home if there is any risk that the laptop might be stolen. Locks are inexpensive and relatively convenient (unless you relocate the laptop frequently). Don't forget that the locking mechanisms really only address the physical security of the remote client computer itself. If your primary concern is the *data* on the client, the hard drive could be removed from the host machine relatively simply and easily. Steps to secure the data are addressed later in this chapter.

Implement Alarm Mechanisms

Alarms are good security mechanisms when traveling. Using a two-part audio alarm is recommended. Two-part audio alarms have one part that is similar to a car alarm button and fits on your key ring. The other part varies in form but is meant to be attached to the laptop. If the two components are separated by more than a set distance, the laptop component sounds an audible alarm. The distance is typically configurable and the alarm can usually be disabled remotely if desired. An example of this type of alarm, TrackIt, can be found at http://www.trackitcorp.com.

Another good solution is an alarm that is triggered by motion. The sensitivity of the motion sensor can be adjusted. The motion sensor is attached to the laptop and triggers an alarm when the laptop is moved. The ability to know when the laptop has been moved is reassuring, and it makes it more difficult for someone to attempt to locate and remove the alarm itself. A well-known maker of the motion alarms, Targus, can be found at http://www.targus.com/us/product_details.asp?sku=PA400U.

Another device, the Caveo Anti-Theft PC Card (http://www.caveo.com/), is similar to the Targus DEFCOM 1 motion sensor. The Anti-Theft PC Card acts as a motion-sensing alarm and encrypts the contents of the hard drive when it is installed. After installation, it decrypts the data as it is accessed. You can configure the alarm either to trigger if the laptop is moved, to trigger if the device is moved outside a designated area, or both. If the device is removed, the entire hard drive contents will be encrypted and unreadable by unauthorized parties. The Anti-Theft PC Card effectively acts as a hardware key to decrypt the contents of the hard drive.

Implement a Physical Security Policy

As always, the technical solutions that you use to make sure that a laptop stays where it is supposed to should be accompanied by a policy that addresses the subject. Your remote access policy should require signoff from anyone who will be accessing company resources remotely. It should specify that the laptop cannot be left unattended, that a motion-sensing alarm must be in place at all times, and that any patches and updates provided by the resource owner must be applied in a timely manner. The policy should distinguish between requirements for laptops and requirements for desktops. Failure to comply with the policy should have consequences that are well defined and have management support.

Control Logical Access

With the machine physically secure, the next step is to control logical access. All remote clients should require authentication to gain access.

Passwords for the local account should be secure and should conform to the password requirements of the corporate security policy. The account used for remote access should not have administrative access to the machine if at all possible. On any of the current versions of major operating systems, this is generally avoidable because you can have programs run in the security context of another user when the application requires escalated privileges. For remote users to have access to sensitive corporate resources, you should require them to reauthenticate via an authentication server on the trusted network, such as a Windows domain server. These credentials should not have the same username or password as the remote client's local authentication account.

The following are some steps you can take to control logical access. Begin with the low-level controls that are easy to implement, such as a BIOS password, and work your way through the available options:

1. Enable a BIOS password.
2. Rename the administrator account.
3. Disable the guest account.
4. Configure the system to lock the screen if left unattended.
5. Clear the name of the last logged-in user.
6. Restrict boot devices in BIOS.
7. Disable autorun for CD-ROMs.
8. Use local policies to clear the swap file and disable the crash dump file.
9. Secure local account passwords.

Enable a BIOS Password

The first step in controlling logical access is to enable a BIOS password. While a BIOS password generally is not terribly hard to bypass, it will stop the casual thief who isn't technically savvy. Although the specific menu varies, typically, once you enter the BIOS configuration menu, you will be able to access a security options submenu in which you can enter a password that will be required before the computer can boot. The procedure to bypass this password generally is not complex but often requires taking the laptop apart to remove a battery or toggle an internal switch. Because an intruder cannot easily take apart the laptop without being noticed, he would likely have to physically take the laptop, which you can prevent by locking the laptop in place.

Rename Administrator Account

You should rename the administrator account. This will stop a lot of the "script kiddies" that attempt to do various manipulations against the administrator account. A lot of these programs have the administrator account name hard coded internally. This means it will only look for an account named Administrator, and will not attack any other account. It's a simple change that can go a long way toward stopping malicious activities.

Disable the Guest Account

You should disable the guest account, which is almost never needed and only serves to provide another way for an attacker to gain access to the system. Since this account generally is not used by any legitimate users, it is often overlooked when permissions and passwords are being audited and secured. There are very few circumstances in which the guest account is truly needed, so best practice is to disable it.

Configure the System to Lock the Screen If Left Unattended

Systems should always have a password-protected screen saver so that if the machine is accidentally left unattended it will revert to a secured state. You should set the screen to lock after a short period of inactivity. Although you will have to evaluate your needs, 10 or 15 minutes is a common setting.

A known tactic is to simply wait until the authorized user leaves their workstation and then grab a seat and impersonate them on the system. The unauthorized user could now access systems data as the authorized user. Although policy should state that machines are to never be left logged in and unattended without the screen locked, this setting will help for those times the user forgets to lock the screen.

Clear the Name of Last Logged-In User

A Windows computer should also be configured not to display the username of the last person who logged on. This only serves to give a hacker one more piece of information he wouldn't otherwise have. If he knows the account name, he has enough to begin trying to brute force the password. While removing this bit of free information doesn't make you impervious, it brings you one step closer to being as secure as possible. For Mac OS X, you must not use automatic logon, and you should check the option Display Logon Window As: Name and Password Entry Fields. A Linux or Unix system should not display the last logged-in user by default.

Restrict Boot Devices in BIOS

You need to disable the ability to boot from any device other than the hard drive. There are many different bootable Linux distributions that allow you to boot off the CD-ROM, a floppy disk, or even a USB drive, and have a complete OS available to you. From this Linux OS, you can mount and access the local hard drive, allowing you to bypass all the OS-level controls that were in place and read and edit the files directly unless you have enabled some form of encryption.

Disable Autorun on the CD-ROM

The autorun feature should be disabled on any CD-ROMs or other removable media. If not disabled, this feature allows programs to start and run without any user intervention beyond popping it in the CD-ROM drive. Suppose an unsuspecting user finds waiting on their desk a CD-ROM labeled "great new game" and proceeds to put it in their machine, thinking that a friend has left it. The CD-ROM automatically starts and runs, installing a Trojan but also kicking off an instance of some game to make the user think it is legitimate. The user never "installed" anything as far as they knew, and everything looks normal from the user's perspective.

Clear the Swap File and Disable the Crash Dump File

Both the crash dump file and the Windows swap file can be sources of information for someone who is looking hard enough. If the data on the client is sensitive or valuable, you should use local settings to disable the creation of a dump file. If a machine is not working properly, the dump file can always be enabled to investigate further. Although the contents of dump files are rarely used to troubleshoot system errors, they are often configured. Since dump files can contain everything that was in memory at the time of a system crash, this could conceivably include a lot of sensitive data. The Windows swap file presents a similar exposure. Though some software such as Pretty Good Privacy is supposed to be coded to prevent the secured data from ever being written to the swap file, good policy is to clear it on shutdown.

You can configure the swap file to be cleared on shutdown via local policies as follows (in this example, on a Windows 2000 Professional machine):

1. Go to Control Panel and select Local Security Settings.
2. Expand Local Policies | Security Options in the left pane.

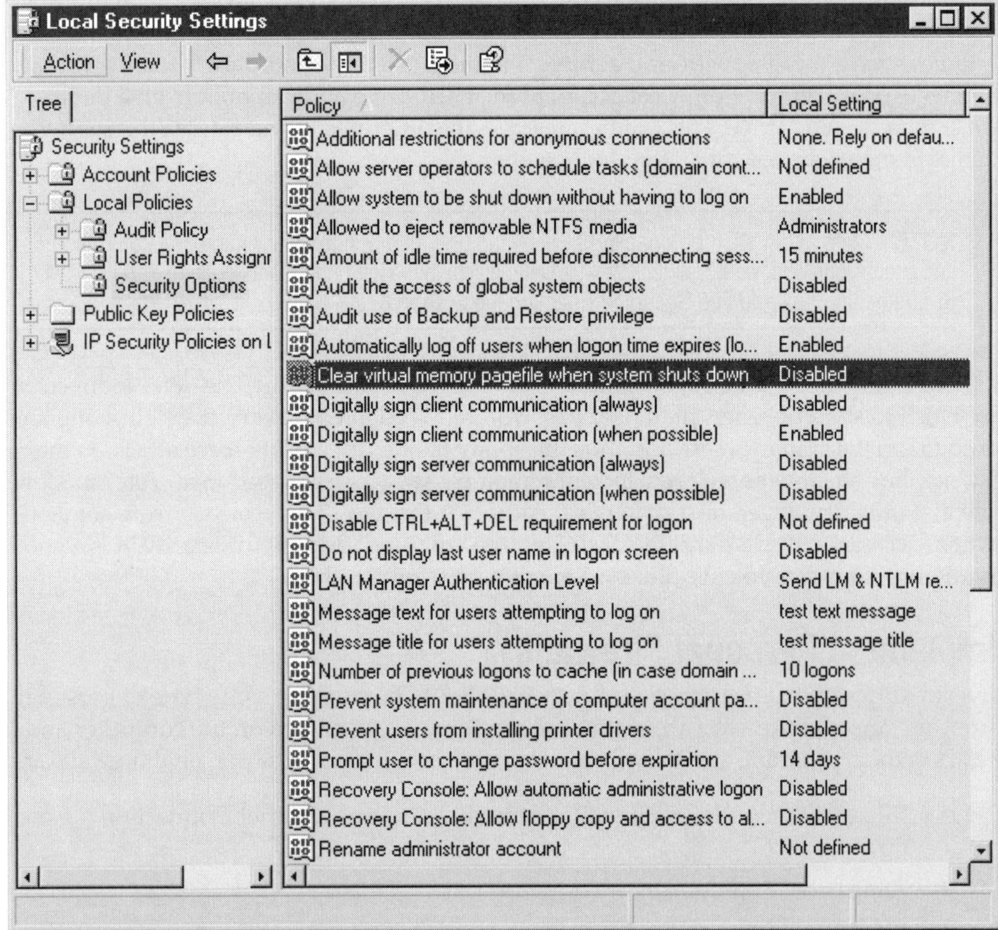

3. Double-click Clear Virtual Memory Pagefile When System Shuts Down in the right pane, and then check Enable.

Use a similar process to configure the following recommended policy settings as well:

- Do not display last user name in login screen
- Message text for users attempting to log on
- Message title for users attempting to log on

Secure Local Account Passwords

Invariably, you will need to have local accounts on the remote client, at the minimum an administrator or root account. Most OSs have steps that you can take to further protect the local accounts beyond the default settings. Where available, you should implement these steps. With Windows, hashes of the account passwords are stored in the Security Accounts Manager (SAM). You can use the windows system key (syskey.exe) utility to encrypt the hashes. This will prevent brute-force attacks against the password hash. Utilities such as ntpassdw (found at http://home.eunet.no/~pnordahl/ntpasswd/) can still be used if you have physical access to the hard drive and can boot from a device other than the hard drive. This utility can access the disk directly and rewrite the password *hashes* to match a password of your choosing.

NOTE More information on enabling syskey can be found at http://www.microsoft.com/resources/documentation/Windows/XP/all/reskit/en-us/Default.asp. In the left-hand menu, choose Part III | Ch 17 | Strengthening Key and File Security | Enabling the Startup Key.

For Linux distributions, you should enable shadow passwords. The default directory in which to store the encrypted user passwords is readable by every user, allowing any account on the system access and thus the ability to attempt a brute-force attack on them. By enabling shadow passwords, the encrypted passwords are placed in an /etc/shadow file that only privileged users can read. Although this won't protect you from someone who is accessing the disk and bypassing your configured file system security, it is a good hardening step that you should implement wherever possible.

Implement Personal Firewalls

Every computer that has access to a network should be running some type of personal firewall. Personal firewalls are software-based firewalls that run on the computer and restrict which programs can talk to the network. The most popular personal firewalls are

- Microsoft's Windows Firewall, formerly known as Internet Connection Firewall (ICF)
- Zone Labs' ZoneAlarm
- Black Ice Software's BlackICE PC Protection Firewall
- iptables/netfilter

Microsoft Windows Firewall

Windows Firewall, also known as ICF in previous versions of Windows, is built into Windows XP, so there is no need to download or install anything. It can be managed and configured via Windows policies and allows you to control what applications are allowed to act as servers on that machine.

To enable WFW, follow these steps:

1. Open Control Panel.
2. Open Network Connections.
3. Right-click the network connection you want to enable WFW for and select Properties.
4. On the Advanced tab, check the "Protect my computer and network…" check box.

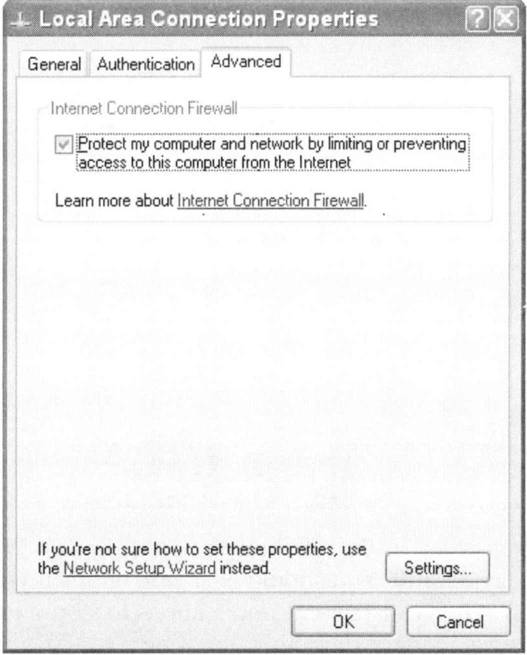

After you complete these steps, if you need to allow inbound connections for various services, you can click the Settings button on the same tab to open the Advanced Settings dialog box. From there you can configure the services that you wish to allow to use that network connection (see Figure 11-4).

Some service definitions are preconfigured. Checking the Web Server (HTTP) option allows the computer to act as an HTTP server on that Internet connection.

Figure 11-4. Enable inbound HTTP within ICF

HEADS UP!

Windows XP ICF is disabled by default through Service Pack 1. Windows XP Service Pack 2 enables ICF by default. You should be aware of this if you plan to roll out SP2 or you if find that ICF causes some applications to stop working properly. If you script or otherwise manage deployments using a configuration file, you can specify whether SP2 turns on the firewall. SP2 also introduces more control over XP's settings via Group Policy, and Group Policy may be used to ensure that laptops are not firewalled while on the corporate network but are firewalled when they cannot authenticate to a domain controller. This means you can have the laptop enable WFW when the computer is not logged into the domain.

Windows Firewall allows inbound traffic only for two reasons:

- If it is in response to a previous outbound request
- If it has been specifically allowed inbound via the procedure just outlined

Windows Firewall does not restrict which programs can talk outbound on your computer. For example, if you enable WFW but do not configure any specific services via the Advanced Settings dialog box, that machine can still go out to the Internet and view web pages. If the remote client is a corporate-owned asset, it should not have *any* services configured in ICF unless there is an approved business need to do so. If the machine is a personally owned computer, it may not be possible to disable any services hosted on the client, though it would be desirable not to have any server processes running if possible. On the Security Logging tab of the Advanced Settings dialog box, you should select both check boxes, Log Dropped Packets and Log Successful Connections. You should change the path of the log file to a directory that only the administrator has access to.

ZoneAlarm Personal Firewall

ZoneAlarm, from Zone Labs (http://www.zonelabs.com/store/content/home.jsp), is an effective way to control all network communications on a Windows computer. Zone Labs offers a free version for private use, and a version with more features for a fee. ZoneAlarm, in its default configuration, prompts you each time a program attempts to access the network. You then have the option to grant access or deny access for that one request, or you can grant or deny access to that program from that point forward. The latter selection enables you to configure ZoneAlarm just once, for example, to allow Internet Explorer to access the Internet, and it won't ask you each time you start Internet Explorer. ZoneAlarm also creates a checksum of the executable so that if a program has the same name as another program on the list, ZoneAlarm treats it as a new program and prompts you to permit or deny access.

ZoneAlarm can protect you from unwanted network communication, both inbound and outbound. Because ZoneAlarm operates off a list of applications that you have designated as either allowed or disallowed (a *whitelist*), if a Trojan were installed on your computer, ZoneAlarm would prompt you for approval when the Trojan attempted to go out on the Internet and speak with the master computer or otherwise receive instructions.

Various default security levels are available, which range from offering little protection, to offering very good protection but also requiring a steep learning curve for the ZoneAlarm users. You need to carefully evaluate the user's skill level and choose ZoneAlarm security settings that are appropriate. Although ZoneAlarm can provide very robust protection, using it effectively requires careful planning and user education.

You can also configure ZoneAlarm to create a log file of program access attempts. Logging should be enabled. Any locally stored log files should be placed in a directory that only the administrator has access to. If you are using the enterprise version of the software, you can log to a central logging repository.

BlackICE PC Protection Firewall

BlackICE PC Protection Firewall is very similar to ZoneAlarm in functionality and is also a Windows-only product. Although BlackICE is no longer available for free, it does include more robust logging options than ZoneAlarm does. One such option is Intrusion Logging, which captures the entire packet if the system detects suspicious activity. As always, the user on the system should not have access to change or delete the log files the personal firewall creates. Most of your view into the state of a remote client will be from locally generated log files. The client will not always be connected to the corporate network when significant log entries are generated. Because of this, you need to implement some method of retrieving and auditing these local log files periodically. You could, for instance, send a copy of the remote log files to a central logging server as part of the remote client's login script.

iptables

For Linux systems, you should implement iptables/netfilter for personal firewall functionality. Previous versions were called ipchains and ipfwadm before that. Newer distributions refer to the package as iptables or netfilter interchangeably.

iptables is built into most current Linux distributions. It allows you to set up various rules to control the flow of network traffic into and out of the box. Setting up and configuring iptables is beyond the scope of this book. If you are interested in doing so, a good resource is *Hardening Linux* (Osborne/McGraw-Hill, 2004). There are also innumerable web sites offering step-by-step instruction and automated hardening scripts available online, one of the most well known of which is Bastille Linux. Bastille Linux is an automated script that prompts the user for confirmation of each step as it changes default settings to make the system more secure. The script is designed to lock down a default install of Unix or Linux and supports a variety of distributions.

You could add the following lines to the iptables configuration file to do some basic filtering:

```
iptables -P INPUT DROP
iptables -P OUTPUT ACCEPT
iptables -P FORWARD ACCEPT
iptables -A INPUT -i eth0 -m state --state ESTABLISHED, RELATED -j
ACCEPT
```

Assuming that eth0 is your externally facing interface, these rules specify the following, respectively:

- Set the default action for inbound traffic to DROP.
- Set the default action for outbound traffic to ACCEPT.
- Set the default action for forwarded traffic to ACCEPT.
- Add a rule for inbound traffic that says to allow it if the traffic is part of an existing connection.

This configuration would function the same as the default behavior of Windows Firewall.

Control Program Execution

Controlling which programs can use the network is a good step toward maintaining a secure remote client. To raise the security of the system to the next level, you should control *all* program execution on the client, not just program access to the network. If the machine is a corporate-owned resource, you should restrict which programs can be run on the machine. By controlling program execution, you can remove or limit the user's ability to install resource-wasting applications such as games or stock trading software. You will also hinder the spread of some virus or Trojan software. If the user can't install the latest patch or update before your testing lab has approved it, it also could save you on downtime and productivity loss. To some degree, you can control program execution via Windows policies. You can also get specialized software that can control program execution.

There are two approaches to controlling program execution:

- **Blacklist** All programs can be run except those that are specifically restricted. The list of restricted items is the blacklist. Most of the available software for program execution control works on the blacklist principle.
- **Whitelist** The opposite of the blacklist approach; no program can be run unless it is approved (included on the whitelist).

Both approaches can be effective, but the blacklist approach blocks only the software that you have identified. A whitelist approach blocks software you are not aware of, so it does a more thorough job of stopping software execution. Although a blacklist stops only the software that you have specifically chosen, it has less potential to accidentally block legitimate applications. A whitelist approach is much more difficult to configure initially. You run into the standard trade-off of administrative overhead versus the levels of protection.

SecureWave's Sanctuary includes the Application Control component. It is available for Windows NT, Windows XP, Windows 2000, and Windows Server 2003. The Application Control component uses the whitelist approach. This means that even if a Trojan horse is downloaded onto the protected computer, it cannot execute. Similarly, if users attempt to run a game from CD-ROM, the setup program and the game itself cannot be run. All software that is allowed has an SHA-1 hash generated to make sure the software hasn't changed from what was approved. This means a virus or worm that tampers with a file will not be able to use that file as a vehicle to execute itself.

SecureWave Sanctuary has two versions, a Desktop version and a custom version. The Desktop version allows the whitelist to be distributed and applied globally to any workstations you choose. The policy must be applied for all machines. If you wish to have very granular control and apply the whitelist by user, group, or workstation, you need the custom version. You can get more information about Sanctuary Application Control at http://www.securewave.com/turcana/securewave/sanctuary_ACD.jsp.

At a minimum, you should use Windows policies and file-level access restrictions to ensure that nonadministrative users cannot run such things as registry editors and other administrative tools. File-level access restriction allows you to remove access for any and all directories that contain system configuration utilities, system security logs, or other administrative tools. While a blacklist approach is much simpler to manage, its primary use is to prevent execution of applications that will waste corporate resources, such as games and file-sharing software. The whitelist approach requires more administration and management, but prevents anything from running except what you think the remote client needs to be running. If you require absolute program control, you should use a whitelist approach.

Similar program execution control can be found in FoolProof Delux from Horizon DataSys, which runs on Windows or Macintosh. It is not as granular in its control but does support Macintosh, whereas the SecureWave product does not. Details on the product can be found at http://www.horizondatasys.com/foolproofsoftware/index.html.

Ensure Software Integrity

Once you have all the software on the remote client running and configured securely, you want to make sure it doesn't change. In the case of a whitelist approach, a change to any software will result in that program no longer running. This ensures security, but it is not always desired, due to the downtime or overhead involved. In some cases, you may just want to be informed of any changes to the system. This information should be reported centrally so that the appropriate parties can be alerted that the software has been altered. Getting information, such as log files, off of the remote client and to the appropriate groups is a common obstacle.

A reoccurring theme is that you need to collect data to judge how effective your control measures are. Though not foolproof, a scheduled script that periodically checks for network connectivity and attempts to offload the log files is a simple and relatively effective method. Additionally, your policy should specify scheduled times at which remote users must bring corporate-owned computers into work so that support staff can perform routine maintenance on them. If bringing in the computer isn't practical due to distance or other factors, you should look into some type of remote cleanup and maintenance process.

ONE STEP FURTHER

Tripwire from Tripwire Inc. (www.tripwire.com) is the de facto standard for integrity monitoring. Tripwire runs on Windows, Linux, and several other OSs. It allows you to specify what should be monitored for changes, and it will report those changes through several different means. It can send logs to a syslog server, generate reports from a Tripwire server, or even send e-mails alerting staff of what changes have been made. It has a flexible configuration that allows you to monitor only what you wish to. Tripwire is generally reserved for use on servers and other mission-critical hosts. If the data and integrity of the remote client is critical, you should consider using a product such as Tripwire.

This routine maintenance should include applying any patches, loading and auditing log files, removing inappropriate files, and performing general system cleanup. Controlling program execution offers the highest level of application control. The next best thing to controlling execution is to at least monitor software integrity.

Protect the Remote Client Data

Once you have the client secured physically and the software access controlled, the next step is to address the critical issue of securing the data on the remote client. This data is typically of more value to a company than the physical asset. The best way to secure the data is to not allow it onto the remote client in the first place and to use a remote access server for accessing company resources. If that isn't possible, though, you want to make sure that the data is safe on the remote client.

Secure remote data by using encryption and by controlling hardware and software access and usage. Because corporate data is often sensitive and important, encryption of data, in storage and during transport, is a necessity. Having control over the hardware enables you to restrict which hardware devices can be used to move or transport data off of the computer system the user is using. Likewise, you must manage the use of required software.

Protect the Data Using Encryption

Encryption is performed either at the device level, where the entire drive is encrypted, or at the file level. File-level encryption is not as secure as encrypting the whole hard drive, but as always, any protection is better than none. You should use a well-tested and documented encryption algorithm. Advanced Encryption Standard (AES) is currently considered the most secure encryption method, and Triple Data Encryption Standard (3DES) is the minimum level of encryption that you should use for any data of importance. The trade-off for encryption is slower performance. The calculations that must be made to encrypt or decrypt data exact a toll on your CPU. As a general rule, the more secure the encryption algorithm, the more CPU intensive it tends to be. Symmetric algorithms, in which the key used to encrypt the data is the same as the one used to decrypt the data, are typically less taxing on the CPU than asymmetric algorithms. Exactly how great the CPU impact of encryption will be is difficult to say, due to the number of variables involved. The most important factor is the CPU horsepower you have to put behind all that number crunching. On an outdated CPU, modern encryption algorithms will likely bring the system to a crawl, while a high-end system won't likely be impacted in any significant way. As an example, on a 650-MHz Pentium 3 machine with 256MB of RAM, 3DES can reduce the network throughput by as much as 65 percent. You should always test a product or solution thoroughly in the lab before implementing it on a large scale.

Stronger encryption is not *always* the best choice. You should weigh the performance cost of encryption with the value of the information you are encrypting. For example, barring special circumstances, it probably isn't efficient for most people to use Advanced Encryption Standard (AES) encryption to encrypt a grocery list. If it were a list of customer account numbers and access codes, however, you would want to make the data as secure as possible. To maintain data confidentiality, you should secure the entire system appropriately for the most secure piece of data that may be on the system. More simply, this means that the hardening steps for the entire system should be appropriate for the most sensitive component of the system.

HEADS UP!

Key escrow refers to entrusting a third party to hold a key that will decrypt the data. By having an additional decryption, you are ensuring the encrypted data won't be lost if the original key is lost. By having a third party hold it, you ensure that it will not be used without proper justification and need. You should not implement *any* form of encryption without ensuring that the encrypted data can be recovered. Authorized parties should be able to decrypt the data without user intervention. If you implement encryption without a good key-escrow or key-management methodology in place, you are far more likely to lose data through a forgotten password or terminated employee than through data theft.

Device-Level Encryption

Encrypting the entire hard drive and all data it contains is the most secure method by far. With good encryption on the entire drive, a would-be data thief cannot simply boot to another OS and access the data directly. He cannot bypass the OS and software that you so carefully hardened. If the entire drive is encrypted, you alleviate many ways that data can find its way into unauthorized hands. Encryption should be 3DES at a minimum, preferably with two-factor authentication, such as a hardware key and password.

Under no circumstances should you employ an encryption methodology without having a system in place to recover the data. Your chosen encryption method should allow for some type of key escrow. This ensures that the data can be decrypted even if the person with the original password/key can no longer decrypt it.

You should define a procedure that specifies how these keys may be used. Pretty Good Privacy (PGP) makes a product called PGP Corporate Disk to encrypt entire volumes on the hard drive. PGP offers other products to encrypt individual files. PGP Corporate Disk will run on Windows and on Mac OS X 10.2.1 or later. It uses AES encryption and supports FAT/FAT32, NTFS, HFS, HFS+, and Journaled HFS+ file systems. PGP also supports the critical feature of allowing a secondary key to recover the data if needed. Other products are available to encrypt the entire hard drive, such as CompuSec from CE-Infosys. CompuSec will run on Windows NT, Windows 2000, and Windows XP. There is a Linux version in development as well. You can download CompuSec for free at http://www.ce-infosys.com.sg/CeiNews_FreeCompuSec.asp.

File-Level Encryption

If you cannot use an encryption method that encrypts the entire hard drive, file-level encryption is an alternative. One product that you can use to encrypt your data is the Windows Encrypting File System (EFS). This Microsoft product is built into Windows 2000, Windows Server 2003, and Windows XP. Once the encrypt attribute is set on a file or folder, EFS allows you to transparently encrypt and decrypt individual files or entire folders in the background. An advantage of this method is that the user may not even be aware that the files being accessed are encrypted. The strengths of EFS are its affordable cost, wide availability, and ease of use.

To use EFS, follow these steps:

1. Right-click the file or folder you wish to encrypt and select Properties.
2. On the General tab, click the Advanced button.
3. At the bottom of the dialog box, check Encrypt Contents to Secure Data.

You can find additional information on using EFS at http://www.microsoft.com/technet/community/columns/5min/5min-202.mspx?.

On Windows 2000, the local administrator can recover the encrypted data by default. If the Windows 2000 machine is part of a domain, the domain administrator will instead be the default recovery agent. If you don't encrypt the entire volume, anyone who finds or steals the laptop can use various offline attacks to gain access to the administrator account and thus gain access to your encrypted files. To combat this, Windows XP by default does not give the local administrator account data recovery access. This means that you risk having your data become unrecoverable if you do not manually create and configure a data recovery agent. There are additional encryption considerations, especially concerning sharing of encrypted files between users and systems. You should have a complete understanding of the implications of using EFS before implementing it.

Encryption is a valuable tool to protect data confidentiality. Encryption should be used only with care and due diligence. You must research and develop policies and procedures to specify when to encrypt, how to encrypt, and how to manage keys and data recovery. Implementing encryption without proper planning could result in the loss of data. For more detailed coverage of EFS, refer to *Hardening Windows Systems* by Roberta Bragg (McGraw-Hill/Osborne, 2004).

Protect the Data Through Hardware Restrictions

If you want to keep your confidential data confidential, you have to control not only how it can be accessed in an attack scenario, but also how it can be intentionally removed from your controlled environment. There is a lot of hardware available to move data, such as floppy disks, CD-ROM burners, Zip disks, and the infamous pen drive. One option is to use products such as SecureWave's Sanctuary Device Control. It allows you to specify which hardware can be used and by whom. You can make a CD-ROM burner read-only for normal users and unrestricted for administrators. Again, working off of a whitelist, the only devices allowed by default are a USB mouse and keyboard. More information on Sanctuary Device Control can be found at http://www.securewave.com/turcana/securewave/sanctuary_DC.jsp.

Protect the Data Through Software Restrictions

Restricting access to parts of approved software is perhaps the most difficult way to protect data. You can prevent users from running applications, prevent them from using specific hardware, and even manage their access to some types of hardware. However, they need to be able to run approved software in order to do their jobs effectively. One of the most difficult tasks is hardening the remote client so that the software that is required doesn't pose a security risk.

Restrict Web Access

Web access might allow users to upload sensitive company information to the Internet or download a virus or Trojan executable. Unfortunately, web access is often a requirement for many jobs. If it is not a requirement, disabling web access completely is a safe precaution. If web access is a requirement, it is necessary to apply restrictions that prevent the user from uploading data to an external web site, or downloading potentially hostile code from a web site. If the remote client is a corporate-owned resource, you should prohibit direct Internet access of any type. You should require the remote client to access a corporate web proxy server. This will give you very granular control over the user's Internet web browsing activities. There are various proxy servers that can stop HTTP uploads, one of which is Blue Coat Secure Proxy Server, from Clearview Systems, http://www.clearview.co.uk/bluecoat_content_security.htm.

If a specialized solution is out of the budget or otherwise unavailable, you can at least filter out high-risk sites at your proxy or firewall, such as web-based e-mail sites and anonymous web browsing sites. Although this won't stop the technically savvy and determined data thief, it will at least make the task more difficult. Each and every step you take toward hardening your systems will make you a less appealing target for attackers.

If someone does succeed in moving the data off the system, and you then wish to pursue legal measures, you have a good case that the user in question went out of their way to circumvent the in-place policies and restrictions, adding to their culpability.

If the remote client is a personally owned computer, you probably can't prohibit direct Internet access while it is *not* connected to the corporate network. Your policy should require web access to be via a proxy server while accessing corporate resources. If the remote client is using a VPN, the VPN should disable access to all networks other than via the VPN tunnel. The user would then use the VPN tunnel to access a corporate web proxy to gain access to Internet web servers. If the user is using a remote access server for access, the remote access server should be configured to only use a proxy server for Internet web access.

HEADS UP!

Be aware that some VPN clients remove access to all networks except the VPN tunnel gateway by simply editing the route table on the remote computer. While functional, this is easily circumvented by the technically minded user with some manual route entries, allowing the remote client to then act as a router between the public Internet and your corporate network.

Protect Against Key Loggers

If your users have permission to install software, another way for data to leak is via a key logger, which logs every keystroke, to be smuggled out later. There are both hardware and software key loggers. About the only way to detect physical key (hardware based) loggers is via inspection. You can detect the existence of a software key logger by using anti–key logger software.

Keystroke logging also has a legitimate use. Key logging, either hardware or software, provides a good way to audit and gather information after a security incident has occurred. Make sure to create a security policy that governs the key logger use and run all the policies through your legal department. Be sure to include the appropriate disclaimers in your corporate security policy as well.

Harden Wireless Access

Wireless is also a serious security concern. More information on securing wireless networks is located in Chapter 12, and in other books in the *Hardening* series. This section concentrates on wireless security for remote clients. Your first defense is to prevent users from using wireless connections that are not owned by your organization. External wireless networks are not under your control. You have no way to control the implementation or the hardware being used. You don't know whether or not the wireless access point (WAP) is logging all traffic, and you certainly have no access to those logs. You cannot harden the WAP or the communications. Basically, you have no control, and control is the essence of remote access client security.

When remote access to your network is provided for those who work at home, the home remote client should not have access to, or be accessible from, any wireless network, including one the employee may have installed for use by family members. Even if the user implements Wired Equivalent Privacy (WEP), which is certainly better than no encryption, it can be defeated with software such as AirSnort after five to ten million packets have been gathered. While this could take some time, the question is, will it take long enough? In the end, encryption is all about making it take so long to decrypt the data that the data is no longer valuable. So, you need to ask yourself, how long is the data the user will be accessing still going to be valuable? If the remote access client is accessing customer data, such as personal information or account information, the data could be valuable for a long time. Ultimately, WEP just is not secure enough to trust any important data to. The key points to remember about wireless security are as follows:

- Do not to allow wireless access, even via WAPs under your organization's control. However, if you must implement wireless access via WAPs under your control, then secure them.
- Restrict wireless access to the remote clients' MAC addresses.
- Configure a custom service set identifier (SSID) and disable SSID broadcasts.
- Implement Microsoft's Extensible Authentication Protocol (EAP) or Cisco's Lightweight Extensible Authentication Protocol (LEAP).

LEAP is a Cisco solution to the security weaknesses of the current wireless standard. Whereas WEP uses a single static key, LEAP uses a new key for every packet. This means that if the attacker discovers the key, she has the data of only a single packet.

LEAP also authenticates the user against a RADIUS server via a username and password, whereas WEP authenticates a device. With WEP, if someone steals a user's laptop, the laptop would allow the thief access to the wireless network it was configured for, without discriminating based on the user who is attempting access.

Maintain Remote Client Security Policies

Once you have the remote computer configured securely and have policies in place to ensure that the resources are used properly, you need some way to make sure things stay that way. No matter how securely you've configured the remote clients, invariably the configuration will stray from policy over time, either because the user has found some new way to customize things to their liking, or simply because of administrative oversight or carelessness. Either way, you need to develop means to know when things are not running properly and to enforce network security polices.

Cisco Network Admission Control (NAC) allows you to enforce policies on resources that want to use the network. Although currently NAC only supports Windows XP, Windows NT, and Windows 2000, it allows you to enforce policy compliance *before* a computer can access network resources. This is a critical difference between it and some other options. Many other solutions allow the host PC to access the network, and then use that network access to determine whether the PC is in compliance with policy. By integrating the enforcement into the network devices themselves, you can potentially prevent some security exposures.

After installing the Cisco Trust Agent, when a host attempts to gain access to the network, the router or switch it is connected to will verify the host's access to network resources by checking the following for policy compliance:

- IP address
- Operating system version and patch level
- Antivirus software, antivirus engine version, and pattern file versions

Based on the results of the comparison, the host can be denied access, quarantined, or given limited network access. You could, for example, after determining that the host is not current on its service pack, redirect it to a web site from which the user can download and install the service pack. More information on NAC can be found at http://www.cisco.com/en/US/netsol/ns466/netqa0900aecd800fdd6f.html.

Similar functionality is included with Microsoft's ISA 2004 server. It offers the ability to quarantine VPN users who do not comply with the policy you have configured. The quarantine tool is included in the Windows Server 2003 Resource Kit, and you can download the quarantine component for Windows 2000 Server and Windows Server 2003. The tool requires a process to run on the client host that communicates policy compliance or noncompliance to the server. The host state is then compared to the defined policy and a configured action is taken in regard to the remote client's request for connectivity.

You should regularly audit the remote client machine. If it is a laptop, you should schedule dates on which the machine must be brought in to headquarters so that support staff can check its status and perform routine maintenance. This audit would also be a good opportunity to apply any needed patches or new software on the remote client. This would limit the amount of time that the machine is operating with an improper configuration, even if you have no automated measures in place.

Chapter 12

Hardening Wireless

by Wes Noonan

- Plan Secure Wireless Networks
- Seek and Destroy Rogue WLANs
- Design Your WLAN Topology
- Harden Your Wireless WAN

Wireless networks on both the LAN and the WAN are becoming increasingly common. Wireless networks in the WAN environment allow us to provide connectivity to physically remote and desolate locations that lack any form of wired infrastructure, such as oil wells or wilderness research facilities. Wireless networks in the LAN environment afford a tremendous amount of flexibility to allow the unbinding of workers from their desks. For example, doctors can roam the hospital floor with a laptop, tablet, or handheld PC to visit patients while staying connected to patient information and records.

Wireless networks are really a microcosm of the bigger struggle in network security, the struggle between usability and security. By design and by their nature, wireless networks have been implemented to provide a highly usable and flexible system of connectivity for users and systems. At the same time, because the data is sent via the airwaves, where anyone can potentially intercept it (and perhaps even obtain resources on your wired network through your wireless network), wireless networks represent a significant security risk to your environment.

The most secure thing that you can do with wireless networks, of course, is to simply not use them. However, many network environments really need the functionality that wireless provides—and thus the struggle. Is security or functionality more important? More often than not, functionality is going to win that struggle; however, there are tasks that you can undertake to provide the required functionality, in the most secure possible manner. This chapter looks at how to harden your wireless networks, by examining the following topics:

- Planning secure wireless networks
- Seeking and destroying rogue wireless LANs (WLANs)
- Designing your WLAN topology
- Hardening your wireless WAN

NOTE For more information about hardening your wireless LAN, see *Hardening Network Infrastructure*, by Wes Noonan (McGraw-Hill/Osborne, 2004).

Plan Secure Wireless Networks

Many forms of technology lend themselves to what is really a pretty "brain dead" approach to installation, which often doesn't require much design effort. As a result, one can simply follow the wizard, clicking Next and Finish without needing to put much thought into planning and design, and the technology works. Not all technologies can be installed in this somewhat nonchalant manner, however, and WLANs in particular defy this simplistic installation method if you want them to be secure. Oh, sure, WLANs can easily be installed on virtually any network, but by default most WLANs are not secure and thus will undermine your security posture if they have not been strictly planned. For example, people make the comment that their wireless network is secure because it was installed behind their firewall—even though wireless transmissions cannot be blocked by the wired firewall. The truth, however, is that installing wireless behind your firewall is potentially the worst place to install it, and planning your wireless network would illustrate the reason for this. The first step in planning your wireless network is to define the security policy that the wireless network should adhere to.

Write a Wireless Security Policy

Before you can design a secure wireless implementation, you have to define what secure wireless means for your organization. Your wireless security policy should define the standards, policies, and non-implementation-specific procedures that will be followed to ensure that any wireless implementation is performed in the most secure fashion possible.

At the same time, it's important to differentiate between your wireless security policy and your implementation procedures. A good way to look at it is that your security policy will tell you what to do, leaving the details of how to do it to be defined in subsequent documents. For example, your wireless security policy can state that smart card authentication is required, without providing the details of the exact implementation procedures for installing and configuring RSA SecurID smart cards. Indeed, this chapter is going to follow that mantra, by defining the details of the security policy components as the chapter progresses. The key elements that you need to define in your wireless security policy are as follows:

- Who has authority over the wireless networks
- Wireless network segregation requirements
- Hardware and software requirements
- An explicit ban on wireless equipment and software without IT approval
- An authentication method
- An encryption method
- The logging and accounting requirements
- Service Set Identifier (SSID) requirements
- Wireless access point (WAP) security requirements
- The enforcement policy

Define Who Has Authority over the Wireless Networks

One of the more critical components of all network security engagements is to clearly and explicitly define who has authority over the engagement. Your wireless network is no different. Designating who is responsible for managing the wireless network provides a central point of leadership, vision, and ultimately decision making to ensure that the proper security measures have been implemented. In addition, if your organization has departmental or remote wireless networks, you want to define who has authority over those systems and how they fit into the global hierarchy.

Define Wireless Network Segregation Requirements

Defining the wireless network segregation requirements is one of the more difficult aspects of wireless network design. Separate your wireless network from your wired network to ensure that a breach on the wireless network does not automatically grant access to the wired network. In this sense your wireless network should be treated as an untrusted network, whereas your wired network is considered a trusted network.

At the same time, providing wireless networks at a remote location can introduce a magnitude of difficulty to the design. For example, it is relatively easy to segment the WLAN in the central office to a dedicated VLAN, but it can be much more difficult and costly to do so at branch offices. If your branch offices have full connectivity to your network, however, the need for segmentation at those remote branches is no less important than at the main office.

Rather than seeking to specify *where* network segmentation is necessary in your wireless network, your wireless security policy should define *whether* network segmentation is required as well as the circumstances where network segmentation is not required. Your wireless security policy should also define how the segmentation should occur; for example, using simple virtual LANs (VLANs), using VLANs with access control lists (ACLs), using VLANs with firewalls, or even requiring all wireless connections to be segmented and utilizing Virtual Private Network (VPN) technologies to provide production network access. The most secure recommendation, as you will see later in this chapter, is to implement physical segmentation and to utilize a VPN to provide access to the trusted network.

Define Hardware and Software Requirements

Standardization is a key element of security. By standardizing the hardware and software that is used on your wireless network, you are better prepared to manage and maintain the system. Standardization also reduces incompatibility issues (which can result in reduced security) and facilitates more efficient and effective troubleshooting by making it easy to compare devices to identify differences between the systems. Finally, standardization makes the wireless network easier to support since your staff does not need to know multiple hardware types and software versions. For example, your wireless security policy should define the exact hardware vendors and models that will be supported on your network. It should also provide a minimum software version requirement, allowing the technical staff to upgrade the software as required to address security and other issues without needing to go through the time-consuming process of updating the security policy solely for a new patch to be deployed.

Explicitly Ban All Wireless Equipment and Software Without IT Approval

Explicitly banning all wireless equipment and software that is implemented without prior IT approval provides the necessary authority to locate and remove any rogue access points that individuals may implement.

Define an Authentication Method

Because your wireless networks provide a potential easy method of access to your internal network, it is critical that you define an appropriate authentication method that will be employed to ensure that only authorized users can connect to the network. There are a number of elements that your wireless security policy should address, including the authentication standards to adhere to, the authentication method, and the implementation requirements.

First, the wireless security policy should define the appropriate authentication standard. By adhering to a nonproprietary standard, you alleviate the risk of implementing proprietary solutions that may lock you into a certain vendor. Second, the wireless security policy should define the authentication method that will be implemented. For example, you need to determine whether you are going to implement certificates, preshared keys, user authentication, etc. Another aspect of the authentication method is whether you are going to perform mutual authentication (authenticating both the client and server to each other) or simply authenticate the client system or the server. It is more secure to perform mutual authentication.

There are a number of common authentication methods for use in wireless networks:

- **Preshared keys (PSKs)** A method that uses manually created and static keys that an administrator uses to identify a user. PSKs are also frequently used to perform encryption functions.
- **IEEE 802.1*x*** A standard that uses the PPP Extensible Authentication Protocol (EAP), which is defined by RFC 2284. Typically, 802.1*x* authentication uses authentication servers such as RADIUS or TACACS+ to provide authentication of the user to the wireless access point (known as the *authenticator*).
- **Certificates** An electronic form of authentication that uses a public key infrastructure (PKI) and trusted Certification Authorities (CAs) to identify a user or device. Certificates also typically contain information required for performing data encryption and decryption. For more information about certificates, see Chapter 10.
- **User authentication** The standard username/password method of authenticating a particular user. While it can be implemented as a stand-alone authentication method, it is more commonly implemented as a component of 802.1*x*.

Finally, the security policy should define the implementation of the authentication solution. For example, you need to determine what user and group levels will be used, how passwords will be managed, and how certificates will be distributed and managed.

Define an Encryption Method

Defining an encryption method is second, after authentication, in the one-two punch of securing your wireless network. Authentication validates the identity of an authorized user and therefore allows them to connect to the network. Encryption ensures that the data being transmitted is kept confidential and, by using supplemental configurations that exist for many encryption protocols, can also ensure the integrity of the data. For more information about how encryption functions, see Chapter 10.

HEADS UP!

Encryption alone will not provide for the integrity of the data. However, most encryption methods implicitly include integrity-checking mechanisms. This is important to understand, because if you do not have any form of integrity checking, someone can still manipulate encrypted data, and that manipulation would be unknown to the user receiving the data. For example, a malicious user could intercept the packet, decrypt and change the data, and send the packet on to the receiver, who would be unaware that the message had been changed. By signing or hashing the data, however, the receiver can be assured that the data is indeed from the source that it claims to be from.

IPSec typically uses SHA1 or MD5 for hashing to ensure the integrity of the data. In addition, SHA1 or MD5 hashing is used as a part of the Internet Security Association Key Management Protocol (ISAKMP) process to ensure the integrity of the key exchange process. WiFi Protected Access (WPA) and 802.11i use the Michael Message Integrity Check (MMIC) process to ensure the integrity of the data. Wired Equivalent Privacy (WEP) has no integrity method, which is one of the numerous reason for using WPA or 802.11i instead of WEP.

Your security policy needs to identify when encryption should be used and how it should be implemented. A number of encryption methods are available to wireless networks, including WEP, WPA, 802.11i, and VPN-based encryption. As you define your encryption method, try to refrain from introducing additional overhead on your data transmission by using multiple encryption methods. For example, if your security policy is going to require all wireless connections to utilize a VPN connection to gain access to the trusted network, you probably don't need to implement wireless-specific encryption, since the VPN technology will, by definition, provide for both encryption and authentication.

There are four common encryption methods available for use on wireless networks:

- **WEP** Designed to provide for privacy of data over a wireless network on par with a wired network. Unfortunately, WEP has been cracked as an encryption technology and should not be used.
- **WPA** A subset of the 802.11i standard that was developed to address the security issues related to WEP before 802.11i was finalized as a standard. WPA uses a combination of technologies that mitigate the problems that WEP exposes: 802.1*x* authentication, to address authentication issues; Temporal Key Integrity Protocol (TKIP), to address encryption issues; and MMIC, to address message integrity.
- **802.11i** Implements all the technologies that WPA uses for encryption, but also includes the use of even stronger encryption technologies such as Advanced Encryption Standard (AES). Since 802.11i was ratified in June of 2004, it has been the preferred encryption method for wireless networks that do not use a VPN.
- **VPN-based encryption** Requires a wireless client to authenticate to and use a VPN to gain access to the trusted network. VPN-based encryption typically implements IPSec over Layer 2 Tunneling Protocol (L2TP), IPSec alone, or, in the case of the Point-to-Point Tunneling (PPTP), Microsoft Point-to-Point encryption (MPPE). Since the wireless client must use the VPN to gain access to the trusted network, it is not always necessary to implement any form of wireless-specific encryption such as WEP, WPA, or 802.11i.

Define the Logging and Accounting Requirements

Logging and accounting are critical components of being able to track activity on your wireless network and detect misuse. Accounting enables you to track who is connecting to the wireless network and when they are connecting. Accounting is typically implemented in conjunction with technologies like RADIUS or TACACS+.

Logging is required to monitor users, debug problems, and detect misuse. For example, you can use the logs to identify failed authentication attempts, which may indicate that an unauthorized person has attempted to gain access to your network. Similarly, you can use the logs to identify and track an intruder who has successfully accessed your network.

In addition to defining the appropriate logging and accounting technology that will be utilized, your security policy should also define how frequently the logs are reviewed, who should review them, and how alerting will be configured to provide event notification for critical events.

Define SSID Requirements

The Service Set Identifier (SSID) is used to uniquely identify and name a WLAN. This enables wireless clients to browse for and locate a WAP that they can use to gain access to the network. At the same time, however, broadcasting the SSID makes it easy for attackers to identify WAPs that can be attacked. Your wireless security policy should define whether you will or will not broadcast your SSID. In addition, the wireless security policy should define a naming convention that can be used to identify the WAP, but should not be so explicit as to allow someone to be able to associate the WAP with your company. For example, if an attacker is trying to gain access to Joe's Widget Corporation and they locate a WAP with an SSID of joeswidgetwap1, they can reasonably conclude that this is an attack point they should attempt to exploit.

Define WAP Security Requirements

As with all of your network devices, you also want your wireless security policy to define the WAP security requirements for providing both physical and logical security of the device. Your security policy needs to define how administrative access will be provided, who is permitted to establish an administrative session with the device, and who can configure the device. The security policy must also define how any device-specific security mechanisms should be configured.

Define the Enforcement Policy

For any security policy to be effective, it needs to have a section that clearly defines the enforcement policy. The enforcement policy needs to define the technical enforcement mechanisms that will be used to ensure compliance, such as using wireless detection hardware to locate rogue or misconfigured wireless networks. In addition, the enforcement policy section needs to define the punishments for violating the security policy. This is where you give the security policy teeth—if setting up a rogue wireless network is grounds for termination, then you need to clearly document this in the enforcement policy section. Work with human resources and your corporate legal team to ensure that the text is legally appropriate.

Seek and Destroy Rogue WLANs

In a perfect world, explicitly banning rogue wireless networks in your wireless security policy would be sufficient to resolve the issue. Because this isn't a perfect world, however, you must take these additional steps to prevent rogue WLANs from being connected to the network and to discover and remove any that exist:

- *Implement and enforce a wireless security policy.* Your wireless security policy defines how wireless will and will not be implemented in your organization. You have to ensure that your security policy has teeth and is enforceable. For example, it needs to define that bringing a rogue WAP online is grounds for termination. It also needs to define what can be done when a rogue WAP is detected and who is responsible for dealing with the incident.

- *Provide for physical security.* Since most WLANs have a limited range, it is important to implement the appropriate security measures to prevent someone from being able to get within range of any rogue WAP that might be brought online. One option is to use paint and window screening that prevents wireless transmissions from passing. These products can ensure that someone outside of your facility will be unable to connect to any wireless networks running in your buildings. Some examples of these types of products are Force Field Wireless DefendAir Radio Shield paint (http://www.forcefieldwireless.com/defendair.html), Emsec Coating (http://www.emsecsystems.com/products_ecs.html), and GlassLock SpyGuard window treatment (http://www.forceprotection.com/SpyGuard%20Signals%20Defense.htm).
- *Provide a supported WLAN infrastructure.* An effective method of preventing rogue WLANs is to provide the appropriate WLAN infrastructure so that your users aren't compelled to go off and do things on their own.
- *Isolate any rogue WLAN by implementing port-based security on your LAN switches.* While port-based security has its own unique issues that need to be addressed, port-based security can be implemented to ensure that only authenticated systems can be connected to your network. Since a rogue WAP will not have this authentication information, it will not work on your network.

Scan for rogue WLANs, remove them, and punish their implementers—policy and lack of need mean nothing to those who put their own convenience above the good of the organization. It's not enough to have a policy, enforce it.

Implement WLAN Discovery Procedures

The knee-jerk reaction at this point might be to say, "Well, if I can't prevent a rogue WLAN from being implemented, it's a lost cause." This isn't the case, however. Just because you can't really prevent unauthorized WAPs from being implemented on the network doesn't mean you can't discover and remove them.

There are two predominant methods of detecting unauthorized WLANs on your network. The first method attempts to detect them wirelessly. The second method attempts to detect them from the wired network.

Detecting Unauthorized WLANs Wirelessly

A surprisingly effective method of detecting unauthorized WLANs is by simply using a wireless client and locating the WAPs broadcasting in your environment. There are a few caveats to be considered when employing this method, however:

- Because WLANs have a limited range, you have to be within range of the WAP in order to detect it.
- It is very difficult to detect a WAP that does not broadcast its SSID.

- It can be difficult to survey remote sites.

Since most unauthorized WAPs are not implemented by malicious users (and oftentimes are implemented by nontechnical users), the odds are high that the SSID broadcast has not been disabled. This leaves you with the problems of needing to be within range of the WAP to detect it and trying to survey remote sites. It is often impractical for someone in IT to spend the day walking around trying to determine if they can detect access points. One of the more creative solutions for this is to recruit someone who on a daily basis must walk around the environment—the mail delivery person. You can outfit this person with a laptop or handheld carrying extra batteries, and while they make their normal rounds delivering the mail, the laptop can sit in the bottom of the mail cart, quietly detecting any WAPs. If that is too costly, another option is to utilize any of the many pocket wireless detectors that simply glow green when they detect a wireless source. While they were developed and marketed to be a quick and easy way for travelers to find a wireless network they can connect to, you can use that same convenience in detecting rogue wireless networks.

ONE STEP FURTHER

A number of wireless analyzers can be used to detect the presence of unauthorized WAPs, including the following:

- AirDefense (http://www.airdefense.net/)
- AirMagnet (http://www.airmagnet.com/)
- Boingo (http://www.boingo.com/)
- NetStumbler (http://www.netstumbler.com)
- Kismet (http://www.kismetwireless.net/)
- Network Associates Sniffer (http://www.mcafeesecurity.com/us/products/home.htm)
- WildPackets AiroPeek NX (http://www.wildpackets.com/products/airopeek_nx)

NetStumbler provides one of the easiest methods for detecting a rogue AP over the wireless network. Once you install NetStumbler, the program automatically begins scanning for WAPs with no configuration required on your part (other than providing the wireless NIC, of course). For example, Figure 12-1 depicts what I was able to capture while driving down a major freeway in the Houston area. NetStumbler captured 175 WAPs, of which 113 were running no encryption whatsoever, and none of which were running WPA. Instead, they were all using WEP.

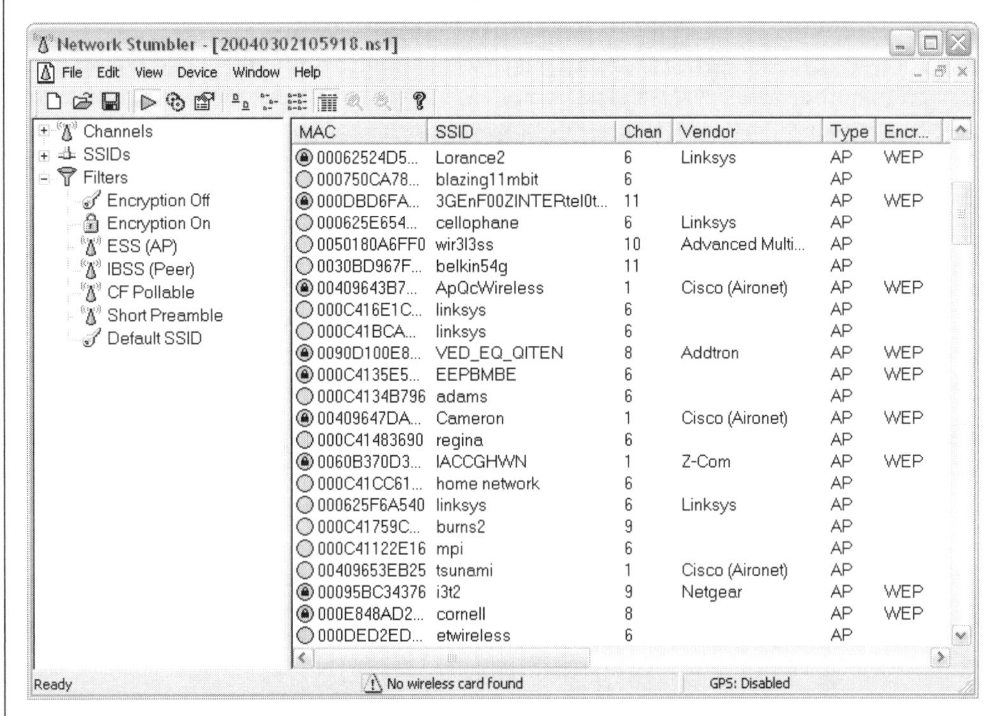

Figure 12-1. NetStumbler capture

ONE STEP FURTHER

A relatively new method of detecting rogue WAPs takes advantage of some of the peer-to-peer networking concepts that allow file-sharing applications to work. This method uses small client software running on every wireless device on your network to collect information on WAPs that they are able to detect, and then report it back to a central location. This effectively turns every wireless client into a rogue WAP detection tool. An example of this technology is the Distributed Wireless Security Auditor (DSWA) from IBM (http://www.research.ibm.com/gsal/dwsa/).

Detecting Unauthorized WAPs from the Wired Network

Using a wired detection process can alleviate some of the disadvantages of trying to detect an unauthorized WAP wirelessly. For example, a wired detection process is not susceptible to missing WAPs that do not broadcast their SSIDs. In addition, a wired detection process can be used to survey remote sites and can even be scheduled and scripted to increase ease of use.

Unfortunately, there are some drawbacks to this method. Locating all the unauthorized access points can be difficult, largely due to the lack of mature or specialized products for this task. Currently, most techniques rely on using the MAC address of the WAP (because all vendors are assigned a MAC address range) or OS fingerprinting to identify the WAP, both of which are an imprecise science. Here are two tools that can assist you in identifying an unauthorized WAP by monitoring MAC addresses:

- **APTools (http://winfingerprint.sourceforge.net/aptools.php)** APTools not only can discover an access point based on the MAC address of the WAP, it can also attempt to check to verify that the access point is a WAP as opposed to any other device that has a MAC address.
- **Arpwatch (http://www-nrg.ee.lbl.gov/)** Arpwatch can monitor the network and maintain a database of MAC address and IP address pairings, allowing you to identify new MAC addresses as well as MAC addresses from nonstandard vendors.

Here are some tools that can assist you in OS fingerprinting:

- **Nmap (http://www.insecure.org/nmap/index.html)** Nmap can be used to identify the OS that a scanned host is running.
- **Xprobe (http://www.sys-security.com/html/projects/X.html)** Xprobe is similar to Nmap in its ability to identify the OS through the use of fingerprinting.
- **Nessus (http://www.nessus.org)** Nessus is a well-known vulnerability-assessment tool that can be used to detect a rogue WAP. You can find an excellent white paper that details the process of using Nessus to detect rogue WAPs at http://www.tenablesecurity.com/white_papers/wap-id-nessus.pdf

Both of these methods, using the MAC address of the WAP and OS fingerprinting, share the common problem of generating false positives. For example, Nmap recognizes a Linksys WAP54G as a Linux device because it actually runs Linux for the OS. This can make it difficult to determine whether the device is indeed a WAP or just a Linux host running on your network. MAC address tools rely on identifying a device based on it having a MAC address that has been assigned to a wireless vendor. That can make it difficult to distinguish between a Cisco AP and a Cisco switch if the database of MAC addresses has not been accurately updated.

Remove Rogue WAPs

Once you have detected a rogue WAP, the next step is to attempt to shut it down. One option is to attempt to physically locate and disconnect the WAP from the network; however, this can be both time consuming and prone to failure. The obvious difficulty of this method is that locating the WAP, usually done through a trial-and-error process, can be very difficult since most WAPs are small and easily hidden.

Another option is to locate the switch port that the MAC address for the WAP is connected to and shut that switch port down. Similarly, you can determine the IP address of the WAP and attempt to block the IP address. You can also shut down the switch port. In many cases, this will cause the person to seek you out, saving you the time and effort of trying to find them.

Design Your WLAN Topology

Once you have written the security policies necessary to define how you will implement wireless in your network, the next step is to design a secure WLAN topology. There are three principle WLAN topology designs:

- Unified wireless and wired network
- Segmented wireless and wired network
- Wireless network with VPN access to wired network

Unified Wireless and Wired Network

While the unified wireless and wired network topology is the most insecure topology, it nonetheless needs to be addressed because in many cases financial implications will prevent you from implementing a more secure topology. As you can see in Figure 12-2, with a unified design, the WLAN is directly connected to the wired LAN infrastructure.

The devices that connect via the WAPs are connected directly to the same network that other clients and servers are connected to. In this type of network design, since there is no separation of trusted and untrusted (or wired and wireless, respectively) resources, it is critical that you take every possible precaution to ensure that only authorized connections are permitted to the wireless network. Specific design recommendations for this topology are to implement the following:

- **Secure authentication** Because nothing stands between a wireless user and your wired resources except the WAP, ensure that you have implemented strict authentication mechanisms. It is recommended to implement 802.1*x* authentication only.

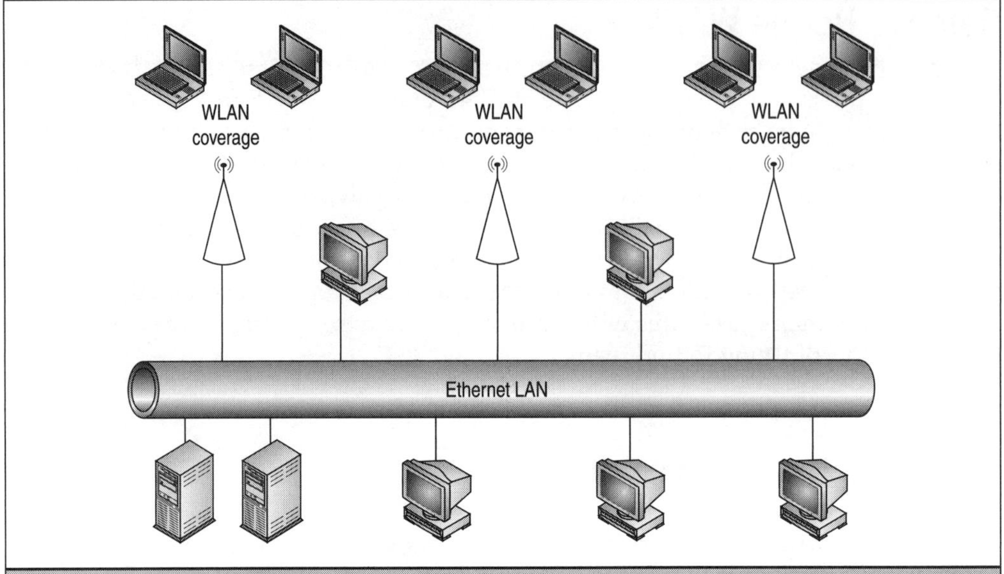

Figure 12-2. Unified wireless and wired network

- **The most stringent encryption** Similarly, the only protection of the data being transmitted over the wireless network will be provided by your WAP configuration. Consequently, you should implement 802.11i for your wireless encryption, or WPA if your devices won't support 802.11i. You should never use WEP in this scenario, because WEP has been cracked.

ONE STEP FURTHER

A frequent point of contention in the industry is my insistence of never recommending WEP. On one hand you have the philosophy that WEP is better than nothing. On the other hand you have the philosophy that since WEP has been cracked, it should never be used in any circumstance. I strongly believe in the latter philosophy. If your wireless equipment only supports WEP, you shouldn't be using the equipment. The absolute minimum encryption method you should permit in your environment is WPA, with 802.11i being the preferred method. If you can't do WPA and the choice is WEP or nothing, you need to elect to go with nothing—no wireless at all, until such time that you can implement WPA or 802.11i. All current WAPs that are designed for a corporate environment support WPA, and as a result, so should you. Anything else is merely providing a false sense of security—and that can be worse than no security at all!

- **Extensive logging** As mentioned previously in this chapter, logging is a critical aspect of detecting misuse. Since there is nothing between the wireless user and your wired network, you need to ensure that you have configured extensive logging and alerting to provide early detection of potential misuse as well as forensic information for investigating incidents.
- **MAC address restrictions** MAC address restrictions allow you to specify which MAC addresses will be allowed to connect to the WAP. While MAC addresses can be spoofed, this still provides a good measure of additional security to ensure that only systems explicitly permitted by you can connect to your WLAN infrastructure.
- **Secure SSID configurations** Because the SSID being broadcast can be easily used to locate a WAP, you should disable the SSID broadcast on the WAP. While most wireless NICs (WNICs) can still connect to the WAP by manually entering the correct SSID, some WNICs have problems connecting in this method. In particular, problems of this nature have been reported with the SanDisk SDIO 802.11b secure digital WNIC. In addition to disabling the SSID broadcast, you should not use any type of company- or location-identifying information in the SSID, as this can be used by an attacker to determine what resources are being attacked.

Segmented Wireless and Wired Network

Separate your network into trusted and untrusted segments. Your wired network is your trusted network and your wireless network is your untrusted network. The objective of this type of network design is to provide a means of restricting traffic from the untrusted network to the trusted network. There are two predominant methods of providing for segmentation between your trusted and untrusted network:

- Implement physical segmentation.
- Implement logical segmentation by using VLANs.

Implement Physical Segmentation

Implementing physical segmentation is as simple as ensuring that the WLAN and the wired LAN are physically separated by either a router or, preferably, a firewall. In this configuration, the WLAN effectively becomes nothing more than a DMZ segment, with the appropriate traffic restrictions. Figure 12-3 illustrates this topology design.

In this topology design, you still want to follow all of the design recommendations for a unified network. Now, your question might be, "If I am going to do the same thing, why not just implement a unified network, since it is simpler and easier to manage?" What physical segmentation buys you is more granular control over the traffic that is to be permitted between the trusted and untrusted networks. By utilizing a physically separated topology, you can implement ACLs at the router or firewall, permitting traffic into the trusted network on the specific ports and to the specific

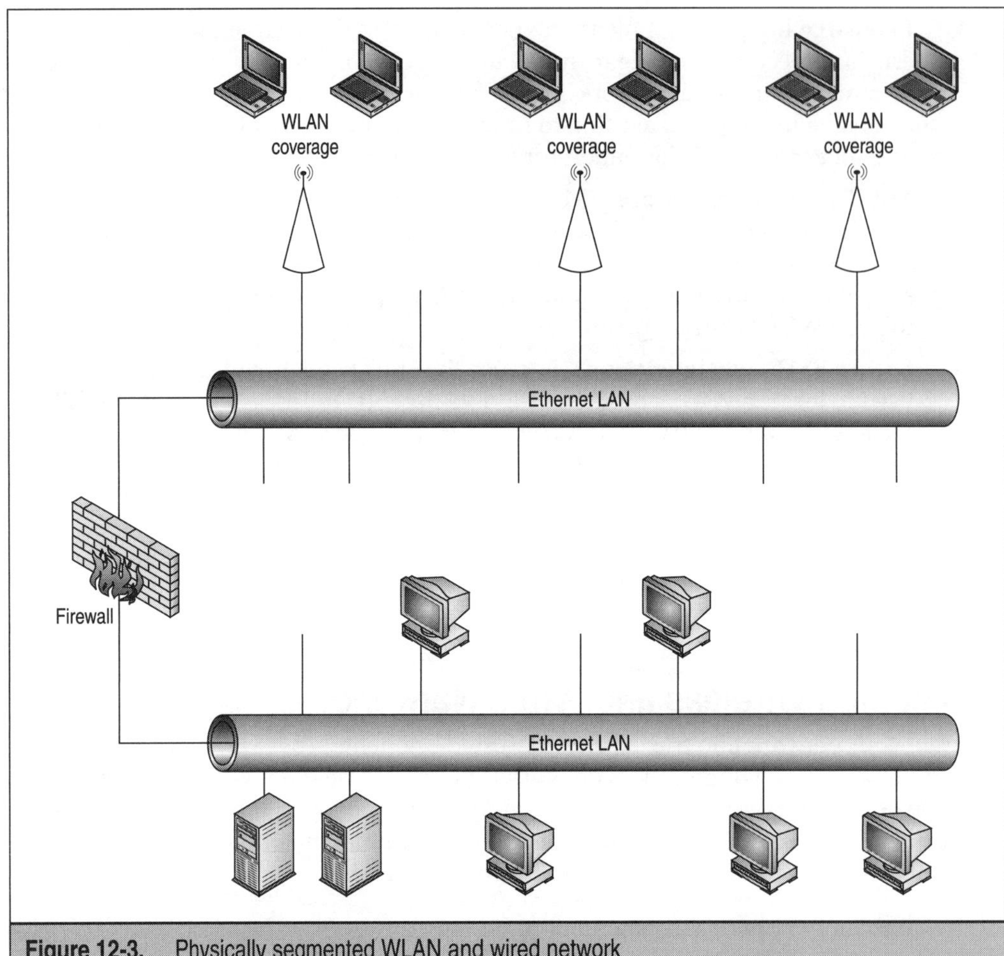

Figure 12-3. Physically segmented WLAN and wired network

hosts that you want to allow. For example, if the wireless hosts need access to only six servers, you can implement an ACL that permits traffic to only those six servers. In addition, you can restrict the traffic to those six servers on the specific TCP or UDP ports required by the applications in use. Figure 12-4 shows a detailed WLAN design that uses redundancy throughout the design to provide secure and highly available wireless access to the trusted network.

In this design, the WLAN is truly treated just like a DMZ, including the deployment of IDS sensors both in front of and behind the firewall to provide additional monitoring and reporting capabilities. Any internal resources must be published through the firewall, and the corresponding ACLs must be configured accordingly to permit the traffic.

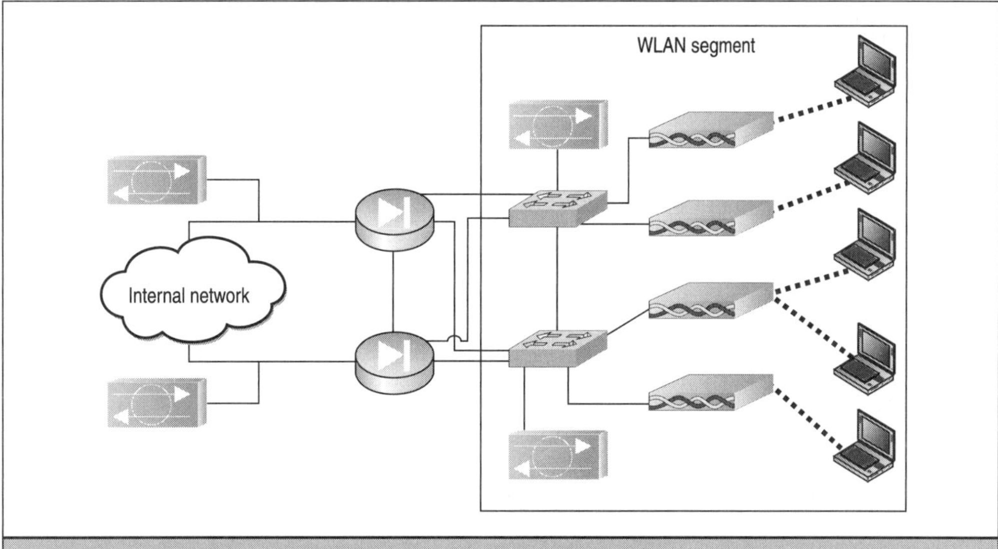

Figure 12-4. Segmented WLAN and wired network using firewalls

Implement Logical Segmentation by Using VLANs

While physical segmentation is the most secure method of segmentation, it is also the most expensive method since it generally requires additional hardware resources. To offset the expense of physical segmentation, you can use VLANs to provide a similar degree of security, while leveraging existing hardware resources. The traffic that must pass between the VLANs still requires a router or firewall and can be secured with the appropriate ACLs and restrictions. Segmentation using VLANs should be secured in the exact manner that physically segmented networks are.

HEADS UP!

While VLANs are a convenient method of segmenting traffic, they are less secure than true physical segmentation because some switches are susceptible to attacks that allow unauthorized traffic to traverse VLANs without going through the router or firewall. Although this situation is rare, it can occur. Consequently, it is important to heavily weigh the cost justification for utilizing VLANs against the potential security threat that VLANs have over true physical segmentation. In most cases with segmenting WLANs, the risk does not justify the additional cost of implementing true physical segmentation.

Wireless Network with VPN Access to Wired Network

The most secure design topology for providing access to the trusted network is to leverage the very mature and reliable VPN technologies in conjunction with your WLANs. In this design, all traffic that is being passed to the trusted network must go through a VPN, thus ensuring that the connection has been authenticated and the data is protected. Figure 12-5 demonstrates a detailed WLAN topology utilizing VPN access.

The wireless clients in this case are configured with the appropriate VPN client. Because the VPN is securing the traffic passing into the trusted network, it is not always necessary to implement wireless security measures such as 802.1*x* or 802.11i. The wireless network in this case really becomes an unsecured medium that allows the clients to establish a VPN connection to the trusted network, similar in practice to how a remote client might establish a VPN connection across the Internet.

ONE STEP FURTHER

Even though the traffic to the trusted network will be secured using a VPN, it still makes sense to implement some form of wireless security, as previously defined. Even though the VPN will protect the traffic passing to the trusted network, it does not protect the wireless client from other wireless clients, unless you configure your VPN clients to not support split tunneling. Therefore, although it will create additional overhead in that the traffic is encrypted first by the WLAN and then by the VPN, if the performance hit is acceptable, it is recommended that you implement both security mechanisms on your WLANs.

Providing Secure WLANs at Remote/Branch Offices

Because of the infrastructure that typically exists in the central office, it is relatively easy to adhere to the design recommendations previously provided. Remote/branch offices represent a problem in that they typically lack the infrastructure or personnel with the appropriate technical expertise to implement the same designs. For example, most branch offices don't have local VPN concentrators to provide for VPN services. At the same time, an attacker that can gain access to a WLAN at the remote office might as well be connected to your main office, since they will likely have access to the same resources.

Now, the knee-jerk reaction might be to say, "I can really only afford to do a unified topology in my remote offices." While this is a perfectly acceptable design in some circumstances, it is less secure than the alternatives. There are some relatively inexpensive ways that you can achieve physical segmentation of your wired and wireless networks, however. Perhaps the most effective solution is to implement a small office firewall such as a Cisco PIX 501 that has the ability to terminate a small number of VPN connections. This not only provides physical or logical segmentation, it also allows you to require VPN access for all wireless-based access to the trusted network.

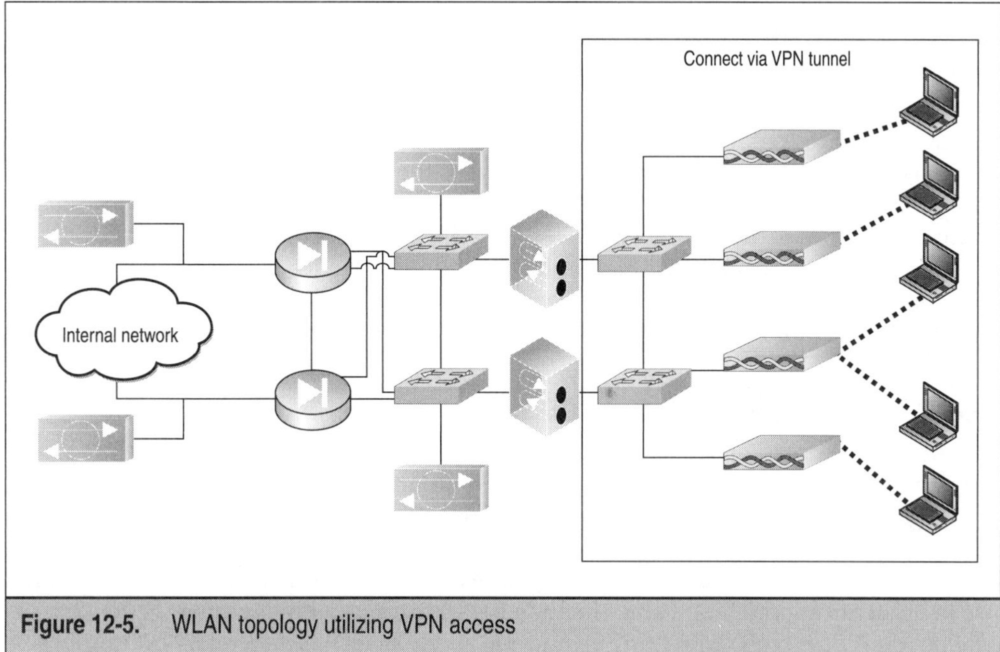

Figure 12-5. WLAN topology utilizing VPN access

Harden Your Wireless WAN

Now that you have looked at how to secure your WLANs, it is time to look at how to harden your wireless WAN (WWAN). The good news is that, compared to a WLAN, WWAN security is a pretty straightforward endeavor. Since WWAN implementations tend to be point-to-point connections, the key to securing them is to implement sound authentication and encryption mechanisms. The downside to WWAN technologies is that, unlike with WLANs, in most cases these security measures are provided by the WWAN vendor, which means that you are at their mercy and must rely on them to provide the necessary WWAN-specific security configurations. This is not always an acceptable answer, however, especially if you are required to manage all of the security in your environment.

An alternative (since you can't really control what the service provider will do) way to ensure the confidentiality and integrity of the data is to implement a VPN or IPSec over the WWAN connection and utilize its authentication and encryption. There are three primary WWAN technologies available to the consumer market:

- Cellular Digital Packet Data (CDPD)
- Code Division Multiple Access (CDMA)
- General Packet Radio Service (GPRS)

Cellular Digital Packet Data

CDPD implements a multitiered security architecture. Device security is handled by implementing unique network entity identifiers (NEIs). Without an NEI, the device cannot connect to the CDPD network. To ensure that CDPD devices cannot be cloned or otherwise manipulated to fraudulently access the network, NEI authentication using Diffie-Hellman electronic key exchange is used to validate three numbers, the Authentication Sequence Number (ASN), the NEI, and the Authentication Random Number (ARN), to generate the credentials the wireless device uses for credentials. Encryption of the data is handled by the CDPD Encryption Service, which uses RSA encryption algorithms to secure the data traffic.

Code Division Multiple Access

CDMA uses a spread-spectrum technology to transmit the data across multiple frequencies. Because the traffic is transmitted on multiple frequencies, eavesdropping on the data is very difficult since the eavesdropper not only must be able to monitor all frequencies, but must also know the proper order in which to put the data back together. Similar to CDPD, CDMA uses a series of values to establish the device credentials for use in authentication. These values include the Electronic Serial Number (ESN), the Mobile Identification Number (MIN), and the A-key, which is a secret 64-bit number used during authentication and encryption of the data on the network.

General Packet Radio Service

GPRS is based on the Global System for Mobile Communication (GSM), which is the most widely implemented global wireless technology. GPRS networks utilize Subscriber Identity Module (SIM) cards to provide access to the network. Authentication is provided by the data contained on the SIM card. Encryption is handled by the GPRS Encryption Algorithm (GEA).

Chapter 13

Hardening a Mixed Unix Network

by Paul Love

- Understand the Basic Problems in a Mixed Unix Environment
- Protect the Root Account

Unix is often seen as one of the more secure operating systems available for the enterprise customer, and it does have the benefit of more than 30 years of active development and production use. However, while it is true that a properly configured and hardened Unix system is a secure, robust operating system, if it is not properly configured it can be a security vulnerability.

One of the unique things about the Unix operating system is that it has forked into many different implementations over the years. They include Solaris Unix, AIX, Linux, FreeBSD, OpenBSD, Mac OS X, and many others. The different Unix implementations share the same concepts, but there are some fundamental under-the-hood implementations that make security configurations much more difficult. While every configuration or under-the-hood implementation is not discussed in this chapter, you will become aware of the more common issues and be directed how to find the fixes. This chapter discusses some of the issues you will face in securing a mixed Unix environment.

Understand the Basic Problems in a Mixed Unix Environment

The differences between the various Unix implementations can be likened to the English language. Consider Solaris Unix a southwestern U.S. dialect, while Linux is a northeastern U.S. dialect, while the other implementations of Unix are other dialects. If you are from one area of the country and visiting the other, you can understand what is being communicated, but you may sometimes stumble because there are differences in how things are said. The same is true when moving from one Unix platform to another; you will not find it difficult to understand the basics of Solaris if you are a Linux guru, but you may find yourself puzzling over exactly how you should configure Solaris to achieve the same effect you can with Linux. You could even consider Windows as part of this analogy; liken the Microsoft operating systems to British English. There are major fundamental differences in how things are said, but the underlying concepts are the same.

All of this means that you do not have to learn too many new concepts to work in a mixed Unix environment, but you do have to resist the tendency to assume identical implementations. If you do not determine the correct configuration for each Unix OS, one or more of them could become the victim of a simple attack that easily could have been repulsed. So keep in mind when configuring security in a mixed Unix environment that Unix systems may not be exactly the same, and thus you always need to refer to the vendor's documentation on specific files and methodologies.

It's the differences noted previously that create a large portion of the errors and confusion that system administrators make when securing a Unix machine. The implementation of a file's locations between the different versions of Unix is different enough to cause some confusion to those who are unfamiliar with the subtitles. For instance, in Solaris and Linux the file that holds all the encrypted passwords is typically kept in the file /etc/shadow, whereas IBM AIX sometimes stores encrypted passwords in /etc/security/shadow. Another instance of these subtle differences is the authentication configuration files these two versions of Unix use, but the overall format is the same (some include the option for longer encrypted strings, etc., by default). In Solaris, they are stored in /etc/pam.conf, whereas in AIX they are stored in /etc/security/user. The different versions of Unix implement configuration files or other system functions a bit differently. The differences can cause even experienced Unix administrators to become confused, so the first step in hardening a mixed Unix environment is to understand something about the different Unix communities.

Understand the Different Distribution and Support Models

As a general observation, Unix experts tend to stick to technical discussions, so nontechnical issues such as support or business use are often overlooked. However, when considering the use of open-source versions of Unix in a business environment, such as the Linux operating system, there are many more things to consider.

Linux (more appropriately GNU/Linux) is a relatively new operating system (since 1991) based on the Unix concepts introduced decades ago. The first obvious difference is the software publication and distribution model. The most prevalent software model in the market today is a commercial model in which the manufacturer sells software licenses, publishes upgrade and new release schedules, and provides support. The source code is not publicly available for review, and certainly not for modification. Microsoft operating systems and most commercial Unix implementations follow this model. This model offers purchasers a degree of assurance that there is a commercial company with a vested interest in the security, reliability, and stability of the product offered. Patches are often deployed in a consistent manner, and if something goes wrong, there is a company to look to for resolution.

There are two major (and many minor) alternatives to this proprietary, commoditized model of software: GNU General Public License (GPL) and BSD License software. GPL (http://www.opensource.org/licenses/gpl-license.php), BSD License (http://www.opensource.org/licenses/bsd-license.php), and other open source–based licenses (http://opensource.org/licenses/) have source code, or "core," that is open for anyone to view. GPL software has the stipulation that if any modifications are made, they must be made available, while the BSD license has no restriction. (There are, however, a lot of nuances between the licenses.) The Open Source Initiative (OSI), which is referenced in this section, is one of the definitive sources for tracking and understanding the different open source licenses and has much more information on the other open source licensing alternatives.

The conventional wisdom is that because the source code is open for review by anyone, weaknesses will be found faster and the code will be better written. This may be true but it is not assured, because not all code will be reviewed by competent security professionals, nor will weaknesses necessarily be found, or corrected faster. It is true, however, that one greatly beneficial aspect of the open-source model is that when problems are found and publicly identified, a patch is usually released immediately. Where there is no dependence on a commercial entity, response can be much more nimble. One example of this is the zlib Compression Library Heap Corruption Vulnerability. The initial vulnerability was identified on March 11, 2002, and most of the major open-source vendors/communities had a patch available within a day of the vulnerability announcement. Sun, on the other hand, took around two weeks to issue a patch for this vulnerability. The length of time for the Solaris patch can be attributed to quality control and research on Sun's side, but the strength of the open-source model is that the code is openly available to everyone, so an army of worldwide developers can work on a patch and provide oversight, while a commercial entity utilizing closed-source methods can only utilize the staff it can afford to assign to work on the patching process.

If your mixed Unix environment includes commercial Unix as well as open-source alternatives, you need to adopt more than one approach to security and documentation. Commercial Unix implementations provide a more rigid, linear approach to security, similar to what previous users of Windows or NetWare-type operating systems are familiar with. The documentation provided typically is straightforward and written by a professional team. Commercial software vendors use a software development model to create software and to make changes to the software, so there is a rigid process around the modification of the software, whereas the open-source model is more unstructured in some cases, but not always.

In the open-source community, some companies deploy rigid software processes, but generally the open-source process model is more decentralized and less rigid. For open source, this lack of rigidity is an advantage, not a detriment, because more programmers can develop the software and improve upon what others have done before them. In many companies, there are strict processes for the implementation of changes, and as more companies adopt project management techniques, there will be more familiarity with the commercial versions of Unix implementation of processes and software change.

One other strong point for the closed-source, commercialized versions of Unix that are so attractive to companies, especially large ones, is that there is a centralized point of contact for training, support, feature requests, and incident response. This may be offered by the commercial open-source companies (SUSE Linux and Red Hat, for example), but this model is still somewhat foreign to most nontechnical business purchasers because the core product or source code is readily available and easy to modify. This ability to communicate in a common business language will come with a price tag, in the form of more expensive hardware (in some cases), software, and support, but it shouldn't be overlooked. Commercial Unix vendors offer extensive support and training, and the systems are usually well documented because their customers expect and pay for this.

Open-source versions do not always have centralized support mechanisms in place; however, a great wealth of information on open-source alternatives is readily available via the Web, books, or Internet newsgroups. In fact, because many versions of open-source Unix implementations exist, and because there may be no commercial vendors to provide a more supportive role, there may be more in-depth public coverage on the implementation of security mechanisms and much more information on alternative methods of doing the same types of tasks. Before you consider implementing commercial or open-source Unix alternatives, you should consider the needs of the business and the availability of support.

Understand Cultural Differences

Within your organization there are cultural differences and expectations among those who administer different operating systems. These differences are fostered by the way in which different operating systems work and how they are supported. These differences can be a serious security problem if they are not recognized. The administrators of Windows, mainframe, Unix, and other OSs have different expectations and are required to work in different ways. They are often viewed by each other as being more or less security conscious, capable, or concerned, by the administrators of the other type of operating system. Administering Unix and mainframe systems typically requires in-depth knowledge of how the systems work; it is generally expected that Unix administrators will look at the systems and try to understand the system internals from a different perspective than administrators of other operating systems. An example of this is how the different OS administrators approach a problem, such as how generally Unix administrators review the internals of the program before implementing or asking questions about a security configuration.

In the Windows world, however, an administrator does not have to read documentation to configure the system, because usually a wizard or other type of easy-to-find tool is available to assist with the administration of security. Ease of administration in the Windows world has often led to the perception that Windows administrators are not expected nor required to understand how the security systems work in order to configure them. While this is a very broad generalization, unfortunately it is the conventional wisdom, although you will find some Unix administrators who only know how to do things through a wizard-type interface and Windows administrators who can tweak the configuration files on all types of programs.

An understanding of the underlying system and what happens behind the scenes and how it happens is crucial to achieving security of the OS. Wizards and scripts are fine for implementing security policy throughout an organization, but without an understanding of what the scripts or wizards do, there is no way to fully understand the security implications of any changes. Nobody has all the answers, and collaboration, especially where security is concerned, is crucial to effectively protecting your systems. This doesn't mean collaborating only with security professionals who have the same background as you, but includes collaborating with those from other backgrounds, such as network security staff, Windows security experts, and so forth.

The Unix world, however, is composed of many communities, one or more for each flavor of Unix that mostly talk among themselves, and a large, open, and vocal open-source community. In the commercial Unix world, it is expected that you will have thoroughly researched the issue and read the man pages and any other associated documentation before asking another Unix administrator a question. In the open-source community, there appears to be a wide range of expectations, from traditional "prove to me you know all the documented stuff before you ask me" to the "help me, how do I do this?" variety. In the Windows world, there is often an expectation on the part of the newer administrator that they are owed an easy path. If it's not intuitive, pop-ups should warn them before they make an error. This attitude is changing, as those responsible for the operation and security of Windows desktops and servers have seen the results of such irresponsibility.

Professionals in all OS communities take on the burden of becoming knowledgeable but most realize that collaborative efforts can combine the knowledge and wisdom of peers into something more than the sum of parts. These differences, however, can lead to problems when administrators of different OSs and OS versions must work together to ensure the security of mixed networks. The problem may be just as difficult within a mixed Unix environment as it may be within a mixed environment of Windows, Unix, and other systems. If each community understands something about the other, and respects that difference while insisting on sound security practice, then the issue can be overcome; if differences are ignored or depreciated, then disaster may be a result to the detriment of all involved.

One way in which the cultural difference between Unix implementations can cause a problem is the requirement that the noncommercial open-source versions of Linux are often primarily supported via research on the Internet instead of a full-time, professional team of support staff. In the commercial Unix world, you can fully expect the vendor to provide patches and a baseline security standard to use on the systems that will provide a modicum of security. In the open-source world, you will find a multitude of information on the different security settings (even information on commercial Linux implementations are widely distributed by sources other than the manufacturer) and other helpful information on securing your systems. Choose the source of security settings carefully, because there is a lot of misleading or poorly constructed information on the Internet. This is true for any operating system, from the commercial Unix implementations to Linux to every other OS. The best sources for information are the vendor or well-established web sites that are known throughout the security community as reputable and factual.

Those with a deep understanding of all Unix cultures and architectures can usually determine which sources are good, and use their knowledge to provide any missing steps or considerations. Those who have little to no experience will find it more difficult. If you are one of the many administrators who have a deep understanding of only closed, proprietary Unix or only open-source Unix and now must understand the other, or if your background is Windows, you will find there is an unusual dichotomy between what would seem to be similar groups. Security within both communities is treated seriously, but the approach to security is vastly different.

In the open-source world, security is a task distributed among a very large user base. Vulnerabilities, for example, can be defined and usually are patched within hours, with sometimes different groups offering different patches for the same vulnerability. The commercial world usually operates at a much slower pace (depending on the vulnerability) and patches can take days or weeks to be released. Some versions of Unix provide patches for free from their web sites, especially security patches, but some are moving to a subscription-based patching service. Red Hat and SuSE provide patches in an easy-to-manage, centralized way for a yearly subscription fee, while Debian Linux provides an easy-to-manage, centralized patching method completely free. There are quality-assurance issues as well, as described previously, in the methods that are used while creating and deploying the patch (such as utilizing a strict quality-control process, etc.). Depending on the source for your patches, code trustworthiness could be an issue, as open-source patches are sometimes available via nontraditional methods (not from the vendor's web site), so keep in mind the famous saying "caveat emptor," or buyer beware, where security patches are concerned.

To overcome some of the issues caused by culture differences, you should utilize trusted sources of information for hardening your Unix system. Vendor web sites are always the best and most authoritative source for trustworthy information (such as those listed later in this chapter in the "Apply Patches" section). Other great sources of information for security information are the better-established, community-supported security web sites, such as SANS (http://www.sans.org) and SecurityFocus (http://www.securityfocus.com). Last but not least, utilize the services of your peers, whether they support Unix systems or not, as their viewpoint may make you think outside the traditional methods.

Protect the Root Account

The major operating systems in use today provide an administrative account or group of administrative accounts that have full access and control of the system. These OSs are not protected from these accounts—they can damage the OS if not properly used. In Unix, this responsibility is held by the root account. The Unix root account must be protected by all means possible from compromise, primarily by using strong passwords, but also by restricting access to the actual root account. One way to limit access to the root account is to use a program called **sudo**, or SUperuser DO.

sudo allows the administrator to delegate a set of usually privileged commands to other users or administrators without giving the user the root password. This means that administrators can be limited to just the privileges they need to do their job, that few if any other administrators will be able to create privileged users, and that privileged access can easily and centrally be controlled. This tool is also a great way to allow the full-time administrators to get tasks done without logging in as root, thereby preserving the root user for true emergencies. The administrator can log on and use a normal user account for mundane work such as reading e-mail or preparing reports, and then **sudo** to root or another privileged account to perform administrative tasks. Requiring delegation, and therefore the use of **sudo**, to perform administrative tasks has two other important security advantages:

- It can prevent mistakes that occur when administrators log in as root and forget they are logged in as root, potentially causing damage to the systems.
- Delegating authority for specific tasks among unique user accounts allows proper accountability for administrative tasks. The logs will record which user did what, not just that the root account was used.

sudo is available for all the Unix implementations (closed and open source) through many means. Most vendors offer a package that can seamlessly install **sudo**, or you can compile it from source if you are so inclined or your version of Unix doesn't include a package for **sudo**.

Add sudo if It Is Not Provided

To add **sudo**, you need a compiler (the GNU Compiler Collection [**gcc**] compiler, available at http://gcc.gnu.org/, is a good choice, but you can use any C compiler) and the source file, available at http://www.courtesan.com/sudo/dist/. You need to run the following commands to **untar** and **gunzip** the file (**untar** is fairly standard on Unix systems, while **gunzip** (GNU zip) is on most open-source and a larger subset of commercial Unix implementations, but if it's not on your system, go to http://www.gnu.org/software/gzip/gzip.html for the latest version). If you download a different version of **sudo** than the one listed here, you need to replace the filename with the filename of the file you downloaded.

```
gunzip sudo-1.6.7.5.tar.gz
tar -zxvf sudo-1.6.7.5.tar
```

Next, you need to read the installation notes provided in the sudo*version* directory and read the file named INSTALL, paying special attention to the version section for your version of Unix. After making note of any special configuration options you may need to enter, type **configure *options***, such as the following for Solaris:

```
./configure --with-CC=/usr/local/bin/gcc
```

Then, you only need to run the **make** and **make install** commands:

```
make
make install
```

Configure sudo Delegation

At this point you are ready to work on the more complicated portion of the **sudo** setup, that being the setup of the sudoers file in order to delegate privileges and nonprivileged commands. This file is installed in /usr/local unless you specified a different directory during configuration. When you open this file, you must keep in mind that your settings in this file will give someone the permission to run programs as the defined user (typically root). Do not give users any of the following:

- **vi**, the interactive text editor, which can enable the user to initiate a shell command from within the **vi** session as the designated user in **sudo** (typically root).
- **gzip**, which can allow someone to gzip the password or shadow file and then unzip it back to it's original location, allowing for a privilege escalation. For instance, someone can modify the /etc/password file and give themselves a

user ID of 0 (or root, which has total administrative control over the system and can cause serious harm to the system) and then uncompress the file back to its original location.

- Any program/application that has the potential for shell access within the program, such as the text editor **vi**, which allows you to run shell commands from within the program.
- Custom-written programs (scripts) or other commands that could give unintended escalated privileges.

Another thing to note about **sudo** is that you should be careful when setting up the configuration file. Sometimes administrators will enter the NOPASSWD option in the sudoers file, allowing commands to be run without having to first enter their user password. This should be avoided at all costs, as someone with access to an unlocked console can then run commands within **sudo** if the logged-in user steps away from their terminal, for instance.

Each man page within **sudo** has a caveat's section that should be thoroughly reviewed, as it will capture many of the common gotcha's for **sudo**.

Configure User Accounts and Passwords

In the next few sections, the discussion turns to technical implementations of some of the more basic hardening steps that are available to the majority of Unix systems. There will be differences in program installations, from the commands to compiling to the installation routines and directories, so those are noted in those cases where referring to the included documentation is appropriate.

Remove or Harden System Accounts

System accounts are one of the most overlooked areas for the typical system administrator because most are installed with the default installation. These accounts represent a potential vulnerability for your system and should be removed or locked down. This is such a problem that it is now part of the SANS Top 20 Internet Security Vulnerabilities (http://www.sans.org/top20/), and there are web sites dedicated to the listing of default system accounts. Default passwords may also be listed. These web sites give an attacker information needed to attack a system but also give the defenders vital security information.

Default system accounts are created to ease administration. While some are needed, most administrators will find that the majority of the accounts are not needed. For instance, in Solaris Unix there is an account named *listen* that is used for backward compatibility with older versions of Solaris. Most environments do not need this account, but it is installed by default on this system. Most Unix vendors provide default accounts for functionality on their systems, the majority of which accounts (to be fair to the Unix vendors) do not allow interactive shell access to the systems. Irrespective, the possibility of a misconfiguration or setting of a weak password always exists as long as the account is available.

One way to secure your system accounts to prevent any type of login until you are sure they are no longer needed is to set the shell in /etc/passwd to **/bin/false** and set a single asterisk, *, in /etc/shadow (the shadow file is different on some implementations of Unix). This prevents anyone trying to log into that account from either getting a shell or logging in with FTP. This is still not the optimal solution, but you can use it to severely restrict any access until the account can be removed. Figure 13-1 shows an example of some of the accounts on a default Solaris 10 installation.

Require Strong Passwords

In addition to removing the vulnerable default system accounts, a policy of strong passwords should be enforced and regularly checked. Strong passwords usually consist of eight or more characters, with at least one or more being nonalphanumeric characters (*, @, #, and so forth), one or more being a number, one or more being an uppercase letter. Furthermore, the password cannot be connected to the user personally (birth date, favorite food, and so forth) and cannot include a sequence or pattern within the password combination (123, abc, etc.). The widely available John the Ripper password-cracking program can quickly check your Unix accounts for weak passwords by attempting to crack the passwords based on predefined dictionaries or through brute force (trying all combinations).

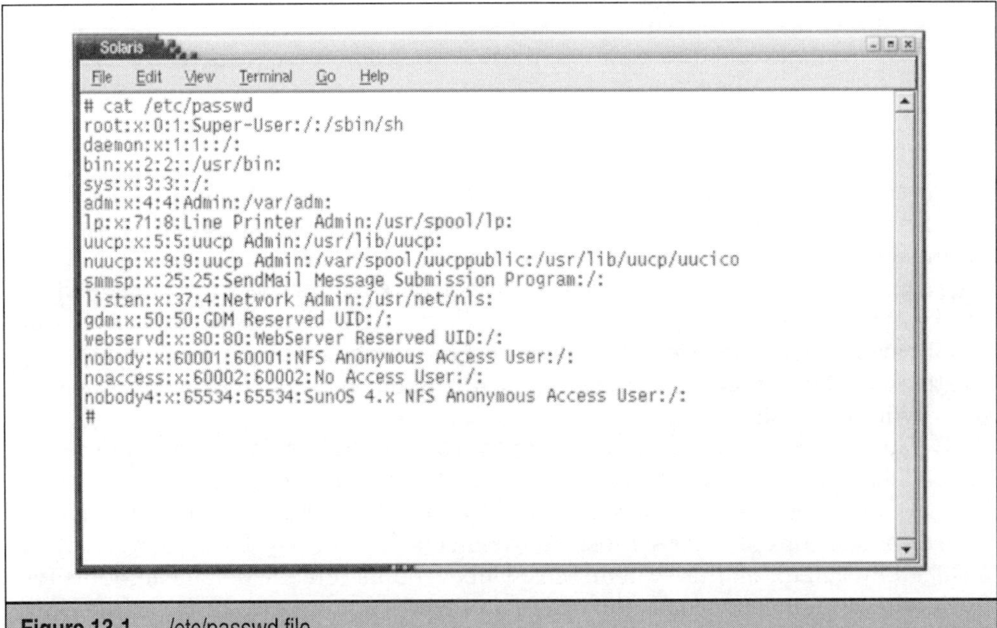

Figure 13-1. /etc/passwd file

NOTE Before you use John the Ripper on any system, you must have prior permission from the system owner/data owner or you could face criminal or civil penalties.

To utilize John the Ripper, you need to download the source code at http://www.openwall.com/john/. After downloading the source, compile the software for your architecture. Then, you only need to acquire the shadow file from the systems you are authorized to check and run John the Ripper. You will begin to see the weak passwords (if any) cracked.

Accommodate Any Nonshadow Password Systems

In the early days of Unix, the /etc/passwd file stored user account names and hashed passwords. This file is world readable, so eventually malicious individuals started to recover the hashed password from /etc/passwd and run cracking programs against the hash. If a password is left long enough and if it isn't changed in a reasonable time period, it is possible to crack any hashed password depending on the password complexity and the processing power dedicated to breaking the password; this could be anywhere from less than a minute for a password as simple as "l1nux" to more than a few weeks for one such as "&1d(zQp!3".

Due to this issue with /etc/passwd, many systems incorporated the /etc/shadow file. This file is restricted from all but the most privileged users and it contains the hashed password, while the /etc/passwd file typically contains an X in the spot where the hashed password was once stored. The use of shadow passwords is the de facto standard on all modern Unix implementations, but you may come across a legacy system that doesn't implement them or you may be required to support a system without shadow passwords. If you are installing a new Unix system, always choose the shadow password options, as these keep the users' passwords in an encrypted file separate from the world-readable password file. If you inherit a system without shadow password support, you may be able to implement shadow passwords. Otherwise, you have to rely upon strictly enforcing a strong password policy in conjunction with a reasonable password change requirement (every 30 to 120 days) to reduce the likelihood of a compromised password. In fact, this should always be done regardless of whether or not shadow passwords are used, because this is considered best practice and provides an additional layer of security to your security program.

Remove Cleartext Services

Unix was initially developed when there wasn't the multitude of computers and the community was small and could be trusted. Because of this, many legacy services were designed for functionality rather than security. This has changed dramatically in the past 20 years, but there are some services that are in use by networks that are not safe from malicious entities. These services include, but are not limited to, the following:

- rcp
- rsh

- rlogin
- ftp
- tftp
- telnet
- smtp
- pop3

These are some of the major nonencrypted services that are still commonly used today, especially in mixed Unix networks, and are the predecessors to the more secure, encrypted protocols, usually developed by following a set of standards among the different implementations. If at all possible, avoid any new implementation of the services listed previously. Once they are integrated into your networks, they are very difficult to weed out because people tend to create scripts dependent on them that are critical to business processes.

If you have inherited systems with these services, the best option is to move to more secure protocols that provide nearly the same functionality, but with stronger authorization mechanisms and encrypted transmission mediums. The most widely used application suite with the same functionality of the r services (**rcp**, **rsh**, **rlogin**, etc.) is the OpenSSH toolset. This is an open-source, free for commercial use toolset that gives the same functionality as the r services. Table 13-1 illustrates the alternatives to unencrypted protocols.

To get OpenSSH, go to http://openssh.org/, where many free versions are available depending on your version of Unix (licensed under GPL and derivatives). If your organization needs a commercially supported version of **ssh**, visit http://www.ssh.com for more information.

For more specifics on installation of **ssh** in Linux (this can also apply to some Unix implementations), refer to *Hardening Linux*, by John Terpstra, Paul Love, Ronald Reck, and Tim Scanlon (McGraw-Hill/Osborne, 2004), Chapter 10.

Unencrypted Protocol	Encrypted Protocol
ftp/tftp	sftp
rsh	ssh
rlogin	ssh
telnet	ssh
rcp	scp

Table 13-1. Unencrypted and Encrypted Protocol Comparison

Reduce the Number of Running Services

Internet services provide specific functionality on the Unix system that is uniform and consistent. Some services are required on machines for the system to do its basic functions, while others run because of legacy applications that no longer require them or that have been turned on by default. Typically, most services on Unix are run from /etc/inetd.conf (a notable exception being that some Linux distributions use xinetd.conf). Many flavors of Unix have some services on by default to provide some basic functionality out of the box for the Unix server. This is contrary to basic security premises, so removing unneeded service functionality is crucially important in the hardening process. For instance, Sun Solaris has typically had a large number of services turned on by default, such as finger, font servers, and a multitude of other services, while most versions of Linux have far fewer services turned on by default, such as SSH only. The fewer services that are running, the fewer potential vulnerable points that exist for an attacker to gain access to the system. Some of these legacy services include **finger, discard, chargen, daytime, time, talkd**, as well as many other vendor-specific services.

When assuming security duties on a system or installing a new system, ensure that you review the services your system is running and disable any unnecessary ones. One word of caution: you should test any changes before implementation, and then confirm with monitoring that the adjusted systems still provide the level of functionality required for business operations.

Apply Patches

Patching is a familiar term to any system administrator, and is one of the most often overlooked, but crucially important security tasks. While Unix is built with security in mind, there will always be new vulnerabilities discovered and new software modifications that may require updates. By keeping systems patched and up to date, you provide vendor corrections to security vulnerabilities and add updated functionality.

Simply subscribing to a security list will show you the number of vulnerabilities documented on the Internet. All organizations must have a plan in place for routine patching as well as what actions to take for critical patches. All Unix vendors provide patches with their products, and some usually provide them for free depending on the patch (security patches are typically free, while upgrade patches are not usually) or whether you have a paid support contract.

The following are major Unix vendors and the sites where their patches are available:

- **SUSE (Linux)** http://portal.suse.com/psdb/index.html
- **Red Hat (Linux)** https://www.redhat.com/security/
- **OpenBSD (BSD)** http://www.openbsd.org/errata.html

- **FreeBSD (BSD)** http://www.freebsd.org/security/
- **Apple (OSX)** http://www.apple.com/support/downloads/
- **Sun (Solaris)** http://sunsolve.sun.com/pub-cgi/show.pl?target=patchpage
- **IBM (AIX)** http://www-1.ibm.com/servers/eserver/support/pseries/aix/solving.html
- **SCO (SCO OpenServer)** http://sco.com/support/security/
- **HP (HP-UX)** http://www.hp.com/products1/unix/operating/security/

Some of these vendors offer the ability to get patches in bundles (most notably Sun and IBM), which enables you to install a large group of patches at once, easing your burden. Most of the commercial Unix vendors offer easy-to-use tools for patch management and monitoring, such as Sun's patchdiag, although some require a subscription or free registration to use the service, so be sure to check out the vendor's home page for more specific information on your flavor of Unix. Some examples of easy-to-use patch management tools are the Red Hat up2date tool, which supports easy patch maintenance from a central location for multiple Red Hat Linux systems.

On a mixed Unix network, patching is more of an issue, because there are few centralized, vendor-supported methods for deploying patches to a large, mixed-vendor network. One product that does is patchlink, but it doesn't cover all versions of Unix, as there are many available. There are different vendor implementations of centralized patching tools, such as PatchPro for Solaris or Red Hat Network for Red Hat Linux. This lack of vendor-agnostic tools for Unix patching can create a major administrative burden and can hamper the timely deployment of patches.

Monitor Log Files

Log files are a security and system administrator's best friend, because they contain information that can assist in determining problems. As with all things Unix, different vendors have decided to implement log files in different ways, although you can generally find most logs of importance to a security administrator in /var/adm or /var/log. These logs contain a treasure trove of information on the operations of the system, from failed and successful logins, to unusual events on the system, such as failed **su** attempts. One great thing about Unix is that almost all implementations have the same format for their logs, allowing you to centralize and analyze the logs from many different Unix systems on one system (which doesn't have to be the same flavor of Unix as the ones sending the logs).

Reviewing the logs on a one-Unix-machine network is not problematic, but when dealing with large numbers of Unix machines, especially with different flavors of Unix, this becomes a very time-consuming process, prone to errors. Unix comes with the capability to send logs to other designated machines on a network via the syslog daemon. A central log server has some of the following advantages over trying to maintain logs over many different systems:

- The logs will be located in the same place regardless of the flavor of Unix.
- The logs can be correlated and analyzed for trends over many machines versus one machine.
- Logs can be backed up easier via a central log server.
- Logs can be secured on a machine specifically hardened for limited access (reducing possibility of log tampering).
- If a machine is compromised, the logs will have been sent to another machine, showing evidence of the beginning of the attack.

Central Log Server Setup

On most versions of Unix, the first step to setting up a secure log server is to edit the /etc/syslog.conf on each of the individual hosts that you want to have logging to the central server. Open the /etc/syslog.conf file and add an entry for the remote log server's IP, such as this:

```
*.debug                                             @192.168.1.2
```

Make sure you use tabs between *.debug and the IP, as this is one of the most common problems for a host to fail to log to the central log server. This level of logging will probably be too aggressive, as you will receive all messages, related to security or not (which can be a lot of unnecessary information). With syslog, two important components determine what is logged, the facility and priority. The facilities and priorities set the conditions for which the syslog daemon will log messages and how verbose the logging will be. Table 13-2 shows the different types of facilities available. Table 13-3 shows the priorities that can be used in syslog.

Facility	Description
auth or authpriv	Authorization messages
cron	Cron/At messages
daemon	System daemon messages
kern	Kernel messages
kpr	Line printer subsystem messages
mail	Mail subsystem messages
news	USENET news subsystem messages
syslog	Internally generated subsystem messages
user	Generic messages
uucp	UUCP subsystem messages
local0-local7	Local messages (open for internal use)

Table 13-2. Facilities Available in syslog

Priority	Meaning
debug	Debug level messages (verbose). This will provide the highest level of logging information for the facility indicated.
info	Informational messages
notice	Normal, yet important messages
warning	Warning messages
err	Error messages
crit	Critically important messages
alert	Urgent messages
emerg	Emergency messages
none	Log no messages for the facility

Table 13-3. Priorities Available in syslog

Although there are many facilities and priorities, for most security administrators the following initial /etc/syslog.conf entry will suffice:

*.info; mail.none;news.none,lpr.none

This configuration logs all informational messages as well as higher-priority messages, but does not log the mail, news, and printer facility messages.

For maximum security, however, it is recommended that everything be logged, as an exploit can occur from anywhere, and more logs are usually better if you have the capacity to sift through the extra information to find the pertinent entries relating to security. Be wary of too much logging, as this will dilute the effectiveness of your security program because it will take more time to review logs, the result of which may be that issues get overlooked because of all the noise in the log.

The last portion of the /etc/syslog.conf line outlines what action is to be taken when the syslog daemon matches the condition outlined in the initial portion of the line. For the central log server, this will be the @ sign followed by the IP address of the central log server or the host name (an /etc/hosts entry must exist for the host name if this option is chosen). If you wanted to log all of the host syslog messages on machine 192.168.1.1 to the central log server you have set up at 192.168.1.2, excluding any line printer messages (the lpr facility), the entry in syslog would be

```
*.debug;lpr.none                                    @192.168.1.2
```

NOTE Make absolutely sure to use tabs between the facility/priority pair and the host designation.

After you make any changes to the /etc/syslog file, you must restart the syslog daemon so that syslogd is prompted to reread the /etc/syslog file (this occurs at reboot as well). You can identify the syslogd process ID (PID) by running the following command:

```
/bin/ps -ef | grep syslogd
```

The first part of the command (`/bin/ps`) calls the **ps** command, which shows all processes. The **–ef** switch provides expanded and full listings of the process. The pipe (|) command redirects the output of the **/bin/ps –ef** command to the **grep** command, which is a pattern-matching the syslogd daemon and searches for the syslogd process. The output will show you the PID, at which point you can **kill –HUP** the PID to restart the daemon. Figure 13-2 shows the output of the **ps –ef** command on a Solaris 10 machine.

The next step is to harden the central log server by removing unneeded accounts, disabling unneeded services (allowing only **ssh** for maintenance and udp 514 for logging, for instance), and taking other steps to restrict access to the machine. Then, you need to set the central log server to accept incoming syslog messages on port 514 (udp), which is the default. The different versions of Unix require different steps to do this; for instance, for Linux and Solaris, you can restart the syslogd daemon with the **–r** option to enable remote logging during the session (for permanent remote logging, you need to edit the init script that starts syslogd and add **–r**). Your central log server should now be receiving log messages.

```
Solaris
File  Edit  View  Terminal  Go  Help
# ps -ef | more
     UID   PID  PPID   C    STIME TTY         TIME CMD
    root     0     0   0 19:22:30 ?           0:03 sched
    root     1     0   0 19:22:31 ?           0:00 /etc/init -
    root     2     0   0 19:22:31 ?           0:00 pageout
    root     3     0   0 19:22:31 ?           0:00 fsflush
    root   357     1   0 19:25:25 ?           0:00 /usr/lib/saf/sac -t 300
    root   470   468   0 19:25:41 pts/2       0:00 /usr/bin/gnome-session
    root   218     1   0 19:24:40 ?           0:00 /usr/sbin/cron
    root    75     1   0 19:24:35 ?           0:00 /usr/lib/sysevent/syseventd
    root    29     1   0 19:22:32 ?           0:00 /sbin/dhcpagent
  daemon    89     1   0 19:24:36 ?           0:00 /usr/lib/crypto/kcfd
    root    92     1   0 19:24:36 ?           0:00 /usr/lib/picl/picld
    root   233     1   0 19:24:41 ?           0:00 /usr/sbin/inetd -s
  daemon   167     1   0 19:24:38 ?           0:00 /usr/sbin/rpcbind
    root   154     1   0 19:24:38 ?           0:00 /usr/sbin/in.routed
    root   213     1   0 19:24:40 ?           0:00 /usr/sbin/syslogd
    root   229     1   0 19:24:41 ?           0:00 /usr/sbin/nscd
    root   271     1   0 19:25:22 ?           0:00 /usr/lib/power/powerd
    root   522   512   0 19:27:14 pts/3       0:00 sh
    root   295   292   0 19:25:22 ?           0:00 /usr/sadm/lib/smc/bin/smcboot
    root   297   292   0 19:25:22 ?           0:00 /usr/sadm/lib/smc/bin/smcboot
    root   282     1   0 19:25:22 ?           0:00 /usr/lib/utmpd
--More--
```

Figure 13-2. ps –ef output

Some other options are to use an encrypted TCP session with Stunnel (http://www.stunnel.org) for your logging, which gives you connection-oriented messaging that is tamper resistant. You can also use syslog-ng (http://www.balabit.com/products/syslog_ng/) to refine your syslog delivery on the central log server to specific directory structures based on the packet contents. Another tool that can extend your logging functionality is the TCP Wrappers daemon available at ftp://ftp.porcupine.org/pub/security/, which initiates a log event for specified events.

Log Monitoring Tools

Logging is great for monitoring system health and security, but you must be vigilant in your monitoring of the logs. A log that isn't monitored is a diminished tool that is not used to its full potential and could be a liability. One of these tools is logcheck, available at http://sourceforge.net/projects/sentrytools.

Logcheck allows the security administrator to monitor the logs in almost real time for specific, user-identifiable events without the drudgery of manually inspecting every line of the log file. You can set up logcheck to e-mail you under certain conditions, as well as configure other notification options.

The first step in the setup of logcheck is to download the necessary files from SourceForge, http://sourceforge.net/projects/sentrytools (logcheck-1.1.1 is recommended).

NOTE Another version of logcheck is available at http://sourceforge.net/projects/logcheck. Version 1.1.2 has the capability to block addresses in conjunction with TCP Wrappers. This version is not covered here because it requires a high level of knowledge of your systems. If you are not completely familiar with your network and its requirements, you should not run this version on a production system, as you could end up creating a denial of service for valid resource users. The version covered here, version 1.1.1, is more benign and alerts security administrators of issues rather than actively blocking perceived threats.

Save the download file in an appropriate directory, such as /opt, and then begin the gunzip and untar the file with

```
tar -zxf logcheck-1.1.1.tar.gz
```

Next, change your directory to logcheck-1.1.1, and you will see the following files and directories:

```
CHANGE
CREDITS
INSTALL
LICENSE
```

```
Makefile
README
README.how.to.interpret
README.keywords
README
src
systems
```

Go into the systems/*unix distribution* directory and open logcheck.sh with your favorite editor. In the logcheck.sh file, go to the #CONFIGURATION SECTION and modify appropriately the variables that apply to your system. You can comment out with the # sign the reference to /var/log/secure and /var/log/maillog because you have all messages going to /var/log/messages from the previous syslog.conf setup earlier in this chapter, unless you find that you need that granularity, in which case you need to edit the /etc/syslog.conf file to send the appropriate messages to the preceding log files. The only variable you probably need to modify is the SYSADMIN variable, which you can change to your pager address or e-mail address for specific paging or notification requirements (be wary that you could get many more e-mails or pages than you initially expect).

After you have configured your logcheck.sh file, do the following:

```
cd ../..
make <unix version>
```

If you receive the following error message,

```
creating temp directory /usr/local/etc/tmp /bin/mkdir:
cannot create directory _/usr/local/etc/tmp_: No such file or directory
```

simply create a directory with the appropriate permissions called /usr/local/etc, which will satisfy the error. You have now compiled logcheck and you need to test it by running /usr/local/etc/logcheck.sh. If it runs with no errors, then it is working properly.

If you receive errors, refer to the README file for more information. Now set up logcheck to run automatically via a **cron** job. To do this, run the **crontab –e** command and add the following line:

```
00 * * * * /usr/local/etc/logcheck.sh
```

This will run logcheck.sh every hour, or you can set it to be more aggressive as needed. Don't pat yourself on the back yet; you still have to edit the various configuration files to meet your specific needs. The default files are a fairly good place to start, but each environment will have specific requirements. The files to edit are identified in Table 13-4.

File	Purpose
/usr/local/etc/logcheck.ignore	Keywords or events specified in the file that should be ignored.
/usr/local/etc/logcheck.hacking	This is where you put keywords related to hacks or attacks to your system.
/usr/local/etc/logcheck.violations	Note any keywords that relate to bad or unwanted events.
/usr/local/etc/logcheck.violations.ignore	Keywords that are checked against the logcheck.violations file and not reported because they are invalid messages.

Table 13-4. Logcheck Configuration Files

After you run the logcheck.sh or have the cronjob report run, you will get an e-mail message similar to the following based on the keywords you added to your configuration files:

```
Active System Attack Alerts
=-=-=-=-=-=-=-=-=-=-=-=-=
Aug  29 21:04:05 linux1 rpc.rstatd[3568]: connect from localhost
Security Violations
=-=-=-=-=-=-=-=-=
Aug  29 21:10:10 linux1 su: _su jsmith_ succeeded for jdoe on /dev/tty3
```

Another tool that accomplishes the same functionality as logcheck is the open-source, GPL-licensed product Swatch (http://swatch.sourceforge.net/), which will watch the log files for specific events identified by the system administrators.

Another great tool for log monitoring is simple event correlator (SEC), available at http://www.estpak.ee/~risto/sec/. This tool has some of the same functionality as the venerable Swatch, but also includes more-defined event matching.

Whatever tool you choose, make sure that the alerting is refined so that administrators don't receive irrelevant messages, which dilutes the impact of the tools by leading to possible lethargy in logfile monitoring.

Physically Secure Your Unix Systems

Unique knowledge of various Unix systems cannot be overlooked when designing and providing physical security. If someone can gain physical access to a system, they can gain root access with very little effort. For Solaris, a simple installation CD-ROM can be mounted during a reboot to change the root password, and for Linux, a bootable disk, CD-ROM, or USB drive can be booted and the file system mounted with full root access to achieve root access. The difference here is that it may be difficult for most people to obtain a Solaris installation CD-ROM, but a bootable Linux disk can be prepared by anyone from code feely available on the Internet, and bootable Linux CD-ROMs are often handed out en masse at conferences. While you cannot prevent access to free software, you can securely store Solaris and other installation disks separately from the system unit. You can be aware of the Linux issue and disable or remove CD-ROM and floppy drives from those systems that must be accessible to many users. Use good physical security to prevent unauthorized access to your Unix system.

Review Vendor-Specific Unix Hardening Resources

There is generally no better place than a vendor's web site to gather more information on specifics to the Unix system you are administering. Here are the major vendors and their security resource sections:

- **Linux (not vendor specific)** http://www.linuxsecurity.com
- **SuSE (Linux)** http://www.suse.de/de/security/
- **Red Hat (Linux)** http://www.redhat.com/security/
- **OpenBSD (BSD)** http://www.openbsd.org/security.html
- **FreeBSD (BSD)** http://www.freebsd.org/security/index.html
- **Apple (OSX)** http://www.info.apple.com/usen/security/index.html
- **Sun (Solaris)** http://sunsolve.sun.com/pub-cgi/show.pl?target=security/sec
- **IBM (AIX)** http://www-1.ibm.com/servers/eserver/pseries/security/
- **SCO (SCO OpenServer)** http://sco.com/support/security/
- **HP (HP-UX)** http://www.hp.com/products1/unix/operating/security/

This is by no means a comprehensive list of security resources, but starting with the vendor pages for the major Unix implementations is a very good move toward securing your Unix system.

These steps are some of the major issues to consider when working with Unix systems, but this list is only the tip of the iceberg in hardening your Unix machines. You should refer to books dedicated to the subject, such as *Hardening Linux,* to get a more comprehensive view of all that is entailed, to ensure maximum security of the Unix OS.

Chapter 14

Intrusion Detection and Response

by Patrick Kelly

- Design the Intrusion Detection/Protection System
- Deploy the Intrusion Detection System
- Harden the Intrusion Detection/Prevention System
- Secure Your IDS Operation
- Develop an Intrusion Reaction Process

Intrusion detection systems (IDSs) provide companies with a constant monitor of network and host access activity. These monitors can be configured to recognize malicious and unwarranted activity and provide an evidentiary audit trail. Properly handled, this audit trail can provide valuable evidence in identification of an attack and determination of a course of remediation. IT professionals need to understand the framework of IDSs and to what extent these systems can assist the organization in maintaining a reliable, safe, and productive technology environment.

When it comes to detecting intrusions, the security industry has developed a number of options. As a result of the different choices and claims, several questions come to the forefront:

- Is intrusion detection enough protection?
- Are intrusion prevention systems mature and accurate enough?
- Should I use host-based or network-based or a combination of both?
- Are signature-based systems current enough or are upgrades to patterns readily available?
- Can anomaly-based systems provide zero-day protection?

Systems that monitor and report any type of intrusion become another layer in your defense-in-depth security strategy. You should look at this class of defense as a monitoring and information tool, not as a prevention tool such as a firewall or content filter. How your systems react to the information you are gathering is a result of your security needs. Because of its role as information provider and auditing base, the information gathered by any monitoring system, the data needs to be irrefutable if used as evidence in a criminal prosecution. This system, like any logging system, must be accurate. The information generated by any monitoring system must be absent of the possibility of tampering, during both transport and storage of the information.

It is important to understand the benefits and expectations as well as the drawbacks and limitations of any monitoring and alarm system. This chapter describes the basics of an intrusion detection system/intrusion prevention system (IDS/IPS) to provide a foundation for you to understand the design elements, deployment challenges, and reaction strategies. For additional information on IDS/IPS, you are encouraged to consult *Hardening Network Infrastructure,* by Wesley J. Noonan (McGraw-Hill/Osborne, 2004).

Design the Intrusion Detection/ Protection System

Designing the IDS/IPS requires an understanding of the types of IDS/IPS and how an IDS/IPS inspects network traffic. Determining how you want your IDS/IPS to react to specific types of information gathered dictates what IDS/IPS components you deploy and where these components are placed in your infrastructure topology. This section introduces the different IDS/IPS components and provides a brief description of each of these technologies.

An IDS is an exploit-analysis system that should be designed to identify any attempts to utilize weaknesses in network and computer systems that could result in a potentially harmful intrusion. The ideal IDS integrates with existing security and network topology and provides a valuable supplement to your current security infrastructure. The IDS will always be working in the background. The notification mechanism and your reaction parameters should accommodate the "always on" paradigm.

An IPS is constructed to have control over the delivery of the network traffic it inspects, regardless of whether the system is inspecting network traffic of protected subnets or traffic of a single system. If the IPS is configured properly, any host producing network traffic with malicious intent will be blocked from communicating or influencing any other system on the protected network. Realizing the potential for internal attacks on the data integrity and availability of your security domain, the implementation of the IPS can become very complex when addressing this internal challenge.

HEADS UP!

There is a continuing line of discussion among security professionals and industry experts concerning the viability of IDSs compared to IPSs. The discussion is based on the value of an IDS compared to the investment of deploying IPS. Market research is beginning to show that although information provided by an IDS is analyzed, little if any further action is taken by the security team (see the sidebar "Tuning an Alert in the Windows Environment"). Critics claim IDSs have failed to provide an additional layer of security and have added complexity to the security management problem.

Proponents of IDSs counter these statements with solid arguments of their own. IDS technology is unlike the other security technology in that the purpose is not to defend from attacks but to monitor and notify of attacks. If other security technologies fail (and that "if" is why you are reading this book), the IDS provides an evidentiary audit trail to assist in determining where the other defenses failed. The ongoing problem with NIPSs is a false sense of security. Administrators using an IPS have an expectation that it is protecting the systems it's associated with. Administrators using an IDS have the expectation that it is monitoring and reporting attacks; no reaction by the IDS is expected to block the attack. If the NIPS blocks all exploits based upon patterns and anomalies, what about the large number of successful attacks based upon configuration errors? Attacks targeted at wrongfully configured systems are not detected or protected by any IDS or IPS.

Understand the Types of IDS/IPS that a Topology May Require

Systems are classified by their topology placement (either network based or host based) or by how they work (signature based or anomaly based):

- **Network-based IDS (NIDS)** A protected node on the network that inspects communication packets as they pass by or through the system.
- **Host-based IDS (HIDS)** An agent installed directly on a computer that is already part of your network.
- **Pattern- or signature-based IDS** Inspects the content of the header and payload sections of the packet, looking for matches with known attacks. Inspection of the payload is referred to as *deep packet inspection.* Manufacturers are also examining new methods of dividing packets to apply specific patterns to matching segments of the packet. Their goal is to reduce the latency caused by buffering the packets to complete the deep packet inspection. In high-volume traffic networks, administrators are pressuring manufacturers to reduce delay caused by filtering systems.
- **Anomaly-based IDS** Looks at the characteristics of the packets to see if they comply with a specific standard that describes normal activity. It alerts on packets that do not match normalcy.

Each of these systems has a place in your IDS design.

Host-Based Intrusion Detection/Prevention Systems

A host-based intrusion detection/prevention system (HIDS/HIPS) is a software package loaded on an individual computer (host) that allows a direct method of monitoring and auditing connections, programs, and activities of the specific machine, program, or service, respectively. A HIDS/HIPS is capable of protecting file integrity by monitoring additions, modifications, and deletoc 1to the file system. Many of these HIDS/HIPSs perform as a host or personal firewall that filters data as it enters the system at the network card hardware driver or the first point of entry into the system. An application-specific HIDS/HIPS recognizes the normal function of system calls to operate in a normal use of the application, such as a web server. If any API calls are triggered outside of this normal activity, the HIDS/HIPS reacts with an alarm, action, or combination, resulting in the denial of the application to continue or complete the malicious request.

Network-Based Intrusion Detection/Prevention Systems

Network-based intrusion detection/prevention systems (NIDS/NIPS) either intercept or promiscuously retrieve network packets from a network segment. The content or payload of the packets is compared to a database of signatures that describe malicious network traffic. If a packet is identified as being potentially malicious, the NIDS/NIPS instigates a notification process and logs the activity. This NIDS/NIPS technology is the target of industry criticism based upon important handicaps. The NIPS is designed to react to any discernable exploit by eliminating the potential delivery of the exploit to the intended target. Further, the NIPS can and should eliminate further exploit attempts from the source against any future targets. This potentially presents a bottleneck for network traffic and results in network latency.

ONE STEP FURTHER

Many NIDSs are attached to networks that use switch technology. Switches direct traffic based upon MAC address routing. Traffic entering a port on a switch will be directed to a specified port based on the recipient's address, to assist in the efficient delivery of traffic to the designated destination host. Hubs, on the other hand, deliver the network traffic to all ports. The hub technology makes deploying NIDS in promiscuous mode as simple as plugging the NIDS into a hub port. In a hub environment, the NIDS has access to all the network packets whose source or destination is any port on the hub.

With switches, you must span or mirror the ports you intend to monitor with the port that the NIDS is connected to. Most configurable switches allow you to designate a single port that will receive traffic from a combination of other ports on the switch. Spanning and mirroring have inherent weaknesses, as they will not forward 100 percent of the traffic to the NIDS port. In addition, the mirrored switch can produce collisions, and the operation of the switch begins to approach the same functionality of a hub.

With the help of a network Test Access Port (TAP) device, your NIDS can gain access to packets traveling on a single wire. For example, you can insert a Net Optics (TAP) device into the network segment you want to monitor. A network TAP will address this packet-loss problem in a switched environment. A TAP allows the insertion of a passive network device into any link (see Figure 14-1). The TAP can be inserted to monitor a single port of a switch or the connections between switches. In effect, it taps the Ethernet cable connection, allowing you to connect the monitor, without degrading network throughput performance. Note that TAPs support copper and fiber links.

Since TAP devices are passive, they will *fail open* (if the power drops, the network traffic will pass through the device like the wire it has tapped into) to eliminate any network outage by the TAP device power failure. Another advantage of a passive device is the lack of requirement to have any identifying addressing schemes. Since the device cannot be addressed, the NIDS is not reachable by any addressing mechanism, neither MAC address nor network IP address. Adding this "hidden from the network" feature, the TAP also may act as a security device for NIDS.

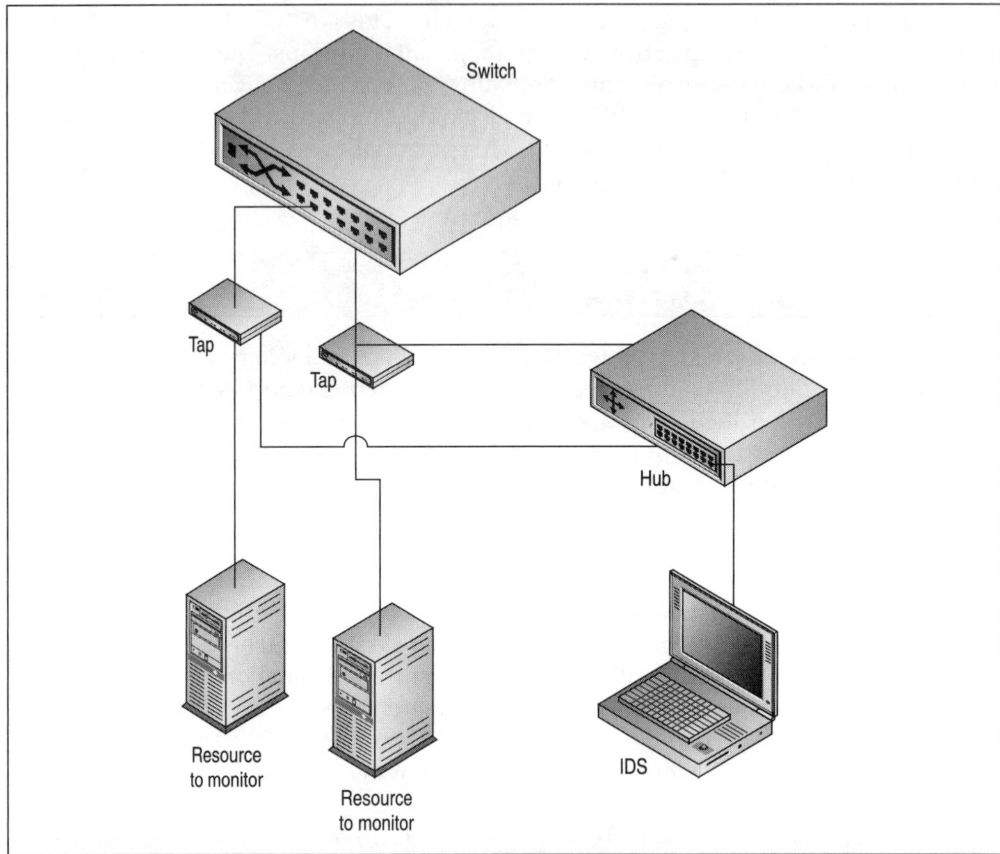

Figure 14-1. Inserting TAP devices into existing network connections to provide access to a network communication segment at the cable level

Signature-Based Intrusion Detection Systems

This method of identifying intrusion attempts uses the content of the attempt itself to trigger the alarm reporting system. The network traffic is processed and compared to a rule base that contains signatures of malicious network traffic instances. A distinguishing pattern either in the packet payload or packet header can trigger a warning if the scanning engine can match the packet pattern to a signature database record. Any alarm that is generated requires prior knowledge of the exploit. Therefore, the signature database must be kept up to date for it to be effective. In addition, many signature-based IDS databases are flexible enough to accommodate custom manipulation to either change the records or extend the database with custom rules.

NIDSs are approaching a new concept of packet inspection. The new approach is to design pattern-type rules that monitor protocol traffic. Any time the packet payload does not match the expectation of the protocol according to RFC specifications, an alarm is triggered.

Anomaly-Based Intrusion Detection Systems

An anomaly-based IDS generates alarms based upon deviations from an operating profile representative of normal, expected network traffic and system operations. A benchmark of normal utilization is established that reflects the normal operations and network traffic patterns for the segment being monitored. Once this normal level is established, the anomaly-based IDS will trigger a warning when this normal level is exceeded. Examples could be defined as an increase in network traffic during normal hours or a burst of traffic during relatively quiet times. Another trigger might be when the IDS notices an unexpected state of an established connection. An example could be an abundance of SYN packets with no matching SYN ACK packets.

Design IDS Selection and Topology to Meet Operational Requirements

The proper selection of and physical location of IDS sensors on the network can maximize their potential. The design of an IDS topology is similar to that of surveillance cameras. Similar challenges and solutions exist for each of these technologies. Just as some IDSs handle traffic and produce a clearer result than others, some surveillance cameras provide a better capture than others of the traffic in front of them. Like the better IDS, the better camera capture increases the value of the camera, as it provides a better audit of past actions. A camera with poor visibility may tell you someone was in the area, but their exact identification may be blurred or impossible to confirm because of the lack of clarity in its gathering of the data available at the time of the capture. Like IDS nodes, cameras also are nodes in a communications network. Cameras must communicate with their recording device. If the data transmission is broken or disturbed, the evidence is lost. A proper surveillance camera topology will provide for the protection of the electronic communication network. A proper IDS topology design will do likewise.

There are design considerations that are unique to the IDS. You need to address these design goals when you are selecting which IDS product is right for your security profile:

- *The IDS must run continually.* You must accommodate for single system outages due to upgrades or equipment failures. You must be able to monitor the IDS monitors as you would any critical security device on your network. Although your users will not notice that a passive network monitoring device has stopped functioning, the security team should find out immediately.
- *The IDS must be capable of updates to signature patterns and anomaly trends.* Failing to keep any security device updated renders it inadequate. These updates are as important as the updates to your antivirus system.

- *The IDS must be flexible and agile enough to allow the administrator to customize the signature patterns and adjust anomaly thresholds to measure expected traffic levels.* The IDS must scale to network bursts without damaging performance. Inline IPSs are susceptible to this limitation. Passive IDSs can use TAP technology to analyze packets with buffers when needed without disrupting traffic. In addition, multiple IDSs can be configured to divide the traffic into specific service threads. Separate IDSs can monitor a subset of the protocols and services traversing the wire without dropping or missing packets. Either your OS interface statistics or the IDS itself can report dropped packets.
- *The IDS should detect malicious payloads in the protocols you need to monitor.* For example, Snort, a free NIDS, will monitor IP, TCP, UDP, and ICMP. Other protocols that you may need to monitor include ARP, IGRP, GRE, OSPF, RIP, IPX, and GBP, among others.

Determine IDS Placement and Monitoring Requirements

To determine the optimal placement of the IDS/IPS, you must determine what systems and connections to monitor. You should also consider only looking for attacks against the specific services and programs supported in your environment.

Select an IPS or IDS Based on Your Needs for Active or Passive Monitoring

An IPS is an active security component in your network. Whether the IPS is using network traffic or host-based functions to inspect potentially malicious traffic, the IPS has direct access to your network and systems. You should expect the IPS to act upon active traffic in real time to send an alarm, alter the delivery of network traffic, or shut off access to a system service. Conversely, the IDS remains a passive network component. The IDS monitors traffic offline. Because the IDS is a passive device, do not expect it to alter network traffic flows or change configurations on systems. The IDS will generate alarms that may lead to manual intervention to adjust network traffic flows or reconfigure systems services and programs.

Select an IDS Based on the Flexibility of Its Three-Module Design

When considering the links and systems to monitor, consider the IDS that is architected in a modular design. Choosing a design with separate modules provides you the flexibility of adjusting and optimizing the placement of the components for performance and efficiency benefits. The IDS is comprised of three separate modules: the sensor, the alarm repository, and the analysis console.

The sensor is the module that directly interfaces with the attack sequence. The sensor is responsible for the following:

- Keeping up with the traffic flow and not dropping packets. Scaling this interface is critical to the success of the IDS.
- Maintaining signature rules or anomaly thresholds.
- Configuring the format and destination for alarms.

HEADS UP!

Scaling the IDS network interface card (NIC) to accommodate the traffic it will see is a complex calculation. Contributing factors to the limited throughput of network cards are memory, buffers, window sizes, and bus speeds if using other hardware, such as writing to a disk. The Pittsburgh Supercomputing Center (http://www.psc.edu/networking/perf_tune.html) has several research projects aimed at providing better utilization of network bandwidth capabilities. Some of the results of this research are to provide a better understanding of how to accomplish better throughput with existing technologies. Understanding the Bandwidth x Delay product (BDP) calculations will assist in network configuration parameter tuning. These parameters are responsible for limits on buffers, window sizes, and protocol manipulations. Command of these configuration parameters will assist in your assurance that each packet you want your IDS to analyze is available to the monitor.

The second component of the NIDS is the alarm repository. Once a network packet is flagged by the sensor rules to trigger an alarm or log entry, the information is sent to the alert log repository. The log repository needs to provide intelligent storage design schemes. The categorization and organization of the alarms and log entries will provide a better tool to act as a basis for alert analysis. The underlying data storage schema should be arranged to provide the query information you need to adequately analyze the alert log entries.

That leads into the third component, the analysis console. This is the component that adds value to the monitor, alert, and storage mechanism of the NIDS. A popular analysis console for the Snort IDS is the Analysis Console for Intrusion Databases (ACID), the GUI for which is shown in Figure 14-2.

Select a NIDS Based on the Ease of Protection of a Self-Contained System

Having all of the NIDS components contained in a single system is a recommended solution and is easier to harden. A self-contained NIDS offers advantages when it comes to hardening the NIDS, as detailed later in this section. It should be used when:

- Access to the console is not burdensome or inconvenient.
- The console can be secured from physical attacks.
- Routing issues, firewall policies, or NAT restrictions may cause interference with the encryption technologies required to protect componentized NIDS.

An alternative to having a completely self-contained NIDS is to have all functions installed in a self-contained system, with the exception of the administrator's analysis console. This deployment strategy may be more practical in smaller environments where a small number of NIDSs would be able to monitor all of the high-risk targets.

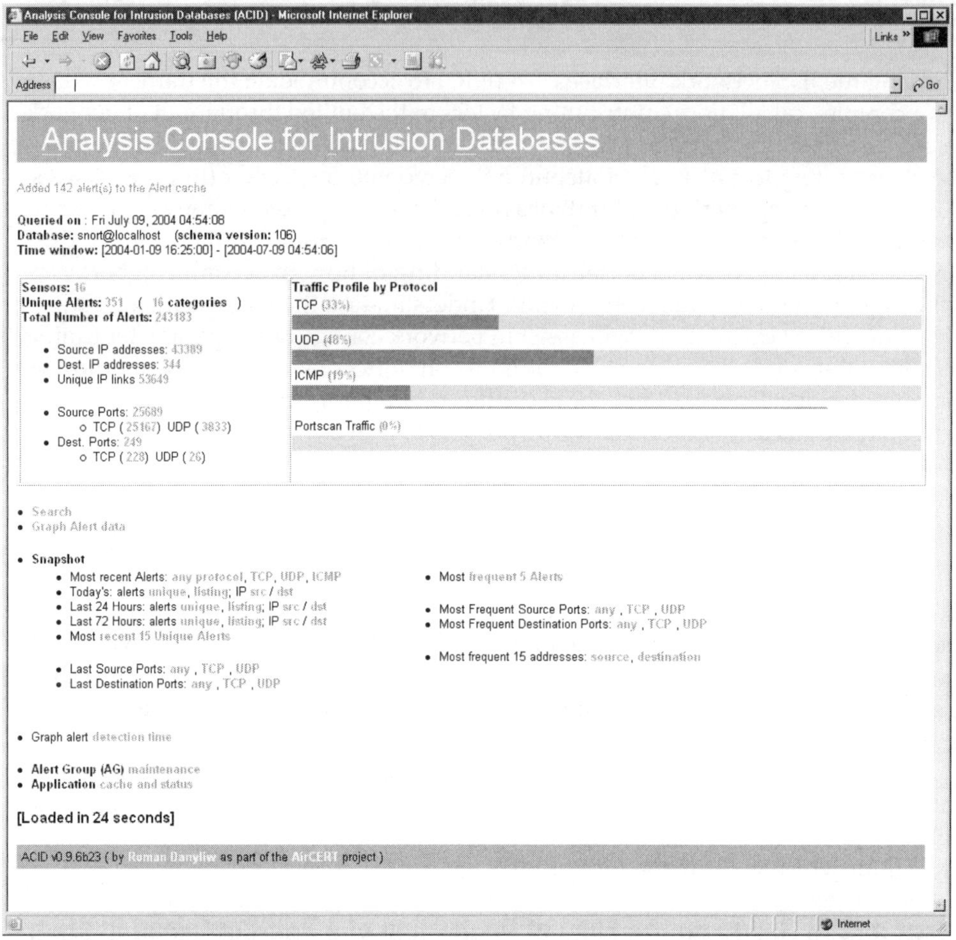

Figure 14-2. ACID categorizes alerts and provides access into packet payload inspection.

Select a Solution with Distributed Sensors and a Central Management Station

In many instances, several sensors can be used. In these particular situations, it is advantageous to have these sensors report to a single console. The main advantage is to have a common view of the information that is gathered by the sensors.

The first instance addresses a situation in which a high volume of traffic passes over a single, common link. Many monitors that are intended to inspect Internet traffic fall into this category. In high-volume circumstances, you can use the divide-and-conquer principle. You can configure the rule sets on multiple sensors to monitor and react only to specific exploit attempts. For instance, you may have one sensor configured for analysis of web traffic, while another sensor may look for mail server or DNS server exploits. All the time, these separate sensors can report to a single consolidation console.

A second instance would be a situation in which multiple sensors are deployed to cover geographically separate monitor locations. In situations where many monitor points are optimal, a distributed deployment may be the best solution to cover a disparate geographic region. The distribution of sensors reporting to a centralized alarm station fits this situation nicely. In the case of a large number of geographically separated monitor points, you can still have a central management station and alarm repository.

The goal in designing the IPS/IDS is to decide which network segments or hosts to monitor. In a small network, you may look at deployment of a single system. But whether you have several systems or just the one, you need to cover these locations to ensure that you are covering all of your other security technologies.

Deploy the Intrusion Detection System

Once you complete the initial design, you can begin to configure the sensors, alert and alarm data repository, and the connections to bring it together. You need a hardware platform for each sensor and alarm repository and, if desired, a network TAP for segment and wire monitoring. If the IDS/IPS is using switch SPAN or mirroring, you also need to monitor the ports and systems directly involved for packet retransmissions both before and after the IDS/IPS installation. This will assist you in the discovery of any network traffic bottlenecks that could result in network performance degradation.

The following is a list of likely deployment locations. These deployment suggestions are based upon the choices of all-inclusive systems combined with multisensor and central alarm repository designs.

- Servers that store proprietary data would be excellent candidates for a NIDS for the network segment and a HIDS for each server to analyze the network traffic originating or terminating at that server.
- Servers that provide authentication are also targets of attacks, especially inside attacks, and thus are good candidates.
- Network links to and from remote access points into your network are good candidates. The more common access points into your network are listed here:
    - Internet access points are more likely to see malicious traffic from attacks and scans than any other points on your network.
    - If you have placed a DMZ in your network design, an IDS/IPS system may be an early-warning system for attacks launched from servers within the DMZ. These alerts may turn a potentially disastrous event into one less critical by stopping the attack at the front door after the attacker has gained

access to the front porch. Also, place HIDS/HIPS systems on servers in the DMZ; at the very least, monitor the services these servers are providing to the outside world.

  - Remote access point defined by VPN devices or RAS servers may be connections to uncontrolled networks. Placement of HIDSs/HIPSs on the exposed servers warns of harmful attempts to compromise these devices.

- Wireless access points (WAPs) connecting to the core network should be mandatory NIDS/NIPS monitor points.
- Visitor areas for temporary employees, vendors, or other short-term guests should be monitored. This will be helpful in spotting rogue workstations and other sources of malicious attacks. Create a VLAN for networks providing access to workers or strangers. Monitor the VLAN for either a planned attack or a system that has been previously compromised seeking to spread the latest attack to the next unsuspecting victims. In addition, monitor your exposed connection to and from this specialized network.
- Monitor both sides of the device providing separation of critical or secured networks, such as a supervisory control and data acquisition (SCADA) system or classified network, within your enterprise network. You will want to monitor attacks that are looking for this critical network's access points, and also monitor any attempts to locate this specialized network's soft spots.
- Monitor both sides of your branch office or other WAN connections. Monitoring remote offices, no matter how small, provides you a source for discovering any rogue WAPs, rogue Internet connections, or other unintentional violations of network security policy.
- Monitor the nontrusted side of your firewalls. There will always be discussion on the value of an IDS placed outside your firewalls. The main argument is that a large volume of attacks should not surprise you at your outer perimeter. There are other security experts who say that any evidence and information you can gather might be beneficial in the face of a serious attack or even a compromise. In looking at the audit trail aspect of an IDS, a well-hidden IDS can provide value if information is needed. You may consider placing a honeypot along with the hidden IDS.

Snort: A Practical NIDS

Snort is presented here as an example of a NIDS because of its relative ease to deploy and its ready accessibility to most administrators (it is open source). If you wish to install and test Snort, the Snort site is at http://www.snort.org.

The Michael Davis and Chris Reid Windows port of Snort is available for download at http://www.snort.org/dl/binaries/win32/. To install and run this version of Snort, you must also download the WinPcap packet driver from http://winpcap.polito.it/install/default.htm. The file winpcap is an executable that will install the driver. This

HEADS UP!

Honeypots or *honeynets* are systems that initially look valuable to attackers and, since they are vulnerable, might be considered a good target. If malicious attacks can be directed to these systems, it may provide a distraction from the more important network components. The hope is that the attacker will try to grab the low-hanging fruit first. Another advantage of honeypots is that they enable you to better understand how the attack works and how the system was compromised. You can then use this information to better protect your production systems. If carefully monitored, attacks against honeypots can be a source of insight not easily gained elsewhere.

There is an important downside to honeypots. If someone uses your honeypot to attack another system, a liability suit could be brought against you or your company.

driver is necessary for the packet-capture function of your network card driver. I have used WinPcap_3_01_a.exe with Snort 2.1.0 on Windows 2000 Server. The Windows 2000 server is up to date with service packs and patches. In the Windows port of both Snort and WinPcap, the installation files are self-executing and follow any defaults during installation. Detailed installation documentation is available on the Snort web site.

The Snort installation creates a Snort directory under C:\ similar to that shown in the following illustration. The ../etc directory is where the snort.conf file is located. In the sections to follow, we will be looking at some settings available in the file.

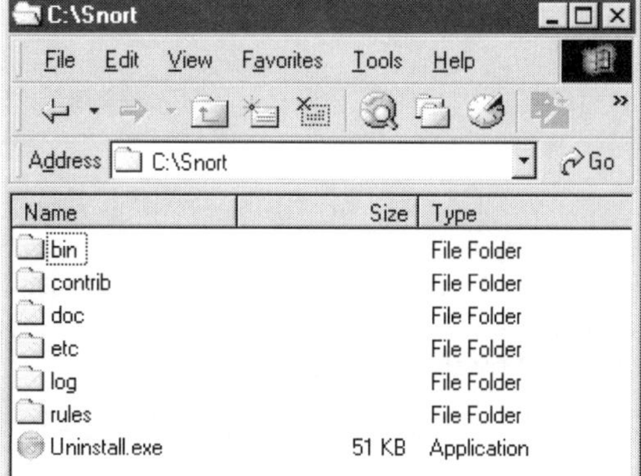

Tune the IDS

Even though you should spend time during implementation to tune your IDS/IPS to your environment, like most security operations, tuning the IDS/IPS is an ongoing process.

Tuning the IDS means adding or removing signatures or constraining signatures so that all known attacks are alerted and yet minimal false alarms are generated. There are several reasons that an IDS requires constant tuning:

- You may be overwhelmed with the volume of alerts. In a busy network with Internet, e-mail, web browsing, and internal broadcast traffic, many alarms will trigger on these events.
- As you begin to analyze the reported alerts and alarms, you will understand the configuration settings in the snort.conf file. Adjusting and refining these system variables and parameters can provide a better picture of the network alarms.
- New attacks are constantly being developed and hence new attack signatures must be added.

Tuning an Alert in the Windows Environment

The following listing is an example of alerts generated by network traffic in a typical Windows 2003 Server environment. The intent of this rule implementation is to identify rogue or misconfigured client computers. This scenario assumes that NetBIOS over TCP/IP is disabled on clients and servers; host resolution comes from DNS settings. Any required NetBIOS traffic takes place over port 445. This rule would not be a good idea on a Windows network with pre-Windows 2000 hosts, because they require the use of NetBIOS over TCP/IP.

```
[**] NETBIOS SMB IPC$ share unicode access [**]
07/15-22:21:17.162819 1.1.1.211:1550 -> 1.1.1.11:139
TCP TTL:128 TOS:0x0 ID:48710 IpLen:20 DgmLen:118 DF
***AP*** Seq: 0xCFB658A4  Ack: 0x4815F8BC  Win: 0xF963  TcpLen: 20
=+=+=+=+=+=+=+=+=+=+=+=+=+=+=+=+=+=+=+=+=+=+=+=+=+=+=+=+=+=+=+=+=+=+=+=+
```

This alert indicates server 1.1.1.211 is sending SMB IPC$ share unicode access traffic to server 1.1.1.11 on port 139. Notice the alert begins with NETBIOS as a designation of the type of alert that has been generated. By matching the type of rule (NETBIOS) to the rule in file \snort\rules\netbios.rules, you can locate the exact rule that was matched by the packet:

```
alert tcp $EXTERNAL_NET any -> $HOME_NET 139 (msg:"NETBIOS SMB IPC$ share
unicode access"; flow:to_server,established; content:"|00|"; depth:1;
content:"|FF|SMBu"; depth:5; offset:4; byte_test:1,>,127,6,relative;
content:"I|00|P|00|C|00 24 00 00|"; distance:32;
nocase; classtype:protocol-command-decode; sid:538; rev:10;)
```

Notice the source is the global variable $EXTERNAL_NET. If you look at the default setting in the etc\snort.conf file, that variable is set to any. This setting would make this rule a candidate for producing an alert no matter what the source computer would be.

Set up the external network addresses as well. A good start may be "any":

```
var EXTERNAL_NET any
```

If you examine other rules in the netbios.rules file, most of the Snort rules are using this $EXTERNAL_NET as the source computer. If it is left to the default `any`, any packet matching this signature will be flagged as an alert. If you are going to consider this normal traffic on your network, you are going to ignore this alert. One way to reduce much of the alert noise and false positives is to look at making this variable in the rules more exact than just any computer. You can make this $EXTERNAL_NET variable any computer not on your network with the example below in the snort.conf file. The exclamation point is an operative expression literally meaning "not."

```
var EXTERNAL_NET !$HOME_NET
```

Provided your $HOME_NET variable is set correctly, now these rules will trigger only if the originating computer is not on your local network. Any attack launched from inside your network would be ignored at this point. If your servers (more specifically, the network hosts you are monitoring) are part of a separate VLAN of 1.1.2.0/24, you could designate that network address for the variable $EXTERNAL_NET in snort.conf for this sensor:

```
var EXTERNAL_NET !1.1.2.0/24
```

This would trigger any traffic matching the attack signature from any network other than the server VLAN. If this sensor monitors only a portion of the servers on the VLAN, you would declare a variable identifying those servers it is monitoring and assign the rest of the networked world with the following configuration in the snort.conf file. You would specifically list the servers in a new variable called SERVERS_NET and assign the negative operator with the new variable to the $EXTERNAL_NET variable, like this:

```
var SERVERS_NET [1.1.2.211/32,1.1.2.202/32,1.1.2.11/32]
var EXTERNAL_NET !$SERVERS_NET
```

This way, any computer that is not a domain controller server generating alerts would be flagged as perhaps the beginning of a malicious attack. This configuration makes more sense if you are going to consider every occurrence of this alert as just another normal Windows server communication and ignore the alert. Now if you see this flag, you will know the origin is not one of your domain controllers and that you should investigate why this alert is triggering.

Harden the Intrusion Detection/ Prevention System

You must harden the IDS/IPS against attack or compromise. As with any security component, you must consider many elements as part of the hardening process. The steps you take will depend on the type (detection or prevention) of system you have installed. Possible hardening tips for NIDS include these:

- If the IDS/IPS is installed on an operating system, harden that OS. Refer to the Hardening Series titles for Windows and Linux for more information.
- Harden the network infrastructure to provide a secure environment within which the IDS/IPS can function. *Hardening Network Infrastructure* in this series can help you there.
- Install Snort or another IDS on a system already hardened on your network. For performance considerations, however, you may find that placing your IDS/IPS on a separate system is best.
- Purchase a self-contained system or appliance that has been hardened and is ready to go.

HEADS UP!

If you purchase a self-contained system or appliance, you must consider the upkeep and patch requirements. Such a system, even though it's a security system, is not immune from attacks and compromises targeted at its OS. Before purchasing an appliance IDS/IPS, investigate the patch and update policy and history. Factor these issues into the overall ownership commitment of this class of solution.

A host-based IDS/IPS requires setup and configuration onto an existing system. To guarantee the system is not compromised, the important factors to consider are physical access to the console as well as remote access. In many OS builds, remote access is available through Terminal Services, Remote Desktop, SSH, and so forth. Consider the convenience of this remote access model when managing a system critical enough to be a candidate for a HIDS, but also consider how to secure it against attack. You should ensure that a HIDS/HIPS will identify, flag, and report an intrusion attempt from remote access services if the supplied credentials are invalid.

Secure Your IDS Operation

Once you have a system prepared, before you place it in production, harden the components as a complete system. The sensors must be protected and must send accurate, unaltered information to the central repository. The data store must be maintained as any other data store in the company.

Protect IDS Communications

Communication between sensors and management stations needs protection as does communication with the administrator's console and the data store. In Figure 14-3, the communication paths between components are represented by arrows and, as noted, are protected with SSL.

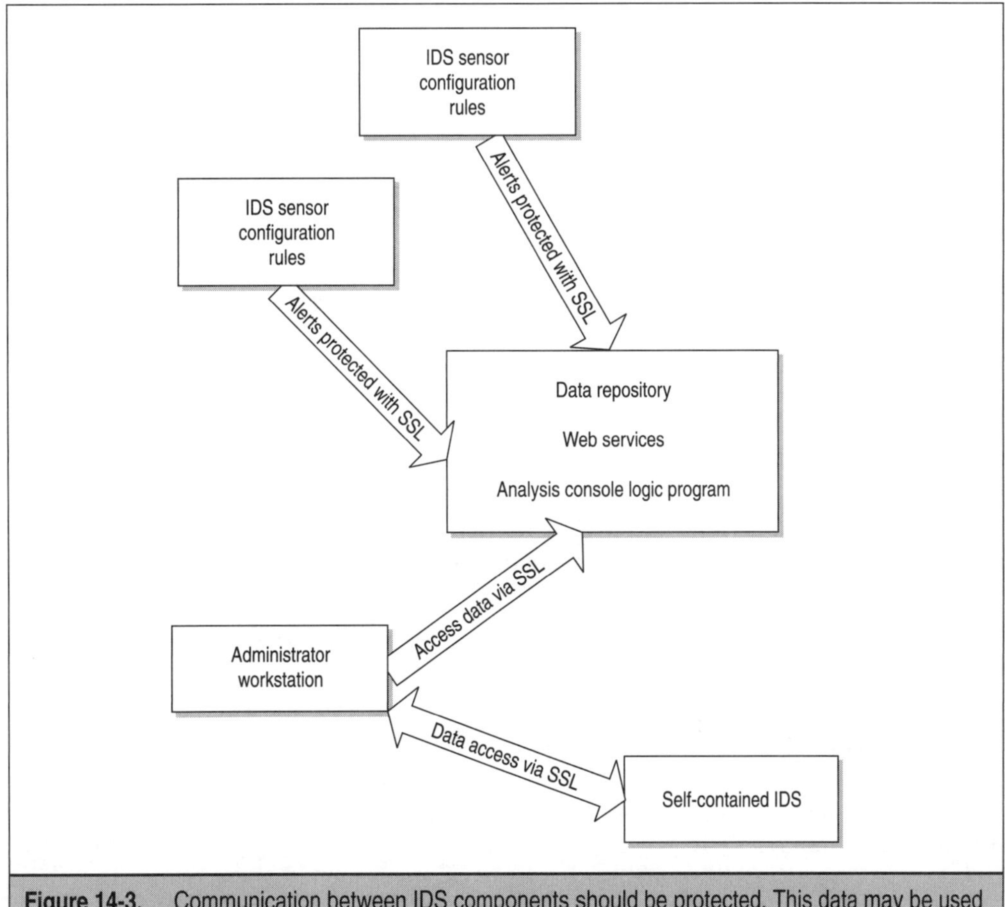

Figure 14-3. Communication between IDS components should be protected. This data may be used as evidence; its integrity must be preserved.

Another area of concern is the access to the alert information during transport from the sensor to the data repository on the management station. This can easily be done with SSL encryption. An example of an SSL encryption system providing protection during communication is Stunnel, which encrypts data communications on a service-by-service basis as needed. Stunnel can redirect communication to a port or service that can be configured with SSL. As the service begins communication over normal ports or services (such as 3306 for MySQL), Stunnel redirects the communication to a port that implements encryption with SSL. Thus, the information being transported between the systems is encrypted with SSL for this service only.

Protect Configuration Files

Configuration files may contain passwords and other sensitive information that should be protected. For example, if you are using Snort with the build directive that uses MySQL (./configure --with-mysql), the snort.conf output plug-in would look like this:

```
output database: log, mysql, user=snort password=PASSWORD dbname=snort
 host=management-server.domain.local
```

In the snort.conf file, the password is stored as plain text. This is a weakness that you need to address. In the case of this Snort installation, the snort.conf is referenced when the process starts. Once the Snort sensor starts, you can safely store this file in a secure area, remove the file entirely, or protect the file with encryption.

NOTE As with any system, the configuration files must be protected. Preserving restricted console access is the first priority. Since IDS sensors are protecting valuable systems, these sensors must follow the same guidelines as the systems they are monitoring.

Protect Database Access Permissions

Database access permissions also need to be protected. Distinguish between the user permissions from the sensors and user permissions from the analysis tools. Only the administrator or DBA will have delete permissions. The account used to attach to the database only needs enough permission to write records to the database.

Develop an Intrusion Reaction Process

All of your work in providing an infrastructure that can detect intrusions is worthless if nothing is done when an intrusion is detected. Therefore, you need to implement an intrusion detection response process.

Reactions to Intrusion Investigation

During investigation of intrusions, I have witnessed some common observations that have been made about the actual process:

- The client found it extremely helpful that they had a plan. The plan did not cover all the subsequent events, but it did provide a direction and sequence of events to follow when emotions were very high.
- Time relating to the sequence of events seemed out of focus. Trying to remember the chronology of events was difficult. Different people had different memories of what had happened.
- The client discovered how good (or bad) their system recovery plan was. Being able to validate the accuracy of their data as they recovered and moved forward was really the most important issue to deal with.

Practice makes perfect is a cliché. I can assure you that your intrusion reaction plan will never be perfect, but as with any recovery system, you should practice.

Understand Intrusion Reaction Stages

Intrusion reaction includes several stages:

- **Discovery and identification of the intrusion** This stage uncovers what information has been "touched." In addition, the team needs access to resources to assist in developing forensic evidence to determine if the information has been seen, moved, altered, or deleted.
- **Recovery** Taking and keeping computer systems offline is expensive, because it moves your system to inactive status. The costs begin to add up exponentially when you factor in lost productivity time combined with the catch-up costs. Making decisions during this phase involves balancing management and productivity pressures, the need to attempt to regain the confidence and integrity of the systems, and the ability to preserve the compromised state for examination and evidentiary needs.
- **Remedy** During this phase, the business decisions are made concerning notification of customers, legal and criminal pursuits, and correction of any discovered weaknesses.

Assemble the Intrusion Response Team

Identify the people who may need to be involved in handling an intrusion. This team includes the core positions involved no matter what the intrusion, how widespread or inclusive. This team must make decisions on what further actions to take.

- **Team leader** It will be very helpful to have a central management contact. Moving through the process, this person will need to coordinate the other team members. Communication between management, internal departments, and the technology team needs to be monitored. Decisions need to be communicated to the appropriate team members in a timely sequence. This position is also responsible for the chronological record of the events.
- **Management** Business decision makers will need to assist in decisions concerning the posturing and philosophy of the company, especially if a crime has been committed. Someone of unquestioned authority needs to be involved from the beginning. What to do with resources is a business decision.
- **Security team** This should include both cyber security and physical security. These people will be responsible for halting any continued intrusion and be prepared to discuss options and decisions with management.
- **Technology staff** This team will be responsible for discovery, recovery, and maintaining the chain of custody for any evidence. It needs to have the processes of maintaining a safe and prosecutorial state of the intrusion. In addition, it needs the resources to recover the system to the production state quickly. If you don't have this expertise in house, you need to contract with someone who has an excellent reputation and experience.
- **Human relations team** It makes sense to include someone from HR on the team; statistics show that a significant number of intrusions originate within the company. Also, in times of crisis, it has proved beneficial to have this perspective involved to assist with communication, interaction among groups, and performance issues.
- **Public relations team** Any official communication either within the company or publicly should be delivered under the discretion of the PR department or partner. California has passed a law whereby companies are required to notify California constituents if their entrusted information is made public. There are ramifications involved with this notification, but any statement to staff, customers, or anyone outside the team should be professionally crafted.
- **Legal staff** This group can provide insight into criminal prosecution. Even before the incident occurs, it can provide resources describing procedures for ensuring the evidentiary integrity of any system or procedure. In addition, it can provide advice on when and what course of action to pursue based upon the facts as presented. Consult with the legal staff prior to releasing any public statements or contacting law enforcement.

HEADS UP!

I have seen companies wrestle with the prospect of notifying customers that their information may have been leaked. In one instance the company believed that it should be honest and forthright with its customers, so it crafted and distributed a confidential letter to customers explaining that its information may have been taken outside the company. As a result of its honesty, no customers filed suit or even left. It even received praise from one customer who appreciated the honesty. On the other hand, some companies have experienced significant negative impact on market prices when their compromises have been publicized.

- **Law enforcement** You should understand any ramifications to contacting law enforcement. Will they seize your equipment? Will their involvement overshadow any attempt from the public relations team? How effective are local law enforcement officials in dealing with cyber crime? Who should be contacted, local, state, or federal agencies? Since this resource is out of your control, it's a good idea to know something about their level and degree of involvement in your situation to benchmark any decision to include them. Under certain circumstances, you may have to include this group.

Prepare for an Intrusion

Intrusion is inevitable. It makes sense to organize defenses based on this assumption. Here are the steps to take:

- *Make sure all your systems are on the same time clock.* Create your own Network Time Protocol (NTP) server and synchronize all of your security and network devices. Having all of your devices on the same time clock will add credibility and accuracy to your side of the chronology of events. Having a well-described series of events with little room for doubt will strengthen your case, should it go to court. At least one of your network devices should synchronize with an authoritative Stratum-level NTP server. There are hundreds of NTP servers available from ntp.org (http://www.ntp.org). Most NTP server administrators require permission to use their server for your time-synchronization server.
- *Keep an updated map of your network.* If you need to bring in outside investigative services or personnel, they will need to know what you have and where it is located. In any large organization, few IT employees will have all this information either.
- *Make sure your company has policies in place to search, monitor, and retrieve information created by employees and contractors.* Is intellectual property that somehow is leaked to a competitor by a former employee or contractor considered an intrusion? This is one example of the issues that the policies should cover.

- *Keep current on laws involving access to information, either stored or transmitted.* Make sure the information you gather for evidence of an intrusion is acquired legally. Make sure you've made it clear to all who attach to your network exactly who owns the data on the network and servers. Include computers on your network that do not belong to your company.
- *Create an Incident Response Supply list.* Some of these items may be on hand but make sure you have your own supply for this type of incident:
  - Extra hard drives for making digital "clones" of any tampered drive. Are your servers operating with RAID 5?
  - Extra backup tapes. You may need to take some out of the rotation that may have valuable information stored.
  - Notebooks and writing instruments. Each team lead and technical members must keep a diary of events. Write in your own words what you have observed and discovered, actions you have taken, and communications concerning facts. Periodically review your chronology. If you need to append notations, initial the notation and timestamp the entry.
  - Blank media, camera, and labels. You may need to take a snapshot of a hard drive file or a physical scene.
  - Forensic tools and the knowledge to use them. Not just any administrator has the experience to perform qualified forensic analysis. Either provide training or consult with someone you can trust. Don't waste time and money preparing evidence that will not withstand cross-examination.

Develop a Plan, Test the Plan, Work the Plan

Building a specific plan to handle an unknown incident may be impossible. Focus more on the tools to provide for flexibility to involve resources you may not be able to identify until you begin the investigation and recovery. Communication will be a key factor. Consensus concerning what direction to follow—gather evidence or restore production—will work to your benefit. A single, poor decision may leave you with damaged data and no recourse for remediation.

The best plan may be to schedule simulated intrusion events based upon actual incidents in the news. Assign team leaders the action item of researching publicized intrusions. If possible, interview some of the players involved to get first-hand knowledge of what it was like and what they could have done better. Experience is a great teacher.

Obtain experience about intrusions before you are faced with that predicament. By then it will be too late. You will wish you had prepared (or be thankful that you have) if you find yourself in that situation. Emotions will be on edge. Remain as calm as possible—you will get through it.

Chapter 15

Managing Malicious Code

by Jason Zann

- Spam: Defend Yourself Against Public Enemy Number One
- Prevent Successful Phishing Attacks
- Protect All Systems from Viruses
- Defend Against Worms
- Engage in Patch-Warfare Tactics
- Protect Against Spyware
- Protect Web Applications from Web-Based Attacks

Malicious code, code that purposefully attempts to annoy system users, corrupt systems, steal data, or otherwise make something harmful happen, may be difficult to detect and difficult to remove. In many cases, malicious code produces an adverse result by using preexisting system settings in a manner in which they were not originally intended to be used. Adverse results range from a threat to privacy, to a compromise of the value of a system, to standard annoyance.

Malicious code in not anything new; in fact, applications that contain it now have their own name: *malware.* This chapter walks you through various types of malware and malicious threats and explains how to detect them, how to deal with them, and how to attempt to block them all together. The types of malware and malicious threats explored in this chapter are as follows:

- Spam
- Phishing
- Viruses and worms
- Zero-day exploits
- Spyware
- Web-based attacks

HEADS UP!

Do not mount a counter offensive. As professionals, we have a responsibility to show some tact when dealing with malicious code on the Internet. Many of us are technically astute enough to identify sources of malicious code (like spam and spyware) and, in many circumstances, to locate the persons or organizations responsible. All of us, at some point or another, have been ready to electronically annihilate the people responsible for the latest piece of malicious code that has affected us. Such attempts do not work and, in fact, usually do more harm to good Internet citizens than to the adversary that you think you are going to destroy. For example, if you load up a few machines and launch a denial of service (DoS) attack on the target, the bandwidth and every hop between you and the target will be taxed, affecting plenty of innocent Internet users. Additionally, in the case of spam, distributed DoS (DDoS) attacks, and so forth, the target that you are aiming at could be a hijacked machine of a person or an organization that is unaffiliated with the spammer or attacker. So, you can never be certain whether the source is actually the perpetrator or a hijacked machine that the real perpetrator used. Besides potentially impacting someone or some organization that is in a similar position to yourself, retaliatory actions of these types are illegal.

Spam: Defend Yourself Against Public Enemy Number One

Soon after sending e-mail messages over the Internet became a globally accepted method of communication, spam entered the e-mail landscape. *Spam* refers to the massive number of unsolicited e-mail messages, generally containing content intended to solicit business (both legal and illegal), that are sent over the Internet every day. For all intents and purposes, spam is the electronic equivalent of the junk mail that you receive in your physical mail box. Message Labs, a managed e-mail security services provider (http://www.messagelabs.com/emailthreats/default.asp), estimates that roughly 60 to 80 percent of the e-mail sent over the Internet is spam.

When dealing with spam, there is one important fact to keep in mind: spam is not going to go away on its own. While some laws and legislation have been (and will continue to be) passed, the most that they can do is deter some of the spam. The primary reason that such laws will not stop spam is the economics behind spam. Even though most of us delete spam, a very small percentage of people actually open and respond to the messages, which makes spamming profitable. Because sending spam is an automated process that does not require much human interaction, and has a very low cost in terms of barrier of entry, it can be rather cost effective even with a very low success rate. Coupled with the fact that the receiver of spam has the largest burden in terms of time, resources, and frustration, any incremental work on the spammers' part is worth it.

Spam is an annoyance, a productivity inhibitor, and a security risk. The annoyance factor is pretty straightforward. We all have better things to do than open our in boxes and sort through e-mail about free porn, debt reduction, or the possibility that we have won $1,000,000. Spam inhibits productivity because it ties up bandwidth, disk space, and administrators' time. Furthermore, users waste significant time sorting through spam, and could potentially overlook or delete an actual business e-mail while cleaning up their in boxes. The security risks posed by spam are a little more complicated:

- **Viruses and malware** When a user opens an unsolicited e-mail, a virus or malware may be launched onto the user's computer and potentially the network.
- **Unavailability of security systems** Enough spam could rise to the level of a DoS attack on an enterprise by consuming too much bandwidth or too much drive space, impairing the availability of the security system.
- **Hostile work environment** If spam that contains material deemed inappropriate by an employee is not blocked by network administrators, that employee might sue the company, claiming that the company has created a hostile work environment through its failure to block the material.

The preceding discussion outlined several high-level reasons why spam is bad and why efforts should be made to block it. If you require more information to build a case for greater support of efforts to block spam in your environment, go to http://www.spamisbad.com/. The rest of this section focuses on methods to deal with spam in your environment.

Antispam Solutions

There are several different ways to address the issue of spam in your environment. To harden your environment against spam, you need to be familiar with what general solutions are available, what to look for in those solutions, and how to evaluate those solutions, as described in the following sections.

Turn Off Open Mail Relaying

An open mail relay is an e-mail server that allows a third party to forward e-mail to another server. The e-mail that is forwarded is not from or to an authorized user of the server. Open mail relays make spam very difficult to prevent. Spammers do not play by the rules. They purposely mislead recipients as to where their e-mail is coming from. They may do so by locating a mail server on the Internet that allows open relay. A misconfigured mail relay service enables someone to connect to a mail server from the Internet, create an e-mail address with bogus From information, and send messages from that address. Essentially, the misconfigured mail server serves as a proxy between the spammer and the individuals who receive the spam. This is why it is important to ensure that your mail relay services are not open to the Internet.

Use a Whitelist

A *whitelist* is a list that is created by you with input from the rest of your organization as to what domains, individuals, mailing lists, and so forth your organization will accept mail from. While in theory this setup is ideal, it is not very practical, primarily because none of us actually has the ability to create comprehensive whitelists and because most organizations need the flexibility to accept mail from multiple unknown addresses or domains. For example, a sales organization most likely does not want to receive e-mails only from preexisting customers, but rather wants new customers to send e-mails as well.

Using a whitelist by itself is not practical; instead, it should be part of your overall antispam strategy. Most products and solutions allow you to place anything that does not match your whitelist into a folder for later review.

Use a Blacklist

Blacklists are the opposite of whitelists. Whereas whitelists allow e-mail only from a predetermined list of addresses or domains, blacklists are lists of addresses and domains from which e-mail is not accepted by your mail system. The biggest issue with blacklists is keeping them updated. Spammers do not disclose where they will be sending from next, what names or domains they might spoof, or if they will even be sending their e-mail from a machine they own. To help you keep your blacklists updated, many vendors offer continuously updated blacklists on a subscription basis. This is beneficial because

ONE STEP FURTHER

Here is a way to verify that your mail server (Microsoft Exchange in this example) is not relaying mail. In the procedure, substitute the name of your e-mail server for *mailservername*. (Note that Microsoft Exchange 5.0 and earlier versions do not provide a method to prevent mail relay if they are connected to the Internet.)

1. Open a command prompt and type **telnet** ***mailservername*** **25**.
2. Press ENTER and type **HELO me**. The server will respond with 250 OK and identify your IP address and possibly your hostname.
3. Press ENTER and type **MAIL FROM:** ***someaddress@yourdomain*.com**. The server will respond with 250 OK.
4. Press ENTER and type **RCPT TO:** ***nobody@anyotherdomain*.com**. The server will respond with 550 Relaying Prohibited.
5. Press ENTER. Using a valid address from your Global Address List, type **RCPT TO:** ***internaladdress@yourdomain*.com**. The server will reply with 250 OK when it accepts the address.

If you have a mail sever other than MS Exchange and would like to verify how to disable mail relay, check out http://www.mail-abuse.com/support/an_sec3rdparty.html.

it offers a way to get updates without having to do your own research. This update process works much the same way that update processes for antivirus solutions work.

Like whitelists, blacklists are not by themselves a complete antispam solution but do have a place in an overall antispam solution.

Review Content to Identify Spam

Many antispam products on the market today offer a form of artificial intelligence that can determine whether or not e-mail is spam. Various methods are used to identify spam, such as

- Text-based analysis
- Keyword matching
- Cryptographic checksums

Text-Based Analysis One of the basic checks that most antispam products do is text-based analysis. They look at the subject line and the body of an e-mail to determine if the content is inappropriate (spam). Text-analysis products rely on word and phrase lists that identify subject lines and topics that are common to spam. If the subject line or content of a message matches the product's lists, the message is classified as spam. The problem with these products is that spammers are aware of their antispam techniques and have developed methods to circumvent them. This is why more and more spam has oddly written subject lines. For example, instead of a subject line of Lower your debt!, you might see L0W3R y0ur D3bt!, 10wer yur d3bt!, or l o w e r y o u r d e b t !, all of which would fool most antispam products. After all, antispam products cannot think. Whereas a human can easily ascertain that e-mails with the preceding subject lines are spam, a program can do so only if it was coded by a human to do so. Because there are so many variations of text and word combinations, the maintenance required to keep these lists current is very time consuming.

Keyword Matching Another way to search content for spam is to use keyword matching. This method uses a scoring system that is based on the types of words and combinations of words that are found in an e-mail. If a particular threshold is hit, the e-mail is flagged as spam. While this method can have a high success factor in stopping spam, it inherently has a high false-positive rate because the e-mail is looked at in terms of content but not context. For example, if a medical research company were to block e-mail with the word *breast*, it could very well block a number of legitimate e-mail messages.

A more advanced type of text-based searching that seems to have lower false-positive results relies on heuristics. Essentially, these products use past known spam in combination with statistical analysis (like Bayesian filters, a technique that uses the entire content of the e-mail and does an analysis of the e-mail's context) and known mechanics of spam—how spammers try to defeat spam detection tools—to try to identify future spam through a learning process.

Cryptographic Checksums One of the more effective techniques of identifying spam is to match cryptographic checksums. These checksums create an electronic representation of the message that allows a comparison to be made with like messages. Because checksums are essentially text and are smaller than the actual message itself, a list of checksums can be distributed to multiple implementations of antispam solutions that use the same technological process for comparison. In other words, the checksums are distributed, the local antispam e-mail processes run incoming mail through the same process, and the checksums of the new mail are compared against the known checksums for spam. In this example, messages are digitally signed and compared. This comparison is done via other messages classified as spam by the product purchased to perform this task. This process is generally proprietary to vendors and, in many cases, is one of the major items that you pay for in an in-house antispam solution. A good example of an open-source antispam solution that uses this process is Vipul's Razor, located at http://razor.sourceforge.net/.

Use Antispam Products

The following are the four basic types of products that can be used to reduce spam in your environment:

- **Client-based** Solutions that reside on the same machine as the client e-mail application

- **Homegrown gateway** Solutions that are designed by your organization for your organization
- **Third-party gateway** Solutions developed by third-party vendors that can be customized for your environment
- **Outsourced** Solutions offered by third-party organizations that perform antispamming functions for your organization

The requirements of your organization ultimately drive which type of solution (or combination of solutions) you should implement. Table 15-1 outlines the pros and cons of the four types of solutions that are available. It also lists examples of each type of solution. Note that in Table 15-1, the term *gateway* refers to the mail gateway. The mail gateway for your organization may be near the Internet connection or nestled further back in your environment. For purposes of this section, think of it as the point directly in front of where all the mail comes into your mail servers.

Figure 15-1 shows what an antivirus and antispam solution may look like in your environment.

Solution	Pros	Cons	Examples
Client-based	Can be customized on a per-user basis. Can be installed on a user-by-user basis, based on which users have the most spam.	Difficult to control from an enterprise perspective. More user education is required.	Norton AntiSpam 2004 (http://www.symantec.com/antispam/) SpamKiller (http://us.mcafee.com)
Gateway: homegrown	Can be more flexible, tightly coupled, and customized to your environment and your security specifications. Cost of implementation can be offset through the use of open-source solutions.	In-house expertise is required for setup, configuration, capacity planning, interoperation with other e-mail solutions (like antivirus), and ongoing management of the solution.	Distributed Checksum Clearinghouse (http://www.rhyolite.com/anti-spam/dcc/) Vipul's Razor (http://razor.sourceforge.net)
Gateway: third party	Can compensate for lack of in-house expertise and time by providing a solution that normally comes as an appliance and can receive updates (decreasing time needed to maintain the solution). Generally, easier to implement and interface with other e-mail solutions (like antivirus).	Generally, more expensive. Once customized for your environment, can be difficult to replace. Flexibility of the solution in your environment is limited to what the vendor can support.	CipherTrust (http://www.ciphertrust.com/) Brightmail, now owned by Symantec (http://www.symantec.com)
Outsourced	Can compensate for lack of in-house expertise and time with experts that focus on spam reduction. Very easy to implement because there are no infrastructure costs and only minor modifications need to be made to take advantage of these solutions.	Lack of local control and ability to address user issues without invoking the vendor. Customization could be limited and force your organization to adopt the vendor's solutions for other e-mail services (like antivirus).	Postini (http://www.postini.com/) FrontBridge Technologies (http://www.frontbridge.com)

Table 15-1. Spam Solution Table

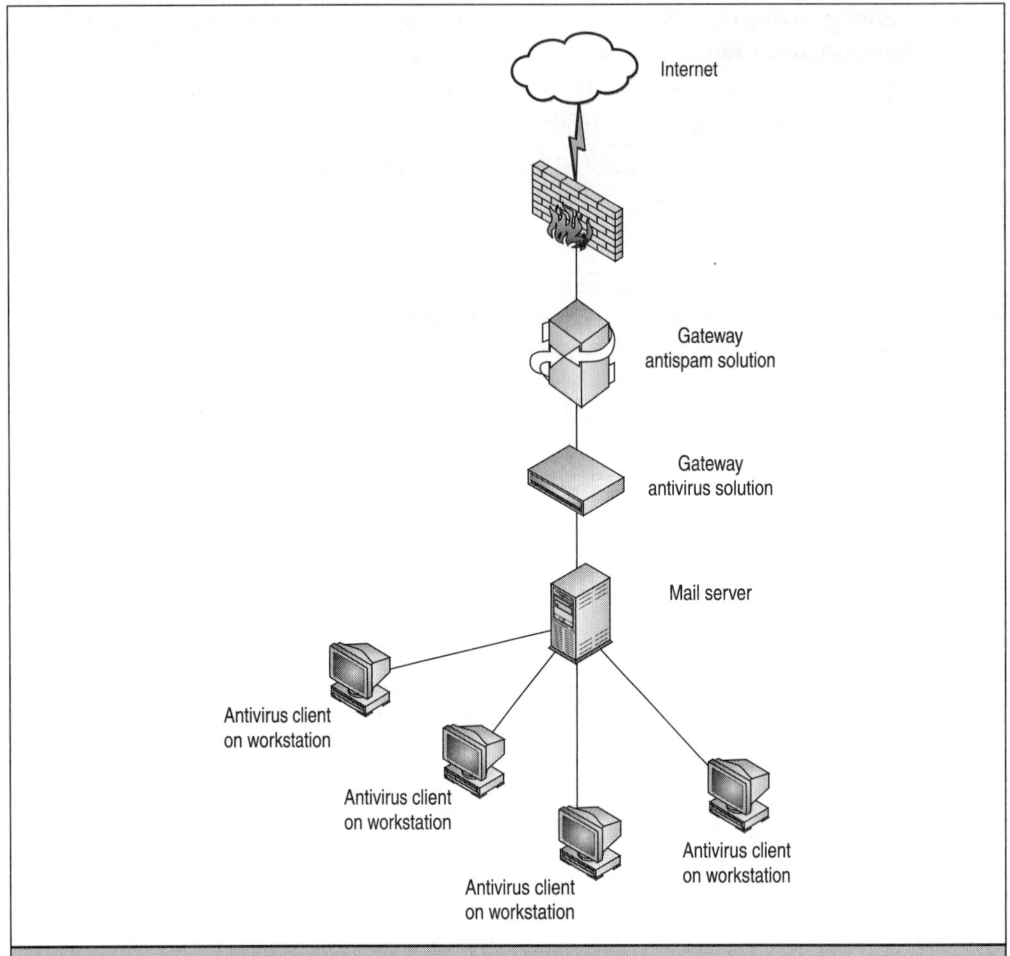

Figure 15-1. Example of layered antivirus and antispam solution

Prevent Successful Phishing Attacks

Phishing (pronounced "fishing") refers to an attempt to fraudulently attain information, such as user IDs and passwords, by sending e-mail that is spoofed to look as if it is being sent by a normally trusted entity. Such e-mail usually mimics e-mail from a legitimate company, both in content and appearance.

Most phishing scams are sent out in bulk (very similar to spam) and lure their victims by imitating e-mail (including branding, language, logos, images, and the like) from a large, trusted entity such as a financial institution or e-mail provider.

Phishing has been around for quite some time on the Internet. Reports dating back to 1996 describe hackers on AOL attempting to fool legitimate AOL users into giving up their user ID and password. Today, phishing has been "perfected" to the point that it is a common practice of online criminal enterprises. In fact, the Anti-Phishing Working Group (http://www.antiphishing.org/) estimates that over 200 unique phishing scams were released in February 2004 alone, which is more than double the number released in February 2003.

In today's environment, you can take additional steps to reduce the effects of phishing in your environment. These steps are described in the sections that follow.

Use Antispam Software to Identify and Quarantine Phishing Attacks

Most commercial antispam software can detect and quarantine phishing e-mail. Once a phishing e-mail message is detected, filters can be established to flag similar e-mail messages.

Train Users to Identify Phishing Attacks

You can make your users better aware of phishing threats and how to detect them by passing along the information presented in this section.

Most reputable organizations do not send e-mail with a link embedded and ask the recipients to follow the link and provide personal information. If your users receive an e-mail that purports to be from a company they do business with and it asks them for personal information, they should attempt to verify that the e-mail is legitimate. They can do so in the following ways:

- Determine whether the link provided looks valid. For example, look for and be suspicious of links that have the @ symbol in them. Most phishers use URL modifications to fake out their victims. An example is described in the Heads Up! following this list.
- Directly visit the web site of the trusted entity by entering the URL in the browser address space (users should not click the link in the e-mail that they receive) and then send an e-mail to the web site's customer service address, requesting confirmation of the e-mail's contents.
- Use out-of-band communications, like calling or sending snail mail to the source, to verify the legitimacy of the e-mail.
- Legitimate companies (banks, utility companies, etc.) will send out links inside of their e-mails. If the link in the e-mail is selected, inform your client that they can double check what they have clicked on by looking for the lock icon in Internet Explorer or the key icon to come together in Netscape. These icons indicate that the site is using SSL, which provides authentication for the site that is being connected to (and also provides encrypted communications). Another quick

way that users can validate SSL connections is to click on the lock or the key to see if the site that is listed on the certificate matches what they expect to see on the site.

NOTE Some phishing scams are rather convincing on the surface and may not immediately ask for personal information. For example, an e-mail could be delivered that makes a statement and tells the user to go to a site to get more information. After reviewing the site, there would be a Login button so the user can verify the information against their actual account. This is an example where there are multiple steps to a phishing scam and where the e-mail is not validated at the time that it is viewed, but is verified based on where it has taken you. This is not a fool-proof mechanism of knowing that the e-mail is not a scam, just another indicator that should be taken into account.

HEADS UP!

As mentioned, most phishers use URL modifications to trick their victims. An example URL modification might be something like http://www.legitimatesite.com@10.10.10.10/login/login.htm, where

- http://www.legitimatesite.com is actually a user ID
- @ redirects the user to another location
- 10.10.10.10 is the IP address of the rogue web site
- login is a password
- login.htm is the page on the web site that the user is being directed to

This attack will work because most users see http://www.legitimatesite.com and assume that it is safe. This method has been used for years by system administrators to play jokes on each other. All major browsers have provided a patch to curb the issue of special characters, like @, being used in the browser Address field. This is another reason to make sure that you patch your applications, such as browsers, and not just your OSs.

Be Aware of New Types of Phishing Attacks

Phishing is becoming more and more difficult to defend against because of the increasingly sophisticated and authentic-looking content of phishing expeditions. Newer attacks are starting to use combinations of multiple types of vulnerabilities to achieve their results. For example, cross-site scripting errors in web development can be used by attackers to launch phishing attacks. Cross-site scripting occurs when a vulnerable web-based application is injected with client-side code, such as JavaScript or VBScript, that gathers user data for malicious and illegitimate purposes. Instead of attempting to gather data, phishers will redirect users to an illegitimate site and attempt to gather legitimate information from them.

If you have a web presence, the best thing that you can do to protect your organization is to never trust user input and always filter metadata. Application layer firewalls, as outlined later in the chapter, also assist in doing this for your organization.

The bottom line is that phishing attacks always attempt to exploit the trust of potential victims. Users should always be paranoid about how and why information is being asked of them online.

ONE STEP FURTHER

The Federal Trade Commission (FTC) enables you to report e-mail scams, like phishing. Simply go to http://www.ftc.gov and click File a Complaint.

Additionally, the Anti-Phishing Working Group, located at http://www.antiphishing.org/, provides a wealth of information on phishing scams and trends as well as samples of past phishing scams.

Protect All Systems from Viruses

Viruses have been plaguing computers since computers have been around and will continue to plague them for the foreseeable future, if not forever. This section focuses on what you need to do now to provide virus protection for your network:

- Install and maintain antivirus software on all computers
- Scan for viruses at the e-mail gateway
- Train users to protect themselves against viruses

Install and Maintain Antivirus Software on All Computers

Because virus scanners are traditionally signature based (i.e., rely on a unique string of bits to identify each virus), an antivirus solution can protect your machines only against malicious code that has been discovered and reported to the antivirus solution. In other words, to have an effective antivirus implementation, you need a way to update virus signatures. Depending on the size of your organization and the requirements that you have for control over machines in your environment, there are two primary methods to handle virus updates:

- *Configure the antivirus application on each user's machine to pull updates from an antivirus site.* You can configure the antivirus application on each user's machine to routinely (e.g., every 24 hours) go out to the Internet to get an updated signature file. Although you can configure the programs to prompt the user to click OK before going through with the update process, this is a risky proposition in corporate environments. Users often are reluctant or complacent with regard to these types of tasks because they may seem intrusive.

Another problem with this method is that servers may not be logged into on a regular basis, so if a virus update fails for some reason, those servers could be vulnerable for a period of time. This could be an issue if you are not able to confirm that an update has been successful on a machine. In corporate deployments, applications such as Microsoft System Management Server (SMS) can send this information for someone to investigate. If the only way to verify the success of an update is to physically log into the machine and check, it becomes a very manual process and is often overlooked.

- *Configure a server in your environment to obtain the updates from the antivirus product site and push them to clients on as close to a real-time basis as possible.* This is done when the machine logs onto the network. If necessary, virus updates could be pushed out to machines in the middle of the day. This flexibility not only enables you to dynamically update machines against virus threats, but also offers consistency regarding what virus protection level every machine is at.

Scan for Viruses at the E-Mail Gateway

As viruses like Melissa and ILOVEYOU have demonstrated over the past few years, e-mail can be one of the largest proliferators of viruses. For this reason, you should make sure that antivirus software is installed not only at hosts but at the mail gateway as well. The mail gateway is located between the Internet and the mail server for your environment. This is a critical place to detect and remove viruses. If all corporate e-mail goes through this point, viruses can be eradicated prior to entering your environment. These solutions can be updated with new signature files without having to start and stop services. It is critical to maintain a current list of virus signatures while also keeping the mail flowing without disruption.

You must keep in mind that not all e-mail-borne viruses that are inbound to your environment will be detected by an e-mail gateway solution. This is the reason you also need to implement a host-based antivirus product and educate your users about how to spot suspicious e-mail attachments.

As an example of how a virus can slip past your gateway virus scanner, suppose that a password-protected Zip file containing a virus is sent into your environment as an attachment to an e-mail message. The virus scanner cannot scan the infected files within the Zip file until after they are unzipped, and it cannot unzip them since it does not have the password and is not programmed to enter one when attempting to scan zipped files. Thus, the attachment will be passed to the user. The body of the e-mail in this scenario would likely display the password and tell the user to enter it when prompted after clicking to open the Zip file. Many users will do so, thereby opening the Zip file and executing the virus. This is why virus protection on the desktop is important: to catch viruses that may not be detected through any other means. One way that organizations have addressed this problem is to not allow Zip files as e-mail attachments.

To protect against viruses inside password-protected Zip files, the e-mail gateway product that you choose must be able to identify that a Zip file is password protected and alert the users that it was unable to scan the file.

Train Users to Protect Themselves Against Viruses

Very few users actually have intent to harm the corporate environment, and even fewer, if any, want to infect their own workstation by allowing a virus to be installed or proliferate. However, users have an undying curiosity to know what happens when they double-click on an attachment. This is the reason why it is very important to train users to be aware of the threats of viruses even though you have controls in place, like host and gateway antivirus solutions. Inform users that it is always best to error on the side of caution. This section provides some training tips.

Instruct Users to Submit Questionable Attachments for Inspection

Instruct users that if they receive a suspicious e-mail attachment, they should not open it but should contact a security administrator. The security administrator can use an offline (not connected to the network) computer, kept up to date with virus scanning software, to inspect the attachment by opening it and scanning it. Although this exercise involves some extra time, the potential benefits, including keeping one more virus out of your environment, are worth it.

The bottom line is that you need to reiterate to users that opening attachments from unknown parties is one of the primary ways in which viruses proliferate. Additionally, just because an e-mail was received from a trusted party, this does not necessarily guarantee that it is safe. It is important for users to look at the content of the subject line and consider whether it makes sense in the context of their relationship with the sender. For example, in the case of the "I love you" virus, a recipient of an e-mail message from a business associate with the subject line "I love you" should be very suspicious.

Instruct Users Not to Proliferate Chain E-Mails

The promises contained in chain letters and hoaxes are another way in which users are induced to proliferate virus-infected e-mail. Hoaxes are e-mails that users pass on knowingly because the e-mail gave them some incentive to do so, such as a statement that a new, very destructive virus is on the loose and that the recipient should warn everyone they know. Chain letters are e-mails that get forwarded because they either promise some reward for continuing the chain or threaten some punishment for breaking the chain. Beyond the annoyance factor, chain letters add to the problem of additional, unwanted mass e-mails in your environment. In one example, a corporate mail server crashed because numerous e-mail messages were sent in response to an e-mail chain letter stating that users would receive a dollar for every message they forwarded. Multiple people forwarded the e-mail to everyone in the corporate address book.

To prevent proliferation of hoaxes and chain e-mails:

- Educate users by familiarizing them with e-mail hoax lists. Probably the most common is the list maintained by DataFellows (F-Secure) at http://www.datafellows.com/news/hoax.htm.
- Make and enforce a corporate policy against sending chain e-mails.
- Configure your mail server so that only certain individuals can send an e-mail to the entire organization.

Defend Against Worms

Worms have many traits that are similar to those of viruses, such as the ability to replicate and infect many other machines. Like viruses, worms may contain code that can corrupt files, crash machines, or do something else that is not desired. The primary difference between viruses and worms is that worms can exist on their own, meaning they do not have to attach themselves to files or programs as do viruses. Worms take advantage of preexisting methods of communication between machines or applications to proliferate. Worms can be a critical threat to an environment if they are released. They often move very fast in terms of their infection rate. For example, the "Slammer" worm, released in 2003, infected hundreds of thousands of computers around the world in less than three hours and affected everything from ATM cash machines to airline flights. The worm did not discriminate based on industry or country and affected organizations both large and small.

With the rapid rate at which worms spread, it is difficult to defend against a specific worm once it has been released and is proliferating. From a preventive standpoint, the following should be uppermost on your list of steps to mitigate the threat of worms:

- *Get rid of any unneeded services and components.* When designing and implementing security for workstations, servers, or entire systems, always keep foremost in your mind this question: What are the absolute minimum things that need to be turned on (services, protocols, and so forth) for this workstation, server, etc. to operate? Answering this question may sometimes be difficult; however, it is a necessary step for securing your environment. If the execution of a worm requires the presence of a service or component that you have disabled or have not installed, not only have you provided a layer of protection, but you can now focus your resources on the machines that might be affected.
- *Install and update your patches.* Patching (discussed in depth next) is something that administrators will be responsible for as long as they run systems. It is part of the "care and feeding" of any electronic system and is one of the best defenses against the potential destruction that worms could wreak within your environment.

Engage in Patch-Warfare Tactics

Patching is a requirement to maintain a base level of security within your environment. Application of patches can prevent successful usage of system exploits and can provide protection against other threats like worms. Patch management is often thought of as operating system maintenance; however, the same process should be adapted for applications as well. The following is a list of steps that will help you to implement an effective patch-management strategy for your environment:

- *Inventory machines, applications, programs, and the like.* This gives you an overview of what you need to protect. Without an accurate list, it is next to impossible to understand the impact of technology vulnerabilities that could expose your environment.
- *Document data flows.* This tells you what applications need access to what services on what machines on what networks in what areas of the organization. This documentation is extremely beneficial in identifying what services and components need to be installed or turned on for an application to work and what types of exploits you need to be vigilant of. As stated in the preceding section, if a function is not required and is not installed or is disabled, you can immediately reduce exposures and therefore provide an additional layer of security.
- *Subscribe to a vulnerability subscription service (VSS).* VSSs are required for anyone who is responsible for patching systems. A free service like the one offered by SecurityFocus (subscribe to bugtraq at http://www.securityfocus.com/) has numerous contributors and is one of the most widely used vulnerability mailing lists on the Internet. Other services, like TruSecure's ntbugtraq (http://ntbugtraq.ntadvice.com/), can be customized to your environment based on the technologies you use and the versions those technologies are on. The catch with VSSs is that they have to be read and acted on to be effective. Often, alerts that are sent out are deleted before they are ever read. It is critical that administrators responsible for a platform understand their role in receiving vulnerability alerts and acting on them.
- *Implement a patch review strategy.* Just because a patch is released does not necessarily mean that it needs to be installed. The patch may not affect your environment or, even worse, may break something that is currently working in your environment. It is critical to establish teams, based on technology, that can obtain documentation and other information to aide in discerning the severity of the vulnerability, evaluate the patch relative to your environment, test the patch application, and determine how and where the patch should be implemented in your environment. In some instances, a team might conclude that immediately

installing a patch could adversely impact a system and that it must be tested first. In other instances, a team may determine that the patch is so critical that it needs to be installed immediately regardless of the potential adverse impact. The bottom line is that you need to obtain a patch management strategy for your organization from the security department and the relevant technology department. They must arrive at a consensus on how and when to implement patches on a case-by-case basis. If the decision is not to implement a patch immediately, everyone involved needs to realize the potential impact of not installing the patch.

- *Subscribe to vendor vulnerability/patch notification services.* You should do this for all products that are used in your organization. Examples of such services include the Microsoft service at http://www.microsoft.com/technet/security/default.mspx and the Cisco service at http://www.cisco.com/security/.

Prepare for "Zero-Day" Exploits

As covered in the previous section, a "window of exposure" exists between when a vulnerability is first reported to a vendor and when it is patched. The goal should be to reduce as much as possible the length of time this window is open. Traditionally, months would pass between when a vulnerability was reported and when it was actually exploited. Today, that window is usually measured in weeks, and it is predicted that in the future, the timeframe between when a vendor first knows about a vulnerability and when it is exploited will be less than one day, giving rise to "zero-day" exploits.

Organizations basically are dependent on vendors to provide security patches, hot fixes, service packs, and the like in a timely manner. In some cases, it just may not be possible for a vendor to respond quickly enough to provide a patch against an exploit that is less than a day old. To counter this, you need to have a layered security approach. This means that you not only have to be vigilant about where your technologies are vulnerable, but also must have in place layered defenses against those vulnerabilities (like the gateway devices described earlier in this chapter) to provide some cover while you are patching your systems. Additionally, make sure to hold your vendors responsible for diligently making patches available.

NOTE If your organization is small to medium sized or has remote offices, several new solutions are available that handle through a single device antivirus and worm protection along with firewalling functions, content filtering, and VPN capabilities. These solutions not only handle multiple functions in a single device (eliminating the need to have multiple solutions to handle the same functions) but also offer an automatic update capability to provide dynamic protection. Examples of players in this space are Check Point Software Technologies' Safe@Office solutions (http://www.checkpoint.com) and Symantec's Integrated Security Solution (http://www.symantec.com). As a point to consider, although integrating many security needs into one appliance is convenient, that one appliance also is a potential single point of failure.

Protect Against Spyware

Spyware is any technology that aids in gathering information about a person or organization without their knowledge. Spyware is often classified according to the intent with which it is used:

- Spyware used for legitimate purposes, such as a keystroke logger, installed by an administrator on a corporate machine to attain information about a user or a system. This type of technology is used to gather evidence or to do PC surveillance and can be hardware or software based.
- Spyware used for illegitimate purposes, such as software that is loaded on a user's machine while the user is browsing the Internet, or a keystroke logger that is loaded on a coworker's machine to spy on them.

Spyware that is loaded on a user's machine when the user is browsing the Internet is an issue for organizations both large and small. The majority of this type of spyware is generally harmless, from a security perspective. In fact, most Internet spyware is usually called *adware* and is used to track browsing habits as users traverse the Internet, the goal being to provide marketing information and to determine where to place banner ads. (Gator, now called Clarion, is a well-known example of a marketing spyware application.) However, you need to consider the larger privacy issues. Your first concern should be that all the web traffic, including everything that a user types into a browser, is sent to an unknown source.

The major issue with spyware downloaded from the Internet is that organizations that use spyware, such as advertising companies, install onto your machines tracking programs that call home over the Internet to report data. Usually, this tracking software reports on users' habits only while they are online. However, such spyware has the capability to report on much more information. True adversaries can capitalize on these technologies to breech security within your environment. The legal implication of companies installing spyware on your machines is murky, so you must be prepared to defend against spyware.

Spyware (including adware) also poses corporate policy and privacy issues that require caution. Most organizations have strict policies that state that unauthorized programs cannot be loaded on workstations (regardless of whether the program is from a CD-ROM or the Internet). Who is held responsible when spyware overloads a machine and slows it down to a crawl or attains information that is private and should not be disclosed? Users usually do not even know that spyware has been loaded on their machine, so how can they be held responsible? Corporate policies should take into account such issues.

Install a Spyware Detection Application

To rid your environment of spyware, you should install a spyware detection application. Most spyware detection applications look through cookies, registry entries, and the like to find tracking software. A free spyware detection and destruction tool that seems to work very well is Spybot Search & Destroy (http://www.safer-networking.org/). If you have never run a spyware detection program and you are using a machine that has seen a fair amount of Internet use, you will probably be in for a surprise when you run a spyware detection application. You will see names of various advertisers, and maybe other culprits, that have loaded tracking software on your machines. The performance impact of running an antispyware application is minimal and can often be done while working in other applications.

CAUTION Spyware, like keystroke loggers, can be loaded on virtually any machine. While you may have measures in place to control spyware within your environment, spyware may be loaded in other areas that can cause a much larger issue. For example, with the proliferation of Internet cafes and public-access machines for web surfing, most individuals look at the Internet as an anytime, anywhere solution to do everything from check their account balances to access corporate resources. If you are using only password authentication to connect to your corporate e-mail system from the Internet, and you use a public-access Internet terminal that you do not control, a keystroke logger could record sites and passwords to your corporate resources.

Managing this type of solution from a corporate perspective is rather difficult at this time, because an element of human interaction is needed. Currently, the only way to effectively handle this from a corporate level is to train users to use a spyware detection and destruction application.

ONE STEP FURTHER

Earlier in this chapter, blacklists were discussed in relation to preventing spam. Blacklists can also be used on firewalls and proxy servers to prevent users from accessing certain sites on the Internet. Blacklists are normally employed to block internal traffic from inappropriate web sites like porn sites and hate sites. Blacklists can also be used to help prevent spyware from leaking information out of your environment.

Spyware normally has a URL associated with it to send information to the "mother ship." squidGuard (http://www.squidguard.org/) maintains an open-source list of spyware sites that you can use to create your own blacklist of spyware sites. While this may not prevent spyware from being loaded on user desktops, it can prevent infected desktops from reporting information to locations outside of your environment.

Protect Web Applications from Web-Based Attacks

Applications are vulnerable to web-based attacks for two reasons. First, most firewalls are not capable of protecting applications from these attacks. Second, many applications are poorly written and unpatched. To protect applications from web-based attacks, ensure that applications are hardened and patched and then do the following:

- Educate developers about typical web attacks
- Train developers to look beyond known coding flaws
- Implement an application layer firewall

Educate Developers About Typical Web Attacks

If your developers do not know what dangerous code looks like or are developing applications that are susceptible to exploitation, the first thing you need to do is educate them. A great way to begin is to introduce the Open Web Application Security Project (OWASP) Top Ten, a compilation of the top ten most critical web application vulnerabilities for 2004. OWASP outlines its Top Ten as follows.

NOTE Reading the full report is strongly recommended. It is available at the OWASP web site, http://www.owasp.org/documentation/topten.html.

1	Unvalidated Input	Information from web requests is not validated before being used by a web application. Attackers can use these flaws to attack backend components through a web application.
2	Broken Access Control	Restrictions on what authenticated users are allowed to do are not properly enforced. Attackers can exploit these flaws to access other users' accounts, view sensitive files, or use unauthorized functions.
3	Broken Authentication and Session Management	Account credentials and session tokens are not properly protected. Attackers that can compromise passwords, keys, session cookies, or other tokens can defeat authentication restrictions and assume other users' identities.
4	Cross Site Scripting (XSS) Flaws	The web application can be used as a mechanism to transport an attack to an end user's browser. A successful attack can disclose the end user's session token, attack the local machine, or spoof content to fool the user.
5	Buffer Overflows	Web application components in some languages that do not properly validate input can be crashed and, in some cases, used to take control of a process. These components can include CGI, libraries, drivers, and web application server components.
6	Injection Flaws	Web applications pass parameters when they access external systems or the local operating system. If an attacker can embed malicious commands in these parameters, the external system may execute those commands on behalf of the web application.

7	Improper Error Handling	Error conditions that occur during normal operation are not handled properly. If an attacker can cause errors to occur that the web application does not handle, they can gain detailed system information, deny service, cause security mechanisms to fail, or crash the server.
8	Insecure Storage	Web applications frequently use cryptographic functions to protect information and credentials. These functions and the code to integrate them have proven difficult to code properly, frequently resulting in weak protection.
9	Denial of Service	Attackers can consume web application resources to a point where other legitimate users can no longer access or use the application. Attackers can also lock users out of their accounts or even cause the entire application to fail.
10	Insecure Configuration Management	Having a strong server configuration standard is critical to a secure web application. These servers have many configuration options that affect security and are not secure out of the box.

If your development community is not familiar with the preceding attacks, including what causes them, how they are exploited, which remedies are used to fix them, and what their relationship is to your environment, you should schedule basic training classes for your development community.

Other vulnerabilities exist (in addition to the OWASP Top Ten) that your developers should be aware of based on the type of applications that your organization uses and how they were developed. As your developers learn about these types of attacks, as described in the following section, they not only need to carry this information forward to future development projects, but also need to analyze their existing applications to see if there are vulnerabilities present and, if so, when and how to address them.

Train Developers to Look Beyond Known Coding Flaws

When training your development community, you must also train developers to "feed themselves." The OWASP Top Ten is a snapshot in time. The goal should be to have developers constantly review and look for ways to make their code more secure. Besides doing their own research, developers can use products (both free and commercial) to assist in reviewing code for vulnerabilities. Nessus (http://www.nessus.org/), which is open source, and SPI Dynamics (http://www.spidynamics.com/), which is commercial, are examples of application scanners that can scan sites for application vulnerabilities.

Code scanners such as these have multiple benefits. First of all, they can be used as a method of quality control in your software development life cycle. Then, as code is being functionally tested, code scanners can be used to scan it for vulnerabilities. Regardless of whether or not you have a programming background, these products offer you a method to audit web-based applications that are currently in production.

Implement an Application Layer Firewall

Firewalls are typically implemented to protect a trusted network from unauthorized access to applications and services. They operate by blocking traffic based on the port numbers used by the applications. Traditional firewalls cannot protect authorized

Internet-facing applications from web-based attacks that utilize the ports authorized for access to the trusted network. As the need to access applications from the Internet has grown, access through many ports is not allowed by firewalls. In addition, many applications are now programmed to allow access over ports 80 and 443, the single most frequently opened ports on firewalls.

To provide protection for Internet-facing applications, firewalls must have the ability to do deep packet inspection. In other words, they must be able to look at more than only the source and destination IP addresses and port; they must also look at the data payload of the packets directed at internal servers. Such firewalls are called application layer firewalls. Implementing an application layer firewall is the primary step with regard to protecting applications from web-based attacks.

Application layer firewalls sit behind a traditional firewall and in front of your web servers. The purpose of an application layer firewall is to thoroughly search all traffic that is going over ports 80 and 443 (the ports through which web traffic travels) and discern whether or not the traffic is hostile. Application layer firewalls provide immediate protection against vulnerabilities such as buffer overflows, cross-site scripting, and the like. This is important because you can instantly insert a layer of protection while you are testing your applications for vulnerabilities and training your development community about application vulnerabilities.

Most application layer firewalls function more as a network device than as a server. This means that they can scale for performance in much the same way as other network devices do, such as traditional firewalls and load balancers. Performance can be increased either by using higher-capacity hardware or by clustering multiple hardware devices in the same data stream.

An additional benefit of an application layer firewall is that it mitigates the factor of human error in future code development. If a trained development group accidentally exposes vulnerable code to the Internet, an application layer firewall provides a safety net. Finally, if a new application vulnerability is discovered on the Internet tomorrow, you can use your application layer firewall to create a global policy change and affect all the applications that are sitting behind the application layer firewall until they can be fixed. Figure 15-2 shows how an application layer firewall would be implemented.

An example of an application layer firewall is Teros (http://www.teros.com). Teros can protect applications based on signatures (for example, match a signature of a vulnerability and block traffic that matches that signature) and do positive rule matches (for example, identify the RFC for HTTP and drop the connection if the traffic traversing the application layer firewall does not match the RFC exactly).

Additionally, Teros offers a unique option on its product that is equally beneficial: the ability to do bidirectional traffic analysis. This means that Teros can validate not only inputs to the web server (signature based or rules based) but also the traffic returning to the client browser. This is beneficial when you want to enforce a policy regardless of how the application is designed to perform.

As an example of the benefit of bidirectional traffic analysis, suppose that you have a web site that handles online ordering for customers, who pay for their goods by submitting

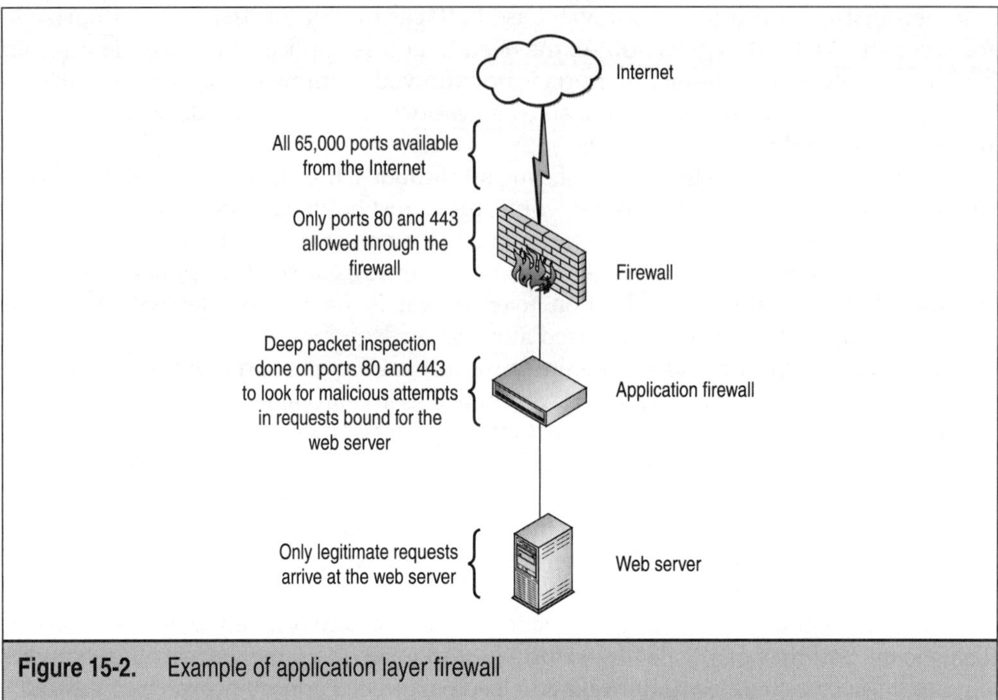

Figure 15-2. Example of application layer firewall

a credit card number. From a security perspective, you know that only one credit card number is associated with each customer. Thus, at the application layer firewall, you can enforce a rule that states there will never be more than one credit card number displayed at a time. Even if the application is accidentally programmed to allow multiple credit card numbers for multiple people to be displayed simultaneously, the application layer firewall will interpret that multiple credit card numbers are going to be displayed in a request and terminate the request before the client can view it.

NOTE Policies and application developers should not disclose entire credit card numbers inside of a web-based application (it is best to use representative values of a credit card, such as listing the last four digits of the credit card number and the type of card, for example Visa 1234). However, in most cases, the credit card numbers are stored in a database and encrypted on the way to the browser. If a developer's programming error or an error in a web-based application could inadvertently allow a full credit card number (or worse yet, multiple credit card numbers) to be disclosed to the browser, the application layer firewall could recognize and deny the request.

Chapter 16

Hardening Wetware

by John Mallery

- End User: Friend or Foe?
- Prepare a Foundation: Policies and Procedures
- Establish a Training Program: The Building of a Team
- Develop Communication Skills

The most overlooked security issue in an enterprise is the hardening of wetware. *Wetware* (or, less commonly, *meatware* or *liveware*) is a slang term for the human side of the security equation. Information technology professionals, due to their interest and background, focus on technology solutions, such as firewalls, system patching, intrusion detection systems, and so forth, often feeling that another department should handle the human factor. And most other departments in an organization feel that the IT staff should handle all network security issues. Because of these attitudes, the human factor is often overlooked and thus can cause some of the most significant security breaches in an enterprise. A firm's employees can be the first line of defense in protecting a network, regardless of the operating systems in use. End users immediately notice network issues, such as slow response times when trying to retrieve files or the inability to access particular systems or devices, and are often the first to notice unauthorized activity or personnel in a facility. All end users in an organization should be considered "tools" in the enterprise security toolbox.

End User: Friend or Foe?

Most IT professionals consider end users to be a necessary evil at best and an extreme annoyance at worst. An IT staff can be extremely intolerant of end users' lack of technical sophistication. Numerous stories are circulated about help desk issues that are logged simply as PEBCAK (problem exists between chair and keyboard) or id-10-t errors. One network administrator was overheard to say, "End users are like ants, they're everywhere and you can't get rid of them." Although these comments are humorous, they indicate a lack of respect for end users. It is important to keep in mind that without end users, IT professionals would not have jobs. Developing respect for end users and opening lines of communication is critical for protecting an enterprise.

Extra Eyes and Ears

How many IT departments have been overheard saying, "We have more staff than we could possibly need and we can easily get our work done in an eight-hour day"? Historically, IT departments are understaffed and overworked. They simply can't be everywhere at once. This is why it is important to include end users as part of the security team.

End users are very often the first-choice target for an attacker. Their perceived lack of sophistication makes them extremely appealing. In addition, end users' computers are not as heavily "guarded" as servers or other network devices. This compounds the attraction of end users as targets. Attackers can use numerous methods to breach a network by exploiting end users. Computer users are constantly being bombarded with requests to "click here," "download this," and "install that." Not only should users be trained to not comply with these requests (specific training issues are addressed later in this chapter, in the section "Establish a Training Program: The Building of a Team"), they should feel comfortable notifying IT staff that they have received such requests. This type of communication can alert the IT staff regarding new threats. The IT staff can then

HEADS UP!

Hardening wetware can be accomplished only if the "wetware" wishes to be hardened. Individuals who have a history of fraud and embezzlement convictions or who are in a precarious financial state may be more difficult, if not impossible, to harden. Businesses need to include pre-employment background checks as part of the hiring process. These checks should also include credit checks if the new hires have the "keys to the castle"—the capability to cut checks, pay vendors, or access proprietary information unfettered. To illustrate the importance of background checks, all one has to do is look at this example: An insurance company that did not perform background checks hired a new claims processor who could authorize the payment of claims up to $2000. This claims processor created a series of dummy claims in the amount of $1999 that were payable to a business P.O. box that was actually owned by the claims processor. The insurance company discovered the fraud after $15,000 had been embezzled. In the investigation that followed, the company learned that the claims processor had two felony convictions for doing the exact same thing at two other insurance companies. The insurance company now conducts pre-employment background checks.

proactively alert the rest of the organization to these new threats. (Obviously, training end users is a significant part of the process, so they know what should be reported to the IT staff; otherwise, the IT staff will be inundated with e-mails and notifications.)

This philosophy of reporting unusual activity extends beyond the desktop. End users can also report other unusual activity. Since having physical access to a computer or network is the easiest way to bypass security, users can report visitors wandering the building that are unescorted or not wearing visitor badges. There have been numerous instances in which employees unwittingly helped an attacker by being a Good Samaritan and providing a stranger with directions to the server room or CEO's office. Some employees have gone so far as to give strangers the combination to numeric keypads because the stranger "forgot" the combination. From these examples alone it should be readily apparent that end users should be part of the security team.

Prepare a Foundation: Policies and Procedures

The first step in hardening wetware is for an organization to determine its security stance regarding its infrastructure, intellectual property, and employees. From this stance, the organization should create a set of policies and procedures outlining expected and approved behavior of its employees. These policies include a listing of inappropriate activities and the consequences for engaging in inappropriate activities. These policies are the foundation for establishing and maintaining security within the organization. There are numerous policies that an organization can employ, and many are industry specific. However, there are several policies that an organization must have in place regardless of the industry or the corporate culture of the enterprise.

Establish an Acceptable Use Policy for All Users

Every organization that utilizes technology must have in place an *acceptable use* policy. This policy outlines specifically what an employee can and cannot do with an organization's computer systems and devices. The main thrust of an acceptable use policy is to inform employees that corporate systems are the property of the corporation or business and only business-related activities may be conducted on these systems. Many organizations utilize an acceptable use policy to control productivity issues, essentially to make sure that employees are using the systems to conduct business and not to research the latest fashion trends on the Internet. However, an acceptable use policy can also be the first line of defense in protecting an organization's data and reputation.

An acceptable use policy can address password issues, such as "an employee shall never share their password with anyone." It should spell out that introducing malicious software and cracking passwords are strictly prohibited. It is important to include all prohibited activities. An acceptable use policy often includes the following:

- A definition of corporate systems and an explanation that they are to be used for business purposes only
- A password policy that defines acceptable and unacceptable passwords
- A prohibition against visiting inappropriate web sites, such as pornographic, racist, gambling, or other offensive sites
- A prohibition against installing software
- A prohibition against distributing copyrighted materials without adhering to appropriate copyright laws
- A prohibition against using company supplied e-mail to post personal opinions on public web sites or newsgroups
- A prohibition against installing unauthorized devices on the network, laptops, PDAs, etc.

Defining acceptable use is critical from a security perspective but it also goes a long way toward helping an organization during some types of HR-related litigation. When employees are terminated for what a firm considers inappropriate activities, the employee must know that their behavior was strictly prohibited. If an employee was not specifically told that a certain behavior was prohibited, they could file (and possibly win) a wrongful termination lawsuit and use the "I didn't know I wasn't supposed to do that" defense.

A mistake some organizations make when creating an acceptable use policy is to overlook peripheral devices that could be used to steal information or introduce malicious code into an organization. Portable devices should be included in the acceptable use policy, including cell phones, personal digital assistants (PDAs), Blackberries, and so forth. Even if an organization does not issue PDAs to its employees, the acceptable use policy should still address them. Many portable devices, such as PDAs, are inexpensive and may be purchased by employees, who will then attach them to their office computer. Customer lists, business plans, and account information could easily "leave" an organization in this way. Some other devices that are often overlooked include digital cameras and MP3 players. The storage media used by these devices do not simply store images and music. They are simply mass storage devices that can store any type of digital data. Allowing users to indiscriminately connect any digital device to the network or systems is simply asking for trouble.

For many organizations, telling users what they can and cannot do is simply not enough. These organizations implement technical controls that protect their systems and remove temptations from users. Many organizations prohibit the transportation of data via removable media. To enforce this restriction, floppy drives are removed from desktop systems and USB ports are disabled. Copying data to removable media such as floppy disks and USB flash drives is no longer possible. If businesses are concerned with the attachment of PDAs or similar devices to desktop systems, they not only disable the USB ports but the serial ports as well. Telling users in the acceptable use policy that downloading executable files is prohibited, combined with blocking executable files at the firewall, can significantly reduce the threat of malicious software. Technical controls add an additional layer of defense and can provide protection from inadvertent violation of the policy. Keep in mind that even if a technical control is in place to prohibit certain behavior, it is still important to include the prohibition in the acceptable use policy. This provides a level of understanding and protection should the technical control fail.

Additional policies may be created that impact specific users or departments. These policies can address issues such as remote access for a mobile workforce, and configuration specifications for specific devices such as routers, firewalls, and wireless technologies. Policies can be written that addresses every aspect of a firm's technology.

But it is important to remember that an endless collection of policies can be ineffective, for several reasons. Managing, reviewing, and enforcing numerous policies can be extremely cumbersome. Plus, an endless collection of policies also increases the likelihood that employees won't read them. In addition, security policies are often perceived as intrusive and an impediment to productivity. Moreover, poorly developed policies can certainly inhibit efficiency. To avoid creating ineffective policies, a team should create all policies. Be sure to include at least one individual from the department or business unit that will be most affected by the new policy. A policy-writing team should include members from the legal, security, and human resources departments.

Guard Against Intellectual Property Theft

Since the creation of policies is the first part of the security process, be sure to include policies that address all threats. Acceptable use policies are designed to tell honest employees what they can and cannot do with company systems and information. These policies also outline consequences for not-so-honest employees in an effort to deter inappropriate activities. It is important to recognize that the digitization of organizational data poses special problems. Because of these issues, it is important to create additional policies that support and work in conjunction with the acceptable use policy.

Most people think that data will be lost through external attacks or some type of disaster, such as hardware failure or an act of God. But it is important to remember that there is an epidemic in the business community. Few see it, few recognize it, and even fewer know how to combat it. It is not deterred by many of the measures put in place by most security professionals, and it can significantly impact an organization's ability to conduct business. This epidemic is the theft of trade secrets. It happens on a regular basis, and it is on the rise due to the fact that nearly all of our business documents and communications are in electronic format and can be disseminated easily with the click of a mouse. It is extremely difficult to keep track of all versions of all files and to keep tabs on the activities of traveling employees when they work on their laptops while on the road. Many people have multiple e-mail accounts—both business and personal. It is a trivial matter for an individual to forward confidential and proprietary files to a personal e-mail account. This may be done as a normal course of business because the individual wants to work on the files while at home. However, if there is a business downturn or the individual becomes disgruntled, these files can easily be sent to a competitor.

Due to these issues, there are additional policies that an organization must have in order to prevent the loss of proprietary information and trade secrets. These policies rarely fall under the authority of the IT department, but the IT department should be aware of these policies or, if they don't exist, enthusiastically encourage the organization to adopt them. Without these policies, companies can lose valuable information, even if the network and systems are secure. These policies are as follows:

- **Nondisclosure agreement** Binds an employee to not disclose trade secret information during and for a specified time after employment.
- **Nonsolicitation agreement** Forbids an employee to solicit business from current clients for a specified time if they begin working for a competitor.
- **Nonrecruitment policy** Prohibits former employees from actively recruiting employees from their previous employer (sometimes called a nonsolicitation of employees policy). This type of policy can help prevent the wholesale departure of a particular department.
- **Noncompete agreement** Prohibits employees from working for a competitor for a specified amount of time. This policy is the most direct but is also the most controversial. Many courts believe that a former employer does not have a right to prevent someone from earning a living and therefore find noncompete agreements unenforceable. It is important to have noncompete agreements even in areas where the courts have ruled them unenforceable, because a noncompete agreement is considered one of the mechanisms used to show that an organization is taking reasonable measures of protection regarding trade secrets and proprietary information.

TIP For those individuals tasked with creating policies, it can appear to be a daunting task. However, there are numerous sample polices available that can provide a starting point for the creation of a customized policy. For technology-related policies, one of the best places to start is The SANS (System Administration and Network Security) Security Policy Project. Over 25 policies are provided and have been reviewed by a knowledgeable staff. They can be found at http://www.sans.org/resources/policies/. For those interested in learning more about trade secret information, Sheryl J. Willert's article, "Safeguarding Trade Secrets in the Information Age" (*The Practical Lawyer*, Feb. 2003) is a great place to start. This document can be found at http://www.wkg.com/media/Safeguarding%20Trade%20Secrets.pdf.

Enforce Polices

Having policies in place is an excellent idea and a first step in beginning to create a culture of security within an organization. However, it is absolutely critical that the policies be enforced. Without enforcement, the policies are worthless.

Require Employees to Read and Sign Off on Acceptable Use Policies

It is recommended that critical policies, especially the acceptable use policy, be presented to employees on their first day of employment. The employee should be given the opportunity to read the policy and ask relevant questions, and should then sign the policy to confirm that they have read and understood the policy. This signed copy of the policy should be placed in the employee's personnel folder. This provides the employer the opportunity to counter the common, "I didn't know I wasn't supposed to do that" defense should a situation ever arise. If revisions are made to the policy, the new version should be distributed, signed, and placed in the employee personnel folders. Policies should not be static documents, especially in a growing company. It is a bad sign when someone asks to see a copy of the acceptable use policy and it requires digging through a closet and pulling out a dust-covered binder that contains all of the company policies.

Provide Evaluation of Employee's Compliance in Annual Review

An employee's ability or inability to adhere to various policies should be included in the annual evaluation process. If an employee has numerous violations of a policy, this should be taken into account when the time comes to determine compensation increases or promotions. This process will quickly lead to employees keeping security issues in mind. Some organizations take this a step further and actively and publicly praise or reward employees who comply with security policies. This type of positive reinforcement is perhaps the best method of ensuring that employees consider the adherence to security policies a good idea.

Establish Penalties for Noncompliance

Establishing and enforcing penalties for noncompliance is absolutely critical to the success of any security program. Many acceptable use policies use vague language in describing penalties for noncompliance, using phrases like "up to and including termination." These penalties are meaningless, especially if no one has ever been terminated. The penalties applied should increase with either the significance or number of violations. One possible series of penalties might include the following:

- **First offense** Verbal warning, with documentation added to the employee's personnel folder.
- **Second offense** Written warning, with documentation added to the employee's personnel folder. Written warnings in a personnel folder will cause a reduction in any bonuses or raises for one year after the infraction.
- **Third offense** Employee is placed on probation for a specified period. If the employee violates any company policy while on probation, they are terminated immediately. No raises or bonuses for one year after the infraction.
- **Fourth offense** Immediate termination.

Another penalty that needs to be considered but is not often utilized is to contact the appropriate law enforcement agency if the employee's conduct warrants it. Some companies find that having an employee on trial for a particular crime can cause undesirable media attention and intensified scrutiny by the board of directors and shareholders.

Establish a Training Program: The Building of a Team

Security professionals often advocate training of employees as one of the first steps to securing a corporation's infrastructure. Although training is an excellent tool, if the training program is not designed properly, the resources used to present the training could be wasted.

Define a Specific Training Goal

The first step in designing a training program is to define a specific goal. The goal should be well defined and easily understood. Simply stating that the goal of the training program is to educate users about security policies and procedures is not enough. Instead, the goal should be to educate users about security policies and procedures so that they can more effectively participate in the protection of corporate assets and information. The phrase "more effectively participate" is the key point here and it should be understood that this participation includes open dialog between the users and the IT staff. This open dialog can begin with the training program itself, since most effective trainers find that they always learn from their students while training.

Establish Requirements for Trainers

For effective training it is important to use someone who is a skilled trainer, not simply a subject matter expert or someone equipped with a PowerPoint presentation. Having a subject matter expert deliver the message in a training program is pointless if the expert is unable to hold an audience's attention. Require trainers to follow the guidelines that follow.

Use Approved Instructional Methods

The trainer should be familiar with approved instructional methods. These methods are outlined and discussed in many train-the-trainer programs and are covered in great detail in the training classes for the CompTIA Certified Technical Trainer (CTT+) certification. It is important to recognize that these are the same skills required to be a certified instructor for many vendor-specific training programs. A great resource for learning some of the skill sets necessary to be a skilled trainer is *How to Be a Successful Technical Trainer* by Terrance Keys and Andrew R. Zeff (McGraw-Hill/Osborne, 2000). Many of the training skills required for certifications are based on the instructor competencies outlined by the International Board of Standards for Training, Performance and Instruction (http://www.ibstpi.org). An individual tasked with training end users should honestly evaluate their training skills by comparing them to the competencies listed in Table 16-1.

Provide Varied Training Materials and Approaches

One of the most critical concepts for a trainer to learn is that a training program does not simply consist of reading bullet points from a PowerPoint presentation. For many in the industry, this is simply referred to as "Death by PowerPoint" and should be avoided at all costs. Although PowerPoint is a valuable tool, it should not be relied upon as the sole delivery mechanism in a training class. Individuals learn differently, so it is important to vary the delivery mechanism frequently. Using printed handouts as a basis for a discussion or question-and-answer period is an excellent way to break up the program and reinforce previously discussed materials. Another popular training mechanism is to use role-playing activities, where the students are given a particular scenario and asked to act out how they would respond in the situation dictated to them by the scenario. The trainer can then evaluate whether the participants responded in accordance with the firm's security policies.

Some individuals reading this section may be thinking that there are other effective mechanisms for training users on security policies and procedures other than instructor-led training. Creating an interactive web site and developing a self-paced program that can be distributed on a CD-ROM are some of the other popular training tools in use today. However, the premise behind instructor-led training is to begin the process of developing open lines of communication between the IT staff and end users. End users are more likely to communicate problems to someone they have met as opposed to simply calling an extension or phone number listed on a corporate roster. Instructor-led training is the first step in building a team focused on protecting corporate assets.

Professional Foundations	
1.	Communicate effectively.
2.	Update and improve one's professional knowledge and skills.
3.	Comply with established ethical and legal standards.
4.	Establish and maintain professional credibility.
Planning and Preparation	
5.	Plan instructional methods and materials
6.	Prepare for instruction.
Instructional Methods and Strategies	
7.	Stimulate and sustain learner motivation and engagement.
8.	Demonstrate effective presentation skills.
9.	Demonstrate effective facilitation skills.
10.	Demonstrate effective questioning skills.
11.	Provide clarification and feedback.
12.	Promote retention of knowledge and skills.
13.	Promote transfer of knowledge and skills.
14.	Use media and technology to enhance learning and performance.
Assessment and Evaluation	
15.	Assess learning and performance.
16.	Evaluate instructional effectiveness.
Management	
17.	Manage an environment that fosters learning and performance.
18.	Manage the instructional process through the appropriate use of technology

Table 16-1. 2003 Instructor Competencies from the International Board of Standards for Training, Performance and Instruction.

An organization that does not have a skilled trainer on staff may want to look at computer-based training as an alternative. It would be worthwhile for an organization in this position to consider hiring a skilled third party to deliver the security training. Internal staff can be on hand to respond to any company-specific questions that may arise. Although using a third party is not ideal, there are some advantages. Attendees will likely learn more from a skilled trainer than from an internal staff member with poor presentation skills. Third parties are unbiased. They are unaffected by internal corporate politics and do not have any preconceived notions regarding particular individuals or departments. But perhaps the most significant thing to consider is that an outside trainer still has the advantage over computer-based training because they are able to put a human face on security issues.

Explain Reasoning Behind Policies

When presenting security-related policies and procedures, the trainer should be in a position to explain the reasons behind each particular policy and procedure. Security policies are often seen as annoying or cumbersome, an intrusion into an already busy workday. Explaining the reasoning behind the policies often makes them seem less intrusive and can assist in demonstrating current threats to an organization. In addition, explaining the reasoning behind the policies avoids the perception of the "Do it because I said so" mentality. Parents learn quickly that this is not an effective way to explain policies to teenagers, and the same holds true with most adults.

Establish Requirements for the Training Program: The Message

A security-training program needs to be customized to the needs and issues that are specific to a particular organization.

Explain Legal Requirements

Some businesses that provide services to government agencies are required to adhere to strict policies and procedures due to security concerns. Other industries may be impacted by other regulations such as the Health Insurance Portability and Accountability Act (HIPAA) or the Gramm-Leach-Bliley Act (GLBA), both of which are discussed in more detail in Chapter 2. Regardless of the industry, there are some common issues that need to be explained and defined.

Provide Personal Reasons for Voluntary Support of Security

The important thing to remember during this training is that the message must not be overbearing (e.g., "Do this or else!") but rather should be designed to elicit support from the end users. Explaining that security mechanisms are implemented to protect the business and keep it solvent is a very good approach. End users are less likely to open suspicious e-mail attachments if they understand that the money used to clean up a virus infection is money that will not be used for raises and bonuses. When the threats are described in a personal manner, it is very easy for people to understand the issues, which increases the likelihood that they will comply with an organization's policies and procedures.

Use Demonstrations

During this training process, be sure to include as many live demonstrations as possible. Employees will much more easily understand the critical importance of having complex passwords if you demonstrate a password-cracking program that cracks a password in a fraction of a second. Demonstrating concepts also goes a long way toward livening up what for some participants might be considered an extremely boring topic. When participants exclaim "Wow!" when a concept is demonstrated, the trainer has hit the target with his or her message.

Provide a Rationale for Web Site Restrictions

Perhaps one of the best places to start security training is to explain the reasoning behind web site restrictions. For businesses with automated web site blocking, this is a good time to explain the policy. But for smaller businesses that do not have the capability to block specific web sites or that cannot block web sites for business reasons, this is a critical discussion. Explaining that surfing to unapproved web sites is restricted due to productivity issues is the normal approach when training on this topic. However, discussing web site restrictions is a great springboard to begin addressing other issues and topics.

Most users do not understand that web sites can contain hostile code or behave in a manner not expected by the user. Brief discussions regarding items such as ActiveX controls, JavaScript, cookies, and spyware can be introduced here. But perhaps the best way to make the point that indiscriminate web surfing is a dangerous pursuit is to demonstrate that HTML is *code* and can perform unwanted actions. Doing the following can create an interesting and hopefully amusing demonstration. (This demonstration is based on an example provided by Ed Skoudis in his book *Malware: Fighting Malicious Code*, Prentice Hall PTR, 2003.)

1. Open your favorite text editor (Notepad, gedit, etc., depending on your OS).
2. Create the following HTML code:

```
<html>
<script>alert("I just stole all of your passwords!")</script>
</html>
```

3. Save the file as index.html.
4. Distribute this file to the computers in the training lab.
5. Have the students double-click the file. Their browser should open and display the following message:

Although the code in this demonstration does not steal passwords, it should get their attention. This discussion of HTML code is an excellent place to address the issue of HTML-formatted e-mail messages. Because HTML-based documents can contain malicious code, many organizations are blocking HTML-formatted e-mail messages at the gateway to their networks. This is an excellent opportunity to explain why and to discuss the advantages of text-based e-mail.

HTML-formatted messages are blocked at the gateway not only because of the possibility of spreading malicious code, but also to block spam messages, since most spam messages use HTML formatting. Educating users on these issues can help them to understand company policies regarding the use of text-based e-mail. If the system in use in the organization does not automatically default to text-based formatting, instructing users on how to select "plain text" when creating messages would be prudent.

Even if sending HTML-formatted messages is permitted, training users on text-based versus HTML-formatted e-mail is important. Clients or business partners may not allow HTML-formatted messages into their systems, so users could have e-mail rejected. Explaining these concepts puts the user in a better position to understand why the message was rejected and how to resend the message so that it will be accepted.

Harden E-Mail Usage

When users create e-mail messages, they often forget the impact the contents of the message may have on the recipient. E-mail messages are "emotionless," because the sender cannot support the meaning of the message with tone, facial expression, or body language as they can with verbal communications. To ensure that their meaning is not misconstrued, users often use *emoticons* (emotion + icon) to convey the tone of a message. In addition, e-mail is nearly instantaneous; once the Send button is clicked, there is no retrieving the message. Users need to understand the legal issues regarding e-mail usage as well as current trends in the use of e-mail. To harden e-mail usage in your organization, you should do the following:

Teach Users to Review Content Before Sending: Avoiding the "Oops, I Wish I Hadn't Said That" Syndrome E-mail has been one of the greatest tools created for quick, efficient communications. However, e-mail is often created hastily and sent without thinking of the consequences. This is why nearly all current business litigation usually includes the examination of e-mail communications. Very often e-mail messages contain the "smoking gun" that supports one party's claim during the litigation. And most users forget that e-mail messages are often archived to backup tapes and can be recovered many years after the e-mail message was created. Very often, the archiving of e-mail messages is not for disaster-recovery purposes but is required to comply with various legislative or legal requirements. Some users try to utilize web-based e-mail such as Hotmail, MSN Mail, Yahoo, and so forth to bypass this archiving process. Unfortunately, they are unfamiliar with the fact that web-based e-mail messages are cached on their local hard drive and can also be recovered years after they were created.

NOTE Many organizations provide to mobile and home users web access to e-mail services on corporate systems. If cached web-based e-mail messages are not deleted on a regular basis, they can pose a threat to an organization during litigation or if the systems are stolen. It may be prudent to show users how to delete cached Internet files or show them how to configure their browser to automatically delete the files for them. Just remember that by doing this you will not be able to utilize cached Internet files during an internal investigation.

The risk of casual e-mail comments is exemplified by this e-mail message from a drug company administrator, which is cited in the book *Dispensing with the Truth* (St. Martin's Press, 2001) by Alicia Mundy: "Can I look forward to my waning years signing checks for fat people who are a little afraid of some silly lung problem...?"

This quote pertains to the fen-phen diet pill litigation. The author of the e-mail is complaining about paying claims to overweight people who took the diet pill fen-phen and developed a "silly lung problem." The silly lung problem referred to here is primary pulmonary hypertension and is nearly always fatal. This e-mail showed that this particular employee had a cavalier attitude regarding a very significant problem. This type of e-mail can prove damaging in litigation.

Teach Users to Review Addressee Before Sending Another point to make when discussing e-mail is that users should verify that they are sending the e-mail to the appropriate recipient prior to clicking the Send button. Many e-mail programs attempt to be helpful by completing an e-mail address after a user types in one or more characters of an address. If users are not careful, they could send proprietary information to the wrong party or, even worse, a distribution list. The normal disclaimer that organizations add to the end of an e-mail message stating that the e-mail is for the "designated recipient only" is useless here because the e-mail did reach the recipient designated in the To field. Many courts have found these disclaimers invalid because they are provided at the end of the e-mail and no one ever reads them anyway. When discussing these issues, some people may not understand their significance. Once again, the issue here is cost. E-mail messages sent hastily can cost a business a client, its reputation, and the loss of proprietary information. These issues affect revenues, which affect users' jobs.

Discuss Spam and Teach Users How It's Managed E-mail discussions can lead into a very controversial topic, spam. Most users are unfamiliar with the fact that registering for a web site using a business e-mail address or subscribing to a nifty new electronic newsletter is one of the surest ways to get an e-mail address added to a spammer's list. This is another opportunity to explain the dangers of a threat from a dollars-and-cents perspective. The following 2003 statistics quoted from Spam Filter Review are extremely enlightening (http://www.spamfilterreview.com/spam-statistics.html):

- Email considered Spam: 40% of all e-mail
- Daily Spam emails sent: 12.4 billion
- Daily Spam received per person: 6
- Annual Spam received per person: 2,200
- Spam costs to all non-corp Internet Users: $255 million
- Spam costs to US corporations in 2002: $8.9 billion
- Email address changes due to Spam: 16%
- Estimated Spam Increase by 2007: 63%
- Annual Spam in 1,000 Employee Company: 2.1 million

Statistics such as these can be used to calculate the volume of spam in your organization. Mind-numbing statistics such as these can go a long way toward convincing users that contributing to the spread of spam is not a good idea. After explaining the costs of spam, it might be prudent to explain other defenses in addition to what has been previously mentioned. Instruct users to

- Not use business addresses to sign up for newsletters that are not business related.
- Never use the unsubscribe feature in a spam message, as it often notifies the sender that the e-mail address is valid.
- Never order anything advertised in a spam message.
- Never use automated out-of-office messages. Because spammers often use fake return e-mail addresses, an automated out-of-office reply generates an undeliverable response, which is additional unwanted traffic on a company's mail server.

NOTE Some companies require automated out-of-office replies for employees who will be out of the office for an extended period. To reduce traffic, firms can utilize automated tools that prevent automated replies from going to external sources. Many e-mail programs or clients have the ability to create rules that can specify when to send automated messages. Creating a rule that sends the automated reply only to messages that arrive with the company's domain name can prove helpful. If this capability exists in your organization, provide training on rule creation.

Provide Proper Instructions for Responding to Malicious Code

Perhaps the biggest threat to an organization is malicious code (viruses, Trojan horses, rootkits, spyware, etc.), which is also the threat least understood by the user population. From a technical perspective, this is a very complex topic and there are complete books on the topic. The tendency for IT professionals is to focus on the technical aspects of malicious code. For the average user, this type of information is neither needed nor wanted. The most valuable information to give end users is how to identify a possible virus and how to react if one is encountered.

NOTE Many organizations have taken steps to block viruses at the gateway, either by blocking specific attachments or through more robust mechanisms. Even in organizations that believe they have robust antivirus programs in place, virus awareness training is still important. Antivirus programs can fail, and new virus-dispersal methods may be created that bypass the antivirus system. In addition, many users work from home and have corporate e-mail contacts in their home address books. Putting end users in a position where they can identify virus threats at home can go a long way in preventing virus problems in the workplace.

Train Users to Identify Virus Indicators Demonstrating these ideas is best presented by a visual demonstration of the key virus indicators that can be located in an e-mail message. Currently, virus-infested e-mails are so common, it should be easy to find an e-mail similar to the one shown in Figure 16-1 to demonstrate key points.

Figure 16-1 shows an e-mail that is carrying a zipped file attachment that contains a virus. The first red flag can be found in the From field. The sender's address is listed as *security@fdic.com*. This appears to be a legitimate e-mail being sent from the Federal Deposit Insurance Corporation, FDIC. The only problem is that the domain name for the FDIC is www.fdic.*gov*. A casual observer might overlook this.

Other warning signs include the lack of a personal salutation or greeting, poor grammar and spelling, and the lack of contact information at the end of the message.

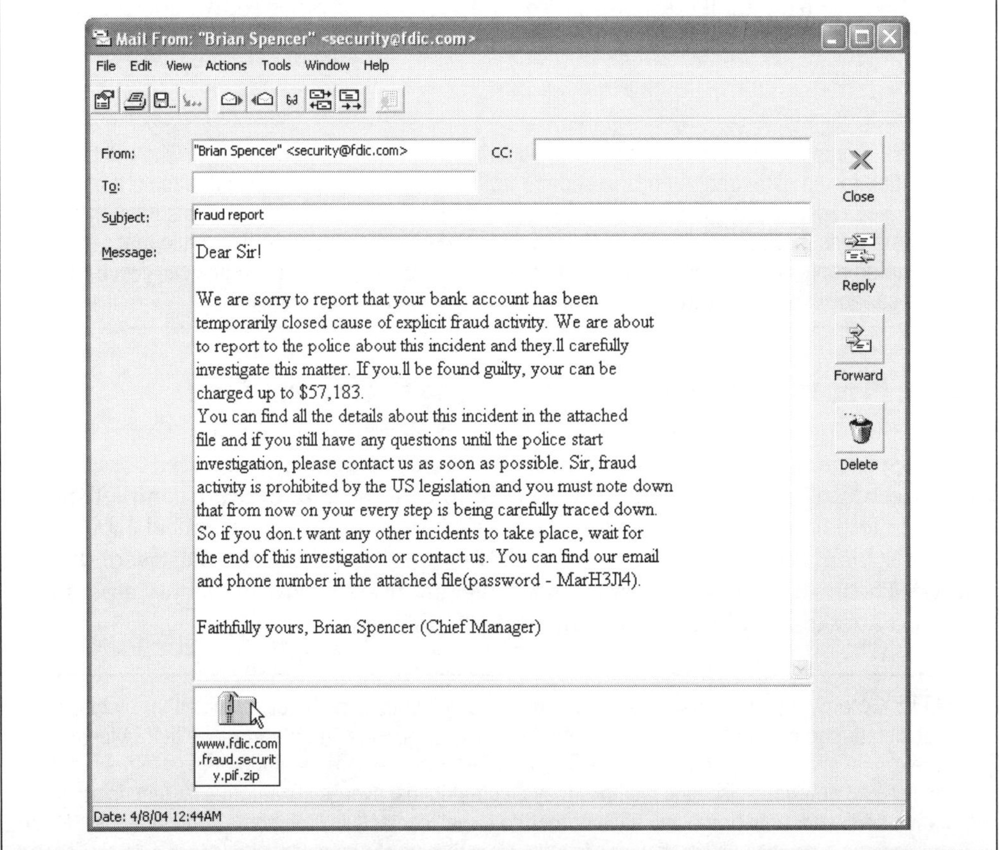

Figure 16-1. An example of a virus-carrying e-mail message

It is hard to imagine that anyone would believe that a message of this significance would be delivered anonymously via e-mail.

The last noteworthy item is that the file attachment contains multiple file extensions, .pif.zip.

Train Users in File Extension Concepts Many users are not familiar with the concept of file extensions. It might be prudent at this point to discuss file extensions and the most commonly exploited file types, such as .bat, .com, .exe, .pif, .vb, .scr, .js, and so forth. Additional information to share with users is that Zip or compressed files are often used to transport malicious code in order to bypass firewall restrictions.

Train Users to Identify Hoaxes No discussion of viruses and other malicious code would be complete without a discussion of hoaxes. Hoaxes can cause nearly as many lost-productivity issues and bandwidth-consumption problems as a well-crafted virus. Nearly all hoaxes instruct a user to forward the hoax's warning to "everyone in their address book." What do viruses do? Replicate themselves by sending copies to everyone in a user's address book. So a hoax simply has the users do the dirty work for them. Instruct users that genuine virus warnings never originate from Microsoft, AOL, or Intel as in, "Microsoft just announced that this is the worst virus ever." Genuine warnings also never include the phrase, "please forward this to everyone in your address book." This may sound trivial but if users follow these directions, the consequences can be significant.

Additional hoax warning signs to pass along to users include the fact that hoaxes often have a sense of urgency, "Do this now or all is lost!" and may include the disclaimer "This is not a hoax!" Numerous resources exist that allow individuals to determine if a particular warning or alert is valid or simply a hoax. The Department of Energy's Computer Incident Advisory Capability has its Hoaxbusters site, http://hoaxbusters.ciac.org, and Purportal.com, http://www.purportal.com, provides the opportunity to submit inquiries to multiple sites. These sites are very useful, but they contain some interesting and humorous information that could prove distracting to the average user. Pass along these sites to your users at your own discretion.

Train Users in Avoiding Mail Storms Immediately after the attacks of September 11, 2001, Americans became extremely patriotic and began exchanging and distributing patriotic sentiments and images across the country. Recipients would forward the most stirring e-mails to *everyone in their address books.* Because of this, the events on the East Coast slowed or stopped many networks and systems across the country even though they were not directly impacted by the attacks. Events such as this are extremely emotional. It is not recommended that you train users to quell their emotions, but it might be beneficial to provide another mechanism to share sentiments. On September 11, some organizations provided an area where users could post printouts of exceptionally patriotic or emotional materials. This allowed the opportunity for users to share their feelings and elicit national pride, but it also helped to reduce network traffic.

Train Users in Password Creation

Security professionals have been telling or forcing users to use complex passwords for years. The user community generally still does not understand the reasoning behind this—they either refuse to create complex passwords or nearly revolt when forced to remember complex passwords. The only way to drive home the point that complex passwords are a requirement is to demonstrate how trivial it is to crack a password. Numerous tools exist to crack passwords, but for demonstration purposes use a simple tool in a context that the users can understand. Cracking an Outlook Express password with SnadBoy's Revelation (http://www.snadboy.com) is quick and simple. Most importantly, the password is cracked immediately, even with complex passwords.

For this demonstration, simply create a dummy e-mail account in Outlook Express:

1. Open Outlook Express.
2. Click Tools | Accounts.
3. In the Internet Accounts window, click Add | Mail.
4. Enter a name for the account.
5. Click Next.
6. Enter an e-mail address and click Next.
7. Enter incoming and outgoing mail server names (they can be the same), something like mail.server.com
8. Enter an account name and a password. For the greatest impact, make the password complex, using numbers, letters, and special characters.
9. Check the Remember Password box.
10. Click Next and, in the last Window, click Finish.
11. The account is now created and can be used for demonstration purposes at any time.

To run the demonstration, follow these steps:

1. Open Outlook Express.
2. Click Tools | Accounts.
3. In the Internet Accounts window, click the Mail tab and double-click the account you created in the preceding steps.
4. When the Account Properties window opens, click the Servers tab.

5. Start SnadBoy's Revelation by double-clicking on Revelation.exe. The exact location of where the executable is located depends on where you have it installed.
6. Drag the cross hairs, which are referred to as the "circled +" in the application, over the password text box. The encrypted password will be displayed immediately.

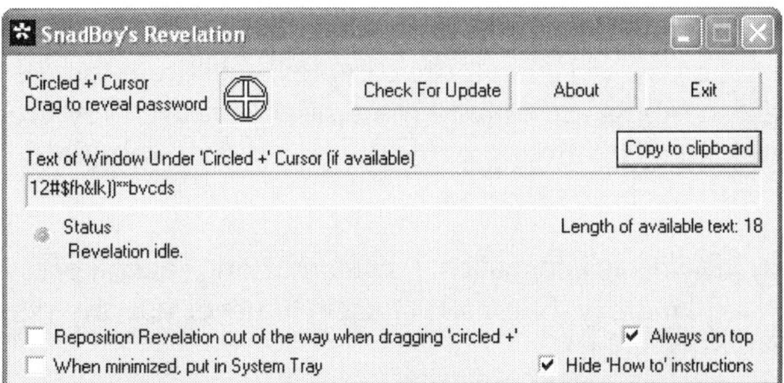

Among the points to make during this presentation is the fact that tools like SnadBoy's Revelation are freely available on the Internet and can be used covertly. SnadBoy's Revelation fits on a floppy disk. In addition, mention that the password could be captured only because the Remember Password box had been checked. But the most powerful point to make is that many people use the same password for multiple accounts, which means that a simple tool like SnadBoy's Revelation could give an attacker access to multiple systems and accounts.

Using a POP3 mail client in this demonstration is effective because most users will be familiar with the program, thus making the demonstration personal. Cracking password-protected Microsoft Office files is another opportunity to make the point. Word Key from LostPassword.com (http://lostpassword.com) allows you to break the password of any Microsoft Word document (except for those using the advanced protection capabilities of Office 2003). There are other password-cracking tools available, and you may have a favorite, but it is important to remember that any tool you demonstrate could be used against you or your organization.

Numerous password-cracking tools exist, and it is important to instill in the users that some of the tools that are capable of cracking network passwords are extremely powerful and have the ability to capture password files remotely or to sniff username and password combinations traveling across the network. Because of this fact, training users on the proper creation of passwords is important. Information that users need to have regarding passwords includes the following.

Create Complex Passwords "Create complex passwords" is the standard instruction for users ... and is extremely vague. Some users think that prepending or appending a number to a word makes the password complex. This is one of the first processes a password-cracking program runs, checking for numbers before or after words. One of the most creative ways to create complex passwords is to create phrases or sentences and then use the first letter of each word to create the password. As an example, take the well known phrase

The quick brown fox jumped over the lazy dog.

If you take the first letter from each word, you have "tqbfjotld," which is a complex password, fairly easy to remember, and somewhat challenging for a password-cracking program. To make the password even more complex, substitute the @ symbol for the *o* and ! for the *l*. These symbols are easy to remember because they are shaped like the letters they are replacing. This now creates the password "tqbfj@t!d." This is easy to remember and difficult to crack or guess.

Do Not Use Personally Identifiable Information After cracking several passwords, this section should be fairly self explanatory, but instruct users to never use any personal information when creating passwords, such as

- Names of spouses, children, or pets
- Birthdates for any family member
- Dates of graduation from educational institutions (many people keep diplomas in their office)
- Other relevant numbers—social security number, drivers license number, license plate number, etc.
- Make of any computer system or peripheral
- Any word that appears in any dictionary, for any language

Many operating systems include mechanisms that force users to create more complex passwords. Passwords must be a certain length, must contain specific characters, can't be the same as the username, and so on. By demonstrating how easily passwords can be cracked, users will understand these technical policies and should no longer see the password policies as oppressive, but rather as a necessity.

Train Users to Report Suspicious Activity

Security professionals like to tell stories of how they were able to accomplish some feat without being detected by a security team or challenged by an employee. A typical story might describe how the security professional was able to tag along behind an employee into a secure area without providing any ID or using an access control device (called *piggybacking* or *tailgating* in the security industry). Once inside the secure area, the security professional attempts to access a computer. They are usually able to find a computer that is turned on, logged in, and unattended. Proprietary information is normally either printed off or downloaded to a floppy disk. The security professional then is able to walk out of the facility with the "stolen" material completely uncontested. In this scenario, there are both physical and IT security breaches described.

Require Challenges to Badgeless Visitors Hardening wetware must include training the employees to confront visitors who are in a secure area without an escort or visitor badge. The term *confront* does not necessarily mean that the employee has to be aggressive; it simply means that the employee should address the individual so that they know they have been recognized. A simple "May I help you?" could be enough to give an intruder second thoughts. Or "I see that you don't have a visitor badge. Why don't I take you to the guard booth to get one?" may thwart an intrusion. If the employee is afraid of being physically harmed, they should call security immediately. Employees should understand that confronting suspicious employees is not "antisocial"; they are simply protecting their jobs and their coworkers. This point can easily be made by comparing the workspace to an employee's home. If an employee were to see a stranger walking around in their backyard, would they simply ignore the stranger, as they might do at work? Probably not.

Provide Anonymous Reporting Mechanisms Reporting suspicious activity of a stranger or nonemployee is pretty straightforward, but how should an employee respond if they see a coworker involved in suspicious activity? Internal politics and corporate culture hold greater significance when a fellow employee is witnessed engaging in questionable activities. Consequences for reporting the activity may be perceived as more significant than the consequences for not reporting the activity, especially if the person engaged in inappropriate activities is a supervisor or member of management. Filing a report on a coworker is extremely difficult, considering we are taught at a young age that no one likes a "snitch" or a "tattletale." Proper anonymous reporting mechanisms need to be employed so that employees can effectively report suspicious activity without the threat of repercussions. End-user training should effectively communicate these mechanisms and reinforce the fact that the reporting is anonymous. Companies that offer a phone number or web-based system for anonymously reporting tips should distribute the phone number or URL during the training session. To learn more about anonymous reporting mechanisms, download The Network's whitepaper, "Best Practices in Ethics Hotlines," which is available at http://www.tnwinc.com/downloads/TNW-HOTWP2-CM.pdf.

Train Users to Resist Social Engineering

Having robust physical and IT security mechanisms in place to protect a corporation's proprietary information is useless if employees can be convinced to give away the information just by asking for it. This is essentially what social engineering accomplishes. It convinces employees either to give away access to proprietary information, by giving up usernames and passwords, or to simply give away the information directly. The art of social engineering is also described as "hacking humans," which is much more accurate, because social engineers take advantage of vulnerabilities in human nature. Everyone likes to be helpful, and it is human nature to provide assistance when it is requested. If a social engineer impersonates a help desk technician and asks an end user for their password, the end user will freely provide the information. End users should understand that they should never give out a password, to anyone, ever.

Many end users believe that there is no way they could be fooled. This misconception needs to be addressed directly during the training process. Social engineers use many tricks to convince people of the legitimacy of their request and position. They will sound authoritative, will have a sense of urgency, will use intimidation, will drop the names of people in management, and so forth. In order for employees to understand the methods used, role-playing scenarios can be an extremely effective part of the training process.

One scenario that has been extremely effective is to have attendees write down their names, usernames, and passwords on a slip of paper. The premise behind this is that the slips of paper will be entered into a drawing for a door prize. Every attendee will provide the information without hesitation. Once the slips are collected, it is then appropriate to point out how quickly and easily they gave up their usernames and passwords.

Another option is to create a survey asking for personally identifiable information, such as name, address, social security number, number and names of children, home address, favorite food, hobbies, and so forth. Present this survey to the training session attendees, as a quality-control mechanism. Once the surveys have been completed and turned in, explain that they need to be more careful in providing personal information, since it can be used to guess passwords or to help create a false identity for someone wishing to break into a company or system.

Discuss Response Outside the Office It is imperative that you include in the social engineering section of the training instructions on how to respond to threats outside of the business. People often let their guard down once they leave the office. Many individuals are proud of their jobs and will freely discuss current projects, favorite customers, planned expansion, and so forth if approached in a social situation after work. The amount of information that they will disseminate expands exponentially if the request for information comes from an attractive member of the opposite sex and alcohol is involved. People often start bragging about their activities to impress prospective dates.

Discuss Proper Disposal of Confidential Information Discuss document shredding as a key part of this program. Social engineers often begin their intelligence gathering by examining a corporation's trash. An activity affectionately referred to as "dumpster diving." What may appear to be innocuous documents to employees can help provide valuable information to attackers. Internal memos and documents can help would-be attackers learn naming conventions and employee names, positions, and phone numbers or extensions. Username and password combinations are often discarded in the trash. Businesses and employees always underestimate the value of particular information. It is best to err on the side of caution and insist that employees always shred their trash.

Identify Privacy Issues

Although courts have recognized that employees have no expectation of privacy in the workplace, it is important to address this topic during the training program because it is an extremely volatile topic and any misunderstandings can have serious consequences. The U.S. District Court for the District of Nebraska ruled in *United States v. Bailey*, 2003 (D. Neb. July 23, 2003) that employees have no expectation of privacy if they are told that their computer activities will be monitored. Many organizations include a statement regarding the monitoring of employee computer activity in the acceptable use policy and provide a banner during the login process that states that by logging into the system, the user consents to the monitoring of their activities. Even with these mechanisms in place, many employees find it extremely offensive that their computer activities could be monitored. During this part of the training program, it is extremely important to inform users that the monitoring of employee activity is designed to evaluate system performance, discover network bottlenecks, and to prevent system failure. Developing a culture of security within an organization requires a certain level of trust between all parties. If users believe that the IT staff is monitoring all user activity, that trust relationship will disappear very quickly. Several great resources to learn more about privacy issues include the Electronic Frontier Foundation, http://www.eff.org, and the Electronic Privacy Information Center, http://www.epic.org.

Identify Information Classification and Its Proper Handling

For many organizations that do not work for government agencies, the concept of information or data classification is completely foreign. For most people the classification of documents as "confidential," "secret," and "top secret" is the stuff of spy movies. However, in order to prevent trade secret information from walking out the door, according to the Uniform Trade Secrets Act, it must be designated as a trade secret and reasonable measures must be taken to protect the information. This is an extremely important concept, because if the proper mechanisms are not put in place to protect trade secrets, they can leave an organization, and the organization may have no recourse to prevent their dissemination.

As part of training on data classification, it is important to discuss related materials, such as document retention policies, and issues regarding removable media, such as USB drives, floppy disks, and CD-Rs and DVD-Rs. Educating users on how and when to store, transport, and destroy data is an important part of the training process.

Identify File Sharing and Instant Messaging Issues

With all of the media attention regarding the copyright issues of sharing music files across the Internet, file sharing should be a short discussion. However, other issues regarding file sharing should be discussed. Music files and video files could contain malicious code, and the downloading of files can utilize significant bandwidth, which can cause efficiency issues. But the most significant issue to address is that both file sharing programs and many instant messaging programs open holes in firewalls, allowing corporate systems to be compromised. This can be presented without going into technical details and an overview should be enough for users to understand the threat. Do not make your only defense of corporate policy the productivity perspective, as in "Don't share or download music files because you are wasting company resources." This comes across as oppressive and does not help open lines of communication.

ONE STEP FURTHER

In an effort to continue to build a positive relationship with users, it might be beneficial to address computer and computer security issues that the users might face on their home computers. By providing information on cookies, online auction do's and don'ts, personal firewall products, and so forth, users will begin to see the IT security team as a valuable resource. These topics would be very important to discuss with those users that use their home computers to access corporate systems. In addition, one of the greatest concerns employees have is how to protect young family members that spend a great deal of time on the Internet. Unfortunately, most people are completely unfamiliar with the scope of the threat of the Internet for children. A member of the Cybercrime Unit of the Kansas City Field Office of the FBI stated that, "If every member of the law enforcement community was tasked with tracking down pedophiles and purveyors of child pornography they would only scratch the surface of the problem." Numerous resources exist, but the FBI's "A Parent's Guide to Internet Safety" is one of the best. It is available in electronic form at http://www.fbi.gov/publications/pguide/pguidee.htm. Hard copies are available through local FBI field offices. Additional resources include GetNetWise, at http://www.getnetwise.org, and Yahoo's "Safe Surfing With Your Family," http://yahooligans.yahoo.com/parents/safety.html. Providing this type of information shows concern for the employees' families and will help keep the relationship with employees strong.

Provide Contact Information

As a final part of the training process, it is important to distribute contact information for the IT security team. End users should feel that the IT security team is approachable and can be contacted easily if there is a problem or a concern. The ability to have efficient communications is an important part of the security process.

Provide Ongoing Training

Training should be ongoing. There are many methods to keep security topics in front of users. Internal web sites, newsletters, and annual training to address new threats and new policies are all valuable methods to "get the word out." Because individuals learn differently, utilizing a combination of different methods is the most effective. One excellent resource that could be used as a giveaway at user training sessions or as a textbook for user training is *Computer Security: 20 Things Every Employee Should Know* by Ben Rothke (McGraw-Hill/Osborne, 2003). This is an inexpensive, well-written manual that could be a very effective supplement to customized internal training.

Develop Communication Skills

Perhaps one of the biggest failures in a comprehensive security program is the inability of security professionals to effectively communicate with other departments or business units within their organization. The ability to communicate well with other departments helps build a level of trust, which in turn makes it easier to roll out new security policies and procedures and, more importantly, can allow for more effective notifications when problems arise or breaches occur. Developing communication skills may require individuals to get out of their comfort zones and learn something new. It is important to recognize that many technology-based professionals pursue a particular career path so that they do not have to work with other people.

Provide Cross-Departmental Training

One of the best ways to open lines of communication is for members of the information technology and the information security teams to participate in cross-departmental training. Spending a day working in another department can provide some great insight for all of the parties involved. The security team can witness the impact of various security mechanisms and policies. They can determine if they are effective or an impediment to efficient workflow. Working within another department also provides the opportunity to learn the needs of the department. If a department is in the process of trying to evaluate various technologies to improve efficiency or performance, having an IT staff member immediately available can be extremely beneficial. The IT staff member may be able to suggest a solution, but they can also ensure that the solutions being evaluated will not cause security problems or vulnerabilities.

Working shoulder to shoulder with other employees can help break down barriers that are based on stereotypes and preconceived ideas of how certain departments function. When participating in cross-departmental training it is important to have an open mind. Most participants will find themselves saying things like, "Wow, he really is a nice guy!" or "I didn't realize how hard they work in that department." This kind of awareness leads to understanding, which allows better communication, which ultimately leads to a more secure environment.

Get IT Staff Out of the IT Box

Another significant issue for IT professionals is that they often eat, sleep, and breathe technology. During the day they may work with business and enterprise technologies, and after hours they may be involved with more personal technologies. But the issue here is that they are so involved with technology that they have a hard time understanding that technology does not exist in a vacuum. Technology is used to support business processes; it does not exist alone. Understanding fundamental business concepts is absolutely critical to being able to support a business effectively and to implement the appropriate security solutions.

There are many training options available to assist the IT professional with learning business concepts. The options range from independent, self-study to full-blown degree programs in business. Self-study programs are often ineffective, and most professionals do not have the time or resources to pursue a business degree. There is an excellent alternative that provides the knowledge in a reasonable timeframe for a reasonable price. Many business schools offer what is called a "Mini MBA" program. These programs vary in length, but usually meet for one night a week for 10 to 14 weeks. The instructors of these programs usually are the same instructors that teach in the full MBA program. Topics covered include business law, accounting, finance, human resources, marketing, information management, and international business. These classes expose the IT professional to the issues faced by all businesses and acquaint them with the terminology used by other departments. This, in turn, enables the IT professional to communicate more effectively, which leads to enhanced security.

Part III

Once Is Never Enough

Chapter 17

Auditing and Testing the Security of a Mixed Network

by Eric Seagren

- Perform the Pre-Assessment Phase
- Perform the Assessment
- Perform the Post Assessment

Computer networks are often extremely complex, including a mixture of products, vendors, and technologies. Developing technological controls and documenting policies to protect your sensitive data can be a daunting task. Extensively documented procedures and racks of the newest technical gadgets will not ensure that your network is secure. Because humans are designing and configuring your network and systems, odds are good that it is *not* perfect. Policy and procedures are great, but how do you know if those policies and procedures are being followed?

A thorough audit allows you to measure policy against what is actually being implemented. An audit is your opportunity to see where policy isn't being followed and take corrective actions, or possibly adjust policy. Under some circumstances, periodic audits might be a legal requirement as well. It is important to differentiate between an audit, a vulnerability assessment, and a penetration test; they are not the same thing. An *audit* in this context is a review and measurement against a defined standard. A *vulnerability assessment* is a review to determine what vulnerabilities are present. During a vulnerability assessment the vulnerabilities are not actually exploited. A *penetration test* is an attempt to gain unauthorized access by exploiting vulnerabilities.

That standard used during an audit could be based only off of internal policy, but could also include industry best practices or even government guidelines. For example, if the purpose of the audit is only to find out if the corporate IT security policy is being adhered to, and policy requires administrator accounts to have a blank password, then finding all the administrator accounts with a blank password would not be an audit exception. In this example scenario, based on the defined policy, all is well from an audit perspective. In reality, part of the value the customer receives from a skilled auditor is the auditor's ability to point out places where the policy is weak and needs adjustment, even if the system in question complies with the policy.

A penetration test is an attempt to find a weakness in a system or process and exploit that weakness. The weakness could be physical, social, or technological. Depending on your objectives, a penetration test can be very invasive. This means that it does not just look at a system or at documentation and declare the system to be secure. Rather, the penetration testers try to actually break into the system. In many cases, the testing can inadvertently cause a service disruption to the target system. The measure of when the system has been compromised can vary and should be explicitly documented beforehand. A vulnerability assessment involves trying to identify security weaknesses without actually exploiting them. A penetration test or vulnerability assessment is part of a thorough audit, but an audit is not generally part of a penetration test or a vulnerability assessment. Throughout this chapter, the discussion assumes that a penetration test is being done rather than a vulnerability assessment; however, many of the steps outlined should apply to either scenario.

The objective of this chapter is to explain what you should do as part of an IT audit. Your circumstances may not require all of the elements that will be discussed, but by being familiar with the things that an audit may include, you can make an informed choice as to what *should* be included. This can be useful for the manager who wants to better understand what is needed from an internal or external audit. It should also be useful to someone who will be performing an audit. You may be performing an audit as part of a regular *internal* process, or as work for another company. By making sure an audit is comprehensive and fits the needs of the customer, you will be able to deliver more value to the customer. A good audit report will prove indispensable when it comes time to harden your network.

Perform the Pre-Assessment Phase

An audit is all about being thorough. The objective of an audit is to discover any flaws or weaknesses that exist in the current environment so that it can be made more secure. These weaknesses may be present due to oversight, absence of policy, or lack of training. In most cases, someone has probably reviewed the system or process before. As an auditor, your task is to scrutinize the same system or process and discover any security weaknesses that others may have missed, and to look for openings that a hostile party might find and exploit.

As part of being thorough, the audit must be well planned and well documented. A lot of work has to be done before inspecting any of the customer's systems. This section discusses all of the components that should go into the pre-assessment phase. These are the things that should be done up front, *before* any actual auditing takes place. These steps are vital, because without the proper planning before the audit is performed, the results will be of little to no value to the customer.

Understand the Customer's Needs

Vital to the success of your audit is that you understand the customer's needs. This includes a working knowledge of both the customer's business itself and the customer's specific needs from an audit. While not exactly the same, these two are tied together. To some degree, the customer's business might dictate auditing requirements, such as for financial institutions or health care providers. In addition to this, the customer will likely have specific areas that they know need special attention during an audit. Perhaps a critical server has been hacked previously and the customer wants to test that system in the particular way it was compromised before.

Understand the Customer's Business

You should have a conversation with the customer's representatives so that they can explain, in general terms, their business functions. If it is a very large company, the conversation might be limited to representatives from a particular business unit or geographic location rather than the whole firm. This conversation should be one of the first communications between the auditor and the customer. Knowing the customer's business functions not only alerts you to any special requirements or regulations that must be met, but also allows you to better understand the key areas for the customer. If you know that a company is manufacturing and selling widgets, then you also know that confidentiality of the widget designs is critical to the company. You also know that the availability of processing systems in its widget factory is critical. By contrast, if the company sells lemonade, they might not have any confidential data on how to make the lemonade. Confidentiality and integrity of its HR data would likely be its most critical area. A customer in the service industry will likely need to protect their employees more than their product, while a manufacturing company will need to protect the product it manufactures.

The auditor or audit team should be prepared for any special considerations, such as automated processing facilities, assembly lines, and security issues dealing with network time keeping. Time keeping issues are especially critical in automated environments where machines rely on accurate time to run properly. Accurate time can be important for logging mechanisms so that accurate timelines can be documented for legal cases or simply to reconstruct what happened during an outage. If the customer instead is a chain of hair salons, then the most vital data would likely be HR information on the company's employees.

While you don't need to know every single detail about a customer's business, having this broad understanding helps you to bring value to the assessment. Armed with this knowledge, you can cater your offerings to better fit the customer's needs. This also allows you to plan to call in any specialists you might need to test a specific type of system. You need to think ahead about what your capabilities are. It is far better to outsource some of the assessment to a specialist than to sell a service to the customer that you are not qualified to perform. As a professional, you will be expected to know what the customer's needs are even when the customer doesn't.

Understand the Customer's Audit Goals

Once you understand the customer's business, you should begin to define its needs from an IT security audit. It's very important to find out from the customer what it wants from the audit and what it expects upon completion of the audit. You cannot overlook this step, because what the customer wants and what the customer needs may not always be the same thing. This could be very generic, like "make us more secure," but really it should be clarified as much as possible. The customer could have *internal* policy requirements or, in some cases, might not really know exactly what it wants. If the customer simply wants to be "more secure," then you need to prepare a plan that defines exactly what the measures of success will be. Will the customer want a follow-up audit at a later date? Will it have another external review or audit of your findings?

Once the customer has defined the requirements it knows about, you need to explore and discuss any external needs that the customer may or may not be aware of. These could include regulatory requirements from sources such as the following (refer to Chapter 2 for more details):

- **Health Insurance Portability and Accountability Act (HIPAA)** Among other things, HIPAA specifies national standards for the security of health care transactions and health care data. More detailed information can be located at the Center for Medicare and Medicaid Services (CMS) web site, http://www.cms.hhs.gov/hipaa/.

- **Gramm-Leach-Bliley Act (GLBA)** Also known as the Financial Services Modernization Act, Title V of this act deals with privacy issues for financial institutions and their customer data. More information is available at http://banking.senate.gov/conf/grmleach.htm.
- **Sarbanes-Oxley Act** Also known as the Public Company Accounting Reform and Investor Protection Act, this act provides guidelines that help ensure accurate accounting practices. This is a very large set of requirements handed down from the U.S. Securities and Exchange Commission (SEC) and covers a large number of areas that will impact audit requirements. To get more information, visit http://www.sarbanes-oxley.com/ or http://www.sec.gov/spotlight/sarbanes-oxley.htm; you can view or download the act in its entirety at http://www.law.uc.edu/ccl/soact/soact.pdf.
- **Computer Security Act of 1987** Requires standards to be created that outline the *minimum* security requirements for *federal* employees and systems dealing with sensitive information. This act requires not only the development of standards but also training for all persons involved in the management, use, or operation of federal computer systems housing sensitive information. The act itself doesn't actually specify the standards, but stipulates that the National Bureau of Standards must create and maintain these standards. One of the many places you can view the act is http://www.cio.gov/archive/computer_security_act_jan_1998.html.

Any of these acts could have a major impact on the audit requirement of an organization. The auditor must be familiar with these requirements in order to perform an effective measurement of the customer's systems. If you are not familiar with the requirements, you are doing a disservice to the customer and could find yourself liable for your findings at a later date. If you are not familiar with the legislative requirements and impact on network security, you should seek the assistance of someone who is, to help with the audit.

Identify Key Points of Contact

For the most part, upper-level management will provide the audit objectives, but you will likely need to speak with many people at other levels of the business as well. In preparation for doing the actual audit, you need to get all the contact information from the customer. This includes area managers, subject matter experts, system operators, and legal contacts. As you are creating the documentation that will be the bases for the assessment plan, you should document what the roles of each contact are going to be.

You should discuss and determine who will be informed of the audit prior to it taking place, and for whom it will be a surprise. In some cases, if people know they are being audited, they might act differently than they normally would, which can invalidate the findings of the audit. Clear escalation paths need to be laid out in case you are not getting what you need from customer staff. Senior management needs to be available in case of security issues, such as an employee reporting a security breach due to activities that are part of the audit. Once you have the contact information of all the right resources, you can begin to perform the next step.

Create a Criticality Matrix of Systems and Information

Once you know who to speak to, you will be able to identify the critical components in the infrastructure. You need to speak with managers from different functional groups. With their help, you can create a matrix of critical systems and sensitive information. This matrix should include system information such as system name, location (city, state, building, floor), network information, system administrator/owner, and a criticality rating of the system relative to business function. You need to note any sensitive data on the system, and its criticality rating. The business structure will influence the organization of this matrix, such as whether it should be grouped by host system, business function, or even by specific file types. The key here is to be flexible and adopt a system that fits the customer and the cope of the assessment.

You should document any special considerations for these systems. This includes things such as special times of the day that you can or cannot access the system. Typically, any invasive access that could adversely affect the system should be performed during non-business hours or during routine maintenance windows. You should also include any specific systems that are not to be touched for any reason and are outside the scope. For example, the customer might house some servers that don't belong to it, in which case the customer probably could not allow the auditor access to these systems at all.

Determine if a Penetration Test Is Needed

This is the point where you should determine if the scope of the audit will include a vulnerability assessment, a penetration test, both, or neither. Typically, a thorough audit includes a vulnerability assessment; a penetration test is optional and generally is performed only on specific systems. Whether or not you choose to include a vulnerability assessment or a penetration test, the audit steps will be relatively unchanged. The key to keep in mind is that a vulnerability assessment doesn't actually compromise any security or break into any system, it only tries to measure whether an attacker could. A penetration test involves actually trying to break into the systems. Because the skills required to perform an audit are very different from those needed to perform a penetration test, you should determine early in the process whether this audit will include a penetration test, so that you can make sure the appropriate experts are available.

Include Audit Only

When the scope of the audit does not include a penetration test (or vulnerability assessment), the audit is typically less invasive and less likely to cause business disruption. The audit consists mostly of speaking with people and requesting and reviewing documentation. It also includes first-hand inspections of systems. Although viewing configuration information is not as thorough a way to measure a system's security as a penetration test, it often results in significant savings in time and money. A penetration test performed by highly skilled testers, coupled with a vulnerability assessment, is the most complete measure of your network security. Of course, as time progresses and software and hardware change, this measure becomes increasingly inaccurate. This is the reason audits should always be repeated on a predetermined schedule.

Include a Penetration Test

Much like an audit may have many different meanings to different people, so may a penetration test. In general, you can break penetration tests down into two major categories: zero-knowledge penetration tests and full-knowledge penetration tests.

- **Zero-knowledge (blind) test** The penetration testers effectively are provided little to no information about the systems they are attacking. For example, to test a publicly available web server, the penetration testers might be provided with nothing but the URL. This type of test simulates an external attacker who has no inside knowledge of the network or systems. The testers have to gather information on the target just like a hacker would, test for weaknesses, and then attempt to exploit any weaknesses they find.
- **Full-knowledge test** The penetration testers are provided with any type of information they need concerning the systems and their controls. The assumption here is that they know how the system works, and the test is purely to ensure that it works *properly*. This would be useful to verify that your VPN implementation is working properly and cannot be compromised. The testers would be provided with the IP addresses of all systems, the protocols being used, and probably even a map of the network in question. They might even be provided with the protocol settings, like frequency of key exchanges and such. In some cases, the testers might launch their attacks from an internal network segment rather than from an outside location like the public Internet. The objectives of the test dictate what information the testers are given.

In most cases, some combination of the two tests is used, or possibly both. If you have had your external firewall tested frequently and recently, you might not need to test from the Internet and instead just focus on attacks against the internal infrastructure. Once you know what type of test you will be doing, you need to determine the measure for success. While it may seem obvious when a system has been compromised, this is actually a critical step. Make certain all parties are aware of the measures for success. A common measure for considering a system "hacked" is that the tester is able to write a file to the root of the drive, which demonstrates that the integrity of the data on the system can be compromised. In other situations, the requirement might be to obtain a copy of some sensitive data, demonstrating that confidentiality of the data has been compromised. You should work with the customer to define exactly what the customer wants to see as evidence, so that it will be satisfied with your findings.

HEADS UP!

It's important to note that running a vulnerability scanner against the network systems is *not* a penetration test. Although some of the vulnerability scanners are very good, that is only a small part of a penetration test. The results from the scan must then be manually verified to rule out any false positives, and possibly to uncover any weaknesses that the scanner wasn't looking for. A false positive in this context is when the vulnerability scanner indicates that a security vulnerability exists when there is none.

Anyone can run a vulnerability scanner with a little effort, and you can and should be running one on your network regularly anyway. The real value of penetration testers is both the hands-on activities that the scanners can't duplicate and the manual verification of those things the scanner does find. Vulnerability scanners look for known vulnerabilities and, as such, generally cannot test unknown protocols or software, such as those developed in-house. The results of the vulnerability scan can be useful information for the manual tester to explore custom settings and configurations for vulnerabilities.

Obtain Customer Signoff

Once you have determined whether of not the audit will include a penetration test and what the measures of success of the penetration test will be, it's time to document in the assessment plan everyone's acceptance of these parameters. It is critical to have signoff from all relevant managers. This absolutely must include senior management. In case there is legal fallout, you want all of this approval documented as completely as possible. Management should understand that a penetration test, or even a simple vulnerability scan, may have unintentional adverse effects on the target system. In most cases the system will only require a reboot to make it functional, but in the case of critical resources, this could be costly. You should include verbiage to protect yourself from liability in case there is a financial loss incurred due to the testing. You should seek legal assistance in wording both the statement of risks, and the customer's acceptance of the assessment parameters. There are some risks around performing a penetration test, and the more thorough the test, the higher the risk of causing a disruption to some of the systems tested. In most cases the customer will also be required to sign an authorization letter that is often referred to as a "get out of jail free" letter. This is basically a standardized letter that states that the tester is protected from legal actions that might arise as a result of testing. The assessment is tailored to a specific customer and will include specific parameters dealing with liability while the authorization letter is usually generic and includes broad statements of authorization.

Identify Systems and Processes to Be Assessed

At this point you know what systems are out there and any special considerations for each system. Creating this inventory is a critical step. Without an accurate inventory you cannot possibly make an educated decision about which systems should be in scope for the audit. If the customer has 20 web servers, will all of them be in scope? Will all user desktops be in scope, or is there a particular group that should not be included? Will DNS servers be covered? Will laptops be included? These are all questions to consider as you define the list of hosts, systems, and processes to be included in the audit.

After defining the list of *systems* to be audited, you need to determine the specific ways in which these systems will be evaluated. The National Security Agency (NSA) has formalized an INFOSEC Assessment Methodology (IAM) found here, http://www.iatrp.com/iam.cfm. This can serve as a useful template to the types of things to be assessed. The NSA is the U.S. federal government agency that is responsible for "protecting U.S. information systems and producing foreign intelligence information."

The IAM breaks down an audit into 18 core subjects:

- Account Management
- Auditing
- Backups
- Configuration Management
- Contingency Planning
- Documentation
- External Connectivity
- Identification & Authentication
- Labeling
- Maintenance
- Media Sanitization/Disposal
- Personnel Security
- Physical Environment
- Roles & Responsibilities
- Session Controls
- Telecommunications
- Training & Awareness
- Virus Protection

These are the broad categories of what could be encompassed by an INFOSEC assessment. The following sections elaborate as to what each of these categories should include, and identify some common pitfalls and things to look for.

Evaluate Account Management

A proper audit ensures that accounts have policies around their creation, access, deletion, and lockouts. Account policy should include the following:

- Regular reviews of all accounts.
- A procedure to systematically shut down inactive accounts after a set period of time.
- Particular attention paid to accounts used for external access, such as by vendors and support personnel.

- A documented password policy and measures in place to ensure the policy is being followed. Most systems have an option to enforce password policies, such as password length, password age, history, and complexity (i.e., must contain numbers, upper- and lowercase letters, etc.).
- Requirements for adequate signoff and verification of account need and access by more than one person.

All of these things should be verified both in policy and in practice (via testing). Review the policies concerning account management and verify settings on all accounts. Check for accounts that have been inactive longer than policy allows but have not been disabled or deleted.

Evaluate Auditing Practices

In addition to periodic evaluations against a set of guidelines, auditing also refers to the process of knowing and documenting what is happening on your systems. Firewalls typically generate log files of activity, recording blocked traffic or other messages according to how they are configured. The recording and periodic review of these logs is a form of auditing. Intrusion detection systems record attacks, and access badge readers log what areas the badge carrier has accessed. These are all valuable logs for auditing purposes. You should verify that there are policies specifying not only *what* to audit, *when* to audit, and *how* to audit, but also how to store the audit data.

Log files may document that a hacker was attempting to break into your network. If legal action against the hacker is ever pursued, you will need to demonstrate that the logs were not modified after being recorded. Thus, you need to implement procedures to verify the integrity of the log data, such as hashes and possibly encryption. You should also ensure that the devices collecting the logs are secure. There should be a written policy on how to handle log data, including how to store it, how to access it, and how to destroy it. Although legal precedent is always evolving, currently a log file derives most of its value as evidence because you can document that the log was collected as part of your everyday standard practices. Often, log data is stored as it is being recorded onto CD-ROM disks or in some cases printed out, ensuring that the data could not be modified at a later date.

All these examples are forms of everyday auditing that a larger audit will verify are taking place. Verify the existence and accuracy of these audit logs by generating audit events (if needed) and then inspecting the logs for accuracy. Accurate log files include proper identification and accurate timestamps of the audit event. There should also be regular requirements for a full audit. The frequency and depth of these audits will be determined by need and, in some cases, legal requirements, such as for financial institutions. Periodic audits allow the auditors to verify that the policies are in place and that audit findings are being acted upon in a timely fashion. Essentially, a good audit ensures that you are far better prepared for any future audits.

Evaluate Backup Policies and Procedures

Backups, by their nature, contain the same data as the original system. Sometimes the original system is well secured but the backups are not. This creates an easily exploitable risk. You should verify all backup procedures, including backup frequency, the functionality of the backups, and who has access to the backup media.

> **HEADS UP!**
>
> I have personally been in situations in which I could call the offsite storage company, request "my tapes," and simply tell them the date of the tape I wanted. They would then deliver it to me without requiring further information. Not only that, but they met me outside on the street and placed the tapes in my hands, and never even asked who I was. You should regularly test the effectiveness of your storage facility's ability to verify the confidentiality and integrity of your backups. As a general rule, the backup tapes should be *at least as secure* as the original machine they were backing up.

Backups and your backup logs could be used during legal proceedings and should be handled with the utmost care. In addition to data confidentiality, keeping the chain of custody is important, and this chain should be clear from the logs and procedures that are in place. For legal proceedings, you must be able to document control of the backup media at all times. The integrity of the backups is the number one priority. If you don't maintain the integrity, then the backups will be worthless. You should consider these factors and evaluate the customer's backup strategy accordingly. The customer's backup policy should specify procedures for backups and handling of backup media. If you identify any risks or areas where the customer's backup policy is not being followed, it should be documented in the audit report.

Evaluate Configuration Management

Configuration management is critical if you want to have any control over the infrastructure. Configuration management includes doing the following:

- Verify that there is a policy for change management and that the policy is being followed. The policy should specify an approval procedure, turnaround time, and change windows for normal changes and emergency changes.
- Verify that the people who are responsible for approving changes are clearly documented.

- Review logs from when changes were made to systems. Ensure that they include information on why the maintenance was needed, and who performed the maintenance. All changes should be documented, especially changes to the physical infrastructure of the network. Over time, changes are made for emergency repairs, and often no one ever goes back to document the changes. When the next emergency arises, no one has an accurate picture of the environment. This causes loss of efficiency, which generally translates into loss of money. The audit will reveal whether or not these processes are working effectively.

Evaluate Contingency Planning Practices

Contingency planning includes both disaster recovery and business continuity. Disaster recovery is a subset of business continuity. A contingency planning audit reviews your procedures for both. You should verify that

- Documented procedures exist that explain recovery steps. Recovery steps should include any information needed to resume business function in the event of a disaster. This could include items such as alternate data centers, alternate processing centers, redundant hardware, and redundant WAN links. The purpose here is to ensure that there are no single points of failure for any critical systems.
- Recovery plans include procedures for dealing with both man-made disasters and any likely natural disasters such as earthquakes, flooding, and fires.
- There is no missing or unclear documentation or procedures. Also note any discrepancies between the plan's assumed or required resources and the actual resources available.
- BC and DR plans are adequate in scope, based on the customer's risks.
- BC and DR plans satisfy any regulatory requirements that might apply.
- BC and DR plans are stored in secured locations and that the handling of these documents is in accordance with the security policy.
- Results from any past business continuity or disaster recovery tests are reviewed. Not only is this a way to walk through their results and see if any of the issues that were documented pose a security risk, but it allows you to verify that the proper paperwork and follow-up has been done for the testing. Remember that the BC and DR plans typically contain highly sensitive information and should be treated as such.

Evaluate Documentation

IT documentation includes all data available on the network and documentation about the network itself. Confidentiality of documentation is usually of the highest priority. In order to evaluate documentation, however, you must verify the documentation's availability, integrity, and confidentiality. To do so:

- Make sure every critical piece of information is not located at one site.

- Evaluate whether you would incur a business disruption if you were to lose all or any part of that documentation.
- Ensure that there are adequate access controls in place.
- Ensure that there is a process for authorizing and documenting changes to the documentation.

HEADS UP!

A common oversight is weak or nonexistent business continuity (BC) and disaster recovery (DR) plans. A surprisingly simple error some people make is to fail to ensure the availability of the BC and DR plans. Frequently, no copy of the DR plan exists other than the one located at work. Many people fail to think that if a disaster strikes, they might not have access to their work location and thus their DR plan. BC and DR documents frequently contain sensitive information about your company's networks and systems, but it is important to make sure to securely store some copies offsite so that they will be readily available should a disaster occur.

- Ensure that sensitive documents are secured with access controls in place to limit who can view them.
- If the documents are sufficiently sensitive, include a mechanism to audit all access to them. Depending on the nature of the documents (digital or hard copies), auditing information could be provided by things such as key cards, video surveillance, and even two-party authentication requirements and file-level audit logs. *Two-party authentication* refers to when each person has only part of what is needed to gain access, such as each having one of two different keys to get into a file cabinet or only a portion of a combination to a safe.
- Ensure that printers in nonsecured areas are not being used for sensitive information. The same cautions apply for fax machines receiving sensitive information as well.
- Control documentation integrity. Changes to sensitive documentation should require a revision history and some information on the nature of and reason for the change.
- Evaluate disposal of documents (see "Evaluate Media Sanitization/Disposal Practices" later in this chapter) and the sensitivity labeling of documents and information (see "Evaluate Labeling Practices" in this chapter).

Evaluate External Connectivity

External connectivity should be a matter of top concern. An external connection is any place that your corporate network connects to another network that you don't have control over. This includes dial-up connections, point-to-point circuits such as T1s, Frame Relay circuits, and even cable modems or DSL. This is a doorway into your network that you must guard and protect. The audit should verify policy adequacy, policy compliance, and policy effectiveness for external connections. This verification requires reviewing documentation as well as hands-on observation and testing. You must ensure that any testing you do does not risk a service disruption for any external systems. If some risk is unavoidable, you must have appropriate, documented approval from both your customer and its external connection partner prior to testing. Look for the following:

- The existence of policies and procedures outlining what the required steps are for making a connection to the corporate network. Procedures should be documented describing how to approve network access, who can approve network access, what types of access are acceptable, and what documentation is required to obtain access.
- Policy stating that a review of proposed external connections is required prior to enabling network connectivity.
- Verify that the approval process for network connectivity includes signoff by responsible parties representing both management and technical staff who can evaluate the security risks involved.
- Verify that the appropriate documentation and approval exists for all current external connections.
- Perform a vulnerability assessment or penetration test to verify that encryption is functioning properly and that the session controls between external and internal entities are working properly. These testing methods will be much the same as listed in the previous sections.

Evaluate Identification and Authentication

Systems should be evaluated for their ability to ensure proper authentication, the process of proving people are who they say they are. Identification and authentication are not the same. Identification is simply a declaration of who a person is. Authentication is verification that the person is who they claim to be. For example, if someone introduces herself as Jane Doe, that is only identification; it doesn't actually offer any way to verify that she really is Jane Doe. To authenticate her identity, you would then request some other proof that she is the real Jane Doe.

Access to sensitive information and systems should require identification and authentication of persons attempting access. Ideally, the minimum requirement for sensitive information is two-factor authentication. Authentication factors are the specific credentials used to prove identity, which are commonly classified in three categories:

- **Something you know** When you ask someone for a password to authenticate them, you are using that one piece of information as your determining factor of whether they are who they say they are. This password is a piece of information that only the real person should know.

- **Something you have** You can also use something the person has, such as a key, identification card, or security token.
- **Something you are** One newer method of authentication that is growing in popularity is the use of biometric technologies. Biometric authentication uses physical characteristics to verify identity. The most common biometric devices are fingerprint scanners. The obvious advantage of biometrics is that, unlike a token or password, you cannot forget or lose your credentials.

Two-factor authentication uses factors from any *two* of these categories to verify a person's identity. Your audit should verify adequate measures are in place to identify and authenticate users. Without proper authentication, any authorization processes will be rendered ineffective.

Evaluate Labeling Practices

Standards for naming and labeling of virtually all components should be present and in use. Of primary concern is the classification and labeling of data and system confidentiality levels. Examine the labeling standards with the following in mind:

- Common data labels are public, internal, confidential, and secret. While these four labels are normally adequate for most organizations, there are a number of labeling schemes, some of which have more or fewer categories. Some organizations also use categories such as sensitive, top secret, and others.
- Ensure that a security policy is in place that documents the organization's labels and how each type of data should be handled. You cannot hope to secure your data if you don't know which data needs what level of security.

Ensure that the labeling methods prescribed are being properly implemented. Data must be labeled before the appropriate security policies can be applied to the data. Review the policy and sample data to ensure that it is labeled properly. Verify that there is a documented process in place for the lowering of data's sensitivity level as well. This process should maintain a separation of duties to ensure that someone cannot lower the sensitivity rating of data or systems for fraudulent purposes.

Evaluate Maintenance Practices

Maintenance for hardware and software will always be necessary. Maintenance should not compromise the security of the network. Review maintenance policies by doing the following.

- Ensure that maintenance windows are clearly documented for all critical systems.
- Require logging of outages and downtimes and regular review of logs.
- Look for a written procedure that documents how maintenance personnel obtain access to facilities. Responsibilities should be clearly defined for who can grant access to critical areas. Verify that these procedures are being followed. Verification can include social engineering attacks where you attempt to gain

access under the guise of a maintenance person. It could also include simply reviewing documentation for someone who has been granted access.

- Check for a procedure that specifies the monitoring of vendor-specific and vendor-neutral sources for new vulnerabilities and a mechanism to get any needed updates into the change-management schedule.
- Record any areas where these procedures are inadequate and identify systems that are not being properly maintained.

Evaluate Media Sanitization/Disposal Practices

Sanitization refers to erasing the media for reuse without destroying it, like *erasing* a floppy diskette. *Disposal,* of course, refers to what you do with media after the media and data are no longer needed. Media sanitization and media destruction render your sensitive data unreadable. After sanitization, the media can still be used to record new data. The following is a list of some media sanitization and disposal areas to audit:

- Review all types of media, such as hard disks, floppy disks, printouts, faxes, and possibly even print ribbons. If the media ever had sensitive data recorded on it, it should be subject to the media sanitization and disposal policies and procedures. Note that many types of media are often overlooked, so make sure that you review all types.
- Check for policies that specify proper sanitization and disposal methods for each data classification level and for each media type. Ensure that policies include timeframes for sanitization and disposal. Confidential data will likely have different disposal methods than secret data.
- Verify that the media sanitization and disposal methods in use actually work properly. Typically, media that once housed secret information, or information of the highest importance, should be destroyed for maximum security. This is because with the proper budget and equipment, you can read data off of a hard drive after it has been erased. If you do not destroy it, and instead use a utility to "wipe" the data, the reliability of that utility should be tested and verified. Just because the software claims it overwrites and destroys all data in three passes does not always mean it really does.
- Observe demonstrations of sanitization and disposal procedures to verify that the policies are being followed. During an observational exercise, the process or procedure is not being performed specifically for you, but rather is being performed in the course of normal business activities. A demonstration, on the other hand, is when the process or procedure is performed specifically for the auditor's benefit.

Evaluate Personnel Security

Personnel security is primarily concerned with risks to the infrastructure from the employees themselves. Your audit in this area should include the following:

- Review the policy for hiring personnel and granting access to sensitive information. If the policy says that a background check must be done, verify that it is being done. If the policy does not require a background check, you should assess whether it should and for what positions.
- Verify that existing staff has all the appropriate documentation on file. This could include system access forms, administrative signoff, and acceptable use agreements for company IT assets.
- Ensure that access to sensitive information requires the appropriate managerial approval and signoff.
- Review potential risks to personnel themselves. Evaluate policies and practices concerning personnel meetings for any risk issues. For example, if the company has an annual meeting at which all senior managers are present, without appropriate security measures in place, a disaster that strikes the meeting place could seriously disrupt the company.

Evaluate the Physical Environment

Securing the physical environment includes the use of cameras, gates, locks, guards, and other protection and enforcement measures. Policy and plans should include securing the physical infrastructure as well as the data center, storage areas, and data. The security of the physical environment also includes threats from natural disasters. Use the following checklist to audit physical security:

- Verify that there is a policy specifying security measures for any areas housing sensitive information and equipment. It should include requirements for locks and alarms.
- Verify that areas housing sensitive information and equipment are secured with locks of the appropriate type, as specified in the security policy.
- Ensure that access to network devices, servers, and telephone equipment is restricted.
- Ensure that support personnel such as cleaning crews and maintenance personnel do not have access to sensitive data.
- Inspect and review the physical security of the grounds, noting key areas such as telco demarcation areas and power supply paths. Verify that these are secured as well. Having a building protected like Fort Knox but with an easily accessible single point of power entry would be a hole in your security.
- Inspect and review security cameras, guards, fences, and badge readers. A parking garage under your data center would be an easy target for someone wanting to interrupt your processing facilities.
- Ensure that data centers located in areas prone to flooding are not housed in basements.

- Ensure that floods, earthquakes, fires, avalanches, and other natural disasters have been considered and that plans are in place to protect data during a natural disaster and to recover from the damage. If these events are likely, they must be considered when your location is being assessed. In the event of one of these disasters, you have to be ready to keep the facilities and the data inside secured.
- Inspect for any indirect risks posed by the physical environment. This includes such things as inadequate cooling for servers and network equipment. Is there emergency cooling available in a timely fashion? Are there water lines near critical electronic equipment? If there are, are there alarms to detect a leak? Are the fire suppression systems of the appropriate type? Are they properly maintained and periodically inspected? These are all factors that could pose a risk to the network's operation.
- Walk around and inspect the external markings. If the customer's entire critical infrastructure is at a single site (a risk in itself), this fact should not be advertised. You wouldn't want a big sign outside that indicates this is the site of your corporate data center.
- Ensure that other critical areas are not easily identified. Your risk can be reduced by not advertising the best places to attack you. This goes for other areas as well, such as where the facility ties into the power grid and where the major telecommunication links are located. If possible, access to the grounds should be restricted and identification and authentication should be required to get on the property.

Evaluate Roles and Responsibilities

The most common security risk to discover when evaluating roles and responsibilities is a conflict of interest. A conflict of interest is the conflict between the private interests and the official responsibilities of a person in a position of trust. The way to combat conflicts of interest is with separation of duties, which means to ensure that no one person has enough authority in a system to compromise the security of the entire system. Sometimes this can be difficult to achieve. For example, the person in HR who changes an employee's status to "terminated" in the computer system should not also have the authority to decide which employees get terminated. The system should require a manager's approval in order to complete the termination processing. That way, the HR person cannot fire someone on a whim, possibly exposing the company to a lawsuit.

These are some common scenarios to watch out for:

- Credentials used by IT support staff to perform maintenance should not allow processing of live transactions.
- The group responsible for making changes to the network should not also be the group responsible for approving changes to the network.

- The people requesting access to sensitive data should not also be able to approve such access.
- HR staff should require approval from management to terminate employees.

By ensuring there are checks and balances, no one person can perform an unauthorized action against sensitive systems or information. By requiring multiple approvals and signoff, a disgruntled employee would need more than one person working together to perform an unauthorized action. This acts as a significant deterrent to fraudulent activities and greatly reduces the likelihood of accidental changes to data and systems. Proper separation of duties not only helps protect the data and systems from unauthorized manipulation, but also helps protect the business from liability and financial loss.

Evaluate Session Controls

Session controls dictate how and by whom a communication session can be established. One of the most common session control examples would be a firewall. Auditing the session controls includes evaluating both policy and the actual device configurations. The audit should look at session control between end devices as well as between internal infrastructure devices like routers and switches. Specifically:

- Inspect and test firewall, router, switch, and other device configuration.
- Don't focus on traffic through a firewall only and overlook traffic *to* the firewall itself.
- Look for controls on internal network traffic to and from critical resources. More and more attacks are originating from inside companies.

The area of session controls is where a penetration test does most of its work. The tests conducted against routers, servers, and other devices ensure that the session controls in place are working as intended. Tests against known vulnerabilities for which a patch has been provided can verify that the policy stating that servers should be patched regularly is being followed. This is also where you ensure that the configurations and functionality of your firewalls follow policy and have the required functionality. The penetration test should include a review of documentation and policy, reviews of device configuration, and hands-on testing and verification that the controls in place are working as intended.

The verification stage should include several tasks. You should attempt to scan through firewalls using several different flag settings. Network Mapper, or Nmap runs on both Windows and Linux and allows you to perform a variety of TCP and UDP scans in which you can specify the source and destination IP addresses. By generating traffic and sniffing for it on the other side of the firewall, you can verify access control lists are working properly. By controlling various flags on the traffic, you can also verify stateful operation of the firewall. Nmap can be downloaded at http://www.insecure.org/nmap/.

Dsniff, http://www.monkey.org/~dugsong/dsniff/, can be used to verify some port-level security settings. Dsniff advertises false DNS or MAC information to impersonate another host and facilitate a man-in-the-middle attack. This behavior causes appropriately configured port security settings to disable the offending port. If the customer does not have an intrusion detection system (IDS), implementing one for the assessment may be useful. An IDS such as Snort (refer to Chapter 14 for more information on Snort) uses signatures and rules to detect unauthorized traffic on a network. This can apply not only to traffic that typically indicates an attack, but also to traffic that violates the security policy. You could use the IDS to detect file-sharing programs, external instant messaging programs, or Trojan software traffic.

You should verify that traffic that *should* be encrypted *is* actually encrypted by inspecting it with a sniffer. If it is encrypted, the data should not be visible as clear text in a sniffer. Many free and commercial sniffers are available. For example, Ethereal (http://www.ethereal.com) is free, runs on Windows or Linux, and includes a GUI. Tcpdump, http://www.tcpdump.org, is a *nix command-line sniffer. Windump, http://windump.polito.it/, is the Windows port.

Evaluate Telecommunications Systems

Telecommunications essentially means any communication over a long distance. In the IT auditing sense, this would cover network links over any media, and links for phone service. The scope of auditing for telecommunications can grow very large. You should have any required experts available to assess specialized equipment or technologies. Although voice networks and data networks are increasingly merging into one, each is addressed separately here.

Voice Network Telecommunications It is important to rely on staff members who are familiar with the equipment and technologies that are being audited. Often, people who are knowledgeable in voice network technologies are not as knowledgeable in data network technologies, and vice versa. Any phone line is a potential back door into your infrastructure. Every modem and fax line should be documented and secured. You should review the documentation and verify that the connection has been through the appropriate approval process. For an attacker to gain access to your network, all it takes is one computer with unauthorized and improperly secured software on it, such as pcAnywhere or some other remote access software, and a phone line. Unused phone lines should *not* be unsecured. They should be disconnected at a physically secured wiring closet or LAN room. Getting a phone line installed and activated should require the appropriate signoff and approvals.

Voice communication equipment should be secured as well. Frequently, the phone switch (PBX) has remote administration capabilities. It must be tested for adequate access controls. Penetration tests can be conducted against the telecommunication equipment in a similar fashion to network devices. The exact hardening steps vary from one vendor's implementation to the next, so the best source of information is likely from vendor support channels. If scope and scale allows, war dialing can be used to identify telephone lines that are connected to network equipment. *War dialing* is using specialized software (and sometimes hardware) to quickly dial large blocks of customer-owned phone numbers. The software used typically attempts to identify what type of device answers the call based on banner information and other characteristics. There are many war-dialing products, such as Sandstorm Enterprises' PhoneSweep (http://www.sandstorm.net/products/phonesweep/). After the war dialing is completed, you can compare the resultant list against a list of authorized connections and take steps to secure or remove the unauthorized connections.

Data Network Telecommunications To audit telecommunications and inspect the routers, traffic, and facilities, you should do the following:

- Verify that the hardware is configured properly. The data telecommunication equipment should have a secure configuration and use secure administration channels.
- Use available tools to test your client's router security in an automated fashion. These tools are similar to network vulnerability scanners but are made for routers specifically. One tool for Cisco routers is Router Audit Tool (RAT). This tool will check a Cisco IOS router configuration and compare it with the NSA's recommended configuration guidelines. RAT is available for free download from the Center for Internet Security, at http://www.cisecurity.org/bench_cisco.html.
- Perform an inventory of external circuits and hardware to locate any rogue connections that were not decommissioned properly or went in without adequate documentation.
- Verify that network documentation matches the physical environment.

NOTE *Hardening Network Infrastructures*, by Wesley Noonan (McGraw-Hill/Osborne, 2004), provides detailed steps on securing your network infrastructure devices and traffic.

Evaluate Virus-Protection Strategy

Virus protection is no longer optional in modern business. Ensure it is in place and review its use, as follows:

- Review virus protection documentation and policy.
- Perform onsite evaluations of the effectiveness of the virus-protection and policy adherence.
- Verify that virus definitions are up to date and are being distributed in a timely manner.
- Document any machines that are not getting virus definitions or engine file updates within the timeframes outlined in the corporate policy.

- Verify policy and procedures for when a virus is detected. Quarantine and notification steps should be clearly documented. There should be a plan to notify senior staff in the event of a virus outbreak on the network.
- Simulate a virus event, such as by having a user call the help desk, in order to evaluate the adequacy of virus training programs and response procedures.

Evaluate Training and Awareness Programs

No security is complete without training and awareness programs. The best policies do not help if no one knows about them or follows them. Review the training and awareness policies and verify that they are being followed. This may include interviewing random personnel and determining if they are aware of the security policies. Ask if they know what to do if they suspect a virus on the network. What do they do if they see suspicious activity in the building? Is there a signature on file indicating the employee has signed an acceptable use statement? Do employees know how to identify and escalate a security incident? Will an employee open an e-mail from an unknown source and then open the attachment? In addition to interviewing employees, you should review any training programs and verify that they are appropriate.

Finalize the Testing Plan

By asking questions prior to the audit and evaluating the information provided in response, you know what to include in the audit and what level of testing needs to be done. You need to be aware of test windows and have contacts for all systems that may be affected. An absolute must is to have a documented escalation path for any security incidents or down time incurred *by* the testing. All of these details should be captured in the testing plan. At this point, the test plan represents the entire scope of work. This test plan should be reviewed and discussed with representatives from the customer. Any final questions or additions should be made, and the scope of work should be explained. Questions or clarifications should be added to the documentation. The completed assessment plan should include all of the following:

- Contact information for both the auditors and the customer
- The organization's mission and background information
- The organization's security policies, and scope of testing for both sensitive data and critical hosts.
- Any customer concerns or caveats
- Contact information of individuals to be interviewed
- Documents that will be reviewed
- A timeline and schedule of all major milestones
- The customer's IT security policy

Once the customer and auditor are satisfied that everything has been captured, both parties sign the plan and testing can begin.

Coordinate Any Final Logistics

With the scope of work clearly documented, testing must begin. This requires contacting the customer and coordinating specific test dates for each area. Arrangements should be made for customer contacts and obtaining access to facilities and documents. In some cases, user accounts may need to be set up, badges issued, and paperwork filled out to request access. Any other scheduling arrangements should be completed at this time. If a penetration test will be performed, any information that was to be disseminated to the auditors should be handed out. Advance notification and coordination needs to be made with the appropriate customer contacts. Some customer staff may have no advance notice of the audit activities.

Perform the Assessment

This is where the actual audit can begin. Depending on the scope, particularly if it is large, the audit may be broken up into an onsite phase and an offsite phase. Much of the initial review and verification deals with policy and documentation. This can often be done remotely, saving time and money. For the things that need to be verified first hand, you have to be onsite. Depending on the size of the engagement, it might require onsite visits to multiple locations. Once this assessment is underway, there should be regularly scheduled correspondence with the customer representatives to advise them of the progress.

Perform Offsite Activities

This stage of the assessment is done from a location other than the customer's location. This can include operating from the auditor's place of business, or even using whatever remote user capabilities the customer might posses. Documentation and some employee interviews can be handled via fax and phone. Some documents can be sent for review via e-mail as well. Generally speaking, the more that can be done offsite the better, but you do want to make sure that anything reviewed remotely is verified when you are onsite.

Request and Review Documentation

Although the exact method you choose to transport information is not really important, how you handle the information is important. If you will be viewing confidential information, you must ensure that the *customer's* policies are being followed with regard to data security, media sanitization, and media disposal. Sensitive information should not be sent to an unsecured fax machine or sent via e-mail unencrypted. For telephone calls, some means should be used to verify the identity of the speakers if sensitive information will be discussed. If controls are not enforced, an audit could represent a prime time to compromise the customer's security.

Perform a Zero-Knowledge Penetration Test

A blind penetration test is done from the perspective of an outside attacker. When you perform a blind penetration test, you evaluate a lot of areas, directly and indirectly. If the customer has intrusion detection systems, the penetration test tests those systems as well. Verify that adequate logs are being generated of any intrusion attempts and that policy is being followed with regard to incident reporting. This portion of the test is often done without the IDS personnel being aware of it. If the staff has not been informed of the penetration test, you can also evaluate incident response procedures at this time. When support staff report the attacks, if policy requires alerting senior personnel, the senior personnel should already be aware of the testing that is in progress. The high-level steps for performing a zero-knowledge penetration test are listed here.

1. Attempt to gather information to augment any that was provided as part of the testing agreement. This includes attempting to gather information on the network and its systems. Attempt to create a topology map of the network(s) using tools such as DNS, finger, whois, ping, Nmap, firewalk, and hping. Vary information-gathering methods in terms of stealth, in order to test the ability of the IDS systems to detect them.
2. Use standardized tests and vulnerability scans to determine what is running on the hosts, then check for the known vulnerabilities in the OS, running services, and any discovered applications.
3. Attempt to exploit vulnerabilities that are discovered and document your test results.
4. If it is in scope for the penetration test, launch social engineering attacks at this point. Social engineering is basically attacking the social security measures instead of the technological ones. A frequently used example is a hacker calling up the help desk and claiming to be the CEO. The hacker yells, rants and raves, and demands that the help desk personnel reset "his" password immediately to a password of his choosing. If the help desk personnel are not properly trained or are not following procedures, they might reset the password without verifying the identity of the "CEO." At this point, the social engineering attack is successful and the attacker now has access to the network, and possibly critical information as well. Social engineering attacks can be defeated with adequate policies and good training and awareness programs.

It is important to make sure that the level of information that will be shared with the testers is agreed upon prior to the test. If someone calls up requesting information and claims to represent the auditors, you could be assisting in a legitimate attack against your systems by providing the information. You could also be talking to the penetration testers themselves as part of the test. Any correspondence with the auditors or their penetration testing team (sometimes called a *tiger team*) should have documented methods to verify the identity of all parties involved. You don't want to let your guard down because a penetration test in is progress. To the contrary, any time of change is a prime time for hackers to strike.

Determine the Onsite Activities

Based on the information obtained up to this point, you can build a plan of the activities to be performed onsite. This could include further testing, additional interviews, or additional documentation whose relevance was previously unknown. As part of the regular updates, you should relay any additional requirements to the customer and obtain management's approval before proceeding. If there is a change of scope that will affect the costs of the audit, this should be included and approved as well. Some of the offsite activities can occur concurrently with some of the onsite activities if that arrangement makes sense.

Perform Onsite Activities

The onsite activities are similar to the offsite ones. The primary difference is that only while onsite can you see how a process works. This is called a *demonstration*. Frequently, it only involves watching over someone's shoulder as they use a system or go through a process. This does a couple of things. It allows you to possibly spot in the process a weakness that was not obvious from the documentation, and it allows you to observe if the process is being followed. You should also inspect systems to ensure that policy is being followed. This can be a very large job and could take some time.

Request and Review Documentation

Since much of the documentation has been reviewed already, this may not be a very big step. Primarily, you ask for and review additional documentation that you haven't seen previously. Also, you inspect any documentation that is sensitive and thus could not be viewed remotely.

You also review document storage and handling at this point. You should ensure that sensitive information and documents are being handled appropriately and in compliance with stated policy. This includes document disposal and storage practices. In some cases, you will be working with people who have had little notice of the audit, the reason for which is that you don't want the procedure to be modified because of your presence or the employees' foreknowledge of the audit.

Perform Interviews

While you may have already interviewed some people by telephone during the offsite activities, you can interview any additional individuals at this time or conduct follow-up interviews to the telephone interviews. Interviewing people enables you to evaluate their knowledge of policies and policy compliance. You should verify that staff is aware of policies regarding information storage, use, and disposal, and security event notification and escalation. Interviews should be conducted privately if possible. Managers or supervisors should not be present, as this may affect the information provided. Employees can also be a valuable source of information regarding inadequate policies or system flaws. It is the person who is doing the day-to-day work that is generally most aware of gaps in the current policies and procedures.

View Demonstrations

You should view demonstrations of systems and processes. This allows you to evaluate processes for weak areas and inadequate controls. If a policy states that Jane needs her manager's approval to process something, that may sound good on paper. By viewing a demonstration, you might discover the "approval" is in the form of a stamp on Jane's manager's desk, located only ten feet away from Jane's desk. This risk would not be obvious without a demonstration of how the process is being applied and an inspection of the premises. Similarly, you should observe system maintenance and system configuration tasks, along with any critical software usage and maintenance. When you evaluate these items, you should keep in mind security, compliance with policy, and, if applicable, legal requirements.

Assess Physical Security

The physical security cannot be assessed remotely. You need to inspect the premises first hand for any security weaknesses. You should verify functionality of locks, ensuring that areas that are required to have locks do have them, and that they actually remain locked. Many times I've seen a door propped open because the lock was inconvenient to use. Locks should be of adequate quality to protect what lies behind them. The lock on your average desk or filing cabinet can be bypassed in less than 60 seconds using only a paper clip. Someone with proper tools can easily bypass some higher-quality locks with little effort.

Verify that security cameras are functioning properly and that surveillance tapes (if preserved) are handled properly. Ensure that security guards are not letting people through without verifying their identity and that they are alert for suspicious activity. This could include things such as documents or hardware leaving the premises without proper approval. Inspect fences and other perimeter barriers to ensure they are in working order and are secured. Doors and gates left propped open and unlocked need to be noted and action taken to remedy the situation.

Assessing the physical security of a site requires a broad set of skills and should not be attempted by someone who does not posses the appropriate skill set. There are plenty of resources for assessing physical security in both printed publications and online. There is even a certification for physical security knowledge. You should ensure that the person(s) responsible for assessing the physical security is knowledgeable in physical security measures and controls.

Perform a Full-Knowledge Penetration Test

The focus of a full-knowledge penetration test is a little different from the focus of a zero-knowledge penetration test. Whereas a blind test aims to test the security from the perspective of an outsider, an inside or full-knowledge test more accurately mirrors what an insider could do. You should inspect internal resources with automated vulnerability scanners and verify the results manually. The purpose of these tests is to determine what an internal attacker could do and how they could negatively impact the confidentiality, integrity, or availability of systems or data.

In addition to using automated vulnerability scanners, you should attempt to circumvent known security measures, such as by bypassing encryption and attacking back-end databases and other systems. The key here is that an adequately protected system is protected from *any* users attempting unauthorized activity, not just external users. Verify that critical systems are protected with a firewall or other access controls even from internal users. Although it is generally impractical to protect critical resources from internal threats as well as they are protected from external threats, if the system is truly critical, you don't want to simply hope that an attacker never gets inside the network or that a disgruntled employee never decides to take action. Access control lists, limited routing, VLANs, and encryption can all help protect systems from internal attackers as well as external ones.

HEADS UP!

Just as you require proper authorization and management of external penetration tests, you should not attempt during internal testing or reviewing to compromise the security in any way without support and signoff from senior management. Employees who discover security weaknesses sometimes face legal actions from their employers. There is no "good Samaritan" law to protect IT security staff or auditors, so don't do *anything* against the security policy without explicit written permission by people who have the authority to give that permission.

If it is in scope, a little social engineering can go a long way. Social engineering may be impractical if all the staff knows who you are. There is no credibility to gaining access if everyone knows you are authorized. Can you walk through secured areas without authorization by closely following someone? Can you show up at the help desk area and get a password changed without authorization? Can you ask a passerby to use their password/ID badge/fingerprint to let you into a secured area? Can you walk out of the building carrying a server? Can you walk out with an entire box of documents? Hopefully you will be stopped, thus demonstrating that the policy is adequate and, more important, being followed. If you are not stopped, the weakness generally boils down to either a shortcoming in the policy or inadequate training and awareness programs. Either way, the findings should be noted in the final assessment. The incident should be documented with as much detail as possible even if those details are not within scope for the final assessment report. You should include details such as the date of incident, time of incident, who was present, and any other conditions of note.

Provide Initial Feedback and Status

At this point you are really just touching base with any final requirements and a status update. This is about the last opportunity to add anything to the scope, drill down on a particular system, or test anything differently. The customer should be informed of any adjusted timelines for receiving the final report. This is also a good time to answer customer questions if any. You should review high-risk issues at a high level as well. Sometimes the customer might want to address an issue immediately and then reassess the system. If you find that the customer is highly exposed to some easily exploitable risk, you have an obligation to inform them as soon as possible rather than leave the customer exposed while you finalize the report.

Perform the Post Assessment

Post assessment consists of any last-minute information gathering or follow-up that might be needed. No matter how good the plan and its execution, unexpected things will come up. If there are any final interviews or inspections that need to be done, this is the time to do them. Once you've finished all the inspection work, you can finalize the report, package it for presentation, and schedule a time to present it to the customer.

Perform Any Needed Follow-Up

Up to this point, you have probably spent most of your time inspecting and testing things. Although you reviewed your data as it was received, now you are sitting down to really analyze it collectively. You might find that something new comes to the surface that you didn't notice before. Perhaps some additional potential weakness in policy that wasn't obvious at first. Request any final documentation at this time. You will ultimately be delivering more value by doing a thorough job. Any final interviews or demonstrations should be completed as well. If any of the information that you requested still hasn't been received, this is your last opportunity to follow up and escalate if necessary. If necessary, complete and document any final penetration tests. Basically, this is the last of the hands-on tasks before you complete the audit report.

Finalize the Audit Report

This is where all the work comes together. Gather and package all your findings into a report to present to the customer. It is important to focus the report toward the intended audience. The technical level of the recipients may vary. Remember, the final report is practically the sole measuring stick of all the work you've done on the audit. This is what the people paying the bill are getting for their money. In the end, senior management wasn't there all the nights and days you spent doing the audit, so all they will see is this final report. The report should look professional and be well thought out. If the scope justifies it, hiring a professional to edit and print it would be a good investment.

The exact layout of the final report is up to you, but it should include three key elements:

- **Executive summary** Outlines the findings at a high level, and perhaps includes some graphics to help drive the point home. It should be simple and not too technical. Risks should be rated according to how easy they are to realize, and the damage that can be done. Any critical security risks should be highlighted under their own heading. If it was part of the original scope, potential losses should be estimated in an easy-to-read format. The executive summary should be at the very beginning of the report, followed by the more detailed and technical explanation of the findings.
- **Technical explanation** Includes *all* the findings. In some cases, the report also explains how the vulnerability was discovered and how it can be verified. In addition to explaining the vulnerability, the report should provide steps to mitigate the risk. Depending on the scope of work that was agreed to, these may be general, such as "implement encryption on server *x*," or very specific, with step-by-step instructions on mitigating the risks. This section is likely to be lengthy and should be well annotated. A breakdown by risk and type would be useful. This should be the battle plan for the customer to systematically remove the risks and harden its network.
- **A means to verify the data integrity of the report itself** You should implement a method to verify the contents of the audit report as presented to the customer. You could generate a hash of the entire report, or enlist the services of a notary. This way, you will know if the report is edited at any stage of its distribution. This will also serve as evidence of the findings of the audit, in case that ever comes into question in the future.

Chapter 18

Change Management

by Patrick Kelly

- Identify and Classify Change Management Scenarios
- Develop a Change Management Framework
- Develop a Change Management Process

Change management is the systematic approach of tracking and defining the evolution of technology systems. Organizing changes to a technology infrastructure focuses upon the resulting functionality. As businesses look to improve, many solutions or changes include technology changes. Security needs to be included as a part of this focus on improvement and change. As a result of any change, the security profile should also be improved.

This chapter shows you the role that security should play in the change management scheme. Change management incorporates a well-defined process built on a customized framework that uses the available resources to accomplish growth. The goal throughout the change process is to maintain the security profile and an acceptable level of risk.

Identify and Classify Change Management Scenarios

There is no one scenario that represents change; hence, there cannot be any one approach to change management. Instead, change should be classified, and each classification of change should be mapped to a different approach to moving it through the change management process. Security changes can range from an isolated change that affects one computer or one individual to change that affects the entire business process. Changes that affect a diverse group of processes and technologies require the full functionality of the change management process. This includes communication throughout both the technology and business process divisions.

The change management framework must recognize these differences by presenting different change scenarios. Being able to identify a place within the change management scheme for different types of changes incorporates the benefits of having a flexible, agile, change management system. Developing a wide range of change management processes means including a process for small or routine jobs that prevents them from slipping through the cracks. Having a change management process that handles changes of varying depths will leverage control and predictability.

Integrating security perspectives into these different categories of changes can be a challenge. If a change is considered too insignificant to place in the change management process, how will security issues be addressed? The answer is identification, classification, and inclusion of all technology changes into a flexible change management system. You can meet this challenge by defining and recognizing change initiatives.

Separate Planned from Unplanned Changes

The first classification step is to identify the changes you can foresee and provide accommodations for those you cannot foresee. You may find that previously unmanaged change that may have challenged your resources can be managed. A good example is the management of patches to operating systems and applications. Regardless of whether a manufacturer releases updates or patches on a timetable or when the need arises, you know that patches and updates are a part of technology operations. When developing a change management plan, plan for regular review of pending updates and allow for an accelerated flow to meet any immediate and critical need for change that may arise. For unforeseen changes, the goal from the security perspective is to resolve a sudden awareness of an elevated level of risk. The plan should recognize the need for an accelerated timetable from discovery through deployment. This quick reaction is an example of an agile change management scheme.

Unplanned changes put strain on the control and predictability of the outcome. Because you cannot know how the change will affect other systems and the security profile, these changes need solid justification in order to be deployed. If immediate change is necessary, the rollback and recovery components of the change process should become a heightened focus. The day-to-day recovery for network components needs to be solid, dependable, and tested. As unplanned changes arise, risk of failure increases, and the ability to recover to a "known good state" is imperative. Backing up a system is only part of the equation. You need to prove you can recover the component. Prepare the recovery and rollback operations for all network components now. Don't wait until a failure to test your ability to recover.

Planned changes start with a clear and defined business or security recognition for necessary change. An example might be a change to a perimeter firewall to allow a business partner to exchange data more efficiently. You identify a business sponsor and begin with a change request document to suit your business atmosphere. Planned changes incorporate the wisdom of the controlled change process, discussed in the rest of this chapter.

NOTE Some environments have a work-ticket mechanism in place that can be utilized to develop, define, assign, and track this type of planned change. Other shops could adopt such a ticketing system. By making a conscious effort to create a repository of change requests, you can establish a method by which you can measure progress and coordination

Minimize Reactive Changes

The goal for successful change management is to minimize the reactive changes and increase the proactive changes. Proactive changes involve acting upon prior recognition of the necessity to change some network component to reduce an identified risk. Reactive changes are changes that must be done because something happened that caused systems to either cease functioning or decrease in performance, confidentiality, availability, or integrity. Reactive changes often result in side effects to other programs or components of the original target computer or other networked component. Many of these reactive changes may have been predictable, but due to lack of communication or proper planning, they were not foreseen. So, the related systems end up requiring immediate and unplanned attention. This type of reactive change perpetuates the unplanned, out-of-control environment that change management can improve.

To assist your organization in reaching its goal of planning for technology changes, you should include in the discussion and implementation business units that are capable of deploying changes to the current technology state. Organizing communication across business units helps your organization to consider the requirements of technology and, more important, security when incorporating changes. Communication of technology changes is a key goal in ensuring the expectations of positive results are realistic when dealing with change.

Manage New Business Initiative Changes

Many technology changes originate with new business initiatives. Representatives from all of the business decision groups should be included in the change management process. While management should include technology representatives early in the planning process, technology professionals recognize that understanding business processes increases their opportunity to be involved in business change, either as a contributor or as a consultant. Your contribution not only makes the change process more complete, but also strengthens your position as a team player. As part of the team, your knowledge of business initiatives will provide an avenue for you to align your necessitated change process with the expectation of the business process changes.

Business Initiatives Spawn Technology Change

Here are a couple of examples of the impact of business initiatives on technology. Suppose the marketing department decides to use e-mail to deliver a message to a target constituency. While some could construe this process as spam, your marketing team believes in the message it is delivering and may only see a marketing strategy.

The marketing department has researched the potential growth in sales and contact response and has adopted e-mail as the methodology for accomplishing its business objectives. You realize that using e-mail may increase information security risks. You can anticipate more exposure to e-mail vulnerabilities by the increased volume of e-mail expected and handled. More pressure and emphasis will be placed on your incoming spam filter accuracy and your antivirus accuracy and currency, and any retaliation could lead to forged or malicious responses or even denial of services.

Another business-generated change may be a requirement to comply with state or federal regulation. Healthcare and financial industries are tightly regulated with regard to protecting personal information. The utility industry is beginning regulatory compliance initiatives. Electric utilities are being required to produce documentation that tracks the evolution of a technology state and provide a roadmap of those changes to be reviewed in case a vulnerability were to be discovered in a future state. In the electric distribution industry, the North American Energy Reliability Counsel (NERC) requires that changes to critical infrastructure systems be documented and defines a timeline for the completion of the documentation. In addition, electric access control changes must be documented. (See the NERC Urgent Action Cyber Security Standard, section 1204.2, "Electronic Access Controls.")

Manage Technical Change

Technical changes can range from adoption of new technology that helps to fill a gap between current acceptance of risk and risk remediation, to a methodology of reducing a specific risk or group of associated risks. Making changes to technology and infrastructure is constant. Technology changes could deploy new authentication systems, new operating systems, and many more systems, all with new security challenges.

All technology changes can introduce new opportunities for security safeguards. They can also lead to a concession of security measures that are viewed as obstacles to progress. An example is the introduction of enterprise software that comes with an application-specific authentication system. The owners of the business initiative may not incorporate authentication and password standards that are currently defined for network access. Changing authentication standards to access significant data is a change to be addressed by security team members. This type of change to the network security profile should be addressed by the change management framework but many times it is not.

If the company is investing in improving business efficiency, improving security efficiency must also be a goal. Solid technology change management will consider these and other origins of change:

- Patch management for security fixes
- Patch management for new features or enhancement to existing ones
- Configuration changes used to improve or define how a system functions
- Additional products used to grow the productivity of the business
- Information access changes

Discover and Monitor for Changes

Routine reconnaissance or proactive network scans may lead you to discover new business assets that need to be classified, assessed, and protected. Asset reconnaissance tools such as Nmap or SMBWalk can provide information on new network nodes. With the proper run-time parameters, these tools are intended to discover open ports and vulnerabilities as well.

Failing to attend to the proper protection and risk reduction of unprotected assets could be catastrophic. The change management philosophy should be developed to identify and accommodate this classification of change. From the security perspective, the use of vulnerability and threat discovery tools is a valuable resource to identify risk. Using the change management process to remediate those risks ensures that the resulting configuration will align with business objectives.

Anticipated Change

Applying a security policy directive is a basic example of a security-related change. At one company, a change was proposed to eliminate access from corporate LAN browsers to nonbusiness web-based e-mail (Hotmail, Yahoo, etc.). Security professionals had found, upon correlating firewall logs, web access logs, and virus quarantine logs, that accessing personal e-mail accounts over the corporate LAN was introducing viruses and Trojans into the company's computer environment. Employee use of these alternate mail paths also circumvented spam-filtering objectives.

In anticipation of user outrage, detailed scripts for help desk personnel, readiness preparation for spam analysis, as well as attention dedicated to virus and Trojan frequency increases were prepared. When the change was put into place with web content filters, the help desk did not receive any complaints referencing the inability of technology users to access their nonbusiness, private web-based e-mail. Instead, some users questioned the usefulness of e-mail as a communication device and began to find alternate, nontechnical methods of communication. Their response opened new avenues that had to be monitored for any "leakage" of proprietary and confidential information. The employees' reaction to change was not on anyone's radarscope.

Because the workers developed different methods of communicating and transmitting information, the company had to address additional security issues. This included policies regarding manufacturing and releasing information in new formats. These new formats for transmitting and exchanging data consisted of CDs, USB drives, drawings, and printed volumes, all of which were difficult to track. The actual changes that the company made in response included enhancing the security policy to define proprietary information and developing an information release procedure. Even a review of the original spam-filtering technology resulted in searching for an alternative. One change made to influence workers' behavior resulted in many changes to accommodate the way the company would do business.

Develop a Change Management Framework

There are several components of a change management plan that are basic and consistent with most theories. These principles can be scaled to fit most environments; it is the process of tying these components together that develops your change management policy. Implementing or improving change management within an organization boils down to process improvement. One approach, investigating the methodologies of Six Sigma, will provide guidance and a starting point to develop a real plan for change. This approach uses DMAIC (Define, Measure, Analyze, Improve, Control). Using this formula with basic practices for a solid change management process will lead to success measured by perception, efficiency, and progress. For more information on these concepts, visit http://www.isixsigma.com/dictionary/DMAIC-57.htm.

Your change management framework can adopt these process improvement concepts. You can build a change management process flow map to outline the steps and resources involved in technology changes. The collection of data involving the change request, change processes, and eventual outcomes will provide an opportunity for an analysis of the specific changes and the change process as a whole. Using this data collection, you can identify any areas that are candidates for improvement and establish documented control over the entire change process.

Change management policy should promote the management of changes in a deliberate and predictable manner in order to reduce the possible negative impact of the change or lack of change. The purpose of developing a framework is to define the components used within the management process. When assembling a puzzle, you organize the pieces before you decide how they fit together. From the security perspective, you need to address the following considerations when integrating security objectives in a changing atmosphere:

- The framework must acknowledge changes that may impact the integrity, confidentiality, and availability of valuable information sources within the company.
- Changes will originate from many sources.
- The framework for managing the change must be agile. Agility allows the process of change to accommodate diverse needs and results of the changes requested.
- The framework must be flexible. Critics of the management processes will cite the awkwardness and rigidity of many change management frameworks. Adding flexibility to accommodate change within the change management processes will strengthen the process in its ability to timely incorporate the change.
- The enterprise adoption and distribution of the framework as a whole will allow any gaps of the existing change management process in the current environment to be filled.
- The framework must address the potential change in the acceptable risk strategy. The last thing the company needs to have is technology and processes that ignore security risks. This type of environment gives firms a false sense of assurance.

When initiating or adjusting an enterprise change management procedure, be patient. There are a number of bases to cover:

- Make sure that you have complied with any company policy, regulatory requirement, or departmental practice on tracking and recording the data in the change management process.
- You may find colleagues who resist spending time documenting, scheduling, and testing changes. They may challenge you based on the fact it may take more time to follow the process than to just make the change. Still others will challenge your security initiatives. Such topics that address nonbelievers are discussed in Chapter 22.
- Instituting security requirements into change management adds overhead and potential delays. Offset the cost of any security delays with the benefits of better control of the risks inherent in change management. Ensuring control over the risks involved with changes will lead to more effective, efficient, and successful changes.

There are many case examples that support a change management system to assist the technologist in maintaining and minimizing the accepted level of vulnerability risk. There are virtually no examples justifying the lack of change control to strengthen the security effort in mitigating risk or loss from poor security initiatives.

Identify and Assign Roles

To guard against developing a system void of checks and balances, involve people from diverse business groups in the change management process. Assigning roles to be used in the process will allow a contribution from these team members to the review and notification processes. You may need to define roles associated with the change process, such as

- **Administrator** Administers the target system
- **Data owner** Responsible for the data, possible data backup and restore, and overall integrity of the data
- **Review body** Comprised of technology input as well as business acumen, assigned to review the feasibility of the pending changes
- **Implementer** Implements the actual change
- **Documentation analyst** Ensures that documentation is completed and stored in a history log and knowledge base
- **Results analyst** Ensures that the change has achieved or will achieve its intended goal

Each role has a responsibility for overseeing the success of any change. The security aspect of changing any system, modifying a configuration or setting, or deploying new technology is that the data and systems must maintain confidentiality, availability, and integrity. The team members filling these roles should be educated on these security principles. Their security awareness should help influence involvement in the change process. If security awareness is lost or neglected, business will be unaware of the risk assumptions adopted as a result of a poorly managed change. This ignorance of the state of operations can be catastrophic and sometimes makes recovery impossible.

Make Change Management Part of Your Security Policy

Incorporate the change management process into your security policy. Identify the change management players and their responsibility to incorporate security policy into the decisions and actions of the change management team. Adjust your security policy to include the approval and testing processes of technology-based changes. Change approval should address more than business functionality and technical improvement. Change approval should also include risk assessment and security policy directives that may influence the change process. Use your security policy statement to address changes to the network infrastructure, configuration changes, and even retired components. The change management process should refer to the security policy statements to assure that the proposed changes are not in violation of the security policy.

Develop a Centralized Change Tracking Mechanism

Change tracking mechanisms range from enterprise-wide ticket-generation systems such as Remedy (see Figure 18-1) to free, open-source tools such as Double Choco Latte (see Figure 18-2), which has a wide range of integration components. Details on installation and operation of Double Choco Latte can be found at http://sourceforge.net/projects/dcl. The product sets associated with the other required components are identified in Table 18-1, which demonstrates the flexibility of open-source change management tools to assist in tracking change requests from initiation to completion. These products cover a wide range of information collection, expanding their usefulness to include trouble ticket tracking, inventory changes, as well as configuration changes.

Integration Component	Product Options
Operating system	Linux, Windows, FreeBSD
Web server	Apache
Scripting language	PHP
Database engine	PostgreSQL, MySQL, Microsoft SQL Server, Sybase

Table 18-1. Open-Source Change Management Options

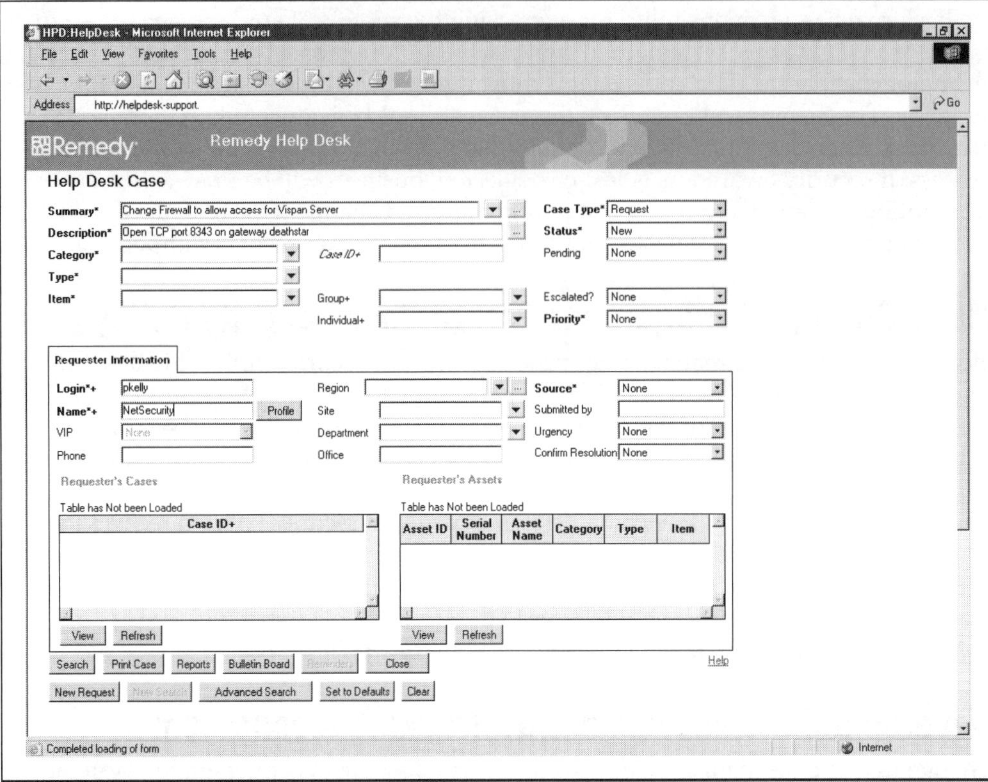

Figure 18-1. Field entries from Remedy for tracking changes capture information that is used to produce reports

Outline the Process Flow from Beginning to End

A clear understanding of the processes by everyone involved in the change process is critical to a successful change management framework. One way to accomplish clear communication is to develop a process flowchart, which should be a cornerstone of the change management framework. This chart should be reviewed periodically for efficiency and should be flexible enough for adjustment to the flow between the steps and incorporation of changes to the order of the steps themselves. Figure 18-3 provides a basic starting point.

You should ensure that you have contingencies defined for each scenario and classification of change. Once you have identified a change scenario that requires rapid deployment, the chart should show the accelerated path. Moving through the approval steps rapidly and moving the documentation steps to post deployment will allow for quicker deployment. The process flow must provide flexibility for rapid deployment.

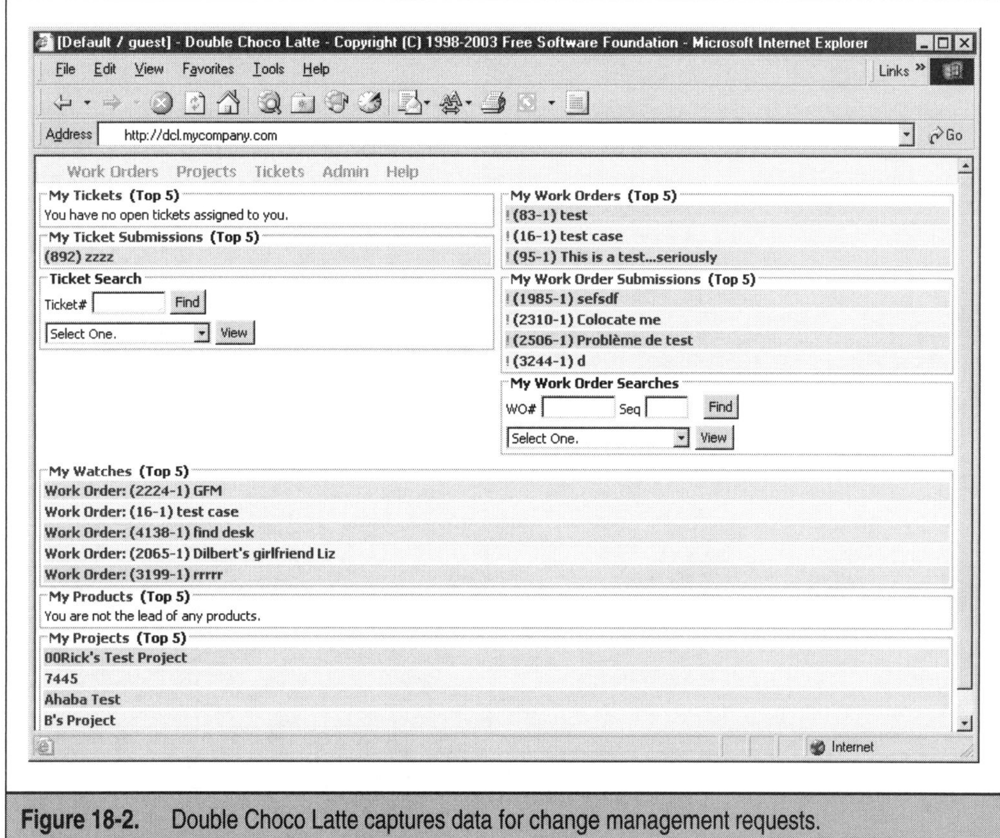

Figure 18-2. Double Choco Latte captures data for change management requests.

Obtain Management Support

The most important component of any change management policy is internal, political support. Building a case for management support varies between organizational structures. Volumes have been written on gaining upper-management support. Fundamentally, change is about cost effectiveness. Begin to document any delays in adoption and implementation of changes affecting the security profile. Don't forget to include risk exposure in determining the cost of delays. Anticipate the negative backlash in requiring technical people to perform nontechnical duties. Prepare even for technicians who do not have documentation and flow control skills. Researching case studies that promote your position on change management processes will help you to support your position.

Even before you make any attempt to secure management support, however, begin some of the practices that will be included in the requirements for your plan. Adoption and implementation of the basic components will familiarize you with what you are attempting to practice.

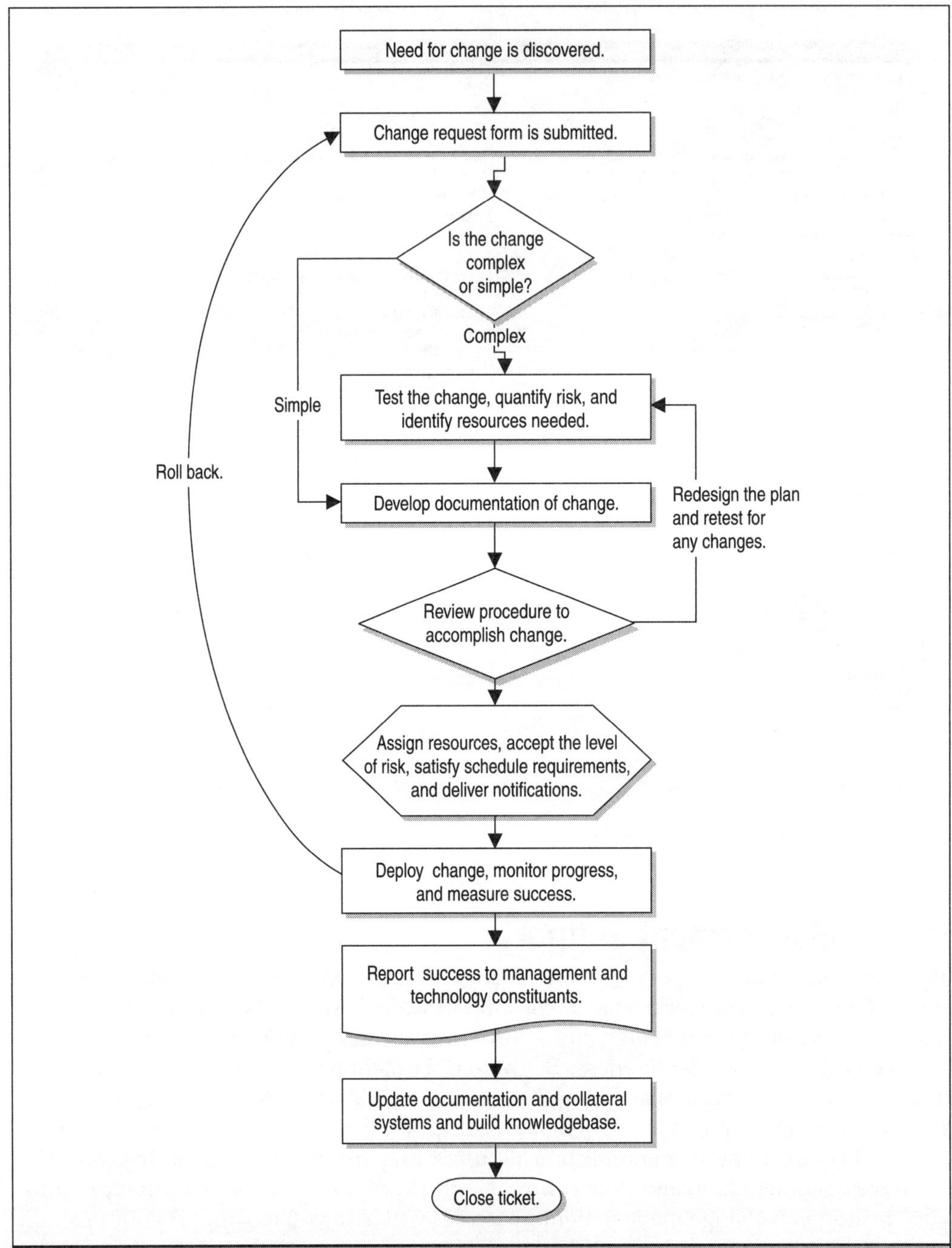

Figure 18-3. Basic change management process flowchart

Establish a Change Notification System

A key element to generation of a documented change request is developing a mechanism to notify the users of the data and systems. Even in emergency situations, notification will assist in setting the expectation of availability. Business processes can be planned or altered to continue productivity when data availability is removed. Also, including the users of systems shows respect and consideration, which will add to your credibility and perceived competency level.

In addition, many organizations fail to document the process of requesting change. This change could be based in technology or in business process. Either of these targets for change can lead to a change in the company's security profile. There are a number of technology tools to assist in this phase of change management.

Provide a Centralized Repository for Change Requests and Fulfillment

Creating a central repository for change will greatly assist you in the communication of the change across business units. Communicating throughout the enterprise the changes that have been made adds visibility to the growth and progress of the technology effort. Incorporating security initiatives into the communication piece of the change process will contribute to the security awareness effort. Using a centralized scheduling and notification tool for changes may allow business unit leaders to check the published schedule and plan work schedules accordingly.

The change request form development will provide an enterprise presence. By including business groups as a possible source for change requests, more communication will exist between technology and business growth objectives.

In addition, providing a central collection of the documentation, plans, reports, results, and so forth will assist a documentation analyst in coordinating the information in a meaningful format to assist with future changes and remedies if the need arises. Collecting the information regarding changes will empower the review process to draw from past experiences to assist in predicting the results and benefits of future change requests. You can organize a central repository to measure successes and report those successes to management. Collecting and collating a history of the changes will provide a great opportunity to develop a trending analysis of the change record and growth.

Develop a Change Management Process

The change process adds structure and continuity to recurring change in the organization. This process will formalize change control to include control over change, communication across technology and business, adjustment of risk acceptance, documentation utilized in reporting success, and measuring growth. By adopting a formal process, different business units, including security, can contribute to the growth and future of the technology and the business.

Document and Benchmark the Existing State

Every change process flow defines a beginning, the change process, and an ending point. Defining and measuring the current state will provide significant results in identifying the effectiveness of the changes you deploy. There are environments that develop this current state as the need for change begins to appear. This current documentation provides not only a starting point, but also the desired target in case a rollback is required. In addition, any operating errors prior to the change that may or may not be corrected by the proposed change need to be documented. A failure of a system or component during the change or configuration process may be the result of a discretely related resource.

Determine the Impact of the Change

Putting a thought process together to discover what systems, processes, and resources the proposed change will influence helps the change management team to determine the risk associated with the proposed change. Defining the different categories of resources will enable the change review body to efficiently recognize the depth of the changes. Associating the resources impacted to the business processes will help the change review team identify the risks and the cost of mistakes and failures. For example, a change to the financial accounting system would affect the accounting system. Scheduling the change during an accounting closing period would raise the risk and cost of failure or delay to complete the change. Accounts payable, receivables, collections, billing, payroll, and purchasing, among others, could be impacted. Many batch jobs are executed in off hours, so planning changes during those off hours may not be practical. Including team members who are familiar with the accounting department processes will minimize the risk to business revenue due to loss of service. Other classes to consider might be hardware, network transport, administration, human resources, sales, and marketing. Input from business process owners will increase the chances for success.

The security input into the change should always prepare a risk analysis of the actual change. You should consider factors such as the following:

- **Complexity of the change** Does this change affect most of the business functions? How much productivity will halt and for how long if the change fails? What is the worst possible scenario and how likely is that to come true?
- **Recovery time from worst disaster to production environment** How much data and time will be lost if we have a disaster recovery scenario? Do I have enough time to perform a backup prior to the change? Will the backup fit into the outage window? At what point in time of the change must I decide to move forward or roll back?
- **Total impact on system constituents** Is production time a total loss if a system is unavailable? Are there administrative or alternative tasks constituents can perform in lieu of system-dependant functions?

Seek Approval for Change

Approval for the change at hand comes from many directions. The path to change approval should consider and answer several questions. Is the business case strong enough to accept the risk? Is the benefit worth the cost, aggravation, and risk of failure? If the upgrade goes terribly wrong, how much productivity loss will be realized getting a working system in place? Results-oriented managers might be resistant to change that involves a steep learning curve for workers. Does she resist the change to protect her staff? Is the manager seeking recognition from staff by fighting the changes? The security team should have questions concerning the changes to the security profile. Remote access is convenient, but are the necessary components for authentication, identification, and protection of the data adequately in place? Carefully listen to the objections and succinctly identify the true obstacles to the changes.

As previously stated, executive support can assist in change. The due diligence of the security team is to bring the changes, good or bad, of the security profile to the approval process. The security directive is to have the change enhance a safe and productive environment.

Adequately Test the Change

Determining whether or not to test a change before moving the change into a production environment is a factor of identifying the comfort level and the assumption of some risk. Routine changes that rely upon a level of knowledge and confidence in the result may not need a rigorous testing regimen. More complex changes to mission-critical systems and networks should not be attempted without a high level of surety. Measuring the cost of reproducing an environment for testing a change may be worthwhile when compared to the risk associated with not testing and a resulting loss of productivity. Look for ways of acquiring even a temporary lab environment. Seek assistance from a vendor for a demo component to test changes against.

Having a lab environment in some situations is a luxury. Dedicating resources to nonproduction environments is difficult for many business units to justify. Testing a change in your firewall rule sets may not be realistic when you only have one production firewall. The application of a fix, update, or patch to a single component in the environment is difficult if not impossible to re-create in a test environment. Ensure that actual change timeframes are within the acceptable parameters of the lowest period of impact of the system and its users. Include target constituents in the review process to discern the best time for down time.

Doing research can diminish some of this risk. The time to seek out public sources of information relating to technologies under your control is now. News groups, mailing lists, and user groups can assist in determining if a change in the form of an update or patch is inciting public outcries. Often, if a change is going to have negative results, those results will be reported. Look for frequent, reliable contributors to the forums as a guide for a favorable or skeptical viewpoint on a specific change.

Configuration changes to existing elements may not be adequately tested in a production environment. Lack of adequate testing will be a factor in the review analysis. It is up to the decision makers included in the review process to weigh the risk of proceeding amid inadequate testing versus the risk of no action.

Document Changes

Documentation of the actual steps to be executed to accomplish the change can be compared to dropping breadcrumbs along a strange path. This documentation of steps will answer the question "What changed?" if a retrace of the steps might be necessary to return a changed system back to its original, working condition. This step should also include the information necessary to roll back a change to a working state. The decision to pull out of a change should be made at this time.

Once the change has been completed, this documentation can be a building block for a knowledge-base system that is used to assist with future changes. This documentation will be used during and after the changes as an exact journal representing the progress that has been accomplished.

NOTE Now that you have begun the documentation process with respect to configuration management, don't forget to protect that data with control lists, formatting conventions, on-document confidentiality notices, and Non-Disclosure Agreements (NDAs) for consultants who may need access to this information.

Review the Proposed Change

To prepare for the presentation of the plan to change, you need to prepare documentation. This can range from a formal, step-by-step form for large change projects to a printout of a web page with instructions on how to apply the latest patch. Once you have gathered this documentation, present it to the change review group. This group can recommend the change as currently planned, ask for clarification of the plan, or reject any proposed changes. The change review group should consist of at least the data owners, security representation, and data or system users.

Planning the change will greatly decrease any negative impact upon the availability of the target system. The plan will identify what is needed to accomplish the change. This could include patch or hotfix files, version update files from a manufacturer, or even a new intrusion detection system for a new network segment. The plan should include a clear timetable to schedule resources.

Another benefit from scheduling is that it enables you to determine the best time to interrupt access or use of a system. This is not always after hours, and some computer and batch jobs may need to run during off hours. Gather input from data owners and users to determine the best scheduling times.

It will be helpful to itemize the steps necessary to complete the change. If other components are needed or additional groups or individuals need notification, this to-do list will help you to identify any missing parts of the proposed change. A step you hope to never use but need to plan for nonetheless is the "return to previous configuration" step. Developing a backout or rollback plan will assist in repairing any unforeseen damage this change may inflict. Decisions that result in uninstalling the patch or hotfix or completely removing the added system may be necessary to stay within any scheduled outage window. The need to reverse the change may not be apparent immediately. It may take some time to discover a new vulnerability or risk resulting from a previous alteration. Documenting the sequence of events of these changes helps you to keep track of all changes to a system. When a new risk is identified by a routine assessment (and you are performing periodic, routine, internal assessments, right?), a history documenting a previous state of the system can be a hero maker. Recognition of these types of risks is made easier when answering the question, "What changed?"

Anticipating the collateral alterations that a given change can make on systems will also assist you in diminishing risks associated with change. A general rule to follow is to balance the risk of not instituting the proposed change versus the risk of implementing the change.

If needed, the documentation should be updated to reflect any refinement in the change plan. Remember, factor in the impact on the security profile when determining if the change as planned meets the goal and objectives of the enterprise. Refer to the security policy statement to ensure that any changes will not violate policy. If there is a conflict, this is the phase of the change to remedy the conflict.

HEADS UP!

A worm is released and discovered and is propagated only by an infected computer making a network connection on a specific port. You study your documentation, and your computers are configured not to use that specific port. Specifically, the worm propagates on port 139 and you have NetBIOS over TCP/IP, the service that uses this port, disabled. The computers with NetBIOS over TCP/IP disabled would not be vulnerable to this exploit. Any urgency to apply this patch or hotfix would be diminished in this environment. An environment where NetBIOS is enabled would need to place more urgency on applying the patch. The point is to evaluate your specific risk and exposure and apply changes appropriately to the risk.

Schedule and Notify Affected Groups

After the review process is complete and the decision to move forward with the proposed change is made, you need to address the details of performing the change. When scheduling changes, you must take into account the total process of the change, by asking questions such as these:

- Should the change take place after hours?
- Is manufacturer support immediately after the change available?
- Should the changes be implemented during a slower period in a high-availability environment?
- Can the change be systematically implemented in mission-critical situations so that availability is undisturbed?
- When was the last backup of the system taken, in case a complete restoration of the system is needed?
- How long will the restore or rollback take?
- At what point during the change must we decide to forge ahead or begin a rollback or restore?

It is helpful to have a periodic, scheduled outage or window within which to implement changes, patches, or upgrades. Find out when users of specific systems can be without access to those systems and schedule accordingly. Set the expectation and perform accordingly. System user tolerance increases if the outage is expected and the results are beneficial.

Once the schedule has been set, post or deliver notification to anyone affected by the changes. You should consider relaying information concerning whether or not end users will be disconnected from the network or e-mail server, or logged out of the target system completely. Will users need to reboot to regain access to a business function? How will users be notified if the results are not as expected? These communication scenarios should be considered when building the notification and communication components of your framework.

Deploy the Change

Once the decision to proceed has been made, the schedule has been set, and proper notification has been conveyed, it is time to perform. Whether the security profile is the direct target of the change or a collateral component, keep the vision of the end result well in focus. All software, hardware, and documentation should be ready for the big event. Follow the working plan as much as possible. Document explicitly any deviations or additions to the original plan. This can be a valuable tool if a system recovery or restoration becomes a reality. Security monitoring devices should be periodically consulted to ensure that the impact of the change is within the expected parameters. If you are fortunate enough to have a network-monitoring tool in place, such as Simple Network Management Protocol (SNMP), unexpected outages will be reported promptly.

Report Success

This may be one of the most important steps in change management: being able to show improvement in security controls. Once the change is accomplished, you must test the target systems for the possibility of mistakenly altering the security profile, resulting in a new and unexpected exposure to vulnerabilities. The results should include the ability to better examine and test systems, if possible. Not only will the technology be updated, but any security risks will be reduced. It is wise to perform an audit of the changes to ensure that the running configuration has adopted the scheduled changes.

Once the change is verified, make sure the documentation is updated and finalized to reflect the new operating configuration. The security policy should be updated if needed. Network diagrams should be updated to incorporate new technologies or additional components. Any changes to contingent systems such as DNS, VLAN structure, or network management tools should be updated. Document all security risks and remediation for inclusion in the security profile documentation.

Monitor the systems for any latent effects that may not be readily apparent. Where changes have moved through the process without adequate testing, there is added importance due to a higher risk of failure. One way to discover latent issues is to monitor mailing lists, newsgroups, and manufacturer bulletins.

Broadcast and publicize reports of successful changes to technology. For security-related changes, a security newsletter can reinforce the goals and objectives of the enterprise security effort to make a safe and productive environment.

Close the Change Procedure

After systems and documentation updates have been completed, move the original request for change to a closed status. Included in the tracking tool should be attachment of documentation, pertinent knowledge discovered in the process, and lessons learned. It is this closure and collection of facts that comprises a report on the success of the change. Also address any reduction of risk and any improved security profile statements as a result of the changes. It is through the measurement process of identifying and reporting success that true improvement can be realized. Improvement is the real basis for all change.

Test for Compliance and Improvement to the Security Profile

Once the change has been implemented, you must test and validate the security profile. The process should be a part of a routine to constantly test systems for potential vulnerabilities and exposure to threats. Each type of change can introduce new security challenges into the technology environment. By using a vulnerability testing tool (see Chapter 17), you can identify the absence of the vulnerability addressed by the change. At the same time, you should be looking for any new security issues generated by the change management system.

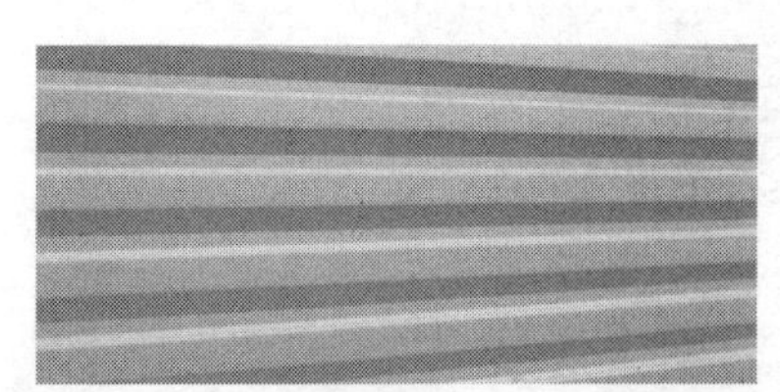

Chapter 19

Security Patching

by Patrick Kelly

- Identify What Needs to Be Patched
- Locate Reliable Sources of Vulnerability Notices and Patch Availabilities
- Obtain Certified Patches
- Verify that Patches Are Authentic
- Determine Which Patches Should Be Applied to Which Systems and When
- Test Patches and Test-Patching Processes
- Install the Security Patches
- Audit the Modifications to Systems Being Patched
- Perform Vulnerability Assessment

Security patching is one of the most important tasks facing system administrators today. Systems administrators are experiencing a tremendous increase in vulnerability discoveries and in the release of exploit code that takes advantage of this new knowledge. Security patching must be kept current to present the best defense against unauthorized access to and destruction of protected networks and information. A critical piece of your security defense is a successful patch management program. You must have the ability to fix known security vulnerabilities in order to maintain a current, safe, and productive environment.

Patching software is not a one-time job. It begins each time software is released and seems to never end. Software is often rushed to market, after which vulnerabilities are discovered, the manufacturer releases a fix, and the administrator applies the fix and waits for the next vulnerability discovery. Ignoring or falling behind with security patches puts the company, its investment in data, and employees' jobs in jeopardy. Maintaining an up-to-date profile on security patches has become a necessity.

This chapter looks at the security-patching process and methods to ensure that the security patch has remedied the threat. The solution you should be looking for will provide a framework that assists you in collecting, testing, planning, deploying, and verifying patch installation. The following steps are part of the process:

- Identify the systems that require patching.
- Verify software and hardware update and patch licenses.
- Provide patch notification in a timely manner.
- Provide the ability to obtain patches.
- Ensure that the patches you acquire are authentic.
- Determine which patches should be applied to which systems.
- Allow time for adequate testing of patch compatibility and to reduce installation problems.
- Provide flexibility in scheduling the distribution and installation of patches.
- Provide a method for installing patches easily across multiple computers.
- Verify that the patch has been applied.
- Test the system to verify that the patch has addressed the vulnerability.
- Provide an efficient recovery or rollback if needed.

Security patch management is a subset of change management, discussed in Chapter 18. Patch management strategies incorporate deployment techniques and processes from your change management framework. Security patching extends the change management scheme by several factors. Security patches can add a level of urgency. The greater the exposure to the threat, the quicker you need to react with the remedy. Because of the added pressure to react quickly, you must apply more attention to accelerating the testing, staging the deployment, and verifying the results.

Identify What Needs to Be Patched

Knowing what systems your company depends upon is crucial to your security-patching and security-update processes. Establishing documentation of your software and hardware inventory provides a foundation for your security-patching process. You can develop software inventories by inspecting purchase records and licensing repositories and, as a last resort, via manual inspection and discovery. Many centralized patching tools are available that help you to discover network components and identify the existing patch levels. For example, HFNetCheckPro (http://www.shavlik.com) can scan domains, networks, and single computers in a mixed Microsoft and Linux environment. The results of the scan identify patches installed and patches not installed. It uses an XML file to identify the patches appropriate for your operating system and installed Microsoft programs.

HEADS UP!

I have heard many people claim that one system is more secure than another. They may even lead you to believe that their systems do not need to be patched. What you really need to determine for yourself are the answers to these two questions: "Do my systems now have or have they ever had vulnerabilities?" and "What's the vendor's history on repairing them?" It would be difficult to find a system on which no exploits have been discovered. You need to be prepared to apply security patches and fixes to all systems you use. The Cassandra project, from the Center for Education and Research in Information Assurance and Security (CERIAS) at Purdue University, provides a compilation of the top 100 vendor vulnerabilities at https://cassandra.cerias.purdue.edu/resource/vendors.php. How many of the systems mentioned can you find in your environment? (You can read more about the Cassandra project in "Search Multiple Vulnerability Data Repositories and Portals" later in this chapter.)

During this research phase, do not forget to identify applications and hardware in addition to operating systems. The ICAT Metabase (http://icat.nist.gov) includes all computer vulnerabilities, including those on commercial applications, OS, and firmware. More information on the ICAT Metabase is provided later in the chapter, in the section "Search Multiple Vulnerability Data Repositories and Portals."

Verify Software and Hardware Update and Patch Licenses

Some vendors provide free patches, updates, and fixes and some do not. You may have to purchase software maintenance contracts or subscriptions in order to receive updates, patches, and fixes. You may find that even free patches and updates will not install if your copy of the OS is not licensed. Part of your patch management strategy must be to determine the current status of product licensing and the manufacturers' requirements for obtaining security fixes. In addition, if your software or hardware manufacturer uses subscription licensing for access to updates and patches, these licenses and subscriptions must be kept current.

CAUTION One form of security patching is to update pattern files in the antivirus products. Without updating the pattern files, your product becomes ineffective in providing protection against newly discovered threats. Licensing for the acquisition of the updated pattern files is essential. Failure to keep this license current can be devastating if a new virus is released and you are not able to incorporate the latest level of protection. Find out now when your license for updates, fixes, and patches will expire for each OS, software, and hardware platform involved in running your company and make sure they are renewed before they expire. Enter the expirations in your calendar to be reminded in plenty of time to renew.

Discover All Technology Products

To identify networked systems and begin the licensing audit, develop a process that systematically discovers networked devices. Running an enumeration tool can do this. Many products can provide cross-platform information concerning OSs, installed programs, and rogue applications. Once a device has been discovered, identified, and enumerated, you can validate the licensing information and verify the availability of patch and update support. While registration and patch licensing of new systems should be one step on their procurement and installation path, periodically use an enumeration tool to discover any gaps in the process. Manual inspection can be automated with software discovery tools.

One of the most popular scanning tools is Nmap from Insecure.Org (http://www.insecure.org/nmap). Nmap can provide information in several forms to assist your search for systems and programs in need of security patching. Figure 19-1 demonstrates that, in addition to the OS (Linux 2.4.*x*), several installed software programs are installed and waiting network connections, including OpenSSH, ISC Bind 9.2.2 (DNS), Webmin Web Server, Sendmail 8.12.10. These applications should also be included in your patch management process. If the applications listen on an open port for connections, that port could also be used for an attack. However, even if an application does not actively provide legitimate remote access to its functionality, it can still contain vulnerable code that might be exploited after an intruder has obtained connection to the system. Protect the system by providing updates for the applications.

Nmap can be installed on and operated from the following OSs:

- Linux: Red Hat, Debian
- FreeBSD
- OpenBSD

- NetBSD
- Solaris
- HP-UX
- Windows

NOTE Mostly known for discovering open ports, Nmap also has one of the best OS fingerprinting systems in place. *Fingerprinting* is the process of remotely identifying characteristics of a computer system.

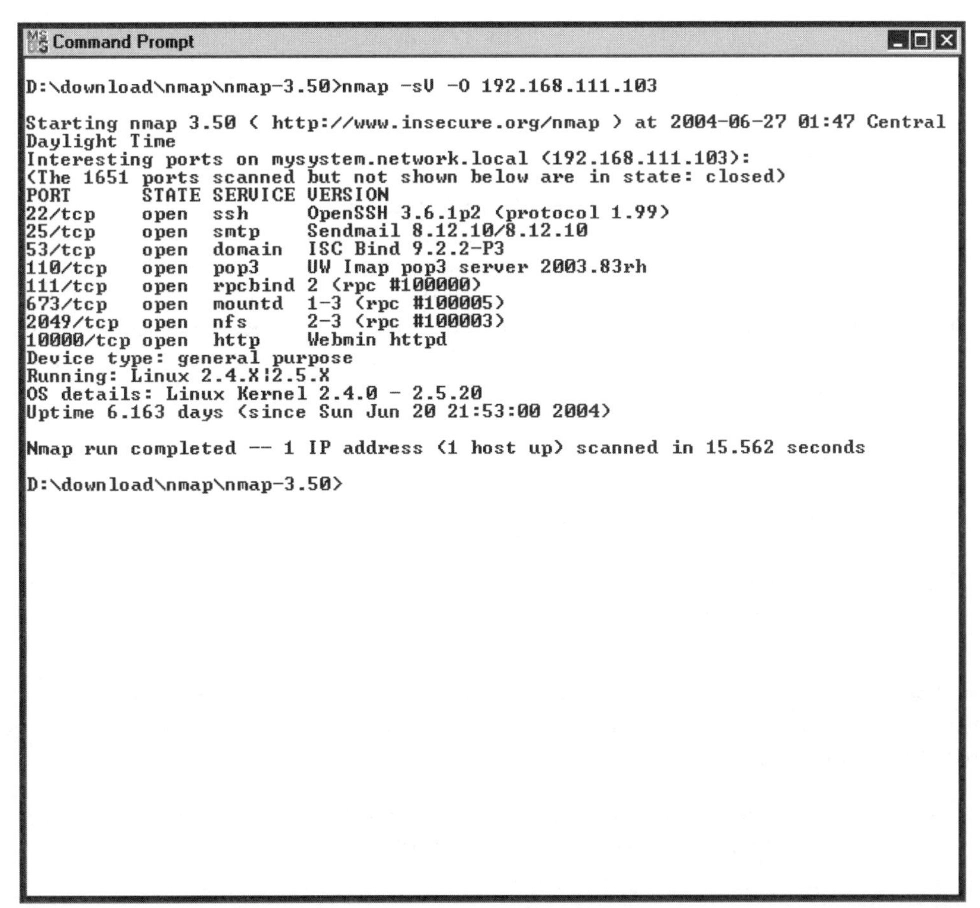
Command Prompt
D:\download\nmap\nmap-3.50>nmap -sV -O 192.168.111.103
Starting nmap 3.50 (http://www.insecure.org/nmap) at 2004-06-27 01:47 Central Daylight Time
Interesting ports on mysystem.network.local (192.168.111.103):
(The 1651 ports scanned but not shown below are in state: closed)
PORT STATE SERVICE VERSION
22/tcp open ssh OpenSSH 3.6.1p2 (protocol 1.99)
25/tcp open smtp Sendmail 8.12.10/8.12.10
53/tcp open domain ISC Bind 9.2.2-P3
110/tcp open pop3 UW Imap pop3 server 2003.83rh
111/tcp open rpcbind 2 (rpc #100000)
673/tcp open mountd 1-3 (rpc #100005)
2049/tcp open nfs 2-3 (rpc #100003)
10000/tcp open http Webmin httpd
Device type: general purpose
Running: Linux 2.4.X|2.5.X
OS details: Linux Kernel 2.4.0 - 2.5.20
Uptime 6.163 days (since Sun Jun 20 21:53:00 2004)
Nmap run completed -- 1 IP address (1 host up) scanned in 15.562 seconds
D:\download\nmap\nmap-3.50>

Figure 19-1. Example Nmap report

HEADS UP!

Most people take for granted the integrity of downloaded files. However, packets traveling through the Internet are exposed to fragmenting, reassembly, and possible corruption. Even the smallest alteration of a patch file can have disastrous results when the file is installed. You should always verify the integrity and authenticity of applications downloaded from the Internet. One way to do this is to validate the vendor-provided hash. For example, download information from the Nmap hackers list on Nmap for Windows indicates that the MD5 hash for the file is

ca0ef17aafb0834c59ea1231b572ee3f nmap-3.50-win32.zip

You can use the md5sum utility to generate your own hash of the downloaded file by using the first command line shown next. You should receive a line similar to the second line shown. Compare the hash listed in this line with the one provided by the download site. If they match, this ensures that the file has not been altered on the download site, during transportation, or during storage on your system.

```
D:\download\nmap>..\md5sum\md5sum.exe nmap-3.50-win32.zip
ca0ef17aafb0834c59ea1231b572ee3f *nmap-3.50-win32.zip
```

If the site where you download software is operated by someone with harmful intent, the site owner might advertise malware as if it were a legitimate product and provide you an MD5 hash of the malware. When you perform your test, you might think everything is okay, only to be infected or "Trojaned." A hash only verifies file integrity; it cannot validate that the file is the software you expected. Once you can ensure that the download site is authentic, then using the hash comparison is useful. You should only download software from trusted sites. If the patch files are digitally signed, you must trust that the owner of the certificate has adequately protected the certificates. You must also ensure that the certificates used to sign the downloaded files are valid by checking the sources of the certificate.

The Windows version is currently a command-line program with the same functionality as the Unix graphical front end. For a Windows installation, you must install these two programs:

- nmap-*X.Y*-win32.zip (*X.Y* being the current release of the Nmap program, i.e., currently 3.50 at the time of this writing)
- Winpcap

Winpcap adds a packet filter driver for Windows 95, 98, Me, NT, 2000, XP, and 2003. The available downloads include an auto-installer for easy installation.

Nmap installation files for Windows are also available at http://www.insecure.org, in the form of WinZip files. Once you extract and save the files to your computer, you are ready to begin OS fingerprinting and identification. Figure 19-2 shows the Nmap command and parameters to fingerprint a class C private network, 192.168.1.1–255. The **–O** option returns the known fingerprint retrieved during the scan from the target network device and provides a match against other known fingerprints.

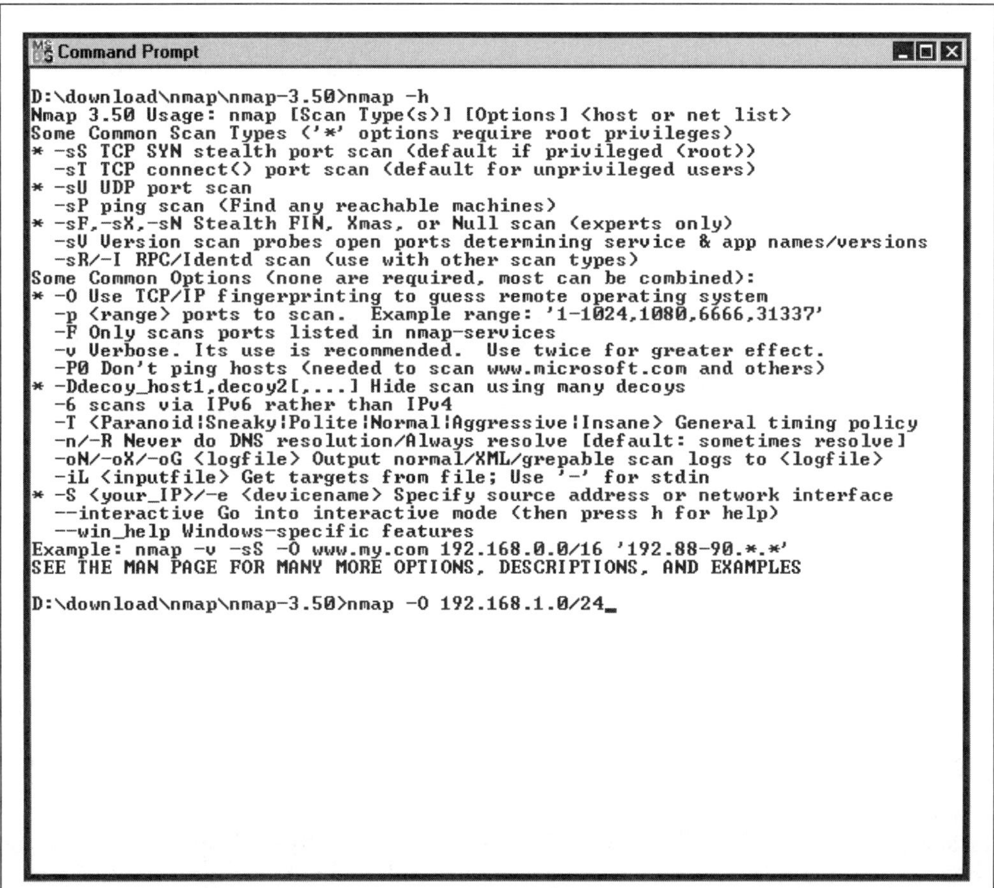

Command Prompt
D:\download\nmap\nmap-3.50>nmap -h
Nmap 3.50 Usage: nmap [Scan Type(s)] [Options] <host or net list>
Some Common Scan Types ('*' options require root privileges)
* -sS TCP SYN stealth port scan (default if privileged (root))
-sT TCP connect() port scan (default for unprivileged users)
* -sU UDP port scan
-sP ping scan (Find any reachable machines)
* -sF,-sX,-sN Stealth FIN, Xmas, or Null scan (experts only)
-sV Version scan probes open ports determining service & app names/versions
-sR/-I RPC/Identd scan (use with other scan types)
Some Common Options (none are required, most can be combined):
* -O Use TCP/IP fingerprinting to guess remote operating system
-p <range> ports to scan. Example range: '1-1024,1080,6666,31337'
-F Only scans ports listed in nmap-services
-v Verbose. Its use is recommended. Use twice for greater effect.
-P0 Don't ping hosts (needed to scan www.microsoft.com and others)
* -Ddecoy_host1,decoy2[,...] Hide scan using many decoys
-6 scans via IPv6 rather than IPv4
-T <Paranoid|Sneaky|Polite|Normal|Aggressive|Insane> General timing policy
-n/-R Never do DNS resolution/Always resolve [default: sometimes resolve]
-oN/-oX/-oG <logfile> Output normal/XML/grepable scan logs to <logfile>
-iL <inputfile> Get targets from file; Use '-' for stdin
* -S <your_IP>/-e <devicename> Specify source address or network interface
--interactive Go into interactive mode (then press h for help)
--win_help Windows-specific features
Example: nmap -v -sS -O www.my.com 192.168.0.0/16 '192.88-90.*.*'
SEE THE MAN PAGE FOR MANY MORE OPTIONS, DESCRIPTIONS, AND EXAMPLES
D:\download\nmap\nmap-3.50>nmap -O 192.168.1.0/24_

Figure 19-2. Fingerprinting a class C network

Locate Reliable Sources of Vulnerability Notices and Patch Availabilities

Once you have identified the systems that you must protect, the next step is to locate vulnerability notifications and remedies or patches. Manufacturers of hardware and software are not always the first to publicize the vulnerabilities of their products. There are a couple of reasons for this. Some software "testers" seek the notoriety of being the first to declare discovery of a vulnerability and will be quick to publicize the information. Usually this is done for fame. Other vulnerabilities may not be publicized upon discovery. If the discovering party wants to exploit this vulnerability for profit, they will want to keep the vulnerability quiet while they harvest data exposed by the security hole. There are a number of alternate sources for this information, as we discuss here.

Use Independent Newsgroups and Lists

Vendor sites may or may not provide the information you need to understand the vulnerability and how to mitigate it. Many third-party monitored and unmonitored newsgroups and lists provide a place for discussion on patching, and on vulnerabilities old and new. They can serve as a place to obtain information on announced vulnerabilities, learn of vulnerabilities to applications and systems that do not provide their own security list, and receive early warning of new exploits.

The following are some current sources (note that at times these lists are quite busy):

- **Bugtraq** http://www.securityfocus.com/archive/1
- **NTBugtraq** http://www.ntbugtraq.com
- **Full-Disclosure** http://lists.netsys.com/mailman/listinfo/full-disclosure
- **Help Net Security** http://www.net-security.org/vuln_main.php

Search Multiple Vulnerability Data Repositories and Portals

The Cassandra project, from the Center for Education and Research in Information Assurance and Security (CERIAS) at Purdue University (https://Cassandra.cerias.purdue.edu/main/), provides a service to assist with tracking multiple vendors and software packages. The Cassandra web site requires registration, including your e-mail address, a username, and a password. The list provides a first-time access code. Once you obtain the code and log in to the site, you can begin to construct searches against the ICAT vulnerability database maintained by NIST.

HEADS UP!

Manufacturers and security companies sponsor some of these lists. As such, the information they provide may be slanted. Monitored lists may only show what the list manager believes is important and information with which he agrees, or may reflect only those comments that follow a company's agenda. On the other hand, they may also be quite fair and impartial, or at least strive for that. Unmonitored lists, and those organized and delivered by those without a cause to push, may inundate you with much meaningless chatter, or possibly copies of exploit code. Be very aware of the circumstances surrounding each list you subscribe to, and filter the commentary. Use caution when opening e-mails and do not open attachments unless you are prepared to deal with the consequences. Read and understand the Privacy Notice, which should accompany your subscription to the list or web site. You may want to subscribe to some lists by using anonymous names or special e-mail addresses that are related to these public lists.

NOTE The ICAT Metabase is a searchable index of information on computer vulnerabilities. It provides search capability at a fine granularity and links users to vulnerability and patch information. ICAT and NIST collaborate with several contributing organizations, one of which is CERIAS at Purdue University. Cassandra enables you to create profile searches that will keep your e-mail inbox up to date on reported or discovered vulnerabilities. The e-mail notification provides links to the vulnerability description and workarounds, updates, and patches.

Once you log in to the Cassandra site, you can construct queries based upon vendor and products. First, you choose a vendor such as Microsoft, Red Hat, or Oracle, to name a few. Next, you select the products from that vendor and add that selection to your profile (see Figure 19-3). Once this query of vendor and product is saved, a script on the server will e-mail the results to the e-mail address in the profile. You may create several profiles. Only new entries since the last time the script ran will be mailed to you. The Incremental setting will find the latest reported vulnerabilities since the last execution of that query. Each profile creates a search that is executed against a data set that is one of these following frequencies that you select for your profile:

- Current month
- 3 months
- 6 months
- 1 year
- Incremental

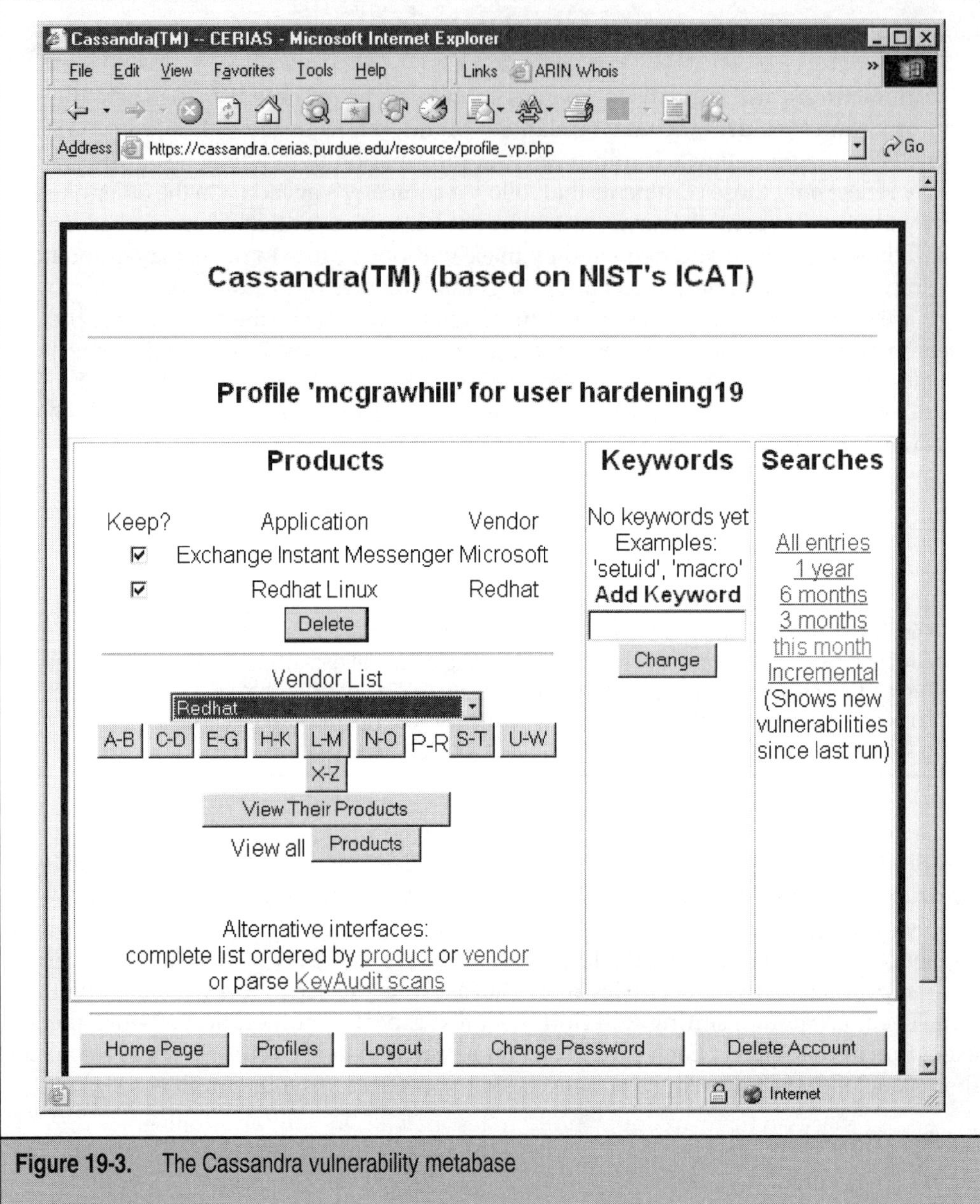

Figure 19-3. The Cassandra vulnerability metabase

The following are some other searchable collections of vulnerabilities:

- **Common Vulnerabilities and Exposures (CVE)** http://cve.mitre.org
- **US-CERT** http://www.us-cert.gov

- **ICAT Metabase** http://icat.nist.gov
- **PacketStormSecurity** http://packetstormsecurity.org
- **Secunia** http://secunia.com

Another method to keep up to date on vulnerabilities is to locate a security news portal. Often, the news of a freshly discovered vulnerability is captured by a security portal. For example, Security News Portal (http://www.securitynewsportal.com) provides current security information and several methods to customize the information you access with RSS feeds, XML feeds, Java Tickers, etc.

Use Vendor Security Sites and Notification Lists

In addition to monitoring the meta notification sites, you should monitor the manufacturer's site for the latest on patches, updates, and fixes. Many of the makers of the software programs and hardware platforms maintain a security section on their web site. For example, Lotus Notes from IBM maintains a history of security-related notices at http://www.lotus.com/ldd/security.

Many of these manufacturers also provide a notification system, usually in the form of a broadcast e-mail system. For example, Microsoft maintains a Security Newsletter. To register, visit http://www.microsoft.com/technet/security/secnews/default.mspx. Cisco Systems supports two mailing lists, one each for notices and discussions on security issues. Each list can be subscribed to by sending an e-mail to majordomo@cisco.com from the mailbox in which you want the announcements and discussions to appear. Include in the message body either **subscribe cust-security-announce** for announcements and notices or **subscribe cust-security-discuss** for customer discussions. Once you have validated that the reply e-mail address is accurate, you will begin to receive the broadcasts from the security announcement and discussion lists.

These are two ways that most manufacturers are assisting their customers through the often-complex security-patching experience.

Obtain Certified Patches

It is important that you separate the patch-obtainment process from the patch-application process so that you have an opportunity to test patches in your environment. Products that both obtain and apply patches in a single step are available, and are actually the best solution for home and small business use and for cases where you have a small number of a specific OSs or applications. If you choose one of these programs, it becomes your patch management program because the vendor takes over the patch-validation and patch-testing processes. Unless you have a testing lab or other nonproduction environment, these downloaded files are applied to your production systems. If this is accomplished in one large single step without testing or analyzing the results, you have to trust that this single patch will work perfectly. If it doesn't, you face the risk of production computers in the enterprise becoming infected. The fallback or rollback plan puts tremendous pressure on your availability requirements for the systems patched. Nevertheless, you assume some risk, and must be prepared to remove patches, recover systems, and obtain help from the vendor if needed.

Applying security updates is much easier today because of the efforts made by many vendors. Many of them provide products that can be used to obtain and/or apply patches. The section "Use Vendor-Supplied Patch-Update Software" later in this chapter introduces and describes some of these tools. In the enterprise, you should consider a product and process that allows you to test patches before their installation and provides a more efficient manner of updating.

To obtain patches for testing and use in your patch management programs, use one of the following techniques:

- *Download patches from the vendor's web site.* For example, Microsoft provides the Windows download site. Check Point Software Technologies provides SmartUpdate for its firewall, VPN, and other security products. Within the SmartUpdate interface, you can manage licensing and product updates. You can download the update from the Check Point site (provided you have purchased the software support) and apply Hotfix Accumulators (HFAs) to your firewall enforcement points from a central management point of reference.
- *Obtain a service pack or security patch CD-ROM directly from the vendor.* You may need to order from a web site, visit a vendor office, or request CD-ROMs from vendor representatives. You can often pick these up at conferences and trade shows at no charge.
- *Subscribe to a vendor program that provides CD-ROMs as part of its package.* For example, Microsoft's MSDN and TechNet programs, though not patching or security programs, provide, in addition to other resources, updated service pack and patching CD-ROMs on a periodic basis.
- *Use a vendor-supplied or third-party patching product that downloads patches to a repository and then allows you to control patch validation, testing, and distribution.* Shavlik, makers of HFNetCheckPro, has partnered with Microsoft to provide many of the same programs, scripts, and features found in free patching tools like Microsoft Software Update Services (SUS). Other patch management vendors, such as PatchLink (http://www.patchlink.com/), provide patching solutions for applications such as Adobe and OSs like Mac OS X, Novell, and Sun.

Often, your options are limited to a specific method of acquiring patches based upon the method supplied by the vendor. Ease of use, time invested, and recovery plans are just some of the operational considerations when looking at the investment in a particular software product. Patching and updating costs should be a consideration as your company invests in new technologies.

There are products and vendors available whose purpose or business is to provide patch management systems. These options range from providing patch availability to providing a patch management and deployment framework. Choosing the right tools to maximize the patching effort will reward companies who have the insight to invest in maintenance technology. Some manufacturers of these tools bundle, consolidate, and simplify the patching and update complexity caused by environments with multiple systems and limited resources. As the IT industry continues to mature, it has become obvious that system ownership must include mechanisms to maintain a safe, secure, and productive environment. Your technology environment needs to acknowledge the necessity of security enhancements to all systems.

Software products that provide a patch framework typically provide a central repository to collect patches. There are major differences in the methodology used in delivering the patches to the end of the line computers, as discussed in the following two sections.

Select Agentless "Push" Patch Management Utilities

One method to deliver patches uses a push technology. The patches are collected on the console server(s) and readied for distribution. The server then initiates a communications stream to the listening client. If the client responds to the initial handshake, the patches are pushed to the client. The server push is usually targeted at a predictable listening port, such as NetBIOS services on a Windows client. If you are striving to lock down your desktops by removing the NetBIOS services, this solution is not practical for you. It presents a catch-22: you need to patch your systems against exploits from NetBIOS attacks but you need NetBIOS running to patch your systems.

Select Agent-Based "Pull" Patch Management Utilities

Another solution to deliver patches is the method whereby the client contacts the server to see if there are any patches available for the originating client's configuration. Most systems can be configured to either schedule the download of patches or manually request them. After the patches have been obtained, you can schedule the automatic installation or perform the installation manually. Figure 19-4 shows the Microsoft Windows pull solution, Automatic Updates (accessed by clicking Automatic Updates in the Control Panel). Before you begin to take steps to change or update programs or files on a computer, check to see if the procedure can be undone. Ensure that you can return the computer to it's previously working condition by either uninstalling the patch or restoring from backup.

In order for the patch server to know what patches to offer the client, some information needs to accompany the client's patch request. In the Windows Update scenario, the following items are transmitted to the Microsoft patch servers:

- Operating system version and Product ID numbers
- Internet Explorer and other software version numbers
- Plug and Play ID number of hardware devices
- Globally Unique Identifier (GUID) to track the client's patch request history

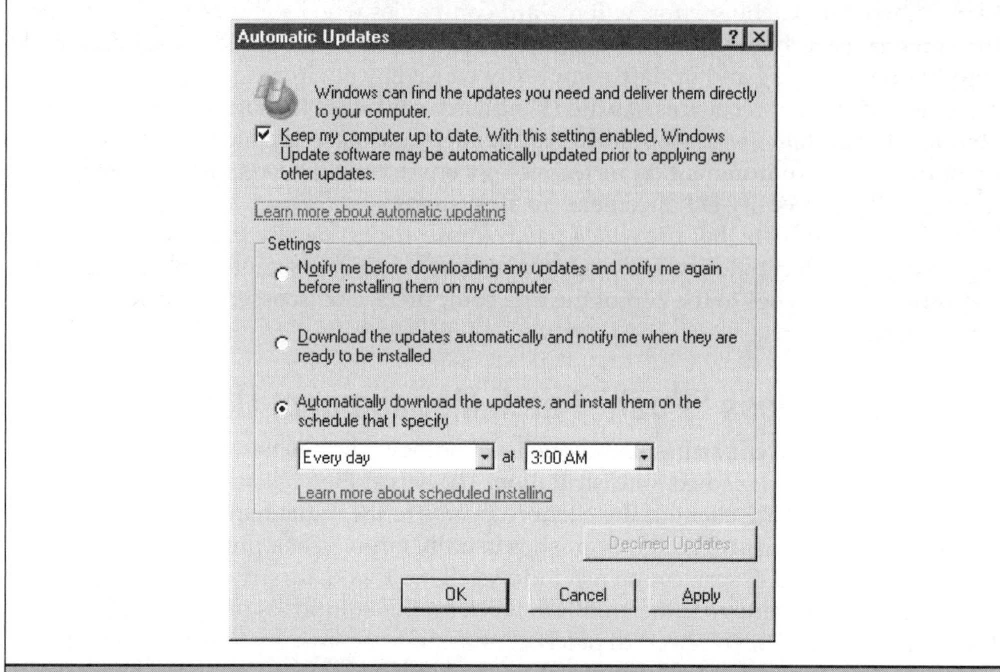

Figure 19-4. Windows Automatic Updates allows you to configure settings for scheduled acquisition of patches and separate scheduling of installation.

Many centralized patch servers obtain their updates by initiating communication with the parent patch server. It is the responsibility of the patch administrator to ensure that the original source of the patches is authentic. Most of these servers are maintained by the manufacturer of the system or program to be patched.

Verify that Patches Are Authentic

You do not want to apply a patch that has been corrupted or, worse, apply what you think is a patch only to find out it is malware masquerading as a patch. Many vendors digitally sign their patches, and the OS looks for this signature before applying the patch. You can also manually inspect the signature. To do so, you need to obtain information on the way the patch is signed and the credentials required to check it. This should be available on the vendor's web site.

You must validate that the acquisition method of obtaining the patch has not exposed the patch to alteration. For example, large downloads could have corrupted the data file. Even the slightest alteration will render the patch useless or dangerous. Most, if not all, manufacturers of patches provide a mechanism to ensure that the patch is authentic. For example, they may publish the MD5 hash on the download site. Other manufacturers digitally sign their patch or update files. Often, the installation package of the patch will validate the digital signature of the file for you.

Once you know how the publicized checksum was created, for instance with MD5, you can use a program such as md5sum to generate a hash digest on the file you are going to apply to your computer systems and compare that to the published value. If the signature matches the one supplied by the vendor you can be assured the file is the same as what the manufacturer has released. A description of how to use md5sum is included in the section "Discover All Technology Products," earlier in this chapter.

Some manufacturers sign their patches. Included in the installation or application of the patch is a signature-checking routine that properly validates the authenticity of the patch you are applying. For example, Sun's patching program can apply both signed and unsigned patches. The digital certificates are issued by Baltimore Technologies through GTE CyberTrust. The public key included as part of the patch is paired with the matching private key held by Sun at the time you commit to applying the patch. The patching program will validate the patch and apply it only if the patch is safe. If the issuer of the patch does not provide a similar level of granularity on patch applications, you must research your situation to fulfill your acceptable standard for safe patch levels.

HEADS UP!

Never accept an e-mail purporting to be from a vendor when it comes with an attachment the e-mail calls a recommended patch. Most vendors never distribute patches in this manner and are straightforward in telling you that. Make sure that you understand the process that each vendor incorporates in its patch-distribution methodology.

Determine Which Patches Should Be Applied to Which Systems and When

There are several criteria to consider when applying changes or patches to your production systems. You have to decide which patches to apply on which computer systems and when to apply them. This section offers some guidelines to assist you with these challenges.

Determine Which Patches Must Be Applied

Knowing which patches to apply requires an analysis of the risk. The risk assessment must determine the best choice among several process scenarios. One such assessment is the comparison of leaving the vulnerability exposed by not applying the patch as opposed to applying the patch with an untested result. To resolve this dilemma analyze the true risk introduced by the new threat to your systems from the vulnerability addressed in the patch. If you have low or no risk from this threat, there is no urgency to apply the patch. It would be considered a higher risk to apply the patch without good cause.

One challenge facing many system administrators who are responsible for keeping systems updated is to cover the wide number of patches available for a system. For example, an open-source OS such as Red Hat Linux has hundreds of packages available for installation. How can anyone keep track of what to update or what is available for an update?

To effectively manage a patching regimen, you must inventory the applications, programs, and add-ins that comprise the complete system. Any system or application that interacts with another system, or data produced or used by another system, is a candidate for a patch procedure. Omitting any subcomponent of a complete system reduces the reliability and safety of the remaining systems. Do not allow a weakness of an application to circumvent an otherwise diligent and thorough security-patching effort.

Understand the Patch-Release Strategy of the Manufacturer

Identify the patch-accumulation practice of the vendor's patching mechanism. Several manufacturers have a patch-accumulation strategy whereby all of the previous patches are part of the new patch-release formula. You may end up applying a patch that you are not completely informed about.

For example, Microsoft combines patches and hotfixes into Service Packs. By the time a Service Pack is assembled, tested, produced, and distributed, Microsoft may need to release a new fix for a recently discovered problem that isn't covered in the Service Pack. This scenario could occur in any manufacturer who assembles rollup patches or hotfix accumulators. After the application of a multiple-fix patch, apprise yourself of any additional patch releases to establish that your patch level state is current.

Determine if a Patch, Fix, Configuration Change, or Workaround Is Necessary

Fixing security vulnerabilities does not always involve just running an executable file to patch your systems. There are times when the proper remedy is to alter a configuration. There are times when exploits do not attack the manufacturer's code. The real attack may be the result of finding a configuration setting that opens a vulnerability of your system. When a warning of an exploit comes from the manufacturer, the configuration setting that causes the vulnerability might be the default setting. The fix might be to change or adjust the default setting to eliminate the threat exposure. You may already have made such adjustments, or doing so may cause other programs to fail. You must still evaluate the risk and the proposed mitigation to determine what to do.

HEADS UP!

Look no further than the events that led to the spread of the Slammer worm for an example of increasing your risk by not applying a "risky" patch. At the time of the Slammer outbreak, Microsoft had released two security patches to prevent this exploit. The first patch released resulted in claims that it disrupted productivity and availability of production service to some configurations and implementations. These claims directly contributed to many administrators' decisions to delay or reject the application of the first patch. When the second patch was released, many administrators were either too confused or too skeptical to implement either patch, fearing the patch would put their productivity and availability at too high a risk. No known exploit was discovered until later. At that time, some administrators still feared the results of the patch. To protect themselves from the Slammer worm, they blocked communication from potentially harmful sources with firewall configuration changes until any patch remediation could be tested and deployed. In some cases, this temporary configuration change imposed a result very much like a denial of service.

Still other warnings about a system weakness may be directly related to a common deployment of the system or feature of the system. You may be instructed to perform an action on a separate but related component to work around the reported exploit. The workaround is generally a precursor to the release of a patch or fix. The manufacturer issues the warning and provides information concerning the threat. Conscientious vendors will issue instructions to remedy the threat before their engineering and development staffs can provide a distributable patch.

Select Computer Systems for Patching

If security patches worked as expected all the time, there would be no doubt that you should apply each patch as soon as it's available to all computer systems. The reality is that any change to a computer system may cause the system to become unstable or, in the worst-case scenario, unusable. This problem may be a faulty patch, an incompatibility with your installed applications or configurations, or some other issue.

The decision to apply a security patch to a system should be made only after balancing the risk of falling victim to the pending threat versus the system becoming unusable due to an unforeseen negative reaction to the applied patch. Keep in mind that the most important goal is to keep your systems operational and your data accurate (and private where required).

Study the severity of the threat as it applies to your environment. If you are vulnerable to a serious threat and have significant exposure, you should consider an accelerated timetable for applying the security patch that will address the threat. An example would be a threat to a publicly accessible server, such as a web server or mail server. If these servers are available to anyone on the Internet, they should be patched as soon as possible. Even if these servers are behind a firewall, they are accessible via open ports on the firewall and therefore are not protected from any vulnerability accessible through that port. Other servers behind a firewall that are not accessible from the Internet are protected from externally mounted attacks. However, they are not protected from internally mounted attacks until the vulnerability is remedied. Patch publicly available systems first. If you determine that the immediate threat of the vulnerability is minimal, you may proceed with more caution.

The Internet is not the only path from which a vulnerability might be exploited. You must consider not only the direct threat from the Internet, but also other delivery methods that might expose you to the threat. For example, during your vigilant monitoring of vulnerability-reporting web sites, suppose you discover a vulnerability found in the web browser that your company has installed on its desktops. If your e-mail client and web browser share components, this vulnerability could be exploited not only when your company's users browse the Internet, but also through your e-mail system. If your e-mail client parses HTML in a message body, reading an e-mail might trigger the vulnerability. An example of this type of exploit is described by the Cross-Domain Vulnerability in MHTML Protocol Handler (see http://www.us-cert.gov–Alert TA04-099A). The lesson is to understand how vulnerability exploits can be launched within your environment and take the necessary patching or other defensive response.

Once you have identified which systems are good candidates for the proposed security patch, you must take steps to test, deploy, and monitor the success of the change.

Determine When to Apply Security Patches

The timing of applying security patches is driven by the urgency of the threat, the availability of systems, and the confidence in the success of the patch. As you analyze the real threat of the vulnerability, you must prioritize the patch application. The priority depends on several factors:

- Does the vulnerability remedied by the patch pose a critical, moderate, or no threat to computer operations?
- Is my risk from the vulnerability decreased because of another security component in my defense-in-depth model?
- Can I isolate a group of computer systems that are more exposed to the threat than others?
- How important to productivity are the computers with the greatest threat?

Involve System Owners in the Planning Process

It is important to notify in advance the users and owners of a system before making a change with a security patch. Just as with any change, the authorization to potentially alter the availability of a system should require input from the owners of those systems. It is imperative that you help the business users/owners of the systems affected by the security threat to understand any urgency of applying any security patch. Business process owners, supervisors, managers, and directors need to be informed and reminded of the potential adverse outcomes of the pending changes. Based upon the potential outage in the worst case, they may assist you in determining the best plan to apply different risk-level patches. They can assist with timing and scheduling based upon a sample group as a precursor to a complete rollout.

Plan for Business Interruption

Many security patches require a reboot or system restart, causing a brief interruption in service. Make sure you have accounted for the lack of availability and be prepared to act quickly and efficiently if a system does not come back online.

Test Patches and Test-Patching Processes

If you have a nonproduction replica of critical network systems, you can and should test patches on those systems before deployment into production. The next best alternative is to deploy on a subset of target systems and closely monitor the results. In addition, monitor the original site of the patch for notices of issues, recalls, re-releases, or adjustments to the original patch. Use these techniques to bridge the gap between holding the patch and deploying it. Do not make the mistake of not applying a patch for reasons of fear, uncertainty, and doubt about applying the patch to your systems. Leaving a system unprotected is the greatest risk of all.

Testing should take place in two phases. First, test to ensure that the patch does not cause new problems. Then, test a patched system to see if the security vulnerability has been repaired. Again, if available, test patches on nonproduction systems. Applying the patch or fix on nonproduction systems prevents you from suffering avoidable consequences from a bad patch or incompatibility. Be sure that test systems are configured exactly the same as production systems. Representative systems of all types of systems on the LAN should be tested, not just for perceived stability after the patch application and to eliminate compatibility concerns, but to verify that the patches have been installed and to validate the patching process.

A test site comprised of nonproduction systems is an excellent environment for patches that will be deployed to mission-critical systems and is imperative. Patches meant for complex systems should also be tested thoroughly on non-critical systems. Complex systems are those with a large number of components, those with a great deal of installed component customization, and those with obscure or disparate components installed. Patching a database server, for example, may be straightforward; however, measuring the interaction between a customized application and the patch changes is tedious and unpredictable. One method used by some companies is to keep a catalog of system command calls and files used by the customized application. If the patch changes any of these files, it is imperative to test the effects of the new file on existing code. No matter how much testing is done, there is still some risk involved in applying any patch to a production system.

After you test systems to ensure that the patch does no harm and does close the vulnerability, it is imperative that you restore the test systems to the prechange state of operation. This allows you to test your recovery strategy, a necessity if patching a production system causes it to break. To ensure recovery, you must understand and practice the vendor procedures for rolling back a patch, and have a good backup that can be used should it prove impossible to remove the patch. Don't just verify the backup, test the restoration and recovery actions periodically. It is not enough that you can restore files from the backup system, you also must be able to completely rebuild the system from scratch. The amount of time it takes to rebuild the target system is the amount of time the system you attempted to patch will potentially be unavailable. Make sure that any outage timeframe can accommodate this complete system rebuild or restore procedure.

Install the Security Patches

Deploying patches to client computers, servers, applications, network equipment, and security components can be a consuming task. The best way to conquer the patch management battle is to automate the process as much as possible. The strategy you choose depends on factors relating to the following:

- System management tools available
- Local user access rights
- Resources available to accomplish the patching process
- The complexity and variety of systems to be supported and patched

Your patching strategy must meet the requirements of securing your systems. The marketplace for patch management tools is evolving to offer comprehensive and flexible solutions. Choose a tool to address as many OSs and applications in your environment as possible. Consolidation of patching tasks will reduce the cost of ownership of any tool you purchase. If you adhere to the concept that patching systems is inevitable, security patching should be considered a contributing factor to the real cost of ownership of those systems.

Patch Remote Clients

Remote clients are more frequently exposed to untrusted networks, yet are more difficult to keep updated. Some remote clients only connect to the corporate network occasionally; hence, it is difficult to provide them with patches from a patching server under corporate control. Installing an update agent on these systems provides a mechanism for them to maintain a current patch history. Protecting these systems is a vital component to a successful security patch management plan.

St. Bernard Software produces UpdateEXPERT, which provides for remote and infrequently connected systems Leaf Agent, client-side agent software that is installed on remote, traveling, or slow WAN (under 512 Kbps line speed) connections. Leaf Agent offers encrypted transport options, Internet download of patches and program updates, and local logging. This agent can act independently of the Master Agent, used in a constantly connected network, to keep this individual node patched. More information on UpdateEXPERT can be found at http://www.stbernard.com

Provide Patching Software that Does Not Require Elevated Privileges to Run

A patch methodology that requires intervention by the system user may contradict your security profile. It is commonplace for administrators to restrict the system configuration capabilities of many system users to reduce system manipulation by untrained users. However, some patching plans may require elevated access control settings to successfully apply security and system patches. A tool that utilizes system agents can be installed and operated by a non-user or service account to circumvent undesirable privilege elevation of users.

Install Quickly to a Large Number of Systems

The process of installing security patches to a large number of systems in a short time requires coordination, timing, and multiprocessing. These characteristics are only found in patch management tools. Configured correctly, these products can mean the difference between unwillingly accepting critical vulnerabilities and fending off the next large-scale computer event.

Use Vendor-Supplied Patch-Update Software

Many vendors provide patching and updating software as part of their product or downloadable from their web sites. Many of them offer excellent tools for patching small numbers of systems. To give you an idea of what is available, this section describes patching and updating software from four major vendors.

Apply Patches in Chronological Order

Prepare and apply patches and hotfixes in the correct chronological order. If you mistakenly apply an older patch after a more current patch, you may unknowingly create a state of vulnerability and false sense of security, because older versions of files may overwrite newer ones. Be careful, as well, if a patch requires reboot. Applying multiple patches without rebooting after each patch might also cause a problem, because open or in-use files are not overwritten by newer files in a patch until the system is rebooted. When multiple patches are applied in the wrong order without a reboot, the wrong version of a file might be applied. In a Windows environment, use the utility qchain.exe to circumvent the requirement to reboot after each patch. Qchain.exe inspects the version information of replacement files "in the queue" and ensures that the latest version of the file is applied after the reboot. Your patch management process should include checking the file versions after patching to verify their correctness. (When a system is updated using Microsoft's online Windows Update site, version inspection in the queue is performed automatically.) Microsoft TechNet Knowledge Base Article 296861 is a solid reference for installing multiple patches.

Red Hat's up2date and Fedora Project yum offer versioning and release checking during the dependency analysis phase of the update. These update processes use Red Hat Package Manager (rpm) as an installation platform that checks for dependency on other programs and updates before the pending package is updated.

Red Hat Package Manager is a utility for installing, updating, and removing programs or packages in Red Hat Linux. The command

```
#rpm -U package.version.release.rpm
```

will update the specific package to the updated version. With command-line parameters, you can force the update and ignore any dependency by issuing

```
#rpm -U package.version.release.rpm --force
```

Sun Microsystems PatchPro

The goal of Sun PatchPro 2.2 and other manufacturers' patching utilities is to simplify the security-patching process. Sun developed the PatchPro product to provide a reliable, easy-to-use product. The acquisition and installation of this patch utility can be summarized in these steps:

1. Download the tar file to the system.
2. Run **./setup**.
3. Specify the connection mechanism to the Internet, proxy or direct.

4. Restart WBEM services:

```
# /etc/init.d/init wbem stop
# /etc/init.d/init wbem start
```

5. Validate the configuration data.
6. Modify your environment path:

```
# PATH=/usr/sadm/bin:/opt/SUNWppro/bin:${PATH}
# export PATH
```

7. Modify your man page path:

```
# MANPATH=/opt/SUNWppro/man:${MANPATH}
# export MANPATH
```

The detailed instructions are available at http://docs.sun.com/db/doc/817-3331/6miuccqn5?a=view. Sun's use of digital certificates to authenticate the patch provides assurance that the patch is authentic. The digital certificates are imported into a protected database on your system that stores keys and certificates from Sun. The protected database is password protected with a system-specific password that you can set.

Red Hat Network up2date

The Red Hat Network up2date utility is included in the installation distribution. Red Hat Enterprise Linux licensees are entitled to receive updates from the Red Hat Network. Registration provides each registered system a profile that is used to provide pertinent updates, fixes, and errata information. You optionally schedule the Red Hat system to visit Red Hat's update site to obtain patches, or you can invoke the Red Hat Network Daemon (rhnsd) program manually. The program will periodically query the Red Hat Network Site for available updates, download the appropriate files, and install them.

To initiate the process:

1. Register Red Hat Enterprise Linux and activate your profile.
2. Schedule the up2date utility to run as a cron job:

   First, create a file named **up2date.cron** and place this file in the /etc/cron.daily directory on your Red Hat systems. Here is the suggested content of the file:

```
#!/bin/bash
address="you@yourdomain.tld"
host='hostname'
subject="Update Log for $host"
tmpfile=/tmp/up2date-cron.log
up2date-nox -u > $tmpfile
if [ -f $tmpfile ]; then
mail -s "$subject" $address < $tmpfile
rm $tmpfile
```

```
else
mail -s "No Update Log File" $address
fi
exit 0
```

Then replace the e-mail address you@yourdomain.tld with an e-mail address you want to use for patch monitoring. An e-mail will be sent to that address each time a patch update is attempted. By receiving and storing these e-mails, you can maintain a chronological e-mail repository for Linux system updates.

Use cron to Schedule Update Tasks

For those unfamiliar with Unix and Linux systems, a *cron job* is a way of scheduling repetitive tasks on a system. cron is a Unix/Linux daemon that initiates every minute on your system. You can schedule on an hourly, daily, weekly, or monthly basis. By editing the crontab file, you can choose what minute, hour, day of the week, and month to execute a command. To execute the file update.cron every day at 3:00 A.M., for example, the crontab entry would look like this:

```
0 3 * * * /path/to/update/command
```

The crontab file has default hourly, daily, weekly, and monthly settings. You can discover more details concerning cron and crontab by typing **man cron** or **man crontab** on the command line in Linux/Unix. Additional help on how-to and documentation for this scheduler can be found at http://www.redhat.com.

Mac Software Update Preferences

Mac OS X systems have an update system similar to the Red Hat Network. Use the Mac OS X Software Update preferences utility to acquire and install updates, including security updates to your systems. Software Update is located in the View menu under System Preferences. You are presented with a listing of possible updates. You must decide which updates apply to your needs. For example, you would mark updates for a foreign language installation as inactive. Once you select the update, it is installed. If you need to reboot the computer, check to see if other updates are available, as some updates are dependent on previously released updates being completely installed and active.

You have the option to schedule an automatic update process or apply updates manually. Some updates require a stand-alone installer. These installers can be reused for future patches. The security patches for Mac OS X systems are located at http://www.apple.com/support/downloads/.

Microsoft Update Tools

Microsoft's patching methodologies have been debated in the security industry for years. Current Microsoft desktop and server OS products have a feature called Automatic Updates to address the large Windows consumer market, the dominant OS in this market. This large market share makes Windows the largest target for exploits. Small, medium, and enterprise-class products range from Software Update Service to Systems Management Server (SMS). By integrating Software Update Services Feature Pack into SMS 2003 and leveraging Microsoft Baseline Security Analyzer, the Windows administrator can coordinate system enumeration, vulnerability assessment and tracking, and deployment of Service Pack and security hotfixes to the Windows enterprise. In 2005, Microsoft promises to release Windows Update Services to provide better control and administration in securing the Windows platform. To keep updated about the future release of Windows Update Services, tune in to http://www.microsoft.com/windowsserversystem/sus/wusfaq.mspx. For more information on hardening Microsoft Windows, refer to *Hardening Windows Systems* by Roberta Bragg (McGraw-Hill/Osborne, 2004).

Use Third-Party Tools for Patching

Many enterprise-class patch tools offer patching for multiple OSs, including Novell, Windows, Red Hat, Solaris, etc. In addition, many of the patch tools offer program application update capabilities. A few examples mentioned earlier are St. Bernard Software and PatchLink. Being able to consolidate security-patching tasks for as many products as possible in the environment is insightful, cost effective, and a way of providing a high level of confidence that the number of outstanding exploits against all systems has be reduced.

A package Yellowdog Updater Modified, or yum, is a patch, or package as they are often referred to in Linux communities, manager for Red Hat 7.3 and above. Yum uses technologies and code from various other sources. Yum has a configuration file, /etc/yum.conf, that is able to search, download, and apply updates to a multitude of packages.

Audit the Modifications to Systems Being Patched

Simply installing patches as presented by the vendor is insufficient. You must understand what the patch will change. This understanding is important so that, prior to patching, you might predict the impact the change will have on dependant systems and, after patching, can ensure that patches were installed correctly. Some patch documentation will provide a list of files that are changed. For others, you may need to inspect the patch to find out for yourself. In addition, if you have a list of changed files, troubleshooting post-implementation issues may be easier. Knowing what changed often solves many problems when trying to restore a system back to operation.

The file integrity feature of a product like Tripwire (http://www.tripwire.com) can readily provide information on file modifications, deletions, and additions. This is important because

- If you monitor changes during patch testing, you establish a benchmark of expectation of what should be completed during the complete patch rollout.
- Documenting changes to files during the updating process enables you to meet the requirement to maintain the integrity of a security change.
- You leverage your investment by providing a host-based intrusion detection system (HIDS). If you periodically review the list of expected changes caused by applying patches, and compare them to unauthorized changes, you may discover an intrusion.

However, it is nearly impossible to track adds, deletes, and modifications to files manually. A product like Tripwire can do that for you. If you are going to use Tripwire or another HIDS that is capable of monitoring file changes, you must start by obtaining a baseline. A baseline is a scan of the system prior to any updates or modifications. Use the HIDS to execute a file enumeration procedure before applying any updates. Once the patch has been deployed, another file integrity check provides a listing of file system changes.

Compare this list with the patch documentation to ensure that the patch completed as expected. If you have a large number of patch target machines, this process for each machine is not realistic. However, auditing enough randomly selected and critical systems will provide a comfort level that you can live with. Once you are comfortable with the changes, you can accept the file system changes created by the patch application.

Test for the Absence of the Threat or Vulnerability

The last step to ensure that the vulnerability or threat has been properly patched is to verify that the patch has been applied. The logical method is to execute the exploit to see if the patch fixed the vulnerability. However, executing an exploit against your production system is not a realistic course of action. The last thing you want is to take down your own system. There are several alternatives.

Many patch management tools are capable of producing an inventory of the current patch state. These tools and features can inspect file systems, registry settings, and system states to ensure that they have been updated by applying the patches.

Use a Patch-Checking Tool

The same tools that inform you of the missing patches and fixes can also be used to validate the installation of the patch. Many patching tools work by identifying the missing patches on a system. After you apply the patch, if you run the tool again, it should indicate that the patch is no longer missing.

One such tool is hfnetchk from Shavlik. The command-line program is adequate for testing the presence of patches or the lack thereof on Windows systems. You can download a free version of the program at http://www.shavlik.com. (A commercial program with more features is also available.) The downloaded file is a self-extracting file that provides the licensing text file, readme text file, the executable, and a winhttp .dll file. Each time you run the program, hfnetchk.exe, it downloads a current version of mssecure.cab and mssecure.xml After downloading the current files, the program searches the local Windows computer for missing patches based on the content of the XML file in place.

Other third-party programs, as well as free Microsoft tools such as Windows Update and Microsoft Security Baseline Analyzer, can also be used to verify patch application. Unfortunately, you may obtain different results depending on the tool you use. This conundrum may be the result of many things:

- Not all applicable patches and hotfixes for your target systems are currently present in the XML file many of these tools use to test. There is no one, centralized, all-inclusive, patch-awareness repository.
- Different products test for patch inclusion in different ways, from examining registry entries to examining file versions.
- Some security fixes do not include patches, but rather are configuration changes, and the patch-testing product does not test for such changes.
- The XML file used is not up to date. This can be the result of using a local copy of the file that is not current. (Many tools check online for the latest version of the file, but if the system does not have Internet connectivity, it cannot do so.)
- A newer version of the file than the one in the security patch is installed. A file may be updated during the installation of a new product or new version of a product. If this file was produced after the patch was released, it may include the patch fix, but not be known to the patching product.

Because of these potential discrepancies, you need more than a single-tool approach. Your security patch assurance strategy may require multiple combinations of existing tools and certainly will require analysis of the results. In many cases, for example, the patch tool may detect an anomaly and provide helpful hints as to why it may exist.

Perform Vulnerability Assessment

To add to your assurance that the threat has been minimized from the latest vulnerability, you should perform a full vulnerability scan against the systems recently patched. The benefit from this action is twofold:

- The results will address the immediate past threats to show the system security profile is intact. Ensure that the scanning tool has incorporated the test for recent vulnerabilities. It is imperative to update the exploit database of the scanner prior to testing the latest patches.

- You have some mechanism to test whether your patches have introduced another vulnerability. This is more apt to happen with workarounds and fixes than with actual patches. A configuration change to a system should always be tested to validate that the correct change was made and the system security profile was improved.

Qualys (http://www.qualys.com) is a vulnerability assessment company that will perform an online scan against publicly accessible IP addresses. You can use a commercial product or an open-source software package such as Nessus (http://www.nessus.org) to accomplish this same goal. Test your systems against known vulnerabilities and threats. Additionally, check and recheck your efforts in areas where mistakes would be costly. As part of an ongoing assessment plan, audit the security changes you make. Validate that the security profile is improving. Remain vigilant to approaching threats by researching vulnerabilities.

Chapter 20

Security Review

by John Mallery

- Evaluate End-User Compliance and Acceptance
- Conduct Post-Event Reviews

Maintaining a secure system or network is a dynamic process. In the information technology world, operating systems and applications cannot be "fixed once, fixed forever." New vulnerabilities and threats are discovered on a regular basis. And end users will always find ways to circumvent policies and procedures. Successful organizations are constantly upgrading or purchasing software in an effort to become more efficient and provide better service to customers. All of these issues mean that you must constantly evaluate and reevaluate to maintain the security of a system or network. Without these evaluations, the initial effort that you put forth to secure systems is time not well spent.

Because of the war in Iraq and the events leading up it, there is a renewed interest in security and security practices. More businesses now conduct regularly scheduled, formal, detailed security audits, similar to the annual financial audits performed on the financial records of the company. These security audits are often performed annually and are often considered to be all that is necessary to protect an organization's infrastructure. But due to the dynamic nature of networks and businesses, this "once yearly is enough" attitude is not effective. Numerous changes occur in an enterprise over the course of a year; employees are hired and terminated, new software is added or upgraded, and new relationships are started with vendors and clients. All of these changes can impact the security of a business. Therefore, you should conduct periodic security reviews to verify that new changes have not significantly altered the security stance of the business. An analogy can be drawn to personal healthcare. Most people go to the doctor once a year for an annual physical to verify that no major issues exist. But if someone is feeling "not quite right," experiencing unexplained rashes, fevers, or pains for example, they will visit the doctor for a quick checkup. The same applies to the corporate network and infrastructure. Networks too can have times when they are acting "not quite right"—unexplained slow downs, erratic performance, and unusual alerts or warnings can cause the need for periodic "checkups."

These periodic security reviews do not have to be complete audits, but rather can focus only on the section of the network or business that is directly impacted by a change (by analogy, a doctor does not search for broken bones if the complaint is an ear ache). These reviews may be either simple, consisting of informal evaluations, or more elaborate, if a significant issue needs to be addressed. Although this chapter focuses primarily on policy and procedure reviews, you may also need to periodically check security settings of different devices and operating systems. Several tools exist that allow you to accomplish this outside of a security audit (Chapter 17 provides detailed information on checking security settings in the enterprise). The Center for Internet Security (http://www.cisecurity.org) provides tools that allow you to compare system configurations to recognized benchmarks. Similarly, Microsoft provides an excellent tool, Microsoft Baseline Security Analyzer (MBSA), to find common system misconfigurations in numerous Microsoft products. You can download MBSA from http://www.microsoft.com/technet/security/tools/mbsahome.mspx.

Evaluate End-User Compliance and Acceptance

Establishing well-written policies and procedures is one of the first steps in securing a corporation's digital assets. However, if end users find the policies and procedures cumbersome or annoying, their productivity may be inhibited and they may find ways to circumvent them.

It is important to periodically review the effectiveness of currently implemented policies and procedures. To determine the frequency at which these reviews should occur, you need to consider a combination of the resources available, compliance issues, and business needs.

Develop and Use a List of Common Infractions

Experienced information systems auditors have stories that illustrate the common ways policies are abused. Gather their stories and your own, and keep a list of these abuses. This provides you with a starting point from which to evaluate end-user compliance. If you do nothing more than ensure that these abuses, if they exist, are uncovered and corrected in your environment, you will have improved the security of your information systems. Several examples of what to evaluate are described next.

Look for Physical Security Breaches

A typical example of how simple noncompliance can impact information security is the common practice of propping open external fire doors to provide extra ventilation or to allow access for smokers who do not want to walk to designated smoking areas. These open fire doors provide additional access points into the facility and significantly increase the potential for unauthorized access by outsiders. Many individuals do not recognize the threat posed by providing access to unauthorized outsiders and feel that leaving fire doors open is "no big deal." However, leaving these doors open provides outsiders access to employees, corporate assets, and the corporate network. Employees can be attacked, property can be stolen (including computers and other digital devices), and proprietary data can be accessed (because everyone leaves their computers turned on and logged in).

Look for Password Sharing

Information security policies and procedures are bypassed frequently. Employees often share usernames and passwords with other employees who have forgotten their passwords. Or employees may provide usernames and passwords to visitors so that they can use the Internet or print off documents for a meeting or presentation. Once again, employees share this information usually only because they don't understand the risks involved. If accounts are shared, it becomes difficult if not impossible to track and log normal employee activity, thereby making it much more difficult (and therefore more expensive) to identify a breach of the network. If the account is shared with multiple people, multiple people can be logged in at different times, but the logs show that only one person has been logging in. Are these logins authorized? What data is being accessed? Sharing accounts with visitors provides them with access to the network while onsite, but will the same username and password grant them access remotely? By sharing an account, users inadvertently provide information on the naming conventions used by their organization. This provides the opportunity to try to log in as another employee; all they need to do is start guessing passwords.

Review Executive Computer Use

Some individuals will not follow policies and procedures because they feel their position grants them the authority to ignore standard protocol. This sort of activity can put systems and businesses at risk. Very often, the worst offenders are those employees who "should know better"—IT staff and executive management, people who have access to critical data and systems.

In one organization, the senior vice president would constantly open questionable e-mail attachments, regularly infecting his computer with a virus. He would also install unauthorized software, often causing necessary work-related software to function erratically. The support and help desk costs for this one individual equaled the support and help desks costs for all other employees combined. In addition, lost productivity from one of the highest-paid employees in the firm added additional costs to his behavior. His attitude and behavior also had a trickle-down effect to other employees. The attitude was, if the senior VP doesn't follow proper procedures and protocols, they shouldn't have to either. The cost to the company was so significant that raises and promotions were suspended and salaries were cut by 10 percent. This example demonstrates why it is critical that executive management support security initiatives, procedures, and protocols.

From an IT perspective, system administrators often require users to have unique and complex passwords, but do not enforce the policy on themselves. Network devices

HEADS UP!

When conducting periodic evaluations, keep in mind that many people will be on their best behavior during the review process. Many people will provide the answers they know the reviewers want to hear, while others will provide the "right" answers so that they look like loyal and dedicated employees. In many organizations, the reviews are conducted on the same dates every year and are announced in advance. It can be extremely valuable to perform these reviews in a random fashion, without any advance notice (although, to avoid problems, they should be conducted with management approval). If the reviews are conducted unexpectedly, the findings of the review will be much more valuable.

often have default passwords or easy-to-guess passwords, making the network extremely vulnerable. Passwords based on *Star Wars*, *Star Trek*, and *The Lord of the Rings* characters are extremely popular, as are terms related to sex, sports, and foul language. Utilizing these types of passwords makes guessing passwords that much easier.

It is important that all members of an organization comply with security policies and procedures. Otherwise, regardless of technical mechanisms put in place, the corporate network and the data it contains is still extremely vulnerable.

Conduct Informal Evaluations

Many organizations conduct periodic reviews of their security processes and procedures but limit the reviews to formal, "between the lines" reviews, conducted by following step-by-step checklists or by using automated tools to check security implementations. Although extremely valuable, these formal reviews should not be the only review process implemented. The following sections discuss some of the informal evaluations that you may find valuable.

Conduct Informal Interviews

Having open lines of communication between users and IT staff is an important part of the security process. Open lines of communication are usually created over a period of time, but the process can be started by informal interviews of users. These "interviews" can be conducted by walking through departments, introducing yourself, and asking questions such as the following:

- *Have you received a copy of the new acceptable use policy? Do you have any questions about it?* These questions can help provide insight as to whether the distribution methods for new policies are effective. If a user has no questions about it, it may mean they either understand it perfectly or have yet to read it.
- *Are you having any problems with your computer?* Although this can lead to "How do I do this?" type questions, responses like "I'm having a hard time accessing my e-mail" or "Our accounting program is extremely slow today" may indicate a security problem. The inability to access resources may be caused by a denial of service attack, corrupted or deleted resources, hardware failure, or malicious code. These comments should be taken seriously and investigated.
- *Did you get the latest virus alert?* This is another question that can demonstrate effectiveness of information distribution methods. It can also provide the opportunity for the user to ask additional questions about viruses and other malware (malicious code).
- *Do you know how to identify and report a security issue?* Users must understand both how to identify a security issue and how to report it. A security issue will remain unresolved if a user can identify it but does not know how to report it, or if a user knows proper reporting procedures but cannot identify the security issue.

Informal interviews should be considered only part of the review process, since they may not cover all departments equally. However, an informal process has numerous advantages, including the following:

- **Spontaneous answers** Since users are unaware that a review is underway, they do not have time to prepare answers.
- **More honest responses** Formal reviews can be intimidating for some people, who may respond more honestly in an informal setting.
- **More numerous responses** Informal interviews make IT professionals more approachable and may provide an opportunity for an employee to proactively report a problem or a concern.

Conduct Periodic Walk-Throughs

Taking the time to periodically walk through departments can be extremely educational. These walk-throughs should be used to look for any policy violations or other security problems. Things to look for include passwords written down and posted in conspicuous locations, computers turned on and logged in when users are not present, and the open sharing of passwords between employees. If numerous policy violations are identified, it may indicate that either enforcement policies are not being followed or additional end-user training is required.

To be effective, walk-throughs should be done randomly, on different days and different times.

NOTE Walk-throughs should not be used to "write up" personnel for policy violations or to confront violators. Walk-throughs should be used as information-gathering tools only. If significant disciplinary action is administered as a result of walk-throughs, they eventually become less effective because violators simply become more covert in their actions. In addition, those who conduct the walk-throughs will be looked upon as "enforcers," which makes them less approachable. Obviously, significant violations have to be handled immediately, especially those that may require criminal prosecution.

Review Help Desk Logs

Reviewing help desk logs can be extremely helpful in determining the effectiveness and acceptance of new security implementations. If help desk logs contain a disproportionate volume of calls regarding problems with security mechanisms and procedures, it may be time to reevaluate those mechanisms and procedures. This does not necessarily mean that you need to change anything, but you should conduct a review to verify that the latest security changes have not created a productivity problem.

Many people will complain about new implementations or procedures simply because they are not comfortable with the changes. Obviously, the number of help desk calls will increase immediately after security mechanisms are added or changed, but should drop off after a period of time. If the number of calls does not drop off after a significant

ONE STEP FURTHER

Since unauthorized wireless access points are a significant threat to an organization, it might be beneficial to carry a wireless access point finder on your periodic walk-throughs. Several devices exist that can be carried covertly if necessary. Products include the following:

- **Chrysalis WiFi Seeker** http://www.wifiseeker.com/
- **Kensington WiFi Finder** http://www.kensington.com/html/3720.html
- **Smart ID WFS-1** http://www.smartid.com.sg/prod01.htm
- **Zap Checker** http://www.zapchecker.com

If a wireless signal is found, document the location and discreetly contact another member of the IT security team and let them conduct a thorough search for the access point. When the access point is discovered, corporate policy regarding the removal of the access point should be followed. If at all possible, the identity of the individual or individuals that installed the access point should be determined, and disciplinary actions should be taken. To maintain the effectiveness of the wireless access point discovery process, be sure that the discovery methodologies are not revealed.

period of time, it could indicate that additional training needs to be conducted or that the new security implementation was misconfigured. It does not mean that the security mechanisms should be removed, just reconfigured. Determining the amount of time to wait to evaluate the volume of help desk calls depends on the complexity of the new security implementations and the size of the organization. But the number of calls should drop off after two to four weeks.

NOTE Reviewing help desk logs can also help identify security problems or breaches. Numerous callers complaining of slow system performance or the inability to access particular system resources may indicate an attack is underway. In environments where intruder lockouts are enabled, numerous callers requesting the resetting of accounts because users are locked out may indicate that a brute-force attack is being conducted.

Conduct Formal Reviews

Informal evaluations are helpful because they can identify any problems and issues that arise in between more formal and in-depth evaluations. But conducting formal, structured evaluations is the best way to identify problems and issues. Formal evaluations provide the opportunity to benchmark security postures and to document good-faith efforts to protect corporate systems and data, as required by government regulations.

Conduct Surveys of Employees

Surveys provide the opportunity to craft relevant questions and to perform statistical analysis on the results. The advantage of conducting surveys is that everyone has participated in a survey at one time or another. Whether filling out a paper form, answering questions during a phone or live interview, or participating in an online survey, surveys have become a large part of an information-based economy. The disadvantages of conducting surveys are that some people consider them intrusive and annoying, and it is extremely difficult to get 100 percent participation. However, for organizations that are large or dispersed over a large geographic area, surveys may be the best method for collecting feedback from employees regarding security issues and mechanisms.

Creating and conducting surveys requires specialized skills and proper planning. Although it is designed to address large-scale public surveys, the *What Is a Survey?* series by the American Statistical Association (ASA) is an excellent place to start, http://www.amstat.org/sections/srms/whatsurvey.html.

There are numerous vendors that provide survey solutions, including Hosted Survey, http://www.hostedsurvey.com, SurveyView, http://www.surveyview.com, and

HEADS UP!

It is extremely important to craft survey questions properly. This excerpt from the ASA brochure *What Is a Survey?* demonstrates this point extremely well (http://www.amstat.org/sections/srms/brochures/survwhat.html):

> For example, a recent NBC/Wall Street Journal poll asked two very similar questions with very different results: (1) Do you favor cutting programs such as social security, Medicare, Medicaid, and farm subsidies to reduce the budget deficit? The results: 23% favor; 66% oppose; 11% no opinion. (2) Do you favor cutting government entitlements to reduce the budget deficit? The results: 61% favor; 25% oppose; 14% no opinion.

Applying this concept to information security–related questions is fairly straightforward. If a company requires users to utilize alphanumeric passwords with a minimum length of eight characters, the company might ask a survey question such as, "Do you find eight-character passwords difficult to remember?" This question might elicit a different percentage of yes and no answers if asked this way, "Do you find eight-character passwords so difficult to remember you must write them down?"

By understanding that questions can be interpreted differently by different people, the results of a survey can be more accurately interpreted. For additional information on designing surveys, see *Designing Surveys: A Guide to Decisions and Procedures* (Pine Forge, 1996) by Ronald Czaja and Johnny Blair. (The second edition of the book is scheduled to be released December 2004.)

Insiteful Surveys, http://www.insitefulsurveys.com/. If you conduct a search on the Internet, you will find numerous other vendors of survey tools and software.

Conduct Regularly Scheduled Meetings

Meeting with different departments at regularly scheduled times provides an excellent opportunity to learn what security issues each department faces and provides the IT staff the opportunity to provide updates and information on currently implemented processes and procedures, and those that will be implemented in the future.

When planning these meetings, be sure to distribute an agenda prior to the meeting so that all members can be prepared and the time allotted for the meeting is used effectively. Topics for discussion may include the following:

- Recent problems or incidents
- Pending legislation, federal or state, that will impact the business
- Future wants and needs of each department, including hardware and software requirements
- If applicable, growth and expansion of particular departments
- Explanation of new policies and procedures

End the meeting with positive comments regarding the department's support of security initiatives. These meetings should be used for both information-gathering purposes and information-dissemination purposes. The frequency with which these meetings are scheduled should depend on the technological sophistication of each department. Departments that utilize and embrace technology require more frequent meetings. Departments that consider technology a necessary evil may require less frequent meetings. To be effective, be sure to respect participants' time, or the value of these meetings could be reduced.

Use Checklists

As part of the review process, it can be extremely useful to compare implemented processes and procedures with a checklist of either required or recommended processes and procedures. Using a checklist of *required* processes and procedures helps to ensure that the required level of security is being maintained and that regulatory compliance is being maintained. Utilizing a checklist of *recommended* processes and procedures can allow a business to determine how its systems compare with industry recommendations and best practices.

Organizations can create their own checklists, but creating checklists from scratch can be an extremely time-consuming process. Numerous published checklists are available that either can be used as a starting point to create a custom checklist or can be used "as is" after being reviewed and approved by the security team. Checklists are available that provide an opportunity to review settings and configurations of specific applications and operating systems, as well as to review the enterprise-wide security posture.

A search on the Internet for the phrase "security checklists" provides thousands of possible resources, among them AuditNet (http://www.auditnet.org). But the most-cited resources are the checklists provided by the National Institute of Standards and Technology (NIST) Computer Security Resource Center (CSRC), which are available for numerous operating systems and applications (http://csrc.nist.gov/pcig/cig.html). In addition, the *Security Self-Assessment Guide for Information Technology Systems*, written by Marianne Swanson of NIST, is an extremely detailed checklist that includes valuable information on conducting self-assessments (http://www.csrc.nist.gov/publications/nistpubs/800-26/sp800-26.pdf). Figure 20-1 shows a section from this checklist.

NIST has taken this checklist and developed an automated process for its completion, ASSET (Automated Security Self-Evaluation Tool). This tool is a freely downloadable software program that includes the questions from the *Security Self-Assessment Guide for Information Systems* and has mechanisms in place to help ensure proper completion of the checklist. In addition, various reports can be created that allow for an accurate review of the assessment results. Figure 20-2 shows the interface for ASSET.

Appendix A
System Questionnaire

11. Data Integrity

Data integrity controls are used to protect data from accidental or malicious alteration or destruction and to provide assurance to the user the information meets expectations about its quality and integrity. The following questions are organized according to two critical elements. The levels for each of these critical elements should be determined based on the answers to the subordinate questions.

Specific Control Objectives and Techniques	L.1 Policy	L.2 Procedures	L.3 Implemented	L.4 Tested	L.5 Integrated	Risk Based Decision Made	Comments	Initials
Data Integrity *OMB Circular A-130, 8B3*								
11.1 Critical Element: Is virus detection and elimination sofware installed and activated?								
11.1.1 Are virus signature files routinely updated? *NIST SP 800-18*								
11.1.2 Are virus scans automatic? *NIST SP 800-18*								
11.2 Critical Element: Are data integrity and validation controls used to provide assurance that the information has not been altered and the system functions as intended?								
11.2.1 Are reconciliation routines used by applications, i.e., checksums, hash totals, record counts? *NIST SP 800-18*								
11.2.2 Is inappropriate or unusual activity reported, investigated, and appropriate actions taken? *FISCAM SS-2.2*								
11.2.3 Are procedures in place to determine compliance with password policies? *NIST SP 800-18*								

A-34

Figure 20-1. Sample questions from the *Security Self Assessment Guide for Information Technology Systems*

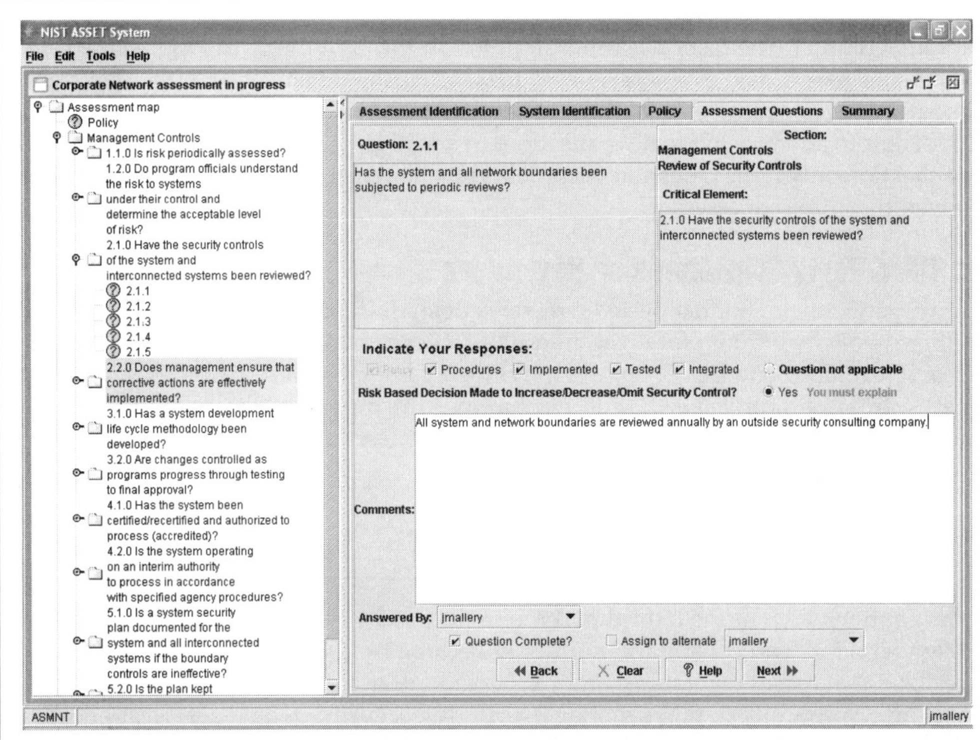

Figure 20-2. ASSET—Automated Security Self-Evaluation Tool

HEADS UP!

Checklists are a great tool to assist with reviewing security policies and procedures. However, as with all other tools, checklists have some limitations. It is important to recognize that a Yes response to a particular question does not necessarily indicate a totally secure environment. For example, a self-assessment checklist/questionnaire might include the following question, "Are all doors to the network operations center equipped with locks?" A Yes answer to this question does not necessarily mean the NOC is secure. Why? The locks may be inadequate or of poor design, or employees may never actually lock the doors. So on the surface, answering Yes, the doors have locks, does not mean the doors are secure.

Because checklists are often not detailed enough, they should never be considered a substitute for a penetration test or network vulnerability assessment. Checklists allow for human frailties such as dishonesty and laziness to impact the results. Automated vulnerability assessments provide more concrete, impartial results. Information on penetration testing and vulnerability assessments can be found in Chapter 17.

When you are answering questions using this tool, it provides guides to ensure that you fully complete the responses and do not rush through them. In Figure 20-2, the question has received a Yes response, next to which is the statement "You must explain." If information is not entered into the Comments text box, the program will not allow the assessor to advance to the next question. In addition, it is possible to advance to the next question only if the Question Complete? box has been checked or the question is assigned to a different assessor.

Use Third-Party Consultants or Reviewers

Many organizations conduct periodic reviews using in-house staff. This can be useful but there is plenty of room for error. Internal staff can be hindered by politics, lack of time and resources, and lack of objectivity. Utilizing objective third parties has significant benefits. Internal political issues do not hamper third parties. They also have the time and resources available to keep abreast of the latest security issues and updates.

HEADS UP!

Use caution when hiring a third party to review security policies and procedures. Many vendors and consultants suddenly became "security experts" when they realized that recent regulations and a renewed interest in security meant that there was an opportunity to make money by offering security-related services. These "experts" often have no formal security training and have no significant experience with security tools and issues. When engaging the services of a consultant, be sure to undertake due diligence to verify that they can properly perform the services requested. Do not take their qualifications and expertise at face value; ask for references and contact those references. Ask for résumés or CVs for the key parties who will be conducting the work. And once the work has been initiated, be sure that the technicians are the ones for whom résumés were presented. Some unscrupulous vendors provide résumés of qualified individuals during the negotiating process but then provide unqualified individuals to perform the work.

Many companies state that they use only "certified technicians." This is extremely vague—certified in what? If your business runs strictly Linux and the technicians are only certified in Windows 2000, be extremely cautious, because they do not have the skill sets needed for the project. Conduct research prior to the engagement to determine what industry-recognized certifications apply to the work you wish to have performed. Be certain that the certifications presented by the consultant are up to date and respected by the industry. Be leery of companies that profess expertise with regulatory compliance, especially if they profess knowledge of a regulated industry but have few if any clients in that industry.

They often have received specialized security training and are provided the opportunity to keep certifications up to date. And most importantly, third parties provide a different perspective that may uncover problems that had been previously overlooked.

Include Physical Security in the Review Process

Restricting physical access to information systems hardware is a critical part of maintaining the security of corporate systems and data. Unfortunately, many IT professionals overlook this fact because they feel physical security is not their responsibility. This is a dangerous and narrow-minded attitude. During the review process, the following issues should be addressed and evaluated:

- **Access control systems and policies** Is access to server rooms, wiring closets, and data centers restricted to only those employees who need access as part of their job responsibilities? Are keys and access cards promptly recovered from terminated employees?
- **CCTV (closed circuit television) and monitoring review** Are critical resources monitored by CCTV cameras? Do security professionals (i.e., guards) monitor those cameras? Are the cameras connected to a recording device? If the cameras are recording activity, are the images detailed enough to allow law enforcement to identify the intruder?
- **Background checks** Are background checks conducted on all employees who have access to data? Are additional background checks conducted at the time of promotion or change in status (e.g., if they are now granted access to financial records)? Are credit checks routinely conducted on employees who have access to financial records or have the ability to pay vendors or business partners?
- **Perimeter security** Is the perimeter of the building completely secure? As an example, is the loading dock door open with only a sleeping security guard on duty?
- **Disaster response and recovery** Are disaster response programs in place and tested on a regular basis? Are the backup generators thoroughly tested under a full load?
- **Placement of equipment** Is critical hardware thoroughly secured? Are servers located against glass walls or windows that could easily be shattered or breached? Is equipment located in areas that are free from environmental hazards—heat, water, and chemicals?
- **Alarm systems** Have alarm systems been thoroughly tested? Are the proper personnel notified in a timely manner when an alarm is triggered? If an alarm notifies the police, what is their response time? (With the incredible number of false alarms that plague police, their response times can be inconsistent at best.)

ONE STEP FURTHER

The trend in the security industry is for security professionals to develop skills in both physical security and information security. This is because the systems that house proprietary data need to be physically protected and many physical security devices are now running on standard TCP/IP networks. Several resources are available to the IT professional who wants to gain an understanding of physical security concepts. These include ASIS International (formerly the American Society for Industrial Security), a trade group that addresses all areas of the security industry. Its publication, *Security Management*, is considered by many to be the leading resource for security professionals. This group also offers regional security-related training. Its annual conference brings in more than 17,000 attendees. To learn more about this group, visit http://www.asisonline.org.

Another valuable free resource is *Security Technology & Design* magazine, for which this author is a contributing editor. Both physical and logical security issues are addressed by this publication. The most recent issue and subscription information can be viewed at http://www.securityinfowatch.com/magazine/std.jsp. There are also several popular books that are extremely useful for those who are new to physical security concepts, including the classic *Introduction to Security, Seventh Edition*, by Robert J. Fischer and Gion Green (Butterworth-Heinemann, 2003), and *Effective Physical Security, Third Edition*, by Lawrence J. Finelly (Butterworth-Heinemann, 2003).

Conduct Post-Event Reviews

Networks and systems do not exist in a vacuum. They are constantly being reconfigured, patched, upgraded, and connected to additional systems. The dynamic nature of networks means that the "once yearly is enough" attitude toward security reviews is unrealistic and impractical. Nor are periodic reviews (such as once a quarter) the only reviews that should be undertaken. Many events have an impact on a system or network and generate the need for an additional security review. Some examples of events that should trigger a security review are discussed in this section.

Conduct a Review After Major Infrastructure Changes

Introducing a new operating system into a network can introduce new vulnerabilities and require changes to policies and procedures. It is important to ensure that all new systems are patched, unnecessary services are removed, unneeded ports are closed, and any other hardening steps advised for that specific OS are followed. The staff that is responsible for supporting the new OS needs to receive additional training. If the new OS is implemented to support a new application, the application requires review as well. If at all possible, the new application should be reviewed in a lab environment prior to being rolled out on production systems. New policies and procedures have to be developed to address the new application.

Additional infrastructure changes that might require a security review include (but are not limited to) the following:

- Adding or moving to a new e-mail server
- Adding or upgrading a database server
- Implementing an enterprise resource planning (ERP) product
- Adding, upgrading, or expanding accounting and human resources software
- Adding new hardware such as routers, switches, and firewalls
- Adding an IP-based CCTV system
- Adding a Voice over IP product
- Adding a new network segment
- Developing and deploying an in-house application

These are only examples, but they demonstrate the types of infrastructure changes that warrant a security review.

Conduct a Review After a Merger or Acquisition

When businesses are combined through either a merger or acquisition, multiple networks and systems are suddenly connected, which can pose a significant threat if a security review is not conducted. Policies and procedures between systems will be completely different; for example, one organization may allow certain activities that the other organization strictly prohibits, or one organization may have a strong security stance while the other organization may not consider security to be a priority.

NOTE Because conducting a security review is critical after businesses combine, budgeting for the review should be part of the planning process of mergers and acquisitions.

Conduct a Review After Discovery of New Threats or Vulnerabilities

New threats and vulnerabilities are discovered on a frequent basis. This fact frustrates many system administrators who feel that operating systems and applications should be secure before they are offered for sale. Although developers should take extra steps to ensure that they create secure code and products, it is unrealistic to expect all software releases to be 100 percent secure. In her May 26, 2003, Forbes.com article, "The Exterminator" (http://www.forbes.com/global/2003/0526/056.html), Victoria Murphy describes part of the problem: "The Windows operating system has 50 million lines of code (a line averages 60 characters) and grows 20% with every release. It's put together by 7,200 people, comes in 34 languages and has to support 190,000 devices—different models of digital cameras, printers, handhelds and so on." With that many lines of code and that many developers, it becomes easier to understand why flaws and issues exist in Microsoft Windows OSs. And because most OSs and enterprise software also include large amounts of code and are developed by teams of programmers, flaws and issues exist in nearly all software. These flaws are often overlooked until the software is installed and utilized in a production environment. When these flaws lead to security issues, one of several things can happen:

- If unscrupulous individuals discover the flaws, they may develop malicious code that exploits those flaws. They may then release this new malicious code on the Internet, making it available to hackers around the world.
- If the product developers or security professionals discover the flaws, they can quickly develop patches or fixes and make them available to users of the vulnerable product. They can post notices of the vulnerabilities and patches on numerous web sites and distribute them electronically as quickly as possible so that the threat can be minimized. Of course, posting these vulnerabilities and threats is a double-edged sword, because it also notifies attackers that they now have another opportunity to compromise a system. Therefore, it is extremely critical to keep up to date on the latest flaws, threats, and vulnerabilities.

There are several methods that allow system administrators and security professionals to keep current with the latest threats and vulnerabilities. One method is to periodically review security-related web sites for the latest threats and vulnerabilities. An excellent place to start is the site belonging to the United States Computer Emergency Readiness Team, US-CERT, http://www.us-cert.gov/cas/techalerts/index.html. This site lists current activities and the latest alerts. Other sites that offer valuable information include SecurityFocus, http://www.securityfocus.com/bid, and the SANS Institute's Internet Storm Center, http://isc.sans.org/.

Most system administrators are too busy to visit web sites to learn about the latest threats and vulnerabilities. Fortunately, several sites provide the opportunity to sign up for newsletters and alerts. For US-CERT, visit http://www.us-cert.gov/cas/signup.html. The SANS Institute provides *@RISK: The Consensus Security Alert*; to subscribe, visit http://www.sans.org/newsletters/.

In addition to subscribing to alerts, it is extremely beneficial to sign up for security-related mailing lists, often referred to as listservs. These provide the opportunity to see what security-related issues and questions other people may be facing. The greatest benefit of subscribing to these mailing lists is that you have the opportunity to post your own questions to the list. Very often, your questions are answered quickly by other list members, which can help you to resolve your problems more efficiently. Two popular mailing lists are Full-Disclosure and bugtraq. To subscribe to Full-Disclosure, sign up at http://lists.netsys.com/mailman/listinfo/full-disclosure. For bugtraq, send an e-mail to bugtraq-subscribe@securityfocus.com.

The alerts and mailing lists previously described cover multiple issues and multiple platforms. You should subscribe to vendor-specific alerts and mailing lists for products that are being utilized in your environment. As an example, Cisco Systems provides an alert mailing list, cust-security-announce@cisco.com, and a discussion mailing list, cust-security-discuss@cisco.com. Information on subscribing to both mailing lists can be found at http://www.cisco.com/en/US/products/products_security_vulnerability_policy.html. All major vendors have alert notification lists and many have other mailing lists as well.

NOTE When determining which resources to utilize to research new vulnerabilities, keep in mind how much time you have available to read material. If you subscribe to every possible mailing list and alert service, you will become overwhelmed and miss significant updates and notifications. Start out with recommended resources and then reduce the volume of information you receive by unsubscribing to the lists you find the least helpful.

Another method to keep up to date with security issues is to subscribe to Really Simple Syndication (RSS) feeds and view them in an aggregator. RSS is an XML standard that allows publishers to quickly and easily share information. A simple-to-use RSS aggregator is BottomFeeder, http://www.cincomsmalltalk.com/BottomFeeder/. (Additional information on RSS readers can be found at http://blogspace.com/rss/readers.) The advantage of using an RSS aggregator is that all alerts and news headlines can be found in one location without having to spend time surfing through numerous web pages. Several useful RSS channels are listed here:

- **US-CERT Technical Cyber Security Alerts** http://www.us-cert.gov/channels/techalerts.rdf
- **SecurityFocus News** http://www.securityfocus.com/rss/news.xml
- **Virus.org** http://www.virus.org/backend.php
- **SANS Security Alerts** http://www.sans.org/alerts/rss/

Regardless of the method used to retrieve information on vulnerabilities and issues, it is important to consistently review these reports and to have a mechanism in place that addresses reported vulnerabilities for software that is used in your organization. Most businesses have patch-management programs in place that address vulnerabilities in OSs and enterprise-wide applications. But it is important to be prepared to address vulnerabilities in applications that are used by single departments or small groups of users, because these applications may be overlooked by the corporate patch-management program. Other programs that are often overlooked include applications that are not officially authorized but are allowed to exist because they appear to be "harmless enough." These applications are usually installed for user convenience, such as desktop weather programs, stock market feeds, etc., which many administrators know are installed but turn a blind eye to because they don't appear to pose a threat to the network.

The person (or persons) who is reviewing vulnerability reports must have the ability to verify what applications are actually used in the organization. A company can put its systems in a precarious position if someone says to him- or herself, "This vulnerability does not apply to us because I don't *think* we use that particular application." They need to know what applications are installed and be in a position to protect them or disable them should they suddenly pose a security threat. As an example, if a stock market feed suddenly poses a threat, the administrator should be able to immediately block the feed at the firewall, either by blocking a particular port or by blocking feed requests from inside the network.

When evaluating new threats, it is extremely important to look beyond your own systems and networks, and often beyond technology, to current global issues. Many businesses began a security review within minutes after the attacks of September 11, 2001. They recognized that if the country was being attacked, their systems might become targets.

In addition, political activists may suddenly target your company because it has released a controversial new product or has merged with a company that is a target. Actions of a country's government or military may cause businesses in that country to become the focus of attacks. For example, after the April 1, 2001, incident in which a U.S. Navy surveillance plane collided with a Chinese military jet and had to make an emergency landing in China, Chinese activists began defacing web sites of U.S. businesses in response.

ONE STEP FURTHER

If your business is involved in activities that draw unwelcome attention from activists, it is a good idea to proactively monitor the activities of well-known activist groups, which includes periodically reviewing their web sites, attending their local public demonstrations, and identifying their local branches or chapters. This monitoring can often provide advance notice of businesses that are going to be targeted for demonstrations or "attacks." The following are some of the groups that have received "recognition" for their aggressive activities:

- **People for the Ethical Treatment of Animals (PETA)**
  http://www.peta.org/alert/index.asp
- **Earth Liberation Front (ELF)**
  http://www.earthliberationfront.com/main.shtml
- **Animal Liberation Front (ALF)**
  http://www.animalliberationfront.com/

If you find that your company is described in an unflattering way on one of these web sites, be concerned. Although these groups have not been known to utilize technology to attack the targets of their ire, it is probably just a matter of time.

Political activists that use technology to forward their goals are often referred to as "hacktivists." One group, The Electronic Disturbance Theatre, encourages the use of "Electronic Civil Disobedience." An example of electronic civil disobedience is the Zapatista FloodNet, which targeted a Mexican government web site and reloaded its web page several times a minute. Hacktivists believe that if enough people utilized the tool at the same time, they could stop or slow legitimate traffic to the site. Slowing traffic is combined with the presentation of a political message, as described by Brett Stalbaum in "The Zapatista Tactical FloodNet" (http://www.thing.net/~rdom/ecd/ZapTact.html):

> As FloodNet performs automatic reloads of the site in the background, slowing or halting access to the targeted server, FloodNet also encourages interaction on the part of individual protesters. Netsurfers may voice their political concerns on a targeted server via the "personal message" form which sends the surfer's own statement to the server error log. Additionally, a mouse click on the applet image (containing a representation of the targeted site), sends a predefined message to the server error log.

Although this tool is believed by many to have had limited impact, it does demonstrate that activists are moving their "demonstrations" to the Internet. Figure 20-3 shows the FloodNet web site as it looked during the Zapatista demonstration.

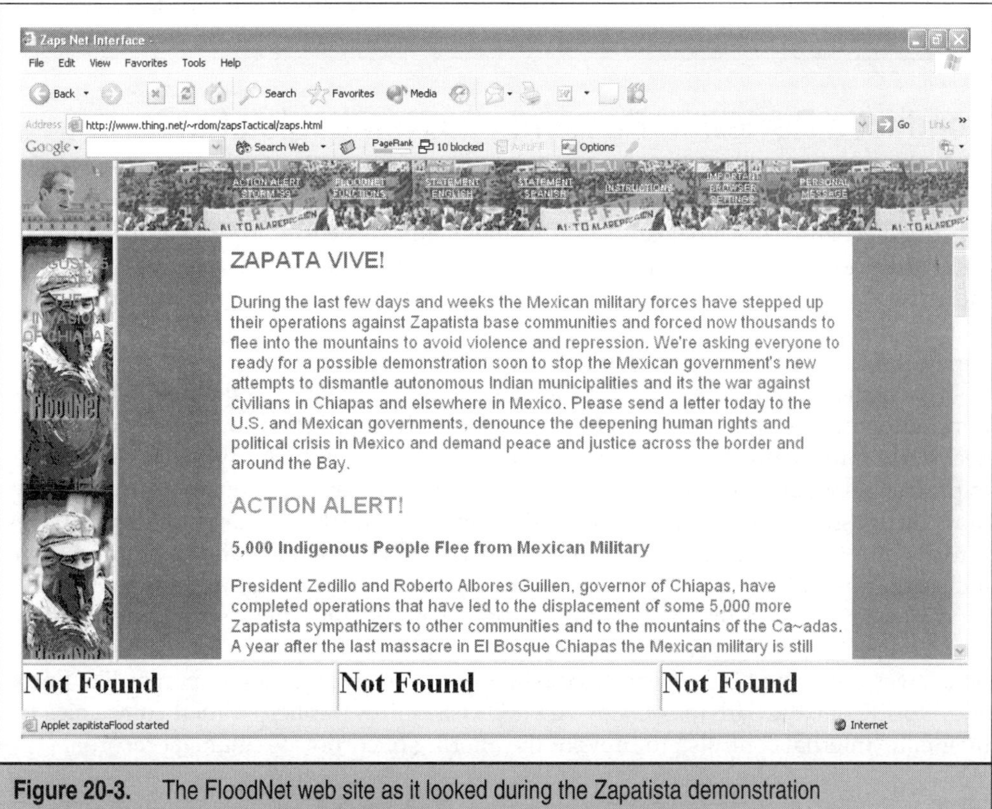

Figure 20-3. The FloodNet web site as it looked during the Zapatista demonstration

Conduct a Review if Employee Productivity Drops

Even with proper planning, it is possible that new security mechanisms, including policies, may slow employee productivity. If system performance is reduced to the point where employees are unable to effectively perform their duties, it would be prudent to conduct another security review. Questions to ask include the following:

- Are the current security mechanisms appropriate or simply overkill?
- Is the poor performance the result of a security mechanism or simply improper configuration of an application?
- Can employee re-education solve the problem?
- Has a security mechanism failed, causing a system breach that allows unwanted traffic into the network?
- Has a networking device such as a router or switch failed?

NOTE Take seriously employee complaints about system performance. This is often easier said than done, because any degradation in performance will elicit complaints. But if you develop a good working relationship with employees, determining when their complaints are legitimate should be much easier.

Conduct a Review in Response to New Legislation

The U.S. government has for a long time been asking businesses to protect their systems and data. Many businesses have complied willingly, while others think that implementing security mechanisms is too costly and thus have done little to comply. Because of the latter attitude, the government has been adopting new legislation requiring specific industries to implement security policies and procedures. The driving force behind many of these acts is the significant rise in identity theft and the inappropriate use of personal information by businesses.

Two of the acts that have received the most attention recently are the Health Insurance Portability and Accountability Act (HIPAA), which is designed to protect personal healthcare information, and the Gramm-Leach-Bliley Act (GLBA), which is designed to protect personal financial information. These acts are far reaching and impact many more businesses than people realize. Initially aimed at the healthcare industry, HIPAA actually impacts any business that maintains records of personal healthcare information, including internal personnel records. Although GLBA was designed to target banks primarily, any business that maintains personal financial information, such as universities and colleges that process student loans, must comply with the act. A more recent act, which was developed in response to the financial shenanigans of companies like Enron and WorldCom, the Sarbanes-Oxley Act (SOX), requires publicly traded companies to maintain "internal controls" to prevent the altering of corporate financial records.

These regulations are quite detailed and impact many industries and businesses. If you are unfamiliar with these regulations, it is recommended that you take the time to learn as much as you can about them. Information on these regulations can be found at the following web sites:

- **Gramm-Leach-Bliley Act** http://www.ftc.gov/privacy/glbact/index.html
- **Health Insurance Portability and Accountability Act** The original statute, which includes the finalized Privacy and Security Rules, can be downloaded at http://www.hhs.gov/ocr/hipaa/
- **Sarbanes-Oxley Act** http://www.pcaobus.org/rules/Sarbanes_Oxley_Act_of_2002.pdf

The federal government is not the only entity enacting security-related acts. The state of California enacted the Security Breach Information Act on July 1, 2003. This act requires "Any agency that owns or licenses computerized data that includes personal information shall disclose any breach of the security of the system following discovery or notification of the breach in the security of the data to any resident of California whose unencrypted personal information was, or is reasonably believed to have been, acquired by an unauthorized person." The entire bill can be found at http://info.sen.ca.gov/pub/01-02/bill/sen/sb_1351-1400/sb_1386_bill_20020926_chaptered.html.

Businesses and their internal IT security teams must be aware of not only enacted legislation but also industry guidelines. Although industry guidelines often are not enforced, if a company has had a security breach or problem that could have been avoided by following industry guidelines, it can quickly find itself embroiled in costly litigation. An example is a guideline released by the U.S. Food and Drug Administration in November of 2003, *Retail Food Stores and Food Service Establishments: Food Security Preventive Measures Guidance* (http://www.cfsan.fda.gov/~dms/secgui11.html). Under the section, "Access to Computer Systems," the guideline states:

> FDA recommends that retail food store and food service establishment operators consider:
>
> - Restricting access to critical computer data systems to those with appropriate clearance (for example, using passwords, firewalls)
> - Eliminating computer access when a staff member is no longer associated with the establishment
> - Establishing a system of traceability of computer transactions
> - Reviewing the adequacy of virus protection systems and procedures for backing up critical computer-based data systems
> - Validating the computer security system

Not only is current legislation going to be modified, additional legislation will be enacted if businesses do not take adequate steps to protect their data and systems. As reported on About.com on July 11, 2003, the chairman of the House Government Reform Subcommittee on Technology, Representative Adam Putnam (R-Florida), "...plans to introduce legislation to mandate minimum baselines security standards for the private sector. Mr. Putnam feels that the private sector has not done enough on its own to secure its networks and it is time for standards to be mandated" (from "Pending Legislation to Mandate Computer Security," http://netsecurity.about.com/b/a/007727.htm). Although Putnam's initial cybersecurity bill was tabled after vendor pressure (http://www.computerworld.com/governmenttopics/government/policy/story/0,10801,86984,00.html), he is still pushing for information security reforms. In June 2004, he and Representative Tom Davis (R-VA) introduced an amendment to the Clinger Cohen Act, bill HR 4570, which will require federal agencies to "...include cybersecurity as a requirement for systems planning and acquisition by agencies and to provide the Office of Management and Budget greater authority in guiding agencies on information security issues" (http://reform.house.gov/TIPRC/News/DocumentPrint.aspx?DocumentID=4289).

Representative Putnam is not the only politician trying to pass computer security–related legislation. In June 2003, Senator Diane Feinstein of California introduced the Notification of Risk to Personal Data Act (S. 1350), which would require government agencies and businesses involved in interstate commerce to disclose unauthorized access of personal information. It is only a matter of time before the federal government enacts cybersecurity legislation. The contents of S. 1350 can be found at http://thomas.loc.gov/cgi-bin/query/z?c108:S.1350.IS:.

As new legislation is enacted, it is important to conduct a security review to analyze whether your business will be impacted directly or indirectly by the legislation and what, if any, new mechanisms need to be implemented to maintain compliance with this legislation.

Conduct a Review in Response to a Failed Compliance Audit

If the government regulates your business sector and your company fails a compliance audit, it is recommended that you conduct a security review. It is important to determine why a particular security requirement was overlooked or misapplied. Has your organization misinterpreted the legislation? Are there gaps in either the security review process or the security audit process? Is your firm lacking the mechanisms to stay informed on current changes in legislation and compliance requirements?

As an example, one part of the Gramm-Leach-Bliley Act requires that the management and board of a financial institution must adequately oversee their organization's information security program. Even if an organization is in the process of improving its information security program, if it does not communicate its progress to management or the board, the organization may fail an audit. If it does fail, it needs to review its reporting processes and procedures to ensure that it does not fail future audits.

Conduct a Review in Response to a Breach or Incident

Perhaps the most critical event for an organization is when systems are breached or security incidents occur. These types of events can cause loss of revenue, loss of reputation, and loss of intellectual property, and can even cause a business to fail. Many businesses focus on the recovery aspect of an incident ("Let's plug the hole, fix the damage, and get back to business"), often forgetting to determine why the incident occurred in the first place. In the book *Incident Response* by E. Eugene Schmeltz and Russell Shumway (Pearson Education, 2002), the authors describe a six-stage incident response methodology, with the last step being "Follow-Up." The first five steps are Preparation, Detection, Containment, Eradication, and Recovery. They describe the follow-up stage in this manner, "This stage is extremely critical, however, so critical that it is hard to envision a successful incident response effort if it is omitted."

After the dust has settled and the business has recovered, it is important to discover why the incident occurred in the first place. Normally, the source of the incident is identified by the incident response team, but during the review process, you need to evaluate what allowed the source to be exploited. Was the incident the result of

- Human error?
- System failure?
- Violation of company policy and procedure?
- Unknown or unpublished vulnerability?
- A fault of the original review process?

Once you have identified the reason, the review can move on to examine whether the incident response plan was effective. Things to examine include the following:

- **Response time** Was the incident identified quickly and promptly?
- **Reporting mechanism** Was the reporting process effective? Did the reporting of the event make it through the chain of command in a timely fashion? If law enforcement was contacted, were the contacts outlined in the incident response plan the correct contacts? Did law enforcement respond?
- **Documentation** Was the incident and the corresponding response well documented so that legal recourse can be initiated if it is warranted?
- **Final report** Was an accurate final report, summarizing the incident, created and submitted to management? Did it include lessons learned and steps to prevent future incidents?

NOTE Conducting periodic reviews is one method of minimizing the impact of security incidents. If policies and procedures are reviewed and updated on a regular basis, an organization can be well prepared when an incident occurs.

Conduct a Review After Key Personnel Leave the Organization

When key personnel, such as C-level (chief technology officer, chief financial officer, etc.) employees and above, leave an organization, it is often prudent to conduct a review to ensure that the appropriate separation policies have been followed. Because these individuals know where the corporate "crown jewels" are kept, it is important to terminate their access to corporate systems promptly. The ability to log in to corporate systems and utilize corporate resources such as e-mail should be disabled immediately upon their departure. Some organizations go so far as to remove the hard drives from key employees' desktop computers when they leave and place them in a safe. Instead of removing the drive, some firms make a forensic image of the drive and place it in a safe. In this manner, the hard drives can be examined at a later date for relevant data if it is discovered that the employee was involved in inappropriate activities prior to their departure.

When key technology personnel leave, it is recommended that, in addition to a review, a complete security audit be conducted on the systems for which they were responsible to ensure that they have not created backdoors or unauthorized accounts.

Part IV

How to Succeed at Hardening

Chapter 21

Politics of Security Management

by John Mallery

- Recognize Fellow Employees as "Customers"
- Identify the Players in the Security Management Game

Since technology impacts all departments within an organization, it is critical to have all departments "on board" with any security implementations. The current trend in the security industry is a concept called *holistic security* or *collaborative security*. The basic premise is that all departments within an organization must work together to secure the organization's infrastructure and assets.

This concept is counterintuitive to many people who have chosen a career that suits their aptitude and personality. The thought of having to work and communicate with people from other career areas is simply unappealing. People would rather work with their "own kind" than have to learn to understand the needs and wishes of other groups. But to secure corporate systems and infrastructure, that is exactly what must happen.

NOTE The concept of security management politics is often addressed in MBA programs in the broader context of organizational behavior. If you are interested in researching this topic further, be sure to look at materials that address this topic. Resources include *Organizational Behavior,* Tenth Edition, by Stephen P. Robbins (Prentice Hall, 2002), and Harvard Business Online, http://hbrarchives.harvardbusinessonline.org.

Recognize Fellow Employees as "Customers"

The first step in the game of security management politics is for IT professionals to identify fellow employees as customers. The IT department is designed to recognize and support an organization's technological needs so that it runs smoothly and efficiently. This concept applies to more than just daily operations; it equally applies to security issues as well. The following are questions that you should ask on a regular basis:

- How can I protect data yet provide seamless access to those that need it?
- What is the most economical yet secure form of remote access for "road warriors?"
- When is the most appropriate time to reconfigure systems to ensure limited business interruption?
- Do we have enough help desk staff scheduled to work after a major software rollout to handle the additional influx of calls?
- Will blocking particular ports at the firewall prevent individuals from doing their work?
- Have the latest configuration changes been fully tested in a lab environment prior to being rolled out in the production environment?
- Can data be recovered and restored in a timely manner after data loss or destruction?

IT professionals should recognize that keeping data properly secure prevents the company from spending additional resources on recovering data or addressing security issues and breaches. These additional resources can be used for raises, bonuses, training, and other benefits. Keeping the infrastructure secure provides job security for all employees. This could be considered excellent customer service.

Identify the Players in the Security Management Game

The second step in the game of security management politics is to recognize and identify the key players in the security management game. Knowing who performs which functions in securing data and the corporate infrastructure plays an important part in maintaining a strong security stance. Each department has an important part to play in the security process, so each department must know what its part is and how to perform it effectively.

NOTE In organizations that do not have a mature security program in place, some departments will not know the role that they play. In these organizations, it is important to educate departments to recognize their role. In some organizations, management is the missing link in the process. In such cases, trying to make security a priority in the organization may be an uphill battle.

The following departments play significant roles in the security process:

- Human resources
- Legal
- Physical security
- IT security
- Management
- End users (not a department but a critical part of the security process)

Start the Security Process with Human Resources

The human resources department (HR) is the front line in the security management process. Its responsibilities cover the entire duration of an employee's tenure within an organization, from the hiring process all the way through to the employee's departure. HR must conduct pre-employment background checks on all potential employees (including executive management) and conduct credit checks on potential or current employees who will have access to or control of financial information.

HR is also responsible for including security training as part of the orientation process, usually in the form of discussing the computer acceptable use policy. HR must also ensure that new employees sign noncompete and nondisclosure statements, where applicable. As part of the hiring process, HR notifies several departments of its intent to hire a new employee and the employee's effective start date. The two critical departments to notify are the physical security department and the information systems department. These departments ensure that the new hire has the proper access credentials to get into the facility and that the appropriate accounts are created on the network. These steps must be performed prior to an employee's start date so that the employee doesn't have any reason to borrow credentials or username/password combinations. If borrowing credentials is required on the first day of employment, the strength of the security posture has already been weakened.

During the course of an employee's tenure at an organization, the human resources department is responsible for several security-related items. These include ensuring that any security-related violations are documented in the employee's personnel file. HR also plans and documents security-related training for the employees.

When an employee leaves an organization, for whatever reason, HR should immediately notify both the physical security and information systems departments to immediately terminate access to facilities and systems. HR should also immediately collect all of the following:

- All corporate-owned portable devices including PDAs, Blackberries, cell phones, and laptop computers
- Access cards or tokens that grant physical access to any facilities
- Parking cards and passes
- Company credit cards
- All keys
- Corporate-owned peripheral devices installed at the employee's home

In addition, the corporation should require that all company-owned software and corporate data be removed from home systems.

Retrieving all of these items in a timely fashion can be difficult. You need to work with HR to implement a mechanism that convinces employees to return items promptly. Withholding a final paycheck or compensation until items are returned works well for some organizations. For situations where a severance package is offered, indicating that the initial payment will begin immediately upon the return of company property can also be effective.

NOTE Deferring payment of a severance package may be illegal in some jurisdictions. Check with legal counsel prior to implementing this procedure.

The termination of an employee requires HR to work closely with the IT security department to ensure that data security issues are addressed. It is important that the terminated employee's access to corporate data be disabled immediately upon termination. This includes both internal and remote network access. The employee's e-mail accounts should be disabled and their web-based access to corporate databases should be terminated.

HR must also work closely with the physical security department to ensure that physical access to assets is also removed. Preventing physical access protects employees from physical harm should the terminated employee decide to return for revenge purposes, but it also protects corporate information systems, because physical access can lead to destruction of equipment or "digital" access to proprietary information.

The importance of having all of these departments involved in the termination process is best exemplified by an organization that terminated a system administrator without involving either the physical or IT security departments. The system administrator returned to the organization after hours and entered the building using his access card—which should have been recovered. He then utilized his knowledge of the network and his rights as a system administrator (which were not revoked) to delete all files belonging to the executive manager that fired him, and then deleted the manager's network and e-mail accounts. Although the system administrator was eventually arrested (based on the logging of the access control system and CCTV recordings), the cost to the organization was significant. The organization could have saved itself money and aggravation if the HR department had simply made two quick phone calls to the physical and IT security departments when it decided to terminate the system administrator.

Additional examples of the importance of working with the physical security department are outlined later in this chapter in the section "Work with the Physical Security Team."

Let the Legal Department Learn What Is Required

The legal department has an extremely difficult task when it comes to its security responsibilities. It must construct all legal documents that pertain to security, which includes noncompete, nondisclosure, and nonsolicitation agreements (which state that departing employees will not solicit business from company clients for a specified period and/or will not solicit employees to leave the firm with them).

The legal department must also ensure that any currently implemented security solutions meet legal requirements, both domestically and abroad. As an example, some businesses utilize monitoring hardware and software to determine the computer activities of employees suspected of inappropriate behavior. Courts in the United States have determined that this is not a civil rights violation, especially if employees are notified in writing that their computer activities will be monitored. This notification is usually provided in the computer acceptable use policy and in a login banner that states "By logging into this system you consent to the monitoring of your activities."

However, if a business has offices in the United Kingdom, the monitoring of employee activities is governed by the Employment Practices Data Protection Code (http://www.informationcommissioner.gov.uk/), which has different legal requirements for what types of monitoring an employer can perform.

NOTE Even if your company does not conduct business in the UK, reading the Employment Practices Data Protection Code can provide some additional insight into data protection and confidentiality issues.

In addition, the legal department must ensure that the organization is maintaining compliance with numerous legislative requirements. A large, publicly traded company may have to comply with all of the latest legislation, including the Health Insurance Portability and Accountability Act, the Gramm-Leach-Bliley Act, and the Sarbanes-Oxley Act. The legal department must also keep track of pending legislation so that it is prepared when new legislation is enacted that impacts the business.

One of the most critical functions of the legal department is to find legal methods of enforcing policies and procedures. When an employee violates a security policy, such as stealing proprietary information and giving or selling it to a competitor, the cost to his employer can be significant due to lost revenues and possibly the loss of competitive advantage. Although many members of an organization would suggest that some ruthless enforcement action be applied to the employee, the legal department must often find unique legal ways to protect a company's assets and enforce policies.

An example of legal creativity is the recent application of the Computer Fraud and Abuse Act (CFAA) to cases of corporate theft of trade secrets. The CFAA was designed to protect corporate trade secrets from hackers and other outside attackers. Essentially, it punishes those people who access computer systems without authorization. It is a federal criminal statute, but some creative attorneys have realized that if an employee establishes a relationship with their firm's competitor prior to leaving their firm, they have breached their loyalty to their employer. This breach of loyalty means that the CFAA now applies and they no longer are authorized to access their firm's computer systems.

To learn more about the CFAA, research the following cases: *Shurgard Storage Centers, Inc. v. Safeguard Self Storage, Inc.*; *Ingenix, Inc. v. Lagalante*; and *EF Cultural Travel BV v. Explorica, Inc.*

Work with the Physical Security Team

It is not possible to secure data or systems without cooperation from the physical security/loss prevention department. If an intruder has physical access to network devices such as file servers, mail servers, database servers, etc., no amount of network security tools, programs, or devices will protect your data. When someone has physical access to servers, they can copy, delete, or modify data; install software, including malware and monitoring programs; change configuration settings or logging capabilities; or simply damage or destroy servers and other network equipment. It is extremely important to recognize that physical security is a very specialized area, and to recognize that most system administrators and network engineers do not have the expertise required to physically protect the corporate infrastructure. What follows are some real-world examples demonstrating this concept.

Install Equipment in Secure Areas

In one organization, a security consultant stood outside a client's locked server room and had an argument over the security of the room. The client claimed that the room was totally secure, the consultant insisted that it was not secure at all. The consultant was unable to convince his client verbally, so he jumped up on the doorknob, pushed up the suspended ceiling, and climbed over the wall and into the server room.

Issues Although the client had state-of-the-art locks and solid walls, the room was not secure because the wall did not actually reach the physical ceiling, providing space for someone to climb over the wall. This issue was resolved by installing a heavy-grade mesh between the wall and the ceiling, thereby preventing access.

Install Equipment in Secure Buildings

An organization decided to move the data center for its global business to a more economical location and chose an old building in an industrial area. Its data center was located on the third floor of the building, above a restaurant with a history of kitchen fires. In addition, the area surrounding the building was under heavy construction, and the organization did not have redundant Internet connectivity. The organization recognized that since the building was in a fairly remote area, it should install an alarm system that automatically notifies the police if someone breaks into the data center.

Issues Moving the data center to this location was nothing short of foolish. Being an old building, it was constructed mostly of wood, and fire doors were not installed to contain a fire should one break out. The alarm system, although a good idea, was simply "window dressing." Due to the high rate of false alarms sent to police departments by alarm systems, police generally have a very slow response time to alarms. In fact, one police officer told me that they referred to alarm calls as "donut runs" because they have plenty of time to stop and get donuts on the way. Therefore, an intruder would have plenty of time to destroy the facility prior to law enforcement arriving to investigate the cause of the alarm.

The root of this problem is very simple: the director of information systems had been allotted a budget to move the data center to a "secure" location. The data center was moved to a new location, but the director decided to find a bargain location and used any leftover money from the budget to set up a series of commercial gaming servers. How could this happen? Management had no valid communication channels with the IT department. In fact, the president of the company did not know the data center had been moved until *one year* after the move.

Don't Overlook Anything

A very large data center spared no expense in securing its facility. Redundant connections to two different power grids, top-of-the-line firewalls and intrusion detection systems, and six diesel generators for backup power were designed to keep the data center up and running regardless of any attacks or disasters. The building was designed with Kevlar in the walls, bullet-proof glass protected the front door, armed guards checked IDs of everyone entering the facility, and a biometric device was used for authentication. However, upon observation, it was realized that packages destined for the facility, and specifically for the inside of the data center, were not scanned or physically checked before entering the center. This meant that it would be a simple task to insert a bomb into the building by concealing it in a "normal" package addressed to the facility. In addition, during a visit, it was noticed that at the back of the building, the loading dock door was open and the security guard watching it was asleep. This would have provided easy access to anyone intent on causing damage to the facility.

Issues Even though the organization had spent hundreds of thousands of dollars protecting its data, it still missed some very basic physical security vulnerabilities. It is extremely important to have physical security experts assist with the design of your protective mechanisms. In addition, security experts should be utilized to audit security mechanisms once they are installed.

Create a First-Rate IT Security Department

Although there are many departments and divisions that are critical to the security of an organization's digital assets, the entire digital security posture starts with the IT security department (for those organizations that are not large enough to support an IT security department, the posture starts with the IT/IS department). The department must set standards for itself that puts it in a position to be respected and considered a contributing part of the organization. Your department has failed if fellow employees are making comments like, "No one understands those geeks downstairs." You can take the steps described next to improve how you and your department are perceived, which in turn will provide the opportunity to enhance the security posture of the organization.

Conduct Yourself with Professionalism

Because many IT professionals spend a great deal of their time in isolated rooms working with technology instead of people, they often let their appearance slide. On the surface, this seems logical, but they forget that they are seen in numerous places throughout the organization during a normal workday, such as in the halls, arriving and departing from the building, and in break- or lunchrooms. In one organization, the IT department was referred to as the "great unwashed" due to the appearance and lack of personal hygiene of its staff.

If your organization has a dress code or dress restrictions, don't push the envelope to see what you can get away with. Wear clean, pressed clothes and dress shoes. If your organization has no dress code, don't utilize your wardrobe to make social or political statements. Accessories should be subtle, which means that large skull-and-crossbones earrings (for men or women) should not appear in the workplace.

NOTE Professional appearance helps with credibility not only from a security perspective, but also when it comes time for evaluations and reviews. A more conservative, professional appearance could translate to larger and more frequent raises.

Develop Good Communication Skills

Although the topic of good communication skills was mentioned briefly in Chapter 16, it is appropriate to mention this topic again and in greater detail. Judith Filek, President of Impact Communications, Inc., states very concisely the importance of good communication skills in her January 2002 *Face-to-Face Communication Skills Newsletter* article "What Technology Consultants Should Know About Communicating" (http://www.impactcommunicationsinc.com/pdf/nwsltr_2002/ICINwsltrff0201.pdf): "It is not what you know that counts but how you communicate it. With good communication skills, people feel they can trust you. They see you as real and confident." These are important concepts in communicating security thoughts, ideas, and issues to other members of the organization. Good communication skills include verbal, nonverbal, and writing skills.

Learn Effective Verbal Communication Skills When communicating technical concepts to nontechnical people, you must use terms and language that the listeners understand. Remove acronyms from your conversation. Be clear and concise; do not muddy the conversation with "ums" and "ahs." If necessary, pause; this allows you to think and gives the listener a chance to absorb what you are saying.

Even if you are able to clearly make your points, you may have weak verbal communication skills if you don't listen to others. Many people forget that communicating is a two-way street, and when they are done speaking, they mentally shut down. Pay attention if your listener asks questions or summarizes your key points. This is an excellent way to ensure that you have been understood and your message was delivered effectively.

Learn Effective Nonverbal Communication Skills Watch successful politicians when they are on the campaign trail. They have excellent posture, they always appear extremely interested in what they are saying and hearing, and they always maintain eye contact. These same skills are important when communicating security concepts in your organization. When speaking with coworkers, it is important to be aware of your nonverbal communication skills. Have you ever had someone speak to you who sounded sincere, but you knew they didn't mean what they were saying? You determined this through nonverbal cues, essentially their body language. Facial expressions, posture, and eye contact can be major factors in face-to-face communications. If an employee is explaining a computer problem to you, it is never appropriate to yawn loudly. You can lose credibility in this manner, which is not helpful when trying to develop the security posture of your business.

Learn Effective Written Communication Skills Very often, the ability to implement new security mechanisms hinges on the ability to convince management through the use of a written proposal. If the proposal does not flow properly and is filled with spelling and grammatical errors, the proposal will not be effective and the likelihood for success will be significantly reduced. With automatic spell checking available as a part of all word processing applications, any spelling errors can cause the reader to stop reading immediately. Why? Many in management believe that if the writer did not think enough of their document to take the time to check the spelling, it is not worth reading.

Two books that can be helpful in refining your written communication skills include the classic *The Elements of Style*, by William Strunk and E. B. White (Longman, 2000), and the *Microsoft Manual of Style for Technical Publications*, Third Edition (Microsoft Press, 2003).

Become a Salesperson

When you are trying to convince your superiors or other departments to support a new security implementation, you are simply acting as a salesperson. This is a frightening concept for some people because of the stigma associated with sales that has been created by obnoxious, in-your-face, "buy or die"–type salespeople. This is unfortunate because, if analyzed closely, sales is nothing more than the ability to convince or persuade someone to come around to your way of thinking. It is essentially the ability to use good communication skills to get your point across.

The mechanism you will be using to conduct "internal sales" is a sales approach often referred to as consultative sales. You are simply identifying problems within your organization and offering solutions in a logical, cohesive manner. When done properly, this approach does not look or feel like a sales pitch, but rather an intelligent business option.

Learning these skills can take some time, and trying to find a valid resource from which to learn these skills can be challenging. Perhaps one of the best places to start is "The Necessary Art of Persuasion," by Jay A. Conger. This is a relatively short article that originally appeared in *Harvard Business Review* and is now available as part of the HBR OnPoint series (this article can be purchased and downloaded at http://harvardbusinessonline.hbsp.harvard.edu/). The key concept in the article is that "Persuasion is not begging or cajoling, selling or convincing. It's learning and negotiating—two powerful leadership tools." Mr. Conger breaks persuasion into four key steps:

1. Establish credibility.
2. Frame goals on common ground.

3. Vividly reinforce your position.
4. Connect emotionally.

These steps are different from how most professionals pitch their security proposals. Most security proposals are made strictly in a "black and white" fashion, using facts and figures. Using the steps outlined by Mr. Conger will greatly enhance your ability to get your security proposals accepted and endorsed.

Gain Allies

One of the biggest issues for many security professionals is gaining access to the decision-makers, those who can authorize the purchase of new security equipment and software. Often-overlooked resources are the administrative assistants that work with these decision-makers. These administrative assistants are often considered "lackeys" by some people, which is a serious strategic mistake. Administrative assistants know the schedules, moods, and attitudes of the executives they support. Gaining their trust and confidence can be one of the most important steps in moving a new security process forward. Treat administrative assistants with the respect they deserve and you will gain a valuable ally in the security process.

Maintain Integrity

Another important personality trait that can impact the security posture of an organization is integrity. Members of the IT security department must maintain integrity at all times if they are going to be considered trusted members of the organization. If an employee is having problems with a security implementation and you promise to help them, do so in a timely manner. If you are going to be delayed, inform the employee of the delay and explain the reason if possible. If you ignore an employee request for help, what do you think their response will be when you ask for assistance or need their cooperation?

Another important aspect of maintaining integrity is to practice what you preach. If you are trying to convince users to conform to various security policies, you must also conform to them. You will have a difficult time convincing anyone of the importance of a security policy or procedure if you don't follow it yourself.

Provide Resources

Another mechanism that can be used to open communications with the rest of the organization is to provide practical technology information via a newsletter. Many employees have personal computers in their homes and know that they need to install antivirus programs, antispyware programs, and firewalls, but they don't understand how to install and run them. They are inundated with spam and have no idea how to reduce it or stop it. Providing information on these topics can help users protect their home systems (which are often used for work purposes) and gives them a better idea of how and why these topics are handled in the corporate environment. To make the newsletter interesting, intersperse other interesting facts, statistics, and anecdotes. For example, including spam statistics, Microsoft Office Tips and Tricks, and the history of the phrase "computer bug" will make for interesting reading. (The history of the phrase "computer bug" is interesting; you can learn about it by researching "Grace Hopper" on the Internet.) If you create a newsletter that people look forward to receiving, you will have accomplished something significant.

HEADS UP!

The line between physical security and IT security is becoming blurred. Many physical security devices are now utilizing computer technologies. CCTV systems are now digital, run on twisted-pair cables, and store their images on hard drives. These cameras are even assigned IP addresses and can be viewed and controlled through a web browser. Additionally, some cameras are wireless and thus have the same issues and concerns as other wireless technologies.

There are now robust security products that run on common operating systems and provide the ability to manage and control multiple security devices. These products include the ability to manage building access control systems, digital video, network access systems, and intrusion detection systems. It is important to recognize that these security products are running on standard IT technologies. Designing, installing, and maintaining these systems are beyond the skills of most "guns, gates, and guards" security professionals. Also, IT professionals understand the technologies but know nothing of physical security concepts. Because of the convergence of physical security technologies and IT technologies, it is important for the physical and IT security departments to work well together and share thoughts, issues, and concerns.

Speak to Management in Their Language

The management team sets the tone for the security posture of an organization. If members of the management team believe security is a priority and are visibly committed to making it a part of the corporate culture, your job will be much easier. When working with management, it helps to understand that its primary responsibility is to maintain and, if possible, improve the profitability of the organization. This means looking at the purchase of new technology with scrutiny. If management can't justify the expense from a business perspective, it will not allow the expense. The purchase has to either help the company make money or help the company save money. Trying to make these types of justifications when requesting resources to purchase, implement, and support security mechanisms can be challenging.

To understand the language of management, one simply has to look in publications like *Forbes* and *Fortune*. For example, in the July 26, 2004, issue of *Forbes*, Quentin Hardy describes the recent reconfiguration of Cisco's infrastructure as follows in his article "What Makes Cisco Run" (p. 68):

> Chambers (Cisco President and CEO) claims this nascent "intelligent information network" saved Cisco $2.1 billion last year in everything from factory operations to worker training. Cisco handled 2.6 million support questions online and took 90% of its orders electronically, saving almost a billion dollars. It put training and meetings online and saved $800 million.

Although many system administrators will not work with projects as large as those mentioned in the article, the concept is the same. Management gets very excited when it can see technology implementations that save the firm money. By focusing on the bottom line, it is easy to turn management into an ally.

NOTE Many IT professionals are proficient when working in hexadecimal and binary, but are extremely lacking when it comes to dollars and cents. To better serve your organization (and to be in a better position to be promoted), learn to speak the language of business, finance, and accounting. You can accomplish this by taking night classes at a local community college, enrolling in a mini-MBA program, or engaging in self-study. One reservation many people have when beginning this area of study is that it will be boring. One book that recognizes this is *The McGraw-Hill 36 Hour Course in Finance for Nonfinancial Managers* by Robert A. Cooke (McGraw-Hill Trade, 1993). The book is filled with humorous anecdotes and equates finance to "business scorekeeping."

Expecting management to be excited about computer security issues without having to explain the financial repercussions is unrealistic. Many people currently in executive management started their business careers before desktop PCs were required in the business world. It is not uncommon to hear executives make comments like, "I don't know anything about computers. I barely know how to send e-mail." There are still executives who have their administrative assistants send and read e-mail messages for them. This attitude is slowly changing as graduate programs begin to include information on security concepts into their MBA programs. James Madison University has even gone one step farther and created an Information Security MBA (http://www.jmu.edu/mba/infosec2.shtml). But until graduates of these programs start entering the ranks of management, you must be prepared to explain security from a financial perspective.

Calculate the Costs of Security Incidents

When trying to justify an expenditure on security products or services, it is often prudent to show the financial impact of a security breach or incident. If you have not had a documented incident for which you can calculate the cost, you may have to confer with other system administrators to have them share their experiences with you. Patrick Sweeney, president and CEO of ServerVault, shared one method of calculating the cost of an incident in a May 2002 *Security Technology & Design* article, "Establishing ROI for Your Upper Management," by Marleah Blades (pp. 20–24). He utilizes the following formula:

Total cost = cost of damage + operations cost + response cost × number of hosts

The parts of this formula can be interpreted as follows:

- **Total cost** The total cost of the incident. This is the number that you use to help support your security implementation requests.
- **Cost of damage** The cost of damaged equipment that must be replaced.
- **Operations cost** The cost due to business interruption.
- **Response cost** The cost to respond to and fix the problems caused by the incident.
- **Number of hosts** The number of devices that were damaged and require repair.

To demonstrate this formula, consider a modified real-world example. A utility company stored detailed maps of all of its power lines and water lines for a large metropolitan area on one file server that utilized a RAID array. Tape backups were done on this system on a weekly basis only, because the data did not change frequently. The system administrators also believed the RAID array would provide them some level of redundancy. Unfortunately, two hard drives and a controller card failed at the same time, after which it was discovered that the backup tapes were blank.

The company immediately called in consultants to help, who then called two data recovery companies. No data could be recovered from the hard drives, and a new file server had to be replaced. All the data had to be manually entered into the new server. Costs for this incident can be broken down in this manner.

- **Cost of damage** Replacement of file server, $25,000.
- **Operations cost** Difficult to calculate because normal maintenance operations were not suspended, they were only delayed. Manual mechanisms had to be implemented, such as searching archived paper documents for power line and water line locations. This labor intensive process increased the response time for work crews.
- **Response cost** This incident required the use of two internal IT staff members for 40 hours at an hourly rate of $35 per hour, $1400 total, plus $5000 for consultant fees. The largest expense was the cost of manually re-entering all the data into the new server, $350,000.
- **Number of hosts** One.

These numbers can now be plugged into the formula:

$\$25,000 + 0 + \$356,400 \times 1 = \$381,400$

You can now use this number, $381,400, as the minimum cost for this incident. This number could be used to help justify the cost of hiring a new staff member to maintain and support this particular server.

This formula is certainly not perfect, but it can help quantify the cost of an incident. Other items that can be included in the costs of responding to an incident are legal fees if the incident causes damage to other systems and networks. This might be the case if a corporation's systems are used to mount a distributed denial of service attack on another business. The company could be held liable for the damages to the other business.

There are other items that can add costs to an incident but are extremely difficult to quantify. These intangible losses include loss of image and loss of faith by customers. The web defacement of an e-commerce web site or the theft of credit cards from an e-commerce server can cause some of these issues. Although it can be difficult to place a solid dollar amount on these types of losses, it is important to factor them into any request for security products.

Calculate the Return on Security Investment

Many executives are used to discussing the return on investment (ROI) for any purchases or acquisitions. They essentially want to know what they are getting for their money. For security purchases, there is a new term, return on security investment (ROSI). In calculating the ROSI, you are justifying the cost of a product by demonstrating how much it can save the business compared to the cost of a security incident or series of incidents. The ROSI can be somewhat difficult to calculate if you are proactively purchasing a product, because you will have no hard figures to compare your purchase to. If you have no data to support your purchase, it may be helpful to reach out to product manufacturers or venders to help you create the ROSI for the purchase of their products. They more than likely have figures already prepared, since ROSI is a valuable marketing tool for them.

NOTE There are unscrupulous salespeople and vendors that inflate the ROSI of their products to help them win business. If at all possible, try to contact some of their previous clients to help validate their ROSI figures.

What you are trying to accomplish with these figures is to show how these products will reduce the number of incidents and reduce the response time (and therefore cost) if an incident does occur.

Calculating the ROSI is not a simple process. It requires an understanding of statistical analysis and the probability that an attack or incident will occur. The New South Wales Office of Information and Communications Technology has created a very detailed guide, *Return on Investment for Information Security*, that includes some sample Excel spreadsheets that can be used to calculate the ROSI. They include random-number generators to help simulate the randomness of attacks. The guide and the spreadsheets can be found at http://www.oict.nsw.gov.au/content/7.1.15.ROSI.asp.

A less-complicated method of calculating the ROSI has been created by a team at the University of Idaho. The team set up an intrusion detection system and calculated the cost benefit of stopping intrusions as opposed to mitigating them. The team created the following formula:

(R – E) + T = ALE, and R – ALE = ROSI

- **R** The cost per year to recover from intrusions
- **E** Savings from implementation of an intrusion detection tool
- **T** The cost of the intrusion detection tool
- **ALE** Annual loss expectancy

Calculating the ROSI is accomplished by subtracting the annual loss expectancy from the cost per year to recover from intrusions:

R – (ALE) = ROSI

These calculations were presented in this format in the February 15, 2002, issue of *CIO* magazine in the article "Finally, a Real Return on Security Spending," by Scott Berinato, http://www.cio.com/archive/021502/security.html. The original research can be found in the paper "Cost-Benefit Analysis for Network Intrusion Detection Systems," by Huaqiang Wei et al., presented at the CSI 28th Annual Computer Security Conference in October 2001. A copy of the research paper can be found at http://wwwcsif.cs.ucdavis.edu/~balepin/new_pubs/costbenefit.pdf.

Use Additional Supporting Material

Trying to quantify the ROSI for a particular product or security implementation can be a time-consuming and somewhat complex process, and the resulting numbers may be challenged as nothing more than a mathematically calculated best guess. Therefore, it is beneficial to have materials to support these numbers. It is also beneficial to have these types of materials available if a current threat or attack doesn't allow you enough time to calculate an ROSI.

Support Proposal with Descriptions of "Probable Threats" as Opposed to "Describable Threats"

There are numerous threats to a corporate network. Malware, hackers, disgruntled employees, and system failures are threats to networks 24 hours a day, 7 days a week. Security professionals know this all too well because they see evidence of it on their systems and are made aware of it by others in the industry. But many executives, lacking the first-hand experience, believe that the threats are exaggerated and that incident statistics are inflated to help sell security products. Because of this attitude, if you are describing a threat or collection of threats, you must be as specific as possible, and if you quote statistics, they should come from reliable sources. If you are trying to convince management to approve the purchase of an enterprise-wide antivirus product, simply stating that it is needed because numerous viruses exist is simply not enough. Providing up-to-date statistics on the current virus threat is much more effective, and these statistics are easy to find since numerous web sites list the current top ten, "in the wild" viruses. As an example, McAfee provides a Regional Virus Info page, which tracks virus threats in different parts of the world within the past 24 hours (http://us.mcafee.com/virusInfo/default.asp?id=regional). These types of "hard" statistics are much more useful in supporting your request for new antivirus products.

NOTE Trend Micro also provides a Virus Map at http://www.trendmicro.com/map/, which shows current virus threats by region. This can help system administrators understand spikes in traffic on various systems as well as allocate resources to protect against particular viruses.

Applying this approach works well when trying to request an intrusion detection system or a second firewall for redundancy purposes. Very often the supporting information that you need will come directly from your current firewall or system logs. Printing out these logs is not practical since they will be meaningless to nontechnical individuals. But if you take a section of the logs and convert the IP addresses of the systems currently scanning your network, you may get some information that is extremely interesting. When one individual performed this, he was surprised to see that his network was being scanned by an IP address belonging to the Ministry of Education, Republic of Taiwan. Not surprisingly, he was able to get a budget approved for an intrusion detection system.

NOTE An excellent tool for determining the name and location of an IP address is VisualRoute from Visualware, which is available at http://www.visualroute.com.

Other resources for finding information on probable threats include trade publications that are directly relevant to your business. If your industry has become the target of attacks, this information can be very helpful when trying to get funds allocated for new security tools.

Explain Security in Quality Assurance Terms For businesses that provide services to clients via the Internet, it may be possible to gain support for security initiatives by demonstrating that properly implemented security will mean greater quality assurance for clients. Explaining that the availability of an online store can be improved with security devices will gain management's attention.

Encourage Compliance of End Users

As discussed in previous chapters, end users often try to bypass security mechanisms. If you follow many of the steps previously outlined in this chapter, you should be well on your way toward gaining the acceptance of end users for currently implemented security policies and procedures. However, there are several additional steps that you can take that should prove extremely helpful in ensuring end-user compliance.

Perhaps the most important process for encouraging end-user compliance is to include adherence to security policies and procedures as part of a user's job responsibilities. If compliance is evaluated during the annual performance review process and users understand that a finding of noncompliance will result in a negative evaluation, they will immediately begin to comply with security policies. Many organizations are beginning to adapt this process; however, they often forget that employees who do comply with security requirements need to be rewarded. These rewards can include additional points during performance reviews or other methods of positive reinforcement such as gift certificates, days off, bonuses, and so forth. This type of positive reinforcement can have a great impact on the user community, including making users more supportive of security efforts.

Compliance can also be encouraged and monitored by using automated compliance tools. Numerous products exist that not only provide policy templates, but also help automate the process of policy and compliance management, allowing for limited loopholes for employees. Several of these products and their associated web sites are listed here:

- **NetIQ VigilEnt Policy Center** http://www.netiq.com/products/vpc/default.asp
- **Polivec Suite** http://www.polivec.com/products.htm
- **NetVision NVPolicy Resource Center** http://www.netvision.com/products/nvpolrsc.html
- **Pedestal Software SecurityExpressions** http://www.pedestalsoftware.com/products/se/

Get All Departments to Work Together

Once you understand the way each department functions, it is time to convince all departments to work together to protect corporate assets and data. The old adage "two heads are better than one" definitely applies here. However, using well worn anecdotes and cliches is not enough to convince skeptics in the corporate environment to work together.

Instead, try to use one of the numerous team-building exercises that exist, many of which are quite valuable. One in particular, "Win as Much as You Can," is incredibly powerful, so much so that the impact of the exercise has stayed with me for more than 20 years. The premise of the exercise is that each "team" should "win as much as they can," and all participants fully accept that premise. The exercise (a game, really) proceeds with competition running rampant. At the end of the game everyone tallies their winnings. A winner is usually announced, but the game's facilitator immediately points out that everyone would have won more had everyone worked together. It is very interesting and intriguing to see people's reactions. If done properly, you can actually see the "light go on" as they realize the implications of working together in the corporate environment. If you can "turn on the light" from a security perspective, the process of implementing security policies, procedures, and mechanisms will be much easier.

NOTE This game is outlined in *Pfeiffers Classic Activities for Managing Conflict at Work*, edited by Jack Gordon. The chapter outlining the game can be downloaded at http://www.pfeiffer.com/WileyCDA/PfeifferTitle/productCd-0787973165,descCd-download.html.

One method of getting divisions to work together is to explain their position in the security organization. Figure 21-1 shows a sample security organizational chart.

NOTE A security organizational chart does not necessarily parallel a managerial organizational chart. A security organizational chart simply outlines the working relationship between departments, not the hierarchical chain of command represented in a managerial organizational chart.

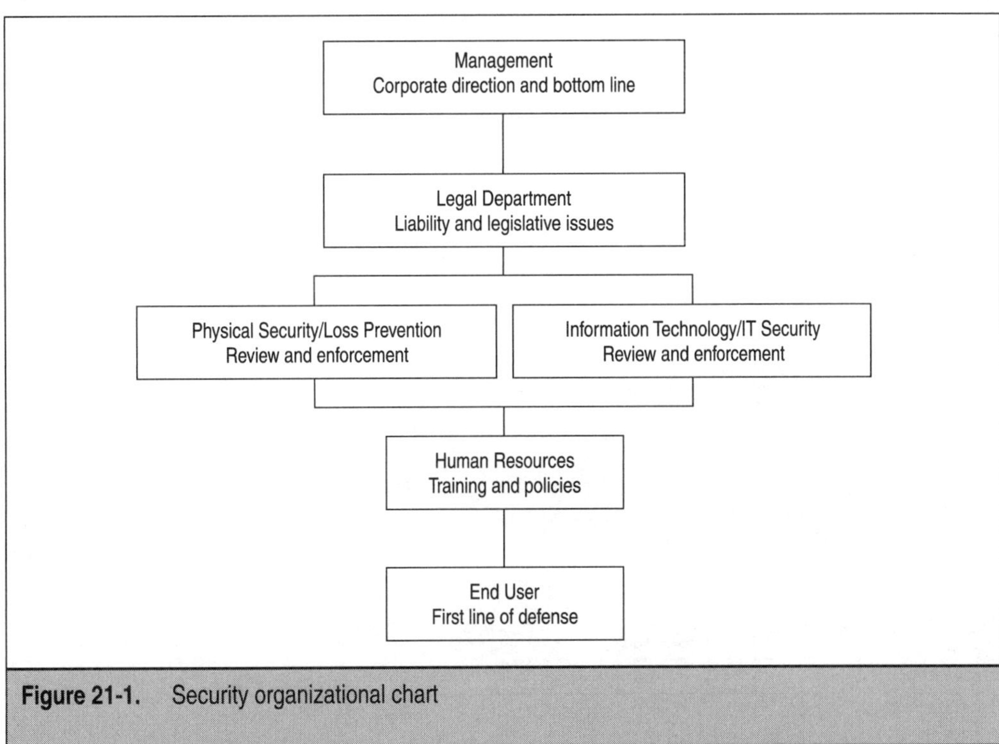

Figure 21-1. Security organizational chart

Chapter 22

Security Apathy

by Patrick Kelly

- Build a Case for Security
- Collect Statistics to Support Your Cause
- Identify What Security Agnostics Believe
- Improve Management's Understanding for the Investment in Security
- Have a Security Policy
- Create a Security-Awareness Program
- Lessons Learned

By far the most dangerous foe we have to fight is apathy—indifference from whatever cause, not from a lack of knowledge, but from carelessness, from absorption in other pursuits, from a contempt bred of self satisfaction.

—Sir William Osler, "Unity, Peace and Concord," *Journal of the American Medical Association* (1905)

Building a technical infrastructure is one step toward a bulletproof network system. Another important step is educating the people who are expected to use the technology. There are two aspects to the human factor in supporting the security profile of your company. On the positive side, vigilant and educated end users can be your best defense against computer compromise. It may well be your users who first notice that data may have been maliciously altered. They may be the first to notice anomalies with the performance and actions of the computer systems they have become familiar with. Properly prepared, they may be your best weapons in defending your critical systems.

On the negative side, end users may be your worst enemy. Unwise decisions when using the company technology can have disastrous results. Opening the wrong attachment, choosing the wrong option from a menu, or writing a destructive line of code could reverse hours of hard work and waste large sums of money representing the company's investment in valuable company information.

Carelessness, ignorance, stubbornness, and greed are among the human traits that can result in defeating your diligent effort toward protecting your data and computer systems from compromise. This chapter provide insight toward understanding why some people refuse to recognize any benefit from computer security. Once you can identify the causes of security apathy, you can outline the path to convert true agnostics into believers.

Build a Case for Security

At some point, everyone has made a decision about his or her commitment to computer security. As technology became an important part of everyday business, many individuals were skeptical of security measures because of the corresponding restrictions and inconveniences of security rules and guidelines. If you have clearly stated rules and guidelines, some individuals will follow along because that is what is expected of them in the role of a good employee. By the same token, there will be other individuals who refuse to follow any direction, holding dear to a rebellious attitude that defines their personality.

No matter what the reason for users not following along with the security rules, you will be required to enforce the security policy of your company. You need to validate your measures against cost justifications, productivity growth, and personal freedoms. Your initial task in handling security apathy is to ensure that users' indifferent actions do not harm the rest of the network systems. Once their current activity is secured, your mission is to alter their viewpoint on security measures in the workplace to reduce future risk. You need to build a compelling story of the corporate and individual benefits of following a comprehensive and thorough security scheme.

Collect Statistics to Support Your Cause

Throughout this book, you have learned how to bulletproof your computer systems to guard against numerous threats. You've studied this book in hopes of gaining a better understanding of what steps and tasks are required to secure and lock down computer systems. The entire *Hardening* series for computer systems was written in hopes that computer systems all over the world would be more secure and less susceptible to the threats, vulnerabilities, and exploits that are growing in sophistication and volume every hour of every day.

Across all products, Microsoft released 51 security advisories in 2003, according to SecurityStats.Com (http://www.securitystats.com). That represents an average of nearly one new security patch per week. Thirty of the MS Security Bulletins released in 2003 pertained to Windows XP. These statistics are not stated to deride Microsoft. These statistics are representative of the efforts of computer crackers, application coders, and security researchers. They are provided here to exemplify the growing need for an expansion of solid, thorough, and diligent computer security practices. The fact that computer systems are continually being compromised points to several conclusive facts:

- The majority of computer users are not affected by malicious attacks on computers.
- The majority of computer users affected by computer virus outbreaks suffer no monetary harm, personal injury, or lasting effects.
- Most people are not *directly* affected by computer crime.

The last point emphasizes *directly* because most people are *indirectly* affected by computer crime and computer security breaches. Companies spend millions of dollars to rectify damage and outages caused by computer tampering or compromise, much of which cost is passed on to consumers through higher prices. The CERT Coordination Center (http://www.cert.org/stats/cert_stats.html) has posted 137,529 incidents reported in the period 2000 to 2003. This represents a dramatic rise in reported computer security incidents. If you want to collect more information on the problem, visit SecurityStats.Com to discover some of the studies and results of estimating costs and occurrences of computer security–related losses.

These statistics are representative of a real need for computer owners and users to take responsibility for protecting their investment of time and money spent on their systems. What additional steps or techniques can you perform or adopt to convey the importance of solid security hardening practices?

ONE STEP FURTHER

Recently, I experienced a truly enlightening experience that visually demonstrated statistics for better comprehension. I was working an engagement that was struggling with methodologies and techniques to effectively deal with unsolicited, commercial e-mail or spam. Management understood the costs involved with end users having to handle and delete the unwanted messages, and understood the liability in having unsolicited communications on everyone's computer system. Users were annoyed at having to delete sometimes hundreds of unwanted messages on a routine basis, and were frustrated about sometimes missing a legitimate message because of the similarity to that of a spam message. The technical staff produced spam statistics in memos, web pages, and e-mails. The problems experienced at this location are universal complaints concerning the handling of unwanted, unsolicited, commercial e-mail:

- Messages that should get to the users are sometimes blocked.
- File attachments are blocked.
- Some spam still gets through.
- The volume of mail is overwhelming to the technical staff.

One day, the order was given to compile and print the spam captured during a 24-hour period. This would be a typical sample of the e-mail tagged and stored as spam. The stack was nearly 30 reams of paper, over six-feet tall. During a management meeting, the stack was visible for all to see. The physical presence made quite an impact. Appealing to a different perception medium put the volume of spam messages into a different perspective. It was no longer a number on a paper but a stack of paper larger than most had previously seen in one place. End users and management began to appreciate the overwhelming burden of successfully handling that quantity of e-mail. Many end users, previously silent or frustrated, began to offer assistance and asked what they could do to assist the technology effort to improve e-mail communications and help cut down on the volume of spam.

Identify What Security Agnostics Believe

There are many reasons and excuses for why individuals do not believe in practicing safe and secure computer systems routines. Identifying why individuals are ignoring your requests to become more security conscious will assist in assembling a treatment to this problem. Once you understand the challenges with regard to individual disregard for the need for security, you can work to present the same point of view and knowledge that converted you into a security proponent.

Their conclusion or belief is based on an understanding of facts. To reach an opinion, a person arranges their fact set to accommodate their belief. Understanding this thought process may assist you in determining if their fact set is based on experience, research, opinion, or misinformation. Once you understand their position, you must be prepared to present conflicting facts that will lead them to reach a different conclusion. Presentation of conflicting facts to an individual's current set of accepted facts is a delicate proposition.

Opinion based on first-hand experience is difficult if not impossible to change. I have interviewed people who have had horrible experience with the implementation of security directives. Some key business issues were poorly addressed, resulting in diminished productivity and waning morale.

Improve Management's Understanding for the Investment in Security

One stumbling block to improving the company security profile is when management cannot be convinced to expend additional resources and funds to cover gaps in the current security effort. Without the support by management to adopt an atmosphere of a safe, secure, and productive technology environment, the security effort will fall short and eventually fail to adequately protect the business. The reasons for management's reluctance may be one or more of many reasons that are commonly offered. Failure to win management's approval can be countered with return on investment (ROI) analysis, proper valuation of the company's investment in stored data, and comparison to the purchase of an insurance policy to protect the expenditure of replacing years of data accumulation and development.

Simply stating to management that the adoption of your ideas and methods will benefit the security posture of the company does not communicate the solutions to the business problems of inadequate security. Treat the expenditure of financial resources for security as an investment in assuring the current investment in information is protected. The more critical the information is to the company, the higher the percentage of security expenditures that must be allocated to protecting that information. Management should understand the principle of financial investment to propel the business venture into profitable areas. The actual burden is on the technology administrator and analyst to apply business principles to justify the improvement of the security and protection of the critical business information.

When quantifying the critical information, factor these items:

- The cost of production and creation of the information
- The cost of nonproductivity during periods when the critical data would become unavailable
- The cost of restoring damaged systems from varying degrees of compromise into usable, reliable data

Have a Security Policy

Products and technologies provide a solid foundation for security initiatives. But products alone will not be enough. Security is a process not a product. Without clear acceptable-use policies, the investment in the technology will be diminished if not wasted. Processes and policies need to be defined by guidelines, standards, and rules. These policies should include descriptions of favorable behavior as well as wrong behavior.

A security policy is a document representing the philosophy of the company. It converts the business vision into procedures, rules, and regulations. Having a tangible, quantitative rule set describing acceptable, secure computing practices will provide guidance that everyone loyal to the company can follow and rally around. Using society as an example, even having rules to govern behavior will still leave room for interpretation and acceptance. An enforceable security policy with the sponsorship of management is the primary step in addressing compliance with security directives.

What Should Be Included in the Security Policy?

When you are creating the security policy, the first question to answer is what to put in the security policy statement. Many companies begin to define a complete depth of security-related issues. Another approach is to keep the security policy statement simple and compile separate documents describing the details of procedures, standards, and guidelines. There are business environments that suit the latter. In some business structures, it may be difficult for upper management to discern what elements of security configurations are best suited for the existing technology situations. It may also take time to stipulate exact security policy if too many executives are responsible for the specific contents of security guidelines and standards. Changes to reflect current issues would be difficult to provide in a timely manner. It may be best to develop the security philosophy to be further described by supporting documents. Identify the creators of the documentation and specify the approval process that is constructed to be agile enough to meet emerging security issues.

Obtain Endorsement from Upper Management

In the course of strengthening your political positioning to enforce rules and regulations, you must have the authority to leverage the threat of repercussions for violations of those rules. You must take careful aim at the executive infrastructure to gain trust and endorsement from key players to enforce the rules and guidelines outlined in the security policy. Without repercussions, there will be no incentive for the rebellious or "rules don't apply to me" type of employee.

When targeting your executive security policy enforcement team, look to different positions to provide a spectrum of enforcement points:

- **Financial executives** Positions such as CFO and finance director are positions valuable to your cause. These individuals control expenditures. These positions carry a sizable amount of respect from other management team members who are responsible for departmental budgeting and divisional purchasing. Traditionally, this group understands the importance of auditing (vulnerability assessments) and compliance with guidelines.
- **Senior positions** Members of this club may have a life-long investment in the success of the corporation. They may have spent most of their adult lives dedicated to the reputation of the company. These individuals understand the importance of protecting the reputation of the company, which can be diminished by any of the following:
  - A public web site that is hacked
  - Leaked proprietary data—private data that has escaped security controls and is now published without permission in the public domain
  - Damage to the image of the company, both internal image and business partner opinion, on dealing with the company
- **Human relations management** This group can assist with the penalty for noncompliance. Engaging this department will assist you in providing realistic punishments and rules of how to apply those punishments within the company code of conduct. If any personnel issues arise in dealing with a troublesome employee, the issue will pass through this group. While HR management will maintain an impartial stance, their familiarity with you and your objectives will formulate their reactions to the issues.

Create Realistic Security Procedures and Guidelines

Creating definitions for acceptable behavior and formulating security standards to follow must coincide with the technology atmosphere. There must be agreement between the security policy and business growth objectives. Requiring complex passwords that users must write on a sticky note is worse than requiring a simpler password that they can remember. There must be justification of your security proposal that strikes a balance and compromise to the goals of getting work done.

In most organizations, business needs outweigh security requirements. Adoption of the security philosophy that the security goal is to provide confidentiality, integrity, and availability (CIA) should assist you in communicating with business units. Work toward educating business units on the virtues of security CIA. Establish security controls to ensure that users can continue to perform tasks that produce a positive bottom-line profit.

Create a Security-Awareness Program

Communication between the security administrator and the technology-user community within the organization is vital to your security initiative. The communication stream must flow in both directions. You must be prepared to listen to the user community to understand any frustrations or problems they may encounter along the way.

Many security-awareness programs include internal newsletters to assist in communication of security ideals and goals. The content of the newsletter should be informative and entertaining. Making security fun to learn will always be more successful than using the newsletter as a soapbox of what you think is right. Examine the concept of reporting current news in a format similar to SANS Newsbites (http://www.sans.org) as a reminder that security is constantly being challenged in all areas of the world and all industries. Include a security quiz with prizes, based upon participation, that employees will value.

Security-awareness programs can build a growing security-aware community within the company. There is strength in numbers. Have security believers discuss the merits of compliance with agnostics. If you are lucky, one of the security believers is a converted agnostic. This person or group can communicate to a level that the recalcitrant can find comfort and familiarity with.

Lessons Learned

The preceding sections of this chapter have provided instructions on how to establish a political infrastructure regarding security initiatives. To convince nonbelievers to join safe and productive security initiatives, you must provide an appealing, irrefutable security organization.

Security professionals should be ready to confront all who question the value of solid security tactics. Many professional organizations empower and encourage membership to champion the cause of technology security. Many professionals are held to a standard of guidelines or recommendations for behavior.

Determine if Resistance to Security Measures Is Masking Genuine Concern for Poor Security Measures

I have worked in organizations that were initiating security policies. I have learned that not all security agnostics are indifferent about security controls. Their real concern is that if the organization implements poor security controls, the end result will be more damage to morale, productivity, and assurance. Their perception and belief is that no actions are better than deployment of incorrect security measures.

ONE STEP FURTHER

The following Objectives for Guidance is from the Certified Information Systems Security Professional code of ethics. It outlines recommended guidelines for behavior. These objectives are for information only and are not intended as a required canon of ethical behavior. More information on security professional certifications can be discovered at the web site of the International Information Systems Security Certification Consortium, or (ISC)^2, at https://www.isc2.org/cgi-bin/index.cgi. You may want to create an informal "certified" group within your company. Include a small "certification" test to measure a level of security understanding. Include a certificate to be displayed in the work area and a notation in the personnel folder of compliance and dedication to security initiatives to be practiced at work and at home.

Objectives for Guidance

These objectives, suggested guidelines of behavior, are targeted to security professionals. This list is crafted by the board of directors of (ISC)^2. I introduce these objectives in the context of providing an example of a framework by which to pattern any internal "certification" program you may initiate. These guidelines should be considered to help the security professional identify and resolve any ethical dilemmas which may present themselves from time to time. The (ISC)^2 Objectives for Guidance are as follows:

- Give guidance for resolving good vs. good and bad vs. bad dilemmas.
- To encourage right behavior such as:
  - Research
  - Teaching
  - Identifying, mentoring, and sponsoring candidates for the profession
  - Valuing the certificate
- To discourage such behavior as:
  - Raising unnecessary alarm, fear, uncertainty, or doubt
  - Giving unwarranted comfort or reassurance
  - Consenting to bad practice
  - Attaching weak systems to the public net
  - Professional association with non-professionals
  - Professional recognition of or association with amateurs
  - Associating or appearing to associate with criminals or criminal behavior

Case Study: Critical Network Security

One organization in which I worked had created a security team that was charged with deploying security technologies throughout the company. The security team began with a mixture of success stories and temporary setbacks in deploying the new technologies and procedures. The team members ran into a dead end when trying to deploy security policy templates to a departmental group of servers. They had taken the position that since they were the security team, they inherently knew what were the best security settings for all computer systems in the organization. I was brought in to validate the security settings and provide assurance to the departmental leaders that the security team was improving the security of the entire organization.

I met with the security team to understand the issues, to try to ascertain the best course of action to secure the organization. I also wanted a private meeting with the departmental administrators to understand the entire picture. The departmental team was labeled as ignorant of sophisticated security influences and of having limited knowledge of security technologies.

While the security team just scoffed and derided the members of the departmental group, I used a different tactic. I gave this "rogue" group the benefit of the doubt and was interested in listening to their ideas on how they approached technology security. I was looking for insight into why the departmental admins thought their approach to security was superior and exactly what it is they were doing that was superior to what the IT/security department had wanted to dictate to them.

Initially, there were two problems with the approach of the security team. First, it didn't want to listen to other employees who also had the same goals in protecting valuable information and technology systems. The security group took the posture that since it consisted of security professionals, it knew more about security initiatives. Second, the security team did not attempt to build a team atmosphere. The group was more interested in imposing its will on everyone, thus the potential for a power struggle overshadowed and virtually eliminated any concept of team membership.

In meeting with the rogue group, initially its members were skeptical of my intentions. I assured them that I had heard one side of the story and that, before I made any recommendations for change, I needed to hear their side of the story. I repeatedly reminded them that I was only interested in the loftier goal of protecting the critical assets and information of the company.

Eventually, I learned that they had a great stake in the acquisition and ownership of the data they were protecting. They had worked and even fought for equipment and software and had dedicated a part of themselves into the work product. They resented someone else taking ownership of their systems. They wanted to remain separate from the rest of the organization.

The end result was the declaration that certain segments of the departmental network, namely the servers, were to be considered a "critical network." Firewall controls were instituted to protect the servers from harm; access to the servers was controlled with firewall rules that needed departmental approval. An IDS and network monitoring was initiated to test and ensure that only qualified employees were accessing the data. Host-based IDS and antivirus solutions were installed on the servers for protection, but the day-to-day administration and final access control settings were administered by the department administrators. This compromise met the goal of information assurance and added the checks and balances required by the departmental administrators.

This case initially looked as if the departmental administrators were resistant to security controls and apathetic to the security requirements of the company. Through open communication and compromise, the security goals of the organization were met.

Clearly Define Repercussions for Noncompliance with Security Policies

In today's workplace, the actions of HR departments are perceived as slow-moving and unresponsive to immediate needs. Much of this perception results from a failure to recognize the deliberate nature of handling potentially litigious situations in preparation for the worst-case scenario. This methodical approach, which may result in employee termination, is comparable to the deliberate nature of scheduled changes to systems. Research is gathered to support the change, and a rollback or contingency plan is developed to replace the asset in a timely manner. The actual deployment is discussed and planned. Once the decision has been made to move forward, scheduling and timing issues are studied and resolved. At this point in time, a solid relationship between corporate security department and HR department is essential.

Unfortunately for the security recalcitrant, one form of remedy for noncompliance with rules is termination. Very few organizations have positions that cannot be retooled with internal promotions or complete replacement with a new candidate. Failure to abide by any company rule can carry serious repercussions. If the failure to follow security policy results in company losses, the company may choose to "set an example of noncompliance with the existing rules."

Many Agnostics Believe Someone Else Should Protect Their Computer

Many computer users believe that security is someone else's job. The rationale follows the belief that the security people are paid to take care of security. Companies are finding

HEADS UP!

Often, employees refer to the computer they use as "their" computer when, in fact, the employer owns the system. It is imperative for the security administrator to always refer to objects, rules, and concepts as the company's asset. It should be referred to as "Acme's security rule" when addressing users. While many companies encourage ownership within the scope of job performance, that task is completed using company procedures and company equipment. To remind employees of ownership rights of equipment, many companies place on the equipment identification logos in the form of stickers, markings, etc., to continually remind workers that the computer is a company asset just like furnishings, carpet, buildings, etc.

that the apathy of the computer user can affect their bottom line. If customers are victims of identity theft, the chances they will become repeat customers diminishes.

ONE STEP FURTHER

Corporations that transact business online have recognized that many of the customers are not security aware. To combat their customers' apathetic view of computer security, the companies have taken proactive steps to protect themselves by assisting customers to identify security shortcomings. They are using a product from WholeSecurity (http://www.wholesecurity.com) to assist users in protecting their identity information on the customer's computer.

Customers are offered the option to have a 300KB ActiveX control downloaded to perform an analysis on their computer. The Confidence Online program, from WholeSecurity, includes a detection engine that examines processes on the computer system. It inspects behavior common to certain types of Trojans, worms, and other remote controls. The behaviors include file manager capabilities, file and information transport, keystroke logging, and network connection behavior.

Passive resistance to security controls can effectively be met with security classifications. Identify unsecured systems as high-risk computers. One foremost example is the mobile computer that will be attached to an unsecured network. Many workers have a habit of transporting the company laptop to the home computer network that may have little or no security controls. Equipping this computer with a software firewall and antivirus software capable of updates from the manufacturer from anywhere on the Internet is the first step in preventing this computer from compromise when not protected by corporate security mechanisms.

Most users are not knowledgeable about security protection for their computer. Once at home, they need the assistance from people like you to protect information on their computer. This includes personal information, financial transactions, and the purchase of goods and services on the Internet.

Many home users are not concerned with computer safety. This issue can be addressed by providing software firewall programs that load as the network interface starts. Check Point's SecureClient enables the security administrator to configure a desktop security policy that the SecureClient program can install on startup. The mobile computer security policy is configured on the management console with the enterprise security policy. The process will start as a service in Windows clients. Administrators need to monitor the computer event logs to ensure that the firewall has not been disabled by a local administrative account.

The Lesson from Security Apathy Can Be Costly

Many agnostics believe that they are too insignificant to be a target of computer hackers. They exhibit cavalier attitudes about their risks and the chances of their systems being the target of malicious attacks. The Internet has eliminated the effectiveness of the security-by-obscurity practice. Anyone looking at firewall logs on an Internet connection is amazed by the continuous attempts at port scanning. There are astounding statistics on port scanning available at the web site of DShield.org, http://www.dshield.org. The point is, no matter how small your business, you are a target of sophisticated attackers looking for bandwidth resources, anonymity, or any information you keep on your computer systems.

Case Study: Small Financial Company

A small financial investment company was implementing a software upgrade to its systems. It hired a consultant to assist the vendor with any network or client computer issues needed for the implementation. The consultant installed a DSL connection to the Internet to access the main server inside the company. Thinking that no one would be interested in the computer systems, the consultant translated the public address to the main server for a period of 30 days, the length of the engagement. One day the backup failed because the tape drive system could not hold the backup data. During the inspection of the system, the consultant noticed files and directories unfamiliar to her experience. As a result of security ignorance, the system had been compromised. The consultant could not believe that anyone would attack that server in just a 30-day period.

Indifference to security puts everyone else at risk. No matter what the excuse or reasoning is, one weak link can lead to system-wide compromise. With the proliferation of malicious attacks, your weaknesses *will* be discovered. Companies need to be proactive in identification of security slackers. In the end, slackers are as dangerous as the hackers and crackers from which you are protecting your assets.

Index

Numbers

A

B

C

D

E

F

G

H

I

J

K

L

O

P

Q

R

S

T

W

X

Y

Z

INTERNATIONAL CONTACT INFORMATION

AUSTRALIA
McGraw-Hill Book Company
Australia Pty. Ltd.
TEL +61-2-9900-1800
FAX +61-2-9878-8881
http://www.mcgraw-hill.com.au
books-it_sydney@mcgraw-hill.com

CANADA
McGraw-Hill Ryerson Ltd.
TEL +905-430-5000
FAX +905-430-5020
http://www.mcgraw-hill.ca

GREECE, MIDDLE EAST, & AFRICA (Excluding South Africa)
McGraw-Hill Hellas
TEL +30-210-6560-990
TEL +30-210-6560-993
TEL +30-210-6560-994
FAX +30-210-6545-525

MEXICO (Also serving Latin America)
McGraw-Hill Interamericana Editores
S.A. de C.V.
TEL +525-1500-5108
FAX +525-117-1589
http://www.mcgraw-hill.com.mx
carlos_ruiz@mcgraw-hill.com

SINGAPORE (Serving Asia)
McGraw-Hill Book Company
TEL +65-6863-1580
FAX +65-6862-3354
http://www.mcgraw-hill.com.sg
mghasia@mcgraw-hill.com

SOUTH AFRICA
McGraw-Hill South Africa
TEL +27-11-622-7512
FAX +27-11-622-9045
robyn_swanepoel@mcgraw-hill.com

SPAIN
McGraw-Hill/
Interamericana de España, S.A.U.
TEL +34-91-180-3000
FAX +34-91-372-8513
http://www.mcgraw-hill.es
professional@mcgraw-hill.es

UNITED KINGDOM, NORTHERN, EASTERN, & CENTRAL EUROPE
McGraw-Hill Education Europe
TEL +44-1-628-502500
FAX +44-1-628-770224
http://www.mcgraw-hill.co.uk
emea_queries@mcgraw-hill.com

ALL OTHER INQUIRIES Contact:
McGraw-Hill/Osborne
TEL +1-510-420-7700
FAX +1-510-420-7703
http://www.osborne.com
omg_international@mcgraw-hill.com